FIFTH EDITION

W9-BUY-261

A HISTORY OF WESTERN SOCIETY

✤ **Volume C**   *From the Revolutionary Era to the Present*

John P. McKay
*University of Illinois at
Urbana–Champaign*

Bennett D. Hill
Georgetown University

John Buckler
*University of Illinois at
Urbana–Champaign*

HOUGHTON MIFFLIN COMPANY
Boston   Toronto
Geneva, Illinois   Palo Alto
Princeton, New Jersey

Sponsoring Editor: Sean W. Wakely
Basic Book Editor: Elizabeth Welch
Senior Associate Editor: Jeffrey Greene
Senior Manufacturing Coordinator: Priscilla Bailey
Marketing Manager: Pamela Shaffer

Cover designer: Harold Burch, Harold Burch Design, New York, New York
Cover image: Carl Olaf Larsson. Self-Portrait. Uffizi, Florence, Italy. Scala/Art Resource, NY

Printed in the U.S.A.
Library of Congress Catalog Card Number: 94-76526
ISBN Student Text: 0–395–70846–X
ISBN Examination Copy: 0–395–71724–8
123456789-VH-98   97   96   95   94

A History of Western Society

About the Authors

John P. McKay Born in St. Louis, Missouri, John P. McKay received his B.A. from Wesleyan University (1961), his M.A. from the Fletcher School of Law and Diplomacy (1962), and his Ph.D. from the University of California, Berkeley (1968). He began teaching history at the University of Illinois in 1966 and became a professor there in 1976. John won the Herbert Baxter Adams Prize for his book *Pioneers for Profit: Foreign Entrepreneurship and Russian Industrialization, 1885–1913* (1970). He has also written *Tramways and Trolleys: The Rise of Urban Mass Transport in Europe* (1976) and has translated Jules Michelet's *The People* (1973). His research has been supported by fellowships from the Ford Foundation, the Guggenheim Foundation, the National Endowment for the Humanities, and IREX. His articles and reviews have appeared in numerous journals, including *The American Historical Review, Business History Review, The Journal of Economic History,* and *Slavic Review*. He edits *Industrial Development and the Social Fabric: An International Series of Historical Monographs.*

Bennett D. Hill A native of Philadelphia, Bennett D. Hill earned an A.B. at Princeton (1956) and advanced degrees from Harvard (A.M., 1958) and Princeton (Ph.D., 1963). He taught history at the University of Illinois at Urbana, where he was department chairman from 1978 to 1981. He has published *English Cistercian Monasteries and Their Patrons in the Twelfth Century* (1968) and *Church and State in the Middle Ages* (1970); and articles in *Analecta Cisterciensia, The New Catholic Encyclopaedia, The American Benedictine Review,* and *The Dictionary of the Middle Ages*. His reviews have appeared in *The American Historical Review, Speculum, The Historian, The Catholic Historical Review,* and *Library Journal.* He has been a fellow of the American Council of Learned Societies and has served on committees for the National Endowment for the Humanities. Now a Benedictine monk of St. Anselm's Abbey, Washington, D.C., he is also a Visiting Professor at Georgetown University.

John Buckler Born in Louisville, Kentucky, John Buckler received his B.A. (*summa cum laude*) from the University of Louisville in 1967. Harvard University awarded him the Ph.D. in 1973. From 1984 to 1986 he was an Alexander von Humboldt Fellow at the Institut für Alte Coschichte, University of Munich. He has lectured at the Fondation Hardt at the University of Geneva, and has participated in numerous international conferences. He is currently the professor of Greek history at the University of Illinois. In 1980 Harvard University Press published his *The Theban Hegemony, 371–362 BC.* He has also published *Philip II and the Sacred War* (Leiden 1989), and co-edited *BOIOTIKA: Vorträge vom 5. International Böotien-Kolloquium* (Munich 1989). He has assisted the National Endowment for the Humanities, and reviews articles for journals in the United States and Europe. His articles have appeared in journals both here and abroad, including the *American Journal of Ancient History, Classical Philology, Rheinisches Museum für Philoloqie, Classical Quarterly, Wiener Studien, Symbolae Osloenses,* and many others.

Contents in Brief

✛ ✛ ✛ ✛ ✛ ✛ ✛ ✛ ✛ ✛

Contents

Maps

Timelines/Genealogies

❖ ❖ ❖ ❖ ❖ ❖ ❖ ❖ ❖

* The comparative timeline, *A History of Western Society: A Brief Overview,* begins on page 1078.

Listening to the Past

✛ ✛ ✛ ✛ ✛ ✛ ✛ ✛ ✛ ✛

Preface

A History of Western Society grew out of the authors' desire to infuse new life into the study of Western civilization. We knew full well that historians were using imaginative questions and innovative research to open up vast new areas of historical interest and knowledge. We also recognized that these advances had dramatically affected the subject of European economic, intellectual, and, especially, social history, while new research and fresh interpretations were also revitalizing the study of the traditional mainstream of political, diplomatic, and religious development. Despite history's vitality as a discipline, however, it seemed to us that both the broad public and the intelligentsia were generally losing interest in the past.

It was our conviction, based on considerable experience introducing large numbers of students to the broad sweep of Western civilization, that a book reflecting current trends could excite readers and inspire a renewed interest in history and our Western heritage. Our strategy was twofold. First, we made social history the core element of our work. Not only did we incorporate recent research by social historians, but also we sought to recreate the life of ordinary people in appealing human terms. At the same time we were determined to give great economic, political, intellectual, and cultural developments the attention they unquestionably deserve. We wanted to give individual readers and instructors a balanced, integrated perspective so that they could pursue—on their own or in the classroom—those themes and questions that they found particularly exciting and significant. In an effort to realize fully the potential of our fresh, yet balanced approach, we made many changes, large and small, in the three editions that followed.

Changes in the New Edition

In preparing the fifth edition we have worked hard to keep our book up-to-date and to strengthen our distinctive yet balanced approach. Six main lines of revision guided our many changes.

Updated Approach to Social History.   First, in a thorough revision of social developments, we have given greater attention to cultural and intellectual life, and somewhat reduced the quantitative and demographic aspects. Increased emphasis on culture and attitudes invigorates our social history core and accurately reflects current scholarship and changing interests within the historical profession. Accordingly, this edition has expanded discussions of religious life including popular religion in Mesopotamia (Chapter 1), classical Greece (Chapter 3), and revolutionary France (Chapter 21); the evolution of Jewish religion (Chapter 2), Eastern monasticism (Chapter 7), and Calvin's Geneva (Chapter 14); and religious revival in the twentieth century (Chapter 28). Consistently greater attention to popular culture includes new sections on medieval music, troubadour poets, and recreation in Chapters 11 and 12; community values in the eighteenth-century (Chapter 20); and the counter-culture in the 1960s (Chapter 30). New material on health and health care features recent research on medieval practices (Chapter 10), early hospitals and the Black Death (Chapter 12), and eighteenth-century practitioners (Chapter 20). Interactions between cultures have also been highlighted, as, for example, the relations between Egyptians and Nubians (Chapter 1), pagans and Christians (Chapter 6), Muslims and Christians (Chapter 7), and educated elites and popular classes (Chapters 18 and 20). In addition, we have carefully revised sections on the life of the people to set social developments consistently in their larger historical context. For example, Chapters 18 through 21 provide a dynamic, thoroughly updated treatment of the eighteenth century that interrelates cultural change, economic expansion, social life, and political revolution.

Integrated Treatment of Women and Gender. Second, we have broadened our treatment of women's history and gender issues and integrated it into the main narrative, rather than reserving it for separate sections. This approach also reflects current scholarly thinking. For example, the updated discussion of Hellenistic women has been integrated into the central narrative (Chapter 4); new material on women in agriculture and commerce during the Middle Ages (Chapters 10 and 11), and on gender roles in the arts (Chapter 15) has been appropriately positioned; elite women in the Enlightenment and peasant women in village communities have been reconsidered in context (Chapters 18 and 20); and women in twentieth-century dictatorships have been compared systematically (Chapter 29). The contemporary women's movement receives expanded separate analysis (Chapter 31) because it emerged as a major cultural and political force.

Organizational Changes. Third, our integrated treatment of women's history is one of several organizational improvements. In addition to the revision of Chapters 18 through 21, Chapter 15 has been thoroughly revised to relate sixteenth-century social and cultural changes consistently to political and religious developments. Chapters 30 and 31 have been completely recast, interrelating political, economic, social, and cultural developments from the new edition's post-Cold War perspective. Chapter 1 has been reorganized to clarify the chronology and the role of writing in Sumerian civilization. The early development of the Kievan principality has been relocated to Chapter 8 to maintain the chronology, and to highlight the integral role of the eastern Slavs in early medieval Europe.

Incorporation of Recent Scholarship. Fourth, every chapter has been carefully revised to reflect recent scholarship. Because the authors are committed to a balanced approach, we have continued to incorporate important new findings on political, economic, and intellectual developments in this edition. Revisions of this nature include the Babylonian Captivity (Chapter 2), democratic ideology in Athens and political background to Plato and Aristotle's thought (Chapter 3), and Roman commerce and frontier relations between Romans and Germans (Chapter 6). Similar revisions in Chapters 7 through 16 incorporate new material on the Spanish *reconquista* (Chapter 7), the medieval origins of the modern state and the power of the church in private life (Chapter 9), economic causes for Magna Carta (Chapter 11), and political violence (Chapter 12). There is new material on banks in continental industrialization and the early labor movement (Chapter 22); the role of class conflict in nineteenth-century domestic politics, imperialism, and the origins of World War One (Chapters 25-27); educational reforms and political culture in Republican France (Chapter 25); Nietzsche and his influence (Chapter 28); and the Nazi state and the origins of Italian fascism (Chapter 29). In short, recent research keeps the broad sweep of our history fresh and up-to-date.

New "Problems of Historical Interpretation." Fifth, the addition of more "problems of historical interpretation" in the fourth edition was well received, so we have increased their number again in this edition. We believe that the problematic element helps our readers develop the critical-thinking skills that are among the most precious benefits of studying history. New examples of this more open-ended, interpretive approach include the debate over the origins of Rome (Chapter 5), the impact of the Renaissance on the lives of ordinary and elite women (Chapter 13), the motives and legacy of Christopher Columbus (Chapter 15), popular reading habits and their significance (Chapter 20), social tensions and the origins of World War One (Chapter 27), and the nature of twentieth-century dictatorships (Chapter 29).

Revised Full-Color Art and Map Programs. Finally, the illustrative component of our work has been carefully revised. We have added many new illustrations to our extensive art program, which includes nearly two hundred color reproductions, letting great art and important events come alive. As in earlier editions, all illustrations have been carefully selected to complement the text, and all carry captions that enhance their value. Artwork remains an integral part of our book; the past can speak in pictures as well as in words. The use of full color throughout this edition also serves to clarify the maps and graphs and to enrich the textual material. The maps and map captions have been updated to correlate directly to the text.

Distinctive Features

Distinctive features, both new and revised, guide the reader in the process of historical understanding. Many of these features also show how historians sift through and evaluate evidence. Our goal is to suggest how historians actually work and think. We want the reader to think critically and to realize that history is neither a list of cut-and-dried facts nor a senseless jumble of conflicting opinions.

New Primary-Source Chapter Feature. To help students and instructors realize this goal, we have added a two-page excerpt from a primary source at the end of each chapter in the fifth edition. This important new feature, entitled "Listening to the Past," extends and illuminates a major historical issue considered in the chapter. For example, in Chapter 4, a selection from *Plutarch's Lives* recounts the sacrifice of a famous queen for her people, while Chapter 9 presents a mind-opening Arab account of the First Crusade. Crime in medieval England is examined through criminal case reports in Chapter 12, and the German traveler Olearius provides a fascinating and influential picture of the Russian state and society in Chapter 17. Writer Stephan Zweig probes the sexuality of young men and women in nineteenth-century Vienna in Chapter 24, and a Jewish doctor who survived Auschwitz describes the horrible inhumanity of Nazi death camps in Chapter 29.

Each primary source opens with a problem-setting introduction and closes with "Questions for Analysis" that invite students to evaluate the evidence as historians would. Drawn from a range of writings addressing a variety of social, cultural, political, and intellectual issues, these sources promote active involvement and critical interpretation. Selected for their interest and importance and carefully fitted into their historical context, these sources do indeed allow the student to "listen to the past" and to observe how history has been shaped by individual men and women, some of them great aristocrats, others ordinary folk.

Improved Chapter Features. Distinctive features from earlier editions have been revised and improved in the fifth edition. To help guide the reader toward historical understanding, we pose specific historical questions at the beginning of each chapter. These questions are then answered in the course of each chapter, and each chapter concludes with a concise summary of its findings. All of the questions and summaries have been reexamined and frequently revised in order to maximize the usefulness of this popular feature.

In addition to posing chapter-opening questions and presenting more problems in historical interpretation, we have quoted extensively from a wide variety of primary sources in the narrative, demonstrating in our use of these quotations how historians evaluate evidence. Thus primary sources are examined as an integral part of the narrative as well as presented in extended form in the new "Listening to the Past" chapter feature. We believe that such an extensive program of both integrated and separate primary source excerpts will help readers learn to interpret and think critically.

Each chapter concludes with carefully selected suggestions for further reading. These suggestions are briefly described to help readers know where to turn to continue thinking and learning about the Western world. Also chapter bibliographies have been revised and updated to keep them current with the vast amount of new work being done in many fields.

Revised Timelines. The timelines appearing in earlier editions have been substantially improved in this edition. In addition to revising the timelines placed within many chapters, we have expanded the comparative timelines previously dispersed throughout the fourth edition and placed them in a unified format in an appendix at the end of the book. Comprehensive and easy to locate, this useful timeline allows students to compare simultaneous political, economic, social, cultural, intellectual, and scientific developments over the centuries.

Flexible Format. Western civilization courses differ widely in chronological structure from one campus to another. To accommodate the various divisions of historical time into intervals that fit a two-quarter, three-quarter, or two-semester period, *A History of Western Society* is being published in four versions, three of which embrace the complete work:

- One-volume hardcover edition, A HISTORY OF WESTERN SOCIETY
- Two-volume paperback, A HISTORY OF WESTERN SOCIETY *Volume I: From Antiquity to the Enlightenment* (Chapters 1–17), *Volume II: From Absolutism to the Present* (Chapters 16–31)
- Three-volume paperback, A HISTORY OF WESTERN SOCIETY *Volume A: From Antiquity to 1500* (Chapters 1–13), *Volume B: From the Renaissance to 1815* (Chapters 12–21), *Volume C: From the Revolutionary Era to the Present* (Chapters 21–31)
- A HISTORY OF WESTERN SOCIETY *Since 1400* (Chapters 13–31), for courses on Europe since the Renaissance

Note that overlapping chapters in both the two- and the three-volume sets permit still wider flexibility in matching the appropriate volume with the opening and closing dates of a course term.

Ancillaries

Learning and teaching ancillaries, listed below, also contribute to the usefulness of the text.

- *Study Guide*
- *Computerized Study Guide*
- *Instructor's Resource Manual*
- *Test Items,*
- *Computerized Test Items*
- *Map Transparencies*
- *Videodisc*
- *Videodisc Guide*

The excellent *Study Guide* has been thoroughly revised by Professor James Schmiechen of Central Michigan University. Professor Schmiechen has been a tower of strength ever since he critiqued our initial prospectus, and he has continued to give us many valuable suggestions as well as his warmly appreciated support. His *Study Guide* contains learning objectives, chapter summaries, chapter outlines, review questions, extensive multiple-choice exercises, self-check lists of important concepts and events, and a variety of study aids and suggestions. The fifth edition also retains the study–review exercises on the interpretation of visual sources and major political ideas as well as suggested issues for

discussion and essay, chronology reviews and sections on studying effectively. These sections take the student through reading and studying activities like underlining, summarizing, identifying main points, classifying information according to sequence, and making historical comparisons. To enable both students and instructors to use the *Study Guide* with the greatest possible flexibility, the guide is available in two volumes, with considerable overlapping of chapters. Instructors and students who use only Volumes A and B of the text have all the pertinent study materials in a single volume, *Study Guide, Volume 1* (Chapters 1–21); likewise, those who use only Volumes B and C of the text also have all the necessary materials in one volume, *Study Guide, Volume 2* (Chapters 12–31). The multiple-choice sections of the *Study Guide* are also available in a *Computerized Study Guide,* a tutorial version that tells students not only which response is correct but also why each of the other choices is wrong; it also provides the page numbers in the text where each question is discussed. These "rejoinders" to the multiple-choice questions also appear in printed form at the end of the *Study Guide.* The *Computerized Study Guide* is available for IBM® computers.

The *Instructor's Resource Manual,* prepared by Professor John Marshall Carter contains instructional objectives, annotated chapter outlines, suggestions for lectures and discussion, paper and class activity topics, primary source exercises, map activities, and lists of audio-visual resources. The accompanying *Test Items,* by Professor Charles Crouch of Georgia Southern University offer identification, multiple-choice, map, and essay questions for a total of approximately 2000 test items. These test items are available to adopters in both IBM® and Macintosh versions, both of which include editing capabilities. To add an exciting multimedia component to lectures and learning laboratories, we have created *The History of Western Civilization Videodisc/Videotape/Slide* program. The program allows the instructor to create customized multimedia classroom presentations using this rich collection of visual images. The program is divided into five chronological periods (ancient, medieval, early modern, modern, and Twentieth Century) and contains over 165 still images, 30 animated maps, and motion footage accompanied by period music. A companion *Videodisc/Videotape* instructor's guide provides descriptions, printed bar codes, bar code stickers to create customized lectures, and numeric codes. The program is available at no cost to adopters of the book. Please contact your local Houghton Mifflin representative for more information about this innovative and exciting multimedia program.

In addition, a set of full-color *Map Transparencies* of all the maps in the text is available on adoption.

Acknowledgments

It is a pleasure to thank the many instructors who have read and critiqued the manuscript through its development:

Anthony Cardoza
Loyola University

Jack Cargill
Rutgers University

Stephanie Christelow
Idaho State University

Jessica Coope
University of Nebraska

George Early
Black Hills State University

Charles Evans
Northern Virginia Community College

Keith Francis
Pacific Union College

David Graf
University of Miami

Barbara Hanawalt
University of Minnesota

Paul Harvey
Penn State University

Charles Ingrao
Purdue University

Gary Johnson
University of Southern Maine

Ellen Kittell
University of Idaho

Harry Liebersohn
University of Illinois

James Masschaele
Rutgers University

Mavis Mate
University of Oregon

Kathryn Norberg
Univlersity of California, Los Angeles

Kathleen Paul
University of South Florida

William M. Reddy
Duke University

Raymond Sickinger
Providence College

Sherill Spaar
East Central University

Ruth Suyama
Mission College, Los Angeles

Bruce Taylor
University of Dayton

Marilyn Yancey
Virginia Union University

It is also a pleasure to thank our editors at Houghton Mifflin for their effort and support over many years. To Elizabeth Welch, Senior Basic Book Editor, who has skillfully guided and encouraged our work since the third edition, we owe a special debt of gratitude and admiration. To Jean Woy, Editor-in-Chief for Social Sciences, who has led us onward for more than a decade, and to Sean Wakely, Sponsoring Editor for History, we express our sincere appreciation. And we thank Leslie Anderson Olney and Carole Frohlich for their contributions in production and photo research.

Many of our colleagues at the University of Illinois continued to provide information and stimulation for our book, often without even knowing it. N. Frederick Nash, Rare Book Librarian, made many helpful suggestions for illustrations, and the World Heritage Museum at the University allowed us complete access to its sizable holdings. James Dengate kindly supplied information on objects from the museum's collection and Caroline Buckler took many excellent photographs of the museum's objects. Such wide-ranging expertise was a great asset for which we are very appreciative. Bennett Hill wishes to express his sincere appreciation to Ramón de la Fuente for his support, encouragement, and research assistance in the preparation of this fifth edition.

Each of us has benefited from the generous criticism of his co-authors, although each of us assumes responsibility for what he has written. John Buckler has written the first six chapters; Bennett Hill has continued the narrative through Chapter 16; and John McKay has written Chapters 17 through 31. Finally, we continue to welcome the many comments and suggestions that have come from our readers, for they have helped us greatly in this ongoing endeavor.

J. P. M.   B. D. H.   J. B.

21

The Revolution in Politics, 1775–1815

The last years of the eighteenth century were a time of great upheaval. A series of revolutions and revolutionary wars challenged the old order of monarchs and aristocrats. The ideas of freedom and equality, ideas that have not stopped shaping the world since that era, flourished and spread. The revolutionary era began in North America in 1775. Then in 1789 France, the most influential country in Europe, became the leading revolutionary nation. It established first a constitutional monarchy, then a radical republic, and finally a new empire under Napoleon. The armies of France also joined forces with patriots and radicals abroad in an effort to establish new governments based on new principles throughout much of Europe. The world of modern domestic and international politics was born.

- What caused this era of revolution?
- What were the ideas and objectives of the men and women who rose up violently to undo the established system?
- What were the gains and losses for privileged groups and for ordinary people in a generation of war and upheaval?

These are the questions underlying this chapter's examination of the revolutionary era.

The mayor of Rouen protects access to the townhall from the on-slaught of a crowd rioting over the lack of bread, August 29, 1792. *(Source: Musée des Beaux Arts, Rouen/Laurie Platt Winfrey, Inc.)*

LIBERTY AND EQUALITY

Two ideas fueled the revolutionary period in both America and Europe: liberty and equality. What did eighteenth-century politicians and other people mean by liberty and equality, and why were those ideas so radical and revolutionary in their day?

The call for liberty was first of all a call for individual human rights. Even the most enlightened monarchs customarily claimed that it was their duty to regulate what people wrote and believed. Liberals of the revolutionary era protested such controls from on high. They demanded freedom to worship according to the dictates of their consciences instead of according to the politics of their monarchs. They demanded an end to censorship and a right to express their beliefs freely in print and at public meetings. They demanded freedom from arbitrary laws and from judges who simply obeyed orders from the government.

These demands for basic personal freedoms, which were incorporated into the American Bill of Rights and other liberal constitutions, were far-reaching. The Declaration of the Rights of Man, issued at the beginning of the French Revolution, proclaimed, "Liberty consists in being able to do anything that does not harm another person." In theory, therefore, a citizen's rights had "no limits except those which assure to the other members of society the enjoyment of these same rights." In the context of the monarchial and absolutist forms of government then dominating Europe, this was a truly radical idea.

The call for liberty was also a call for a new kind of government. Revolutionary liberals believed that the people were sovereign—that is, that the people alone had the authority to make laws limiting the individual's freedom of action. In practice, this system of government meant choosing legislators who represented the people and were accountable to them. Moreover, liberals of the revolutionary era believed that every nation, every "people"—that is, every ethnic group—had this right of self-determination and thus a right to form a free nation.

Equality was a more ambiguous idea. Eighteenth-century liberals argued that, in theory, all citizens should have identical rights and civil liberties. Above all, the nobility had no right to special privileges based on an accident of birth, and such privileges were abolished with great fanfare in the French Revolution. Other well-established distinctions were more easily accepted by liberals.

First, most eighteenth-century liberals were *men* of their times. They generally shared with other men the belief that equality between men and women was neither practical nor desirable. Thus when the men of the French Revolution came to power, they brushed aside the idea that women should have the same rights as men. Above all, they limited formal political rights—the right to vote, to run for office, to participate in government—to men, although women did play an important political role in the the French Revolution at several points.

Second, liberals never believed that everyone should be equal economically. Quite the contrary. As Thomas Jefferson wrote in an early draft of the American Declaration of Independence, before changing "property" to the more noble-sounding "happiness," everyone was equal in "the pursuit of property." Jefferson and other liberals certainly did not expect equal success in that pursuit. Great differences in wealth and income between rich and poor were perfectly acceptable to liberals. The essential point was that everyone should legally have an equal chance.

Such equality of opportunity was a truly revolutionary idea in eighteenth-century Europe. Legal inequality between classes and groups was the rule, not the exception. Society was still legally divided into groups with special privileges, such as the nobility and the clergy, and groups with special burdens, such as the peasantry. In most countries, various middle-class groups—professionals, business people, townspeople, and craftsmen—also enjoyed privileges that allowed them to monopolize all sorts of economic activity. It was this kind of economic inequality based on artificial legal distinctions that liberals criticized, not economic inequality itself.

The Roots of Liberalism

The ideas of liberty and equality—the central ideas of classical liberalism—had deep roots in Western history. The ancient Greeks and the Judeo-Christian tradition had affirmed for hundreds of years the sanctity and value of the individual human being. The Judeo-Christian tradition, reinforced by the Reformation, had long stressed personal responsibility on the part of both common folk and exalted rulers, thereby promoting the self-discipline without which liberty becomes anarchy. The hounded and persecuted Protestant radicals of the later sixteenth century had died for the revolutionary idea that individuals were entitled to their own religious beliefs.

Although the liberal creed was rooted in the Western tradition, classical liberalism first crystallized at the end of the seventeenth century and during the Enlightenment of the eighteenth century. Liberal ideas reflected the Enlightenment's stress on human dignity and human happiness on earth. Liberals shared the Enlightenment's general faith in science, rationality, and progress: the adoption of liberal principles meant better government and a better society for all. Almost all the writers of the Enlightenment were passionately committed to greater personal liberty. They preached religious toleration, freedom of press and speech, and fair and equal treatment before the law.

Certain English and French thinkers were mainly responsible for joining the Enlightenment's concern for personal freedom and legal equality to a theoretical justification of liberal self-government. The two most important were John Locke and the baron de Montesquieu, both considered earlier. Locke (see page 548) maintained that England's long political tradition rested on "the rights of Englishmen" and on representative government through Parliament. Locke admired especially the great Whig nobles who had made the bloodless revolution of 1688 to 1689, and he argued that if a government oversteps its proper function of protecting the natural rights of life, liberty, and private property, it becomes a tyranny. Montesquieu (see page 602) was also inspired by English constitutional history. He, too, believed that powerful "intermediary groups"—such as the judicial nobility of which he was a proud member—offered the best defense of liberty against despotism.

The Attraction of Liberalism

The belief that representative institutions could defend their liberty and interests appealed powerfully to well-educated, prosperous groups, which historians have traditionally labeled as the bourgeoisie. Yet liberal ideas about individual rights and political freedom also appealed to much of the hereditary nobility, at least in western Europe and as formulated by Montesquieu. Representative government did not mean democracy, which liberal thinkers tended to equate with mob rule. Rather, they envisioned voting for representatives as being restricted to those who owned property, those with "a stake in society." England had shown the way. After 1688 it had combined a parliamentary system and considerable individual liberty with a restricted franchise and unquestionable aristocratic pre-eminence. In the course of the eighteenth century, many leading French nobles, led by

a judicial nobility inspired by the doctrines of Montesquieu, were increasingly eager to follow the English example. Thus eighteenth-century liberalism found broad support among the prosperous, well-educated elites in western Europe.

What liberalism lacked from the beginning was strong popular support. At least two reasons account for the people's wary attitude. First, for comfortable liberals, the really important questions were theoretical and political; they had no need to worry about their stomachs and the price of bread. For common people, the great questions were immediate and economic; getting enough to eat was a crucial challenge. Second, some of the traditional practices and institutions that liberals wanted to abolish were dear to peasants and urban workers.

❖ **The Marquis de Lafayette** was the most famous great noble to embrace the liberal revolution. Shown here directing a battle in the American Revolution, he returned to champion liberty and equality in France. The elegant black is Lafayette's servant, a free man in an age of widespread slavery. *(Source: Jean-Loup Charmet)*

Comfortable elites had already come into conflict with the people in the eighteenth century over the enclosure of common lands and the regulation of food prices. This conflict would sharpen in the revolutionary era as differences in outlook and well-being led to many misunderstandings and disappointments for both groups.

✣ THE AMERICAN REVOLUTION, 1775–1789

The era of liberal political revolution began in the New World. The thirteen mainland colonies of British North America revolted against their home country and then succeeded in establishing a new unified government.

Americans have long debated the meaning of their revolution. Some have even questioned whether it was a real revolution, as opposed to a war for independence. According to some scholars, the Revolution was conservative and defensive in that its demands were for the traditional liberties of English citizens; Americans were united against the British, but otherwise they were a satisfied people, not torn by internal conflict. Other scholars have argued that, on the contrary, the American Revolution was quite radical. It split families between patriots and Loyalists and divided the country. It achieved goals that were fully as advanced as those obtained by the French in their great revolution a few years later.

How does one reconcile these positions? Both contain large elements of truth. The American revolutionaries did believe that they were demanding only the traditional rights of English men and women. But those traditional rights were liberal rights, and in the American context they had very strong democratic and popular overtones. Thus the American Revolution was fought in the name of established ideals that were still quite radical in the context of the times. And in founding a government firmly based on liberal principles, the Americans set an example that had a forceful impact on Europe and sped up political development there.

The Origins of the Revolution

The American Revolution had its immediate origins in a squabble over increased taxes. The British government had fought and decisively won the Seven Years' War (see page 643) on the strength of its professional army and navy. The American colonists had furnished little real aid. The high cost of the war to the British, however, had led to a doubling of the British national debt. Anticipating further expense defending its recently conquered western lands from native American uprisings, the British government in London set about reorganizing the empire with a series of bold, largely unprecedented measures. Breaking with tradition, the British decided to maintain a large army in North America after peace was restored in 1763. Moreover, they sought to exercise strict control over their newly conquered western lands and to tax the colonies directly. In 1765 the government pushed through Parliament the Stamp Act, which levied taxes on a long list of commercial and legal documents, diplomas, pamphlets, newspapers, almanacs, dice, and playing cards. A stamp glued to each article indicated the tax had been paid.

This effort to increase taxes as part of a tightening up of the empire seemed perfectly reasonable to the British. Heavier stamp taxes had been collected in Great Britain for two generations, and Americans were being asked only to pay a share of their own defense costs. Moreover, Americans had been paying only very low local taxes. The Stamp Act would have doubled taxes to about 2 shillings per person per year. No other people in the European or colonial world (except the Poles) paid so little. Meanwhile, the British paid the highest taxes in the Western world—26 shillings per person. It is not surprising that taxes per person in the newly independent American nation were much higher in 1785 than in 1765, when the British no longer subsidized American defense. The colonists protested the Stamp Act vigorously and violently, however, and after rioting and boycotts against British goods, Parliament reluctantly repealed the new tax.

As the fury over the Stamp Act revealed, much more was involved than taxes. The key questions were political. To what extent could the home government refashion the empire and reassert its power while limiting the authority of colonial legislatures and their elected representatives? Accordingly, who should represent the colonies, and who had the right to make laws for Americans? While a troubled majority of Americans searched hard for a compromise, some radicals began to proclaim that "taxation without representation is tyranny." The British government replied that Americans were represented in Parliament, albeit indirectly (like most English people themselves), and that the absolute supremacy of Parliament throughout the empire could not be questioned. Many Americans felt otherwise. As John Adams put it, "A Parliament of Great Britain can have no more rights to tax the colonies than a Parliament of Paris." Thus imperial reorganization and parliamentary supremacy came to appear as grave threats to Americans' existing liberties and time-honored institutions.

Americans had long exercised a great deal of independence and gone their own way. In British North America, unlike England and Europe, no powerful established church existed, and personal freedom in questions of religion was taken for granted. The colonial assemblies made the important laws, which were seldom overturned by the home government. The right to vote was much more widespread than in England. In many parts of colonial Massachusetts, for example, as many as 95 percent of the adult males could vote.

Moreover, greater political equality was matched by greater social and economic equality. Neither a hereditary nobility nor a hereditary serf population existed, although the slavery of the Americas consigned blacks to a legally oppressed caste. Independent farmers were the largest group in the country and set much of its tone. In short, the colonial experience had slowly formed a people who felt themselves separate and distinct from the home country. The controversies over taxation intensified those feelings of distinctiveness and separation and brought them to the fore.

In 1773 the dispute over taxes and representation flared up again. The British government had permitted the financially hard-pressed East India Company to ship its tea from China directly to its agents in the colonies rather than through London middlemen who sold to independent merchants in the colonies. Thus the company secured a vital monopoly on the tea trade, and colonial merchants were suddenly excluded from a highly profitable business. The colonists were quick to protest.

In Boston men disguised as Indians had a rowdy "tea party" and threw the company's tea into the harbor. This led to extreme measures. The so-called Coercive Acts closed the port of Boston, curtailed local elections and town meetings, and greatly expanded the royal governor's power. County conventions in Massachusetts protested vehemently and urged that the acts be "rejected as

❖ **Toward Revolution in Boston** The Boston Tea Party was only one of many angry confrontations between British officials and Boston patriots. On January 27, 1774, an angry crowd seized a British customs collector and then tarred and feathered him. This French engraving of 1784 commemorates the defiant and provocative action. *(Source: The Granger Collection, New York)*

the attempts of a wicked administration to enslave America." Other colonial assemblies joined in the denunciations. In September 1774, the First Continental Congress met in Philadelphia, where the more radical members argued successfully against concessions to the Crown. Compromise was also rejected by the British Parliament, and in April 1775 fighting began at Lexington and Concord.

Independence

The fighting spread, and the colonists moved slowly but inevitably toward open rebellion and a declaration of independence. The uncompromising attitude of the British government and its use of German mercenaries went a long way toward dissolving long-standing loyalties to the home country and rivalries among the separate colonies. *Common Sense* (1775), a brilliant attack by the recently arrived English radical Thomas Paine (1737–1809), also mobilized public opinion in favor of independence. A runaway best seller with sales of 120,000 copies in a few months, Paine's tract ridiculed the idea of a small island ruling a great continent. In his call for freedom and republican government, Paine expressed Americans' growing sense of separateness and moral superiority.

On July 4, 1776, the Second Continental Congress adopted the Declaration of Independence. Written by Thomas Jefferson, the Declaration of Independence boldly listed the tyrannical acts committed by George III (r. 1760–1820) and confidently proclaimed the natural rights of mankind and the sovereignty of the American states. Sometimes called the world's greatest political edi-torial, the Declaration of Independence in effect universalized the traditional rights of English people and made them the rights of all mankind. It stated that "all men are created equal. . . . They are endowed by their Creator with certain unalienable rights. . . . Among these are life, liberty, and the pursuit of happiness." No other American political document has ever caused such excitement, either at home or abroad.

Many American families remained loyal to Britain; many others divided bitterly. After the Declaration of Independence, the conflict often took the form of a civil war pitting patriot against Loyalist. The Loyalists tended to be wealthy and politically moderate. Many patriots, too, were wealthy—individuals such as John Hancock and George Washington—but willingly allied themselves with farmers and artisans in a broad coalition. This coalition harassed the Loyalists and confiscated their prop-

The Signing of the Declaration, July 4, 1776 John Trumbull's famous painting shows the dignity and determination of America's revolutionary leaders. An extraordinarily talented group, they succeeded in rallying popular support without losing power to more radical forces in the process. *(Source: Yale University Art Gallery)*

erty to help pay for the American war effort. The broad social base of the revolutionaries tended to make the liberal revolution democratic. State governments extended the right to vote to many more men (but not to any women) in the course of the war and re-established themselves as republics.

On the international scene, the French sympathized with the rebels from the beginning. They wanted revenge for the humiliating defeats of the Seven Years' War. Officially neutral until 1778, they supplied the great bulk of guns and gunpowder used by the American revolutionaries, very much as foreign great powers have supplied weapons for "wars of national liberation" in our time. By 1777 French volunteers were arriving in Virginia, and a dashing young nobleman, the marquis de Lafayette (1757–1834), quickly became one of Washington's most trusted generals. In 1778 the French government offered a formal alliance to the American ambassador in Paris, Benjamin Franklin, and in 1779 and 1780 the Spanish and Dutch declared war on Britain. Catherine the Great of Russia helped organize the League of Armed Neutrality in order to protect neutral shipping rights, which Britain refused to recognize.

Thus by 1780 Great Britain was engaged in an imperial war against most of Europe as well as the thirteen colonies. In these circumstances, and in the face of severe reverses in India, the West Indies, and at Yorktown in Virginia, a new British government decided to cut its losses. American negotiators in Paris were receptive. They feared that France wanted a treaty that would bottle up the new United States east of the Allegheny Mountains and give British holdings west of the Alleghenies to France's ally, Spain. Thus the American negotiators separated themselves from their French allies and accepted the extraordinarily favorable terms Britain offered.

By the Treaty of Paris of 1783, Britain recognized the independence of the thirteen colonies and ceded all its territory between the Allegheny Mountains and the Mississippi River to the Americans. Out of the bitter rivalries of the Old World, the Americans snatched dominion over almost half a continent.

Framing the Constitution

The liberal program of the American Revolution was consolidated by the federal Constitution, the Bill of Rights, and the creation of a national republic. Assembling in Philadelphia in the summer of 1787, the delegates to the Constitutional Convention were determined to end the period of economic depression, social uncertainty, and very weak central government that had followed independence. The delegates decided, therefore, to grant the federal, or central, government important powers: regulation of domestic and foreign trade, the right to levy taxes, and the means to enforce its laws.

Strong rule would be placed squarely in the context of representative self-government. Senators and congressmen would be the lawmaking delegates of the voters, and the president of the republic would be an elected official. The central government would operate in Montesquieu's framework of checks and balances. The executive, legislative, and judicial branches would systematically balance one another. The power of the federal government would in turn be checked by the powers of the individual states.

When the results of the secret deliberations of the Constitutional Convention were presented to the states for ratification, a great public debate began. The opponents of the proposed constitution—the Anti-Federalists—charged that the framers of the new document had taken too much power from the individual states and made the federal government too strong. Moreover, many Anti-Federalists feared for the personal liberties and individual freedoms for which they had just fought. In order to overcome these objections, the Federalists solemnly promised to spell out these basic freedoms as soon as the new constitution was adopted. The result was the first ten amendments to the Constitution, which the first Congress passed shortly after it met in New York in March 1789. These amendments formed an effective bill of rights to safeguard the individual. Most of them—trial by jury, due process of law, right to assemble, freedom from unreasonable search—had their origins in English law and the English Bill of Rights of 1689. Others—the freedoms of speech, the press, and religion—reflected natural-law theory and the American experience.

The American Constitution and the Bill of Rights exemplified the great strengths and the limits of what came to be called "classical liberalism." Liberty meant individual freedoms and political safeguards. Liberty also meant representative government but did not necessarily mean democracy, with its principle of one person, one vote.

Equality—slaves excepted—meant equality before the law, not equality of political participation or economic well-being. Indeed, economic inequality was resolutely defended by the elite that framed the Constitution. The right to own property was guaranteed by the Fifth Amendment, and if the government took private property, the owner was to receive "just compensation." The radicalism of liberal revolution in America was primarily legal and political, *not* economic or social.

The Revolution's Impact on Europe

Hundreds of books, pamphlets, and articles analyzed and romanticized the American upheaval. Thoughtful Europeans noted, first of all, its enormous long-term implications for international politics. A secret report by the Venetian ambassador to Paris in 1783 stated what many felt: "If only the union of the Provinces is preserved, it is reasonable to expect that, with the favorable effects of time, and of European arts and sciences, it will become the most formidable power in the world."[1] More generally, American independence fired the imaginations of those aristocrats who were uneasy with their hereditary privileges and those commoners who yearned for equality. Many Europeans believed that the world was advancing and that America was leading the way. As one French writer put it in 1789, "This vast continent which the seas surround will soon change Europe and the universe."

Europeans who dreamed of a new era were fascinated by the political lessons of the American Revolution. The Americans had begun with a revolutionary defense against tyrannical oppression, and they had been victorious. They had then shown how rational beings could assemble together to exercise sovereignty and write a permanent constitution—a new social contract. All this gave greater reality to the concepts of individual liberty and representative government and reinforced one of the primary ideas of the Enlightenment: that a better world was possible.

✤ THE FRENCH REVOLUTION, 1789–1791

No country felt the consequences of the American Revolution more directly than France. Hundreds of French officers served in America and were in-

spired by the experience. The most famous of these, the young and impressionable marquis de Lafayette, left home as a great aristocrat determined only to fight France's traditional foe, England. He returned with a love of liberty and firm republican convictions. French intellectuals and publicists engaged in passionate analysis of the federal Constitution as well as the constitutions of the various states of the new United States. The American Revolution undeniably hastened upheaval in France.

Yet the French Revolution did not mirror the American example. It was more radical and more complex, more influential and more controversial, more loved and more hated. For Europeans and most of the rest of the world, it was the great revolution of the eighteenth century, *the* revolution that opened the modern era in politics.

The Breakdown of the Old Order

Like the American Revolution, the French Revolution had its immediate origins in the financial difficulties of the government. As we noted in Chapter 18, the efforts of Louis XV's ministers to raise taxes had been thwarted by the Parlement of Paris, strengthened in its opposition by widespread popular support (see pages 615–616). When renewed efforts to reform the tax system met a similar fate in 1776, the government was forced to finance all of its enormous expenditures during the American war with borrowed money. As a result, the national debt and the annual budget deficit soared. By the 1780s, fully 50 percent of France's annual budget went for ever-increasing interest payments on the ever-increasing debt. Another 25 percent went to maintain the military, while 6 percent was absorbed by the costly and extravagant king and his court at Versailles. Less than 20 percent of the entire national budget was available for the productive functions of the state, such as transportation and general administration. This was an impossible financial situation.

One way out would have been for the government to declare partial bankruptcy, forcing its creditors to accept greatly reduced payments on the debt. The powerful Spanish monarchy had regularly repudiated large portions of its debt in earlier times, and France had done likewise after an attempt to establish a French national bank had ended in financial disaster in 1720. Yet by the

1780s, the French debt was being held by an army of aristocratic and bourgeois creditors, and the French monarchy, though absolute in theory, had become far too weak for such a drastic and unpopular action.

Nor could the king and his ministers, unlike modern governments, print money and create inflation to cover their deficits. Unlike England and Holland, which had far larger national debts relative to their populations, France had no central bank, no paper currency, and no means of creating credit. French money was good gold coin. Therefore, when a depressed economy and a lack of public confidence made it increasingly difficult for the government to obtain new gold loans in 1786, it had no alternative but to try increasing taxes. And since France's tax system was unfair and out of date, increased revenues were possible only through fundamental reforms. Such reforms, which would affect all groups in France's complex and fragmented society, opened a Pandora's box of social and political demands.

Legal Orders and Social Realities

As in the Middle Ages, France's twenty-five million inhabitants were still legally divided into three orders, or "estates"—the clergy, the nobility, and everyone else. As the nation's first estate, the clergy numbered about 100,000 and had important privileges. It owned about 10 percent of the land and paid only a "voluntary gift," rather than regular taxes, to the government every five years. Moreover, the church levied a tax (the tithe) on landowners, which averaged somewhat less than 10 percent. Much of the church's income was actually drained away from local parishes by political appointees and worldly aristocrats at the top of the church hierarchy—to the intense dissatisfaction of the poor parish priests.

The second legally defined estate consisted of some 400,000 noblemen and noblewomen—the descendents of "those who had fought" in the Middle Ages. The nobles owned outright about 25 percent of the land in France, and they, too, were taxed very lightly. Moreover, nobles continued to enjoy certain manorial rights, or privileges of lordship, that dated back to medieval times and allowed them to tax the peasantry for their own profit. This was done by means of exclusive rights to hunt and fish, village monopolies on baking

❖ **France and America** Made in France about 1784, this figurine commemorates the vital support that France gave to the colonists in the American Revolution. Arrayed in Roman armor, a majestic Louis XVI hands documents entitled "American independence" and "freedom of the seas" to Benjamin Franklin. Franklin was lionized as a sage and a liberator while American ambassador to France. *(Source: The Providence Athenaeum, Providence, Rhode Island)*

bread and pressing grapes for wine, fees for justice, and a host of other "useful privileges." In addition, nobles had "honorific privileges," such as the right to precedence on public occasions and the right to wear a sword. These rights conspicuously proclaimed the nobility's legal superiority and exalted social position.

Everyone else was a commoner, legally a member of the third estate. A few commoners—prosperous merchants or lawyers and officials—were well educated and rich, and might even buy up manorial rights as profitable investments. Many more commoners were urban artisans and unskilled day laborers. The vast majority of the third estate consisted of the peasants and agricultural workers in the countryside. Thus the third estate was a conglomeration of vastly different social groups united only by their shared legal status as distinct from the nobility and clergy.

In discussing the long-term origins of the French Revolution, historians have long focused on growing tensions between the nobility and the comfortable members of the third estate, usually known as the *bourgeoisie,* or middle class. A dominant historical interpretation, which has held sway for at least two generations, maintains that the bourgeoisie was basically united by economic position and class interest. Aided by the general economic expansion discussed in Chapter 19, the middle class grew rapidly in the eighteenth century, tripling to about 2.3 million persons, or about 8 percent of France's population. Increasing in size, wealth, culture, and self-confidence, this rising bourgeoisie became progressively exasperated by archaic "feudal" laws restraining the economy and by the growing pretensions of a reactionary nobility, which was closing ranks against middle-class needs and aspirations. As a result, the French bourgeoisie eventually rose up to lead the entire third estate in a great social revolution, a revolution that destroyed feudal privileges and established a capitalist order based on individualism and a market economy.

In recent years, a flood of new research has challenged these accepted views, and once again the French Revolution is a subject of heated scholarly debate. Above all, revisionist historians have questioned the existence of a growing social conflict between a progressive capitalistic bourgeoisie and a reactionary feudal nobility in eighteenth-century France. Instead, these historians see both bourgeoisie and nobility as highly fragmented, riddled with internal rivalries. The great nobility, for example, was profoundly separated from the lesser nobility by differences in wealth, education, and world-view. Differences within the bourgeoisie—between wealthy financiers and local lawyers, for example—were no less profound. Rather than standing as unified blocs against each other, nobility and bourgeoisie formed two parallel social ladders increasingly linked together at the top by wealth, marriage, and Enlightenment culture.

Revisionist historians stress three developments in particular. First, the nobility remained a fluid and relatively open order. Throughout the eighteenth century, substantial numbers of successful commoners continued to seek and obtain noble status through government service and purchase of expensive positions conferring nobility. Thus the nobility of the robe continued to attract the wealthiest members of the middle class and to permit social mobility. Second, key sections of the nobility and the prosperous bourgeoisie formed together the core of the book-hungry Enlightenment public discussed in Chapter 18. Both groups saw themselves as forming part of the educated elite and standing well above the common people—the peasants and the urban poor. Both groups were also equally liberal until revolution actually began, and they generally supported the judicial opposition to the government led by the Parlement of Paris. Third, the nobility and the bourgeoisie were not really at odds in the economic sphere. Both looked to investment in land and government service as their preferred activities, and the ideal of the merchant capitalist was to gain enough wealth to retire from trade, purchase estates, and live nobly as a large landowner. At the same time, wealthy nobles often acted as aggressive capitalists, investing especially in mining, metallurgy, and foreign trade.

The revisionists have clearly shaken the belief that the bourgeoisie and the nobility were inevitably locked in growing conflict before the Revolution. But in stressing the similarities between the two groups, especially at the top, revisionists have also reinforced the view, long maintained by historians, that the Old Regime had ceased to correspond with social reality by the 1780s. Legally, society was still based on rigid orders inherited from the Middle Ages. In reality, France had already moved far toward being a society based on wealth and education, where an emerging elite that included both aristocratic and bourgeois notables was frustrated by a bureaucratic monarchy that continued to claim the right to absolute power.

The Formation of the National Assembly

The Revolution was under way by 1787, though no one could have realized what was to follow. Spurred by a depressed economy and falling tax receipts, Louis XVI's minister of finance revived old proposals to impose a general tax on all landed property as well as provincial assemblies to help administer the tax, and he convinced the king to call an assembly of notables to gain support for the idea. The assembled notables, who were mainly important noblemen and high-ranking clergy, were not in favor of it. In return for their support, they demanded that control over all government spending be given to the provincial assemblies. When the government refused, the notables responded that such sweeping tax changes required the approval of the Estates General, the representative body of all three estates, which had not met since 1614.

Facing imminent bankruptcy, the king tried to reassert his authority. He dismissed the notables and established new taxes by decree. In stirring language, the Parlement of Paris promptly declared the royal initiative null and void. The Parlement went so far as to specify some of the "fundamental laws" against which no king could transgress, such as national consent to taxation and freedom from arbitrary arrest and imprisonment. When the king tried to exile the judges, a tremendous wave of protest swept the country. Frightened investors also refused to advance more loans to the state. Finally in July 1788, a beaten Louis XVI bowed to public opinion and called for a spring session of the Estates General. Absolute monarchy was collapsing.

What would replace it? Throughout the unprecedented election campaign of 1788 and 1789, that question excited France. All across the country, clergy, nobles, and commoners came together in their respective orders to draft petitions for change and to elect their respective delegates to the Estates General. The local assemblies of the clergy showed considerable dissatisfaction with the church hierarchy, and two-thirds of the delegates were chosen from among the poorer parish priests, who were commoners by birth. The nobles, already badly split by wealth and education, remained politically divided. A conservative majority was drawn from the poorer and more numerous provincial nobility, but fully one-third of the nobility's representatives were liberals committed to major changes.

As for the third estate, there was great popular participation in the elections. Almost all male commoners twenty-five years or older had the right to vote. However, voting required two stages, which meant that most of the representatives finally selected by the third estate were well-educated, prosperous members of the middle class. Most of them were not businessmen, but lawyers and government officials. Social status and prestige were mat-

ters of particular concern to this economic elite. There were no delegates elected from the great mass of laboring poor, an exclusion that would encourage the peasants and also the urban artisans to intervene directly and dramatically at numerous points in the Revolution, as we shall see.

The petitions for change coming from the three estates showed a surprising degree of consensus on most issues, as recent research has clearly revealed. There was general agreement that royal absolutism should give way to constitutional monarchy, in which laws and taxes would require the consent of the Estates General meeting regularly. All agreed that in the future individual liberties would have to be guaranteed by law and that the economic position of the parish clergy would have to be improved. It was generally acknowledged that economic development required reforms, such as the abolition of internal trade barriers. The striking similarities in the grievance petitions of the clergy, nobility, and third estate reflected the broad commitment of France's educated elite to liberalism.

Yet an increasingly bitter quarrel undermined this consensus during the intense electoral campaign: *how* would the Estates General vote, and precisely *who* would lead in the political reorganization that was generally desired? The Estates General of 1614 had sat as three separate houses. Any action had required the agreement of at least two branches, a requirement that had virtually guaranteed control by the nobility and the clergy. Immediately after the victory over the king, the aristocratic Parlement of Paris, mainly out of respect for tradition but partly out of a desire to enhance the nobility's political position, ruled that the Estates General should once again sit separately. The ruling was quickly denounced by certain middle-class intellectuals and some liberal nobles. They demanded instead a single assembly dominated by representatives of the third estate to ensure fundamental reforms. Reflecting increased political competition and a growing hostility toward aristocratic aspirations, the abbé Emmanuel Joseph Sieyès argued in 1789 in his famous pamphlet *What Is the Third Estate?* that the nobility was a tiny, overprivileged minority and that the neglected third estate constituted the true strength of the French nation. When the government agreed that the third estate should have as many delegates as the clergy and the nobility combined, but then rendered this act meaningless by upholding voting by separate

✦ **The Oath of the Tennis Court** This painting, based on an unfinished work by Jacques-Louis David (1748–1825), enthusiastically celebrates the revolutionary rupture of June 20, 1789. Locked out of their assembly hall at Versailles and joined by some sympathetic priests, the delegates of the third estate have moved to an indoor tennis court and are swearing never to disband until they have written a new constitution and put France on a firm foundation. *(Source: Musée Carnavalet/Photographie Bulloz)*

order, middle-class leaders saw fresh evidence of an aristocratic conspiracy.

In May 1789 the twelve hundred delegates of the three estates paraded in medieval pageantry through the streets of Versailles to an opening session resplendent with feudal magnificence. The estates were almost immediately deadlocked. Delegates of the third estate refused to transact any business until the king ordered the clergy and nobility to sit with them in a single body. Finally, after a six-week war of nerves, a few parish priests began to go over to the third estate, which on June 17 voted to call itself the "National Assembly." On June 20, the delegates of the third estate, excluded from their hall because of "repairs," moved to a large indoor tennis court. There they swore the

famous Oath of the Tennis Court, pledging not to disband until they had written a new constitution.

The king's actions were then somewhat contradictory. On June 23 he made a conciliatory speech urging reforms to a joint session and then ordered the three estates to meet together. At the same time, the vacillating and indecisive monarch apparently followed the advice of relatives and court nobles, who urged him to dissolve the Estates General by force. The king called an army of eighteen thousand troops toward Versailles, and on July 11 he dismissed his finance minister and his other more liberal ministers. Faced with growing opposition since 1787, Louis XVI had resigned himself to bankruptcy. Now he belatedly sought to reassert his historic "divine right" to rule. The middle-class delegates and their allies from the liberal nobility had done their best, but they were resigned to being disbanded at bayonet point. One third-estate delegate reassured a worried colleague, "You won't hang—you'll only have to go back home."[2]

The Revolt of the Poor and the Oppressed

While the educated delegates of the third estate pressed for symbolic equality with the nobility and clergy in a single legislative body at Versailles, economic hardship gripped the common people of France in a tightening vise. Grain was the basis of the diet of ordinary people in the eighteenth century, and in 1788 the harvest had been extremely poor. The price of bread, which had been rising gradually since 1785, began to soar. By July 1789 it had climbed as high as 8 sous per pound in the provinces. In Paris, where bread was regularly subsidized by the government in an attempt to prevent popular unrest, the price rose to 4 sous. The poor could scarcely afford to pay 2 sous per pound, for even at that price a laborer with a wife and three children had to spend half of his wages to buy the family's bread.

Harvest failure and high bread prices unleashed a classic economic depression of the preindustrial age. With food so expensive and with so much uncertainty, the demand for manufactured goods collapsed. Thousands of artisans and small traders were thrown out of work. By the end of 1789, almost half of the French people would be in need of relief. One person in eight was a pauper living in extreme want. In Paris the situation was so desperate in July 1789 that perhaps 150,000 of the city's 600,000 people were without work.

Against this background of dire poverty and excitement generated by the political crisis, the people of Paris entered decisively onto the revolutionary stage. They believed in a general, though ill-defined, way that the economic distress had human causes. They believed that they should have steady work and enough bread at fair prices to survive. Specifically, they feared that the dismissal of the king's moderate finance minister would put them at the mercy of aristocratic landowners and grain speculators. Stories like that quoting the wealthy financier Joseph François Foulon as saying that the poor "should eat grass, like my horses" and rumors that the king's troops would sack the

city began to fill the air. Angry crowds formed, and passionate voices urged action. On July 13 the people began to seize arms for the defense of the city, and on July 14 several hundred of the most determined people marched to the Bastille to search for gunpowder.

A medieval fortress with walls 10 feet thick and eight great towers each 100 feet high, the Bastille had long been used as a prison. It was guarded by eighty retired soldiers and thirty Swiss mercenaries. The governor of the fortress-prison refused to hand over the powder, panicked, and ordered his men to fire, killing ninety-eight people attempting to enter. Cannon were brought to batter the main gate, and fighting continued until the prison surrendered. The governor of the prison was later hacked to death, and his head and that of the mayor of Paris, who had been slow to give the crowd arms, were stuck on pikes and paraded through the streets. The next day a committee of citizens appointed the marquis de Lafayette commander of the city's armed forces. Paris was lost to the king, who was forced to recall the finance minister and disperse his troops. The popular uprising had saved the National Assembly.

As the delegates resumed their long-winded and inconclusive debates at Versailles, the people in the countryside sent them a radical and unmistakable message. All across France, peasants began to rise in spontaneous, violent, and effective insurrection against their lords, ransacking manor houses and burning feudal documents that recorded the peasants' obligations. Neither middle-class landowners, who often owned manors and village monopolies, nor the larger, more prosperous farmers were spared. In some areas, peasants reinstated traditional village practices, undoing recent enclosures and reoccupying old common lands. Peasants seized forests and taxes went unpaid. Fear of vagabonds and outlaws—called the Great Fear by contemporaries—seized the countryside and fanned the flames of rebellion. The long-suffering peasants were doing their best to free themselves from manorial rights and exploitation.

Faced with chaos, yet afraid to call on the king to restore order, some liberal nobles and middle-class delegates at Versailles responded to peasant demands with a surprise maneuver on the night of August 4, 1789. The duke of Aiguillon, also notably one of France's greatest noble landowners, declared that *in several provinces the whole people forms a kind of league for the destruction of the manor houses, the ravaging of the lands, and especially for the seizure of the archives where the title deeds to feudal properties are kept. It seeks to throw off at last a yoke that has for many centuries weighted it down.*[3]

He urged equality in taxation and the elimination of feudal dues. In the end, all the old exactions imposed on the peasants—serfdom where it still existed, exclusive hunting rights for nobles, fees for justice, village monopolies, the right to make peasants work on the roads, and a host of other dues— were abolished, generally without compensation. Though a clarifying law passed a week later was less generous, the peasants ignored the "fine print."

They never paid feudal dues again. Thus the French peasantry, which already owned about 30 percent of all the land, achieved a great and unprecedented victory in the early days of revolutionary upheaval. Henceforth, the French peasants would seek mainly to protect and consolidate their triumph. As the Great Fear subsided in the countryside, they became a force for order and stability.

A Limited Monarchy

The National Assembly moved forward. On August 27, 1789, it issued the Declaration of the Rights of Man, which stated, "Men are born and remain free and equal in rights." The declaration also maintained that mankind's natural rights are

✤ **Storming the Bastille** This representation by an untrained contemporary artist shows civilians and members of the Paris militia—the "conquerors of the Bastille"— on the attack. This successful action had enormous practical and symbolic significance, and July 14 has long been France's most important national holiday. *(Source: Musée Carnavalet/Photo Hubert Josse)*

"To Versailles" This print is one of many commemorating the women's march on Versailles. Notice on the left that the artist has depicted—and criticized—the fashionable lady from the well-to-do as a most reluctant revolutionary. *(Source: Photo Flammarion)*

"liberty, property, security, and resistance to oppression" and that "every man is presumed innocent until he is proven guilty." As for law, "it is an expression of the general will; all citizens have the right to concur personally or through their representatives in its formation. . . . Free expression of thoughts and opinions is one of the most precious rights of mankind: every citizen may therefore speak, write, and publish freely." In short, this clarion call of the liberal revolutionary ideal guaranteed equality before the law, representative government for a sovereign people, and individual freedom. This revolutionary credo, only two pages long, was propagandized throughout France and Europe and around the world.

Moving beyond general principles to draft a constitution proved difficult. The questions of how much power the king should retain and whether he could permanently veto legislation led to another deadlock. Once again the decisive answer came from the poor—in this instance, the poor women of Paris.

Women customarily bought the food and managed the poor family's slender resources. In Paris great numbers of women also worked for wages, often within the putting-out system, making garments and beautiful luxury items destined for an aristocratic and international clientele. Immediately after the fall of the Bastille, many of France's great court nobles began to leave Versailles for foreign lands so that a plummeting demand for luxuries intensified the general economic crisis; international markets also declined. The church was no longer able to give its traditional grants of food and money to the poor. Increasing unemployment and hunger put tremendous pressure on household managers, and the result was another popular explosion.

On October 5 some seven thousand desperate women marched the 12 miles from Paris to Versailles to demand action. A middle-class deputy looking out from the Assembly saw "multitudes arriving from Paris including fishwives and bullies from the market, and these people wanted nothing but bread." This great crowd invaded the Assembly, "armed with scythes, sticks and pikes." One tough old woman directing a large group of younger women defiantly shouted into the debate,

"Who's that talking down there? Make the chatterbox shut up. That's not the point: the point is that we want bread."[4] Hers was the genuine voice of the people, essential to any understanding of the French Revolution.

The women invaded the royal apartments, slaughtered some of the royal bodyguards, and furiously searched for the queen, Marie Antoinette, who was widely despised for her frivolous and supposedly immoral behavior. "We are going to cut off her head, tear out her heart, fry her liver, and that won't be the end of it," they shouted, surging through the palace in a frenzy. It seems likely that only the intervention of Lafayette and the National Guard saved the royal family. But the only way to calm the disorder was for the king to go and live in Paris, as the crowd demanded.

The next day, the king, the queen, and their son left for Paris in the midst of a strange procession. The heads of two aristocrats, stuck on pikes, led the way. They were followed by the remaining members of the royal bodyguard, unarmed and surrounded and mocked by fierce men holding sabers and pikes. A mixed and victorious multitude surrounded the king's carriage, hurling crude insults at the queen. There was drinking and eating among the women, who had clearly emerged as a major and enduring element in the Parisian revolutionary crowd.[5]

The National Assembly followed the king to Paris, and the next two years, until September 1791, saw the consolidation of the liberal Revolution. Under middle-class leadership, the National Assembly abolished the French nobility as a legal order and pushed forward with the creation of a constitutional monarchy, which Louis XVI reluctantly agreed to accept in July 1790. In the final constitution, the king remained the head of state, but all lawmaking power was placed in the hands of the National Assembly, elected by the economic upper half of French males.

New laws broadened women's rights to seek divorce, to inherit property, and to obtain financial support from fathers for illegitimate children. But women were not allowed to vote or hold political office for at least two reasons. First, the great majority of comfortable, well-educated males in the National Assembly believed that women should be limited to child raising and domestic duties and should leave politics and most public activities to men. This was, of course, a hoary idea, but it had

been dressed up and re-energized by Rousseau in his influential *Émile* (see page 665). Second, the delegates to the National Assembly were convinced that political life in absolutist France had been profoundly corrupt and that a prime example of this corruption was the way that some talented but immoral aristocratic women had used their sexual charms to manipulate weak rulers and their ministers. Delegates therefore believed that excluding women from politics would help create the civic virtue that had been missing: the political system would be freed from the harmful effects of sexual favors; and pure, home-focused wives would raise the high-minded sons needed to govern and defend the nation.

The National Assembly replaced the complicated patchwork of historic provinces with eighty-three departments of approximately equal size. The jumble of weights and measures that varied from province to province was reformed, leading to the introduction of the simple, rational metric system in 1793. The National Assembly promoted the liberal concept of economic freedom. Monopolies, guilds, and workers' combinations were prohibited, and barriers to trade within France were abolished in the name of economic liberty. Thus the National Assembly applied the critical spirit of the Enlightenment to reform France's laws and institutions completely.

The Assembly also imposed a radical reorganization on the Catholic church. It nationalized the church's property and abolished monasteries as useless relics of a distant past. The government used all former church property as collateral to guarantee a new paper currency, the *assignats,* and then sold these properties in an attempt to put the state's finances on a solid footing. Although the church's land was sold in large blocks, a procedure that favored nimble speculators and the rich, peasants eventually purchased much of this land when it was subdivided. These purchases strengthened their attachment to the revolutionary state.

The most unfortunate aspect of the reorganization of France was that it brought the new government into conflict with the Catholic church and many sincere Christians, especially in the countryside. Many delegates to the National Assembly, imbued with the rationalism and skepticism of the eighteenth-century philosophes, harbored a deep distrust of popular piety and "superstitious religion." They were interested in the church only to the extent that they could seize its land and use the church to strengthen the new state. Thus they established a national church, with priests chosen by voters. In the face of widespread resistance, the National Assembly then required the clergy to take a loyalty oath to the new government. The Catholic clergy became just so many more employees of the state. The pope formally condemned this attempt to subjugate the church, and only half the priests of France took the oath of allegiance. The result was a deep division within both the country and the clergy on the religious question; confusion and hostility among French Catholics were pervasive. The attempt to remake the Catholic church, like the Assembly's abolition of guilds and workers' combinations, sharpened the conflict between the educated classes and the common people that had been emerging in the eighteenth century. This policy toward the church was the revolutionary government's first important failure.

✤ WORLD WAR AND REPUBLICAN FRANCE, 1791–1799

When Louis XVI accepted the final version of the completed constitution in September 1791, a young and still obscure provincial lawyer and member of the National Assembly named Maximilien Robespierre (1758–1794) evaluated the work of two years and concluded, "The Revolution is over." Robespierre was both right and wrong. He was right in the sense that the most constructive and lasting reforms were in place. Nothing substantial in the way of liberty and equality would be gained in the next generation. He was wrong in the sense that a much more radical stage lay ahead. New heroes and new ideologies were to emerge in revolutionary wars and international conflict.

Foreign Reactions and the Beginning of War

The outbreak and progress of revolution in France produced great excitement and a sharp division of opinion in Europe and the United States. Liberals and radicals saw a mighty triumph of liberty over despotism. In Great Britain especially, they hoped that the French example would lead to a fundamental reordering of the political system. That system, which had been consolidated in the revolu-

tion of 1688 to 1689, placed Parliament in the hands of the aristocracy and a few wealthy merchants; the great majority of people had very little say in the government. After the French Revolution began, conservative leaders such as Edmund Burke (1729–1797) were deeply troubled by the aroused spirit of reform. In 1790 Burke published *Reflections on the Revolution in France,* one of the great intellectual defenses of European conservatism. He defended inherited privileges in general and those of the English monarchy and aristocracy. He glorified the unrepresentative Parliament and predicted that thoroughgoing reform like that occurring in France would lead only to chaos and tyranny. Burke's work sparked vigorous debate.

One passionate rebuttal came from a young writer in London, Mary Wollstonecraft (1759–1797). Born into the middle class, Wollstonecraft was schooled in adversity by a mean-spirited father who beat his wife and squandered his inherited fortune. Determined to be independent in a society that generally expected women of her class to become homebodies and obedient wives, she struggled for years to earn her living as a governess and teacher—practically the only acceptable careers for single, educated women—before attaining success as a translator and author. Interested in politics and believing that "a desperate disease requires a powerful remedy" in Great Britain as well as France, Wollstonecraft was incensed by Burke's book. She immediately wrote a blistering, widely read attack, *A Vindication of the Rights of Man* (1790).

Then, fired up on controversy and commitment, she made a daring intellectual leap. She developed for the first time the logical implications of natural-law philosophy in her masterpiece, *A Vindication of the Rights of Woman* (1792). To fulfill the still-unrealized potential of the French Revolution and to eliminate the many-sided sexual inequality she had felt so keenly, she demanded that

the Rights of Women be respected . . . [and] JUSTICE for one-half of the human race. . . . It is time to effect a revolution in female manners, time to restore to them their lost dignity, and make them, as part of the human species, labor, by reforming themselves, to reform the world.

Setting high standards for women—"I wish to persuade women to endeavor to acquire strength,

like foreign invaders. International tensions mounted. In February 1793 the National Convention, at war with Austria and Prussia, declared war on Britain, Holland, and Spain as well. Republican France was now at war with almost all of Europe, a great war that would last almost without interruption until 1815.

As the forces of the First Coalition drove the French from the Austrian Netherlands, peasants in western France revolted against being drafted into the army. They were supported and encouraged in their resistance by devout Catholics, royalists, and foreign agents.

In Paris the quarrelsome National Convention found itself locked in a life-and-death political struggle between the Girondists and the Mountain. The two groups were in general agreement on questions of policy. Sincere republicans, they hated privilege and wanted to temper economic liberalism with social concern. Yet personal hatreds ran deep. The Girondists feared a bloody dictatorship by the Mountain, and the Mountain was no less convinced that the more moderate Girondists would turn to conservatives and even royalists in order to retain power. With the middle-class delegates so bitterly divided, the laboring poor of Paris emerged as the decisive political factor.

The laboring men and women of Paris always constituted—along with the peasantry in the summer of 1789—the elemental force that drove the Revolution forward. It was the artisans, day laborers, market women, and garment workers who had stormed the Bastille, marched on Versailles, driven the king from the Tuileries, and carried out the September Massacres. The petty traders and laboring poor were often known as the *sans-culottes,* "without breeches," because sans-culottes men wore trousers instead of the knee breeches of the aristocracy and the solid middle class. The immediate interests of the sans-culottes were mainly eco-

The End of Louis XVI The condemned monarch looks down at the basket into which his severed head will fall. The execution of the king was a victory for the radicals in Paris, but it horrified Europe's monarchs and conservatives and strengthened their opposition to the French Revolution. *(Source: Musée Carnavalet/Laurie Platt Winfrey, Inc.)*

nomic, and in the spring of 1793 the economic situation was as bad as the military situation. Rapid inflation, unemployment, and food shortages were again weighing heavily on poor families.

Moreover, by the spring of 1793, the sans-culottes had become keenly interested in politics. Encouraged by the so-called angry men, such as the passionate young ex-priest and journalist Jacques Roux, sans-culottes men and women were demanding radical political action to guarantee them their daily bread. At first the Mountain joined the Girondists in violently rejecting these demands. But in the face of military defeat, peasant revolt, and hatred of the Girondists, the Mountain and especially Robespierre became more sympathetic. The Mountain joined with sans-culottes activists in the city government to engineer a popular uprising, which forced the Convention to arrest thirty-one Girondist deputies for treason on June 2. All power passed to the Mountain.

Robespierre and others from the Mountain joined the recently formed Committee of Public Safety, to which the Convention had given dictatorial power to deal with the national emergency. These developments in Paris triggered revolt in leading provincial cities, such as Lyons and Marseilles, where moderates denounced Paris and demanded a decentralized government. The peasant revolt spread, and the republic's armies were driven back on all fronts. By July 1793 only the areas around Paris and on the eastern frontier were firmly controlled by the central government. Defeat appeared imminent.

Total War and the Terror

A year later, in July 1794, the Austrian Netherlands and the Rhineland were once again in the hands of conquering French armies, and the First Coalition was falling apart. This remarkable change of fortune was due to the revolutionary government's success in harnessing, for perhaps the first time in history, the explosive forces of a planned economy, revolutionary terror, and modern nationalism in a total war effort.

Robespierre and the Committee of Public Safety advanced with implacable resolution on several fronts in 1793 and 1794. First, in an effort to save revolutionary France, they collaborated with the fiercely patriotic and democratic sans-culottes, who retained the common people's traditional faith in fair prices and a moral economic order and who distrusted most wealthy capitalists and all aristocrats. Thus Robespierre and his co-workers established, as best they could, a planned economy with egalitarian social overtones. Rather than let supply and demand determine prices, the government decreed the maximum allowable prices for a host of key products. Though the state was too weak to enforce all its price regulations, it did fix the price of bread in Paris at levels the poor could afford. Rationing was introduced and quality was also controlled. Bakers were permitted to make only the "bread of equality"—a brown bread made of a mixture of all available flours. White bread and pastries were outlawed as frivolous luxuries. The poor of Paris may not have eaten well, but at least they ate.

They also worked, mainly to produce arms and munitions for the war effort. Craftsmen and small manufacturers were told what to produce and when to deliver. The government nationalized many small workshops and requisitioned raw materials and grain from the peasants. Sometimes planning and control did not go beyond orders to meet the latest emergency: "Ten thousand soldiers lack shoes. You will take the shoes of all the aristocrats in Strasbourg and deliver them ready for transport to headquarters at 10 A.M. tomorrow." Failures to control and coordinate were failures of means and not of desire: seldom if ever before had a government attempted to manage an economy so thoroughly. The second revolution and the ascendancy of the sans-culottes had produced an embryonic emergency socialism, which thoroughly frightened Europe's propertied classes and had great influence on the subsequent development of socialist ideology.

Second, while radical economic measures supplied the poor with bread and the armies with weapons, the Reign of Terror (1793–1794) was solidifying the home front. Special revolutionary courts responsible only to Robespierre's Committee of Public Safety tried rebels and "enemies of the nation" for political crimes. Drawing on popular, sans-culottes support centered in the local Jacobin clubs, these local courts ignored normal legal procedures and judged severely. Some 40,000 French men and women were executed or died in prison. Another 300,000 suspects crowded the prisons and often brushed close to death in a revolutionary court.

❖ **The Last Roll Call** Prisoners sentenced to death by revolutionary courts listen to an official solemnly reading the names of those selected for immediate execution. After being bound, the prisoners will ride standing up in a small cart through the streets of Paris to the nearby guillotine. As this painting highlights, both women and men were executed for political crimes under the Terror. *(Source: Mansell Collection)*

Robespierre's Reign of Terror was one of the most controversial phases of the French Revolution. Most historians now believe that the Reign of Terror was not directed against any single class. Rather, it was a political weapon directed impartially against all who might oppose the revolutionary government. For many Europeans of the time, however, the Reign of Terror represented a terrifying perversion of the generous ideals that had existed in 1789. It strengthened the belief that France had foolishly replaced a weak king with a bloody dictatorship.

The third and perhaps most decisive element in the French republic's victory over the First Coalition was its ability to continue drawing on the explosive power of patriotic dedication to a national state and a national mission. This is the essence of modern nationalism, and it was something new in history. With a common language and a common tradition newly reinforced by the ideas of popular sovereignty and democracy, the French people were stirred by a common loyalty. The shared danger of foreign foes and internal rebels unified all classes in a heroic defense of the nation.

In such circumstances, war was no longer the gentlemanly game of the eighteenth century, but a life-and-death struggle between good and evil. Everyone had to participate in the national effort. According to a famous decree of August 23, 1793:

The young men shall go to battle and the married men shall forge arms. The women shall make tents and clothes, and shall serve in the hospitals; children shall tear rags into lint. The old men will be guided to the public places of the cities to kindle the courage of the young warriors and to preach the unity of the Republic and the hatred of kings.

Like the wars of religion, war in 1793 was a crusade. This war, however, was fought for a secular, rather than a religious, ideology.

Because all unmarried young men were subject to the draft, the French armed forces swelled to one million men in fourteen armies. A force of this size was unprecedented in the history of European warfare. The soldiers were led by young, impetuous generals who had often risen rapidly from the ranks and personified the opportunities the Revolution seemed to offer gifted sons of the people.

May 5, 1789	Estates General convene at Versailles
June 17, 1789	Third Estate declares itself the National Assembly
June 20, 1789	Oath of the Tennis Court
July 14, 1789	Storming of the Bastille
July–Aug. 1789	The Great Fear in the countryside
August 4, 1789	National Assembly abolishes feudal privileges
August 27, 1789	National Assembly issues Declaration of the Rights of Man
October 5, 1789	Women march on Versailles and force royal family to return to Paris
November 1789	National Assembly confiscates church lands
July 1790	Civil Constitution of the Clergy establishes a national church Louis XVI reluctantly agrees to accept a constitutional monarchy
June 1791	Arrest of the royal family while attempting to flee France
August 1791	Declaration of Pillnitz by Austria and Prussia
April 1792	France declares war on Austria
August 1792	Parisian mob attacks palace and takes Louis XVI prisoner
September 1792	September Massacres National Convention declares France a republic and abolishes monarchy
January 1793	Execution of Louis XVI
February 1793	France declares war on Britain, Holland, and Spain Revolts in provincial cities
March 1793	Bitter struggle in the National Convention between Girondists and the Mountain
April–June 1793	Robespierre and the Mountain organize the Committee of Public Safety and arrest Girondist leaders
September 1793	Price controls to aid the sans-culottes and mobilize war effort
1793–1794	Reign of Terror in Paris and the provinces
Spring 1794	French armies victorious on all fronts
July 1794	Execution of Robespierre Thermidorean Reaction begins
1795–1799	The Directory
1795	End of economic controls and suppression of the sans-culottes
1797	Napoleon defeats Austrian armies in Italy and returns triumphant to Paris
1798	Austria, Great Britain, and Russia form the Second Coalition against France
1799	Napoleon overthrows the Directory and seizes power

These generals used mass attacks at bayonet point by their highly motivated forces to overwhelm the enemy. By the spring of 1794, French armies were victorious on all fronts. The republic was saved.

The Thermidorian Reaction and the Directory, 1794–1799

The success of the French armies led Robespierre and the Committee of Public Safety to relax the emergency economic controls, but they extended the political Reign of Terror. Their lofty goal was increasingly an ideal democratic republic where justice would reign and there would be neither rich nor poor. Their lowly means were unrestrained despotism and the guillotine, which struck down any who might seriously question the new order. In March 1794, to the horror of many sans-culottes, Robespierre's Terror wiped out many of the angry men, who had been criticizing Robespierre for being soft on the wealthy and who were led by the radical social democrat Jacques Hébert. Two weeks later, several of Robespierre's long-standing collaborators, led by the famous orator Danton, marched up the steps to the guillotine. A strange assortment of radicals and moderates in the Convention, knowing that they might be next, organized a conspiracy. They howled down Robespierre when he tried to speak to the National Convention on 9 Thermidor (July 27, 1794). On the following day, it was Robespierre's turn to be shaved by the revolutionary razor.

As Robespierre's closest supporters followed their leader, France unexpectedly experienced a thorough reaction to the despotism of the Reign of Terror. In a general way, this "Thermidorian reaction" recalled the early days of the Revolution. The respectable middle-class lawyers and professionals who had led the liberal revolution of 1789 reasserted their authority, drawing support from their own class, the provincial cities, and the better-off peasants. The National Convention abolished many economic controls, printed more paper currency, and let prices rise sharply. It severely restricted the local political organizations where the sans-culottes had their strength. And all the while, wealthy bankers and newly rich speculators celebrated the sudden end of the Terror with an orgy of self-indulgence and ostentatious luxury, an orgy symbolized by the shockingly low-cut gowns that quickly became the rage among their wives and mistresses.

The collapse of economic controls, coupled with runaway inflation, hit the working poor very hard. The gaudy extravagance of the rich wounded their pride. The sans-culottes accepted private property, but they believed passionately in small business, decent wages, and economic justice. Increasingly disorganized after Robespierre purged radical leaders, the common people of Paris finally revolted against the emerging new order in early 1795. The Convention quickly used the army to suppress these insurrections. For the first time since the fall of the Bastille, bread riots and uprisings by Parisians living on the edge of starvation were effectively put down by a government that made no concessions to the poor. In the face of all these catastrophes, the revolutionary fervor of the laboring poor in Paris finally subsided. Excluded and disillusioned by the triumphant return of the comfortable educated classes, the urban poor would have little interest in and influence on politics until 1830.

In villages and small towns there arose a great cry for peace and a turning toward religion, especially from women, who had seldom experienced the political radicalization of sans-culottes women in the big cities. Instead, these women had frequently and tenaciously defended their culture and religious beliefs against the often heavy-handed attacks of antireligious revolutionary officials after 1789. As the frustrated government began to retreat on the religious question from 1796 to 1801, the women of rural France brought back the Catholic church and the open worship of God. In the words of a leading historian, these women worked constructively and effectively for a return to a normal and structured lifestyle:

Peacefully but purposefully, they sought to re-establish a pattern of life punctuated by a peeling bell and one in which the rites of passage—birth, marriage, and death—were respected and hallowed. The state had intruded too far and women entered the public arena to push it back and won. It was one of the most resounding political statements made by the populace in the entire history of the Revolution.[9]

As for the middle-class members of the National Convention, in 1795 they wrote yet another constitution, which they believed would guarantee their economic position and political supremacy. The mass of the population voted only for electors, who were men of means. Electors then elected the members of a reorganized legislative assembly, as well as key officials throughout France. The new assembly also chose a five-man executive—the Directory.

The Directory continued to support French military expansion abroad. War was no longer so much a crusade as a means to meet ever-present, ever-unsolved economic problems. Large, victorious French armies reduced unemployment at home and were able to live off the territories they conquered and plundered.

The unprincipled action of the Directory reinforced widespread disgust with war and starvation. This general dissatisfaction revealed itself clearly in the national elections of 1797, which returned a large number of conservative and even monarchist deputies who favored peace at almost any price. The members of the Directory, fearing for their skins, used the army to nullify the elections and began to govern dictatorially. Two years later, Napoleon Bonaparte ended the Directory in a *coup d'état* and substituted a strong dictatorship for a weak one. The effort to establish stable representative government had failed.

✤ THE NAPOLEONIC ERA, 1799–1815

For almost fifteen years, from 1799 to 1814, France was in the hands of a keen-minded military dictator of exceptional ability. One of history's most fascinating leaders, Napoleon Bonaparte (1769–1821) realized the need to put an end to civil strife in France, in order to create unity and consolidate his rule. And he did. But Napoleon saw himself as a man of destiny, and the glory of war and the dream of universal empire proved irresistible. For years he spiraled from victory to victory; but in the end he was destroyed by a mighty coalition united in fear of his restless ambition.

Napoleon's Rule of France

In 1799 when he seized power, young General Napoleon Bonaparte was a national hero. Born in Corsica into an impoverished noble family in 1769, Napoleon left home and became a lieutenant in the French artillery in 1785. After a brief and unsuccessful adventure fighting for Corsican independence in 1789, he returned to France as a

French patriot and a dedicated revolutionary. Rising rapidly in the new army, Napoleon was placed in command of French forces in Italy and won brilliant victories there in 1796 and 1797. His next campaign, in Egypt, was a failure, but Napoleon made his way back to France before the fiasco was generally known. His reputation remained intact.

Napoleon soon learned that some prominent members of the Legislative Assembly were plotting against the Directory. The dissatisfaction of these plotters stemmed not so much from the fact that the Directory was a dictatorship as from the fact that it was a weak dictatorship. Ten years of upheaval and uncertainty had made firm rule much more appealing than liberty and popular politics to these disillusioned revolutionaries. The abbé Sieyès personified this evolution in thinking. In 1789 he had written that the nobility was grossly over-

David: Napoleon Crossing the Alps Bold and commanding, with flowing cape and surging stallion, the daring young Napoleon Bonaparte leads his army across the Alps from Italy to battle the Austrians in 1797. This painting by the great Jacques-Louis David (1748–1825) is a stirring glorification of Napoleon, a brilliant exercise in mythmaking. (*Source: Louvre/Cliché des Musées Nationaux, Paris*)

privileged and that the entire people should rule the French nation. Now Sieyès's motto was "Confidence from below, authority from above."

Like the other members of his group, Sieyès wanted a strong military ruler. The flamboyant thirty-year-old Napoleon was ideal. Thus the conspirators and Napoleon organized a takeover. On November 9, 1799, they ousted the Directors, and the following day soldiers disbanded the Assembly at bayonet point. Napoleon was named first consul of the republic, and a new constitution consolidating his position was overwhelmingly approved in a plebiscite in December 1799. Republican appearances were maintained, but Napoleon was already the real ruler of France.

The essence of Napoleon's domestic policy was to use his great and highly personal powers to maintain order and put an end to civil strife. He did so by working out unwritten agreements with powerful groups in France whereby these groups received favors in return for loyal service. Napoleon's bargain with the solid middle class was codified in the famous Civil Code of 1804, which reasserted two of the fundamental principles of the liberal and essentially moderate revolution of 1789: equality of all male citizens before the law and absolute security of wealth and private property. Napoleon and the leading bankers of Paris established the privately owned Bank of France, which loyally served the interests of both the state and the financial oligarchy. Napoleon's defense of the new economic order also appealed successfully to the peasants, who had gained both land and status from the revolutionary changes. Thus Napoleon reconfirmed the gains of the peasantry and reassured the solid middle class, which had already lost a large number of its revolutionary illusions in the face of social upheaval.

At the same time, Napoleon accepted and strengthened the position of the French bureaucracy. Building on the solid foundations that revolutionary governments had inherited from the Old Regime, he perfected a thoroughly centralized state. A network of prefects, subprefects, and centrally appointed mayors depended on Napoleon and served him well. Nor were members of the old nobility slighted. In 1800 and again in 1802, Napoleon granted amnesty to one hundred thousand émigrés on the condition that they return to France and take a loyalty oath. Members of this returning elite soon ably occupied many high posts in the expanding centralized state. Only one thousand die-hard monarchists were exempted and remained abroad. Napoleon also created a new imperial nobility in order to reward his most talented generals and officials.

Napoleon's great skill in gaining support from important and potentially hostile groups is illustrated by his treatment of the Catholic church in France. In 1800 the French clergy was still divided into two groups: those who had taken an oath of allegiance to the revolutionary government and those in exile or hiding who had refused to do so. Personally uninterested in religion, Napoleon wanted to heal the religious division so that a united Catholic church in France could serve as a bulwark of order and social peace. After long and arduous negotiations, Napoleon and Pope Pius VII (1800–1823) signed the Concordat of 1801. The pope gained for French Catholics the precious right to practice their religion freely, but Napoleon gained political power: his government now nominated bishops, paid the clergy, and exerted great influence over the church in France.

The domestic reforms of Napoleon's early years were his greatest achievement. Much of his legal and administrative reorganization has survived in France to this day. More generally, Napoleon's domestic initiatives gave the great majority of French people a welcome sense of order and stability. And when Napoleon added the glory of military victory, he rekindled a spirit of national unity that would elude France throughout most of the nineteenth century.

Order and unity had their price: Napoleon's authoritarian rule. Women, who had often participated in revolutionary politics without having legal equality, lost many of the gains they had made in the 1790s under the new Napoleonic Code. Under the law, women were dependents, of either their fathers or their husbands, and they could not make contracts or even have bank accounts in their own names. Indeed, Napoleon and his advisers aimed at re-establishing a "family monarch," where the power of the husband and father was as absolute over the wife and the children as that of Napoleon was over his subjects.

Free speech and freedom of the press—fundamental rights of the liberal revolution enshrined in the Declaration of the Rights of Man—were continually violated. Napoleon constantly reduced the number of newspapers in Paris. By 1811 only four were left, and they were little more than organs of government propaganda. The occasional elections were a farce. Later laws prescribed harsh penalties for political offenses.

These changes in the law were part of the creation of a police state in France. Since Napoleon was usually busy making war, this task was largely left to Joseph Fouché, an unscrupulous opportunist who had earned a reputation for brutality during the Reign of Terror. As minister of police, Fouché organized a ruthlessly efficient spy system, which kept thousands of citizens under continual police surveillance. People suspected of subversive activities were arbitrarily detained, placed under house arrest, or even consigned to insane asylums. After 1810 political suspects were held in state prisons, as they had been during the Terror. There were about twenty-five hundred such political prisoners in 1814.

Napoleon's Wars and Foreign Policy

Napoleon was above all a military man, and a great one. After coming to power in 1799, he sent peace feelers to Austria and Great Britain, the two remaining members of the Second Coalition, which had been formed against France in 1798. When these overtures were rejected, French armies led by Napoleon decisively defeated the Austrians. In the Treaty of Lunéville (1801) Austria accepted the loss of almost all its Italian possessions, and German territory on the west bank of the Rhine was incorporated into France. Once more, as in 1797, the British were alone, and war-weary, like the French.

Still seeking to consolidate his regime domestically, Napoleon concluded the Treaty of Amiens with Great Britain in 1802. France remained in control of Holland, the Austrian Netherlands, the west bank of the Rhine, and most of the Italian peninsula. Napoleon was free to reshape the German states as he wished. The Treaty of Amiens was clearly a diplomatic triumph for Napoleon, and peace with honor and profit increased his popularity at home.

In 1802 Napoleon was secure but unsatisfied. Ever a romantic gambler as well as a brilliant administrator, he could not contain his power drive. Aggressively redrawing the map of Germany so as to weaken Austria and attract the secondary states of southwestern Germany toward France, Napoleon threatened British interests in the eastern Mediterranean and tried to restrict British trade with all of Europe. Deciding to renew war with Britain in May 1803, Napoleon concentrated his armies in the French ports on the Channel in the fall of 1803 and began making preparations to invade England. Yet Great Britain remained dominant on the seas. When Napoleon tried to bring his Mediterranean fleet around Gibraltar to northern France, a combined French and Spanish fleet was, after a series of mishaps, virtually annihilated by Lord Nelson at the Battle of Trafalgar on October 21, 1805. Invasion of England was henceforth impossible. Renewed fighting had its advantages, however, for the first consul used the wartime atmosphere to have himself proclaimed emperor in late 1804.

Austria, Russia, and Sweden joined with Britain to form the Third Coalition against France shortly before the Battle of Trafalgar. Actions such as Napoleon's assumption of the Italian crown had convinced both Alexander I of Russia and Francis II of Austria that Napoleon was a threat to their interests and to the European balance of power. Yet the Austrians and the Russians were no match for Napoleon, who scored a brilliant victory over them at the Battle of Austerlitz in December 1805. Alexander I decided to pull back, and Austria accepted large territorial losses in return for peace as the Third Coalition collapsed.

Victorious at Austerlitz, Napoleon proceeded to reorganize the German states to his liking. In 1806 he abolished many of the tiny German states as well as the ancient Holy Roman Empire, whose emperor had traditionally been the ruler of Austria. Napoleon established by decree the German Confederation of the Rhine, a union of fifteen German states minus Austria, Prussia, and Saxony. Naming himself "protector" of the confederation, Napoleon firmly controlled western Germany.

Napoleon's intervention in German affairs alarmed the Prussians, who mobilized their armies after more than a decade of peace with France. Napoleon attacked and won two more brilliant victories in October 1806 at Jena and Auerstädt, where the Prussians were outnumbered two to one. The war with Prussia, now joined by Russia, continued into the following spring, and after Napoleon's larger armies won another victory, Alexander I of Russia wanted peace.

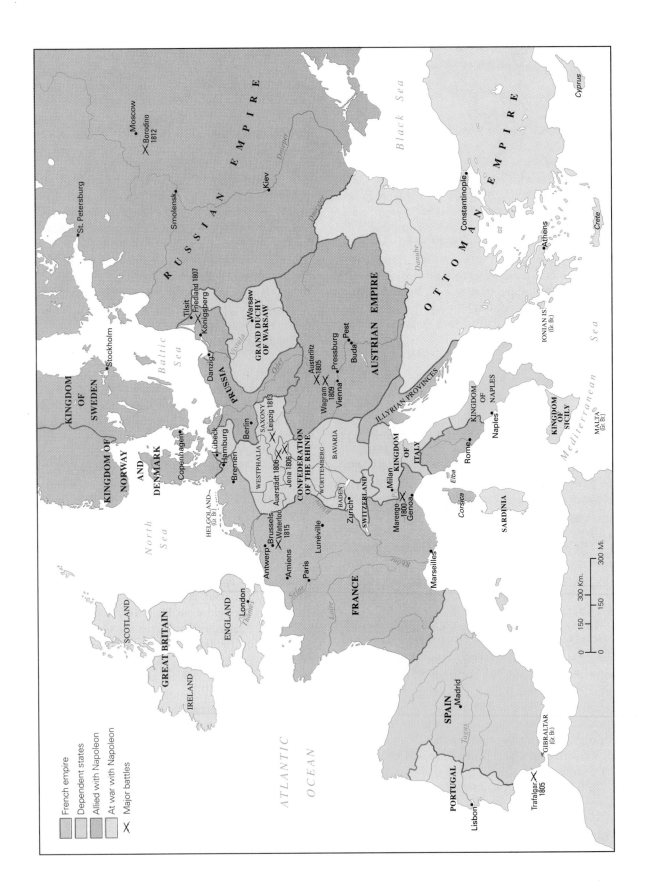

French empire
Dependent states
Allied with Napoleon
At war with Napoleon
X Major battles

RUSSIAN EMPIRE
OTTOMAN EMPIRE
AUSTRIAN EMPIRE
GRAND DUCHY OF WARSAW
PRUSSIA
KINGDOM OF SWEDEN
KINGDOM OF NORWAY AND DENMARK
GREAT BRITAIN
SCOTLAND
IRELAND
ENGLAND
FRANCE
SPAIN
PORTUGAL
CONFEDERATION OF THE RHINE
KINGDOM OF ITALY
KINGDOM OF NAPLES
KINGDOM OF SICILY
WESTPHALIA
SAXONY
BAVARIA
WÜRTTEMBERG
BADEN
SWITZERLAND
ILLYRIAN PROVINCES

Moscow
•Borodino 1812
St. Petersburg
•Smolensk
Kiev•
Tilsit
Friedland 1807
Königsberg
Warsaw•
Danzig•
Stockholm•
Copenhagen•
Lübeck•
Hamburg•
Bremen•
Berlin•
Auerstädt 1806
Jena 1806
Leipzig 1813
Austerlitz 1805
Pressburg•
Pest•
Buda•
Wagram 1809
Vienna•
Constantinople•
Athens•
Crete
Cyprus
IONIAN IS. (Gr. Br.)
MALTA (Gr. Br.)
Naples•
Rome•
Milan•
Genoa•
Marengo 1800
Elba
Corsica
SARDINIA
Zürich•
Lunéville•
Paris•
Amiens•
Brussels•
Waterloo 1815
Antwerp•
Marseilles•
London•
HELGOLAND (Gr. Br.)
Lisbon•
Madrid•
GIBRALTAR (Gr. Br.)
Trafalgar 1805

Black Sea
Baltic Sea
North Sea
ATLANTIC OCEAN
Mediterranean Sea

Dnieper
Dniester
Danube
Vistula
Oder
Elbe
Rhine
Rhône
Loire
Seine
Thames
Tagus

0   150   300 Km.
0   150   300 Mi.

For several days in June 1807, the young tsar and the French emperor negotiated face to face on a raft anchored in the middle of the Niemen River. All the while, the helpless Frederick William III of Prussia rode back and forth on the shore anxiously awaiting the results. As the German poet Heinrich Heine said later, Napoleon had but to whistle and Prussia would have ceased to exist. In the subsequent treaties of Tilsit, Prussia lost half of its population, while Russia accepted Napoleon's reorganization of western and central Europe. Alexander also promised to enforce Napoleon's recently decreed economic blockade against British goods.

After the victory of Austerlitz and even more after the treaties of Tilsit, Napoleon saw himself as the emperor of Europe and not just of France. The so-called Grand Empire he built had three parts. The core, or first part, was an ever-expanding France, which by 1810 included Belgium, Holland, parts of northern Italy, and much German territory on the east bank of the Rhine. Beyond French borders Napoleon established the second part: a number of dependent satellite kingdoms, on the thrones of which he placed (and replaced) the members of his large family. The third part comprised the independent but allied states of Austria, Prussia, and Russia. Both satellites and allies were expected after 1806 to support Napoleon's continental system and cease trade with Britain.

The impact of the Grand Empire on the peoples of Europe was considerable. In the areas incorporated into France and in the satellites (Map 21.1), Napoleon introduced many French laws, abolishing feudal dues and serfdom where French revolutionary armies had not already done so. Some of the peasants and middle class benefited from these reforms. Yet while he extended progressive measures to his cosmopolitan empire, Napoleon had to put the prosperity and special interests of France first in order to safeguard his power base. Levying heavy taxes in money and men for his armies, Napoleon came to be regarded more as a conquering tyrant than as an enlightened liberator.

⁕ **MAP 21.1 Napoleonic Europe in 1810** Only Great Britain remained at war with Napoleon at the height of the Grand Empire. Many British goods were smuggled through Helgoland, a tiny but strategic British possession off the German coast.

The first great revolt occurred in Spain. In 1808 a coalition of Catholics, monarchists, and patriots rebelled against Napoleon's attempts to make Spain a French satellite with a Bonaparte as its king. French armies occupied Madrid, but the foes of Napoleon fled to the hills and waged uncompromising guerrilla warfare. Spain was a clear warning: resistance to French imperialism was growing.

Yet Napoleon pushed on, determined to hold his complex and far-flung empire together. In 1810 when the Grand Empire was at its height, Britain still remained at war with France, helping the guerrillas in Spain and Portugal. The continental system, organized to exclude British goods from the Continent and force that "nation of shopkeepers" to its knees, was a failure. Instead, it was France that suffered from Britain's counter-blockade, which created hard times for French artisans and the middle class. Perhaps looking for a scapegoat, Napoleon turned on Alexander I of Russia, who had been giving only lukewarm support to Napoleon's war of prohibitions against British goods.

Napoleon's invasion of Russia began in June 1812 with a force that eventually numbered 600,000, probably the largest force yet assembled in a single army. Only one-third of this force was French, however; nationals of all the satellites and allies were drafted into the operation. Originally planning to winter in the Russian city of Smolensk if Alexander did not sue for peace, Napoleon reached Smolensk and recklessly pressed on. The great battle of Borodino that followed was a draw, and the Russians retreated in good order. Alexander ordered the evacuation of Moscow, which then burned, and he refused to negotiate. Finally, after five weeks in the burned-out city, Napoleon ordered a retreat. That retreat was one of the great military disasters in history. The Russian army and the Russian winter cut Napoleon's army to pieces. Only 30,000 men returned to their homelands.

Leaving his troops to their fate, Napoleon raced to Paris to raise yet another army. Possibly he might still have saved his throne if he had been willing to accept a France reduced to its historical size—the proposal offered by Austria's foreign minister, Prince Klemens von Metternich. But Napoleon refused. Austria and Prussia deserted Napoleon and joined Russia and Great Britain in the Fourth Coalition. All across Europe patriots called for a "war of liberation" against Napoleon's oppression, and the well-disciplined regular armies of

THE NAPOLEONIC ERA

November 1799	Napoleon overthrows the Directory
December 1799	French voters overwhelmingly approve Napoleon's new constitution
1800	Napoleon founds the Bank of France
1801	France defeats Austria and acquires Italian and German territories in the Treaty of Lunéville Napoleon signs a concordat with the pope
1802	Treaty of Amiens with Britain
December 1804	Napoleon crowns himself emperor
October 1805	Battle of Trafalgar: Britain defeats the French and Spanish fleets
December 1805	Battle of Austerlitz: Napoleon defeats Austria and Prussia
1807	Treaties of Tilsit: Napoleon redraws the map of Europe
1810	Height of the Grand Empire
June 1812	Napoleon invades Russia with 600,000 men
Winter 1812	Disastrous retreat from Russia
March 1814	Russia, Prussia, Austria, and Britain form the Quadruple Alliance to defeat France
April 1814	Napoleon abdicates and is exiled to Elba
Feb.–June 1815	Napoleon escapes from Elba and rules France until suffering defeat at Battle of Waterloo

Napoleon's enemies closed in for the kill. This time the coalition held together, cemented by the Treaty of Chaumont, which created a Quadruple Alliance intended to last for twenty years. Less than a month later, on April 4, 1814, a defeated, abandoned Napoleon abdicated his throne. After this unconditional abdication, the victorious allies granted Napoleon the island of Elba off the coast of Italy as his own tiny state. Napoleon was even allowed to keep his imperial title, and France was required to pay him a large yearly income of 2 million francs.

The allies also agreed to the restoration of the Bourbon dynasty, in part because demonstrations led by a few dedicated French monarchists indicated some support among the French people for that course of action. The new monarch, Louis XVIII (r. 1814–1824), tried to consolidate that support by issuing the Constitutional Charter, which accepted many of France's revolutionary changes and guaranteed civil liberties. Indeed, the Charter gave France a constitutional monarchy roughly similar to that established in 1791, although far fewer people had the right to vote for representatives to the resurrected Chamber of Deputies. Moreover, in an attempt to strengthen popular support for Louis XVIII's new government, France was treated leniently by the allies, which agreed to meet in Vienna to work out a general peace settlement.

Yet Louis XVIII—old, ugly, and crippled by gout—totally lacked the glory and magic of Napo-

✤ **Goya: The Third of May, 1808** This great painting screams in outrage at the horrors of war, which Goya witnessed in Spain. Spanish rebels, focused around the Christ-like figure at the center, are gunned down by anonymous French soldiers, grim forerunners of modern death squads and their atrocities. (*Source: Museo del Prado, Madrid*)

leon. Hearing of political unrest in France and diplomatic tensions in Vienna, Napoleon staged a daring escape from Elba in February 1815. Landing in France, he issued appeals for support and marched on Paris with a small band of followers. French officers and soldiers who had fought so long for their emperor responded to the call. Louis XVIII fled, and once more Napoleon took command. But Napoleon's gamble was a desperate long shot, for the allies were united against him. At the end of a frantic period known as the Hundred Days, they crushed his forces at Waterloo on June 18, 1815, and imprisoned him on the rocky island of St. Helena, far off the western coast of Africa. Old Louis XVIII returned again—this time "in the baggage of the allies," as his detractors scornfully put it—and recommenced his reign. The allies now dealt more harshly with the apparently incorrigible French (see Chapter 22). And Napoleon, doomed to suffer crude insults at the hands of sadistic English jailers on distant St. Helena, could take revenge only by writing his memoirs, skillfully nurturing the myth that he had been Europe's revolutionary liberator, a romantic hero whose lofty work had been undone by oppressive reactionaries. An era had ended.

SUMMARY

The French Revolution left a compelling and many-sided political legacy. This legacy included, most notably, liberalism, assertive nationalism, radical democratic republicanism, embryonic socialism, and self-conscious conservatism. It also left a rich and turbulent history of electoral competition, legislative assemblies, and even mass politics. Thus the French Revolution and conflicting interpretations of its significance presented a whole range of political options and alternative visions of the future. For this reason it was truly the revolution in modern European politics.

The revolution that began in America and spread to France was a liberal revolution. Revolutionaries on both sides of the Atlantic wanted to establish civil liberties and equality before the law within the framework of representative government, and they succeeded. In France liberal nobles and an increasingly class-conscious middle class overwhelmed declining monarchial absolutism and feudal privilege, thanks to the intervention of the common people—the sans-culottes and the peasants. Featuring electoral competition and civil equality, the government established by the Declaration of the Rights of Man and the French constitution of 1791 was remarkably similar to that created in America by the federal Constitution and the Bill of Rights. France's new political system reflected a social structure based increasingly on wealth and achievement rather than on tradition and legal privileges.

After the establishment of the Republic, the radical phase of the revolution during the Terror, and the fall of Robespierre, the educated elites and the solid middle class reasserted themselves under the Directory. And though Napoleon sharply curtailed representative institutions and individual rights, he effectively promoted the reconciliation of old and new, of centralized bureaucracy and careers open to talent, of noble and bourgeois in a restructured property-owning elite. Louis XVIII had to accept the commanding position of this restructured elite, and in granting representative government and civil liberties to facilitate his restoration to the throne in 1814, he submitted to the rest of the liberal triumph of 1789 to 1791. The liberal core of the French Revolution had successfully survived a generation of war and dictatorship.

Revolution in France, as opposed to in the United States, also left a multiplicity of legacies that extended well beyond the triumphant liberalism of 1789. Indeed, the lived experience of the French Revolution and the wars that went with it exercised a pervasive influence on politics and the political imagination in the nineteenth century, not only in France but throughout Europe and even the rest of the world. First, there was the radical legacy of the embattled republic of 1793 and 1794, with its sans-culottes democratic republicanism and its egalitarian ideology and embryonic socialism. This legacy would inspire republicans, democrats, and early socialists. Second, there was the legacy of a powerful and continuing reaction to the French Revolution and to aggressive French nationalism. Monarchists and traditionalists now believed that 1789 had been a tragic mistake. They concluded that democratic republicanism and sans-culottes activism led only to war, class conflict, and savage dictatorship. And even though revolutionary upheaval encouraged generations of radicals to believe that political revolution might remake society and even create a new humanity, conservatives and many comfortable moderates were profoundly disillusioned by the revolutionary era. They looked with nostalgia toward the supposedly ordered world of benevolent monarchy, firm government, and respectful common people.

NOTES

1. Quoted in R. R. Palmer, *The Age of the Democratic Revolution,* vol. 1 (Princeton, N.J.: Princeton University Press, 1959), p. 239.

2. G. Lefebvre, *The Coming of the French Revolution* (New York: Vintage Books, 1947), p. 81.

3. P. H. Beik, ed., *The French Revolution* (New York: Walker, 1970), p. 89.

4. G. Pernoud and S. Flaisser, eds., *The French Revolution* (Greenwich, Conn.: Fawcett, 1960), p. 61.

5. O. Hufton, *Women and the Limits of Citizenship in the French Revolution* (Toronto: University of Toronto Press, 1992), pp. 3–22.

6. Quotations from Wollstonecraft are drawn from E. W. Sunstein, *A Different Face: The Life of Mary Wollstonecraft* (New York: Harper & Row, 1975), pp. 208, 211; and H. R . James, *Mary Wollstonecraft: A Sketch* (London: Oxford University Press, 1932), pp. 60, 62, 69.

7. L. Gershoy, *The Era of the French Revolution, 1789–1799* (New York: Van Nostrand, 1957), p. 150.

8.   Pernoud and Flaisser, pp. 193–194.
9.   Hufton, p. 130.

SUGGESTED READING

For fascinating eyewitness reports on the French Revolution, see the edited works by Beik and by Pernoud and Flaisser mentioned in the Notes. In addition, A. Young's *Travels in France During the Years 1787, 1788 and 1789* (1969) offers an engrossing contemporary description of France and Paris on the eve of revolution. E. Burke, *Reflections on the Revolution in France,* first published in 1790, is the classic conservative indictment. The intense passions the French Revolution has generated may be seen in nineteenth-century French historians, notably the enthusiastic J. Michelet, *History of the French Revolution;* the hostile H. Taine; and the judicious A. de Tocqueville, whose masterpiece, *The Old Regime and the French Revolution,* was first published in 1856. Important general studies on the entire period include the work of R. R. Palmer, cited in the Notes, which paints a comparative international picture; E. J. Hobsbawm, *The Age of Revolution, 1789–1848* (1962); C. Breunig, *The Age of Revolution and Reaction, 1789–1850* (1970); O. Connelly, *French Revolution—Napoleonic Era* (1979); and L. Dehio, *The Precarious Balance: Four Centuries of the European Power Struggle* (1962).

Recent years have seen a wealth of new scholarship and interpretation. A. Cobban, *The Social Interpretation of the French Revolution* (1964), and F. Furet, *Interpreting the French Revolution* (1981), are major reassessments of long-dominant ideas, which are admirably presented in N. Hampson, *A Social History of the French Revolution* (1963), and in the volume by Lefebvre listed in the Notes. E. Kennedy, *A Cultural History of the French Revolution* (1989), beautifully written and handsomely illustrated, and W. Doyle, *Origins of the French Revolution,* 3d ed. (1988), are excellent on long-term developments. Among recent studies, which generally are often quite critical of revolutionary developments, several are noteworthy: J. Bosher, *The French Revolution* (1988); S. Schama, *Citizens: A Chronicle of the French Revolution* (1989); W. Doyle, *The Oxford History of the French Revolution* (1989); and D. Sutherland, *France, 1789–1815: Revolution and Counterrevolution* (1986).

Two valuable anthologies concisely presenting a range of interpretations are F. Kafker and J. Laux, eds., *The French Revolutions: Conflicting Interpretations,* 4th ed. (1989), and G. Best, ed., *The Permanent Revolution: The French Revolution and Its Legacy, 1789–1989* (1988). G. Rude makes the men and women of the great days of upheaval come alive in his *The Crowd in the French Revolution* (1959), whereas R. R. Palmer studies sympathetically the leaders of the Terror in *Twelve Who Ruled* (1941). Four other particularly interesting, detailed works are D. Jordan, *The Revolutionary Career of Maximilien Robespierre* (1985); J. P. Bertaud, *The Army of the French Revolution: From Citizen-Soldier to Instrument of Power* (1988); C. L. R. James, *The Black Jacobins* (1938, 1980), on black slave revolt in Haiti; and J. C. Herold, *Mistress to an Age* (1955), on the remarkable Madame de Staël. Other signifcant studies on aspects of revolutionary France include P. Jones's pathbreaking *The Peasantry in the French Revolution* (1979); W. Sewell, Jr.'s imaginative *Work and Revolution in France: The Language of Labor from the Old Regime to 1848* (1980); and L. Hunt's innovative *Politics, Culture, and Class in the French Revolution* (1984).

An ongoing explosion of studies on women in the French Revolution is increasing knowledge and also raising conflicting interpretations. This may be seen be comparing two particularly important works: J. Landes, *Women and the Public Sphere in the Age of the French Revolution* (1988), and O. Hufton, listed in the Notes. D. Outram, *The Body and the French Revolution: Sex, Class and Political Culture* (1989), and L. Hunt, *The Family Romance of the French Revolution* (1992), provide innovative analyses of the gender-related aspects of revolutionary politics and are highly recommended. D. Levy, H. Applewhite, and M. Johnson, eds., *Women in Revolutionary Paris, 1789–1795* (1979), is a valuable collection of contemporary documents with helpful commentaries. Mary Wollstonecraft's dramatic life is the subject of several good biographies, including those by Sunstein and James cited in the Notes.

Two important works placing political developments in a comparative perspective are P. Higonnet, *Sister Republics: The Origins of French and American Republicanism* (1988), and E. Morgan, *Inventing the People: The Rise of Popular Sovereignty in England and America* (1988). B. Bailyn, *The Ideological Origins of the American Revolution* (1967), is also noteworthy.

The best synthesis on Napoleonic France is L. Bergeron, *France Under Napoleon* (1981). P. Geyl, *Napoleon: For and Against* (1949), is a delightful discussion of changing political interpretations of Napoleon, which may be compared with a more recent treatment by R. Jones, *Napoleon: Man and Myth* (1977). Good biographies are J. Thompson, *Napoleon Bonaparte: His Rise and Fall* (1952); F. Markham, *Napoleon* (1964); and V. Cronin, *Napoleon Bonaparte* (1972). Wonderful novels inspired by the period include Raphael Sabatini's *Scaramouche,* a swashbuckler of revolutionary intrigue with accurate historical details; Charles Dickens's fanciful *Tale of Two Cities;* and Leo Tolstoy's monumental saga of Napoleon's invasion of Russia (and much more), *War and Peace.*

Revolution and Women's Rights

The 1789 Declaration of the Rights of Man was a revolutionary call for legal equality, representative government, and individual freedom. But the new rights were strictly limited to men; Napoleon tightened further the subordination of French women.

Among those who saw the contradiction in granting supposedly universal rights to only half the population was Marie Gouze (1748–1793), known to history as Olympe de Gouges. The daughter of a provincial butcher and peddler, she pursued a literary career in Paris after the death of her husband. Between 1790 and 1793 she wrote more than two dozen political pamphlets under her new name. De Gouges's great work was her "Declaration of the Rights of Women" (1791). Excerpted here, de Gouges's manifesto went beyond the 1789 Rights of Man. It called on males to end their oppression of women and give women equal rights. A radical on women's issues, de Gouges sympathized with the monarchy and criticized Robespierre in print. Convicted of sedition, she was guillotined in November 1793.

. . . Man, are you capable of being just? . . . Tell me, what gives you sovereign empire to oppress my sex? Your strength? Your talents? Observe the Creator in his wisdom . . . and give me, if you dare, an example of this tyrannical empire. Go back to animals, consult the elements, study plants . . . and distinguish, if you can, the sexes in the administration of nature. Everywhere you will find them mingled; everywhere they cooperate in harmonious togetherness in this immortal masterpiece.

Man alone has raised his exceptional circumstances to a principle. . . . he wants to command as a despot a sex which is in full possession of its intellectual faculties; he pretends to enjoy the Revolution and to claim his rights to equality in order to say nothing more about it.

DECLARATION OF THE RIGHTS OF WOMAN AND THE FEMALE CITIZEN

For the National Assembly to decree in its last sessions, or in those of the next legislature:

Preamble

Mothers, daughters, sisters and representatives of the nation demand to be constituted into a national assembly. Believing that ignorance, omission, or scorn for the rights of woman are the only causes of public misfortunes and of the corruption of governments, [the women] have resolved to set forth in a solemn declaration the natural, inalienable, and sacred rights of woman. . . .

. . . the sex that is as superior in beauty as it is in courage during the sufferings of maternity recognizes and declares in the presence and under the auspices of the Supreme Being, the following Rights of Woman and of Female Citizens:

I. Woman is born free and lives equal to man in her rights. Social distinctions can be based only on the common utility.

II. The purpose of any political association is the conservation of the natural and imprescriptible rights of woman and man; these rights are liberty, property, security, and especially resistance to oppression.

III. The principle of all sovereignty rests essentially with the nation, which is nothing but the union of woman and man. . . .

IV. Liberty and justice consist of restoring all that belongs to others; thus, the only limits on the exercise of the natural rights of woman are perpetual male tyranny; these limits are to be reformed by the laws of nature and reason.

V. Laws of nature and reason proscribe all acts harmful to society. . . .

VI. The law must be the expression of the general will; all female and male citizens must representations to its formation; it must be the same for all: male and female citizens, being equal in the eyes of the law, must be equally admitted to all honors, positions, and public employment according to their capacity and without other ·distinctions besides those of their virtues and talents.

VII. No woman is an exception; she is accused, arrested, and detained in cases determined by law. Women, like men, obey this rigorous law.

VIII. The law must establish only those penalties that are strictly and obviously necessary. . . .

IX. Once any woman is declared guilty, complete rigor is [to be] exercised by the law.

X. No one is to be disquieted for his very basic opinions; woman has the right to mount the scaffold; she must equally have the right to mount the rostrum, provided that her demonstrations do not disturb the legally established public order.

XI. The free communication of thoughts and opinions is one of the most precious rights of woman, since that liberty assures the recognition of children by their fathers. Any female citizen thus may say freely, I am the mother of a child which belongs to you, without being forced by a barbarous prejudice to hide the truth. . . .

XIII. For the support of the public force and the expenses of administration, the contributions of woman and man are equal; she shares all the duties . . . and all the painful tasks; therefore, she must have the same share in the distribution of positions, employment, offices, honors, and jobs. . . .

XIV. Female and male citizens have the right to verify, either by themselves or through their representatives, the necessity of the public contribution. This can only apply to women if they are granted an equal share, not only of wealth, but also of public administration. . . .

XV. The collectivity of women, joined for tax purposes to the aggregate of men, has the right to demand an accounting of his administration from any public agent.

XVI. No society has a constitution without the guarantee of rights and the separation of powers; the constitution is null if the majority of individuals comprising the nation have not cooperated in drafting it.

XVII. Property belongs to both sexes whether united or separate; for each it is an inviolable and sacred right. . . .

Postscript

⚜ Late 18th-century French painting, *La Liberté*. (Source: Bibliothèque Nationale/Giraudon/Art Resource, NY)

Women, wake up. . . . Discover your rights. . . . Oh, women, women! When will you cease to be blind? What advantage have you received from the Revolution? A more pronounced scorn, a more marked disdain. . . . [If men persist in contradicting their revolutionary principles,] courageously oppose the force of reason to the empty pretensions of superiority . . . and you will soon see these haughty men, not groveling at your feet as servile adorers, but proud to share with you the treasure of the Supreme Being. Regardless of what barriers confront you; it is in your power to free yourselves; you have only to want to. . . .

Questions for Analysis

1. On what basis did de Gouges argue for gender equality? Did she believe in natural law?

2. What consequences did "scorn for the rights of women" have for France, according to de Gouges?

3. Did de Gouges stress political rights at the expense of social and economic rights? If so, why?

Source: Olympe de Gouges, "Declaration of the Rights of Woman" in Darline G. Levy, Harriet B. Applewhite, and Mary D. Johnson, eds., *Women in Revolutionary Paris, 1789–1795* (Urbana, University of Illinois Preess, 1979), pp. 87–96. Copyright © 1979 by the Board of Trustees, University of Illinois. Used with permission.

22

The Revolution in Energy and Industry

A colored engraving by J. C. Bourne of the Great Western Railway emerging from a tunnel. *(Source: Science and Picture Library, London)*

While the revolution in France was opening a new political era, another revolution was beginning to transform economic and social life. This was the Industrial Revolution, which began in England around the 1780s and started to influence continental Europe after 1815. Because the Industrial Revolution was less dramatic than the French Revolution, some historians see industrial development as basically moderate and evolutionary. But from a longer perspective, it was rapid and brought about radical changes. Perhaps only the development of agriculture during Neolithic times had a similar impact and significance.

The Industrial Revolution profoundly modified much of human experience. It changed patterns of work, transformed the social class structure and the way people thought about class, and eventually even altered the international balance of political power. The Industrial Revolution also helped ordinary people gain a higher standard of living as the widespread poverty of the preindustrial world was gradually reduced.

Unfortunately, the improvement in the European standard of living was quite limited until about 1850 for at least two reasons. First, even in England only a few key industries experienced a technological revolution. Many more industries continued to use old methods, especially on the Continent, and this held down the increase in total production. Second, the increase in total population, which began in the eighteenth century (see page 000), continued all across Europe as the era of the Industrial Revolution unfolded. As a result, the rapid growth in population threatened to eat up the growth in production and to leave individuals poorer than ever. Thus rapid population growth formed a somber background for European industrialization and made the wrenching transformation more difficult.

- What, then, was the Industrial Revolution?
- What were its origins, and how did it develop?
- How did the changes it brought affect people and society in an era of continued rapid population growth?

These are the questions this chapter will seek to answer.

THE INDUSTRIAL REVOLUTION IN ENGLAND

The Industrial Revolution began in England. It was something new in history, and it was quite unplanned. With no models to copy and no idea of what to expect, England had to pioneer not only in industrial technology but also in social relations

❖ **MAP 22.1 Cottage Industry and Transportation in Eighteenth-Century England** England had an unusually good system of navigable waterways even before river-linking canals made it better.

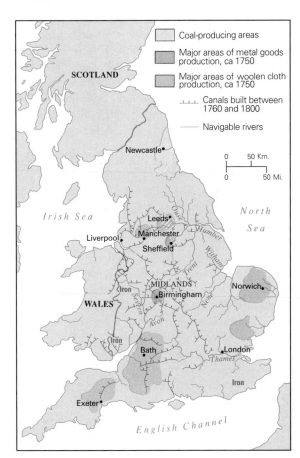

and urban living. Between 1793 and 1815, these formidable tasks were complicated by almost constant war with France. As the trailblazer in economic development, as France was in political change, England must command special attention.

Eighteenth-Century Origins

Although many aspects of the English Industrial Revolution are still matters for scholarly debate, it is generally agreed that the industrial changes that did occur grew out of a long process of development. First, the expanding Atlantic economy of the eighteenth century served mercantilist England remarkably well. The colonial empire that England aggressively built, augmented by a strong position in Latin America and in the African slave trade, provided a growing market for English manufactured goods. So did England itself. In an age when it was much cheaper to ship goods by water than by land, no part of England was more than 20 miles from navigable water. Beginning in the 1770s, a canal-building boom greatly enhanced this natural advantage (Map 22.1). Rivers and canals provided easy movement of England's enormous deposits of iron and coal, resources that would be critical raw materials in Europe's early industrial age. Nor were there any tariffs within the country to hinder trade, as there were in France before 1789 and in politically fragmented Germany.

Second, agriculture played a central role in bringing about the Industrial Revolution in England. English farmers were second only to the Dutch in productivity in 1700, and they were continually adopting new methods of farming as the century went on. The result, especially before 1760, was a period of bountiful crops and low food prices. The ordinary English family did not have to spend almost everything it earned just to buy bread. It could spend more on, for example, manufactured goods—leather shoes or a razor for the man, a bonnet or a shawl for the woman, toy soldiers for the son, and a doll for the daughter. Thus demand for goods within the country complemented the demand from the colonies.

Third, England had other assets that helped give rise to industrial leadership. Unlike eighteenth-century France, England had an effective central bank and well-developed credit markets. The monarchy and the aristocratic oligarchy, which had jointly ruled the country since 1688, provided stable and predictable government. At the same time, the government let the domestic economy operate with few controls, encouraging personal initiative, technical change, and a free market. Finally, England had long had a large class of hired agricultural laborers, rural proletarians whose numbers were further increased by the enclosure movement of the late eighteenth century. These rural wage earners were relatively mobile—compared to village-bound peasants in France and western Germany, for example—and along with cottage workers they formed a potential industrial labor force for capitalist entrepreneurs.

All these factors combined to initiate the Industrial Revolution, a term first coined by awed contemporaries in the 1830s to describe the burst of major inventions and technical changes they had witnessed in certain industries. This technical revolution went hand in hand with an impressive quickening in the annual rate of industrial growth in England. Whereas industry had grown at only 0.7 percent between 1700 and 1760 (before the Industrial Revolution), it grew at the much higher rate of 3 percent between 1801 and 1831 (when industrial transformation was in full swing).[1] The decisive quickening of growth probably came in the 1780s, after the American war for independence and just before the French Revolution.

Therefore, the great economic and political revolutions that shaped the modern world occurred almost simultaneously, though they began in different countries. The Industrial Revolution was, however, a longer process than the political upheavals. It was not complete in England until 1850, and it had no real impact on continental countries until after 1815.

The First Factories

The pressure to produce more goods for a growing market was directly related to the first decisive breakthrough of the Industrial Revolution—the creation of the world's first large factories in the English cotton textile industry. Technological innovations in the manufacture of cotton cloth led to a new system of production and social relationships. Since no other industry experienced such a rapid or complete transformation before 1830, these trailblazing developments deserve special consideration.

Although the putting-out system of merchant capitalism (see pages 636–638) was expanding all

Hargreave's Spinning Jenny The loose cotton strands on the slanted bobbins passed up to the sliding carriage and then on to the spindles in back for fine spinning. The worker, almost always a woman, regulated the sliding carriage with one hand and with the other she turned the crank on the wheel to supply power. By 1783 one woman could spin by hand a hundred threads at a time on an improved model. *(Source: Science Museum, London/Michael Holford)*

across Europe in the eighteenth century, this pattern of rural industry was most fully developed in England. Under the pressure of growing demand, the system's limitations first began to outweigh its advantages. This was especially true in the textile industry after about 1760.

A constant shortage of thread in the textile industry focused attention on ways of improving spinning. Many a tinkering worker knew that a better spinning wheel promised rich rewards. It proved hard to spin the traditional raw materials—wool and flax—with improved machines, but cotton was different. Cotton textiles had first been imported into England from India by the East India Company, and by 1760 there was a tiny domestic industry in northern England. After many experiments over a generation, a gifted carpenter and jack-of-all-trades, James Hargreaves, invented his cotton-spinning jenny about 1765. At almost the same moment, a barber-turned-manufacturer named Richard Arkwright invented (or possibly pirated) another kind of spinning machine, the water frame. These breakthroughs produced an explosion in the infant cotton textile industry in the 1780s, when it was increasing the value of its output at an unprecedented rate of about 13 percent each year. By 1790 the new machines were producing ten times as much cotton yarn as had been made in 1770.

Hargreaves's jenny was simple and inexpensive. It was also hand operated. In early models, from six to twenty-four spindles were mounted on a sliding carriage, and each spindle spun a fine, slender thread. The woman moved the carriage back and forth with one hand and turned a wheel to supply power with the other. Now it was the male weaver who could not keep up with the vastly more efficient female spinner.

Arkwright's water frame employed a different principle. It quickly acquired a capacity of several hundred spindles and demanded much more power—waterpower. The water frame thus required large specialized mills, factories that employed as many as one thousand workers from the very beginning. The water frame could spin only coarse, strong thread, which was then put out for respinning on hand-powered cottage jennies. Around 1790 an alternative technique invented by Samuel Crompton also began to require more power than the human arm could supply. After that time, all cotton spinning was gradually concentrated in factories.

The first consequences of these revolutionary developments were more beneficial than is generally believed. Cotton goods became much cheaper, and they were bought and treasured by all classes. In the past, only the wealthy could afford the comfort and cleanliness of underwear, which was called "body linen" because it was made from expensive linen cloth. Now millions of poor people, who had earlier worn nothing underneath their coarse, filthy outer garments, could afford to wear cotton slips and underpants as well as cotton dresses and shirts.

Families using cotton in cottage industry were freed from their constant search for adequate yarn from scattered, part-time spinners since all the thread needed could be spun in the cottage on the jenny or obtained from a nearby factory. The wages of weavers, now hard pressed to keep up with the spinners, rose markedly until about 1792. Weavers were among the best-paid workers in England. They were known to walk proudly through the streets with 5-pound notes stuck in their hatbands, and they dressed like the middle class.

One result of this unprecedented prosperity was that large numbers of agricultural laborers became handloom weavers. The growth of handloom cotton weaving was an outstanding example of how breakthroughs in factory production normally stimulated complementary increases in handicraft output. It was also an example of how further mechanization threatened certain groups of handicraft workers, for mechanics and capitalists soon sought to invent a power loom to save on labor costs. This Edmund Cartwright achieved in 1785. But the power looms of the factories worked poorly at first, and handloom weavers continued to receive good wages until at least 1800.

Working conditions in the early factories were less satisfactory than those of cottage weavers and spinners. But until the late 1780s, most English factories were in rural areas, where they had access to waterpower. These factories employed a relatively small percentage of all cotton textile workers. People were reluctant to work in them, partly because they resembled the poorhouses where destitute inmates had to labor for very little pay. Therefore, factory owners turned to young children as a source of labor. More precisely, they turned to children who had been abandoned by their parents and put in the care of local parishes. Parish officers often "apprenticed" such unfortunate orphans to factory owners. The parish thus saved money, and the factory owners gained workers over whom they exercised almost the authority of slaveowners.

Apprenticed as young as five or six years of age, boy and girl workers were forced by law to labor for their "master" for as many as fourteen years. Housed, fed, and locked up nightly in factory dormitories, the young workers received little or no pay. Hours were appalling—commonly thirteen or fourteen hours a day, six days a week. Harsh physical punishment maintained brutal discipline. To be sure, poor children typically worked long hours from an early age in the eighteenth century and frequently outside the home for a brutal master. But the wholesale coercion of orphans as factory apprentices constituted exploitation on a truly unprecedented scale. This exploitation ultimately piqued the conscience of reformers and reinforced humanitarian attitudes toward children and their labor in the early nineteenth century.

The creation of the world's first modern factories in the English cotton textile industry in the 1770s and 1780s, which grew out of the putting-out system of cottage production, was a major historical development. Both symbolically and substantially, the big new cotton mills marked the beginning of the Industrial Revolution in England. By 1831 the largely mechanized cotton textile industry towered above all others, accounting for fully 22 percent of the country's entire industrial production.

The Problem of Energy

The growth of the cotton textile industry might have been stunted or cut short, however, if water from rivers and streams had remained the primary source of power for the new factories. But this did not occur. Instead, an epoch-making solution was found to the age-old problem of energy and power. It was this solution to the energy problem (a problem that reappeared in recent times) that permitted continued rapid development in cotton textiles, the gradual generalization of the factory system, and the triumph of the Industrial Revolution in England and Scotland.

Human beings, like all living organisms, require energy. Adult men and women need 2,000 to 4,000 calories (units of energy) daily simply to fuel their bodies, work, and survive. Energy comes from a variety of sources; energy also takes different forms, and one form may be converted into another. Plants have been converting solar energy into caloric matter for eons. And human beings have used their toolmaking abilities to construct machines that convert one form of energy into another for their own benefit.

Prehistoric people relied on plants and plant-eating animals as their sources of energy. With the development of agriculture, early civilizations were able to increase the number of useful plants and thus the supply of energy. Some plants could be fed to domesticated animals, such as the horse. Stronger than human beings, these animals converted the energy in the plants into work.

In the medieval period, people began to develop water mills to grind their grain and windmills to pump water and drain swamps. More efficient use of water and wind in the sixteenth and seventeenth centuries enabled human beings to accomplish more; intercontinental sailing ships were a prime example. Nevertheless, even into the eighteenth century, society continued to rely for energy mainly on plants, and human beings and animals continued to perform most work. This dependence meant that Western civilization remained poor in energy and power.

Lack of power lay at the heart of the poverty that afflicted the large majority of people. The man behind the plow and the woman at the spinning wheel could employ only horsepower and human muscle in their labor. No matter how hard they worked, they could not produce very much. What people needed were new sources of energy and more power at their disposal. Then they would be able to work more efficiently, produce more, and live better.

Where was more energy to be found? Almost all energy came directly or indirectly from plants and therefore from the land: grain for people, hay for animals, and wood for heat. The land was also the principal source of raw materials needed for industrial production: wool and flax for clothing, leather for shoes, wood for housing, tools, and ironmaking. And though swamps could be drained and marshes reclaimed from the sea, it was difficult to expand greatly the amount of land available. True, its yield could be increased, as by the elimination of fallow; nonetheless, there were definite limits to such improvements.

The shortage of energy had become particularly severe in England by the eighteenth century. Because of the growth of population, most of the great forests of medieval England had long ago been replaced by fields of grain and hay. Wood was in ever-shorter supply. Yet it remained tremendously important: it was the primary source of heat for all homes and industries and the key to transportation since ships and wagons were made of wood. Moreover, wood was, along with iron ore, the basic raw material of the iron industry. Processed wood (charcoal) was the fuel that was mixed with iron ore in the blast furnace to produce pig iron. The iron industry's appetite for wood was enormous, and even very modest and constant levels of iron production had gone far toward laying bare the forests of England as well as parts of continental Europe. By 1740 the English iron industry was stagnating. Vast forests enabled Russia in the eighteenth century to become the world's leading producer of iron, much of which was exported to England. But Russia's potential for growth was limited, too, and in a few decades

Henry Cort developed the puddling furnace, which allowed pig iron to be refined in turn with coke. Strong, skilled ironworkers—the puddlers—"cooked" molten pig iron in a great vat, raking off globs of refined iron for further processing. Cort also developed heavy-duty, steam-powered rolling mills, which were capable of spewing out finished iron in every shape and form.

The economic consequence of these technical innovations was a great boom in the English iron industry. In 1740 annual British iron production was only 17,000 tons. With the spread of coke smelting and the first impact of Cort's inventions, production reached 68,000 tons in 1788, 125,000 tons in 1796, and 260,000 tons in 1806. In 1844 Britain produced 3 million tons of iron. This was a truly amazing expansion. Once scarce and expensive, iron became the cheap, basic, indispensable building block of the economy.

The Coming of the Railroads

Sailing ships had improved noticeably since the Age of Discovery, and the second half of the eighteenth century saw extensive construction of hard and relatively smooth roads, particularly in France before the Revolution. Yet it was passenger traffic that benefited most from this construction. Overland shipment of freight, relying solely on horsepower, was still quite limited and frightfully expensive; shippers used rivers and canals for heavy freight whenever possible. It was logical, therefore, that inventors would try to use steampower.

As early as 1800, an American ran a "steamer on wheels" through city streets. Other experiments followed. In the 1820s, English engineers created steam cars capable of carrying fourteen passengers at 10 miles an hour—as fast as the mail coach. But the noisy, heavy steam automobiles frightened passing horses and damaged themselves as well as the roads with their vibrations. For the rest of the century, horses continued to reign on highways and city streets.

The coal industry had long been using plank roads and rails to move coal wagons within mines and at the surface. Rails reduced friction and allowed a horse or a human being to pull a heavier load. Thus once a rail capable of supporting a heavy locomotive was developed in 1816, all sorts of experiments with steam engines on rails went forward. In 1825 after ten years of work, George Stephenson built an effective locomotive. In 1830

his *Rocket* sped down the track of the just-completed Liverpool and Manchester Railway at 16 miles per hour. This was the world's first important railroad, fittingly steaming in the heart of industrial England.

The line from Liverpool to Manchester was a financial as well as a technical success, and many private companies were quickly organized to build more rail lines. These companies had to get permission for their projects from Parliament and pay for the rights of way they needed; otherwise, their freedom was great. Within twenty years, they had completed the main trunk lines of Great Britain. Other countries were quick to follow.

The significance of the railroad was tremendous. The railroad dramatically reduced the cost and uncertainty of shipping freight overland. This advance had many economic consequences. Previously, markets had tended to be small and local; as the barrier of high transportation costs was lowered, they became larger and even nationwide. Larger markets encouraged larger factories with more sophisticated machinery in a growing number of industries. Such factories could make goods more cheaply and gradually subjected most cottage workers and many urban artisans to severe competitive pressures.

In all countries, the construction of railroads contributed to the growth of a class of urban workers. Cottage workers, farm laborers, and small peasants did not generally leave their jobs and homes to go directly to work in factories. However, the building of railroads created a strong demand for labor, especially unskilled labor, throughout a country. Hard work on construction gangs was done in the open air with animals and hand tools. Many landless farm laborers and poor peasants, long accustomed to leaving their villages for temporary employment, went to build railroads. By the time the work was finished, life back home in the village often seemed dull and unappealing, and many men drifted to towns in search of work—with the railroad companies, in construction, in factories. By the time they sent for their wives and sweethearts to join them, they had become urban workers.

The railroad changed the outlook and values of the entire society. The last and culminating invention of the Industrial Revolution, the railroad dramatically revealed the power and increased the speed of the new age. Racing down a track at 16 miles per hour or, by 1850, at a phenomenal 50

❖ **Turner: Rain, Steam, and Speed: The Great Western Railway (1844)** This masterpiece, which conveys the excitement people felt about the new means of transportation, grew out of an unforgettable personal experience. While riding through a rainstorm, Turner stuck his head out of a train window and for ten minutes he watched the locomotive race along. The train on his canvas speeds across the bridge, a streak of motion in a landscape blurred by the rain. *(Source: National Gallery, London/Erich Lessing/Art Resource, NY)*

miles per hour was a new and awesome experience. As a noted French economist put it after a ride on the Liverpool and Manchester in 1833, "There are certain impressions that one cannot put into words!"

Some great painters, notably Joseph M. W. Turner (1775–1851) and Claude Monet (1840–1926), succeeded in expressing this sense of power and awe. So did the massive new train stations, the cathedrals of the industrial age. Leading railway engineers such as Isambard Kingdom Brunel and Thomas Brassey, whose tunnels pierced mountains and whose bridges spanned valleys, became public idols—the astronauts of their day. Everyday speech absorbed the images of railroading. After you got up a "full head of steam," you "highballed" along. And if you didn't "go off the track," you might "toot your own whistle." The railroad fired the imagination.

Industry and Population

In 1851 London was the site of a famous industrial fair. This Great Exposition was held in the newly built Crystal Palace, an architectural masterpiece made entirely of glass and iron, both of which were now cheap and abundant. For the millions who visited, one fact stood out: the little island of Britain—England, Wales, and Scotland—was the "workshop of the world." It alone produced two-thirds of the world's coal and more than one-half of its iron and cotton cloth. More generally, it has been carefully estimated that in 1860 Britain produced a truly remarkable 20 percent of the entire world's output of industrial goods, whereas it had produced only about 2 percent of the world total in 1750.[2] Experiencing revolutionary industrial change, Britain became the first industrial nation (Map 22.2).

✦ **The Crystal Palace** The Great Exhibition of 1851 attracted more than six million visitors, many of whom journeyed to London on the newly built railroads. Companies and countries displayed their products and juries awarded prizes in the strikingly modern Crystal Palace. Are today's malls really different? *(Source: Courtesy of the Trustees of the British Museum)*

As the British economy significantly increased its production of manufactured goods, the gross national product (GNP) rose roughly fourfold at constant prices between 1780 and 1851. In other words, the British people as a whole increased their wealth and their national income dramatically. At the same time, the population of Great Britain boomed, growing from about nine million in 1780 to almost twenty-one million in 1851. Thus growing numbers consumed much of the increase in total production. According to one recent study, average consumption per person increased by only 75 percent between 1780 and 1851, as the growth in the total population ate up a large part of the fourfold increase in GNP in those years.[3]

Although the question is still debated, many economic historians now believe that rapid population growth in Great Britain was not harmful because it facilitated industrial expansion. More people meant a more mobile labor force, with a wealth of young workers in need of employment and ready to go where the jobs were. Contemporaries were much less optimistic. In his famous and influential *Essay on the Principle of Population* (1798), Thomas Malthus (1766–1834) argued that population would always tend to grow faster than the food supply. In Malthus's opinion, the only hope of warding off such "positive checks" to population growth as war, famine, and disease was "prudential restraint." That is, young men and women had to limit the growth of population by the old tried-and-true means of marrying late in life. But Malthus was not optimistic about this possibility. The powerful attraction of the sexes would cause most people to marry early and have many children.

Wealthy English stockbroker and leading economist David Ricardo (1772–1823) coldly spelled out the pessimistic implications of Malthus's thought. Ricardo's depressing "iron law of wages" posited that because of the pressure of population growth, wages would always sink to subsistence level. That is, wages would be just high enough to keep workers from starving. With Malthus and Ricardo setting the tone, economics was soon dubbed "the dismal science."

Malthus, Ricardo, and their many followers were proved wrong—in the long run. However, as the great economist Keynes quipped during the Great Depression of the 1930s, "we are all dead in the long run." Those who lived through the Industrial Revolution could not see the long run in advance. As modern quantitative studies show, until the 1820s, or even the 1840s, contemporary observers might reasonably have concluded that the economy and the total population were racing neck and neck, with the outcome very much in doubt. The closeness of the race added to the difficulties inherent in the unprecedented journey toward industrial civilization.

There was another problem as well. Perhaps workers, farmers, and ordinary people did not get their rightful share of the new wealth. Perhaps only the rich got richer, while the poor got poorer or made no progress. We will turn to this great issue after looking at the process of industrialization in continental countries in the nineteenth century.

✠ INDUSTRIALIZATION IN CONTINENTAL EUROPE

The new technologies developed in the British Industrial Revolution were adopted rather slowly by businesses in continental Europe. Yet by the end of the nineteenth century, several European countries as well as the United States had also industrialized their economies to a considerable but variable degree. This meant that the process of Western industrialization proceeded gradually, with uneven jerks and national (and regional) variations.

Scholars are still struggling to explain these variations, especially since good answers may offer valuable lessons in our own time for poor countries seeking to improve their material condition through industrialization and economic development. The latest findings on the Western experience are encouraging. They suggest that there were alternative paths to the industrial world in the nineteenth century and that, today as then, there was no need to follow a rigid, predetermined British model.

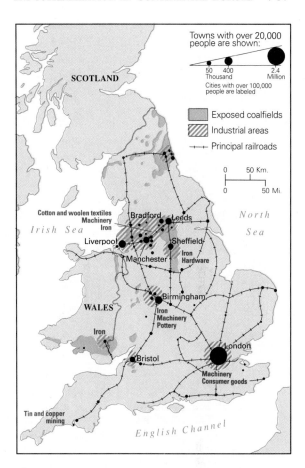

✤ **MAP 22.2 The Industrial Revolution in England, ca 1850** Industry concentrated in the rapidly growing cities of the north and the midlands, where rich coal and iron deposits were in close proximity.

National Variations

European industrialization, like most economic developments, requires some statistical analysis as part of the effort to understand it. Comparative data on industrial production in different countries over time help give us an overview of what happened. One set of data, the work of a Swiss scholar, compares the level of industrialization on a per capita basis in several countries from 1750 to 1913. These data are far from perfect because there are gaps in the underlying records. But they reflect basic trends and are presented in Table 22.1 for closer study.

As the heading of Table 22.1 makes clear, this is a per capita comparison of levels of industrialization—a comparison of how much industrial product was available, on average, to each person in a

TABLE 22.1 PER CAPITA LEVELS OF INDUSTRIALIZATION, 1750–1913

	1750	1800	1830	1860	1880	1900	1913
Great Britain	10	16	25	64	87	100	115
Belgium	9	10	14	28	43	56	88
United States	4	9	14	21	38	69	126
France	9	9	12	20	28	39	59
Germany	8	8	9	15	25	52	85
Austria-Hungary	7	7	8	11	15	23	32
Italy	8	8	8	10	12	17	26
Russia	6	6	7	8	10	15	20
China	8	6	6	4	4	3	3
India	7	6	6	3	2	1	2

Note: All entries are based on an index value of 100, equal to the per capita level of industrialization in Great Britain in 1900.

Source: P. Bairoch, "International Industrialization Levels from 1750 to 1980," *Journal of European Economic History* 11 (Fall 1982): 294. Data for Great Britain are actually for the United Kingdom, thereby including Ireland with England, Wales, and Scotland.

given country in a given year. Therefore, all the numbers in Table 22.1 are expressed in terms of a single index number of 100, which equals the per capita level of industrial goods in Great Britain (and Ireland) in 1900. Every number is thus a percentage of the 1900 level in Great Britain and is directly comparable. The countries are listed in roughly the order that they began to use large-scale, power-driven technology.

What does this overview of European industrialization tell us? First, and very significantly, one sees that in 1750 all countries were fairly close together and that Britain was only slightly ahead of its archenemy, France. Second, Britain had opened up a noticeable lead over all continental countries by 1800, and that gap progressively widened as the British Industrial Revolution accelerated to 1830 and reached full maturity by 1860. The British level of per capita industrialization was twice the French level in 1830, for example, and

more than three times the French level in 1860. All other large countries (except the United States) had fallen even further behind Britain than France had at both dates. Sophisticated quantitative history confirms the primacy and relative rapidity of Britain's Industrial Revolution.

Third, variations in the timing and in the extent of industrialization in the continental powers and the United States are also apparent. Belgium, independent in 1831 and rich in iron and coal, led in adopting Britain's new technology. France developed factory production more gradually, and most historians now detect no burst in French mechanization and no acceleration in the growth of overall industrial output that may accurately be called revolutionary. They stress instead France's relatively good pattern of early industrial growth, which was unjustly tarnished by the spectacular rise of Germany and the United States after 1860. By 1913 Germany was rapidly closing in on Britain, while the United States had already passed the first industrial nation in per capita production.

Finally, all European states (as well as the United States, Canada, and Japan) managed to raise per capita industrial levels in the nineteenth century. These continentwide increases stood in stark contrast to the large and tragic decreases that occurred at the same time in most non-Western countries, most notably in China and India. European countries industrialized to a greater or lesser extent even as most of the non-Western world de-industrialized. Thus differential rates of wealth- and power-creating industrial development, which heightened disparities within Europe, also greatly magnified existing inequalities between Europe and the rest of the world. We shall return to this momentous change in Chapter 26.

The Challenge of Industrialization

The different patterns of industrial development suggest that the process of industrialization was far from automatic. Indeed, building modern industry was an awesome challenge. To be sure, throughout Europe the eighteenth century was an era of agricultural improvement, population increase, expanding foreign trade, and growing cottage industry. England led in these developments, but other countries participated in the general trend. Thus when the pace of English industry began to accelerate in the 1780s, continental businesses began to adopt the new methods as they proved their profitability. English industry enjoyed clear superiority, but at first the Continent was close behind.

By 1815, however, the situation was quite different. In spite of wartime difficulties, English industry maintained the momentum of the 1780s and continued to grow and improve between 1789 and 1815. On the Continent, the unending political and economic upheavals that began with the French Revolution had another effect: they disrupted trade, created runaway inflation, and fostered social anxiety. War severed normal communications between England and the Continent, severely handicapping continental efforts to use new British machinery and technology. Moreover, the years from 1789 to 1815 were, even for the privileged French economy, a time of "national catastrophe"—in the graphic words of a leading French scholar.[4] Thus whatever the French Revolution and the Napoleonic era meant politically, economically and industrially they meant that France and the rest of Europe were further behind Britain in 1815 than in 1789.

This widening gap made it more difficult, if not impossible, for other countries to follow the British pattern in energy and industry after peace was restored in 1815. Above all, in the newly mechanized industries British goods were being produced very economically, and these goods had come to dominate world markets completely while the continental states were absorbed in war between 1792 and 1815. Continental firms had little hope of competing with mass-produced British goods in foreign markets for a long time. In addition, British technology had become so advanced and complicated that very few engineers or skilled technicians outside England understood it. Moreover, the technology of steampower had grown much more expensive. It involved large investments in the iron and coal industries and, after 1830, required the existence of railroads, which were very costly. Continental business people had great difficulty finding the large sums of money the new methods demanded, and there was a shortage of laborers accustomed to working in factories. Landowners and government officials were often so suspicious of the new form of industry and the changes it brought that they did little at first to encourage it. All these disadvantages slowed the spread of modern industry (Map 22.3).

After 1815, however, when continental countries began to face up to the British challenge, they had at least three important advantages. First, most continental countries had a rich tradition of putting-out enterprise, merchant capitalists, and skilled urban artisans. Such a tradition gave continental firms the ability to adapt and survive in the face of new market conditions. Second, continental capitalists did not need to develop, ever so slowly and expensively, their own advanced technology. Instead, they could simply "borrow" the new methods developed in Great Britain as well as engineers and some of the financial resources these countries lacked. European countries such as France and Russia also had a third asset that many non-Western areas lacked in the nineteenth century. They had strong independent governments, which did not fall under foreign political control. These governments could fashion economic policies to serve their own interests, as they proceeded to do. They would eventually use the power of the state to promote the growth of industry and catch up with Britain.

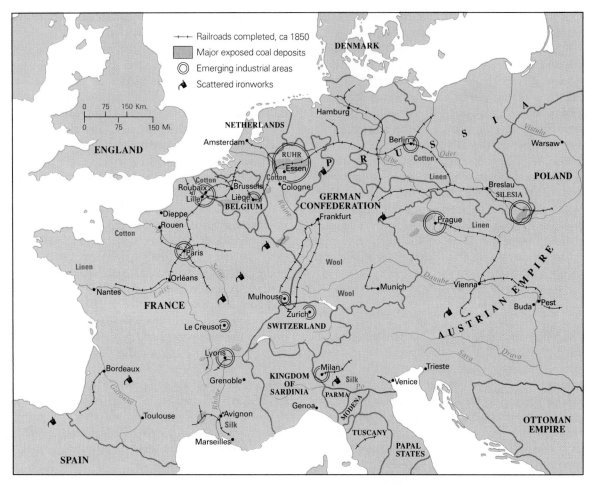

❖ **MAP 22.3 Continental Industrialization, ca 1850** Although continental countries were beginning to make progress by 1850, they still lagged far behind England. For example, continental railroad building was still in an early stage, whereas the English rail system was essentially complete.

Agents of Industrialization

The British realized the great value of their technical discoveries and tried to keep their secrets to themselves. Until 1825 it was illegal for artisans and skilled mechanics to leave Britain; until 1843 the export of textile machinery and other equipment was forbidden. Many talented, ambitious workers, however, slipped out of the country illegally and introduced the new methods abroad.

One such man was William Cockerill, a Lancashire carpenter. He and his sons began building cotton-spinning equipment in French-occupied Belgium in 1799. In 1817 the most famous son, John Cockerill, purchased the old summer palace of the deposed bishops of Liège in southern Belgium. Cockerill converted the palace into a large

industrial enterprise, which produced machinery, steam engines, and then railway locomotives. He also established modern ironworks and coal mines.

Cockerill's plants in the Liège area became an industrial nerve center, continually gathering new information and transmitting it across Europe. Many skilled British workers came illegally to work for Cockerill, and some went on to found their own companies throughout Europe. Newcomers brought the latest plans and secrets, so Cockerill could boast that ten days after an industrial advance occurred in Britain, he knew all about it in Belgium. Thus British technicians and skilled workers were a powerful force in the spread of early industrialization.

A second agent of industrialization were talented entrepreneurs such as Fritz Harkort, a business pioneer in the German machinery industry. Serving in England as a Prussian army officer during the Napoleonic wars, Harkort was impressed and enchanted with what he saw. He concluded that Germany had to match all these English achievements as quickly as possible. Setting up shop in an abandoned castle in the still-tranquil Ruhr Valley, Harkort felt an almost religious calling to build steam engines and become the "Watt of Germany."

Harkort's basic idea was simple, but it was enormously difficult to carry out. Lacking skilled laborers to do the job, Harkort turned to England for experienced, though expensive, mechanics. He could not be choosy, and he longed for the day when he could afford to replace the haughty foreigners with his fellow Germans. Getting materials also posed a great problem. He had to import the thick iron boilers that he needed from England at great cost. Moreover, German roads were so bad that steam engines had to be built at the works, completely dismantled and shipped piece by piece to the buyer, and then reassembled by Harkort's technicians. In spite of all these problems, Harkort built and sold engines, winning fame and praise. His ambitious efforts over sixteen years also resulted in large financial losses for himself and his partners, and in 1832 he was forced out of his company by his financial backers, who cut back

operations to reduce losses. His career illustrates both the great efforts of a few important business leaders to duplicate the British achievement and the difficulty of the task.

Entrepreneurs like Harkort were obviously exceptional. Most continental businesses adopted factory technology slowly, and handicraft methods lived on. Indeed, as recent research on France has shown, continental industrialization usually brought substantial but uneven expansion of handicraft industry in both rural and urban areas for a time. Artisan production of luxury items grew in France as the rising income of the international middle class created foreign demand for silk scarfs, embroidered needlework, perfumes, and fine wines.

A third force for industrialization was government, which often helped business people in continental countries to overcome some of their difficulties. Tariff protection was one such support. For example, after Napoleon's wars ended in 1815, France was suddenly flooded with cheaper and better English goods. The French government responded by laying high tariffs on many English imports in order to protect the French economy. After 1815 continental governments bore the cost of building roads and canals to improve transportation.

❖ **A Silesian Ironworks, 1841** This plant is using the new British method of smelting iron with coke. Silesia and the Ruhr region emerged as the main centers of German heavy industry in the nineteenth century, but that development was only beginning when this picture was painted. *(Source: Deutsches Museum Munich)*

They also bore to a significant extent the cost of building railroads. Belgium led the way in the 1830s and 1840s. In an effort to tie the newly independent nation together, the Belgian government decided to construct a state-owned system. Built rapidly as a unified network, Belgium's state-owned railroads stimulated the development of heavy industry and made the country an early industrial leader. Several of the smaller German states also built state systems.

The Prussian government provided another kind of invaluable support. It guaranteed that the state treasury would pay the interest and principal on railroad bonds if the closely regulated private companies in Prussia were unable to do so. Thus railroad investors in Prussia ran little risk and capital was quickly raised. In France the state shouldered all the expense of acquiring and laying roadbed, including bridges and tunnels. Finished roadbed was leased to a carefully supervised private company, which usually benefited from a state guarantee of its debts and which needed to provide only the rails, cars, and management. In short, governments helped pay for railroads, the all-important leading sector in continental industrialization.

The career of German journalist and thinker Friedrich List (1789–1846) reflects government's greater role in industrialization on the Continent than in England. List considered the growth of modern industry of the utmost importance because manufacturing was a primary means of increasing people's well-being and relieving their poverty. Moreover, List was a dedicated nationalist. He wrote that the "wider the gap between the backward and advanced nations becomes, the more dangerous it is to remain behind." For an agricultural nation was not only poor but also weak, increasingly unable to defend itself and maintain its political independence. To promote industry was to defend the nation.

The practical policies that List focused on in articles and in his influential *National System of Political Economy* (1841) were railroad building and the tariff. List supported the formation of a customs union, or *Zollverein*, among the separate German states. Such a tariff union came into being in 1834. It allowed goods to move between the German member states without tariffs, and a single uniform tariff was erected against all other nations. List wanted a high protective tariff, which would encourage infant industries, allowing them to develop and eventually hold their own against their more advanced British counterparts. List denounced the English doctrine of free trade as little more than England's attempt "to make the rest of the world, like the Hindus, its serfs in all industrial and commercial relations." By the 1840s List's economic nationalism had become increasingly popular in Germany and elsewhere.

Finally, banks, like governments, also played a larger and more creative role on the Continent than in England. Previously, almost all banks in Europe had been private, organized as secretive partnerships. All the active partners were liable for all the debts of the firm, which meant that in the event of a disastrous bankruptcy each partner could lose all of his or her personal wealth in addition to all the money invested in the partnership. Because of the possibility of unlimited financial loss, the partners of private banks tended to be quite conservative and were content to deal with a few rich clients and a few big merchants. They generally avoided industrial investment as being too risky.

In the 1830s two important Belgian banks pioneered in a new direction. They received permission from the growth-oriented government to establish themselves as corporations enjoying limited liability. That is, a stockholder could lose only his or her original investment in the bank's common stock and could not be assessed for any additional losses. Publicizing the risk-reducing advantage of limited liability, these Belgian banks were able to attract many shareholders, large and small. They mobilized impressive resources for investment in big industrial companies, became industrial banks, and successfully promoted industrial development.

Similar corporate banks became important in France and Germany in the 1850s and 1860s. Usually working in collaboration with governments, they established and developed many railroads and many companies working in heavy industry, which were increasingly organized as limited liability corporations. The most famous such bank was the Crédit Mobilier of Paris, founded by Isaac and Émile Pereire, two young Jewish journalists from Bordeaux. The Crédit Mobilier advertised extensively. It used the savings of thousands of small investors as well as the resources of big ones. The activities of the bank were far-reaching; it built railroads all over France and Europe. As Émile Pereire had said in 1835, "It is not enough to outline gigantic programs on paper. I must write my ideas on the earth."

 The Third-Class Carriage The French artist Honoré Daumier was fascinated by the railroad and its human significance. This great painting focuses on the peasant grandmother, absorbed in memories. The nursing mother represents love and creativity; the sleeping boy, innocence. *(Source: The Metropolitan Museum of Art. Bequest of Mrs. H. O. Havemeyer, 1929. The H. O. Havemeyer Collection (29.100.129))*

The combined efforts of skilled workers, entrepreneurs, governments, and industrial banks meshed successfully between 1850 and the financial crash of 1873. This was a period of unprecedentedly rapid economic growth on the Continent. In Belgium, Germany, and France, key indicators of modern industrial development—such as railway mileage, iron and coal production, and steam-engine capacity—increased at average annual rates of 5 to 10 percent compounded. As a result, rail networks were completed in western and much of central Europe and the leading continental countries mastered the industrial technologies that had first been developed in Great Britain. In the early 1870s, Britain was still Europe's most industrial nation, but a select handful of countries was clos-

ing the gap that had been opened up by the Industrial Revolution.

CAPITAL AND LABOR

Industrial development brought new social relations and intensified long-standing problems between capital and labor in both urban workshops and cottage industry (see pages 636–640). A new group of factory owners and industrial capitalists arose. These men and women and their families strengthened the wealth and size of the middle class, which had previously been made up mainly of merchants and professional people. The nineteenth century became the golden age of the middle class. Modern industry also created a much larger group, the factory workers. For the first time, large numbers of men, women, and children came together under one roof to work with complicated machinery for a single owner or a few partners in large companies.

The growth of new occupational groups in industry stimulated new thinking about social relations. Often combined with reflections on the French Revolution, this thinking led to the development of a new overarching interpretation—a new paradigm—regarding social relationships (see Chapter 23). Briefly, this paradigm argued, with considerable success, that individuals were members of economically determined classes, which had conflicting interests. Accordingly, the comfortable, well-educated "public" of the eighteenth century came increasingly to see itself as the backbone of the middle class (or the middle classes), and the "people" gradually transformed themselves into the modern working class (or working classes). And if the new class interpretation was more of a deceptive simplification than a fundamental truth for some critics, it appealed to many because it seemed to explain what was happening. Therefore, conflicting classes existed, in part, because many individuals came to believe they existed and developed an appropriate sense of class feeling—what Marxists call "class consciousness."

What, then, was the relationship between capital and labor in the early Industrial Revolution? Did the new industrial middle class ruthlessly exploit the workers, as Karl Marx and others have charged?

The New Class of Factory Owners

Early industrialists operated in a highly competitive economic system. As the careers of Watt and Harkort illustrate, there were countless production problems, and success and large profits were by no means certain. Manufacturers therefore waged a constant battle to cut their production costs and stay afloat. Much of the profit had to go back into the business for new and better machinery. "Dragged on by the frenzy of this terrible life," according to one of the dismayed critics, the struggling manufacturer had "no time for niceties. He must conquer or die, make a fortune or drown himself."[5]

The early industrialists came from a variety of backgrounds. Many, such as Harkort, were from well-established merchant families, which provided capital and contacts. Others, such as Watt and Cockerill, were of modest means, especially in the early days. Artisans and skilled workers of exceptional ability had unparalleled opportunities. The ethnic and religious groups that had been discriminated against in the traditional occupations controlled by the landed aristocracy jumped at the new chances. Quakers and Scots were tremendously important in England; Protestants and Jews dominated banking in Catholic France. Many of the industrialists were newly rich, and, not surprisingly, they were very proud and self-satisfied.

As factories grew larger, opportunities declined, at least in well-developed industries. It became considerably harder for a gifted but poor young mechanic to end up as a wealthy manufacturer. Formal education became more important as a means of advancement, and formal education at the advanced level was expensive. In England by 1830 and in France and Germany by 1860, leading industrialists were more likely to have inherited their well-established enterprises, and they were financially much more secure than their fathers and grandfathers had been. They also had a greater sense of class consciousness, fully aware that ongoing industrial development had widened the gap between themselves and their workers.

The New Factory Workers

The social consequences of the Industrial Revolution have long been hotly debated. The condition of English workers during the transformation has always generated the most controversy among historians because England was the first country to industrialize and because the social consequences seemed harshest there. Before 1850 other countries had not proceeded very far with industrialization, and almost everyone agrees that the economic conditions of European workers improved after 1850. The countries that followed England were able to benefit from English experience in social as well as technical matters. Thus the experience of English workers to about 1850 deserves special attention. (Industrial growth also promoted rapid urbanization, with its own awesome problems, as will be shown in Chapter 24.)

From the beginning, the Industrial Revolution in England had its critics. Among the first were the romantic poets. William Blake (1757–1827) called the early factories "satanic mills" and protested against the hard life of the London poor. William

Wordsworth (1770–1850) lamented the destruction of the rural way of life and the pollution of the land and water. Some handicraft workers—notably the Luddites, who attacked whole factories in northern England in 1812 and after—smashed the new machines, which they believed were putting them out of work. Doctors and reformers wrote eloquently of problems in the factories and new towns, while Malthus and Ricardo concluded that workers would earn only enough to stay alive.

This pessimistic view was accepted and reinforced by Friedrich Engels (1820–1895), the future revolutionary and colleague of Karl Marx. After studying conditions in northern England, this young middle-class German published in 1844 *The Condition of the Working Class in England,* a blistering indictment of the middle classes. "At the bar of world opinion," he wrote, "I charge the English middle classes with mass murder, wholesale robbery, and all the other crimes in the calendar."[6] The new poverty of industrial workers was worse than the old poverty of cottage workers and agricultural laborers, according to Engels. The culprit was industrial capitalism, with its relentless competition and constant technical change. Engels's extremely influential charge of middle-class exploitation and increasing worker poverty was embellished by Marx and later socialists.

Meanwhile, other observers believed that conditions were improving for the working people. Andrew Ure wrote in 1835 in his study of the cotton industry that conditions in most factories were not harsh and were even quite good. Edwin Chadwick, a great and conscientious government official well acquainted with the problems of the working population, concluded that the "whole mass of the laboring community" was increasingly able "to buy more of the necessities and minor luxuries of life."[7] Nevertheless, if all the contemporary assessments had been counted up, those who thought conditions were getting worse for working people would probably have been the majority.

In an attempt to go beyond the contradictory judgments of contemporaries, some historians have looked at different kinds of sources. Statistical evidence is one such source. If working people suffered a great economic decline, as Engels and later socialists asserted, then they must have bought less and less food, clothing, and other necessities as time went on. The purchasing power of the working person's wages must have declined drastically.

Scholarly statistical studies, which continue to multiply rapidly in an age of easy calculations with computer technology, have weakened the idea that the condition of the working class got much worse with industrialization. But the most recent studies also confirm the view that the early years of the Industrial Revolution were hard ones for English and Scottish workers. There was little or no increase in the purchasing power of the average British worker from about 1780 to about 1820. The years from 1792 to 1815, a period of almost constant warfare with France, were particularly difficult. Food prices rose faster than wages, and the living conditions of the laboring poor declined. Only after 1820, and especially after 1840, did real wages rise substantially, so that the average worker earned and consumed roughly 50 percent more in real terms in 1850 than in 1770.[8] In short, there was considerable economic improvement for workers throughout Great Britain by 1850, but that improvement was hard won and slow in coming.

This important conclusion must be qualified, however. Increased purchasing power meant more goods, but not necessarily greater happiness. More goods may have provided meager compensation for work that was dangerous and monotonous, for example. Also, statistical studies do not say anything about how the level of unemployment may have risen for the simple reason that there are no good unemployment statistics from this period. Furthermore, the hours in the average workweek increased; to an unknown extent, workers earned more simply because they worked more. Finally, the wartime decline was of great importance. The war years were formative years for the new factory labor force. They were also some of the hardest yet experienced. They colored the early experience of modern industrial life in somber tones.

Another way to consider the workers' standard of living is to look at the goods that they purchased. Again the evidence is somewhat contradictory. Speaking generally, workers ate somewhat more food of higher nutritional quality as the Industrial Revolution progressed, except during wartime. Diets became more varied; people ate more potatoes, dairy products, fruits, and vegetables. Clothing improved, but housing for working people probably deteriorated somewhat. In short, per capita use of specific goods supports the position that the standard of living of the working classes rose, at least moderately, after the long wars with France.

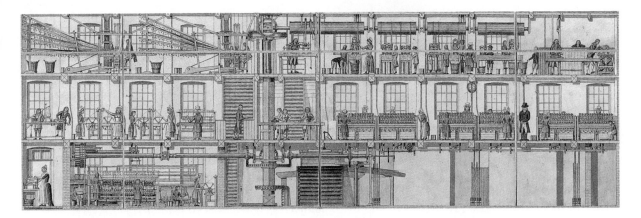

❖ **A Woolen Mill in 1800** This drawing of a mill near Birmingham highlights the complexity, discipline, and family character of the early factory system. To the right on the top floor workers turn raw wool into long ropes, which are then drawn out into slivers (lower left) prior to power spinning (center right) and handloom weaving (upper left). The pace and noise are unrelenting. Men, women, and children, often under the supervision of their parents, labor throughout the mill. A giant water wheel provides power to the entire factory by a system of belts and shafts. *(Source: Warwickshire County, Record office, Warwick, Courtesy of Lord Daventry)*

Conditions of Work

What about working conditions? Did workers eventually earn more only at the cost of working longer and harder? Were workers exploited harshly by the new factory owners?

The first factories were cotton mills, which began functioning along rivers and streams in the 1770s. Cottage workers, accustomed to the putting-out system, were reluctant to work in factories even when they received relatively good wages because factory work was different from what they were used to and was unappealing. In the factory, workers had to keep up with the machine and follow its tempo. They had to show up every day and work long, monotonous hours. Factory workers had to adjust their daily lives to the shrill call of the factory whistle.

Cottage workers were not used to that kind of life and discipline. All members of the family worked hard and long, but in spurts, setting their own pace. They could interrupt their work when they wanted to. Women and children could break up their long hours of spinning with other tasks. On Saturday afternoon the head of the family delivered the week's work to the merchant manufacturer and got paid. Saturday night was a time of relaxation and drinking, especially for the men. Recovering from his hangover on Tuesday, the weaver bent to his task on Wednesday and then worked frantically to meet his deadline on Saturday. Like some students today, he might "pull an all-nighter" on Thursday or Friday in order to get his work in.

Also, early factories resembled English poorhouses, where totally destitute people went to live on welfare. Some poorhouses were industrial prisons where the inmates had to work in order to receive their food and lodging. The similarity between large brick factories and large stone poorhouses increased the cottage workers' fear of factories and their hatred of factory discipline.

It was cottage workers' reluctance to work in factories that prompted the early cotton mill owners to turn to abandoned and pauper children for their labor. As we have seen, these owners contracted with local officials to employ large numbers of these children, who had no say in the matter. Pauper children were often badly treated and terribly overworked in the mills, as they were when they were apprenticed as chimney sweeps, market girls, shoemakers, and so forth. In the eighteenth century, semiforced child labor seemed necessary and was socially accepted. From our modern point of view, it was cruel exploitation and a blot on the record of the new industrial system.

By 1790 the early pattern was rapidly changing. The use of pauper apprentices was in decline, and in 1802 it was forbidden by Parliament. Many more factories were being built, mainly in urban areas, where they could use steampower rather than waterpower and attract a workforce more easily than in the countryside. The need for workers was great. Indeed, people came from near and far to work in the cities, both as factory workers and as laborers, builders, and domestic servants. Yet as they took these new jobs, working people did not simply give in to a system of labor that had formerly repelled them. Rather, they helped modify the system by carrying over old, familiar working traditions.

For one thing, they often came to the mills and the mines as family units. This was how they had worked on farms and in the putting-out system. The mill or mine owner bargained with the head of the family and paid him or her for the work of the whole family. In the cotton mills, children worked for their mothers or fathers, collecting wastes and "piecing" broken threads together. In the mines, children sorted coal and worked the ventilation equipment. Their mothers hauled coal in the narrow tunnels below the surface, while their fathers hewed with pick and shovel at the face of the seam.

The preservation of the family as an economic unit in the factories from the 1790s on made the new surroundings more tolerable, both in Great Britain and in other countries, during the early stages of industrialization. Parents disciplined their children, making firm measures socially acceptable, and directed their upbringing. The presence of the whole family meant that children and adults worked the same long hours (twelve-hour shifts were normal in cotton mills in 1800). In the early years, some very young children were employed solely to keep the family together. Jedediah Strutt, for example, believed children should be at least ten years old to work in his mills, but he reluctantly employed seven-year-olds to satisfy their parents. Adult workers were not particularly interested in limiting the minimum working age or hours of their children as long as family members worked side by side. Only when technical changes threatened to place control and discipline in the hands of impersonal managers and foremen did adult workers protest against inhuman conditions in the name of their children.

Some enlightened employers and social reformers in Parliament definitely felt otherwise. They argued that more humane standards were necessary, and they used widely circulated parliamentary reports to influence public opinion (see Listening

to the Past). For example, Robert Owen (1771–1858), a very successful manufacturer in Scotland, testified in 1816 before an investigating committee on the basis of his experience. He stated that "very strong facts" demonstrated that employing children under ten years of age as factory workers was "injurious to the children, and not beneficial to the proprietors." The parliamentary committee asked him to explain, and the testimony proceeded as follows:

"Seventeen years ago, a number of individuals, with myself, purchased the New Lanark establishment from the late Mr Dale, of Glasgow. At that period I find that there were 500 children, who had been taken from poor-houses, chiefly in Edinburgh. . . . The hours of work at that time were thirteen, inclusive of meal times, and an hour and a half was allowed for meals. I very soon discovered that although those children were very well fed, well clothed, well lodged, and very great care taken of them when out of the mills, their growth and their minds were materially injured by being employed at those ages within the cotton mills for eleven and a half hours per day. . . . Their limbs were generally deformed, their growth was stunted, and although one of the best school-masters upon the old plan was engaged to instruct those children every night, in general they made but a very slow progress, even in learning the common alphabet. . . ."

"Do you think the age of ten the best period for the admission of children into full and constant employment for ten or eleven hours per day, within woollen, cotton, and other mills or manufactories?"

"I do not."

"What other period would you recommend for their full admission to full work?"

"Twelve years."[9]

Owen's testimony rang true because he had already raised the age of employment in his mills and was promoting education for young children. Workers also provided graphic testimony at such hearings as the reformers pressed Parliament to pass corrective laws. They scored some important successes.

Their first major accomplishment was the Factory Act of 1833. It limited the factory workday for children between nine and thirteen to eight hours and that of adolescents between fourteen and eighteen to twelve hours, although the act made no effort to regulate the hours of work for children at home or in small businesses. The law also prohibited the factory employment of children

collapse of Owen's national trade union, a great deal of the energy of working people went into the Chartist movement, whose goal was political democracy. The key Chartist demand—that all men be given the right to vote—became the great hope of millions of aroused people. Workers were also active in campaigns to limit the workday in factories to ten hours and to permit duty-free importation of wheat into Great Britain to secure cheap bread. Thus working people developed a sense of their own identity and played an active role in shaping the new industrial system. Clearly, they were neither helpless victims nor passive beneficiaries.

SUMMARY

Western society's industrial breakthrough grew out of a long process of economic and social change in which the rise of capitalism, overseas expansion, and the growth of rural industry stood out as critical preparatory developments. Eventually taking the lead in all of these developments, and also profiting from stable government, abundant natural resources, and a flexible labor force, England experienced between the 1780s and the 1850s an epoch-making transformation, one that is still aptly termed the Industrial Revolution.

Building on technical breakthroughs, power-driven equipment, and large-scale enterprise, the Industrial Revolution in England greatly increased output in certain radically altered industries, stimulated the large handicraft and commercial sectors, and speeded up overall economic growth. Rugged Scotland industrialized at least as fast as England, and Great Britain became the first industrial nation. By 1850 the level of British per capita industrial production was surpassing continental levels by a growing margin, and Britain savored a near monopoly in world markets for mass-produced goods.

Continental countries inevitably took rather different paths to the urban industrial society. They relied more on handicraft production in both towns and villages. Only in the 1840s did railroad construction begin to create the strong demand for iron, coal, and railway equipment that speeded up the process of industrialization in the 1850s and 1860s.

The rise of modern industry had a profound impact on people and their lives. In the early stages Britain again led the way, experiencing in a striking manner the long-term social changes accompanying the economic transformation. Factory discipline and Britain's stern capitalist economy weighed heavily on working people, who, however, actively fashioned their destinies, refusing to be passive victims. Improvements in the standard of living came slowly, although they were substantial by 1850. The era of industrialization fostered new attitudes toward child labor, encouraged protective factory legislation, and called forth a new sense of class feeling and an assertive labor movement. It also promoted a more rigid division of roles and responsibilities within the family that was detrimental to women, another gradual but profound change of revolutionary proportions.

NOTES

1. N. F. R. Crafts, *British Economic Growth During the Industrial Revolution* (Oxford: Oxford University Press, 1985), p. 32. These estimates are for Great Britain as a whole.

2. P. Bairoch, "International Industrialization Levels from 1750 to 1980," *Journal of European Economic History* 11 (Spring 1982): 269–333.

3. Crafts, pp. 45, 95–102.

4. M. Lévy-Leboyer, *Les banques européennes et l'industrialisation dans la première moitié du XIXe siècle* (Paris: Presses Universitaires de France, 1964), p. 29.

5. J. Michelet, *The People,* trans. with an introduction by J. P. McKay (Urbana: University of Illinois Press, 1973; original publication, 1846), p. 64.

6. F. Engels, *The Condition of the Working Class in England,* trans. and ed. W. O. Henderson and W. H. Chaloner (Stanford, Calif.: Stanford University Press, 1968), p. xxiii.

7. Quoted in W. A. Hayek, ed., *Capitalism and the Historians* (Chicago: University of Chicago Press, 1954), p. 126.

8. Crafts, p. 95.

9. Quoted in E. R. Pike, *"Hard Times": Human Documents of the Industrial Revolution* (New York: Praeger, 1966), p. 109.

10. See, especially, J. Brenner and M. Rama, "Rethinking Women's Oppression," *New Left Review* 144 (March-April 1984): 33–71, and sources cited there.

11. J. Humphries, ". . . 'The Most Free from Objection' . . .: The Sexual Division of Labor and Women's Work in Nineteenth-Century Eng-

land," *Journal of Economic History* 47 (December 1987): 948.

12. Ibid., p. 941; Pike, p. 266.
13. Quoted in Pike, p. 208.
14. Quoted in D. Geary, ed., *Labour and Socialist Movements in Europe Before 1914* (Oxford: Berg, 1989), p. 29.

SUGGESTED READING

There is a vast and exciting literature on the Industrial Revolution. R. Cameron, *A Concise Economic History of the World* (1989), provides an introduction to the issues and has a carefully annotated bibliography. J. Goodman and K. Honeyman, *Gainful Pursuits: The Making of Industrial Europe, 1600–1914* (1988), D. S. Landes, *The Unbound Prometheus: Technological Change and Industrial Development in Western Europe from 1750 to the Present* (1969), and S. Pollard, *Peaceful Conquest: The Industrialization of Europe* (1981), are excellent general treatments of European industrial growth. These studies also suggest the range of issues and interpretations. T. Kemp, *Industrialization in Europe,* 2d ed. (1985), is also useful. M. Berg, *The Age of Manufactures: Industry, Innovation and Work in Britain, 1700–1820* (1985), P. Mathias, *The First Industrial Nation: An Economic History of Britain, 1700–1914* (1969), and P. Mantoux, *The Industrial Revolution in the Eighteenth Century* (1961), admirably discuss the various aspects of the English breakthrough and offer good bibliographies, as does the work by Crafts mentioned in the Notes. W. Rostow, *The Stages of Economic Growth: A Non-Communist Manifesto* (1960), is a popular, provocative study.

H. Kirsh, *From Domestic Manufacturing to Industrial Revolution: The Case of the Rhineland Textile Districts* (1989), and M. Neufield, *The Skilled Metalworkers of Nuremberg: Craft and Class in the Industrial Revolution* (1985), examine the persistence and gradual transformation of handicraft techniques. R. Cameron traces the spread of railroads and industry across Europe in *France and the Economic Development of Europe, 1800–1914* (1961). The works of A. S. Milward and S. B. Saul, *The Economic Development of Continental Europe, 1780–1870* (1973) and *The Development of the Economies of Continental Europe, 1850–1914* (1977), may be compared with J. Clapham's old-fashioned classic, *Economic Development of France and Germany* (1963). C. Kindleberger, *Economic Growth in France and Britain, 1851–1950* (1964), is a stimulating study, especially for those with some background in economics.

Other important works in recent years on industrial developments are C. Tilly and E. Shorter, *Strikes in France, 1830–1848* (1974); D. Ringrose, *Transportation and Economic Stagnation in Spain, 1750–1850* (1970); L. Schofer, *The Formation of a Modern Labor Force* (1975), which focuses on the Silesian part of Germany; and W. Blackwell, *The Industrialization of Russia,* 2d ed. (1982). L. Moch, *Paths to the City: Regional Migration in Nineteenth-Century France* (1983), and W. Schivelbusch, *Disenchanted Night: The Industrialization of Light in the Nineteenth Century* (1983), imaginatively analyze quite different aspects of industrialization's many consequences.

The debate between "optimists" and "pessimists" about the consequences of industrialization in England goes on. P. Taylor, ed., *The Industrial Revolution: Triumph or Disaster?* (1970), is a useful introduction to different viewpoints; Hayek's collection of essays, cited in the Notes, stresses positive aspects. It is also fascinating to compare F. Engels's classic condemnation, cited in the Notes, with Andrew Ure's optimistic defense, *The Philosophy of Manufactures,* first published in 1835 and reprinted recently. J. Rule, *The Labouring Classes in Early Industrial England, 1750–1850* (1987), is a recommended synthesis, whereas E. P. Thompson continues and enriches the Engels tradition in *The Making of the English Working Class* (1963), an exciting book rich in detail and early working-class lore. E. R. Pike's documentary collection, cited in the Notes, provides fascinating insights into the lives of working people. An unorthodox but moving account of a doomed group is D. Bythell, *The Handloom Weavers* (1969). F. Klingender, *Art and the Industrial Revolution,* rev. ed. (1968), is justly famous, and M. Ignatieff, *A Just Measure of Pain* (1980), is an engrossing study of prisons during English industrialization. D. S. Landes, *Revolution in Time: Clocks and the Making of the Modern World* (1983), is a brilliant integration of industrial and cultural history.

Among general studies, G. S. R. Kitson Clark, *The Making of Victorian England* (1967), is particularly imaginative. A. Briggs, *Victorian People* (1955), provides an engrossing series of brief biographies. H. Ausubel discusses a major reformer in *John Bright* (1966), and B. Harrison skillfully illuminates the problem of heavy drinking in *Drink and the Victorians* (1971). The most famous contemporary novel dealing with the new industrial society is Charles Dickens's *Hard Times,* an entertaining but exaggerated story. *Mary Barton* and *North and South* by Elizabeth Gaskell are more realistic portrayals, and both are highly recommended.

The Testimony of Young Mining Workers

The use of child labor in British industrialization quickly attracted the attention of humanitarians and social reformers. This interest led to investigations by parliamentary commissions, which resulted in laws limiting the hours and the ages of children working in large factories. Designed to build a case for remedial legislation, parliamentary inquiries gave large numbers of workers a rare chance to speak directly to contemporaries and to historians.

The moving passages that follow are taken from testimony gathered in 1841 and 1842 by the Ashley Mines Commission. Interviewing employers and many male and female workers, the commissioners focused on the physical condition of the youth and on the sexual behavior of workers far underground. The subsequent Mines Act of 1842 sought to reduce immoral behavior and sexual bullying by prohibiting underground work for all women (and for boys younger than ten).

Mr. Payne, coal master:

That children are employed generally at nine years old in the coal pits and sometimes at eight. In fact, the smaller the vein of coal is in height, the younger and smaller are the children required; the work occupies from six to seven hours per day in the pits; they are not ill-used or worked beyond their strength; a good deal of depravity exists but they are certainly not worse in morals than in other branches of the Sheffield trade, but upon the whole superior; the morals of this district are materially improving; Mr. Bruce, the clergyman, has been zealous and active in endeavoring to ameliorate their moral and religious education. . . .

Ann Eggley, hurrier, 18 years old:

I'm sure I don't know how to spell my name. We go at four in the morning, and sometimes at half-past four. We begin to work as soon as we get down. We get out after four,

sometimes at five, in the evening. We work the whole time except an hour for dinner, and sometimes we haven't time to eat. I hurry [move coal wagons underground] by myself, and have done so for long. I know the corves [small coal wagons] are very heavy, they are the biggest corves anywhere about. The work is far too hard for me; the sweat runs off me all over sometimes. I am very tired at night. Sometimes when we get home at night we have not power to wash us, and then we go to bed. Sometimes we fall asleep in the chair. Father said last night it was both a shame and a disgrace for girls to work as we do, but there was naught else for us to do. I began to hurry when I was seven and I have been hurrying ever since. I have been 11 years in the pits. The girls are always tired. I was poorly twice this winter; it was with headache. I hurry for Robert Wiggins; he is not akin to me. . . . We don't always get enough to eat and drink, but we get a good supper. I have known my father go at two in the morning to work . . . and he didn't come out till four. I am quite sure that we work constantly 12 hours except on Saturdays. We wear trousers and our shifts in the pit and great big shoes clinkered and nailed. The girls never work naked to the waist in our pit. The men don't insult us in the pit. The conduct of the girls in the pit is good enough sometimes and sometimes bad enough. I never went to a day-school. I went a little to a Sunday-school, but I soon gave it over. I thought it too bad to be confined both Sundays and week-days. I walk about and get the fresh air on Sundays. I have not learnt to read. I don't know my letters. I never learnt naught. I never go to church or chapel; there is no church or chapel at Gawber, there is none nearer than a mile. . . . I have never heard that a good man came into the world who was God's son to save sinners. I never heard of

Christ at all. Nobody has ever told me about him, nor have my father and mother ever taught me to pray. I know no prayer; I never pray.

Patience Kershaw, aged 17:

My father has been dead about a year; my mother is living and has ten children, five lads and five lasses; the oldest is about thirty, the youngest is four; three lasses go to mill; all the lads are colliers, two getters and three hurriers; one lives at home and does nothing; mother does nought but look after home.

All my sisters have been hurriers, but three went to the mill. Alice went because her legs swelled from hurrying in cold water when she was hot. I never went to day-school; I go to Sunday-school, but I cannot read or write; I go to pit at five o'clock in the morning and come out at five in the evening; I get my breakfast of porridge and milk first; I take my dinner with me, a cake, and eat it as I go; I do not stop or rest any time for the purpose; I get nothing else until I get home, and then have potatoes and meat, not every day meat. I hurry in the clothes I have now got on, trousers and ragged jacket; the bald place upon my head is made by thrusting the corves; my legs have never swelled, but sisters' did when they went to mill; I hurry the corves a mile and more under ground and back; they weigh 300; I hurry 11 a day; I wear a belt and chain at the workings to get the corves out; the putters [miners] that I work for are *naked* except their caps; they pull off all their clothes; I see them at work when I go up; sometimes they beat me, if I am not quick enough, with their hands; they strike me upon my back; the boys take liberties with me, sometimes, they pull me about; I am the only girl in the pit; there are about 20 boys and 15 men; all the men are naked; I would rather work in mill than in coal-pit.

Isabel Wilson, 38 years old, coal putter:

When women have children thick [fast] they are compelled to take them down early. I have been married 19 years and have had 10 bairns [children]; seven are in life. When on Sir John's work was a carrier of coals, which caused me to miscarry five times from the strains, and was gai [very] ill after each. Putting is no so oppressive; last child was born on Saturday morning, and I was at work on the Friday night.

Once met with an accident; a coal brake my cheek-bone, which kept me idle some weeks.

❖ Female mine worker, from a Parliamentary Report, 1842. *(Source: Mary Evans Picture Library/Photo Researchers, Inc.)*

I have wrought below 30 years, and so has the guid man; he is getting touched in the breath now.

None of the children read, as the work is no regular. I did read once, but no able to attend to it now; when I go below lassie 10 years of age keeps house and makes the broth or stir-about.

Questions for Analysis

1. To what extent are the testimonies of Ann Eggley and Patience Kershaw in harmony with that of Payne?

2. Describe the work of Eggley and Kershaw. What do you think of their work? Why?

3. What strikes you most about the lives of these workers?

4. The witnesses were responding to questions from middle-class commissioners. What did the commissioners seem interested in? Why?

Source: J. Bowditch and C. Ramsland, eds., *Voices of the Industrial Revolution.* Copyright © 1961, 1989 by the University of Michigan. Reprinted by permission.

23

Ideologies and Upheavals, 1815–1850

The momentous economic and political transformation of modern times began in the late eighteenth century with the Industrial Revolution in England and then the French Revolution. Until about 1815, these economic and political revolutions were separate, involving different countries and activities and proceeding at very different paces. The Industrial Revolution created the factory system and new groups of capitalists and industrial workers in northern England, but almost continual warfare with France checked the spread of that revolution to continental Europe. Meanwhile, England's ruling aristocracy suppressed all forms of political radicalism at home and joined with crowned heads abroad to oppose and eventually defeat revolutionary and Napoleonic France. The economic and political revolutions worked at cross-purposes and even neutralized each other.

After peace returned in 1815, the situation changed. Economic and political changes tended to fuse, reinforcing each other and bringing about what historian Eric Hobsbawm has incisively called the "dual revolution." For instance, the growth of the industrial middle class encouraged the drive for representative government, and the demands of the French sans-culottes in 1793 and 1794 inspired many socialist thinkers. Gathering strength and threatening almost every aspect of the existing political and social framework, the dual revolution rushed on to alter completely first Europe and then the world. Much of world history in the last two centuries can be seen as the progressive unfolding of the dual revolution.

Yet in Europe in the nineteenth century, as in Asia and Africa in more recent times, the dual revolution was not some inexorable mechanical monster grinding peoples and cultures into a homogenized mass. The economic and political transformation it wrought was built on complicated histories, strong traditions, and highly diverse cultures. Radical change was eventually

A painting by J. P. Laurens of revolutionary upheaval in Paris in 1848. *(Source: Ville de Paris/Photographie Bulloz)*

757

their independence during and after the Napoleonic wars and were a growing market for British manufactured goods. Encouraged by the British position (and the powerful British navy resting off Latin American coasts), the young United States proclaimed its celebrated Monroe Doctrine in 1823. This bold document declared that European powers were to keep their hands off the New World and in no way attempt to re-establish their political system there. In the United States, constitutional liberalism, an ongoing challenge to the conservatism of continental Europe, retained its cutting edge.

In the years following the crushing of liberal revolution in southern Italy in 1821 and in Spain in 1823, Metternich continued to battle against liberal political change. Sometimes he could do

Metternich This portrait by Sir Thomas Lawrence reveals much about Metternich the man. Handsome, refined, and intelligent, Metternich was a great aristocrat who was passionately devoted to the defense of his class and its interests. *(Source: Copyright reserved to Her Majesty Queen Elizabeth II)*

little, as in the case of the new Latin American republics. Nor could he undo the dynastic changes of 1830 and 1831 in France and Belgium. Nonetheless, until 1848 Metternich's system proved quite effective in central Europe, where his power was the greatest.

Metternich's policies dominated not only Austria and the Italian peninsula but also the entire German Confederation, which the peace settlement of Vienna had called into being. The confederation was composed of thirty-eight independent German states, including Prussia and Austria. (Neither Prussia's eastern territories nor the Hungarian half of the Austrian Empire was included in the confederation.) These states met in complicated assemblies dominated by Austria, with Prussia a willing junior partner in the planning and execution of repressive measures.

It was through the German Confederation that Metternich had the infamous Carlsbad Decrees issued in 1819. These decrees required the thirty-eight German member states to root out subversive ideas in their universities and newspapers. The decrees also established a permanent committee with spies and informers to investigate and punish any liberal or radical organizations. Metternich's ruthless imposition of repressive internal policies on the governments of central Europe contrasted with the intelligent moderation he had displayed in the general peace settlement of 1815.

Metternich and Conservatism

Metternich's determined defense of the status quo made him a villain in the eyes of most progressive, optimistic historians of the nineteenth century. Yet rather than denounce the man, we can try to understand him and the general conservatism he represented.

Born into the middle ranks of the landed nobility of the Rhineland, Prince Klemens von Metternich (1773–1859) was an internationally oriented aristocrat. In 1795 his splendid marriage to Eleonora von Kaunitz, granddaughter of a famous Austrian statesman and heiress to vast estates, opened the door to the highest court circles and a brilliant diplomatic career. Austrian ambassador to Napoleon's court in 1806 and Austrian foreign minister from 1809 to 1848, the cosmopolitan Metternich always remained loyal to his class and jealously defended its rights and privileges to the day he died. Like most other conservatives of his time, he did so with a clear conscience. The nobility was one of Europe's most ancient institutions, and conservatives regarded tradition as the basic source of human institutions. In their view, the proper state and society remained those of pre-1789 Europe, which rested on a judicious blend of monarchy, bureaucracy, aristocracy, and respectful commoners.

Metternich's commitment to conservatism was coupled with a passionate hatred of liberalism. He firmly believed that liberalism, as embodied in revolutionary America and France, had been responsible for a generation of war with untold bloodshed and suffering. Liberal demands for representative government and civil liberties had unfortunately captured the imaginations of some middle-class lawyers, business people, and intellectuals. Metternich thought that these groups had been and still were engaged in a vast conspiracy to impose their beliefs on society and destroy the existing order. Like many other conservatives then and since, Metternich blamed liberal revolutionaries for stirring up the lower classes, which he believed to be indifferent or hostile to liberal ideas, desiring nothing more than peace and quiet.

The threat of liberalism appeared doubly dangerous to Metternich because it generally went with national aspirations. Liberals, especially liberals in central Europe, believed that each people, each national group, had a right to establish its own independent government and seek to fulfill its own destiny. The idea of national self-determination was repellent to Metternich. It not only threatened the existence of the aristocracy; it also threatened to destroy the Austrian Empire and revolutionize central Europe.

The vast Austrian Empire of the Habsburgs was a great dynastic state. Formed over centuries by war, marriage, and luck, it was made up of many peoples speaking many languages (Map 23.2). The Germans, long the dominant element, had supported and profited by the long-term territorial expansion of Austria; yet they accounted for only a quarter of the population. The Magyars (Hungarians), a substantially smaller group, dominated the kingdom of Hungary—which was part of the Austrian Empire—though they did not account for a majority of the population even there.

The Czechs, the third major group, were concentrated in Bohemia and Moravia. There were also large numbers of Italians, Poles, and Ukrainians as well as smaller groups of Slovenes, Croats, Serbs, Ruthenians, and Rumanians. The various Slavic peoples, together with the Italians and the Rumanians, represented a widely scattered and completely divided majority in an empire dominated by Germans and Hungarians. Different ethnic groups often lived in the same provinces and even the same villages. Thus the different parts and provinces of the empire differed in languages, customs, and institutions. They were held together primarily by their ties to the Habsburg emperor.

The multinational state Metternich served was both strong and weak. It was strong because of its large population and vast territories; it was weak because of its many and potentially dissatisfied nationalities. In these circumstances, Metternich virtually had to oppose liberalism and nationalism, for Austria was simply unable to accommodate those ideologies of the dual revolution. Other conservatives supported Austria because they could imagine no better fate for the jumble of small nationalities wedged precariously between masses of Germans and hordes of Russians in east-central Europe. Castlereagh even went so far as to say that Austria was the "great hinge upon which the fate of Europe must ultimately depend." Metternich's repressive conservatism may not hold appeal for many people today, but it had understandable roots in the dilemma of a multinational state in an age of rising nationalism.

✤ RADICAL IDEAS AND EARLY SOCIALISM

The years following the peace settlement of 1815 were years of profound intellectual activity. Intellectuals and social observers were seeking to understand the revolutionary changes that had occurred and were still taking place. These efforts led to ideas that still motivate the world.

Almost all of these basic ideas were radical. In one way or another they opposed the old, deeply felt conservatism that Metternich exemplified so well. Revived conservatism, with its stress on tradition, a hereditary monarchy, a strong and privileged landowning aristocracy, and an official they generally wanted property qualifications attached to the right to vote. In practice, this meant limiting the vote to well-to-do aristocratic land-owners, substantial businessmen, and successful members of the professions. Workers and peasants as well as the lower middle class of shopkeepers, clerks, and artisans did not own the necessary property and thus could not vote.

As liberalism became increasingly identified with the middle class after 1815, some intellectuals and foes of conservatism felt that liberalism did not go nearly far enough. Inspired by memories of the French Revolution and the contemporary example of exuberant Jacksonian democracy in the young American republic, they called for universal voting rights, at least for males. Giving all men the vote, they felt, would allow the masses to join in government and would lead to democracy.

Many people who believed in democracy also believed in the republican form of government. They detested the power of the monarchy, the privileges of the aristocracy, and the great wealth of the upper middle class. These democrats and republicans were more radical than the liberals. Taking for granted much of the liberal program, they sought to go beyond it. Democrats and republicans were also more willing than most liberals to endorse violent upheaval to achieve goals. All of this meant that liberals and radical, democratic republicans could join forces against conservatives only up to a point.

Nationalism

Nationalism was a second radical idea in the years after 1815, an idea destined to have an enormous influence in the modern world. In this complex ideology, three points stand out. First, nationalism has normally evolved from a real or imagined *cultural* unity, manifesting itself especially in a common language, history, and territory. Second, nationalists have usually sought to turn this cultural unity into *political* reality so that the territory of each people coincides with its state boundaries. It was this goal that made nationalism so potentially explosive in central and eastern Europe after 1815, when there were either too few states (Austria, Russia, and the Ottoman Empire) or too many (the Italian peninsula and the German Confederation) and when different peoples overlapped and

intermingled. Third, modern nationalism had its immediate origins in the French Revolution and the Napoleonic wars. Nationalism was effectively harnessed by the French republic during the Reign of Terror to help repel foreign foes, and all across Europe patriots tried to kindle nationalist flames in the war against Napoleon. Thus by 1815 there were already hints of nationalism's remarkable ability to spread and develop.

Between 1815 and 1850, most people who believed in nationalism also believed in either liberalism or radical, democratic republicanism. In more recent times, however, many governments have been very nationalistic without favoring liberty and democracy. Why, then, was love of liberty almost synonymous with love of nation in the early nineteenth century?

A common faith in the creativity and nobility of the people was perhaps the single most important reason for the linking of these two concepts. Liberals and especially democrats saw the people as the ultimate source of all government. The people (or some of them) elected their officials and governed themselves within a framework of personal liberty. Yet such self-government would be possible only if the people were united by common traditions and common loyalties. In practice, common loyalties rested above all on a common language. Thus liberals and nationalists agreed that a shared language forged the basic unity of a people, a unity that transcended local or provincial interests and even class differences.

Early nationalists usually believed that every nation, like every citizen, had the right to exist in freedom and to develop its character and spirit. They were confident that the independence and freedom of other nations, as in the case of other citizens within a nation, would not lessen the freedom of their own country. Rather, the symphony of nations would promote the harmony and ultimate unity of all peoples. As French historian Jules Michelet put it in *The People* in 1846, each citizen "learns to recognize his country . . . as a note in the grand concert; through it he himself participates and loves the world." Similarly, the great Italian patriot Giuseppe Mazzini (see Listening to the Past) believed that "in laboring according to the true principles of our country we are laboring for Humanity." Thus the liberty of the individual and the love of a free nation overlapped greatly in the early nineteenth century.

Nationalism also had a negative side. Even as early nationalists talked of serving the cause of humanity, they stressed the differences among peoples. German pastor and philosopher Johann Herder (1744–1803) had argued that every people has its own particular spirit and genius, which it expresses through culture and language. Yet Herder (and others after him) could not define the uniqueness of the French, German, and Slavic peoples without comparing and contrasting one people with another. Thus even early nationalism developed a strong sense of "we" and "they."

"They" were often the enemy. The leader of the Czech cultural revival, the passionate democrat and nationalist historian Francis Palacký, is a good example of this tendency. In his histories he lauded the Czech people's achievements, which he characterized as a long struggle against brutal German domination. To this "we-they" outlook, it was all too easy for nationalists to add two other highly volatile ingredients: a sense of national mission and a sense of national superiority. As Mazzini characteristically wrote, "Peoples never stop before they have achieved the ultimate aim of their existence, before having fulfilled their mission." Even Michelet, so alive to the aspirations of other peoples, could not help speaking in 1846 of the "superiority of France"; the principles espoused in the French Revolution had made France the "salvation of mankind."

German and Spanish nationalists had a very different opinion of France. To them, the French often seemed as oppressive as the Germans seemed to the Czechs, as hateful as the Russians seemed to the Poles. The despised enemy's mission might seem as oppressive as the American national mission seemed to the Mexicans after the U.S. annexation of Texas. In 1845 American journalist and strident nationalist John Louis O'Sullivan wrote that taking land from an "imbecile and distracted Mexico" was a laudable step in the "fulfillment of our manifest destiny to overspread the continent allotted by Providence for the free development of our yearly multiplying millions."[2]

Early nationalism was thus ambiguous. Its main thrust was liberal and democratic. But below the surface lurked ideas of national superiority and national mission, which could lead to aggressive crusades and counter-crusades, as had happened in the French Revolution and in the "wars of liberation" against Napoleon.

French Utopian Socialism

Socialism was the new radical doctrine after 1815, and to understand it one must begin with France. Despite the fact that France lagged far behind Great Britain in developing modern industry, almost all the early socialists were French. Although they differed on many specific points, these French thinkers were acutely aware that the political revolution in France and the rise of modern industry in England had begun a transformation of society. Yet they were disturbed by what they saw. Liberal practices in politics, such as competition for votes, and in economics, such as free markets and the end of guild regulation, appeared to be fomenting selfish individualism and splitting the community into isolated fragments. There was, they believed, an urgent need for a further reorganization of society to establish cooperation and a new sense of community. Starting from this shared outlook, individual French thinkers went in many different directions. They searched the past, analyzed existing conditions, and fashioned luxurious utopias. Yet certain ideas tied their critiques and visions together.

Early French socialists believed in economic planning. Inspired by the emergency measures of 1793 and 1794 in France, they argued that the government should rationally organize the economy and not depend on destructive competition to do the job. Early socialists also shared an intense desire to help the poor and protect them from the rich. With passionate moral fervor, they preached that the rich and the poor should be more nearly equal economically. Finally, socialists believed that private property should be strictly regulated by the government or that it should be abolished and replaced by state or community ownership. Planning, greater economic equality, and state control of property—these were the key ideas of early French socialism and of all socialism since.

One of the most influential early socialist thinkers was a nobleman, Count Henri de Saint-Simon (1760–1825). A curious combination of radical thinker and successful land speculator, Saint-Simon optimistically proclaimed the tremendous possibilities of industrial development: "The age of gold is before us!" The key to progress was proper social organization. Such an arrangement of society required the "parasites"—the court, the aristocracy, lawyers, churchmen—to give way, once and for all,

❖ **Fourier's Utopia** The vision of a harmonious planned community freed from capitalism and selfish individualism radiates from this 1847 illustration of Fourier's principles. *(Source: Mary Evans Picture Library/Photo Researchers)*

to the "doers"—the leading scientists, engineers, and industrialists. The doers would carefully plan the economy and guide it forward by undertaking vast public works projects and establishing investment banks. Saint-Simon also stressed in highly moralistic terms that every social institution ought to have as its main goal improved conditions for the poor. Saint-Simon's stress on industry and science inspired middle-class industrialists and bankers such as the Pereire brothers, founders of the Crédit Mobilier (see page 742).

After 1830 the socialist critique of capitalism became sharper. Charles Fourier (1772–1837), a lonely, saintly man with a tenuous hold on reality, described a socialist utopia in lavish mathematical detail. Hating the urban wage system, Fourier envisaged self-sufficient communities of 1,620 people living communally on 5,000 acres devoted to a combination of agriculture and industry. Although

Fourier waited in vain each day at noon in his apartment for a wealthy philanthropist to endow his visionary schemes, he was very influential. Several utopian communities were founded along the lines he prescribed. The majority were founded in the United States.

Fourier was also an early proponent of the total emancipation of women. Extremely critical of middle-class family life, Fourier believed that most marriages were only another kind of prostitution. According to Fourier, young single women were shamelessly "sold" to their future husbands for dowries and other financial considerations. Therefore, Fourier called for the abolition of marriage, free unions based only on love, and sexual freedom. Many middle-class men and women found these ideas, which were shared and even practiced by some followers of Saint-Simon, shocking and immoral. The socialist program for the liberation of women as well as workers appeared to them as doubly dangerous and revolutionary.

Louis Blanc (1811–1882), a sharp-eyed, intelligent journalist, was much more practical. In his *Organization of Work* (1839), he urged workers to agitate for universal voting rights and to take control of the state peacefully. Blanc believed that the full power of the state should be directed at setting up government-backed workshops and factories to guarantee full employment. The right to work had to become as sacred as any other right.

Finally, there was Pierre Joseph Proudhon (1809–1865), a self-educated printer who wrote a pamphlet in 1840 entitled *What Is Property?* His answer was that it was nothing but theft. Property was profit that was stolen from the worker, who was the source of all wealth. Unlike most socialists, Proudhon feared the power of the state and was often considered an anarchist.

Of great importance, the message of French utopian socialists interacted with the experiences of French urban workers. In Paris especially, workers cherished the memory of the radical phase of the French Revolution and its efforts to regulate economic life and protect the poor. Skilled artisans, with a long tradition of guilds, apprenticeship, and control of quality and wage rates, became violently opposed to laissez-faire laws that denied workers the right to organize and promoted brutal, unrestrained competition instead. Trying to maintain some control of their trades and conditions of work and developing a sense of class in the process, workers favored collective action and government intervention in economic life. Thus the aspirations of workers and utopian theorists reinforced each other, and a genuine socialist movement emerged in Paris in the 1830s and 1840s.

French utopian ideas had some influence outside France. But the economic arguments of the French utopians were weak, and their specific programs often seemed too fanciful to be taken seriously. To Karl Marx was left the task of establishing firm foundations for modern socialism.

The Birth of Marxian Socialism

In 1848 the thirty-year-old Karl Marx (1818–1883) and the twenty-eight-year-old Friedrich Engels (1820–1895) published the *Communist Manifesto,* which became the bible of socialism.

The son of a Jewish lawyer who had converted to Christianity, the atheistic young Marx had studied philosophy at the University of Berlin before turning to journalism and economics. He read widely in French socialist thought and was influenced by it. He shared Fourier's view of middle-class marriage as legalized prostitution, and he, too, looked forward to the emancipation of women and the abolition of the family. But by the time Marx was twenty-five, he was developing his own socialist ideas.

Early French socialists often appealed to the middle class and the state to help the poor. Marx ridiculed such appeals as naive. He argued that the interests of the middle class and those of the

Karl Marx Active in the Revolution of 1848, Marx fled from Germany in 1849 and settled in London. There he wrote *Capital,* the weighty exposition of his socialist theories, and worked to organize the working class. Marx earned a modest living as a journalist, supplemented by financial support from his coauthor, Friedrich Engels. *(Source: Istar-Tass/Sovfoto)*

industrial working class were inevitably opposed to each other. Indeed, according to the *Manifesto,* the "history of all previously existing society is the history of class struggles." In Marx's view, one class had always exploited the other, and with the advent of modern industry, society was split more clearly than ever before: between the middle class (the bourgeoisie) and the modern working class (the proletariat). Moreover, the bourgeoisie had reduced everything to a matter of money and "naked self-interest." "In a word, for exploitation, veiled by religious and political illusions, the bourgeoisie had substituted naked, shameless, direct brutal exploitation."

Just as the bourgeoisie had triumphed over the feudal aristocracy, Marx predicted, the proletariat would conquer the bourgeoisie in a violent revolution. While a tiny minority owned the means of production and grew richer, the ever-poorer proletariat was constantly growing in size and in class consciousness. In this process, the proletariat was aided, according to Marx, by a portion of the bourgeoisie who had gone over to the proletariat and who (like Marx and Engels) "had raised themselves to the level of comprehending theoretically the historical moment." And the critical moment was very near. "Let the ruling classes tremble at a Communist revolution. The proletarians have nothing to lose but their chains. They have a world to win. WORKING MEN OF ALL COUNTRIES, UNITE!" So ends the *Communist Manifesto.*

In brief outline, Marx's ideas may seem to differ only slightly from the wild and improbable ideas of the utopians of his day. Yet whatever one may think of the validity of Marx's analysis, he must be taken seriously. He united sociology, economics, and all human history in a vast and imposing edifice. He synthesized in his socialism not only French utopian schemes but also English classical economics and German philosophy—the major intellectual currents of his day. Moreover, after the young Marx fled to England as a penniless political refugee following the revolutions of 1848, he continued to show a rare flair for combining complex theorization with both lively popular writing and practical organizational ability. This combination of theoretical and practical skills contributed greatly to the subsequent diffusion of Marx's socialist synthesis after 1860, as will be shown in Chapter 25.

Marx's debt to England was great. He was the last of the classical economists. Following David Ricardo, who had taught that labor was the source of all value, Marx went on to argue that profits were really wages stolen from the workers. Moreover, Marx incorporated Engels's charges of terrible oppression of the new class of factory workers in England; thus Marx's doctrines seemed to be based on hard facts.

Marx's theory of historical evolution was built on the philosophy of the German Georg Hegel (1770–1831). Hegel believed that history is "ideas in motion": each age is characterized by a dominant set of ideas, which produces opposing ideas and eventually a new synthesis. The idea of being had been dominant initially, for example, and it had produced its antithesis, the idea of nonbeing. This idea in turn had resulted in the synthesis of becoming. Thus history has pattern and purpose.

Marx retained Hegel's view of history as a dialectic process of change but made economic relationships between classes the driving force. This dialectic explained the decline of agrarian feudalism and the rise of industrial capitalism. And Marx stressed again and again that the "bourgeoisie, historically, has played a most revolutionary part. . . . During its rule of scarcely one hundred years the bourgeoisie has created more massive and more colossal productive forces than have all preceding generations together." Here was a convincing explanation for people trying to make sense of the dual revolution. Marx's next idea, that it was now the bourgeoisie's turn to give way to the socialism of revolutionary workers, appeared to many the irrefutable capstone of a brilliant interpretation of humanity's long development. Thus Marx pulled together powerful ideas and insights to create one of the great secular religions out of the intellectual ferment of the early nineteenth century.

✥ THE ROMANTIC MOVEMENT

Radical concepts of politics and society were accompanied by comparable changes in literature and other arts during the dual revolution. The early nineteenth century marked the acme of the romantic movement, which profoundly influenced the arts and enriched European culture immeasurably.

The romantic movement was in part a revolt against classicism and the Enlightenment. Classicism was essentially a set of artistic rules and standards that went hand in glove with the Enlightenment's belief in rationality, order, and restraint. The classicists believed that the ancient Greeks and Romans had discovered eternally valid aesthetic rules and that playwrights and painters should continue to follow them. Classicists could enforce these rules in the eighteenth century because they dominated the courts and academies for which artists worked.

Forerunners of the romantic movement appeared from about 1750 on. Of these, Rousseau (see page 606)—the passionate advocate of feeling, freedom, and natural goodness—was the most influential. Romanticism then crystallized fully in the 1790s, primarily in England and Germany. The French Revolution kindled the belief that radical reconstruction was also possible in cultural and artistic life (even though many early English and German romantics became disillusioned with events in France and turned from liberalism to conservatism in politics). Romanticism gained strength until the 1840s.

Romanticism's Tenets

Romanticism was characterized by a belief in emotional exuberance, unrestrained imagination, and spontaneity in both art and personal life. In Germany early romantics of the 1770s and 1780s called themselves the "Storm and Stress" (*Sturm und Drang*) group, and many romantic artists of the early nineteenth century lived lives of tremendous emotional intensity. Suicide, duels to the death, madness, and strange illnesses were not uncommon among leading romantics. Romantic artists typically led bohemian lives, wearing their hair long and uncombed in preference to powdered wigs and living in cold garrets rather than frequenting stiff drawing rooms. They rejected materialism and sought to escape to lofty spiritual heights through their art. Great individualists, the romantics believed the full development of one's unique human potential to be the supreme purpose in life. The romantics were driven by a sense of an unlimited universe and by a yearning for the unattained, the unknown, the unknowable.

Nowhere was the break with classicism more apparent than in romanticism's general conception of nature. Classicism was not particularly interested in nature. In the words of eighteenth-century English author Samuel Johnson, "A blade of grass is always a blade of grass; men and women are my subjects of inquiry." Nature was portrayed by classicists as beautiful and chaste, like an eighteenth-century formal garden. The romantics, in contrast, were enchanted by nature. Sometimes they found it awesome and tempestuous, as in Théodore Géricault's painting *The Raft of the Medusa,* which shows the survivors of a shipwreck adrift in a turbulent sea. Others saw nature as a source of spiritual inspiration. As the great English landscape artist John Constable declared, "Nature is Spirit visible."

Most romantics saw the growth of modern industry as an ugly, brutal attack on their beloved nature and on the human personality. They sought escape—in the unspoiled Lake District of northern England, in exotic North Africa, in an idealized Middle Ages. Yet some romantics found a vast, awesome, terribly moving power in the new industrial landscape. In ironworks and cotton mills they saw the flames of hell and the evil genius of Satan himself. One of John Martin's last and greatest paintings, *The Great Day of His Wrath,* vividly depicts the Last Judgment foretold in Revelation 6, when the "sun became black as sackcloth of hair, and the moon became as blood; and the stars of heaven fell unto the earth." Martin's romantic masterpiece was inspired directly by a journey through the "Black country" of the industrial Midlands in the dead of night. According to Martin's son:

The glow of the furnaces, the red blaze of light, together with the liquid fire, seemed to him truly sublime and awful. He could not imagine anything more terrible even in the regions of everlasting punishment. All he had done or attempted in ideal painting fell far short, very far short, of the fearful sublimity.[3]

Fascinated by color and diversity, the romantic imagination turned toward the study and writing of history with a passion. For romantics, history was not a minor branch of philosophy from which philosophers picked suitable examples to illustrate their teachings. History was beautiful, exciting,

✤ **John Martin: The Great Day of His Wrath** The combination of the terrible and the sublime fascinated English romantic artist John Martin, and he painted wild visions of hell for a popular illustrated edition of John Milton's great epic poem, *Paradise Lost*. But the reality of ironworks blazing in the night seemed to him even more awesome and inspired this image of the Last Judgment and the end of human history. (Source: Tate Gallery, London/Art Resource, NY)

and important in its own right. It was the art of change over time—the key to a universe that was now perceived to be organic and dynamic. It was no longer perceived to be mechanical and static, as it had to the philosophes of the eighteenth-century Enlightenment.

Historical studies supported the development of national aspirations and encouraged entire peoples to seek in the past their special destinies. This trend was especially strong in Germany and other eastern European countries. As the famous English historian Lord Acton put it, the growth of historical thinking associated with the romantic movement was a most fateful step in the story of European thought.

Literature

Britain was the first country where romanticism flowered fully in poetry and prose, and the British romantic writers were among the most prominent in Europe. Wordsworth, Coleridge, and Scott were all active by 1800, to be followed shortly by Byron, Shelley, and Keats. All were poets: romanticism found its distinctive voice in poetry, as the Enlightenment had in prose.

A towering leader of English romanticism, William Wordsworth (1770–1850) traveled in France after his graduation from Cambridge. There he fell passionately in love with a French woman, who bore him a daughter. He was deeply influenced by the philosophy of Rousseau and the spirit of the early French Revolution. Back in England, prevented by war and the Terror from returning to France, Wordsworth settled in the countryside with his sister, Dorothy, and Samuel Taylor Coleridge (1772–1834).

In 1798 the two poets published their *Lyrical Ballads,* one of the most influential literary works in the history of the English language. In defiance of classical rules, Wordsworth and Coleridge abandoned flowery poetic conventions for the language of ordinary speech, simultaneously endowing simple subjects with the loftiest majesty. This twofold rejection of classical practice was at first ignored and then harshly criticized, but by 1830 Wordsworth had triumphed.

One of the best examples of Wordsworth's romantic credo and genius is "Daffodils":

I wandered lonely as a cloud
That floats on high o'er vales and hills,
When all at once I saw a crowd,
A host, of golden daffodils;
Beside the lake, beneath the trees,
Fluttering and dancing in the breeze.

Continuous as the stars that shine
And twinkle on the Milky Way,
They stretched in never-ending line
Along the margin of a bay:
Ten thousand saw I at a glance,
Tossing their heads in sprightly dance.

The waves beside them danced, but they
Out-did the sparkling waves in glee:
A poet could not but be gay,
In such a jocund company:
I gazed—and gazed—but little thought
What wealth the show to me had brought:

For oft, when on my couch I lie
In vacant or in pensive mood,
They flash upon that inward eye
Which is the bliss of solitude;
And then my heart with pleasure fills,
And dances with the daffodils.

Here indeed are simplicity and love of nature in commonplace forms, which could be appreciated, very democratically, by everyone and not just by an intellectual elite. Here, too, is Wordsworth's romantic conviction that nature has the power to elevate and instruct. Wordsworth's conception of poetry as the "spontaneous overflow of powerful feeling recollected in tranquility" is well illustrated by the last stanza.

Born in Edinburgh, Walter Scott (1771–1832) personified the romantic movement's fascination with history. Raised on his grandfather's farm, Scott fell under the spell of the old ballads and tales of the Scottish border. He was also deeply influenced by German romanticism, particularly by the immortal poet and dramatist Johann Wolfgang von Goethe (1749–1832). Scott translated Goethe's famous *Gotz von Berlichingen,* a play about a sixteenth-century knight who revolted against centralized authority and championed individual freedom—at least in Goethe's romantic drama. A natural storyteller, Scott then composed long narrative poems and a series of historical novels. Scott excelled in faithfully recreating the spirit of bygone ages and great historical events, especially those of Scotland.

At first, the strength of classicism in France inhibited the growth of romanticism there. Then between 1820 and 1850, the romantic impulse broke through in the poetry and prose of Lamartine, de Vigny, Hugo, Dumas, and Sand. Of these, Victor Hugo (1802–1885) was the greatest in both poetry and prose.

Son of a Napoleonic general, Hugo achieved an amazing range of rhythm, language, and image in his lyric poetry. His powerful novels exemplified the romantic fascination with fantastic characters, strange settings, and human emotions. The hero of Hugo's famous *Hunchback of Notre Dame* (1831) is the great cathedral's deformed bellringer, a "human gargoyle" overlooking the teeming life of fifteenth-century Paris. A great admirer of William Shakespeare, whom classical critics had derided as undisciplined and excessive, Hugo also championed romanticism in drama. His play *Hernani* (1830) consciously broke all the old rules, as Hugo renounced his early conservatism and equated freedom in literature with liberty in politics and society. Hugo's political evolution was thus exactly the opposite of Wordsworth's, in whom youthful radicalism gave way to middle-aged caution. As the contrast between the two artists suggests, romanticism was a cultural movement compatible with many political beliefs.

Amandine Aurore Lucie Dupin (1804–1876), a strong-willed and gifted woman generally known by her pen name, George Sand, defied the narrow conventions of her time in an unending search for self-fulfillment. After eight years of unhappy marriage in the provinces, she abandoned her dullard of a husband and took her two children to Paris to pursue a career as a writer. There Sand soon achieved fame and wealth, eventually writing over eighty novels on a variety of romantic and social themes. All were shot through with a typically romantic love of nature and moral idealism. George Sand's striking individualism went far beyond her flamboyant preference for men's clothing and cigars and her notorious affairs with poet Alfred de Musset and composer Frédéric Chopin, among others. Her semi-autobiographical novel *Lélia* was shockingly modern, delving deeply into her tortuous quest for sexual and personal freedom.

In central and eastern Europe, literary romanticism and early nationalism often reinforced each other. Seeking a unique greatness in every people, well-educated romantics plumbed their own histories and cultures. Like modern anthropologists, they turned their attention to peasant life and transcribed the folk songs, tales, and proverbs that the cosmopolitan Enlightenment had disdained. The brothers Jacob and Wilhelm Grimm were particularly successful at rescuing German fairy tales from oblivion. In the Slavic lands, romantics played a decisive role in converting spoken peasant languages into modern written languages. The greatest of all Russian poets, Aleksander Pushkin (1799–1837), rejecting eighteenth-century attempts to force Russian poetry into a classical straitjacket, used his lyric genius to mold the modern literary language.

Art and Music

The greatest and most moving romantic painter in France was Eugène Delacroix (1798–1863), probably the illegitimate son of French foreign minister Talleyrand. Delacroix was a master of dramatic, colorful scenes that stirred the emotions. He was fascinated with remote and exotic subjects, whether lion hunts in Morocco or the languishing, sensuous women of a sultan's harem. Yet he was also a passionate spokesman for freedom. His masterpiece, *Liberty Leading the People,* celebrated the nobility of popular revolution in general and revolution in France in particular.

In England the most notable romantic painters were Joseph M. W. Turner (1775–1851) and John Constable (1776–1837). Both were fascinated by nature, but their interpretations of it contrasted sharply, aptly symbolizing the tremendous emotional range of the romantic movement. Turner depicted nature's power and terror; wild storms and sinking ships were favorite subjects. Constable painted gentle Wordsworthian landscapes in which human beings were at one with their environment, the comforting countryside of unspoiled rural England.

It was in music that romanticism realized most fully and permanently its goals of free expression and emotional intensity. Whereas the composers of the eighteenth century had remained true to well-defined structures, such as the classical symphony, the great romantics used a great range of forms to create a thousand musical landscapes and evoke a host of powerful emotions. Romantic composers also transformed the small classical orchestra, tripling its size by adding wind instruments, percussion, and more brass and strings. The crashing chords evoking the surge of the masses in Chopin's "Revolutionary" etude, the bottomless despair of the funeral march in Beethoven's Third Symphony, the solemn majesty of a great religious event in Schumann's Rhenish Symphony—such were the modern orchestra's musical paintings that plumbed the depths of human feeling.

This range and intensity gave music and musicians much greater prestige than in the past. Music no longer simply complemented a church service or helped a nobleman digest his dinner. Music became a sublime end in itself. It became for many the greatest of the arts, precisely because it achieved the most ecstatic effect and most perfectly realized the endless yearning of the soul. It was worthy of great concert halls and the most dedicated sacrifice. The unbelievable one-in-a-million performer—the great virtuoso who could transport the listener to ecstasy and hysteria—became a cultural hero. The composer Franz Liszt (1811–1886) vowed to do for the piano what Nicolo Paganini (1784–1840) had done for the violin, and he was lionized as the greatest pianist of his age.

❖ **Heroes of Romanticism** Observed by a portrait of Byron and bust of Beethoven, Liszt plays for friends in this painting by Josef Danhauser. From left to right sit Alexander Dumas, George Sand (characteristically wearing men's garb), and Marie d'Agoult, Liszt's mistress. Standing are Victor Hugo, Paganini, and Rossini. In fact, this gathering of geniuses was actually imaginary, part of an advertising campaign by a German piano manufacturer to sell pianos to the comfortable middle class. *(Source: Bildarchiv Preussischer Kulturbesitz)*

People swooned for Liszt as they scream for rock stars today.

Though romanticism dominated music until late in the nineteenth century, no composer ever surpassed its first great master, Ludwig van Beethoven (1770–1827). Extending and breaking open classical forms, Beethoven used contrasting themes and tones to produce dramatic conflict and inspiring resolutions. As the contemporary German novelist Ernst Hoffmann (1776–1822) wrote, "Beethoven's music sets in motion the lever of fear, of awe, of horror, of suffering, and awakens just that

infinite longing which is the essence of Romanticism." Beethoven's range was tremendous; his output included symphonies, chamber music, sonatas for violin and piano, masses, an opera, and a great many songs.

At the peak of his fame, in constant demand as a composer and recognized as the leading concert pianist of his day, Beethoven began to lose his hearing. He considered suicide but eventually overcame despair: "I will take fate by the throat; it will not bend me completely to its will."[4] Beethoven continued to pour out immortal music.

Among other achievements, he fully exploited for the first time the richness and beauty of the piano. Beethoven never heard much of his later work, including the unforgettable choral finale to the Ninth Symphony, for his last years were silent, spent in total deafness.

⁜ REFORMS AND REVOLUTIONS

While the romantic movement was developing, liberal, national, and socialist forces battered against the conservatism of 1815. In some countries, change occurred gradually and peacefully. Elsewhere, pressure built up like steam in a pressure cooker without a safety valve and eventually caused an explosion in 1848. Three important countries—Greece, Great Britain, and France—experienced variations on this basic theme.

National Liberation in Greece

National, liberal revolution, frustrated in Italy and Spain by conservative statesmen, succeeded first after 1815 in Greece. Since the fifteenth century, the Greeks had been living under the domination of the Ottoman Turks. In spite of centuries of foreign rule, the Greeks had survived as a people, united by their language and the Greek Orthodox religion. It was perfectly natural that the general growth of national aspirations and a desire for independence would inspire some Greeks in the early nineteenth century. This rising national movement led to the formation of secret societies and then to revolt in 1821, led by Alexander Ypsilanti, a Greek patriot and a general in the Russian army.

The Great Powers, particularly Metternich, were opposed to all revolution, even revolution against the Islamic Turks. They refused to back Ypsilanti and supported the Ottoman Empire. Yet for many Europeans, the Greek cause became a holy one. Educated Americans and Europeans were in love with the culture of classical Greece; Russians were stirred by the piety of their Orthodox brethren. Writers and artists, moved by the romantic impulse, responded enthusiastically to the Greek struggle. The flamboyant, radical poet Lord Byron went to Greece and died there in the struggle "that Greece might still be free." Turkish atrocities to-

ward the rebels fanned the fires of European outrage and Greek determination. One of Delacroix's romantic masterpieces memorialized the massacre at Chios, where the Turks had slaughtered nearly 100,000 Greeks.

The Greeks, though often quarreling among themselves, battled on against the Turks and hoped for the eventual support of European governments. In 1827 Great Britain, France, and Russia responded to popular demands at home and directed Turkey to accept an armistice. When the Turks refused, the navies of these three powers trapped the Turkish fleet at Navarino and destroyed it. Russia then declared another of its periodic wars of expansion against the Turks. This led to the establishment of a Russian protectorate over much of present-day Rumania, which had also been under Turkish rule. Great Britain, France, and Russia finally declared Greece independent in 1830 and installed a German prince as king of the new country in 1832. In the end the Greeks had won: a small nation had gained its independence in a heroic war against a foreign empire.

Liberal Reform in Great Britain

Eighteenth-century British society had been both flexible and remarkably stable. It was dominated by the landowning aristocracy, but that class was neither closed nor rigidly defined. Successful business and professional people could buy land and become gentlefolk, while the common people had more than the usual opportunities of the preindustrial world. Basic civil rights for all were balanced by a tradition of deference to one's social superiors. Parliament was manipulated by the king and was thoroughly undemocratic. Only about 6 percent of the population could vote for representatives to Parliament, and by the 1780s there was growing interest in some kind of political reform.

But the French Revolution threw the British aristocracy into a panic for a generation, making it extremely hostile to any attempts to change the status quo. The Tory party, completely controlled by the landed aristocracy, was particularly fearful of radical movements at home and abroad. Castlereagh initially worked closely with Metternich to restrain France and restore a conservative balance in central Europe. This same intense conservatism motivated the Tory government at home. After

1815 the aristocracy defended its ruling position by repressing every kind of popular protest.

The first step in this direction began with revision of the Corn Laws in 1815. Corn Laws to regulate the foreign grain trade had long existed, but they were not needed during a generation of war with France because the British had been un-able to import cheap grain from eastern Europe. As shortages occurred and agricultural prices sky-rocketed, a great deal of marginal land had been brought under cultivation. This development had been a bonanza for the landed aristocracy, whose fat rent rolls became even fatter. Peace meant that grain could be imported again and that the price

Delacroix: Massacre at Chios The Greek struggle for freedom and independence won the enthusiastic support of liberals, nationalists, and romantics. The Ottoman Turks were seen as cruel oppressors who were holding back the course of history, as in this moving masterpiece by Delacroix. *(Source: Louvre/Cliché des Musées Nationaux, Paris)*

THE PRELUDE TO 1848

March 1814	Russia, Prussia, Austria, and Britain form the Quadruple Alliance to defeat France
April 1814	Napoleon abdicates
May–June 1814	Restoration of Bourbon monarchy; Louis XVIII issues Constitutional Charter providing for civil liberties and representative government First Peace of Paris: allies combine leniency with defensive posture toward France
October 1814–June 1815	Congress of Vienna peace settlement: establishes balance-of-power principle and creates the German Confederation
February 1815	Napoleon escapes from Elba and marches on Paris
June 1815	Battle of Waterloo
September 1815	Austria, Prussia, and Russia form the Holy Alliance to repress liberal and revolutionary movements
November 1815	Second Peace of Paris and renewal of Quadruple Alliance: punishes France and establishes the European "congress system"
1819	Carlsbad Decrees: Metternich imposes harsh measures throughout the German Confederation
1820	Revolution in Spain and the Kingdom of the Two Sicilies Congress of Troppau: Metternich and Alexander I of Russia proclaim principle of intervention to maintain autocratic regimes
1821	Austria crushes liberal revolution in Naples and restores the Sicilian autocracy Greek revolt against the Ottoman Turks
1823	French armies restore the Spanish regime United States proclaims the Monroe Doctrine
1824	Reactionary Charles X succeeds Louis XVIII in France
1830	Charles X repudiates the Constitutional Charter; insurrection and collapse of government; Louis Philippe succeeds to the throne and maintains a narrowly liberal regime until 1848 Greece wins independence from the Ottoman Empire
1832	Reform Bill expands British electorate and encourages the middle class
1839	Louis Blanc, *Organization of Work*
1840	Pierre Joseph Proudhon, *What Is Property?*
1846	Jules Michelet, *The People*
1848	Karl Marx and Friedrich Engels, *The Communist Manifesto*

of wheat and bread would go down. To almost everyone except the aristocracy, lower prices seemed highly desirable. The aristocracy, however, rammed far-reaching changes in the Corn Laws through Parliament. The new regulation prohibited the importation of foreign grain unless the price at home rose above 80 shillings per quarter-ton—a level reached only in time of harvest disaster before 1790. Seldom has a class legislated more selfishly for its own narrow economic advantage or done more to promote a class-based interpretation of political action.

The change in the Corn Laws, coming at a time of widespread unemployment and postwar adjustment, led to protests and demonstrations by urban laborers. They were supported by radical intellectuals, who campaigned for a reformed House of Commons that would serve the nation and not just the aristocracy. In 1817 the Tory government responded by temporarily suspending the traditional rights of peaceable assembly and habeas corpus. Two years later, Parliament passed the infamous Six Acts, which, among other things, controlled a heavily taxed press and practically eliminated all mass meetings. These acts followed an enormous but orderly protest, at Saint Peter's Fields in Manchester, that had been savagely broken up by armed cavalry. Nicknamed the "Battle of Peterloo," in scornful reference to the British victory at Waterloo, this incident expressed the government's determination to repress and stand fast.

Ongoing industrial development was not only creating urban and social problems but also strengthening the upper middle classes. The new manufacturing and commercial groups insisted on a place for their new wealth alongside the landed wealth of the aristocracy in the framework of political power and social prestige. They called for many kinds of liberal reform: reform of town government, organization of a new police force, more rights for Catholics and dissenters, and reform of the Poor Laws that provided aid to some low-paid workers. In the 1820s a less frightened Tory government moved in the direction of better urban administration, greater economic liberalism, and civil equality for Catholics. The prohibition on imports of foreign grain was replaced by a heavy tariff. These actions encouraged the middle classes to press on for reform of Parliament so they could have a larger say in government and perhaps repeal

the latest revision of the Corn Laws, that symbol of aristocratic domination.

The Whig party, though led like the Tories by great aristocrats, had by tradition been more responsive to commercial and manufacturing interests. In 1830 a Whig ministry introduced "an act to amend the representation of the people of England and Wales." Defeated, then passed by the House of Commons, this reform bill was rejected by the House of Lords. But when in 1832 the Whigs got the king to promise to create enough new peers to pass the law, the House of Lords reluctantly gave in rather than see its snug little club ruined by upstart manufacturers and plutocrats. A mighty surge of popular protest had helped the king and lords make up their minds.

The Reform Bill of 1832 had profound significance. The House of Commons had emerged as the all-important legislative body. In the future, an obstructionist House of Lords could always be brought into line by the threat of creating new peers. The new industrial areas of the country gained representation in the Commons, and many old "rotten boroughs"—electoral districts with very few voters that the landed aristocracy had bought and sold—were eliminated.

The redistribution of seats reflected the shift in population to the northern manufacturing counties and the gradual emergence of an urban society. As a result of the Reform Bill of 1832, the number of voters increased by about 50 percent, giving about 12 percent of the total population the right to vote. Comfortable middle-class groups in the urban population as well as some substantial farmers who leased their land received the vote. Thus the pressures building in Great Britain were successfully—though only temporarily—released. A major reform had been achieved peacefully, without revolution or civil war. More radical reforms within the system appeared difficult but not impossible.

The principal radical program was embodied in the "People's Charter" of 1838 and the Chartist movement (see page 752). Partly inspired by the economic distress of the working class, the Chartists' core demand was universal male (but not female) suffrage. They saw complete political democracy and rule by the common people as the means to a good and just society. Hundreds of thousands of people signed gigantic petitions calling on Parliament to grant all men the right to vote, first and most seriously in 1839, again in 1842, and yet again in 1848. Parliament rejected all three petitions. In the short run, the working poor failed with their Chartist demands, but they learned a valuable lesson in mass politics.

While calling for universal male suffrage, many working-class people joined with middle-class manufacturers in the Anti–Corn Law League, founded in Manchester in 1839. Mass participation made possible a popular crusade against the tariff on imported grain and against the landed aristocracy. People were fired up by dramatic popular orators such as John Bright and Richard Cobden. These fighting liberals argued that lower food prices and more jobs in industry depended on repeal of the Corn Laws. Much of the working class agreed. The climax of the movement came in 1845. In that year Ireland's potato crop failed, and rapidly rising food prices marked the beginning of

the Irish famine. Famine prices for food and even famine itself also seemed likely in England. To avert the impending catastrophe, Tory prime minister Robert Peel joined with the Whigs and a minority of his own party to repeal the Corn Laws in 1846 and allow free imports of grain. England escaped famine. Thereafter, the liberal doctrine of free trade became almost sacred dogma in Great Britain.

The following year, the Tories passed a bill designed to help the working classes, but in a different way. This was the Ten Hours Act of 1847, which limited the workday for women and young people in factories to ten hours. Tory aristocrats continued to champion legislation regulating factory conditions. They were competing vigorously with the middle class for the support of the working class. This healthy competition between a still-vigorous aristocracy and a strong middle class was

The Chartist Movement   In 1842, for the second of three times, a long procession of workers marched peaceably through London to present Parliament with demands for democratic reform, as shown here. The Chartists wanted universal manhood suffrage, vote by secret ballot, no property qualifications for members of Parliament, pay for serving in Parliament, equal electoral districts, and annual elections. *(Source: The Fotomas Index)*

❖ **Evictions of Irish Peasants** who could not pay their rent continued for decades after the Great Famine. Surrounded by a few meager possessions, this family has been turned out of its cottage in the 1880s. The door is nailed shut to prevent their return. *(Source: Lawrence Collection, National Library of Ireland, Dublin)*

a crucial factor in Great Britain's peaceful evolution. The working classes could make temporary alliances with either competitor to better their own conditions.

The people of Ireland did not benefit from this political competition. Long ruled as a conquered people, the great mass of the population (outside the northern counties of Ulster, which were partly Presbyterian) were Irish Catholic peasants who rented their land from a tiny minority of Church of England Protestants, many of whom lived in England (see Chapter 20). Ruthlessly exploited and growing rapidly in numbers, Irish peasants had come to depend on the potato crop, the size of which varied substantially from year to year. Potato failures could not be detected in time to plant other crops, nor could potatoes be stored for more

than a year. Moreover, Ireland's precarious potato economy was a subsistence economy, which therefore lacked a well-developed network of roads and trade capable of distributing other foods in time of disaster. When the crop failed in 1845, the Irish were very vulnerable.

In 1846, 1848, and 1851, the potato crop failed again in Ireland and throughout much of Europe. The general result was high food prices, widespread suffering, and, frequently, social upheaval. In Ireland the result was unmitigated disaster—the Great Famine. Blight attacked the young plants, and the tubers rotted. Widespread starvation and mass fever epidemics followed. Total losses of population were staggering. Fully 1 million emigrants fled the famine between 1845 and 1851, going primarily to the United States and Great

Britain, and at least 1.5 million people died or went unborn because of the disaster. The British government's efforts at famine relief were too little and too late. At the same time, the government energetically supported heartless landowner demands with armed force. Tenants who could not pay their rents were evicted and their homes broken up or burned. Famine or no, Ireland remained a conquered province, a poor agricultural land that had gained little from the liberal reforms and the industrial developments that were transforming Great Britain.

The Revolution of 1830 in France

Louis XVIII's Constitutional Charter of 1814—theoretically a gift from the king but actually a response to political pressures—was basically a liberal constitution (see page 720). The economic and social gains made by sections of the middle class and the peasantry in the French Revolution were fully protected, great intellectual and artistic freedom was permitted, and a real parliament with upper and lower houses was created. Immediately after Napoleon's abortive Hundred Days, the moderate, worldly king refused to bow to the wishes of die-hard aristocrats such as his brother Charles, who wished to sweep away all the revolutionary changes and return to a bygone age of royal absolutism and aristocratic pretension. Instead, Louis appointed as his ministers moderate royalists, who sought and obtained the support of a majority of the representatives elected to the lower Chamber of Deputies between 1816 and Louis's death in 1824.

Louis XVIII's charter was anything but democratic. Only about 100,000 of the wealthiest people out of a total population of 30 million had the right to vote for the deputies who, with the king and his ministers, made the laws of the nation. Nonetheless, the "notable people" who did vote came from very different backgrounds. There were wealthy businessmen, war profiteers, successful professionals, ex-revolutionaries, large landowners from the old aristocracy and the middle class, Bourbons, and Bonapartists.

The old aristocracy, with its pre-1789 mentality, was a minority within the voting population. It was this situation that Louis's successor, Charles X (r. 1824–1830), could not abide. Crowned in a lavish, utterly medieval, five-hour ceremony in the cathedral of Reims in 1824, Charles was a true reactionary. He wanted to re-establish the old order in France. Increasingly blocked by the opposition of the deputies, Charles finally repudiated the Constitutional Charter in an attempted coup in July 1830. He issued decrees stripping much of the wealthy middle class of its voting rights, and he censored the press. The immediate reaction, encouraged by journalists and lawyers, was an insurrection in the capital by printers, other artisans, and small traders. In "three glorious days" the government collapsed. Paris boiled with revolutionary excitement, and Charles fled. Then the upper middle class, which had fomented the revolt, skillfully seated Charles's cousin, Louis Philippe, duke of Orléans, on the vacant throne.

Louis Philippe (r. 1830–1848) accepted the Constitutional Charter of 1814; adopted the red, white, and blue flag of the French Revolution; and admitted that he was merely the "king of the French people." In spite of such symbolic actions, the situation in France remained fundamentally unchanged. Casimir Périer, a wealthy banker and Louis Philippe's new chief minister, bluntly told a deputy who complained when the vote was extended only from 100,000 to 170,000 citizens, "The trouble with this country is that there are too many people like you who imagine that there has been a revolution in France."[5] The wealthy notable elite actually tightened its control as the old aristocracy retreated to the provinces to sulk harmlessly. For the upper middle class, there had been a change in dynasty in order to protect the status quo and the narrowly liberal institutions of 1815. Republicans, democrats, social reformers, and the poor of Paris were bitterly disappointed. They had made a revolution, but it seemed for naught.

THE REVOLUTIONS OF 1848

In 1848 revolutionary political and social ideologies combined with economic crisis and the romantic impulse to produce a vast upheaval. Only the most advanced and the most backward major countries—reforming Great Britain and immobile Russia—escaped untouched. Governments toppled; monarchs and ministers bowed or fled. National independence, liberal-democratic constitutions, and social reform: the lofty aspirations of a generation seemed at hand. Yet in the end the revolutions failed. Why was this so?

A Democratic Republic in France

The late 1840s in Europe were hard economically and tense politically. The potato famine in Ireland in 1845 and in 1846 had echoes on the Continent. Bad harvests jacked up food prices and caused misery and unemployment in the cities. "Prerevo-

lutionary" outbreaks occurred all across Europe: an abortive Polish revolution in the northern part of Austria in 1846, a civil war between radicals and conservatives in Switzerland in 1847, and an armed uprising in Naples, Italy, in January 1848. Revolution was almost universally expected, but it took revolution in Paris—once again—to turn expectations into realities.

From its beginning in 1830, Louis Philippe's "bourgeois monarchy" was characterized by stubborn inaction. There was a glaring lack of social

❖ **Delacroix: Liberty Leading the People** This famous romantic painting glorifies the July Revolution in Paris in 1830. Raising high the revolutionary tricolor, Liberty unites the worker, bourgeois, and street child in a righteous crusade against privilege and oppression. The Revolution of 1848 began as a similar crusade, but class warfare in Paris soon shattered the hope of rich and poor joined together for freedom. *(Source: Louvre/Cliché des Musées Nationaux, Paris)*

legislation, and politics was dominated by corruption and selfish special interests. The king's chief minister in the 1840s, François Guizot, was complacency personified. Guizot was especially satisfied with the electoral system. Only the rich could vote for deputies, and many of the deputies were docile government bureaucrats. The government's stubborn refusal to consider electoral reform heightened a sense of class injustice among urban working people, and it eventually touched off a popular revolt in Paris. Barricades went up on the night of February 22, 1848, and by February 24 Louis Philippe had abdicated in favor of his grandson. But the common people in arms would tolerate no more monarchy. This refusal led to the proclamation of a provisional republic, headed by a ten-man executive committee and certified by cries of approval from the revolutionary crowd.

In the flush of victory, there was much about which Parisian revolutionaries could agree. A generation of historians and journalists had praised the First French Republic, and their work had borne fruit: the revolutionaries were firmly committed to a republic as opposed to any form of constitutional monarchy, and they immediately set about drafting a constitution for France's Second Republic. Moreover, they wanted a truly popular and democratic republic so that the healthy, life-giving forces of the common people—the peasants and the workers—could reform society with wise legislation. In practice, building such a republic meant giving the right to vote to every adult male, and this was quickly done. Revolutionary compassion and sympathy for freedom were expressed in the freeing of all slaves in French colonies, the abolition of the death penalty, and the establishment of a ten-hour workday for Paris.

Yet there were profound differences within the revolutionary coalition in Paris. On the one hand, there were the moderate, liberal republicans of the middle class. They viewed universal male suffrage as the ultimate concession to be made to popular forces and strongly opposed any further radical social measures. On the other hand, there were the radical republicans. Influenced by the critique of capitalism and unbridled individualism elaborated by a generation of utopian socialists, and appalled by the poverty and misery of the urban poor, the radical republicans were committed to socialism. To be sure, socialism came in many utopian shapes and sizes for the Parisian working poor and their

leaders, but that did not make their commitment to it any less real. Finally, wedged in between these groups were individuals such as the poet Alphonse Lamartine (1790–1869) and the democrat Alexandre Ledru-Rollin (1807–1874), who were neither doctrinaire socialists nor stand-pat liberals and who sought to escape an impending tragedy.

Worsening depression and rising unemployment brought these conflicting goals to the fore. Louis Blanc, who along with a worker named Albert represented the republican socialists in the provisional government, pressed for recognition of a socialist right to work. Blanc asserted that permanent government-sponsored cooperative workshops should be established for workers. Such workshops would be an alternative to capitalist employment and a decisive step toward a new, noncompetitive social order.

The moderate republicans wanted no such thing. They were willing to provide only temporary relief. The resulting compromise set up national workshops—soon to become a vast program of pick-and-shovel public works—and established a special commission under Blanc to "study the question." This satisfied no one. As bad as the national workshops were, however, they were better than nothing. An army of desperate poor from the French provinces and even from foreign countries streamed into Paris to sign up. The number enrolled in the workshops soared from 10,000 in March to 120,000 by June, and another 80,000 were trying unsuccessfully to join.

While the workshops in Paris grew, the French masses went to the election polls in late April. Voting in most cases for the first time, the people elected to the new Constituent Assembly about five hundred moderate republicans, three hundred monarchists, and one hundred radicals who professed various brands of socialism. One of the moderate republicans was the author of *Democracy in America,* Alexis de Tocqueville (1805–1859), who had predicted the overthrow of Louis Philippe's government. To this brilliant observer, socialism was the most characteristic aspect of the revolution in Paris.

This socialist revolution was evoking a violent reaction not only among the frightened middle and upper classes but also among the bulk of the population—the peasants. The French peasants owned land, and according to Tocqueville, "private property had become with all those who owned it

THE REVOLUTIONS OF 1848

February	Revolt in Paris against Louis Philippe's "bourgeois monarchy"; Louis Philippe abdicates; proclamation of a provisional republic
February–June	Establishment and rapid growth of government-sponsored workshops in France
March 3	Hungarians under Kossuth demand autonomy from Austrian Empire
March 13	Uprising of students and workers in Vienna; Metternich flees to London
March 19–21	Frederick William IV of Prussia is forced to salute the bodies of slain revolutionaries in Berlin and agrees to a liberal constitution and merger into a new German state
March 20	Ferdinand I of Austria abolishes serfdom and promises reforms
March 26	Workers in Berlin issue a series of socialist demands
April 22	French voters favor moderate republicans over radicals 5 : 1
May 15	Parisian socialist workers invade the Constitutional Assembly and unsuccessfully proclaim a new revolutionary state
May 18	Frankfurt Assembly begins writing a new German constitution
June 17	Austrian army crushes working-class revolt in Prague
June 22–26	French government abolishes the national workshops, provoking an uprising June Days: republican army defeats rebellious Parisian working class
October	Austrian army besieges and retakes Vienna from students and working-class radicals
December	Conservatives force Ferdinand I of Austria to abdicate in favor of youngFrancis Joseph Frederick William IV disbands Prussian Constituent Assembly and grants Prussia a conservative constitution Louis Napoleon wins a landslide victory in French presidential elections
March 1849	Frankfurt Assembly elects Frederick William IV of Prussia emperor of the new German state; Frederick William refuses and reasserts royal authority in Prussia
June–August 1849	Habsburg and Russian forces defeat the Hungarian independence movement

a sort of bond of fraternity."[6] The countryside, Tocqueville wrote, had been seized with a universal hatred of radical Paris. Returning from Normandy to take his seat in the new Constituent Assembly, Tocqueville saw that a majority of the members were firmly committed to the republic and strongly opposed to the socialists, and he shared their sentiments.

This clash of ideologies—of liberal capitalism and socialism—became a clash of classes and arms after the elections. The new government's executive committee dropped Blanc and thereafter included no representative of the Parisian working class. Fearing that their socialist hopes were about to be dashed, the workers invaded the Constituent Assembly on May 15 and tried to proclaim a new revolutionary state. But the government was ready and used the middle-class National Guard to squelch this uprising. As the workshops continued to fill and grow more radical, the fearful but powerful propertied classes in the Assembly took the offensive. On June 22 the government dissolved the national workshops in Paris, giving the workers the choice of joining the army or going to workshops in the provinces.

The result was a spontaneous and violent uprising. Frustrated in attempts to create a socialist society, masses of desperate people were now losing even their life-sustaining relief. As a voice from the crowd cried out when the famous astronomer François Arago counseled patience, "Ah, Monsieur Arago, you have never been hungry!"[7] Barricades sprang up in the narrow streets of Paris, and a terrible class war began. Working people fought with the courage of utter desperation, but the government had the army and the support of peasant France. After three terrible "June Days" and the death or injury of more than ten thousand people, the republican army under General Louis Cavaignac stood triumphant in a sea of working-class blood and hatred.

The revolution in France thus ended in spectacular failure. The February coalition of the middle and working classes had in four short months become locked in mortal combat. In place of a generous democratic republic, the Constituent Assembly completed a constitution featuring a strong executive. This allowed Louis Napoleon, nephew of Napoleon Bonaparte, to win a landslide victory in the election of December 1848. The appeal of his great name as well as the desire of the propertied classes for order at any cost had produced a semi-authoritarian regime.

The Austrian Empire in 1848

Throughout central Europe, news of the upheaval in France evoked feverish excitement and eventually revolution. Liberals demanded written constitutions, representative government, and greater civil liberties from authoritarian regimes. When governments hesitated, popular revolts followed. Urban workers and students served as the shock troops, but they were allied with middle-class liberals and peasants. In the face of this united front, monarchs collapsed and granted almost everything. The popular revolutionary coalition, having secured great and easy victories, then broke down as it had in France. The traditional forces—the monarchy, the aristocracy, and the regular army—recovered their nerve, reasserted their authority, and took back many, though not all, of the concessions. Reaction was everywhere victorious.

The revolution in the Austrian Empire began in Hungary. Nationalism had been growing among Hungarians since about 1790, and in 1848, under the leadership of Louis Kossuth, the Hungarians demanded national autonomy, full civil liberties, and universal suffrage. When the monarchy in Vienna hesitated, Viennese students and workers took to the streets on March 13 and added their own demands. Peasant disorders broke out in parts of the empire. The Habsburg emperor Ferdinand I (r. 1835–1848) capitulated and promised reforms and a liberal constitution. Metternich fled in disguise toward London. The old absolutist order seemed to be collapsing with unbelievable rapidity.

The coalition of revolutionaries was not completely stable, however. The Austrian Empire was overwhelmingly agricultural, and serfdom still existed. On March 20, as part of a capitulation before upheaval, the monarchy abolished serfdom, with its degrading forced labor and feudal services. Peasants throughout the empire felt they had won a victory reminiscent of that in France in 1789. Newly free men and women of the land then lost interest in the political and social questions agitating the cities. The government had in the peasants a potential ally of great importance, especially since, in central Europe as in France, the army was largely composed of peasants.

The coalition of March was also weakened, and ultimately destroyed, by conflicting national aspirations. In March the Hungarian revolutionary leaders pushed through an extremely liberal, almost democratic, constitution granting widespread voting rights and civil liberties and ending feudal obligations. So far, well and good. Yet the Hungarian revolutionaries were also nationalists with a mission. They wanted the ancient Crown of Saint

❖ **Revolutionary Justice in Vienna** As part of the conservative resurgence, in October 1848 the Austrian minister of war ordered up reinforcements for an army that was marching on Hungary. In a last defiant gesture the outraged revolutionaries in Vienna seized the minister and lynched him from a lamppost for treason. The army then reconquered the city in a week of bitter fighting. *(Source: Mary Evans Picture Library/Photo Researchers)*

Stephen, with its mosaic of provinces and nationalities, transformed into a unified, centralized, Hungarian nation. To the minority groups that formed half the population of the kingdom of Hungary—the Croats, Serbs, and Rumanians—such unification was completely unacceptable. Each felt entitled to political autonomy and cultural independence. The Habsburg monarchy in Vienna exploited the fears of the minority groups,

and they were soon locked in armed combat with the new Hungarian government.

In a somewhat different way, Czech nationalists based in Bohemia and the city of Prague, led by Czech historian Palacký, came into conflict with German nationalists. Like the minorities in Hungary, the Czechs saw their struggle for autonomy as a struggle against a dominant group, the Germans. Thus the national aspirations of different peoples in the Austrian Empire came into sharp conflict, and the monarchy was able to play off one group against the other.

Nor was this all. The urban working classes of poor artisans and day laborers were not as radical in the Austrian Empire as they were in France, but then neither were the middle class and lower middle class. Throughout Austria and the German states, where Metternich's brand of absolutism had so recently ruled supreme, the middle class wanted liberal reform complete with constitutional monarchy, limited voting rights, and modest social measures. It wanted a central European equivalent of the English Reform Bill of 1832 and the Corn Laws repeal of 1846. When the urban poor rose in arms—as they did in the Austrian cities of Vienna, Prague, and Milan and throughout the German Confederation as well, presenting their own demands for socialist workshops and universal voting rights for men—the prosperous middle classes recoiled in alarm. As in Paris, the union of the urban poor and the middle class was soon a mere memory, and a bad memory at that.

Finally, the conservative aristocratic forces gathered around Emperor Ferdinand I regained their nerve and reasserted their great strength. The archduchess Sophia, a conservative but intelligent and courageous Bavarian princess married to the emperor's brother, provided a rallying point. Deeply ashamed of the emperor's collapse before a "mess of students," she insisted that Ferdinand, who had no heir, abdicate in favor of her eighteen-year-old son, Francis Joseph.[8] Powerful nobles who held high positions in the government, the army, and the church agreed completely. They organized around Sophia in a secret conspiracy to reverse and crush the revolution.

Their first breakthrough came when one of the most dedicated members of the group, Prince Alfred Windischgrätz, bombarded Prague and savagely crushed a working-class revolt there on June 17. Other Austrian officials and nobles began to lead the minority nationalities of Hungary against the revolutionary government proclaimed by the Hungarian patriots. In late July 1848 another Austrian army reconquered Austria's possessions in northern Italy, where Italian patriots had seized power in March. Thus revolution failed as miserably in Italy as everywhere else. At the end of October, the well-equipped, predominantly peasant troops of the regular Austrian army attacked the student and working-class radicals in Vienna and retook the city at the cost of more than four thousand casualties. Thus the determination of the Austrian aristocracy and the loyalty of its army were the final ingredients in the triumph of reaction and the defeat of revolution.

Francis Joseph (r. 1848–1916) was crowned emperor of Austria immediately after his eighteenth birthday in December 1848. Only in Hungary were the Austrian forces at first unsuccessful in establishing control on the new emperor's behalf. Yet another determined conservative, Nicholas I of Russia (r. 1825–1855), obligingly lent his iron hand. On June 6, 1849, 130,000 Russian troops poured into Hungary. After bitter fighting—in which the Hungarian army supported the revolutionary Hungarian government—they subdued the country. For a number of years, the Habsburgs ruled Hungary as a conquered territory.

Prussia and the Frankfurt Assembly

The rest of the states in the German Confederation generally recapitulated the ebb and flow of developments in France and Austria. The key difference was the additional goal of unifying the thirty-eight states of the German Confederation, with the possible exception of Austria, into a single sovereign nation. Therefore, events in Germany were extraordinarily complex since they were occurring not only in the individual principalities but also at the all-German level.

After Austria, Prussia was the largest and most influential German kingdom. Prior to 1848, the goal of middle-class Prussian liberals had been to transform absolutist Prussia into a liberal constitutional monarchy. Such a monarchy would then take the lead in merging itself and all the other German states into a liberal, unified nation. The agitation following the fall of Louis Philippe encouraged Prussian liberals to press their demands. When these were not granted, the artisans and factory workers in Berlin exploded, joining temporarily with the middle-class liberals in the struggle against the monarchy. The autocratic yet paternalistic Frederick William IV (r. 1840–1861), already displaying the instability that later became insanity, vacillated. Humiliated by the revolutionary crowd, which forced him to salute from his balcony the blood-spattered corpses of workers who had fallen in an uprising on March 18, the nearly hysterical king finally caved in. On March 21 he promised to grant Prussia a liberal constitution and to merge it into a new national German state that was to be created. He appointed two wealthy businessmen from the Rhineland—perfect representatives of moderate constitutional liberalism—to form a new government.

The situation might have stabilized at this point if the workers had not wanted much more and the Prussian aristocracy much less. On March 26 the workers issued a series of radical and vaguely socialist demands that troubled their middle-class allies: universal voting rights, a ministry of labor, a minimum wage, and a ten-hour day. At the same time, a wild-tempered Prussian landowner and aristocrat, Otto von Bismarck, joined the conservative clique gathered around the king to urge counter-revolution. While these tensions in Prussia were growing, an elected assembly met in Berlin to write a constitution for the Prussian state.

To add to the complexity of the situation, a self-appointed committee of liberals from various German states successfully called for the formation of a national constituent assembly to begin writing a federal constitution for a unified German state. That body met for the first time on May 18 in Saint Paul's Church in Frankfurt. The Frankfurt National Assembly was a most curious revolutionary body. It was really a serious middle-class body whose 820 members included some 200 lawyers; 100 professors; many doctors, judges, and officials; and 140 businessmen for good measure.

Convened to write a constitution, the learned body was soon absorbed in a battle with Denmark over the provinces of Schleswig and Holstein. Jurisdiction over them was a hopelessly complicated issue from a legal point of view. Britain's foreign minister, Lord Palmerston, once said that only three people had ever understood the Schleswig-Holstein question, and of those one had died, another had gone mad, and he himself had forgotten the answer. The provinces were inhabited primarily by Germans but were ruled by the king of Denmark, although Holstein was a member of the German Confederation. When Frederick VII, the new nationalistic king of Denmark, tried to integrate both provinces into the rest of his state, the Germans there revolted.

Hypnotized by this conflict, the National Assembly at Frankfurt debated ponderously and finally called on the Prussian army to oppose Denmark in the name of the German nation. Prussia responded

Street Fighting in Frankfurt, 1848 Workers and students could tear up the cobblestones, barricade a street, and make it into a fortress. But urban revolutionaries were untrained and poorly armed. They were no match for professional soldiers led by tough officers who were sent against them after frightened rulers had recovered their nerve. *(Source: The Granger Collection, NY)*

and began war with Denmark. As the Schleswig-Holstein issue demonstrated, the national ideal was a crucial factor motivating the German middle classes in 1848.

Almost obsessed with the fate of Germans under Danish rule, many members of the National Assembly also wanted to bring the German-speaking provinces of Austria into the new German state. Yet resurgent Austria resolutely opposed any division of its territory. Once this Austrian action made a "big German state" impossible, the National Assembly completed its drafting of a liberal constitution. Finally, in March 1849 the Assembly elected King Frederick William of Prussia emperor of the new German national state (minus Austria and Schleswig-Holstein).

By early 1849, however, reaction had been successful almost everywhere. Frederick William had reasserted his royal authority, disbanded the Prussian Constituent Assembly, and granted his subjects a limited, essentially conservative constitution. Reasserting that he ruled by divine right, Frederick William contemptuously refused to accept the "crown from the gutter." The reluctant revolutionaries in Frankfurt had waited too long and acted too timidly.

When Frederick William, who really wanted to be emperor but only on his own authoritarian terms, tried to get the small monarchs of Germany to elect him emperor, Austria balked. Supported by Russia, Austria forced Prussia to renounce all its schemes of unification in late 1850. The German Confederation was re-established. After two turbulent years, the political map of the German states remained unchanged. Attempts to unite the Germans—first in a liberal national state and then in a conservative Prussian empire—had failed completely.

SUMMARY

In 1814 the victorious allied powers sought to restore peace and stability in Europe. Dealing moderately with France and wisely settling their own differences, the allies laid the foundations for beneficial international cooperation throughout much of the nineteenth century. Led by Metternich, the conservative powers also sought to prevent the spread of subversive ideas and radical changes in domestic politics. Yet European thought has seldom been more powerfully creative than after 1815, and ideologies of liberalism, nationalism, and socialism all developed to challenge the existing order. The Romantic movement, breaking decisively with the dictates of classicism, reinforced the spirit of change and revolutionary anticipation.

All of these forces culminated in the liberal and nationalistic revolutions of 1848. Political, economic, and social pressures that had been building since 1815 exploded dramatically, but the upheavals of 1848 were abortive, and very few revolutionary goals were realized. The moderate, nationalistic middle classes were unable to consolidate their initial victories in France or elsewhere in Europe. Instead, they drew back when artisans, factory workers, and radical socialists rose up to present their own much more revolutionary demands. This retreat facilitated the efforts of dedicated aristocrats in central Europe and made possible the crushing of Parisian workers by a coalition of solid bourgeoisie and landowning peasantry in France. A host of fears, a sea of blood, and a torrent of disillusion had drowned the lofty ideals and utopian visions of a generation. The age of romantic revolution was over.

NOTES

1. Quoted in A. J. May, *The Age of Metternich, 1814–1848,* rev. ed. (New York: Holt, Rinehart & Winston, 1963), p. 11.
2. Quoted in H. Kohn, *Nationalism* (New York: Van Nostrand, 1955), pp. 141–142.
3. Quoted in F. D. Klingender, *Art and the Industrial Revolution* (St. Albans, Eng.: Paladin, 1972), p. 117.
4. Quoted in F. B. Artz, *From the Renaissance to Romanticism: Trends in Style in Art, Literature, and Music, 1300–1830* (Chicago: University of Chicago Press, 1962), pp. 276, 278.
5. Quoted in G. Wright, *France in Modern Times,* 4th ed. (Chicago: Rand McNally, 1987), p. 145.
6. A. de Tocqueville, *Recollections* (New York: Columbia University Press, 1949), p. 94.
7. M. Agulhon, *1848* (Paris: Éditions du Seuil, 1973), pp. 68–69.
8. Quoted in W. L. Langer, *Political and Social Upheaval, 1832–1852* (New York: Harper & Row, 1969), p. 361.

SUGGESTED READING

All of the works cited in the Notes are highly recommended. May's is a good brief survey, and Kohn has written perceptively on nationalism in many books. Wright's work is a lively introduction to French history with stimulating biographical discussions; Langer's is a balanced synthesis with an excellent bibliography. Among general studies, C. Morazé, *The Triumph of the Middle Classes* (1968), a wide-ranging procapitalist interpretation, may be compared with E. J. Hobsbawm's flexible Marxism in *The Age of Revolution, 1789–1848* (1962). For English history, A. Briggs's socially oriented *The Making of Modern England, 1784–1867* (1967), and D. Thomson's *England in the Nineteenth Century, 1815–1914* (1951), are excellent. Restoration France is sympathetically portrayed by G. de Bertier de Sauvigny in *The Bourbon Restoration* (1967), whereas R. Price, *A Social History of Nineteenth-Century France* (1987), is a fine synthesis incorporating recent research. T. Hamerow studies the social implications of the dual revolution in Germany in *Restoration, Revolution, Reaction, 1815–1871* (1966), which may be compared with H. Treitschke's bombastic, pro-Prussian *History of Germany in the Nineteenth Century* (1915–1919), a classic of nationalistic history, and L. Snyder, *Roots of German Nationalism* (1978). H. James, *A German Identity, 1770–1990* (1989), and J. Sheehan, *Germany, 1770–1866* (1989), are stimulating general histories that skillfully incorporate recent research. Two important reconsiderations of nationalism are B. Anderson, *Imagined Communities,* 2d ed. (1991), and E. Hobsbawm and T. Ranger, *The Invention of Tradition* (1990). E. Kedourie, *Nationalism* (1960), is an influential historical critique of the new faith. H. Kissinger, *A World Restored* (1957), offers not only a provocative interpretation of the Congress of Vienna but also insights into the mind of Richard Nixon's famous secretary of state. Compare that volume with H. Nicolson's entertaining *The Congress of Vienna* (1946). On 1848, L. B. Namier's highly critical *1848: The Revolution of the Intellectuals* (1964), and P. Robertson's *Revolutions of 1848: A Social History* (1960), are outstanding. I. Deak, *The Lawful Revolution: Louis Kossuth and the Hungarians, 1848–49* (1979), is a noteworthy study of an interesting figure.

On early socialism and Marxism, there are A. Lindemann's stimulating survey, *A History of European Socialism* (1983), and W. Sewell, Jr.'s *Work and Revolution in France: The Language of Labor from the Old Regime to 1848* (1980) as well as G. Lichtheim's highpowered *Marxism* (1961), and his *Short History of Socialism* (1970). J. Seigel, *Marx's Fate: The Shape of a Life* (1978), is an outstanding biography. Fourier is treated sympathetically in J. Beecher, *Charles Fourier* (1986). J. Schumpeter, *Capitalism, Socialism and Democracy* (1947), is magnificent but difficult, a real mind-stretcher. Also highly recommended is B. Taylor, *Eve and the New Jerusalem: Socialism and Feminism in the Nineteenth Century* (1983), which explores fascinating English attempts to emancipate workers and women at the same time. On liberalism, there are R. Heilbroner's entertaining *The Worldly Philosophers* (1967), and G. de Ruggiero's classic *History of European Liberalism* (1959). J. Barzun, *Classic, Romantic and Modern* (1961), skillfully discusses the emergence of romanticism, and J. Seigel, *Bohemian Paris; Culture, Politics, and the Boundaries of Bourgeois Life* (1986), imaginatively places romantic aspirations in a broad cultural framework. R. Stromberg, *An Intellectual History of Modern Europe,* 3d ed. (1981), and F. Baumer, *Modern European Thought: Continuity and Change in Ideas, 1600–1950* (1970), are valuable surveys. The important place of religion in nineteenth-century thought is considered from different perspectives in H. McLeod, *Religion and the People of Western Europe* (1981), and O. Chadwick, *The Secularization of the European Mind in the Nineteenth Century* (1976). Two good church histories with useful bibliographies are J. Altholz, *The Churches in the Nineteenth Century* (1967), and A. Vidler, *The Church in an Age of Revolution: 1789 to the Present Day* (1961).

The thoughtful reader is strongly advised to delve into the incredibly rich writing of contemporaries. J. Bowditch and C. Ramsland, eds., *Voices of the Industrial Revolution* (1961), is an excellent starting point, with well-chosen selections from leading economic thinkers and early socialists. H. Hugo, ed., *The Romantic Reader,* is another fine anthology. Mary Shelley's *Frankenstein,* a great romantic novel, draws an almost lovable picture of the famous monster and is highly recommended. Jules Michelet's compassionate masterpiece *The People,* a famous historian's anguished examination of French social divisions on the eve of 1848, draws one into the heart of the period and is highly recommended. Alexis de Tocqueville covers some of the same ground less romantically in his *Recollections,* which may be compared with Karl Marx's white-hot "instant history," *Class Struggles in France, 1848–1850* (1850). Great novels that accurately portray aspects of the times are Victor Hugo, *Les Misérables,* an exciting story of crime and passion among France's poor; Honoré de Balzac, *La Cousine Bette* and *Le Père Goriot;* and Thomas Mann, *Buddenbrooks,* a wonderful historical novel that traces the rise and fall of a prosperous German family over three generations during the nineteenth century.

24

Life in the Changing Urban Society

✣ The era of intellectual and political upheaval that culminated in the revolutions of 1848 was also an era of rapid urbanization. After 1848 Western political development veered off in a novel and uncharted direction, but the growth of towns and cities rushed forward with undiminished force. Thus Western society was urban and industrial in 1900 as surely as it had been rural and agrarian in 1800. The urbanization of society was both a result of the Industrial Revolution and a reflection of its enormous long-term impact.

- What was life like in the cities, and how did it change?
- What did the emergence of urban industrial society mean for rich and poor and those in between?
- How did families change as they coped with the challenges and the opportunities of the developing urban civilization?
- What changes in science and thought reflected and influenced this new civilization?

These are the questions this chapter will investigate.

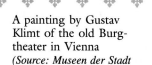

A painting by Gustav Klimt of the old Burg-theater in Vienna *(Source: Museen der Stadt Wien)*

✣ TAMING THE CITY

The growth of industry posed enormous challenges for all elements of Western society, from young factory workers confronting relentless discipline to aristocratic elites maneuvering to retain political power. As we saw in Chapter 22, the early consequences of economic transformation were mixed and far-reaching and by no means wholly negative. By 1850 at the latest,

A COURT FOR KING CHOLERA.

❖ **Filth and Disease** This 1852 drawing from *Punch* tells volumes about the unhealthy living conditions of the urban poor. In the foreground children play with a
dead rat and a woman scavenges a dungheap. Cheap rooming houses provide shelter for the frightfully overcrowded population. *(Source: The British Library)*

horror not surpassed by the rookeries of London.
. . . The evidence shows that the decent cottage
was the exception, the hovel the rule."[4] Thus
housing was far down on the newcomer's list of
priorities, and it is not surprising that many people
carried the filth of the mud floor and the dung of
the barnyard with them to the city.

Indeed, ordinary people generally took dirt and
filth for granted. One English miner told an inves-
tigator, "I do not think it usual for the lasses [in
the coal mines] to wash their bodies; my sisters
never wash themselves." As for the men, "their legs
and bodies are as black as your hat."[5]

The Public Health Movement

Although cleanliness was not next to godliness in
most people's eyes, it was becoming so for some

reformers. The most famous of these was Edwin
Chadwick, one of the commissioners charged with
the administration of relief to paupers under the
revised Poor Law of 1834. Chadwick was a good
Benthamite—that is, a follower of radical philosopher Jeremy Bentham (1748–1832). Bentham had
taught that public problems ought to be dealt with
on a rational, scientific basis and according to the
"greatest good for the greatest number." Applying
these principles, Chadwick soon saw that much
more than economics was involved in the problems
of poverty and the welfare budget. He became
convinced that disease and death actually caused
poverty simply because a sick worker was an unemployed worker and orphaned children were
poor children. Most important, Chadwick believed
that disease could be prevented by cleaning up the
urban environment. That was his "sanitary idea."

Building on a growing number of medical and sociological studies, Chadwick collected detailed reports from local Poor Law officials on the "sanitary conditions of the laboring population." After three years of investigation, these reports and Chadwick's hard-hitting commentary were published in 1842 to wide publicity. This mass of evidence proved that disease was related to filthy environmental conditions, which were in turn caused largely by lack of drainage, sewers, and garbage collection. Putrefying, smelly excrement was no longer simply disgusting. For reformers like Chadwick, it was a threat to the entire community. It polluted the atmosphere and caused disease.

The key to the energetic action Chadwick proposed was an adequate supply of clean piped water. Such water was essential for personal hygiene, public bathhouses, street cleaning, firefighting, and industry. Chadwick correctly believed that the stinking excrement of communal outhouses could be dependably carried off by water through sewers at less than one-twentieth the cost of removing it by hand. The cheap iron pipes and tile drains of the industrial age would provide running water and sewerage for all sections of town, not just the wealthy ones. In 1848, with the cause strengthened by the cholera epidemic of 1846, Chadwick's report became the basis of Great Britain's first public health law, which created a national health board and gave cities broad authority to build modern sanitary systems.

The public health movement won dedicated supporters in the United States, France, and Germany from the 1840s on. As in Great Britain, governments accepted at least limited responsibility for the health of all citizens. Moreover, they adopted increasingly concrete programs of action that broke decisively with the age-old fatalism of urban populations in the face of shockingly high mortality. Thus, despite many people's skepticism about sanitation, European cities were making real progress toward adequate water supplies and sewerage systems by the 1860s and 1870s. And city dwellers were beginning to reap the reward of better health.

The Bacterial Revolution

Effective control of communicable disease required a great leap forward in medical knowledge and biological theory as well as in clean water supply and good sewers. In the early nineteenth century,

reformers such as Chadwick were seriously handicapped by the prevailing *miasmatic theory* of disease—the belief that people contract disease when they breathe the bad odors of decay and putrefying excrement; in short, the theory that smells cause disease. The miasmatic theory was a reasonable deduction from empirical observations: cleaning up filth did produce laudable results. Yet the theory was very incomplete.

Keen observation by doctors and public health officials in the 1840s and 1850s pinpointed the role of bad drinking water in the transmission of disease and suggested that contagion was *spread through* filth and not caused by it. Moreover, some particularly horrid stenches, such as that of the sewage-glutted Thames River at London in 1858, did not lead to widely feared epidemics, and this fact also weakened the miasmatic idea.

The breakthrough was the development of the *germ theory* of disease by Louis Pasteur (1822–

◆ **Louis Pasteur** Shown here working in his laboratory, Pasteur made fundamental discoveries in biology and chemistry. A symbol of scientific achievement, he was—and is—greatly revered by all classes in France. *(Source: Institut Pasteur)*

1895), a French chemist who began studying fermentation in 1854. For ages people had used fermentation to make bread and wine, beer and cheese, but without really understanding what was going on. And from time to time, beer and wine would mysteriously spoil for no apparent reason. Responding to the calls of big brewers for help, Pasteur used his microscope to develop a simple test that brewers could use to monitor the fermentation process and avoid spoilage. Continuing his investigations, Pasteur found that fermentation depended on the growth of living organisms and that the activity of these organisms could be suppressed by heating the beverage—by "pasteurizing" it. The breathtaking implication was that specific diseases were caused by specific living organisms—germs—and that those organisms could be controlled in people as well as in beer, wine, and milk.

By 1870 the work of Pasteur and others had demonstrated the general connection between germs and disease. When, in the middle of the 1870s, German country doctor Robert Koch and his coworkers developed pure cultures of harmful bacteria and described their life cycles, the dam broke. Over the next twenty years, researchers—mainly Germans—identified the organisms responsible for disease after disease, often identifying several in a single year. These discoveries led to the development of a number of effective vaccines and the emergence of modern immunology in the late nineteenth century.

Acceptance of the germ theory brought about dramatic improvements in the deadly environment of hospitals and surgery. English surgeon Joseph Lister (1827–1912) had noticed that patients with simple fractures were much less likely to die than those with compound fractures, in which the skin was broken and internal tissues were exposed to the air. In 1865 when Pasteur showed that the air was full of bacteria, Lister immediately grasped the connection between aerial bacteria and the problem of wound infection. He reasoned that a chemical disinfectant applied to a wound dressing would "destroy the life of the floating particles." Lister's "antiseptic principle" worked wonders. In the 1880s, German surgeons developed the more sophisticated practice of sterilizing not only the wound but also everything—hands, instruments, clothing—that entered the operating room.

The achievements of the bacterial revolution coupled with the ever-more-sophisticated public health movement saved millions of lives, particularly after about 1890. Mortality rates began to decline dramatically in European countries (Figure 24.1) as the awful death sentences of the past—diphtheria, typhoid, typhus, cholera, yellow fever—became vanishing diseases. City dwellers benefited especially from these developments. By 1910 the death rates for people of all ages in urban areas were generally no greater than in rural areas, and sometimes they were less. Particularly striking was the decline in infant mortality in the cities after 1890. By 1910 in many countries, an urban mother was less likely than a rural mother to see her child die before its first birthday. A great silent revolution had occurred: the terrible ferocity of death from disease-carrying bacteria in the cities had almost been tamed.

Urban Planning and Public Transportation

If public health was greatly improved in the course of the nineteenth century, that was only part of the urban challenge. Overcrowding, bad housing, and

❖ **FIGURE 24.1 The Decline of Death Rates in England and Wales, Germany, France, and Sweden, 1840–1913** A rising standard of living, improvements in public health, and better medical knowledge all contributed to the dramatic decline of death rates in the nineteenth century.

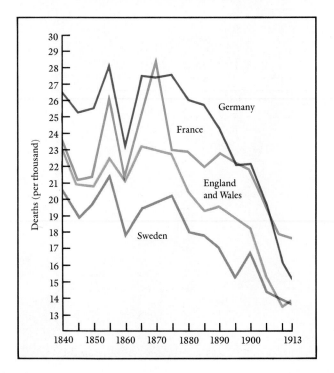

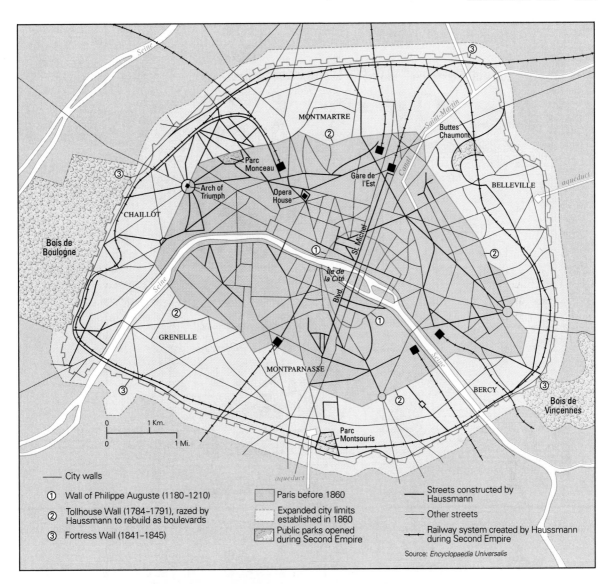

MONTMARTRE

Buttes
Chaumont

Parc
Monceau

Arch of
Triumph

Gare de
l'Est

BELLEVILLE

Opera
House

CHAILLOT

aqueduct

Bois de
Boulogne

Seine

Île de
la Cité

St-Michel

Blvd

GRENELLE

Canal Saint-Martin

BERCY

MONTPARNASSE

Bois de
Vincennes

Parc
Montsouris

0   1 Km.

0   1 Mi.

aqueduct

——— City walls

① Wall of Philippe Auguste (1180–1210)

② Tollhouse Wall (1784–1791), razed by
   Haussmann to rebuild as boulevards

③ Fortress Wall (1841–1845)

▢ Paris before 1860

▢ Expanded city limits
   established in 1860

▢ Public parks opened
   during Second Empire

——— Streets constructed by
     Haussmann

——— Other streets

╫╫╫ Railway system created by Haussmann
     during Second Empire

Source: *Encyclopaedia Universalis*

✤ **MAP 24.2 The Modernization of Paris, ca 1850–1870** Broad boulevards,
large parks, and grandiose train stations transformed Paris. The cutting of the new
north-south axis—known as the Boulevard Saint-Michel—was one of Haussmann's
most controversial projects. It razed much of Paris's medieval core and filled the
Île de la Cité with massive government buildings.

lack of transportation could not be solved by sewers and better medicine; yet in these areas, too,
important transformations significantly improved
the quality of urban life after midcentury.

More effective urban planning was one of the
keys to improvement. Urban planning was in decline by the early nineteenth century, but after
1850 its practice was revived and extended. France
took the lead during the rule of Napoleon III
(r. 1848–1870), who sought to stand above class

conflict and promote the welfare of all his subjects
through government action. He believed that rebuilding much of Paris would provide employment, improve living conditions, and testify to the
power and glory of his empire. In the baron Georges Haussmann (1809–1884), an aggressive, impatient Alsatian whom he placed in charge of Paris,
Napoleon III found an authoritarian planner capable of bulldozing both buildings and opposition.
In twenty years Paris was transformed (Map 24.2).

Apartment Living in Paris This drawing shows how different social classes lived close together in European cities about 1850. Passing the middle-class family on the first (American second) floor, the economic condition of the tenants declined until one reached abject poverty in the garret. *(Source: Bibliothèque Nationale, Paris)*

The Paris of 1850 was a labyrinth of narrow, dark streets, the results of desperate overcrowding. In a central city not twice the size of New York's Central Park lived more than one-third of the city's one million inhabitants. Terrible slum conditions and extremely high death rates were facts of life. There were few open spaces and only two public parks for the entire metropolis. Public transportation played a very small role in this enormous walking city.

Haussmann and his fellow planners proceeded on many interrelated fronts. With a bold energy that often shocked their contemporaries, they razed old buildings in order to cut broad, straight, tree-lined boulevards through the center of the city as well as in new quarters on the outskirts. These boulevards, designed in part to prevent the easy construction and defense of barricades by revolutionary crowds, permitted traffic to flow freely. Their creation also demolished some of the worst slums. New streets stimulated the construction of better housing, especially for the middle classes. Small neighborhood parks and open spaces were created throughout the city, and two very large parks suitable for all kinds of holiday activities were developed—one on the wealthy west side and one on the poor east side of the city. The city also improved its sewers, and a system of aqueducts more than doubled the city's supply of good fresh water.

Haussmann and Napoleon III tried to make Paris a more beautiful city, and to a large extent they succeeded. The broad, straight boulevards, such as those radiating out like the spokes of a wheel from the Arch of Triumph and those centering on the new Opera House, afforded impressive vistas. If for most people Paris remains one of the world's most beautiful and enchanting cities, it is in part because of the transformations of Napoleon III's Second Empire.

Rebuilding Paris provided a new model for urban planning and stimulated modern urbanism throughout Europe, particularly after 1870. In city after city, public authorities mounted a coordinated attack on many of the interrelated problems of the urban environment. As in Paris, improvements in public health through better water supply and waste disposal often went hand in hand with new boulevard construction. Cities such as Vienna and Cologne followed the Parisian example of tearing down old walled fortifications and replacing them with broad, circular boulevards on which office buildings, town halls, theaters, opera houses, and museums were erected. These ring roads and the new boulevards that radiated out from them toward the outskirts eased movement and encouraged urban expansion (see Map 24.2). *Zoning expropriation laws,* which allowed a majority of the owners of land in a given quarter of the city to impose major street or sanitation improvements on a reluctant minority, were an important mechanism of the new urbanism.

The development of mass public transportation was also of great importance in the improvement of urban living conditions. Such transportation came late, but in a powerful rush. In the 1870s, many European cities authorized private companies to operate horse-drawn streetcars, which had been developed in the United States, to carry riders along the growing number of major thoroughfares. Then in the 1890s the real revolution occurred: European countries adopted another American transit innovation, the electric streetcar.

Electric streetcars were cheaper, faster, more dependable, and more comfortable than their horse-drawn counterparts. Service improved dramatically. Millions of Europeans—workers, shoppers, schoolchildren—hopped on board during the workweek. And on weekends and holidays, streetcars carried millions on happy outings to parks and countryside, racetracks and music halls. In 1886 the horse-drawn streetcars of Austria-Hungary, France, Germany, and Great Britain were carrying about 900 million riders. By 1910 electric streetcar systems in the four countries were carrying 6.7 billion riders.[6] Each man, woman, and child was using public transportation four times as often in 1910 as in 1886.

Good mass transit helped greatly in the struggle for decent housing. The new boulevards and horse-drawn streetcars had facilitated a middle-class move to better housing in the 1860s and 1870s; similarly, after 1890 electric streetcars gave people of modest means access to new, improved housing. The still-crowded city was able to expand and become less congested. In England in 1901, only 9 percent of the urban population was "overcrowded" in terms of the official definition of more than two persons per room. On the Continent, many city governments in the early twentieth century were building electric streetcar systems that provided transportation to new public and private housing developments in outlying areas of the city for the working classes. Poor, overcrowded hous-

✣ **Urban Transportation in the 1880s** Horse-drawn streetcars in big cities usually added an upper deck in order to jam more passengers onto the car. But horsecars were slow, relatively expensive, and killers for horses. Horsecars lacked the modernity of railroads, which were honored with monumental buildings like the magnificent neo-Gothic St. Pancras train station and hotel in London, bathed in soft sunlight in this evocative painting by John O'Connor. *(Source: Museum of London)*

ing, long one of the blackest blots on the urban landscape, was in retreat—another example of the gradual taming of the urban environment.

✣ RICH AND POOR AND THOSE IN BETWEEN

General improvements in health and in the urban environment had beneficial consequences for all kinds of people. Yet differences in living conditions among social classes remained gigantic.

Social Structure

How much did the almost-completed journey to an urban, industrialized world change the social framework of rich and poor and those in between?

The first great change was a substantial and undeniable increase in the standard of living for the average person. The real wages of British workers, for example, which had already risen by 1850, almost doubled between 1850 and 1906. Similar increases occurred in continental countries as industrial development quickened after 1850. Ordinary people took a major step forward in the centuries-old battle against poverty, reinforcing efforts to improve many aspects of human existence.

There is another side to the income coin, however, and it must be stressed as well. Greater economic rewards for the average person did *not* eliminate hardship and poverty, nor did they make the wealth and income of the rich and the poor significantly more equal. In almost every advanced country around 1900, the richest 5 percent of all households in the population received 33 percent of all national income. The richest 20 percent of households received anywhere from 50 to 60 percent of all national income, while the entire bottom 80 percent received only 40 to 50 percent. Moreover, the bottom 30 percent of households received 10 percent or less of all income. These enormous differences are illustrated in Figure 24.2.

The middle classes, smaller than they are today, accounted for less than 20 percent of the population; thus the statistics show that the upper and middle classes alone received more than 50 percent of all income. The poorest 80 percent—the working classes, including peasants and agricultural laborers—received less altogether than the two richest classes. Moreover, income taxes on the wealthy were light or nonexistent. Thus the gap between rich and poor remained enormous at the beginning of the twentieth century. It was probably almost as great as it had been in the age of agriculture and aristocracy before the Industrial Revolution.

The great gap between rich and poor endured, in part, because industrial and urban development made society more diverse and less unified. By no means did society split into two sharply defined opposing classes, as Marx had predicted. Instead, economic specialization enabled society to produce more effectively and in the process created more new social groups than it destroyed. There developed an almost unlimited range of jobs, skills, and earnings; one group or subclass shaded off into another in a complex, confusing hierarchy. Thus the tiny elite of the very rich and the sizable mass of the dreadfully poor were separated from each other by a range of subclasses, each filled with individuals struggling to rise or at least to hold their own in the social order. In this atmosphere of competition and hierarchy, neither the middle classes nor the working classes acted as a unified force. This social and occupational hierarchy developed enormous variations, but the age-old pattern of great economic inequality remained firmly intact.

The Middle Classes

By the beginning of the twentieth century, the diversity and range within the urban middle class were striking. Indeed, it is more meaningful to think of a confederation of middle classes loosely united by occupations requiring mental, rather than physical, skill. At the top stood the upper middle class, composed mainly of the most success-

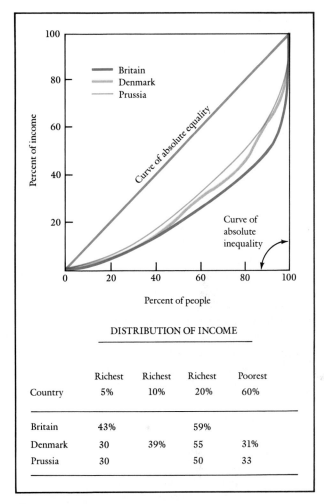

DISTRIBUTION OF INCOME

Country	Richest 5%	Richest 10%	Richest 20%	Poorest 60%
Britain	43%		59%	
Denmark	30	39%	55	31%
Prussia	30		50	33

FIGURE 24.2 The Distribution of Income in Britain, Denmark, and Prussia in 1913 The so-called Lorenz curve is useful for showing the degree of economic inequality in a given society. The closer the actual distribution of income lies to the (theoretical) curve of absolute equality, where each 20 percent of the population receives 20 percent of all income, the more incomes are nearly equal. European society was very far from any such equality before World War One. Notice that incomes in Prussia were somewhat more equal than those in Britain. *(Source: S. Kuznets, Modern Economic Growth, Yale University Press, New Haven, 1966, pp. 208–209)*

ful business families from banking, industry, and large-scale commerce. These families were the prime beneficiaries of modern industry and scientific progress. As people in the upper middle class gained in income and progressively lost all traces of radicalism after the trauma of 1848, they were almost irresistibly drawn toward the aristocratic

806 CHAPTER 24 LIFE IN THE CHANGING URBAN SOCIETY

lifestyle. And although the genuine hereditary aristocracy constituted only a tiny minority in every European country, it retained imposing wealth, unrivaled social prestige, and substantial political influence. This was especially true in central and eastern Europe, where the monarch—the highest-ranking noble of them all—continued to hold great political power.

As the aristocracy had long divided the year between palatial country estates and lavish town-houses during "the season," so the upper middle class purchased country places or built beach houses for weekend and summer use. (Little wonder that a favorite scenario in late-nineteenth-century middle-class novels was a mother and children summering gloriously in the country home, with only sporadic weekend intrusions by a distant, shadowy father.) The number of servants was an important indicator of wealth and standing for the middle class, as it had always been for the aristocracy. Private coaches and carriages, ever expensive items in the city, were also signs of rising social status. More generally, the rich businessman and certainly his son devoted less time to business and more to "culture" and easy living than was the case in less wealthy or well-established commercial families.

The topmost reaches of the upper middle class tended to shade off into the old aristocracy to form a new upper class. This was the 5 percent of the population that, as we have seen, received roughly 33 percent of the national income in European countries before 1914. Much of the aristocracy welcomed this development. Having experienced a sharp decline in its relative income in the course of industrialization, the landed aristocracy had met big business coming up the staircase and was often delighted to trade titles, country homes, and snobbish elegance for good hard cash. Some of the best bargains were made through marriages to American heiresses. Correspondingly, wealthy aristocrats tended increasingly to exploit their agricultural and mineral resources as if they were business people. Bismarck was not the only proud nobleman to make a fortune distilling brandy on his estates.

Below the wealthy upper middle class were much larger, much less wealthy, and increasingly diversified middle-class groups. Here one found the moderately successful industrialists and merchants as well as professionals in law and medicine. This was the middle middle class, solid and quite comfortable but lacking great wealth. Below it were independent shopkeepers, small traders, and tiny manufacturers—the lower middle class. Both of these traditional elements of the middle class expanded modestly in size with economic development.

Meanwhile, the traditional middle class was gaining two particularly important additions. The expansion of industry and technology created a growing demand for experts with specialized knowledge. The most valuable of the specialties became solid middle-class professions. Engineering, for example, emerged from the world of skilled labor as a full-fledged profession of great importance, considerable prestige, and many branches. Architects, chemists, accountants, and surveyors, to name only a few, first achieved professional standing in this period. They established criteria for advanced training and certification and banded together in organizations to promote and defend their interests.

Management of large public and private institutions also emerged as a kind of profession as governments provided more services and as very large corporations such as railroads came into being. Government officials and many private executives were not capitalists in the sense that they owned business enterprises. But public and private managers did have specialized knowledge and the capacity to earn a good living. And they shared most of the values of the business-owning entrepreneurs and the older professionals.

Industrialization also expanded and diversified the lower middle class. The number of independent, property-owning shopkeepers and small business people grew, and so did the number of white-collar employees—a mixed group of traveling salesmen, bookkeepers, store managers, and clerks who staffed the offices and branch stores of large corporations. White-collar employees were propertyless and often earned no more than the better-paid skilled or semiskilled workers did. Yet white-collar workers were fiercely committed to the middle class and to the ideal of moving up in society. In the Balkans, for example, clerks let their fingernails grow very long to distinguish themselves from people who worked with their hands. The tie, the suit, and soft, clean hands were no-less-subtle marks of class distinction than wages.

Relatively well educated but without complex technical skills, many white-collar groups aimed at achieving professional standing and the accompanying middle-class status. Elementary school teachers largely succeeded in this effort. From being miserably paid part-time workers in the early nineteenth century, teachers rode the wave of mass education to respectable middle-class status and income. Nurses also rose from the lower ranks of unskilled labor to precarious middle-class standing. Dentistry was taken out of the hands of working-class barbers and placed in the hands of highly trained (and middle-class) professionals.

In spite of growing occupational diversity and conflicting interests, the middle classes were loosely united by a certain style of life. Food was the largest item in the household budget, for middle-class people liked to eat very well. In France and Italy, the middle classes' love of good eating meant that even in large cities, activity ground almost to a halt between half past twelve and half past two on weekdays as husbands and schoolchildren returned home for the midday meal. Around eight in the evening, the serious business of eating was taken up once again.

The English were equally attached to substantial meals, which they ate three times a day if income allowed. The typical English breakfast of bacon and eggs, toast and marmalade, and stewed fruits—not to mention sardines, kidneys, or fresh fish—always astonished French and German travelers, though large-breakfast enthusiasts such as the Dutch and Scandinavians were less awed. The European middle classes consumed meat in abundance, and a well-off family might spend 10 percent of its substantial earnings on meat alone. In the 1890s, even a very prosperous English family—with an income of, say, 10,000 dollars a year (the average working-class family earned perhaps 400 dollars a year)—spent fully 25 percent of its income on food and drink.

Spending on food was also great because the dinner party was this class's favored social occasion. A wealthy family might give a lavish party for eight to twelve almost every week, whereas more modest households would settle for once a month. Throughout middle-class Europe, such dinners were served in the "French manner" (which the French had borrowed from the Russian aristocracy): eight or nine separate courses, from appetizers at the beginning to coffee and liqueurs at the end. In summer, a picnic was in order. But what a picnic! For a party of ten, one English cookbook suggested 5 pounds of cold salmon, a quarter of a lamb, 8 pounds of pickled brisket, a beef tongue, a chicken pie, salads, cakes, and 6 pounds of strawberries. An ordinary family meal normally consisted of only four courses—soup, fish, meat, and dessert.

The middle-class wife could cope with this endless procession of meals, courses, and dishes because she had both servants and money at her disposal. The middle classes were solid members of what some contemporary observers called the "servant-keeping classes." Indeed, the employment of at least one enormously helpful full-time maid to cook and clean was the best single sign that a family had crossed the vague line separating the working classes from the middle classes. The greater a family's income, the greater the number of servants it employed. The all-purpose servant gave way to a cook and a maid, then to a cook, a maid, and a boy, and so on. A prosperous English family, far up the line with 10,000 dollars a year, in 1900 spent fully 25 percent of its income on a hierarchy of ten servants: a manservant, a cook, a kitchen maid, two housemaids, a serving maid, a governess, a gardener, a coachman, and a stable boy. Domestic servants were the second largest item in the budget of the middle classes. Food and servants together absorbed about 50 percent of income at all levels of the middle classes.

Well fed and well served, the middle classes were also well housed by 1900. Many quite prosperous families rented, rather than owned, their homes. Apartment living, complete with tiny rooms for servants under the eaves of the top floor, was commonplace, and wealthy investors and speculative builders found good profits in middle-class housing. By 1900 the middle classes were also quite clothes conscious. The factory, the sewing machine, and the department store had all helped reduce the cost and expand the variety of clothing. Middle-class women were particularly attentive to the fickle dictates of fashion.

Education was another growing expense, as middle-class parents tried to provide their children with ever-more-crucial advanced education. The keystones of culture and leisure were books, music, and travel. The long realistic novel, the heroics of Wagner and Verdi, the diligent striving of the dutiful daughter at the piano, and the packaged tour to a foreign country were all sources of middle-class pleasure.

❖ **"A Corner of the Table"** With photographic precision this 1904 oil painting by the French academic artist Paul-Émile Chabas (1867–1937) skillfully idealizes the elegance and intimacy of a sumptuous dinner party. *(Source: Bibliothèque des Arts Décoratifs/Jean-Loup Charmet)*

Finally, the middle classes were loosely united by a shared code of expected behavior and morality. This code was strict and demanding. It laid great stress on hard work, self-discipline, and personal achievement. Men and women who fell into crime or poverty were generally assumed to be responsible for their own circumstances. Traditional Christian morality was reaffirmed by this code and was preached tirelessly by middle-class people who took pride in their own good conduct and regular church attendance. Drinking and gambling were denounced as vices; sexual purity and fidelity were celebrated as virtues. In short, the middle-class person was supposed to know right from wrong and was expected to act accordingly.

The Working Classes

About four out of five people belonged to the working classes at the turn of the century. Many members of the working classes—that is, people whose livelihoods depended on physical labor and who did not employ domestic servants—were still small landowning peasants and hired farm hands. This was especially true in eastern Europe. In western and central Europe, however, the typical worker had left the land. In Great Britain, less than 8 percent of the people worked in agriculture, while in rapidly industrializing Germany only 25 percent were employed in agriculture and forestry. Even in less industrialized France, less than 50 percent of the people depended on the land in 1900.

The urban working classes were even less unified and homogeneous than the middle classes. In the first place, economic development and increased specialization expanded the traditional range of working-class skills, earnings, and experiences. Meanwhile, the old sharp distinction between highly skilled artisans and unskilled manual workers gradually broke down. To be sure, highly skilled printers and masons as well as unskilled dockworkers and common laborers continued to exist. But between these extremes there appeared ever-more semiskilled groups, many of which were composed of factory workers and machine tenders (Figure 24.3).

In the second place, skilled, semiskilled, and unskilled workers developed widely divergent lifestyles and cultural values, and their differences contributed to a keen sense of social status and hierarchy within the working classes. The result was great variety and limited class unity.

Highly skilled workers, who made up about 15 percent of the working classes, became a real "labor aristocracy." By 1900 they were earning about 2 pounds per week in Great Britain, or roughly 10 dollars per week and 500 dollars per year. This was only about two-thirds the income of the bottom ranks of the servant-keeping classes. But it was fully twice as much as the earnings of unskilled workers, who averaged about 5 dollars per week, and substantially more than the earnings of semiskilled workers, who averaged perhaps 7 dollars per week. Other European countries had a similar range of earnings.

The most "aristocratic" of the highly skilled workers were construction bosses and factory foremen, men who had risen from the ranks and were fiercely proud of their achievement. The labor aristocracy also included members of the traditional highly skilled handicraft trades that had not been mechanized or placed in factories. These included makers of scientific and musical instruments, cabinetmakers, potters, jewelers, bookbinders, engravers, and printers. This group as a whole was under constant long-term pressure. Irregularly but inexorably, factory methods were being extended to more crafts, and many skilled artisans were being replaced by lower-paid semiskilled factory workers. In the second half of the nineteenth century, traditional woodcarvers and watchmakers virtually

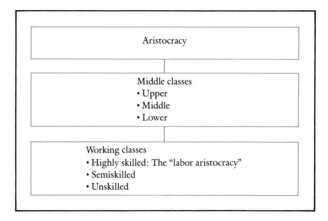

❖ **FIGURE 24.3 The Urban Social Hierarchy**

disappeared, for example, as the making of furniture and timepieces was put into the factory.

At the same time, a contrary movement was occurring. The labor aristocracy was consistently being enlarged by the growing need for highly skilled workers such as shipbuilders, machine-tool makers, railway locomotive engineers, fine cotton textile spinners, and some metalworkers. Thus the labor elite remained in a state of flux as individuals and whole crafts moved in and out of it.

To maintain this precarious standing, the upper working class adopted distinctive values and straitlaced, almost puritanical behavior. Like the middle classes, the labor aristocracy was strongly committed to the family and to economic improvement. Families in the upper working class saved money regularly, worried about their children's education, and valued good housing. Despite these similarities, which superficial observers were quick to exaggerate, skilled workers viewed themselves not as aspirants to the middle class but as the pacesetters and natural leaders of all the working classes. Well aware of the degradation not so far below them, they practiced self-discipline and stern morality.

The upper working class in general frowned on heavy drinking and sexual permissiveness. An organized temperance movement was strong in the countries of northern Europe, such as Great Britain, where a generation advocated tea as the "cup that cheers but does not inebriate." As one German labor aristocrat somberly warned, "The path to the brothel leads through the tavern" and from there quite possibly to drastic decline or total ruin for person and family.[7]

Men and women of the labor aristocracy were quick to find fault with those below them who failed to meet their standards. In 1868 William Lovett, an English labor aristocrat if ever there was one, denounced "this ignorant recklessness and improvidence that produce the swarms of half-starved, neglected, and ignorant children we see in all directions; who mostly grow up to become the burdens and often the pests of society, which the industrious and frugal have to support."[8] Finally, many members of the labor aristocracy had definite political and philosophical beliefs, whether Christian or socialist or both. Such beliefs further strengthened the firm moral code of the upper working class.

Below the labor aristocracy stood semiskilled and unskilled urban workers. The enormous complexity of this sector of the world of labor is not easily summarized. Workers in the established crafts—carpenters, bricklayers, pipefitters—stood near the top of the semiskilled hierarchy, often flirting with (or having backslid from) the labor elite. A large number of the semiskilled were factory workers who earned highly variable but relatively good wages and whose relative importance in the labor force was increasing.

Below the semiskilled workers was a larger group of unskilled workers that included day laborers such as longshoremen, wagon-driving teamsters, teen-agers, and every kind of "helper." Many of these people had real skills and performed valuable services, but they were unorganized and divided, united only by the common fate of meager earnings. The same lack of unity characterized street vendors and market people—self-employed workers who competed savagely with each other and with the established shopkeepers of the lower middle class.

One of the largest components of the unskilled group was domestic servants, whose numbers grew steadily in the nineteenth century. In advanced Great Britain, for example, one out of every seven employed persons was a domestic servant in 1911. The great majority were women; indeed, one out

❖ **A School for Servants** Although domestic service was poorly paid, there was always plenty of competition for the available jobs. Schools sprang up to teach young women the manners and the household skills that employers in the "servant-keeping classes" demanded. *(Source: Greater London Council Photograph Library)*

of every three girls in Britain between the ages of fifteen and twenty was a domestic servant. Throughout Europe and America, a great many female domestics in the cities were recent migrants from rural areas. As in earlier times, domestic service was still hard work at low pay with limited personal independence. For the full-time general maid in a lower-middle-class family, there was an unending routine of baby-sitting, shopping, cooking, and cleaning. In the great households, the girl was at the bottom of a rigid hierarchy; status-conscious butlers and housekeepers were determined to stand almost as far above her as the wealthy master and mistress.

Nonetheless, domestic service had real attractions for "rough country girls" with strong hands and few specialized skills. Marriage prospects were better, or at least more varied, in the city. And though wages were low, they were higher and more regular than in hard agricultural work. Finally, as one London observer noted, young girls and other migrants were drawn to the city by

the contagion of numbers, the sense of something going on, the theaters and the music halls, the brightly lighted streets and busy crowds—all, in short, that makes the difference between the Mile End fair on a Saturday night, and a dark and muddy country lane, with no glimmer of gas and with nothing to do.[9]

Many young domestics from the countryside made a successful transition to working-class wife and mother. Yet with an unskilled or unemployed husband and a growing family, such a woman often had to join the broad ranks of working women in the "sweated industries." These industries flowered after 1850 and resembled the old putting-out and cottage industries of the eighteenth and early nineteenth centuries. The women normally worked at home, though sometimes together in some loft or garret, for tiny merchant manufacturers. Paid by the piece and not by the hour, these women (and their young daughters), for whom organization and collective action were virtually impossible, earned pitiful wages and lacked any job security.

Some women did hand-decorating of every conceivable kind of object; the majority, however, made clothing, especially after the advent of the sewing machine. Foot-powered sewing machines allowed the poorest wife or widow in the foulest dwelling to rival and eventually supplant the most

highly skilled male tailor. By 1900 only a few such tailors lingered on in high-priced "tailor-made" shops. An army of poor women accounted for the bulk of the inexpensive "ready-made" clothes displayed on department store racks and in tiny shops. All of these considerations graphically illustrate the rise and fall of groups and individuals within the working classes.

The urban working classes sought fun and recreation, and they found both. Across the face of Europe, drinking remained unquestionably the favorite leisure-time activity of working people. For many middle-class moralists as well as moralizing historians since, love of drink has been a curse of the modern age—a sign of social dislocation and popular suffering. Certainly, drinking was deadly serious business. One English slum dweller recalled that "drunkenness was by far the commonest cause of dispute and misery in working class homes. On account of it one saw many a decent family drift down through poverty into total want."[10]

Generally, however, heavy "problem" drinking declined in the late nineteenth century as it became less and less socially acceptable. This decline reflected in part the moral leadership of the upper working class. At the same time, drinking became more public and social, especially as on-the-job drinking, an ancient custom of field laborers and urban artisans, diminished. Cafés and pubs became increasingly bright, friendly places. Working-class political activities, both moderate and radical, were also concentrated in taverns and pubs. Moreover, social drinking in public places by married couples and sweethearts became an accepted and widespread practice for the first time. This greater participation by women undoubtedly helped civilize the world of drink and hard liquor.

The two other leisure-time passions of the working classes were sports and music halls. A great decline in "cruel sports," such as bullbaiting and cockfighting, had occurred throughout Europe by the late nineteenth century. Their place was filled by modern spectator sports, of which racing and soccer were the most popular. There was a great deal of gambling on sports events, and for many a working person a desire to decipher racing forms provided a powerful incentive toward literacy. Music halls and vaudeville theaters, the working-class counterparts of middle-class opera and classical theater, were enormously popular throughout Europe. In 1900 there were more than fifty such

❖ **Renoir: Le Moulin de la Galette à Montmartre** In this 1876 masterpiece, the impressionist painter Auguste Renoir (1841–1919) has transformed a popular outdoor dance hall of the Parisian masses into an enchanted fairyland. Renoir was a joyous artist, and his work optimistically affirmed the beauty and value of modern life. *(Source: Musée d'Orsay/Cliché des Musées Nationaux, Paris)*

halls and theaters in London alone. Music hall audiences were thoroughly mixed, which may account for the fact that drunkenness, sexual intercourse and pregnancy before marriage, marital difficulties, and problems with mothers-in-law were favorite themes of broad jokes and bittersweet songs.

In more serious moments, religion and Christian churches continued to provide working people with solace and meaning. The eighteenth-century vitality of popular religion in Catholic countries and the Protestant rejuvenation exemplified by German Pietism and English Methodism (see pages 678–681) carried over into the nineteenth century. Indeed, many historians see the early nine-

teenth century as an age of religious revival. Yet historians also recognize that by the last two or three decades of the nineteenth century, a considerable decline in both church attendance and church donations was occurring in most European countries. And it seems clear that this decline was greater for the urban working classes than for their rural counterparts or for the middle classes.

What did the decline in working-class church attendance really mean? Some have argued that it accurately reflected a general decline in faith and religious belief. Others disagree, noting correctly that most working-class families still baptized their children and considered themselves Christians. Although more research is necessary, it appears that the urban working classes in Europe did become more secular and less religious in the late nineteenth and early twentieth centuries. They rarely repudiated the Christian religion, but it tended to play a diminishing role in their daily lives.

Part of the reason for this change was that the construction of churches failed to keep up with the rapid growth of urban population, especially in new working-class neighborhoods. Thus the vibrant, materialistic urban environment undermined popular religious impulses, which were poorly served in the cities. Equally important, however, was the fact that throughout the nineteenth century both Catholic and Protestant churches were normally seen as they saw themselves—as conservative institutions defending social order and custom. Therefore, as the European working classes became more politically conscious, they tended to see the established (or quasi-established) "territorial church" as defending what they wished to change and as allied with their political opponents. Especially the men of the urban working classes developed vaguely antichurch attitudes, even though they remained neutral or positive toward religion. They tended to regard regular church attendance as "not our kind of thing"—not part of urban working-class culture.

The pattern was different in the United States. There, most churches also preached social conservatism in the nineteenth century. But because church and state had always been separate and because there was always a host of competing denominations and even different religions, working people identified churches much less with the political and social status quo. Instead, individual churches in the United States were often closely identified with an ethnic group rather than with a social class; and churches thrived, in part, as a means of asserting ethnic identity. This same process did occur in Europe if the church or synagogue had never been linked to the state and served as a focus for ethnic cohesion. Irish Catholic churches in Protestant Britain and Jewish synagogues in Russia were outstanding examples.

✤ THE CHANGING FAMILY

Urban life wrought many fundamental changes in the family. Although much is still unknown, it seems clear that in the second half of the nineteenth century the family had stabilized considerably after the disruption of the late eighteenth and early nineteenth centuries. The home became more important for both men and women. The role of women and attitudes toward children underwent substantial change, and adolescence emerged as a distinct stage of life. These are but a few of the transformations that affected all social classes in varying degrees.

Premarital Sex and Marriage

By 1850 the preindustrial pattern of lengthy courtship and mercenary marriage was pretty well dead among the working classes. In its place, the ideal of romantic love had triumphed. Couples were ever-more likely to come from different, even distant, towns and to be more nearly the same age, further indicating that romantic sentiment was replacing tradition and financial considerations.

Economic considerations in marriage remained more important to the middle classes than to the working classes after 1850. In France dowries and elaborate legal marriage contracts were common practice among the middle classes in the later nineteenth century, and marriage was for many families one of life's most crucial financial transactions. A popular author advised young Frenchmen that "marriage is in general a means of increasing one's credit and one's fortune and of insuring one's success in the world."[11] This preoccupation with money led many middle-class men in France and elsewhere to marry late, after they had been established economically, and to choose women considerably younger and less sexually experienced than themselves. These differences between husband and wife became a source of tension in many middle-class marriages.

A young woman of the middle class found her romantic life carefully supervised by her well-meaning mother, who schemed for a proper marriage and guarded her daughter's virginity like the family's credit (see Listening to the Past). After marriage, middle-class morality sternly demanded fidelity.

Middle-class boys were watched, too, but not as vigilantly. By the time they reached late adolescence, they had usually attained considerable sexual experience with maids or prostitutes. With marriage a distant, uncertain possibility, it was all too easy for the young man of the middle classes to turn to the urban underworld of prostitution and sexual exploitation to satisfy his desires.

In the early nineteenth century, sexual experimentation before marriage also triumphed, as did illegitimacy. There was an "illegitimacy explosion" between 1750 and 1850 (see page 661). By the 1840s, as many as one birth in three was occurring outside of wedlock in many large cities. Although poverty and economic uncertainty undoubtedly prevented many lovers from marrying, there were also many among the poor and propertyless who saw little wrong with having illegitimate offspring. One young Bavarian woman answered happily when asked why she kept having illegitimate children, "It's O.K. to make babies. . . . The king has o.k.'d it!"[12] Thus the pattern of romantic ideals, premarital sexual activity, and widespread illegitimacy was firmly established by midcentury among the urban working classes.

It is hard to know how European couples managed sex, pregnancy, and marriage after 1850 because such questions were considered improper both in polite conversation and in public opinion polls. Yet there are many telltale clues. In the second half of the century the rising rate of illegitimacy was reversed: more babies were born to married mothers. Some observers have argued that this shift reflected the growth of puritanism and a lessening of sexual permissiveness among the unmarried. This explanation, however, is unconvincing.

The percentage of brides who were pregnant continued to be high and showed little or no tendency to decline after 1850. In many parts of urban Europe around 1900, as many as one woman in three was going to the altar an expectant mother. Moreover, unmarried people almost certainly used the cheap condoms and diaphragms the industrial age had made available to prevent pregnancy, at least in predominately Protestant countries.

Thus unmarried young people were probably engaging in just as much sexual activity as their parents and grandparents who had created the illegitimacy explosion of 1750 to 1850. But in the later nineteenth century, pregnancy for a young single woman led increasingly to marriage and the establishment of a two-parent household. This important development reflected the growing respectability of the working classes as well as their gradual economic improvement. Skipping out was less acceptable, and marriage was less of an economic challenge. Thus the urban working-class couple became more stable, and that stability strengthened the family as an institution.

Prostitution

In Paris alone, 155,000 women were registered as prostitutes between 1871 and 1903, and 750,000 others were suspected of prostitution in the same years. Men of all classes visited prostitutes, but the middle and upper classes supplied much of the motivating cash. Thus, though many middle-class men abided by the publicly professed code of stern puritanical morality, others indulged their appetites for prostitutes and sexual promiscuity.

My Secret Life, the anonymous eleven-volume autobiography of an English sexual adventurer from the servant-keeping classes, provides a remarkable picture of such a man. Beginning at an early age with a maid, the author becomes progressively obsessed with sex and devotes his life to living his sexual fantasies. In almost every one of his innumerable encounters all across Europe, this man of wealth simply buys his pleasure. Usually meetings are arranged in a businesslike manner: regular and part-time prostitutes quote their prices; working-class girls are corrupted by hot meals and baths.

At one point, he offers a young girl a sixpence for a kiss and gets it. Learning that the pretty, unskilled working girl earns nine pence a day, he offers her the equivalent of a week's salary for a few moments of fondling. When she finally agrees, he savagely exults that "*her* want was my opportunity." Later he offers more money for more gratification, and when she refuses, he tries unsuccessfully to rape her in a hackney cab. On another occasion he takes a farm worker by force: "Her tears ran down. If I had not committed a rape, it looked uncommonly like one." He then forces his victim to take money to prevent a threatened lawsuit, while the foreman advises the girl to keep quiet and realize that "you be in luck if he likes you."[13]

Obviously atypical in its excesses, *My Secret Life,* in its encyclopedic thoroughness, does reveal the dark side of sex and class in urban society. Frequently thinking of their wives largely in terms of money, family, and social position, the men of the comfortable classes often purchased sex and even affection from poor girls both before and after marriage. Moreover, the great continuing differences between rich and poor made for every kind of debauchery and sexual exploitation, including the brisk trade in poor virgins that the author of *My Secret Life* particularly relishes. Brutal sexist behavior was part of life—a part the sternly moral women (and men) of the upper working class detested and tried to shield their daughters from. For many poor young women, prostitution, like domestic service, was a stage of life and not a permanent employment. Having chosen it for two or three years in their twenties, they went on to marry (or live with) men of their own class and establish homes and families.

Kinship Ties

Within working-class homes, ties to relatives after marriage—kinship ties—were in general much stronger than superficial social observers have recognized. Most newlyweds tried to live near their parents, though not in the same house. Indeed, for many married couples in later-nineteenth-century cities, ties to mothers and fathers, uncles and aunts, were more important than ties to nonrelated acquaintances.

People turned to their families for help in coping with sickness, unemployment, death, and old age. Although governments were generally providing more welfare services by 1900, the average couple and its children inevitably faced crises. Funerals, for example, brought sudden demands, requiring a sudden large outlay for special clothes, carriages,

and burial services. Unexpected death or desertion could leave the bereaved or abandoned, especially widows and orphans, in need of financial aid or perhaps a foster home. Relatives responded to such cries, knowing full well that their time of need and repayment would undoubtedly come.

Relatives were also valuable at less tragic moments. If a couple was very poor, an aged relation often moved in to cook and mind the children so that the wife could earn badly needed income outside the home. Sunday dinners were often shared, as were outgrown clothing and useful information. Often the members of a large family group all lived in the same neighborhood.

Sex Roles and Family Life

Industrialization and the growth of modern cities brought great changes to the lives of European women. These changes were particularly consequential for married women, and most women did marry in the nineteenth century.

After 1850 the work of most wives became increasingly distinct and separate from that of their husbands. Husbands became wage earners in factories and offices, while wives tended to stay home and manage households and care for children. The preindustrial pattern among both peasants and cot-

✤ **Spitzweg: The Sunday Outing** Families often shared life's pleasures as well as its hardships with relatives and in-laws, who provided mutual support in the complex urban society. Holiday outings were a favorite way to bring large family groups together, like these Germans strolling happily in the open air on a Sunday afternoon. *(Source: Archiv für Kunst and Geschichte, Berlin)*

tage workers, in which husbands and wives worked together and divided up household duties and child rearing, declined. Only in a few occupations, such as retail trade, did married couples live where they worked and struggle together to make their mom-and-pop operations a success. Factory employment for married women also declined as the early practice of hiring entire families in the factory disappeared.

As economic conditions improved in the later nineteenth century, married women tended to work outside the home only in poor families. One old English worker recalled that "the boy wanted to get into a position that would enable him to keep a wife and family, as it was considered a thoroughly unsatisfactory state of affairs if the wife had to work to help maintain the home."[14] The ideal became a strict division of labor by sex: the wife as mother and homemaker, the husband as wage earner.

This rigid division of labor meant that married women faced great injustice if they tried to move into the man's world of employment outside the home. Husbands were unsympathetic or hostile. Well-paying jobs were off limits to women, and a woman's wage was almost always less than a man's, even for the same work.

Moreover, married women were subordinated to their husbands by law and lacked many basic legal rights. In England the situation in the early nineteenth century was summed up in a famous line from jurist William Blackstone: "In law husband and wife are one person, and the husband is that person." Thus a wife in England had no legal identity and hence no right to own property in her own name. Even the wages she might earn belonged to her husband. In France the Napoleonic Code also enshrined the principle of female subordination and gave the wife few legal rights regarding property, divorce, and custody of the children. Legal inferiority for women permeated Western society.

With middle-class women suffering, sometimes severely, from a lack of legal rights and with all women facing discrimination in education and employment, there is little wonder that some women rebelled and began the long-continuing fight for equality of the sexes and the rights of women. Their struggle proceeded on two main fronts. First, following in the steps of women such as Mary Wollstonecraft (see page 707), organizations founded by middle-class feminists campaigned for equal legal rights for women as well as access to higher education and professional employment. In the later nineteenth century, these organizations scored some significant victories, such as the 1882 law giving English married women full property rights. In the years before 1914, middle-class feminists increasingly shifted their attention to securing the right to vote for women.

Women inspired by utopian and especially Marxian socialism blazed a second path. Often scorning the programs of middle-class feminists, socialist women leaders argued that the liberation of (working-class) women would come only with the liberation of the entire working class through revolution. In the meantime, they championed the cause of working women and won some practical improvements, especially in Germany, where the socialist movement was most effectively organized. In a general way, these different approaches to women's issues reflected the diversity of classes in urban society.

If the ideology and practice of rigidly separate roles undoubtedly narrowed women's horizons and caused some women to rebel, there was a brighter side to the same coin. As home and children became the typical wife's main concerns in the later nineteenth century, her control and influence there apparently became increasingly strong throughout Europe. Among the English working classes, it was the wife who generally determined how the family's money was spent. In many families the husband gave all his earnings to his wife to manage, whatever the law might read. She returned to him only a small allowance for carfare, beer, tobacco, and union dues. All the major domestic decisions, from the children's schooling and religious instruction to the selection of new furniture or a new apartment, were hers. In France women had even greater power in their assigned domain. One English feminist noted in 1908 that "though legally women occupy a much inferior status than men [in France], in practice they constitute the superior sex. They are the power behind the throne." Another Englishwoman believed that "in most French households, women reign with unchallenged sway."[15]

Women ruled at home partly because running the urban household was a complicated, demanding, and valuable task. Twice-a-day food shopping, penny-pinching, economizing, and the growing

❖ **Women Workers** Founded in 1869, the German Social Democratic party became the strongest socialist party in Europe. Women were active in the socialist movement, as this engraving from 1890 of a meeting of workers in Berlin illustrates. Some women activists committed their lives to working for socialism. (See Listening to the Past, Chapter 25.) *(Source: Bildarchiv Preussischer Kulturbesitz)*

crusade against dirt—not to mention child rearing—were a full-time occupation. Nor were there any laborsaving appliances to help. Working yet another job for wages outside the home had limited appeal for most married women unless such earnings were essential for family survival. Many married women in the working classes did make a monetary contribution to family income by taking in boarders or doing piecework at home in the sweated industries (see page 811).

The wife also guided the home because a good deal of her effort was directed toward pampering her husband as he expected. In countless humble households, she saw that he had meat while she ate bread, that he relaxed by the fire while she did the dishes.

The woman's guidance of the household went hand in hand with the increased emotional importance of home and family. The home she ran was idealized as a warm shelter in a hard and impersonal urban world. For a child of the English slums in the early 1900s,

home, however poor, was the focus of all love and interests, a sure fortress against a hostile world. Songs about its beauties were ever on people's lips. "Home, sweet home," first heard in the 1870s, had become "almost a second national anthem." Few walls in lower-working-class houses lacked "mottoes"—colored strips of paper, about nine inches wide and eighteen inches in length, attesting to domestic joys: EAST, WEST, HOME'S BEST; BLESS OUR HOME; GOD IS MASTER OF THIS HOUSE; HOME IS THE NEST WHERE ALL IS BEST.[16]

By 1900 home and family were what life was all about for millions of people of all classes.

Married couples also developed stronger emotional ties to each other. Even in the comfortable classes, marriages in the late nineteenth century were increasingly based on sentiment and sexual attraction as money and financial calculation declined in importance. Affection and eroticism became more central to the couple after marriage. Gustave Droz, whose best seller *Mr., Mrs., and Baby*

SUNDAY MORNING
WORKMANS HOME
LEATHER LANE

❖ **A Working-class Home, 1875** Emotional ties within ordinary families grew stronger in the nineteenth century. Parents gave their children more love and better care. (*Source:* Illustrated London News, *LXVI, 1875. Photo courtesy of Boston Public Library*)

went through 121 editions between 1866 and 1884, saw love within marriage as the key to human happiness. He condemned men who made marriage sound dull and practical, men who were exhausted by prostitutes and rheumatism and who wanted their young wives to be little angels. He urged women to follow their hearts and marry a man more nearly their own age:

A husband who is stately and a little bald is all right, but a young husband who loves you and who drinks out of your glass without ceremony, is better. Let him, if he ruffles your dress a little and places a kiss on your neck as he passes. Let him, if he undresses you after the ball, laughing like a fool. You have fine spiritual qualities, it is true, but your little body is not bad either and when one loves, one loves completely. Behind these follies lies happiness.[17]

Many French marriage manuals of the late 1800s stressed that women had legitimate sexual needs, such as the "right to orgasm." Perhaps the French were a bit more enlightened in these matters than other nationalities. But the rise of public socializing by couples in cafés and music halls as well as

franker affection within the family suggests a more erotic, pleasurable intimate life for women throughout Western society. This, too, helped make the woman's role as mother and homemaker acceptable and even satisfying.

Child Rearing

One of the most striking signs of deepening emotional ties within the family was the growing love and concern that mothers gave their tiny infants. This was a sharp break with the past. Although it may seem hard to believe today, the typical mother in preindustrial Western society was frequently indifferent toward her baby. This indifference—an unwillingness to make real sacrifices for the welfare of the infant—was beginning to give way among the comfortable classes by the end of the eighteenth century, but the ordinary mother of modest means adopted new attitudes only as the nineteenth century progressed. The baby became more important, and women became better mothers.

Mothers increasingly breast-fed their infants, for example, rather than paying wet nurses to do so. Breast-feeding involved sacrifice—a temporary loss of freedom, if nothing else. Yet in an age when there was no good alternative to mother's milk, it saved lives. This surge of maternal feeling also gave rise to a wave of specialized books on child rearing and infant hygiene, such as Droz's phenomenally successful book. Droz urged fathers to get into the act and pitied those "who do not know how to roll around on the carpet, play at being a horse and a great wolf, and undress their baby."[18] Another sign, from France, of increased affection is that fewer illegitimate babies were abandoned as foundlings after about 1850. Moreover, the practice of swaddling disappeared completely. Instead, ordinary mothers allowed their babies freedom of movement and delighted in their spontaneity.

The loving care lavished on infants was matched by greater concern for older children and adolescents. They, too, were wrapped in the strong emotional ties of a more intimate and protective family. For one thing, European women began to limit the number of children they bore in order to care adequately for those they had. It was evident by the end of the century that the birthrate was declining across Europe, as Figure 24.4 shows, and it continued to do so until after World War Two. The Englishwoman who married in the 1860s, for example, had an average of about six children; her daughter marrying in the 1890s had only four; and her granddaughter marrying in the 1920s had only two or possibly three.

The most important reason for this revolutionary reduction in family size, in which the comfortable and well-educated classes took the lead, was parents' desire to improve their economic and social position and that of their children. Children were no longer an economic asset in the later nineteenth century. By having fewer youngsters, parents could give those they had valuable advantages, from music lessons and summer vacations to long, expensive university educations and suitable dowries. A young German skilled worker with only one child spoke for many in his class when he said, "We want to get ahead, and our daughter should have things better than my wife and sisters did."[19] Thus the growing tendency of couples in the late nineteenth century to use a variety of contraceptive methods—rhythm, withdrawal, and mechanical devices—certainly reflected increased concern for children.

Indeed, many parents, especially in the middle classes, probably became *too* concerned about their

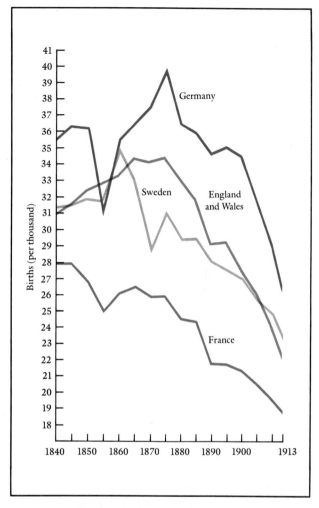

FIGURE 24.4 The Decline of Birthrates in England and Wales, France, Germany, and Sweden, 1840–1913 Women had fewer babies for a variety of reasons, including the fact that their children were increasingly less likely to die before reaching adulthood. Compare with Figure 24.1 on page 800.

children, unwittingly subjecting them to an emotional pressure cooker of almost unbearable intensity. The result was that many children and especially adolescents came to feel trapped and in desperate need of greater independence.

Prevailing biological and medical theories led parents to believe in the possibility that their own emotional characteristics were passed on to their offspring and that they were thus directly responsible for any abnormality in a child. The moment the child was conceived was thought to be of enor-

The triumph of science and technology had at least three significant consequences. First, though ordinary citizens continued to lack detailed scientific knowledge, everyday experience and innumerable popularizers impressed the importance of science on the popular mind.

Second, as science became more prominent in popular thinking, the philosophical implications of science formulated in the Enlightenment spread to broad sections of the population. Natural processes appeared to be determined by rigid laws, leaving little room for either divine intervention or human will. Yet scientific and technical advances had also fed the Enlightenment's optimistic faith in human progress, which now appeared endless and automatic to many middle-class minds.

Third, the methods of science acquired unrivaled prestige after 1850. For many, the union of careful experiment and abstract theory was the only reliable route to truth and objective reality. The "unscientific" intuitions of poets and the revelations of saints seemed hopelessly inferior.

Social Science and Evolution

From the 1830s onward, many thinkers tried to apply the objective methods of science to the study of society. In some ways these efforts simply perpetuated the critical thinking of the philosophes. Yet there were important differences. The new "social scientists" had access to the massive sets of numerical data that governments had begun to collect on everything from children to crime, from population to prostitution. In response, social scientists developed new statistical methods to analyze these facts "scientifically" and supposedly to test their theories. And the systems of the leading nineteenth-century social scientists were more unified, all-encompassing, and dogmatic than those of the philosophes. Marx was a prime example (see pages 769–770).

Another extremely influential system builder was French philosopher Auguste Comte (1798–1857). Initially a disciple of the utopian socialist Saint-Simon (see page 767–768), Comte wrote the six-volume *System of Positive Philosophy* (1830–1842), which was largely overlooked during the romantic era. But when the political failures of 1848 completed the swing to realism, Comte's philosophy came into its own. Its influence has remained great to this day.

Comte postulated that all intellectual activity progresses through predictable stages:

The great fundamental law . . . is this:—that each of our leading conceptions—each branch of our knowledge—passes successively through three different theoretical conditions: the Theological, or fictitious; the Metaphysical, or abstract; and the Scientific, or positive. . . . The first is the necessary point of departure of human understanding, and the third is the fixed and definitive state. The second is merely a transition.[21]

By way of example, Comte noted that the prevailing explanation of cosmic patterns had shifted, as knowledge of astronomy developed, from the will of God (the theological) to the will of an orderly nature (the metaphysical) to the rule of unchanging laws (the scientific). Later, this same intellectual progression took place in increasingly complex fields—physics, chemistry, and, finally, the study of society. By applying the scientific or *positivist* method, Comte believed, his new discipline of sociology would soon discover the eternal laws of human relations. This colossal achievement would in turn enable expert social scientists to impose a disciplined harmony and well-being on less enlightened citizens. Dismissing the "fictions" of traditional religions, Comte became the chief priest of the religion of science and rule by experts.

Comte's stages of knowledge exemplify the nineteenth-century fascination with the idea of evolution and dynamic development. Thinkers in many fields, such as the romantic historians and "scientific" Marxists, shared and applied this basic concept. In geology, Charles Lyell (1797–1875) effectively discredited the long-standing view that the earth's surface had been formed by short-lived cataclysms, such as biblical floods and earthquakes. Instead, according to Lyell's principle of uniformitarianism, the same geological processes that are at work today slowly formed the earth's surface over an immensely long time. The evolutionary view of biological development, first proposed by the Greek Anaximander in the sixth century B.C., re-emerged in a more modern form in the work of Jean Baptiste Lamarck (1744–1829). Lamarck asserted that all forms of life had arisen through a long process of continuous adjustment to the environment.

Lamarck's work was flawed—he believed that the characteristics parents acquired in the course of their lives could be inherited by their children—and was not accepted, but it helped prepare the way for Charles Darwin (1809–1882), the most influential of all nineteenth-century evolutionary thinkers. As the official naturalist on a five-year scientific cruise to Latin America and the South Pacific beginning in 1831, Darwin carefully collected specimens of the different animal species he encountered on the voyage. Back in England, convinced by fossil evidence and by his friend Lyell that the earth and life on it were immensely ancient, Darwin came to doubt the general belief in a special divine creation of each species of animals. Instead, he concluded, all life had gradually evolved from a common ancestral origin in an unending "struggle for survival." After long hesitation, Darwin published his research, which immediately attracted wide attention.

Darwin's great originality lay in suggesting precisely *how* biological evolution might have occurred. His theory is summarized in the title of his work *On the Origin of Species by the Means of Natural Selection* (1859). Decisively influenced by Malthus's gloomy theory that populations naturally grow faster than their food supplies, Darwin argued that chance differences among the members of a given species help some survive while others die. Thus the variations that prove useful in the struggle for survival are selected naturally and gradually spread to the entire species through reproduction. Darwin did not explain why such variations occurred in the first place, and not until the early twentieth century did the study of genetics and the concept of mutation provide some answers.

As the capstone of already widespread evolutionary thinking, Darwin's theory had a powerful and many-sided influence on European thought and the European middle classes. Darwin was hailed as the great scientist par excellence, the "Newton of biology," who had revealed once again the powers of objective science. Darwin's findings also reinforced the teachings of secularists such as Comte and Marx, who scornfully dismissed religious belief in favor of agnostic or atheistic materialism. In the great cities especially, religion was on the defensive. Finally, many writers applied the theory of biological evolution to human affairs. Herbert Spencer (1820–1903), an English disciple of Auguste Comte, saw the human race as driven forward to

❖ **Attracting Females** was an integral part of the struggle for survival, according to Darwin. He theorized that those males who were most attractive to females would have the most offspring, like this type of monkey that had developed ornamental hair, giving him devastating sex appeal. Darwin used this illustration in *The Descent of Man* (1871). *(Source: Library of Congress)*

ever-greater specialization and progress by the brutal economic struggle that efficiently determined the "survival of the fittest." The poor were the ill-fated weak; the prosperous, the chosen strong. Understandably, Spencer and other Social Darwinists were especially popular with the upper middle class.

Realism in Literature

In 1868 Émile Zola (1840–1902), the giant of the realist movement in literature, defended his violently criticized first novel against charges of pornography and corruption of morals. Such accusations were meaningless, Zola claimed: he was only a purely objective scientist using *the modern method, the universal instrument of inquiry of which this age makes such ardent use to open up the future. . . . I chose characters completely dominated by their nerves and their blood, deprived of free-will, pushed to each action of their lives by the fatality of their flesh. . . . I have simply done on living bodies the work of analysis which surgeons perform on corpses.*[22]

Zola's literary manifesto articulated the key themes of realism, which had emerged in the 1840s and continued to dominate Western culture and style until the 1890s. Realist writers believed that literature should depict life exactly as it was. Forsaking poetry for prose and the personal, emotional viewpoint of the romantics for strict, scientific objectivity, the realists simply observed and recorded—content to let the facts speak for themselves.

The major realist writers focused their extraordinary powers of observation on contemporary everyday life. Emphatically rejecting the romantic search for the exotic and the sublime, they energetically pursued the typical and the commonplace.

Degas: Women Ironing Realism replaced romanticism as the dominant trend in the visual arts for a long generation after 1850. This French work by Edgar Degas (1834–1917) accurately captures the hard work and fatigue of unskilled labor. *(Source: Musée d'Orsay copyright photo R.M.N.)*

Beginning with a dissection of the middle classes, from which most of them sprang, many realists eventually focused on the working classes, especially the urban working classes, which had been neglected in imaginative literature before this time. The realists put a microscope to many unexplored and taboo subjects—sex, strikes, violence, alcoholism—and hastened to report that slums and factories teemed with savage behavior. Many shocked middle-class critics denounced realism as ugly sensationalism wrapped provocatively in pseudoscientific declarations and crude language.

The realists' claims of objectivity did not prevent the elaboration of a definite world-view. Unlike the romantics, who had gloried in individual freedom and an unlimited universe, realists such as Zola were strict determinists. Human beings, like atoms, were components of the physical world, and all human actions were caused by unalterable natural laws. Heredity and environment determined human behavior; good and evil were merely social conventions.

The realist movement began in France, where romanticism had never been completely dominant, and three of its greatest practitioners—Balzac, Flaubert, and Zola—were French. Honoré de Balzac (1799–1850) spent thirty years writing a vastly ambitious panorama of postrevolutionary French life. Known collectively as *The Human Comedy,* this series of nearly one hundred books vividly portrays more than two thousand characters from virtually all sectors of French society. Balzac pictures urban society as grasping, amoral, and brutal, characterized by a Darwinian struggle for wealth and power. In *Le Père Goriot* (1835), the hero, a poor student from the provinces, eventually surrenders his idealistic integrity to feverish ambition and society's all-pervasive greed.

Madame Bovary (1857), the masterpiece of Gustave Flaubert (1821–1880), is far narrower in scope than Balzac's work but unparalleled in its depth and accuracy of psychological insight. Unsuccessfully prosecuted as an outrage against public morality and religion, Flaubert's carefully crafted novel tells the ordinary, even banal, story of a frustrated middle-class housewife who has an adulterous love affair and is betrayed by her lover. Without moralizing, Flaubert portrays the provincial middle class as petty, smug, and hypocritical.

Zola was most famous for his seamy, animalistic view of working-class life. But he also wrote gripping, carefully researched stories featuring the stock exchange, the big department store, and the army as well as urban slums and bloody coal strikes. Like many later realists, Zola sympathized with socialism, a sympathy evident in his overpowering *Germinal* (1885).

Realism quickly spread beyond France. In England, Mary Ann Evans (1819–1880), who wrote under the pen name George Eliot, brilliantly achieved a more deeply felt, less sensational kind of realism. "It is the habit of my imagination," George Eliot wrote, "to strive after as full a vision of the medium in which a character moves as one of the character itself." Her great novel *Middlemarch: A Study of Provincial Life* examines masterfully the ways in which people are shaped by their social medium as well as their own inner strivings, conflicts, and moral choices. Thomas Hardy (1840–1928) was more in the Zola tradition. His novels, such as *Tess of the D'Urbervilles* and *Return of the Native,* depict men and women frustrated and crushed by fate and bad luck.

The greatest Russian realist, Count Leo Tolstoy (1828–1910), combined realism in description and character development with an atypical moralizing, which came to dominate his later work. Tolstoy's greatest work was *War and Peace,* a monumental novel set against the historical background of Napoleon's invasion of Russia in 1812. Tolstoy probed deeply into the lives of a multitude of unforgettable characters, such as the ill-fated Prince Andrei; the shy, fumbling Pierre; and the enchanting, level-headed Natasha. Tolstoy went to great pains to develop his fatalistic theory of history, which regards free will as an illusion and the achievements of even the greatest leaders as only the channeling of historical necessity. Yet Tolstoy's central message was one that most of the people discussed in this chapter would have readily accepted: human love, trust, and everyday family ties are life's enduring values.

Thoroughgoing realism (or "naturalism," as it was often called) arrived late in the United States, most arrestingly in the work of Theodore Dreiser (1871–1945). His first novel, *Sister Carrie* (1900), a story of an ordinary farm girl who does well going wrong in Chicago, so outraged conventional morality that the publisher withdrew the book. The United States subsequently became a bastion of literary realism in the twentieth century after the movement had faded away in Europe.

SUMMARY

The Industrial Revolution had a decisive influence on the urban environment. The populations of towns and cities grew rapidly because it was economically advantageous to locate factories and offices in urban areas. This rapid growth worsened long-standing overcrowding and unhealthy living conditions and posed a frightening challenge for society. Eventually government leaders, city planners, reformers, scientists, and ordinary citizens responded. They took effective action in public health and provided themselves with other badly needed urban services. Gradually they tamed the ferocious savagery of the traditional city.

As urban civilization came to prevail, there were major changes in family life. Especially among the working classes, family life became more stable, more loving, and less mercenary. These improvements had a price, however. Sex roles for men and women became sharply defined and rigidly separate. Women especially tended to be locked into a subordinate and stereotypical role. Nonetheless, on balance, the quality of family life improved for all family members. Better, more stable family relations reinforced the benefits for the masses of higher real wages, increased social security, political participation, and education.

While the quality of urban and family life improved, the class structure became more complex and diversified than before. Urban society featured many distinct social groups, which existed in a state of constant flux and competition. The gap between rich and poor remained enormous and really quite traditional in mature urban society, although there were countless gradations between the extremes. Large numbers of poor women in particular continued to labor as workers in sweated industries, as domestic servants, and as prostitutes in order to satisfy the demands of their masters in the servant-keeping classes. Urban society in the late nineteenth century represented a great step forward for humanity, but it remained very unequal.

Inequality was a favorite theme of realist novelists such as Balzac and Zola. More generally, literary realism reflected Western society's growing faith in science, material progress, and evolutionary thinking. The emergence of urban, industrial civilization accelerated the secularization of the Western world-view.

NOTES

1. A. Weber, *The Growth of Cities in the Nineteenth Century* (New York: Columbia University Press, 1899), p. 1.

2. Quoted in W. Ashworth, *The Genesis of Modern British Town Planning* (London: Routledge & Kegan Paul, 1954), p. 17.

3. S. Marcus, "Reading the Illegible," in *The Victorian City: Images and Realities,* ed. H. J. Dyos and Michael Wolff, vol. 1 (London: Routledge & Kegan Paul, 1973), p. 266.

4. E. Gauldie, *Cruel Habitations: A History of Working-Class Housing, 1780–1918* (London: George Allen & Unwin, 1974), p. 21.

5. Quoted in E. Chadwick, *Report on the Sanitary Condition of the Labouring Population of Great Britain,* ed. M. W. Flinn (Edinburgh: University of Edinburgh Press, 1965; original publication, 1842), pp. 315–316.

6. J. P. McKay, *Tramways and Trolleys: The Rise of Urban Mass Transport in Europe* (Princeton, N.J.: Princeton University Press, 1976), p. 81.

7. Quoted in R. P. Neuman, "The Sexual Question and Social Democracy in Imperial Germany," *Journal of Social History* 7 (Winter 1974): 276.

8. Quoted in B. Harrison, "Underneath the Victorians," *Victorian Studies* 10 (March 1967): 260.

9. Quoted in J. A. Banks, "The Contagion of Numbers," in Dyos and Wolff, p. 112.

10. Quoted in R. Roberts, *The Classic Slum: Salford Life in the First Quarter of the Century* (Manchester, Eng.: University of Manchester Press, 1971), p. 95.

11. Quoted in T. Zeldin, *France, 1848–1945* (Oxford: Clarendon Press, 1973), vol. 1, p. 288.

12. Quoted in J. M. Phayer, "Lower-Class Morality: The Case of Bavaria," *Journal of Social History* 8 (Fall 1974): 89.

13. Quoted in S. Marcus, *The Other Victorians: A Study of Sexuality and Pornography in Mid-Nineteenth-Century England* (New York: Basic Books, 1966), p. 142.

14. Quoted in G. S. Jones, "Working-Class Culture and Working-Class Politics in London, 1870–1900: Notes on the Remaking of a Working Class," *Journal of Social History* 7 (Summer 1974): 486.

15. Quoted in Zeldin, p. 346.

16. Roberts, p. 35.

17. Quoted in Zeldin, p. 295.

18. Ibid., p. 328.

19. Quoted in Neuman, p. 281.

20. Quoted by S. Kern, "Explosive Intimacy: Psychodynamics of the Victorian Family," *History of Childhood Quarterly* 1 (Winter 1974): 439.

21. A. Comte, *The Positive Philosophy of Auguste Comte,* trans. H. Martineau, vol. 1 (London: J. Chapman, 1853), pp. 1–2.

22. Quoted in G. J. Becker, ed., *Documents of Modern Literary Realism* (Princeton, N.J.: Princeton University Press, 1963), p. 159.

SUGGESTED READING

All of the books and articles cited in the Notes are highly recommended; the *Journal of Social History,* which has a strong European orientation, is excellent both for its articles and reviews of new books. T. Zeldin, *France, 1848–1945,* 2 vols. (1973, 1977), is a pioneering social history that opens many doors, as is the ambitious synthesis by T. Hamerow, *The Birth of a New Europe: State and Society in the Nineteenth Century* (1983). P. Pillbeam, *The Middle Classes in Europe, 1789–1914: France, Germany, Italy, and Russia* (1990), is a stimulating introduction.

On the European city, D. Harvey, *Consciousness and the Urban Experience* (1985), is provocative. D. Silverman, *Art Nouveau in Fin-de-Siècle France: Politics, Psychology, and Style* (1989), and D. Pickney, *Napoleon III and the Rebuilding of Paris* (1972), are fascinating, as are G. Masur, *Imperial Berlin* (1970), and M. Hamm, ed., *The City in Russian History* (1976). So also are N. Evenson's beautifully illustrated *Paris: A Century of Change, 1878–1978* (1979), and D. Grew's authoritative *Town in the Ruhr: A Social History of Bochum, 1860–1914* (1979). T. Clark, *The Painting of Modern Life: Paris in the Age of Manet and His Followers* (1985), and J. Merriman, *Margins of City Life: Explorations on the French Urban Frontier* (1991), are important works on France. The outstanding study by J. Schmiechen, *Sweated Industries and Sweated Labor: The London Clothing Trades* (1984), complements H. Mayhew's wonderful contemporary study, *London Labour and the Labouring Poor* (1861), reprinted recently. Michael Crichton's realistic historical novel on organized crime, *The Great Train Robbery* (1976), is excellent. J. J. Tobias, *Urban Crime in Victorian England* (1972), is a lively, scholarly approach to declining criminal activity in the nineteenth century, with a wealth of detail. J. P. Goubert, *The Conquest of Water: The Advent of Health in the Industrial Age* (1989), and G. Rosen, *History of Public Health* (1958), are excellent introductions to sanitary and medical developments. For society as a whole,

J. Burnett, *History of the Cost of Living* (1969), cleverly shows how different classes spent their money, and B. Tuchman, *The Proud Tower* (1966), draws an unforgettable portrait of people and classes before 1914. J. Laver's handsomely illustrated *Manners and Morals in the Age of Optimism, 1848–1914* (1966) investigates the urban underworld and relations between the sexes. Sexual attitudes are also examined by J. Walkowitz, *Prostitution and Victorian Society: Women, Class and State* (1890); J. Phayer, *Sexual Liberation and Religion in Nineteenth-Century Europe* (1977); and L. Engelstein, *The Key to Happiness: Sex and the Search for Modernity in Fin-de-Siècle Russia* (1992). G. Alter, *Family and Female Life Course: The Women of Verviers, Belgium, 1849–1880* (1988), and A. McLaren, *Sexuality and Social Order: Birth Control in Nineteenth-Century France* (1982), explore attitudes toward family planning.

Women have come into their own in historical studies. In addition to the general works by Shorter, Wrigley, Stone, and Tilly and Scott cited in Chapter 20, there are a growing number of eye-opening specialized investigations. These include L. Davidoff, *The Best Circles* (1973), and P. Jalland, *Women, Marriage and Politics, 1860–1914* (1986), on upper-class society types; O. Banks, *Feminism and Family Planning in Victorian England* (1964); and P. Branca, *Women in Europe Since 1750* (1978). M. J. Peterson, *Love and Work in the Lives of Victorian Gentlewomen* (1989), L. Holcombe, *Victorian Ladies at Work* (1973), and M. Vicinus, *Independent Women: Work and Community for Single Women, 1850–1920* (1985), examine women at work. M. Vicinus, ed., *Suffer and Be Still* (1972) and *A Widening Sphere* (1981), are far-ranging collections of essays on women's history, as is R. Bridenthal, C. Koonz, and S. Stuard, eds., *Becoming Visible: Women in European History,* 2d ed. (1987). Feminism is treated perceptively in R. Evans, *The Feminists: Women's Emancipation in Europe, America, and Australia* (1979); K. Blair, *The Clubwoman as Feminist: True Womanhood Redefined, 1868–1914* (1980); and C. Moses, *French Feminism in the Nineteenth Century* (1984). L. Tickner, *The Spectacle of Women: Imagery*

of the Suffrage Campaign, 1907–1914 (1988), perceptively discusses Britain. J. Gillis, *Youth and History* (1974), is a good introduction. D. Ransel, ed., *The Family in Imperial Russia* (1978), is an important work on the subject, as is J. Donzelot, *The Policing of Families* (1979), which stresses the loss of family control of all aspects of life to government agencies.

Among studies of special groups, J. Scott, *The Glass-Workers of Carmaux* (1974), is outstanding on skilled French craftsmen, and D. Lockwood, *The Blackcoated Worker* (1958), carefully examines class consciousness in the English lower middle class. J. R. Wegs, *Growing Up Working Class: Continuity and Change Among Viennese Youth, 1890–1938* (1989), is recommended. Two fine studies on universities and their professors are S. Rothblatt, *Revolution of the Dons: Cambridge and Society in Victorian England* (1968), and F. Ringer, *The Decline of the German Mandarins* (1969). Servants and their employers receive excellent treatment in T. McBride, *The Domestic Revolution: The Modernization of Household Service in England and France, 1820–1920* (1976), and B. Smith, *Ladies of the Leisure Class: The Bourgeoises of Northern France in the Nineteenth Century* (1981), which may be compared with the innovative study by M. Miller, *The Bon Marché: Bourgeois Culture and the Department Store, 1869–1920* (1981).

On Darwin, M. Ruse, *The Darwinian Revolution* (1979), is a good starting point, as are P. Bowler, *Evolution: The History of an Idea,* rev. ed. (1989), and G. Himmelfarb, *Darwin and the Darwinian Revolution* (1968). O. Chadwick, *The Secularization of the European Mind in the Nineteenth Century* (1976), analyzes the impact of science (and other factors) on religious belief. The masterpieces of the great realist social novelists remain one of the best and most memorable introductions to nineteenth-century culture and thought. In addition to the novels discussed in this chapter and those cited in the Suggested Reading for Chapters 22 and 23, Ivan Turgenev's *Fathers and Sons* and Émile Zola's *The Dram-Shop* are especially recommended.

CHAPTER

25

The Age of Nationalism, 1850–1914

The revolutions of 1848 closed one era and opened another. Urban industrial society began to take strong hold on the Continent and in the young United States, as it already had in Great Britain. Internationally, the repressive peace and diplomatic stability of Metternich's time were replaced by a period of war and rapid change. In thought and culture, exuberant romanticism gave way to hardheaded realism. In the Atlantic economy, the hard years of the 1840s were followed by good times and prosperity throughout most of the 1850s and 1860s. Perhaps most important of all, Western society progressively found, for better or worse, a new and effective organizing principle capable of coping with the many-sided challenge of the dual revolution and the emerging urban civilization. That principle was nationalism—dedication to and identification with the nation-state.

The triumph of nationalism is an enormously significant historical development that was by no means completely predictable. After all, nationalism had been a powerful force since at least 1789. Yet it had repeatedly failed to realize its goals, most spectacularly so in 1848.

A painting of the Italian patriot Garibaldi entering Naples, in 1861, after his military victory in southern Italy. *(Source: Museo del Risorgimento/ Scala/Art Resource, NY)*

- Why, then, did nationalism become in one way or another an almost universal faith in Europe and in the United States between 1850 and 1914?

- More specifically, how did nationalism evolve so that it appealed not only to predominately middle-class liberals but also to the broad masses of society?

These are the weighty questions this chapter will seek to answer.

831

NAPOLEON III IN FRANCE

Early nationalism was at least liberal and idealistic and often democratic and radical as well. The ideas of nationhood and popular sovereignty posed an awesome revolutionary threat to conservatives like Metternich. Yet from the vantage point of the twentieth century, it is clear that nationalism wears many masks: it may be democratic and radical, as it was for Mazzini and Michelet; but it can also flourish in dictatorial states, which may be conservative, fascist, or communist. Napoleon I's France had already combined national devotion with authoritarian rule. Significantly, it was Napoleon's nephew, Louis Napoleon, who revived and extended this merger. He showed how governments could reconcile popular and conservative forces in an authoritarian nationalism. In doing so, he provided a model for political leaders elsewhere.

The Second Republic and Louis Napoleon

The overwhelming victory of Louis Napoleon Bonaparte in the French presidential election of December 1848 has long puzzled historians. The nephew of Napoleon I and the heir to the family's dynastic claims after the death of Napoleon I's son in 1832, Louis Napoleon had lived most of his life outside of France and played no part in French politics before 1848. Why did universal male suffrage give such an unproven nobody 5.5 million votes, while the runner-up, General Cavaignac of June Days fame (see page 786), polled only 1.5 million and the other three candidates (including the poet Lamartine) received insignificant support?

The usual explanation is that, though Louis Napoleon had only his great name in common with his uncle, that was enough. According to some historians, the Napoleonic legend—a monument to the power of romanticism between 1820 and 1848—had transformed a dictator into a demigod in the minds of the unsophisticated French masses. Another explanation, popularized by Karl Marx, has stressed the fears of middle-class and peasant property owners in the face of the socialist challenge of urban workers. These classes wanted protection. They wanted a tough cop with a big stick on the beat. They found him in Louis Napoleon, who had indeed served briefly as a special constable in London at the height of the Chartist agitation.

These explanations are not wrong, but there was more to Louis Napoleon's popularity than stupid-

ity and fear. In late 1848 Louis Napoleon had a positive "program" for France, which was to guide him throughout most of his long reign. This program had been elaborated earlier in two pamphlets, *Napoleonic Ideas* and *The Elimination of Poverty,* which Louis Napoleon had written while imprisoned for a farcical attempt to overthrow Louis Philippe's government. The pamphlets had been widely circulated prior to the presidential election.

Louis Napoleon believed that the government should represent the people and that it should try hard to help them economically. How were these tasks to be done? Parliaments and political parties were not the answer, according to Louis Napoleon. Politicians represented special-interest groups, particularly middle-class ones. When they ran a parliamentary government, they stirred up class hatred because they were not interested in helping the poor. This had occurred under Louis Philippe, and it was occurring again under the Second Republic. The answer was a strong, even authoritarian, national leader, like the first Napoleon, who would serve all the people, rich and poor. This leader would be linked to the people by direct democracy and universal male suffrage. Sovereignty would flow from the entire population to the leader and would not be diluted or corrupted by politicians and legislative bodies.

These political ideas went hand in hand with Louis Napoleon's vision of national unity and social progress. Rather than doing nothing or providing only temporary relief for the awful poverty of the poor, the state and its leader had a sacred duty to provide jobs and stimulate the economy. All classes would benefit by such action.

Louis Napoleon's political and social ideas were at least vaguely understood by large numbers of French peasants and workers in December 1848. To many common people he appeared to be a strong man *and* a forward-looking champion of their interests, and that is why they voted for him.

Elected to a four-year term, President Louis Napoleon had to share power with a conservative National Assembly. With some misgivings he signed a bill to increase greatly the role of the Catholic church in primary and secondary education. In France, as elsewhere in Europe after 1848, the anxious well-to-do saw religion as a bulwark against radicalism. As one leader of the church in France put it, "There is only one recipe for making those who own nothing believe in property-rights: that is to make them believe in God, who dictated

❖ **The Official Inauguration of the Second Republic** was marked by joyful celebration. The Second Republic established a presidential system based on universal male suffrage, which led to the unexpected victory of Louis Napoleon, the nephew of Napoleon I. This bird's-eye view of the festivities looks eastward across the Louvre palace. The Seine and the Latin Quarter are on the right. *(Source: Musée Carnavalet/Photographie Bulloz)*

the Ten Commandments and who promises eternal punishment to those who steal."[1] Very reluctantly, Louis Napoleon also signed another law depriving many poor people of the right to vote. He took these conservative measures for two main reasons: he wanted the Assembly to vote funds to pay his personal debts, and he wanted it to change the constitution so he could run for a second term.

The Assembly did neither. Thus in 1851 Louis Napoleon began to organize a conspiracy with key army officers. On December 2, 1851, he illegally dismissed the Assembly and seized power in a *coup d'état*. There were some armed resistance in Paris and widespread insurrection in the countryside in southern France, but these protests were quickly crushed by the army. Restoring universal male suffrage, Louis Napoleon called on the French people, as his uncle had done, to legalize his actions. They did: 92 percent voted to make him a strong president for ten years. A year later, 97 percent agreed in a national plebiscite to make him heredi-

tary emperor; for the third time, and by the greatest margin yet, the authoritarian Louis Napoleon was overwhelmingly elected to lead the French nation.

Napoleon III's Second Empire

Louis Napoleon—now proclaimed Emperor Napoleon III—experienced both success and failure between 1852 and 1870. His greatest success was with the economy, particularly in the 1850s. His government encouraged the new investment banks and massive railroad construction that were at the heart of the Industrial Revolution on the Continent. The government also fostered general economic expansion through an ambitious program of public works, which included the rebuilding of Paris to improve the urban environment. The profits of business people soared with prosperity, and the working classes did not fare poorly either. Their wages more than kept up with inflation, and jobs were much easier to find.

Louis Napoleon always hoped that economic progress would reduce social and political tensions. This hope was at least partially realized. Until the mid-1860s, there was little active opposition and there was even considerable support for his government from France's most dissatisfied group, the urban workers. Napoleon III's regulation of pawnshops and his support of credit unions and better housing for the working class were evidence of positive concern in the 1850s. In the 1860s, he granted workers the right to form unions and the right to strike—important economic rights denied by earlier governments.

At first, political power remained in the hands of the emperor. He alone chose his ministers, and they had great freedom of action. At the same time, Napoleon III restricted but did not abolish the Assembly. Members were elected by universal male suffrage every six years, and Louis Napoleon and his government took the parliamentary elections very seriously. They tried to entice notable people, even those who had opposed the regime, to stand as government candidates in order to expand the base of support. Moreover, the government used its officials and appointed mayors to spread the word that the election of the government's candidates—and the defeat of the opposition—was the key to roads, schools, tax rebates, and a thousand other local concerns.

In 1857 and again in 1863, Louis Napoleon's system worked brilliantly and produced overwhelming electoral victories. Yet in the 1860s, Napoleon III's electoral system gradually disintegrated. France's problems in Italy and the rising power of Prussia led to increasing criticism at home from his Catholic and nationalist supporters. With increasing effectiveness, the middle-class liberals who had always wanted a less authoritarian regime continued to denounce his rule.

Napoleon was always sensitive to the public mood. Public opinion, he once said, always wins the last victory. Thus in the 1860s, he progressively liberalized his empire. He gave the Assembly greater powers and the opposition candidates greater freedom, which they used to good advantage. In 1869 the opposition, consisting of republicans, monarchists, and liberals, polled almost 45 percent of the vote.

The next year, a sick and weary Louis Napoleon again granted France a new constitution, which combined a basically parliamentary regime with a hereditary emperor as chief of state. In a final great plebiscite on the eve of a disastrous war with Prussia, 7.5 million Frenchmen voted in favor of the new constitution, and only 1.5 million opposed it. Napoleon III's attempt to reconcile a strong national state with universal male suffrage was still evolving and was doing so in a democratic direction.

 # NATION BUILDING IN ITALY AND GERMANY

Louis Napoleon's triumph in 1848 and his authoritarian rule in the 1850s provided the old ruling classes of Europe with a new model in politics. To what extent might the expanding urban middle classes and even the growing working classes, like people in rural areas, rally to a strong and essentially conservative national state? This was one of the great political questions in the 1850s and 1860s. In central Europe, a resounding answer came with the national unification of Italy and Germany.

Italy to 1850

Italy had never been a united nation prior to 1860. Part of Rome's great empire in ancient times, the Italian peninsula was divided in the Middle Ages into competing city-states, which led the commercial and cultural revival of the West with amazing creativity. A battleground for great powers after 1494, Italy was reorganized in 1815 at the Congress of Vienna. The rich northern provinces of Lombardy and Venetia were taken by Metternich's Austria. Sardinia and Piedmont were under the rule of an Italian monarch, and Tuscany, with its famous capital of Florence, shared north-central Italy with several smaller states. Central Italy and Rome were ruled by the papacy, which had always considered an independent political existence necessary to fulfill its spiritual mission. Naples and Sicily were ruled, as they had been for almost a hundred years, by a branch of the Bourbons. Metternich was not wrong in dismissing Italy as "a geographical expression" (Map 25.1).

Between 1815 and 1848, the goal of a unified Italian nation captured the imaginations of increasing numbers of Italians. There were three basic approaches. The first was the radical program of the idealistic patriot Guiseppe Mazzini, who preached a centralized democratic republic based on universal suffrage and the will of the people (see

Kingdom of Sardinia before 1859
To Kingdom of Sardinia, 1859
To Kingdom of Sardinia, 1860
To Kingdom of Italy, 1866, 1870
× Major battles
— Boundary of Kingdom of Italy after unification

❖ **MAP 25.1 The Unification of Italy, 1859–1870** The leadership of Sardinia-Piedmont and nationalist fervor were decisive factors in the unification of Italy.

pages 766). The second was that of Vincenzo Gioberti, a Catholic priest, who called for a federation of existing states under the presidency of a progressive pope. The third was the program of those who looked for leadership toward the autocratic kingdom of Sardinia-Piedmont, much as many Germans looked toward Prussia.

The third alternative was strengthened by the failures of 1848, when Austria smashed and discredited Mazzini's republicanism. Almost by accident, Sardinia's monarch, Victor Emmanuel, retained the liberal constitution granted under duress in March 1848. This constitution provided for a fair degree of civil liberties and real parliamentary

With Russian diplomatic support, Austria had blocked the halfhearted attempt of Frederick William IV of Prussia (r. 1840–1861) to unify Germany "from above." This action contributed to a growing tension between Austria and Prussia as each power sought to block the other within the reorganized German Confederation, made up of thirty-eight sovereign states after 1815 (see pages 761–790). Stalemate also prevailed in the domestic politics of the individual states as Austria, Prussia, and the smaller German kingdoms entered a period of reaction and immobility in the 1850s.

At the same time, powerful economic forces were undermining the political status quo. As we have seen, modern industry grew rapidly in Europe throughout the 1850s. Nowhere was this growth more rapid than within the German customs union (Zollverein). Developing gradually under Prussian leadership after 1818 and founded officially in 1834 to stimulate trade and increase the revenues of member states, the Zollverein had not included Austria. After 1848 this exclusion became a crucial factor in the Austro-Prussian rivalry.

Tariff duties were substantially reduced so that Austria's highly protected industry could not bear to join. In retaliation, Austria tried to destroy the Zollverein by inducing the south German states to leave it, but without success. Indeed, by the end of 1853 all the German states except Austria had joined the customs union. A new Germany excluding Austria was becoming an economic reality. Middle-class and business groups in the Zollverein were enriching themselves and finding solid economic reasons to bolster their idealistic support of national unification. The growing economic integration of the states within the Zollverein gave Prussia a valuable advantage in its struggle against Austria's supremacy in German political affairs.

The national uprising in Italy in 1859 made a profound impression in the German states. In Prussia, great political change and war—perhaps with Austria, perhaps with France—seemed quite possible. Along with his top military advisers, the tough-minded William I of Prussia (r. 1861–1888), who had replaced the unstable Frederick William IV as regent in 1858 and become king himself in 1861, was convinced of the need for major army reforms. William I wanted to double the size of the highly disciplined regular army. He also wanted to reduce the importance of the reserve militia, a semipopular force created during the Napoleonic wars. Army reforms meant a bigger defense budget and higher taxes.

Prussia had emerged from 1848 with a parliament of sorts, which was in the hands of the liberal middle class by 1859. The wealthy middle class, like the landed aristocracy, was greatly overrepresented by the Prussian electoral system, and it wanted society to be less, not more, militaristic. Above all, middle-class representatives wanted to establish once and for all that the parliament, not the king, had the ultimate political power. They also wanted to ensure that the army was responsible to Prussia's elected representatives and was not a "state within a state." These demands were popular. The parliament rejected the military budget in 1862, and the liberals triumphed so completely in new elections that the conservatives "could ride to the parliament building in a single coach." King William considered abdicating in favor of his more liberal son. In the end, William called on Count Otto von Bismarck to head a new ministry and defy the parliament. This was a momentous choice.

Bismarck Takes Command

The most important figure in German history between Luther and Hitler, Otto von Bismarck (1815–1898) has been the object of enormous interest and debate. A great hero to some, a great villain to others, Bismarck was above all a master of politics. Born into the Prussian landowning aristocracy, the young Bismarck was a wild and tempestuous student given to duels and drinking. Proud of his Junker heritage—"my fathers have been born and have lived and died in the same rooms for centuries"—and always devoted to his Prussian sovereign, Bismarck had a strong personality and an unbounded desire for power.

Bismarck entered the civil service, which was the only socially acceptable career except the army for a Prussian aristocrat. But he soon found bureaucratic life unbearable and fled to his ancestral estate. "My pride," he admitted, "bids me command rather than obey."[2] Yet in his drive to secure power for himself and for Prussia, Bismarck was extraordinarily flexible and pragmatic. "One must always have two irons in the fire," he once said. He kept his options open, pursuing one policy and then another as he moved with skill and cunning toward his goal.

Bismarck first honed his political skills as a diplomat. Acquiring a reputation as an ultraconservative in the Prussian assembly in 1848, he fought against Austria as the Prussian ambassador to the German Confederation from 1851 to 1859. Transferred next to St. Petersburg and then to Paris, he worked toward a basic goal that was well known by 1862—to build up Prussia's strength and consolidate Prussia's precarious Great Power status.

To achieve this goal, Bismarck was convinced that Prussia had to control completely the northern, predominately Protestant part of the German Confederation. He saw three possible paths open before him. He might work with Austria to divide up the smaller German states lying between them. Or he might combine with foreign powers—France and Italy or even Russia—against Austria. Or he might ally with the forces of German nationalism to defeat and expel Austria from German affairs. He explored each possibility in many complicated diplomatic maneuvers, but in the end the last path was the one Bismarck took.

That Bismarck would join with the forces of German nationalism to increase Prussia's power seemed unlikely when he took office as chief minister in 1862. Bismarck's appointment made a strong but unfavorable impression. His speeches were a sensation and a scandal. Declaring that the government would rule without parliamentary consent, Bismarck lashed out at the middle-class opposition: "The great questions of the day will not be decided by speeches and resolutions—that was the blunder of 1848 and 1849—but by blood and iron." In 1863 he told the Prussian parliament, "If a compromise cannot be arrived at and a conflict arises, then the conflict becomes a question of power. Whoever has the power then acts according to his opinion." Denounced for this view that "might makes right," Bismarck had the Prussian bureaucracy go right on collecting taxes, even though the parliament refused to approve the budget. Bismarck reorganized the army. And for four years, from 1862 to 1866, the voters of Prussia continued to express their opposition by sending large liberal majorities to the parliament.

The Austro-Prussian War, 1866

Opposition at home spurred the search for success abroad. The ever-knotty question of Schleswig-Holstein provided a welcome opportunity. When the Danish king tried again, as in 1848, to bring the provinces into a centralized Danish state against the will of the German Confederation, Prussia joined Austria in a short and successful war

✤ **Otto von Bismarck** The commanding presence and the haughty pride of the Prussian statesman are clearly evident in this photo taken shortly before he came to power. Dressed in formal diplomatic attire as Prussia's ambassador in Paris, Bismarck is perhaps on his way to see Emperor Louis Napoleon and size up his future adversary once again. *(Source: Archiv Für Kurst und Geschichte, Berlin)*

against Denmark in 1864. Then Bismarck maneuvered Austria into a tricky position. Prussia and Austria agreed to joint administration of the conquered provinces, thereby giving Bismarck a weapon he could use either to force Austria into peacefully accepting Prussian domination in northern Germany or to start a war against Austria.

Bismarck knew that a war with Austria would have to be a localized one. He had to be certain that Prussian expansion would not provoke a mighty armed coalition, such as the coalition that had almost crushed Frederick the Great in the eighteenth century. Russia, the great bear to the east, was no problem. Bismarck had already gained Alexander II's gratitude by supporting Russia's repression of a Polish uprising in 1863. Napoleon III—the "sphinx without a riddle," according to Bismarck—was another matter. But Bismarck charmed Napoleon into neutrality with vague promises of more territory along the Rhine. Thus when Austria proved unwilling to give up its historic role in German affairs, Bismarck was in a position to engage in a war of his own making.

The Austro-Prussian War of 1866 lasted only seven weeks. Utilizing railroads to mass troops and the new breechloading needle gun to achieve maximum firepower, the reorganized Prussian army overran northern Germany and defeated Austria decisively at the Battle of Sadowa in Bohemia. Anticipating Prussia's future needs, Bismarck offered Austria realistic, even generous, peace terms. Austria paid no reparations and lost no territory to Prussia, although Venice was ceded to Italy. But the German Confederation was dissolved, and Austria agreed to withdraw from German affairs. The states north of the Main River were grouped in the new North German Confederation, led by an expanded Prussia. The mainly Catholic states of the south remained independent while forming alliances with Prussia. Bismarck's fundamental goal of Prussian expansion was being realized (Map 25.2).

The Taming of the Parliament

Bismarck had long been convinced that the old order he so ardently defended should make peace, on its own terms, with the liberal middle class and the nationalist movement. Inspired somewhat by Louis Napoleon, Bismarck realized that nationalism was not necessarily hostile to conservative, authoritarian government. Moreover, Bismarck believed that because of the events of 1848, the German middle class could be led to prefer the reality of national unity under conservative leadership to a long, uncertain battle for truly liberal institutions. During the constitutional struggle over army reform and parliamentary authority, he had delayed but not abandoned this goal. Thus during the attack on Austria in 1866, he increasingly identified Prussia's fate with the "national development of Germany."

In the aftermath of victory, Bismarck fashioned a federal constitution for the new North German Confederation. Each state retained its own local government, but the king of Prussia became president of the confederation and the chancellor—Bismarck—was responsible only to the president. The federal government—William I and Bismarck—controlled the army and foreign affairs. There was also a legislature consisting of two houses that shared equally in the making of laws. Delegates to the upper house were appointed by the different states, but members of the lower house were elected by universal, single category, male suffrage. With this radical innovation, Bismarck opened the door to popular participation and the possibility of going over the head of the middle class directly to the people, much as Napoleon III had done in France. All the while, however, ultimate power rested as securely as ever in the hands of Prussia and its king and army.

Events within Prussia itself were even more significant than those at the federal level. In the flush of victory, the landed nobility and the ultraconservatives expected Bismarck to suspend the Prussian constitution or perhaps abolish the Prussian parliament altogether. Yet he did nothing of the sort. Instead, he held out an olive branch to the parliamentary opposition. Marshaling all his diplomatic skill, Bismarck asked the parliament to pass a special indemnity bill to approve after the fact all of the government's spending between 1862 and 1866. Most of the liberals snatched at the chance to cooperate. For four long years, they had opposed and criticized Bismarck's "illegal" measures. And what had happened? Bismarck, the king, and the army with its aristocratic leadership had persevered, and in the end these conservative forces had succeeded beyond the wildest dreams of the liberal middle class. In 1866 German unity was in sight, and the people were going to be allowed to participate actively in the new state. Many liberals repented their "sins" and were overjoyed that Bismarck would forgive them.

None repented more ardently or more typically than Hermann Baumgarten, a mild-mannered, thoroughly decent history professor and member of the liberal opposition. In his essay "A Self–Criticism of German Liberalism," he confessed in 1866:

We thought by agitation we could transform Germany. But . . . almost all the elements of our political system have been shown erroneous by the facts themselves. . . . Yet we have experienced a miracle almost without parallel. The victory of our principles would have brought us misery, whereas the defeat of our principles has brought boundless salvation.[3]

MAP 25.2 The Unification of Germany, 1866–1871 This map deserves careful study. Note how Prussian expansion, Austrian expulsion from the old German Confederation, and the creation of a new German Empire went hand in hand. Austria lost no territory but Prussia's neighbors in the north suffered grievously or simply disappeared. The annexation of Alsace-Lorraine turned France into a lasting enemy of Germany before 1914.

The constitutional struggle was over. The German middle class was bowing respectfully before Bismarck and the monarchial authority and aristocratic superiority he represented. The middle class never stood again in the years before 1914.

The Franco-Prussian War, 1870–1871

The rest of the story of German unification is anticlimactic. In 1867 Bismarck brought the four south German states into the Zollverein and estab-

"**His First Thought**" This 1896 cartoon provides a brilliant commentary on German middle-class attitudes. Suddenly crippled, the man's first thought is "Disaster! Now I can no longer be a reserve army officer." Being a part-time junior officer and serving under the dominant aristocratic career officers became a great middle-class status symbol. (*Source:* Simplicissimus/*Caroline Buckler*)

lished a customs parliament. But the south Germans were reluctant to go further because of their different religious and political traditions. Bismarck realized that a patriotic war with France would drive the south German states into his arms. The French obligingly played their part. The apparent issue—whether a distant relative of Prussia's William I (and France's Napoleon III) might become king of Spain—was only a diplomatic pretext. By 1870 the French leaders of the Second Empire, alarmed by their powerful new neighbor on the Rhine, had decided on a war to teach Prussia a lesson.

As soon as war against France began in 1870, Bismarck had the wholehearted support of the south German states. With other governments standing still—Bismarck's generosity to Austria in 1866 was paying big dividends—German forces under Prussian leadership decisively defeated Louis Napoleon's armies at Sedan on September 1, 1870. Three days later, French patriots in Paris proclaimed yet another French republic and vowed to continue fighting. But after five months, in January 1871, a starving Paris surrendered, and France went on to accept Bismarck's harsh peace terms. By this time, the south German states had agreed to join a new German empire. The victorious William I was proclaimed emperor of Germany in the Hall of Mirrors in the palace of Versailles. Europe had a nineteenth-century German "sun king." As in the 1866 constitution, the king of Prussia and his ministers had ultimate power in the new German Empire, and the lower house of the legislature was elected by universal male suffrage.

The Franco-Prussian War, which Europeans generally saw as a test of nations in a pitiless Darwinian struggle for existence, released an enormous surge of patriotic feeling in Germany. Bismarck's genius, the invincible Prussian army, the solidarity of king and people in a unified nation—these and similar themes were trumpeted endlessly during and after the war. The weakest of the Great Powers in 1862 (after Austria, Britain, France, and Russia), Prussia had become, with fortification by the other Germans states, the most powerful state in Europe in less than a decade. Most Germans were enormously proud, enormously relieved. And they were somewhat drunk with success, blissfully imagining themselves the fittest and best of the European species. Semi-authoritarian nationalism and a "new conservatism," which was based on an alliance of the propertied classes and sought the active support of the working classes, had triumphed in Germany. Only a few critics remained dedicated to the liberal ideal of truly responsible parliamentary government.

NATION BUILDING IN THE UNITED STATES

Closely linked to general European developments in the nineteenth century, the United States experienced the full drama of midcentury nation building and felt the power of nationalism to refashion politics and remake states. Yet in the United States competing national aspirations served first to divide rather than unite. Only after a bitter civil war was nationalism successfully harnessed to the building of a transcontinental giant.

Slavery and Territorial Expansion

Formed in the process of revolt against Great Britain, the young "United" States was divided by slavery from its birth. As the new federal Constitution was being written, the Northwest Ordinance of 1787 effectively extended the seaboard patterns of free and slave labor into the vast area west of the Allegheny Mountains and east of the Mississippi, with the Ohio River serving as the fatal dividing line. The purchase of the entire Louisiana Territory from France in 1803 opened another enormous area for settlement as the native American Indians continued to be pushed to the fringes or decimated. Thus the stage was set for growing regional tensions as American economic development carried the free and the slaveholding states in very different directions.

In the North, white settlers broke the soil north of the Ohio and extended the pattern of family farm agriculture. Ingenious Yankees began building English-model factories, drawing first on New England farm girls housed in company dormitories and then on families of Irish immigrants. By 1850 an industrializing, urbanizing North was also building an efficient system of canals and railroads and attracting most of the rising tide of European immigrants.

In the South, by contrast, industry and cities did not develop, and newcomers avoided the region. And even though fully three-quarters of all Southern white families were small farmers and owned no slaves in 1850, plantation owners holding twenty or more slaves and producing a market crop dominated the economy and the society, as they had since colonial times. Turning increasingly from tobacco, sugar cane, and rice, the rich, profit-minded slaveowners used gangs of black slaves to claim a vast new kingdom where cotton was the king. Expanding into fertile virgin lands and relying after 1793 on Eli Whitney's newly invented cotton engine (or "gin," for short), which separated the sticky green seeds from the fluffy fiber and did the work of fifty people, the cotton kingdom eventually stretched across most of the Deep South, from the Carolinas westward to Arkansas and eastern Texas. By 1850, this kingdom was producing 5 million bales a year (as opposed to only 4,000 bales in 1791) and was profitably satisfiying an apparently insatiable demand from

Slavery and Cotton The intense activity and the systematic exploitation of slave labor on large cotton plantations come alive in this contemporary painting. Slaves of both sexes and of all ages pick the cotton and transport it to smoke-belching worksheds, shown in the background, for later processing in cotton gins. *(Source: Courtesy Jay P. Altmayer)*

✤ **The Battle of Gettysburg, July 1–3, 1863** marked the high point of the Confederate advance and was the greatest battle of the war. This painting commemorates the climax on the third day, when Confederate General Robert E. Lee commanded Pickett's division to charge the Union center. Coming toward the viewer in the face of terrible fire, the brave Southerners have reached the first Union line. But General Hancock, shown with arm extended in the left foreground, is ordering the Northern counterattack that will decimate Pickett's troops and force the Confederates back into Virginia. *(Source: Photograph by Al Freni © 1985 Time-Life Books, Inc. Courtesy, The Seventh Regiment Fund, Inc.)*

blacks were generally forced to continue laboring for white landowners, but now as tenants under unfavorable sharecropping conditions. Blacks also faced very pervasive discrimination. Thus as a result of war and reunification, the life of blacks in the Southern states moved much closer to that of the small number of blacks in the North, who had long been free but unequal citizens.

✤ THE MODERNIZATION OF RUSSIA

Russia also experienced a profound midcentury crisis of nation building. This crisis was unlike those occurring in Italy and Germany, for Russia had no need to build a single state out of a jumble of principalities. The Russian Empire was already an enormous multinational state that contained all the ethnic Russians and many other nationalities as well. Rather, as in the United States, the long-term challenge facing the government was to hold the existing state together, either by means of political compromise or by military force. Thus Russia's rulers saw national self-determination as a subversive ideology in the early nineteenth century, and they tried with some success to limit its development among their non-Russian subjects.

Yet old autocratic Russia found itself in serious trouble after 1853. It became clear to Russia's leaders that the country had to embrace the process of *modernization*. A vague and often overworked term, modernization is a great umbrella under which some writers place most of the major developments of the last two hundred or even five hundred years. Yet defined narrowly—as changes that enable a country to compete effectively with the leading countries at a given time—modernization can be a useful concept. It fits Russia after the Crimean War particularly well.

The "Great Reforms"

In the 1850s Russia was a poor agrarian society. Industry was little developed, and almost 90 percent of the population lived on the land. Agricultural techniques were backward: the ancient open-field system reigned supreme. Serfdom was still the basic social institution. Bound to the lord on a hereditary basis, the peasant serf was little more than a slave. Individual serfs and serf families were regularly sold, with and without land, in the early nineteenth century. Serfs were obliged to furnish labor services or money payments as the lord saw fit. Moreover, the lord could choose freely among the serfs for army recruits, who had to serve for twenty-five years, and he could punish a serf with deportation to Siberia. Sexual exploitation of female serfs by their lords was common.

Serfdom had become the great moral and political issue for the government by the 1840s, but it might still have lasted many more years had the Crimean War of 1853 to 1856 not occurred. The war began as a dispute with France over who should protect certain Christian shrines in the Ottoman Empire. Because the fighting was concentrated in the Crimean peninsula on the Black Sea, Russia's transportation network of rivers and wagons failed to supply the distant Russian armies adequately. France and Great Britain, aided by Sardinia and the Ottoman Empire, inflicted a humiliating defeat on Russia.

This military defeat marked a turning point in Russian history. The Russian state had been built on the military, and Russia had not lost a major war for a century and a half. This defeat demonstrated that Russia had fallen behind the rapidly industrializing nations of western Europe in many areas. At the very least, Russia needed railroads, better armaments, and reorganization of the army if it was to maintain its international position. Moreover, the disastrous war had caused hardship and raised the specter of massive peasant rebellion. Reform of serfdom was imperative. And as the new tsar, Alexander II (r. 1855–1881), told the serf owners, it would be better if reform came from above. Military disaster thus forced Alexander II and his ministers along the path of rapid social change and general modernization.

The first and greatest of the reforms was the freeing of the serfs in 1861. Human bondage was abolished forever, and the emancipated peasants received, on average, about half of the land. Yet they had to pay fairly high prices for their land, and because the land was owned collectively, each peasant village was jointly responsible for the payments of all the families in the village. The government hoped that collective responsibility would strengthen the peasant village as a social unit and prevent the development of a class of landless peasants. In practice, collective ownership and responsibility made it very difficult for individual peasants to improve agricultural methods or leave their villages. Thus the effects of the reform were limited, for it did not encourage peasants to change their old habits and attitudes.

Most of the later reforms were also halfway measures. In 1864 the government established a new institution of local government, the *zemstvo*. Members of this local assembly were elected by a three-class system of towns, peasant villages, and noble landowners. A zemstvo executive council

❖ **The Limits of Russian Modernization** The business and professional classes grew stronger and became more prosperous in the era of reform, but the hard life of Russian peasants changed slowly. The striking contrast between the rugged old peasant and the elegant middle-class women in this photo aptly symbolizes the widening gap between the two sections of the population. *(Source: Sovfoto/Eastfoto)*

dealt with local problems. The establishment of the zemstvos marked a significant step toward popular participation, and Russian liberals hoped it would lead to an elected national parliament. They were soon disappointed. The local zemstvo remained subordinate to the traditional bureaucracy and the local nobility, which were heavily favored by the property-based voting system. More successful was reform of the legal system, which established independent courts and equality before the law. Education was also liberalized somewhat, and censorship was relaxed but not removed.

The Industrialization of Russia

Until the twentieth century, Russia's greatest strides toward modernization were economic rather than political. Industry and transport, both so vital to the military, were transformed in two industrial surges. The first of these came after 1860. The government encouraged and subsidized private railway companies, and construction boomed. In 1860 the empire had only about 1,250 miles of railroads; by 1880 it had about 15,500 miles. The railroads enabled agricultural Russia to export grain and thus earn money for further industrialization. Domestic manufacturing was stimulated, and by the end of the 1870s Russia had a well-developed railway-equipment industry. Industrial suburbs grew up around Moscow and St. Petersburg, and a class of modern factory workers began to take shape.

Industrial development strengthened Russia's military forces and gave rise to territorial expansion to the south and east. Imperial expansion greatly excited many ardent Russian nationalists and superpatriots, who became some of the government's most enthusiastic supporters. Industrial development also contributed mightily to the spread of Marxian thought and the transformation of the Russian revolutionary movement after 1890.

In 1881 Alexander II was assassinated by a small group of terrorists. The era of reform came to an abrupt end, for the new tsar, Alexander III (r. 1881–1894), was a determined reactionary. Russia, and indeed all of Europe, experienced hard times economically in the 1880s. Political modernization remained frozen until 1905, but economic modernization sped forward in the massive industrial surge of the 1890s. Nationalism played a decisive role, as it had after the Crimean War. The key leader was Sergei Witte, the tough, competent minister of finance from 1892 to 1903. Early in his career, Witte found in the writings of Friedrich List (see page 742) an analysis and a program for action. List had stressed the peril for Germany of remaining behind England in the 1830s and 1840s. Witte saw the same threat of industrial backwardness threatening Russia's power and greatness.

Witte moved forward on several fronts. A railroad manager by training, he believed that railroads were "a very powerful weapon . . . for the direction of the economic development of the country."[6] Therefore, the government built state-owned railroads rapidly, doubling the network to 35,000 miles by the end of the century. The gigantic trans-Siberian line connecting Moscow with Vladivostok on the Pacific Ocean 5,000 miles away was Witte's pride, and it was largely completed during his term of office. Following List's advice, Witte established high protective tariffs to build Russian industry, and he put the country on the gold standard of the "civilized world" in order to strengthen Russian finances.

Witte's greatest innovation, however, was to use the West to catch up with the West. He aggressively encouraged foreigners to use their abundant capital and advanced technology to build great factories in backward Russia. As he told the tsar, "The inflow of foreign capital is . . . the only way by which our industry will be able to supply our country quickly with abundant and cheap products."[7] This policy was brilliantly successful, especially in southern Russia. There, in eastern Ukraine, foreign capitalists and their engineers built an enormous and very modern steel and coal industry almost from scratch in little more than a decade. By 1900 only the United States, Germany, and Great Britain were producing more steel than Russia. The Russian petroleum industry had even pulled up alongside that of the United States and was producing and refining half the world's output of oil.

Witte knew how to keep foreigners in line. Once a leading foreign businessman came to him and angrily demanded that the Russian government fulfill a contract it had signed and pay certain debts immediately. Witte asked to see the contract. He read it and then carefully tore it to pieces and threw it in the wastepaper basket without a word of explanation. It was just such a fiercely autocratic and independent Russia that was catching up with the advanced nations of the West.

The Revolution of 1905

Catching up partly meant vigorous territorial expansion, for this was the age of Western imperialism. By 1903 Russia had established a sphere of influence in Chinese Manchuria and was casting greedy eyes on northern Korea. When the diplomatic protests of equally imperialistic Japan were ignored, the Japanese launched a surprise attack in February 1904. To the amazement of self-confident Europeans, Asian Japan scored repeated victories, and Russia was forced in August 1905 to accept a humiliating defeat.

As is often the case, military disaster abroad brought political upheaval at home. The business and professional classes had long wanted to match economic with political modernization. Their minimal goal was to turn the last of Europe's absolutist monarchies into a liberal, representative regime. Factory workers, strategically concentrated in the large cities, had all the grievances of early industrialization and were organized in a radical and still illegal labor movement. Peasants had gained little from the era of reforms and were suffering from poverty and overpopulation. At the same time, nationalist sentiment was emerging among the empire's minorities. The politically and culturally dominant ethnic Russians were only about 45 percent of the population, and by 1900 some intellectuals among the subject nationalities were calling for self-rule and autonomy. Separatist nationalism was strongest among the Poles and Ukrainians. With the army pinned down in Manchuria, all these currents of discontent converged in the revolution of 1905.

The beginning of the revolution pointed up the incompetence of the government. On a Sunday in January 1905, a massive crowd of workers and their families converged peacefully on the Winter Palace in St. Petersburg to present a petition to the tsar. The workers were led by a trade-unionist priest named Father Gapon, who had been secretly supported by the police as a preferable alternative to more radical unions. Carrying icons and respectfully singing, "God save the tsar," the workers did not know Nicholas II had fled the city. Suddenly troops opened fire, killing and wounding hundreds. The "Bloody Sunday" massacre turned ordinary workers against the tsar and produced a wave of general indignation.

Outlawed political parties came out into the open, and by the summer of 1905 strikes, peasant

Bloody Sunday This print from a contemporary French newspaper shows the tragic conclusion of the effort to present a petition to the tsar on January 22, 1905. Soldiers on the left fire directly into the crowd of unarmed workers led by Father Gapon, who holds the petition and an upraised cross. A Cossack brigade charges another group of peaceful demonstrators on the bridge. *(Source: Jean-Loup Charmet)*

uprisings, revolts among minority nationalities, and troop mutinies were sweeping the country. The revolutionary surge culminated in October 1905 in a great paralyzing general strike, which forced the government to capitulate. The tsar issued the October Manifesto, which granted full civil rights and promised a popularly elected duma (parliament) with real legislative power. The manifesto split the opposition. It satisfied most moderate and liberal demands, but the Social Democrats rejected it and led a bloody workers' uprising in Moscow in December 1905. Frightened middle-class leaders helped the government repress the uprising and survive as a constitutional monarchy.

On the eve of the opening of the first Duma in May 1906, the government issued the new constitution, the Fundamental Laws. The tsar retained great powers. The Duma, elected indirectly by universal male suffrage, and a largely appointive upper house could debate and pass laws, but the tsar had an absolute veto. As in Bismarck's Germany, the emperor appointed his ministers, who did not need to command a majority in the Duma.

The disappointed, predominately middle-class liberals, the largest group in the newly elected Duma, saw the Fundamental Laws as a step backward. Efforts to cooperate with the tsar's ministers soon broke down. The tsar then dismissed the Duma, only to find that a more hostile and radical opposition was elected in 1907. After three months of deadlock, the tsar dismissed the second Duma. Thereupon he and his reactionary advisers unilaterally rewrote the electoral law so as to increase greatly the weight of the propertied classes at the expense of workers, peasants, and national minorities.

The new law had the intended effect. With landowners assured half the seats in the Duma, the government secured a loyal majority in 1907 and again in 1912. Thus armed, the tough, energetic chief minister, Peter Stolypin, pushed through important agrarian reforms designed to break down collective village ownership of land and to encourage the more enterprising peasants—a strategy known as the "wager on the strong." On the eve of the First World War, Russia was partially modernized, a conservative constitutional monarchy with a peasant-based but industrializing economy.

✣ THE RESPONSIVE NATIONAL STATE, 1871–1914

For central and western Europe, the unification of Italy and Germany by "blood and iron" marked the end of a dramatic period of nation building. After 1871 the heartland of Europe was organized into strong national states. Only on the borders of Europe—in Ireland and Russia, in Austria-Hungary and the Balkans—did subject peoples still strive for political unity and independence. Despite national differences, European domestic politics after 1871 had a common framework, the firmly established national state. The common themes within that framework were the emergence of mass politics and growing mass loyalty toward the national state.

For good reason, ordinary people—the masses of an industrializing, urbanizing society—felt increasing loyalty to their governments. More people could vote. By 1914 universal male suffrage had become the rule rather than the exception. This

development had as much psychological as political significance. Ordinary men were no longer denied the right to vote because they lacked wealth or education. They felt that they counted; they could influence the government to some extent. They were becoming "part of the system."

Women also began to demand the right to vote. The women's suffrage movement achieved its first success in the western United States, and by 1913 women could vote in twelve states. Europe, too, moved slowly in this direction. In 1914 Norway gave the vote to most women. Elsewhere, women such as the English Emmeline Pankhurst were very militant in their demands. They heckled politicians and held public demonstrations. These efforts generally failed before 1914, but they prepared the way for the triumph of the women's suffrage movement immediately after World War One.

As the right to vote spread, politicians and parties in national parliaments represented the people more responsively. The multiparty system prevailing in most countries meant that parliamentary majorities were built on shifting coalitions, which gave parties leverage to obtain benefits for their supporters. Governments also passed laws to alleviate general problems, thereby acquiring greater legitimacy and appearing more worthy of support.

There was a less positive side to building support for strong nation-states after 1871. Governments, often led by conservatives inspired by the examples of Cavour and Bismarck, found that they could manipulate national feeling to create a sense of unity and to divert attention away from underlying class conflicts. For example, conservative and moderate leaders who despised socialism found that workers who voted socialist would still rally around the flag in a diplomatic crisis or that they would cheer enthusiastically when distant territory of doubtful value was seized in Africa or Asia (see Chapter 26). Therefore, governing elites frequently channeled national sentiment in an antiliberal and militaristic direction after 1871. This policy helped manage domestic conflicts, but only at the expense of increasing the international tensions that erupted in 1914 in cataclysmic war and revolution (see Chapter 27).

The German Empire

Politics in Germany after 1871 reflected many of the general developments. The new German Empire was a federal union of Prussia and twenty-four smaller states. Much of the everyday business of government was conducted by the separate states, but there was a strong national government with a chancellor—until 1890, Bismarck—and a popularly elected parliament, called the *Reichstag*. Although Bismarck refused to be bound by a parliamentary majority, he tried nonetheless to maintain one. This situation gave the political parties opportunities. Until 1878 Bismarck relied mainly on the National Liberals, who had rallied to him after 1866. They supported legislation useful for further economic and legal unification of the country.

Less wisely, they backed Bismarck's attack on the Catholic church, the so-called *Kulturkampf,* or "struggle for civilization." Like Bismarck, the middle-class National Liberals were particularly alarmed by Pius IX's declaration of papal infallibility in 1870. That dogma seemed to ask German Catholics to put loyalty to their church above loyalty to their nation. Only in Protestant Prussia did the Kulturkampf have even limited success. Catholics throughout the country generally voted for the Catholic Center party, which blocked passage of national laws hostile to the church. Finally, in 1878 Bismarck abandoned his attack. Indeed, he and the Catholic Center party entered into an uneasy but mutually advantageous alliance. Their reasons for doing so were largely economic.

After a worldwide financial bust in 1873, European agriculture was in an increasingly difficult position. Wheat prices plummeted as cheap grain poured in from the United States, Canada, and Russia. New lands were opening up in North America and Russia, and the combination of railroads and technical improvements in shipping cut freight rates for grain drastically. European peasants, with their smaller, less efficient farms, could not compete in cereal production, especially in western and southern Germany. The peasantry there was largely Catholic, and the Catholic Center party was thus converted to higher tariffs to protect the economic interests of its supporters.

The same competitive pressures caused the Protestant Junkers, who owned large estates in eastern Germany, to embrace the cause of higher tariffs. These noble landowners were joined by some of the iron and steel magnates of the Prussian Rhineland and Westphalia who had previously favored free trade. With three such influential groups lobbying energetically, Bismarck was happy to go along with a new protective tariff in 1879. In doing so, he won new supporters in the Reich-

stag—the Center party of the Catholics and the Conservative party of the Prussian landowners—and he held on to most of the National Liberals.

Bismarck had been looking for a way to increase taxes and raise more money for the government. The solution he chose was higher tariffs. Many other governments acted similarly. The 1880s and 1890s saw a widespread return to protectionism. France, in particular, established very high tariffs to protect agriculture and industry, peasants and manufacturers, from foreign competition. Thus the German government and other governments responded effectively to a major economic problem and won greater loyalty. The general rise of protectionism in the late nineteenth century was also an outstanding example of the dangers of self-centered nationalism: high tariffs led to international name calling and nasty trade wars.

As for socialism, Bismarck tried to stop its growth in Germany because he genuinely feared its revolutionary language and allegiance to a movement transcending the nation-state. In 1878, after two attempts on the life of William I by radicals (though not socialists), Bismarck used a carefully orchestrated national outcry to ram through the Reichstag a law that strictly controlled socialist meetings and publications and outlawed the Social Democratic party, which was thereby driven underground. However, German socialists displayed a discipline and organization worthy of the Prussian army itself. Bismarck decided to try another tack.

Thus Bismarck's essentially conservative nation-state pioneered with social measures designed to win the support of working-class people. In 1883 he pushed through the Reichstag the first of several modern social security laws to help wage earners. The laws of 1883 and 1884 established national sickness and accident insurance; the law of 1889 established old-age pensions and retirement benefits. Henceforth sick, injured, and retired workers could look forward to some regular benefits from the state. This national social security system, paid for through compulsory contributions by wage earners and employers as well as grants from the state, was the first of its kind anywhere. (The United States would not take similar measures for fifty years.) Bismarck's social security system did not wean workers from voting socialist, but it did give them a small stake in the system and protect them from some of the uncertainties of the complex urban industrial world. This enormously significant development was a product of political

❖ **Captain Alfred Dreyfus**
Leaving an 1899 reconsideration of his original court martial, Dreyfus receives an insulting "guard of dishonor" from soldiers whose backs are turned. Top army leaders were determined to brand Dreyfus as a traitor. *(Source: Bibliothèque Nationale, Paris)*

Although the educational reforms of the 1880s disturbed French Catholics, many of them rallied to the republic in the 1890s. The limited acceptance of the modern world by the more liberal Pope Leo XIII (1878–1903) eased tensions between church and state. Unfortunately, the Dreyfus affair changed all that.

Alfred Dreyfus, a Jewish captain in the French army, was falsely accused and convicted of treason. His family never doubted his innocence and fought to reopen the case, enlisting the support of prominent republicans and intellectuals such as novelist Émile Zola. In 1898 and 1899, the case split France apart. On one side was the army, which had manufactured evidence against Dreyfus, joined by anti-Semites and most of the Catholic establishment. On the other side stood the civil libertarians and most of the more radical republicans.

This battle, which eventually led to Dreyfus's being declared innocent, revived republican feeling against the church. Between 1901 and 1905, the government severed all ties between the state and the Catholic church after centuries of close relations. The salaries of priests and bishops were no longer paid by the government, and all churches were given to local committees of lay Catholics. Catholic schools were put completely on their own financially, and in a short time they lost a third of their students. The state school system's power of indoctrination was greatly strengthened. In France only the growing socialist movement, with its very different and thoroughly secular ideology, stood in opposition to patriotic, republican nationalism.

Great Britain and Ireland

Britain in the late nineteenth century has often been seen as a shining example of peaceful and successful political evolution. Germany was stuck with a manipulated parliament that gave an irresponsible emperor too much power; France had a quarrelsome parliament that gave its presidents too little power. Great Britain, in contrast, seemed to enjoy an effective two-party parliament that skillfully guided the country from classical liberalism to full-fledged democracy with hardly a misstep.

This view of Great Britain is not so much wrong as incomplete. After the right to vote was granted to males of the solid middle class in 1832, opinion leaders and politicians wrestled with the uncertainties of a further extension of the franchise. In his famous essay *On Liberty*, published in 1859, philosopher John Stuart Mill (1806–1873), the leading heir to the Benthamite tradition (see page 798), probed the problem of how to protect the rights of individuals and minorities in the emerging age of mass electoral participation. Mill pleaded eloquently for the practical and moral value inherent in safeguarding individual differences and unpopular opinions. In 1867 Benjamin Disraeli and the Conservatives extended the vote to all middle-class males and the best-paid workers. The son of a Jewish stockbroker and himself a novelist and urban dandy, the ever-fascinating Disraeli (1804–1881) was willing to risk this "leap in the dark" in order to gain new supporters. The Conservative party, he believed, needed to broaden its traditional base of aristocratic and landed support if it was to survive. After 1867 English political parties and electoral campaigns became more modern, and the "lower orders" appeared to vote as responsibly as their "betters." Hence the Third Reform Bill of 1884 gave the vote to almost every adult male.

While the House of Commons was drifting toward democracy, the House of Lords was content to slumber nobly. Between 1901 and 1910, however, that bastion of aristocratic conservatism tried to reassert itself. Acting as supreme court of the land, it ruled against labor unions in two important decisions. And after the Liberal party came to power in 1906, the Lords vetoed several measures passed by the Commons, including the so-called People's Budget. The Lords finally capitulated, as they had done in 1832, when the king threatened to create enough new peers to pass the bill.

Aristocratic conservatism yielded to popular democracy once and for all. The result was that extensive social welfare measures, slow to come to Great Britain, were passed in a spectacular rush between 1906 and 1914. During those years, the Liberal party, inspired by the fiery Welshman David Lloyd George (1863–1945), substantially raised taxes on the rich as part of the People's Budget. This income helped the government pay for national health insurance, unemployment benefits, old-age pensions, and a host of other social measures. The state was integrating the urban masses socially as well as politically.

This record of accomplishment was only part of the story, however. On the eve of World War One, the ever-emotional, ever-unanswered question of Ireland brought Great Britain to the brink of civil war. In the 1840s, Ireland had been decimated by famine, which fueled an Irish revolutionary movement. Thereafter, the English slowly granted concessions, such as the abolition of the privileges of the Anglican church and rights for Irish peasants. Liberal prime minister William Gladstone (1809–1898), who had proclaimed twenty years earlier that "my mission is to pacify Ireland," introduced bills to give Ireland self-government in 1886 and in 1893. They failed to pass. After two decades of relative quiet, Irish nationalists in the British Parliament saw their chance. They supported the Liberals in their battle for the People's Budget and received a home-rule bill for Ireland in return.

Thus Ireland, the emerald isle, achieved self-government—but not quite, for Ireland was (and is) composed of two peoples. As much as the Irish Catholic majority in the southern counties wanted home rule, precisely that much did the Irish Protestants of the northern counties of Ulster come to oppose it. Motivated by the accumulated fears and hostilities of generations, the Protestants of Ulster refused to submerge themselves in a Catholic Ireland, just as Irish Catholics had refused to submit to a Protestant Britain.

The Ulsterites vowed to resist home rule in northern Ireland. By December 1913 they had raised 100,000 armed volunteers, and they were supported by much of English public opinion. Thus in 1914 the Liberals in the House of Lords introduced a compromise home-rule bill that did not apply to the northern counties. This bill, which openly betrayed promises made to Irish nationalists, was rejected, and in September the original home-rule bill was passed but simultaneously suspended for the duration of the hostilities—the momentous Irish question had been overtaken by an earth-shattering world war in August 1914.

Irish developments illustrated once again the power of national feeling and national movements in the nineteenth century. Moreover, they were proof that governments could not elicit greater loyalty unless they could capture and control that elemental current of national feeling. Though Great Britain had much going for it—power, Parliament, prosperity—none of these availed in the face of the conflicting nationalisms espoused by

NO HOME RULE

LET OUR FLAG
RUN OUT STRAIGHT
IN THE WIND,
THE OLD RED
SHALL BE
FLOATED
AGAIN

WHEN THE RANKS
THAT
ARE THINNED SHALL
BE THINNED,
WHEN THE NAMES
THAT ARE
TWENTY ARE TEN.

ULSTER !

❖ **"No Home Rule"** Posters like this one helped to foment pro-British, anti-Catholic sentiment in the northern Irish counties of Ulster before the First World War. The rifle raised defiantly and the accompanying rhyme are a thinly veiled threat of armed rebellion and civil war. *(Source: Courtesy, Ulster Museum, Belfast)*

Catholics and Protestants in northern Ireland. Similarly, progressive Sweden was powerless to stop the growth of the Norwegian national movement, which culminated in Norway's breaking away from Sweden and becoming a fully independent nation in 1905. In this light, one can also see how hopeless was the case of the Ottoman Empire in Europe in the later nineteenth century. It was only a matter of time before the Serbs, Bulgarians, and Rumanians would break away, and they did.

The Austro-Hungarian Empire

The dilemma of conflicting nationalisms in Ireland also helps one appreciate how desperate the situation in the Austro-Hungarian Empire had become by the early twentieth century. In 1849 Magyar nationalism had driven Hungarian patriots to declare an independent Hungarian republic, which was savagely crushed by Russian and Austrian armies (see pages 786–788). Throughout the 1850s, Hungary was ruled as a conquered territory, and Emperor Francis Joseph and his bureaucracy tried hard to centralize the state and Germanize the language and culture of the different nationalities.

Then in the wake of defeat by Prussia in 1866, a weakened Austria was forced to strike a compromise and establish the so-called dual monarchy. The empire was divided in two, and the nationalistic Magyars gained virtual independence for Hungary. Henceforth each half of the empire agreed to deal with its own "barbarians"—its own minorities—as it saw fit. The two states were joined only by a shared monarch and common ministries for finance, defense, and foreign affairs. After 1867 the disintegrating force of competing nationalisms continued unabated, for both Austria and Hungary had several "Irelands" within their borders.

In Austria ethnic Germans were only one-third of the population, and by 1895 many Germans saw their traditional dominance threatened by Czechs, Poles, and other Slavs. A particularly emotional issue in the Austrian parliament was the language used in government and elementary education at the local level. From 1900 to 1914, the parliament was so divided that ministries generally could not obtain a majority and ruled instead by decree. Efforts by both conservatives and socialists to defuse national antagonisms by stressing economic issues that cut across ethnic lines—endeavors that led to the introduction of universal male suffrage in 1907—proved largely unsuccessful.

One aspect of such national antagonisms was anti-Semitism, which was particularly virulent in Austria. The Jewish populations of Austrian cities grew very rapidly after Jews obtained full legal equality in 1867, and by 1900 Jews constituted 10 percent of the population of Vienna. Many Jewish business people were quite successful in banking and retail trade, while Jewish artists, intellectuals, and scientists, such as the world-famous Sigmund Freud, played a major role in making Vienna a leading center of European culture and modern thought. When extremists charged the Jews with controlling the economy and corrupting German culture with alien ideas and ultramodern art, anxious Germans of all classes tended to listen. The popular mayor of Vienna from 1897 to 1910, Dr. Karl Lueger, combined anti-Semitic rhetoric with calls for "Christian socialism" and municipal ownership of basic services. Lueger appealed especially to the German lower middle class—and to an unsuccessful young artist named Adolf Hitler.

In Hungary the Magyar nobility in 1867 restored the constitution of 1848 and used it to dominate both the Magyar peasantry and the minority populations until 1914. Only the wealthiest one-fourth of adult males had the right to vote, making the parliament the creature of the Magyar elite. Laws promoting use of the Magyar (Hungarian) language in schools and government were rammed through and bitterly resented, especially by the Croatians and Rumanians. While Magyar extremists campaigned loudly for total separation from Austria, the radical leaders of the subject nationalities dreamed in turn of independence from Hungary. Unlike most major countries, which harnessed nationalism to strengthen the state after 1871, the Austro-Hungarian Empire was progressively weakened and destroyed by it.

✤ MARXISM AND THE SOCIALIST MOVEMENT

Nationalism served, for better or worse, as a new unifying principle. But what about socialism? Did the rapid growth of socialist parties, which were generally Marxian parties dedicated to an international proletarian revolution, mean that national states had failed to gain the support of workers? Certainly, many prosperous and conservative citizens were greatly troubled by the socialist movement. And numerous historians have portrayed the years before 1914 as a time of increasing conflict between revolutionary socialism, on the one hand, and a nationalist alliance of the conservative aristocracy and the prosperous middle class, on the other. This question requires close examination.

The Socialist International

Socialism appealed to large numbers of working men and women in the late nineteenth century (see Listening to the Past), and the growth of socialist parties after 1871 was phenomenal. Neither Bismarck's antisocialist laws nor his extensive social security system checked the growth of the German Social Democratic party, which espoused

✦ **The Language Ordinances of 1897,** which were intended to satisfy the Czechs by establishing equality between German and the local language in non-German districts of Austria, produced a powerful backlash among Germans. This wood engraving shows troops dispersing German protesters of the new law before the parliament building. *(Source: Österreichische Nationalbibliothek)*

the Marxian ideology. By 1912 it had millions of followers and was the largest party in the Reichstag. Socialist parties also grew in other countries, though nowhere else with such success. In 1883 Russian exiles in Switzerland founded the Russian Social Democratic party, which grew rapidly after 1890 despite internal disputes. In France various socialist parties re-emerged in the 1880s after the carnage of the Commune. They were finally unified in 1905 in an increasingly powerful Marxian party called the French Section of the Workers International. Belgium and Austria-Hungary also had strong socialist parties.

As the name of the French party suggests, Marxian socialist parties were eventually linked together in an international organization. As early as 1848, Marx had laid out his intellectual system in the *Communist Manifesto* (see pages 769–770). He had declared that "the working men have no country," and he had urged proletarians of all nations to unite against their governments. Joining the flood of radicals and republicans who fled continental Europe for England and America after the unsuccessful revolutions of 1848, Marx settled in London. Poor and depressed, he lived on his meager earnings as a journalist and on the gifts of his friend Engels. Marx never stopped thinking of revolution. Digging deeply into economics and history, he concluded that revolution follows economic crisis and tried to prove this position in *Critique of Political Economy* (1859) and in his greatest theoretical work, *Capital* (1867).

The bookish Marx also excelled as a practical organizer. In 1864 he played an important role in founding the First International of socialists—the International Working Men's Association. In the following years, he battled successfully to control the organization and used its annual meetings as a means of spreading his realistic, "scientific" doctrines of inevitable socialist revolution. Then Marx enthusiastically embraced the passionate, vaguely radical patriotism of the Paris Commune and its terrible conflict with the French National Assembly as a giant step toward socialist revolution. This impetuous action frightened many of his early supporters, especially the more moderate British labor leaders. The First International collapsed.

Yet international proletarian solidarity remained an important objective for Marxists. In 1889, as the individual parties in different countries grew stronger, socialist leaders came together to form the Second International, which lasted until 1914.

The International was only a federation of national socialist parties, it had great psychological impact. Every three years, delegates from the different parties met to interpret Marxian doctrines and plan coordinated action. May 1 (May Day) was declared an annual international one-day strike, a day of marches and demonstrations. A permanent executive for the International was established. Many feared and many others rejoiced in the growing power of socialism and the Second International.

Unions and Revisionism

Was socialism really radical and revolutionary in these years? On the whole, it was not. Indeed, as socialist parties grew and attracted large numbers of members, they looked more and more toward gradual change and steady improvement for the working class and less and less toward revolution. The mainstream of European socialism became militantly moderate; that is, socialists increasingly combined radical rhetoric with sober action.

Workers themselves were progressively less inclined to follow radical programs. There were several reasons for this. As workers gained the right to vote and to participate politically in the nation-state, their attention focused more on elections than on revolutions. And as workers won real, tangible benefits, this furthered the process. Workers were also not immune to patriotic education and indoctrination during military service, and many responded positively to drum-beating parades and aggressive foreign policy as they loyally voted for socialists. Nor were workers a unified social group.

Perhaps most important of all, workers' standard of living rose gradually but substantially after 1850 as the promise of the Industrial Revolution was at least partially realized. In Great Britain, for example, workers could buy almost twice as much with their wages in 1906 as in 1850, and most of the increase came after 1870. Workers experienced similar gradual increases in most continental countries after 1850, though much less strikingly in late-developing Russia. Improvement in the standard of living was much more than merely a matter of higher wages. The quality of life improved dramatically in urban areas. For all these reasons, workers tended more and more to become militantly moderate: they demanded gains, but they were less likely to take to the barricades in pursuit of them.

❖ **May Day in Dresden, 1890** As this print from a German newspaper suggests, workers participated enthusiastically in the one-day strike honoring international socialist solidarity. But May Day was also a happy holiday, a celebration of working-class respectability and an independent working-class culture. *(Source: Archiv Für Kurst und Geschichte, Berlin)*

The growth of labor unions reinforced this trend toward moderation. In the early stages of industrialization, modern unions were generally prohibited by law. A famous law of the French Revolution had declared all guilds and unions illegal in the name of "liberty" in 1791. In Great Britain attempts by workers to unite were considered criminal conspiracies after 1799. Other countries had similar laws, and these obviously hampered union development. In France, for example, about two hundred workers were imprisoned each year between 1825 and 1847 for taking part in illegal combinations. Unions were considered subversive bodies, only to be hounded and crushed.

From this sad position workers struggled to escape. Great Britain led the way in 1824 and 1825 when unions won the right to exist but (generally) not the right to strike. After the collapse of Robert Owen's attempt to form one big union in the 1830s (see page 747), new and more practical kinds of unions appeared. Limited primarily to highly skilled workers such as machinists and carpenters, the "new model unions" avoided both radical politics and costly strikes. Instead, their sober, respectable leaders concentrated on winning better wages and hours for their members through collective bargaining and compromise. This approach helped pave the way to full acceptance in Britain in the 1870s, when unions won the right to strike without being held legally liable for the financial damage inflicted on employers. After

1890 unions for unskilled workers developed, and between 1901 and 1906 the legal position of British unions was further strengthened.

Germany was the most industrialized, socialized, and unionized continental country by 1914. German unions were not granted important rights until 1869, and until the antisocialist law was repealed in 1890, they were frequently harassed by the government as socialist fronts. Nor were socialist leaders particularly interested in union activity, believing as they did in the iron law of low wages and the need for political revolution. The result was that as late as 1895, there were only about 270,000 union members in a male industrial workforce of nearly 8 million. Then with German industrialization still storming ahead and almost all legal harassment eliminated, union membership skyrocketed, reaching roughly 3 million in 1912.

This great expansion both reflected and influenced the changing character of German unions. Increasingly, unions in Germany focused on bread-and-butter issues—wages, hours, working conditions—rather than on the dissemination of pure socialist doctrine. Genuine collective bargaining, long opposed by socialist intellectuals as a "sell-out," was officially recognized as desirable by the German Trade Union Congress in 1899. When employers proved unwilling to bargain, a series of strikes forced them to change their minds.

Between 1906 and 1913, successful collective bargaining gained a prominent place in German industrial relations. In 1913 alone, over ten thousand collective bargaining agreements affecting 1.25 million workers were signed. Gradual improvement, not revolution, was becoming the primary goal of the German trade-union movement.

The German trade unions and their leaders were in fact, if not in name, thoroughgoing revisionists. *Revisionism*—that most awful of sins in the eyes of militant Marxists in the twentieth century—was an effort by various socialists to update Marxian doctrines to reflect the realities of the time. Thus the socialist Edward Bernstein (1850–1932) argued in 1899 in his *Evolutionary Socialism* that Marx's predictions of ever-greater poverty for workers and ever-greater concentration of wealth in ever-fewer hands had been proved false. Therefore, Bernstein suggested, socialists should reform their doctrines and tactics. They should combine with other progressive forces to win gradual evolutionary gains for workers through legislation, unions, and further economic development. These views were denounced as heresy by the German Social Democratic party and later by the entire Second International. Yet, the revisionist, gradualist approach continued to gain the tacit acceptance of many German socialists, particularly in the trade unions.

Moderation found followers elsewhere. In France the great socialist leader Jean Jaurès (1859–1914) formally repudiated revisionist doctrines in order to establish a unified socialist party, but he remained at heart a gradualist. Questions of revolution split Russian Marxists.

Socialist parties before 1914 had clear-cut national characteristics. Russians and socialists in the Austro-Hungarian Empire tended to be the most radical. The German party talked revolution and practiced reformism, greatly influenced by its enormous trade-union movement. The French party talked revolution and tried to practice it, unrestrained by a trade-union movement that was both very weak and very radical. In England the socialist but non-Marxian Labour party, reflecting the well-established union movement, was formally committed to gradual reform. In Spain and Italy Marxian socialism was very weak. There anarchism, seeking to smash the state rather than the bourgeoisie, dominated radical thought and action.

In short, socialist policies and doctrines varied from country to country. Socialism itself was to a large extent "nationalized" behind the imposing façade of international unity. This helps explain

why when war came in 1914, almost all socialist leaders supported their governments.

SUMMARY

From the mid-nineteenth century on, Western society became nationalistic as well as urban and industrial. Nation-states and strong-minded national leaders gradually enlisted widespread support and gave men and women a greater sense of belonging. Even socialism became increasingly national in orientation, gathering strength as a champion of working-class interests in domestic politics. Yet even though nationalism served to unite peoples, it also drove them apart. Though most obvious in the United States before the Civil War and in Austria-Hungary and Ireland, this was in a real sense true for all of Western civilization. The universal national faith, which reduced social tensions within states, promoted a bitter, almost Darwinian competition between states and thus threatened the progress and unity it had helped to build.

NOTES

1. Quoted in G. Wright, *France in Modern Times,* 4th ed. (New York: W. W. Norton, 1987), p. 138.
2. Quoted in O. Pflanze, *Bismarck and the Development of Germany: The Period of Unification, 1815–1871* (Princeton, N.J.: Princeton University Press, 1963), p. 60.
3. Quoted in H. Kohn, *The Mind of Germany: The Education of a Nation* (New York: Charles Scribner's Sons/Macmillan, 1960), p. 159.
4. Quoted in R. Sewell, *A House Divided: Sectionalism and Civil War, 1848–1865* (Baltimore: Johns Hopkins University Press, 1988), p. 79.
5. Ibid., p. 124.
6. Quoted in T. von Laue, *Sergei Witte and the Industrialization of Russia* (New York: Columbia University Press, 1963), p. 78.
7. Quoted in J. P. McKay, *Pioneers for Profit: Foreign Entrepreneurship and Russian Industrialization, 1885–1913* (Chicago: University of Chicago Press, 1970), p. 11.

SUGGESTED READING

In addition to the general works mentioned in the Suggested Reading for Chapter 23, which treat the entire nineteenth century, G. Craig, *Germany, 1866–1945* (1980), and B. Moore, *Social Origins of Dictatorship and Democracy* (1966), are outstanding. R. Anderson, *France, 1870–1914* (1977), provides a good introduction and has a useful bibliography.

D. Harvey, *Napoleon III and His Comic Empire* (1988), and R. Williams, *Gaslight and Shadows* (1957), bring the world of Napoleon III vibrantly alive, whereas K. Marx's *The Eighteenth Brumaire of Louis Napoleon* is a famous denunciation of the *coup d'état*. E. Weber, *France, Fin de Siècle* (1986), and the engaging collective biography by R. Shattuck, *The Banquet Years* (1968), capture the spirit of Paris at the end of the century. E. Weber, *Peasants into Frenchmen* (1976), stresses the role of education and modern communications in the transformation of rural France after 1870. E. Thomas, *The Women Incendiaries* (1966), examines radical women in the Paris Commune. G. Chapman, *The Dreyfus Case: A Reassessment* (1955), and D. Johnson, *France and the Dreyfus Affair* (1967), are careful examinations of the famous case. In *Jean Barois,* Nobel Prize–winner Roger Du Gard accurately recreates in novel form the Dreyfus affair, and Émile Zola's novel *The Debacle* treats the Franco-Prussian War realistically.

D. M. Smith has written widely on Italy, and his *Garibaldi* (1956) and *Italy: A Modern History,* rev. ed. (1969) are recommended. P. Schroeder, *Austria, Great Britain and the Crimean War* (1972), is an outstanding and highly original diplomatic study. In addition to the important studies on Bismarck and Germany by Pflanze and Kohn cited in the Notes, see E. Eyck, *Bismarck and the German Empire* (1964). H. Wehler, *The German Empire, 1871–1918* (1985), stresses the strength of the landed nobility and the weakness of the middle class in an influential synthesis, which is challenged by D. Blackbourn and G. Eley, *The Peculiarities of German History: Bourgeois Society and Politics in 19th–Century Germany* (1984). F. Stern, *Gold and Iron* (1977), is a fascinating examination of relations between Bismarck and his financial adviser, the Jewish banker Bleichröder. L. Cecil, *Wilhelm II: Prince and Emperor, 1859–1900* (1989), probes the character and politics of Germany's ruler. G. Iggers, *The German Conception of History* (1968); K. D. Barkin, *The Controversy over German Industrialization, 1890–1902* (1970); and E. Spencer, *Management and Labor in Imperial Germany: Ruhr Industrialists as Employers* (1984), are valuable in-depth investigations. H. Glasser, ed., *The German Mind in the Nineteenth Century* (1981), is an outstanding anthology, as are R. E. Joeres and M. Maynes, eds., *German Women in the Eighteenth and Nineteenth Centuries* (1986), and P. Mendes-Flohr, ed., *The Jew in the Modern World: A Documentary History* (1980). C. Schorske, *Fin de Siècle Vienna: Politics and Culture* (1980), and P. Gay,

Freud, Jews, and Other Germans (1978), are brilliant on aspects of modern culture. A. Sked, *The Decline and Fall of the Habsburg Empire, 1815–1918* (1989), and R. Kann, *The Multinational Empire,* 2 vols. (1950, 1964), probe the intricacies of the nationality problem in Austria-Hungary. Southern nationalism has been interpreted from different perspectives by P. Escott, *After Secession: Jefferson Davis and the Failure of Confederate Nationalism* (1974), and D. Faust, *The Creation of Confederate Nationalism* (1988). E. Foner, *A Short History of Reconstruction* (1989), is recommended.

In addition to the studies on Russian industrial development by von Laue and McKay cited in the Notes, P. Gatrell, *The Tsarist Economy, 1850–1917* (1986), and A. Rieber, *Merchants and Entrepreneurs in Imperial Russia* (1982), are recommended. Among fine studies on Russian development, H. Rogger, *Russia in the Age of Modernization and Revolution, 1881–1917* (1983), which has an excellent bibliography; T. Emmons, *The Russian Landed Gentry and the Peasant Emancipation of 1861* (1968); and H. Troyat, *Daily Life in Russia Under the Last Tsar* (1962), are especially recommended. T. Friedgut, *Iuzovka and Revolution: Life and Work in Russia's Donbass, 1869–1924* (1989); R. Zelnik, *Labor and Society in Tsarist Russia, 1855–1870* (1971); and R. Johnson, *Peasant and Proletarian: The Working Class of Moscow at the End of the Nineteenth Century* (1979), skillfully treat different aspects of working-class life and politics. W. E. Mosse, *Alexander II and the Modernization of Russia* (1958), discusses midcentury reforms, whereas C. Black, ed., *The Transformation of Russian Society* (1960), offers a collection of essays on Russian modernization.

G. Dangerfield, *The Strange Death of Liberal England* (1961), brilliantly examines social tensions in Ireland as well as Englishwomen's struggle for the vote before 1914. D. Boyce, *Nationalism in Ireland,* 2d ed. (1991), provides an excellent account of the Irish struggle for nationhood. The theme of aristocratic strength and survival is expanded in A. Mayer's provocative *Persistence of the Old Regime: Europe to the Great War* (1981).

J. Seigel, *Marx's Fate: The Shape of a Life* (1978), is an outstanding biography. C. Schorske, *German Social Democracy, 1905–1917* (1955), is a modern classic. V. Lidtke, *The Alternative Culture: Socialist Labor in Imperial Germany* (1985), and J. Quataert, *Reluctant Feminists in German Social Democracy, 1885–1917* (1979), are also recommended for the study of the German socialists. H. Goldberg, *The Life of Jean Jaurès* (1962), is a sympathetic account of the great French socialist leader. D. Geary, ed., *Labour and Socialist Movements in Europe Before 1914* (1989), contains excellent studies on developments in different countries and has up-to-date references.

The Making of a Socialist

Nationalism and socialism appeared locked in bitter competition in Europe before 1914, but they actually complemented each other in many ways. Both faiths were secular as opposed to religious, and both fostered political awareness. A working person who became interested in politics and developed nationalist beliefs might well convert to socialism at a later date.

This was the case for Adelheid Popp (1869–1939), a self-taught working woman who became an influential socialist leader. Born into a desperately poor working-class family in Vienna and remembering only a "hard and gloomy childhood," she was forced by her parents to quit school at age ten to begin full-time work. She struggled with low-paying piecework for years before she landed a solid factory job, as she recounts in the following selection from her widely read autobiography.

Always an avid reader, Popp became the editor of a major socialist newspaper for German working women. She then told her life story so that all working women might share her truth: "Socialism could change and strengthen others, at it did me."

[Finally] I found work again; I took everything that was offered me in order to show my willingness to work, and I passed through much. But at last things became better. [At age fifteen] I was recommended to a great factory which stood in the best repute. Three hundred girls and about fifty men were employed. I was put in a big room where sixty women and girls were at work. Against the windows stood twelve tables, and at each sat four girls. We had to sort the goods which had been manufactured, others had to count them, and a third set had to brand on them the mark of the firm. We worked from 7 A.M. to 7 P.M. We had an hour's rest at noon,

half-an-hour in the afternoon. . . . I had never yet been paid so much. . . .

I seemed to myself to be almost rich. . . . [Yet] from the women of this factory one can judge how sad and full of deprivation is the lot of a factory worker. In none of the neighbouring factories were the wages so high; we were envied everywhere. Parents considered themselves fortunate if they could get their daughters of fourteen in there on leaving school. . . . And even here, in this paradise, all were badly nourished. Those who stayed at the factory for the dinner hour would buy themselves for a few pennies a sausage or the leavings of a cheese shop. . . . In spite of all the diligence and economy, every one was poor, and trembled at the thought of losing her work. All humbled themselves, and suffered the worst injustice from the foremen, not to risk losing this good work, not to be without food. . . .

I did not only read novels and tales; I had begun . . . to read the classics and other good books. I also began to take an interest in public events. . . . I was not democratically inclined. I was full of enthusiasm then for emperors, and kings and highly placed personages played no small part in my fancies. . . . I bought myself a strict Catholic paper, that criticised very adversely the workers' movement, which was attracting notice. Its aim was to educate in a patriotic and religious direction. . . . I took the warmest interest in the events that occurred in the royal families, and I took the death of the Crown Prince of Austria so much to heart that I wept a whole day. . . . Political events [also] held me in suspense. The possibility of a war with Russia roused my patriotic enthusiasm. I saw my brother already returning from the battlefield covered with glory. . . .

When a particularly strong anti-Semitic feeling was noticeable in political life, I sympathised with it for a time. A broad sheet, "How Israel Attained Power and Sovereignty over all the Nations of the Earth," fascinated me. . . .

About this time an Anarchist group was active. Some mysterious murders which had taken place were ascribed to the Anarchists, and the police made use of them to oppress the rising workmen's movement. . . . I followed the trial of the Anarchists with passionate sympathy. I read all the speeches, and because, as always happens, Social Democrats, whom the authorities really wanted to attack, were among the accused, I learned their views. I became full of enthusiasm. Every single Social Democrat . . . seemed to me a hero. . . .

There was unrest among the workers . . . and demonstrations of protest followed. When these were repeated the military entered the "threatened" streets. . . . In the evenings I rushed in the greatest excitement from the factory to the scene of the disturbance. The military did not frighten me; I only left the place when it was "cleared."

Later on my mother and I lived with one of my brothers who had married. Friends came to him, among them some intelligent workmen. One of these workmen was particularly intelligent, and . . . could talk on many subjects. He was the first Social Democrat I knew. He brought me many books, and explained to me the difference between Anarchism and Socialism. I heard from him, also for the first time, what a republic was, and in spite of my former enthusiasm for royal dynasties, I also declared myself in favour of a republican form of government. I saw everything so near and so clearly, that I actually counted the weeks which must still elapse before the revolution of state and society would take place.

From this workman I received the first Social Democratic party organ. . . . I first learned from it to understand and judge of my own lot. I learned to see that all I had suffered was the result not of a divine ordinance, but of an unjust organization of society. . . .

In the factory I became another woman. . . . I told my [female] comrades all that I had read of the workers' movement. Formerly I had often told stories when they had begged me for them. But instead of narrating . . . the fate of some queen, I now held forth on oppression and exploitation. I told of accumulated wealth in the hands of a few, and introduced as a contrast the shoemakers who

1890 engraving of a meeting of workers in Berlin. *(Source: Bildarchiv Preussischer Kulturbesitz)*

had no shoes and the tailors who had no clothes. On breaks I read aloud the articles in the Social Democratic paper and explained what Socialism was as far as I understood it. . . . [While I was reading] it often happened that one of the clerks passing by shook his head and said to another clerk: "The girl speaks like a man."

Questions for Analysis

1. How did Popp describe and interpret work in the factory?

2. To what extent did her socialist interpretation of factory life fit the facts she described?

3. What were Popp's political interests before she became a socialist?

4. How and why did she become a Social Democrat?

5. Was this account likely to lead other working women to socialism? Why or why not?

Source: Slightly adapted from A. Popp, *The Autobiography of a Working Woman,* trans. E. C. Harvey (Chicago: F. G. Browne, 1913), pp. 29, 34–35, 39, 66–69, 71, 74, 82–90.

CHAPTER 26

The West and the World

✤ While industrialization and nationalism were transforming urban life and Western society, Western society itself was reshaping the world. At the peak of its power and pride, the West entered the third and most dynamic phase of the aggressive expansion that had begun with the Crusades and continued with the great discoveries and the rise of seaborne colonial empires. An ever-growing stream of products, people, and ideas flowed out of Europe in the nineteenth century. Hardly any corner of the globe was left untouched. The most spectacular manifestations of Western expansion came in the late nineteenth century when the leading European nations established or enlarged their far-flung political empires. The political annexation of territory in the 1880s—the "new imperialism," as it is often called by historians—was the capstone of a profound underlying economic and technological process.

- How and why did this many-sided, epoch-making expansion occur in the nineteenth century?

- What were some of its consequences for the West and the rest of the world?

These are the questions this chapter will examine.

The Emigrant Ship by the British painter Charles J. Staniland, 1898. *(Source: Bridgeman Art Library, London)*

✤ INDUSTRIALIZATION AND THE WORLD ECONOMY

The Industrial Revolution created, first in Great Britain and then in continental Europe and North America, a growing and tremendously dynamic economic system. In the course of the nineteenth century, that system was extended across the face of the earth. Some of this extension into non-Western areas was peaceful and beneficial for all concerned, for the West had

865

many products and techniques the rest of the world desired. If peaceful methods failed, however, Europeans did not stand on ceremony. They used their superior military power to force non-Western nations to open their doors to Western economic interests. In general, Westerners fashioned the global economic system so that the largest share of the ever-increasing gains from trade, technology, and migration flowed to the West and its propertied classes.

The Rise of Global Inequality

The Industrial Revolution in Europe marked a momentous turning point in human history. Indeed, it is only by placing Europe's economic breakthrough in a global perspective that one can truly appreciate its revolutionary implications and consequences.

From such a global perspective, the ultimate significance of the Industrial Revolution was that it allowed those regions of the world that industrialized in the nineteenth century to increase their wealth and power enormously in comparison to those that did not. As a result, a gap between the industrializing regions (mainly Europe and North America) and the nonindustrializing ones (mainly Africa, Asia, and Latin America) opened up and grew steadily throughout the nineteenth century. Moreover, this pattern of uneven global development became institutionalized, or built into the structure of the world economy. Thus we evolved a "lopsided world," a world of rich lands and poor.

Historians have long been aware of this gap, but it is only recently that historical economists have begun to chart its long-term evolution with some precision. Their findings are extremely revealing, although one must understand that they contain a margin of error and other limitations as well. The findings of one such study are summarized in Figure 26.1. This figure compares the long-term evolution of average income per person in today's "developed" (or industrialized) regions—defined as western and eastern Europe, North America, and Japan—with that found in the "Third World," a term that is now widely used by international organizations and by scholars to group Africa, Asia, and Latin America into a single unit. To get these individual income figures, researchers estimate a country's gross national product (GNP) at different points in time, convert those estimates to some

common currency, and divide by the total population.

Figure 26.1 highlights three main points. First, in 1750 the average standard of living was no higher in Europe as a whole than in the rest of the world. In 1750 Europe was still a poor agricultural society. Moreover, the average per-person income in the wealthiest European country (Great Britain) was less than twice that in the poorest non-Western land. By 1970, however, the average person in the wealthiest countries had an income fully twenty-five times as great as that received by the average person in the poorest countries of Africa and Asia.

Second, it was industrialization that opened the gaps in average wealth and well-being among countries and regions. One sees that Great Britain had jumped well above the European average by 1830, when the first industrial nation was well in advance of its continental competitors. One also sees how Great Britain's lead gradually narrowed as other European countries and the United States successfully industrialized in the course of the nineteenth century.

Third, income per person stagnated in the Third World before 1913, in striking contrast to the industrializing regions. Only after 1945, in the era of political independence and decolonization, did Third World countries finally make some real economic progress, beginning in their turn the critical process of industrialization.

The rise of these enormous income disparities, which are poignant indicators of equal disparities in food and clothing, health and education, life expectancy and general material well-being, has generated a great deal of debate. One school of interpretation stresses that the West used science, technology, capitalist organization, and even its critical world-view to create its wealth and greater physical well-being. Another school argues that the West used its political and economic power to steal much of its riches, continuing in the nineteenth (and twentieth) century the rapacious colonialism born of the era of expansion.

These issues are complex, and there are few simple answers. As noted in Chapter 22, the wealth-creating potential of technological improvement and more intensive capitalist organization was indeed great. At the same time, those breakthroughs rested, in part, on Great Britain's having already used political force to dominate the world economy in the nineteenth century. Wealth—unprecedented wealth—was indeed created, but the lion's share of that new wealth flowed to the West and its propertied classes.

The World Market

Commerce between nations has always been a powerful stimulus to economic development. Never was this more true than in the nineteenth century, when world trade grew prodigiously. World trade grew modestly until about 1840, and then it took off. After a slowdown in the last years of the century, another surge lasted until World War One. In 1913 the value of world trade was roughly $38 billion, or about *twenty-five* times what it had been in 1800. (This amount actually understates the growth since average prices of both manufactured goods and raw materials were lower in 1913 than in 1800.) In a general way, the enormous increase in international commerce summed up the growth of an interlocking world economy centered in and directed by Europe.

Great Britain played a key role in using trade to tie the world together economically. In 1815 Britain already had a colonial empire, for India, Canada, Australia, and other scattered areas remained British possessions after American independence. The technological breakthroughs of the Industrial Revolution allowed Britain to manufacture cotton textiles, iron, and other goods more cheaply and to far outstrip domestic demand for such products. Thus British manufacturers sought export markets first in Europe and then around the world.

Take the case of cotton textiles. By 1820 Britain was exporting 50 percent of its production. Europe bought 50 percent of these cotton textile exports, while India bought only 6 percent. Then as European nations and the United States erected protective tariff barriers and promoted domestic industry, British cotton textile manufacturers aggressively sought and found other foreign markets in non-Western areas. By 1850 India was buying 25 percent and Europe only 16 percent of a much larger total. As a British colony, India could not raise tariffs to protect its ancient cotton textile industry, and thousands of Indian weavers lost their livelihoods.

After the repeal of the Corn Laws in 1846 (see page 780), Britain also became the world's single best market. The decisive argument in the battle against tariffs on imported grain had been, "We

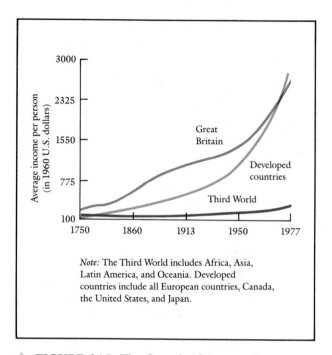

FIGURE 26.1 The Growth of Average Income per Person in the Third World, Developed Countries, and Great Britain, 1750–1970, in 1960 U.S. dollars and prices. *(Source: P. Bairoch and M. Léboyer, eds.,* Disparities in Economic Development Since the Industrial Revolution. *New York: St. Martin's Press, 1981, pp. 7–8, 10)*

must give if we mean honestly to receive, and we must buy as well as sell." Until 1914 Britain thus remained the world's emporium, where not only agricultural products and raw materials but also manufactured goods entered freely. Free access to Britain's enormous market stimulated the development of mines and plantations in many non-Western areas.

The growth of trade was facilitated by the conquest of distance. The earliest railroad construction occurred in Europe (including Russia) and in America north of the Rio Grande; other parts of the globe saw the building of rail lines after 1860. By 1920 more than one-quarter of the world's railroads were in Latin America, Asia, Africa, and Australia. Wherever railroads were built, they drastically reduced transportation costs, opened new economic opportunities, and called forth new skills and attitudes. Moreover, in the areas of massive European settlement—North America and Australia—they were built in advance of the population and provided a means of settling the land.

The power of steam revolutionized transportation by sea as well as by land. In 1807 inhabitants of the Hudson Valley in New York saw the "Devil on the way to Albany in a saw-mill," as Robert Fulton's steamship *Clermont* traveled 150 miles upstream in thirty-two hours. Steampower, long used to drive paddle-wheelers on rivers, particularly in Russia and North America, finally began to supplant sails on the oceans of the world in the late 1860s. Lighter, stronger, cheaper steel replaced iron, which had replaced wood. Screw propellers superseded paddle wheels, while mighty compound steam engines cut fuel consumption by half. Passenger and freight rates tumbled, and the intercontinental shipment of low-priced raw materials became feasible. In addition to the large passenger liners and freighters of the great shipping companies, there were innumerable independent tramp steamers searching endlessly for cargo around the world.

An account of an actual voyage by a typical tramp freighter highlights nineteenth-century developments in global trade. The ship left England in 1910 carrying rails and general freight to western Australia. From there it carried lumber to Melbourne in southeastern Australia, where it took on harvester combines for Argentina. In Buenos Aires it loaded wheat for Calcutta, and in Calcutta it took on jute for New York. From New York it carried a variety of industrial products to Australia before returning to England with lead, wool, and wheat after a voyage of approximately 72,000 miles to six continents in seventeen months.

The revolution in land and sea transportation helped European pioneers open up vast new territories and produce agricultural products and raw materials there for sale in Europe. Moreover, the development of refrigerated railway cars and, from the 1880s, refrigerator ships enabled first Argentina and then the United States, Australia, and New Zealand to ship mountains of chilled or frozen beef and mutton to European (mainly British) consumers. From Asia, Africa, and Latin America came not only the traditional tropical products—spices, tea, sugar, coffee—but also new raw materials for industry, such as jute, rubber, cotton, and coconut oil.

Intercontinental trade was enormously facilitated by the Suez and Panama canals. Of great importance, too, was large and continual investment in modern port facilities, which made loading and unloading cheaper, faster, and more dependable. Finally, transoceanic telegraph cables inaugurated rapid communications among the financial centers of the world. While a British tramp freighter steamed from Calcutta to New York, a broker in London was arranging by telegram for it to carry an American cargo to Australia. World commodity prices were also instantaneously conveyed by the same network of communications.

The growth of trade and the conquest of distance encouraged the expanding European economy to make massive foreign investments. Beginning about 1840, European capitalists started to invest large sums in foreign lands. They did not stop until the outbreak of World War One in 1914. By that year, Europeans had invested more than $40 billion abroad. Great Britain, France, and Germany were the principal investing countries, although by 1913 the United States was emerging as a substantial foreign investor. The sums involved were enormous (Map 26.1). In the decade before 1914, Great Britain was investing 7 percent of its annual national income abroad, or slightly more than it was investing in its entire domestic economy. The great gap between rich and poor within Europe meant that the wealthy and moderately well-to-do could and did send great sums abroad in search of interest and dividends.

Most of the capital exported did not go to European colonies or protectorates in Asia and Africa. About three-quarters of total European investment went to other European countries, the United States and Canada, Australia and New Zealand, and Latin America. Europe found its most profitable opportunities for investment in construction of the railroads, ports, and utilities that were necessary to settle and develop the almost-vacant lands in such places as Australia and the Americas. By lending money for a railroad in Argentina or in Canada's prairie provinces, for example, Europeans not only collected interest but also enabled white settlers to buy European rails and locomotives, developed sources of cheap wheat, and opened still more territory for European settlement. Much of this investment—such as in American railroads, fully a third of whose capital in 1890 was European, or in Russian railroads, which drew heavily on loans from France—was peaceful and mutually beneficial for lenders and borrowers. The victims were native American Indians and Australian aborigines, who were decimated by the dis-

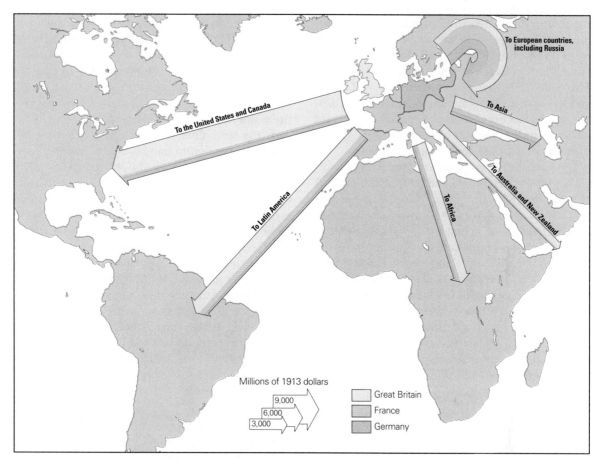

❖ **MAP 26.1 European Investment to 1914** Foreign investment grew rapidly after 1850, and Britain, France, and Germany were the major investing nations. As this map suggests, most European investment was not directed to the African and Asian areas seized by the "new imperialism" after 1880.

eases, liquor, and weapons of an aggressively expanding Western society.

The Opening of China and Japan

Europe's relatively peaceful development of robust offshoots in sparsely populated North America, Australia, and much of Latin America absorbed huge quantities of goods, investments, and migrants. From a Western point of view, that was the most important aspect of Europe's global thrust. Yet Europe's economic and cultural penetration of old, densely populated civilizations was also profoundly significant, especially for the non-European peoples affected by it. With such civilizations Europeans also increased their trade and profit. Moreover, as had been the case ever since

Vasco da Gama and Christopher Columbus, the expanding Western society was prepared to use force, if necessary, to attain its desires. This was what happened in China and Japan, two crucial examples of the general pattern of intrusion into non-Western lands.

Traditional Chinese civilization was self-sufficient. For centuries China had sent more goods and inventions to Europe than it had received, and this was still the case in the eighteenth century. Europeans and the English in particular had developed a taste for Chinese tea, but they had to pay for it with hard silver since China was supremely uninterested in European wares. Trade with Europe was carefully regulated by the Chinese imperial government—the Manchu Dynasty—which was more interested in isolating and controlling the strange "sea barbarians" than in pursuing commercial exchange. The imperial government refused to establish diplomatic relations with the "inferior" European states, and it required all foreign merchants to live in the southern city of Canton and to buy from and sell to only the local merchant monopoly. Practices considered harmful to Chinese interests, such as the sale of opium and the export of silver from China, were strictly forbidden.

For years the little community of foreign merchants in Canton had to accept the Chinese system. By the 1820s, however, the dominant group, the British, were flexing their muscles. Moreover, in the smoking of opium—that "destructive and ensnaring vice" denounced by Chinese decrees—they had found something the Chinese really wanted. Grown legally in British-occupied India, opium was smuggled into China by means of fast ships and bribed officials. The more this rich trade developed, the greedier British merchants became, and the more they resented the patriotic attempts of the Chinese government to stem the tide of drug addiction. By 1836 the aggressive goal of the

British merchants in Canton was an independent British colony in China and "safe and unrestricted liberty" in trade. Spurred on by economic motives, they pressured the British government to take decisive action and enlisted the support of British manufacturers with visions of vast Chinese markets to be opened.

At the same time, the Manchu government decided that the opium trade had to be stamped out. It was ruining the people and stripping the empire of its silver, which was going to British merchants to pay for the opium. The government began to prosecute Chinese drug dealers vigorously and in 1839 sent special envoy Lin Tse-hsü to Canton. Lin Tse-hsü ordered the foreign merchants to obey China's laws, "for our great unified Manchu Empire regards itself as responsible for the habits and morals of its subjects and cannot rest content to see any of them become victims of a deadly poison."[1] The British merchants refused and were expelled, whereupon war soon broke out.

Using troops from India and being in control of the seas, the British occupied several coastal cities

Britain and China at War, 1841 Britain capitalized on its overwhelming naval superiority, and this British aquatint celebrates a dramatic moment in a crucial battle near Canton. Having received a direct hit from a steam-powered British ironclad, a Chinese sailing ship explodes into a wall of flame. The Chinese lost eleven ships and 500 men in the two-hour engagement; the British suffered only minor damage. (*Source: National Maritime Museum, London*)

✦ **East Meets West** This painting gives a Japanese view of the first audience of the American Consul and his staff with the shogun, Japan's hereditary military governor, in 1859. The Americans appear strange and ill at ease. *(Source: Laurie Platt Winfrey, Inc.)*

and forced China to surrender. In the Treaty of Nanking in 1842, the imperial government was forced to cede the island of Hong Kong to Britain forever, pay an indemnity of 100 million dollars, and open up four large cities to foreign trade with low tariffs.

Thereafter the opium trade flourished, and Hong Kong developed rapidly as an Anglo-Chinese enclave. China continued to nurture illusions of superiority and isolation, however, and refused to accept foreign diplomats in Peking, the imperial capital. Finally, there was a second round of foreign attack between 1856 and 1860, culminating in the occupation of Peking by seventeen thousand British and French troops and the intentional burning of the emperor's summer palace. Another round of harsh treaties gave European merchants and missionaries greater privileges and protection. Thus did Europeans use military aggression to blow a hole in the wall of Chinese seclusion and open the country to foreign trade and foreign ideas. Blasting away at Chinese sovereignty as well, they forced the Chinese to accept trade and investment on unfavorable terms for the foreseeable future.

China's neighbor Japan had its own highly distinctive civilization and even less use for Westerners. European traders and missionaries first arrived in Japan in the sixteenth century. By 1640 Japan had reacted quite negatively to their presence. The government decided to seal off the country from all European influences in order to preserve traditional Japanese culture and society. Officials ruthlessly persecuted Japanese Christians and expelled all but a few Dutch merchants, who were virtually imprisoned in a single port and rigidly controlled. When American and British whaling ships began to appear off Japanese coasts almost two hundred years later, the policy of exclusion was still in effect. An order of 1825 commanded Japanese officials to "drive away foreign vessels without second thought."[2]

Japan's unbending isolation seemed hostile and barbaric to the West, particularly to the United States. It complicated the practical problems of shipwrecked American sailors and the provisioning of whaling ships and China traders sailing in the eastern Pacific. It also thwarted the hope of trade and profit. Moreover, Americans shared the self-confidence and dynamism of expanding Western society. They had taken California from Mexico in 1848, and Americans felt destined to play a great role in the Pacific. It seemed, therefore, the duty of the United States to force the Japanese to share their ports and behave as a "civilized" nation.

After several unsuccessful American attempts to establish commercial relations with Japan, Commodore Matthew Perry steamed into Edo (now Tokyo) Bay in 1853 and demanded diplomatic negotiations with the emperor. Japan entered a grave crisis. Some Japanese warriors urged resistance, but senior officials realized how defenseless their cities were against naval bombardment. Shocked and humiliated, they reluctantly signed a treaty with the United States that opened two ports and permitted trade. Over the next five years, more treaties spelled out the rights and privileges of the Western nations and their merchants in Japan. Japan was "opened." What the British had done in China with war, the Americans had done in Japan with the threat of war.

Western Penetration of Egypt

Egypt's experience illustrates not only the explosive power of the expanding European economy and society but also their seductive appeal in non-Western lands. European involvement in Egypt also led to a new model of formal political control, which European powers applied widely in Africa and Asia after 1882.

Of great importance in African and Middle Eastern history, the ancient land of the pharaohs had since 525 B.C. been ruled by a succession of foreigners, most recently by the Ottoman Turks. In 1798 French armies under young General Napoleon Bonaparte invaded the Egyptian part of the Ottoman Empire and occupied the territory for three years. Into the power vacuum left by the French withdrawal stepped an extraordinary Albanian-born Turkish general, Muhammad Ali (1769–1849).

First appointed governor of Egypt by the Turkish sultan, Muhammad Ali soon disposed of his political rivals and set out to build his own state on the strength of a large, powerful army organized along European lines. He drafted for the first time the illiterate, despised peasant masses of Egypt, and he hired French and Italian army officers to train these raw recruits and their Turkish officers. The government was also reformed, new

lands were cultivated, and communications were improved. By the time of his death in 1849, Muhammad Ali had established a strong and virtually independent Egyptian state, to be ruled by his family on a hereditary basis within the Turkish empire.

Muhammad Ali's policies of modernization attracted large numbers of Europeans to the banks of the Nile. As one Arab sheik of the Ottoman Empire remarked in the 1830s, "Englishmen are like ants; if one finds a bit of meat, hundreds follow."[3] The port city of Alexandria had more than fifty thousand Europeans by 1864, most of them Italian, Greek, French, or English. Europeans served not only as army officers but also as engineers, doctors, high government officials, and police officers. Others found their "meat" in trade, finance, and shipping.

To pay for a modern army as well as for European services and manufactured goods, Muhammad Ali encouraged the development of commercial agriculture geared to the European market. This development had profound implications. Egyptian peasants had been poor but largely self-sufficient, growing food for their own consumption on state-owned lands allotted to them by tradition. Faced with the possibility of export agriculture, high-ranking officials and members of Muhammad Ali's family began carving large private landholdings out of the state domain. The new landlords made the peasants their tenants and forced them to grow cash crops for European markets. Borrowing money from European lenders at high rates and still making good profits, Egyptian landowners "modernized" agriculture, but to the detriment of peasant well-being.

These trends continued under Muhammad Ali's grandson Ismail, who in 1863 began his sixteen-year rule as Egypt's *khedive,* or prince. Educated at France's leading military academy, Ismail was a westernizing autocrat. He dreamed of using European technology and capital to modernize Egypt quickly and build a vast empire in northeast Africa. The large irrigation networks he promoted caused cotton production and exports to Europe to boom. Ismail also borrowed large sums to install modern communications, and with his support the Suez Canal was completed by a French company in 1869. The Arabic of the masses, rather than the Turkish of the conquerors, became the official language, and young Egyptians educated in Europe helped spread new skills and new ideas in the bureaucracy. Cairo acquired modern boulevards, Western hotels, and an opera house. As Ismail proudly declared, "My country is no longer in Africa, we now form part of Europe."[4]

Yet Ismail was too impatient and too reckless. His projects were enormously expensive, and the sale of his stock in the Suez Canal to the British government did not relieve the situation. By 1876 Egypt owed foreign bondholders a colossal 450 million dollars and could not pay the interest on its debt. Rather than let Egypt go bankrupt and repudiate its loans, as had some Latin American countries and U.S. state governments in the early nineteenth century, the governments of France and Great Britain intervened politically to protect the European bankers who held the Egyptian bonds. They forced Ismail to appoint French and British commissioners to oversee Egyptian finances so that the Egyptian debt would be paid in full. This was a momentous decision. It implied direct European political control and was a sharp break with the previous pattern of trade and investment. Throughout most of the nineteenth century, Europeans had used naked military might and political force primarily to make sure that non-Western lands would accept European trade and investment. Now Europeans were going to determine the state budget and effectively rule Egypt.

Foreign financial control evoked a violent nationalistic reaction among Egyptian religious leaders, young intellectuals, and army officers. In 1879, under the leadership of Colonel Ahmed Arabi, they formed the Egyptian Nationalist party. Continuing diplomatic pressure, which forced Ismail to abdicate in favor of his weak son, Tewfiq (r. 1879–1892), resulted in bloody anti-European riots in Alexandria in 1882. A number of Europeans were

✧ **A Western Hotel in Cairo** This photo suggests both the reality and the limits of modernization in Ismail's Egypt. An expensive hotel, complete with terrace cafe and gaslight, now adorns the Egyptian capital. But the hotel is for foreigners, and the native Egyptians are servants and outsiders. *(Source: Popperfoto)*

killed, and Tewfiq and his court had to flee to British ships for safety. When the British fleet bombarded Alexandria, more riots swept the country, and Colonel Arabi declared that "an irreconcilable war existed between the Egyptians and the English." But a British expeditionary force decimated Arabi's forces and as a result occupied all of Egypt.

The British said their occupation was temporary, but British armies remained in Egypt until 1956. They maintained the façade of the khedive's government as an autonomous province of the Ottoman Empire, but the khedive was a mere puppet. The able British consul, General Evelyn Baring, later Lord Cromer, ruled the country after 1883. Once a vocal opponent of involvement in Egypt, Baring was a paternalistic reformer who had come to believe that "without European interference and initiative reform is impossible here." Baring's rule did result in tax reforms and better conditions for peasants, while foreign bondholders tranquilly

clipped their coupons and Egyptian nationalists nursed their injured pride.

In Egypt Baring and the British reluctantly but spectacularly provided a new model for European expansion in densely populated lands. Such expansion was based on military force, political domination, and a self-justifying ideology of beneficial reform. This model was to predominate until 1914. Thus did Europe's Industrial Revolution lead to tremendous political as well as economic expansion throughout the world.

✦ THE GREAT MIGRATION

A poignant human drama was interwoven with economic expansion: millions of people pulled up stakes and left their ancestral lands in the course of history's greatest migration. To millions of ordinary people, for whom the opening of China and the interest on the Egyptian debt had not the slightest significance, this great movement was the central experience in the saga of Western expansion. It was, in part, because of this great migration that the West's impact on the world in the nineteenth century was so powerful and many-sided.

The Pressure of Population

In the early eighteenth century, the growth of European population entered its third and decisive stage, which continued unabated until the twentieth century (see Chapter 19). Birthrates eventually declined in the nineteenth century, but so did death rates, mainly because of the rising standard of living and secondarily because of the medical revolution. Thus the population of Europe (including Asiatic Russia) more than doubled, from approximately 188 million in 1800 to roughly 432 million in 1900.

These figures actually understate Europe's population explosion, for between 1815 and 1932 more than sixty million people left Europe. These migrants went primarily to the "areas of European settlement"—North and South America, Australia, New Zealand, and Siberia—where they contributed to a rapid growth in numbers. The population of North America (the United States and Canada) alone grew from six million to eighty-one million between 1800 and 1900 because of continual immigration and high fertility rates. Since population grew more slowly in Africa and Asia than in

✦ **FIGURE 26.2 The Increase of European and World Populations, 1750–1980** *(Source: W. Woodruff,* Impact of Western Man: A Study of Europe's Role in the World Economy. *St. Martin's Press, New York, 1967, p. 103; United Nations.* Statistical Yearbook, 1982, *1985, pp. 2–3.)*

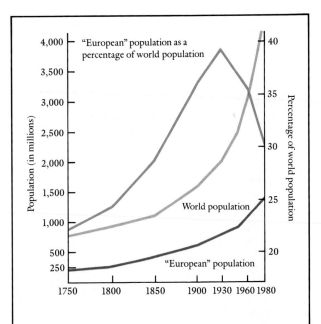

Note: "European" population includes Europe and also areas of predominately European settlement—Asiatic Russia, North America, South America, and Australia/New Zealand.

Europe, as Figure 26.2 shows, Europeans and people of European origin jumped from about 22 percent of the world's total to about 38 percent on the eve of World War One.

The growing number of Europeans provided further impetus for Western expansion. It was a driving force behind emigration. As in the eighteenth century, the rapid increase in numbers put pressure on the land and led to land hunger and relative overpopulation in area after area. In most countries, migration increased twenty years after a rapid growth in population, as many children of the baby boom grew up, saw little available land and few opportunities, and migrated. This pattern was especially prevalent when rapid population increase predated extensive industrial development, which offered the best long-term hope of creating jobs within the country and reducing poverty. Thus millions of country folk went abroad as well as to nearby cities in search of work and economic opportunity. The case of the Irish, who left in large numbers for Britain during the Industrial Revolution and for the United States after the potato famine, was extreme but not unique.

Before looking at the people who migrated, let us consider three facts. First, the number of men and women who left Europe increased rapidly before World War One. As Figure 26.3 shows, more than eleven million left in the first decade of the twentieth century, over five times the number departing in the 1850s. The outflow of migrants was clearly an enduring characteristic of European society for the entire period.

Second, different countries had very different patterns of movement. As Figure 26.3 also shows, people left Britain and Ireland (which are not distinguished in the British figures) in large numbers from the 1840s on. This emigration reflected not only rural poverty but also the movement of skilled, industrial technicians and the preferences shown to British migrants in the British Empire. Ultimately, about one-third of all European migrants between 1840 and 1920 came from the British Isles. German migration was quite different. It grew irregularly after about 1830, reaching a first peak in the early 1850s and another in the early 1880s. Thereafter it declined rapidly, for Germany's rapid industrialization was providing adequate jobs at home. This pattern contrasted sharply with that of Italy. More and more Italians left the country right up to 1914, reflecting severe problems in Italian villages and relatively slow industrial

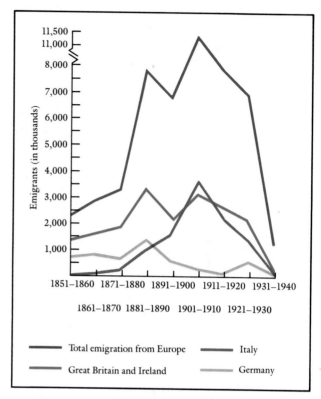

FIGURE 26.3 Emigration from Europe by Decades, 1851–1940 *(Source: W. Woodruff, Impact of Western Man: A Study of Europe's Role in the World Economy. St. Martin's Press, New York, 1967, pp. 106–107 and references cited therein.)*

growth. Thus, migration patterns mirrored social and economic conditions in the various European countries and provinces.

Third, although the United States absorbed the largest number of European migrants, less than half of all migrants went to the United States. Asiatic Russia, Canada, Argentina, Brazil, and Australia also attracted large numbers, as Figure 26.4 shows. Moreover, migrants accounted for a larger proportion of the total population in Argentina, Brazil, and Canada than in the United States. Between 1900 and 1910, for example, new arrivals represented 3 percent of Argentina's population each year, as opposed to only 1 percent for the United States. The common American assumption that European migration meant migration to the United States is quite inaccurate.

European Migrants

What kind of people left Europe, and what were their reasons for doing so? Most were poor people

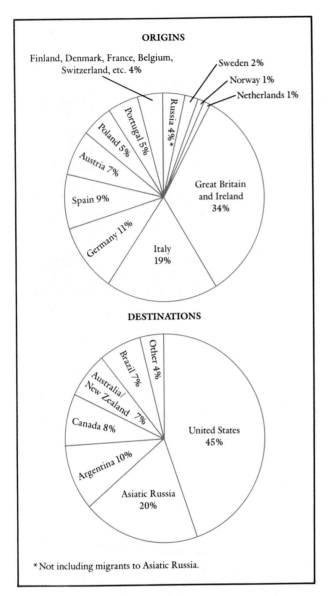

ORIGINS

Finland, Denmark, France, Belgium, Switzerland, etc. 4%

Sweden 2%
Norway 1%
Netherlands 1%

Russia 4%*
Portugal 5%
Poland 5%
Austria 7%
Spain 9%
Germany 11%
Italy 19%

Great Britain and Ireland 34%

DESTINATIONS

Other 4%
Brazil 7%
Australia/New Zealand 7%
Canada 8%
Argentina 10%

United States 45%

Asiatic Russia 20%

*Not including migrants to Asiatic Russia.

✦ **FIGURE 26.4 Origin and Destination of European Emigrants, 1851–1960** *(Source: W. Woodruff,* Impact of Western Man: A Study of Europe's Role in the World Economy. *St. Martin's Press, New York, 1967, pp. 108–109 and references cited therein.)*

from rural areas, though seldom from the poorest classes. Indeed, the European migrant was most often a small peasant landowner or a village crafts- man whose traditional way of life was threatened by too little land, estate agriculture, and cheap, factory-made goods. German peasants who left the Rhineland and southwestern Germany between 1830 and 1854, for example, felt trapped by what

Friedrich List called the "dwarf economy," with its tiny landholdings and declining craft industries. Selling out and moving to buy much cheaper land in the American Midwest became a common re- sponse. Contrary to what is often said, the Euro- pean migrant was generally not a desperately im- poverished landless peasant or urban proletarian, but an energetic small farmer or skilled artisan trying hard to stay ahead of poverty.

Determined to maintain or improve their status, migrants were a great asset to the countries that received them. This was doubly so because the vast majority were young and very often unmarried. Fully 67 percent of those admitted to the United States were under thirty-one years of age, and 90 percent were under forty. They came in the prime of life and were ready to work hard in the new land, at least for a time. Many Europeans moved but remained within Europe, settling temporarily or permanently in another European country. Jews from eastern Europe and peasants from Ireland migrated to Great Britain, Russians and Poles sought work in Germany, and Latin peoples from Spain, Portugal, and Italy entered France. As in the case of migration to North and South America, the vast bulk of this movement within Europe was legal.

Even in the New World, many Europeans, espe- cially by the end of the nineteenth century, were truly migrants as opposed to immigrants—that is, they returned home after some time abroad. One in two migrants to Argentina and probably one in three to the United States eventually returned to their native land. The likelihood of repatriation varied greatly by nationality. Seven out of eight people who migrated from the Balkans to the United States in the late nineteenth century re- turned to their countries. At the other extreme, only one person in ten from Ireland and only one in twenty among eastern European Jews returned to the country of origin.

Once again, the possibility of buying land in the old country was of central importance. Land in Ireland (as well as in England and Scotland) was tightly held by large, often absentee landowners, and little land was available for purchase. In Russia Jews were left in relative peace until the assassina- tion of Alexander II by non-Jewish terrorists in 1881 brought a new tsar and an official policy of pogroms and savage discrimination. Russia's five million Jews were already confined to the market

The Drama of Migration These Italian migrants are passing through the port of Naples circa 1900, heading for both temporary work and permanent settlement in North and South America. Naples was the principal outlet for large-scale migration from southern Italy, and it handled more passengers than all other Italian ports combined. *(Source: Touring Club Italiano, Milan)*

towns and small cities of the so-called Pale of Settlement, where they worked as artisans and petty traders. Most land was held by non-Jews. Therefore, when Russian Jewish artisans began in the 1880s to escape both factory competition and oppression by migrating—a migration that eventually totaled two million people—this was basically a once-and-for-all departure. Non-Jewish migrants from Russia, who constituted a majority of those leaving the tsar's empire after 1905, had access to land and thus returned much more frequently to their peasant villages in central Russia, Poland, and Ukraine.

The mass movement of Italians illustrates many of the characteristics of European migration. As late as the 1880s, which was for Italians, as for Russian Jews, the first decade of substantial exodus, three in every four Italians depended on agri-

culture. With the influx of cheap North American wheat, the long-standing problems of the Italian village became more acute. And since industry was not advancing fast enough to provide jobs for the rapidly growing population, many Italians began to leave their country for economic reasons. Most Italian migrants were not landless laborers from areas dominated by large estates; such people tended to stay in Italy and turned increasingly toward radical politics. Instead, most were small landowning peasants whose standard of living was falling because of rural overpopulation and agricultural depression. Migration provided them with an escape valve and possible income to buy more land.

Many Italians went to the United States, but before 1900 more went to Argentina and Brazil; indeed, two out of three migrants came from Italy. In Brazil the large coffee planters, faced with the

❖ **The Jewish Market** on New York's lower East Side was a bustling center of economic and social life in 1900. Jewish immigrants could usually find work with Jewish employers, and New York's Jewish population soared from 73,000 in 1880 to 1.1 million in 1910. (*Source: The Granger Collection*)

collapse of black slavery, attracted Italians to their plantations with subsidized travel and promises of relatively high wages.

Many Italians had no intention of settling abroad permanently. Some called themselves "swallows": after harvesting their own wheat and flax in Italy, they "flew" to Argentina to harvest wheat between December and April. Returning to Italy for the spring planting, they repeated this exhausting process. This was a very hard life, but a frugal worker could save 250 to 300 dollars in the course of a season. A one-way passage from Latin America to Italy usually cost only 25 to 30 dollars and sometimes as little as 8 dollars. Italian migrants also dominated the building trades and the architectural profession in Latin America and succeeded in giving a thoroughly Italian character to many Latin American cities.

Other Italians migrated to other European countries. France was a favorite destination. In 1911 the Italian-born population of France was roughly a third as large as that in the United States.

Ties of family and friendship played a crucial role in the movement of peoples. Many people from a given province or village settled together in rural enclaves or tightly knit urban neighborhoods thousands of miles away. Very often a strong individual—a businessman, a religious leader—would blaze the way and others would follow, forming a "migration chain."

Many landless young European men and women were spurred to leave by a spirit of revolt and independence. In Sweden and in Norway, in Jewish Russia and in Italy, these young people felt frustrated by the small privileged classes, which often controlled both church and government and resisted demands for change and greater opportunity. Many a young Norwegian seconded the passionate cry of Norway's national poet, Bjørnson: "Forth will I! Forth! I will be crushed and consumed if I stay."[5]

Many young Jews wholeheartedly agreed with a spokesman of Kiev's Jewish community in 1882, who declared, "Our human dignity is being trampled upon, our wives and daughters are being dishonored, we are looted and pillaged: either we get decent human rights or else let us go wherever our eyes may lead us."[6] Thus for many, migration was a radical way to "get out from under." Migration slowed down when the people won basic political and social reforms, such as the right to vote and social security.

Asian Migrants

Not all migration was from Europe. A substantial number of Chinese, Japanese, Indians, and Filipi-nos—to name only four key groups—responded to rural hardship with temporary or permanent migration. At least three million Asians (as opposed to more than sixty million Europeans) moved abroad before 1920. Most went as indentured laborers to work under incredibly difficult conditions on the plantations or in the gold mines of Latin America, southern Asia, Africa, California, Hawaii, and Australia. White estate owners very often used Asians to replace or supplement blacks after the suppression of the slave trade.

In the 1840s, for example, there was a strong demand for field hands in Cuba, and the Spanish government actively recruited Chinese laborers. They came under eight-year contracts, were paid about twenty-five cents a day, and were fed potatoes and salted beef. Between 1853 and 1873, when such migration was stopped, more than 130,000 Chinese laborers went to Cuba. The majority spent their lives as virtual slaves. The great landlords of Peru also brought in more than

✦ **"Is She Hardworking?"** Entering the United States in their colorful kimonos, these Japanese women are "picture brides." Their marriages to Japanese men in the United States have already been arranged by friends and marriage brokers, who have used pictures and references to strike a bargain with prospective husbands. About 600 Japanese picture brides entered annually until the U.S. government outlawed the practice in 1921. *(Source: California Department of Parks and Recreation)*

100,000 workers from China in the nineteenth century, and there were similar movements of Asians elsewhere.

Such migration from Asia would undoubtedly have grown to much greater proportions if planters and mine owners in search of cheap labor had had their way. But they did not. Asians fled the plantations and gold mines as soon as possible, seeking greater opportunities in trade and towns. There they came into conflict with brown-skinned peoples—as in Malaya and East Africa—and with white settlers in areas of European settlement.

These settlers demanded a halt to Asian migration. One Australian brutally summed up the typical view: "The Chinaman knows nothing about Caucasian civilization. . . . It would be less objectionable to drive a flock of sheep to the poll than to allow Chinamen to vote. The sheep at all events would be harmless."[7] By the 1880s Americans and Australians were building "great white walls"—discriminatory laws designed to keep Asians out. Thus a final, crucial factor in the migrations before 1914 was the general policy of "whites only" in the open lands of possible permanent settlement. This, too, was part of Western dominance in the increasingly lopsided world. Largely successful in monopolizing the best overseas opportunities, Europeans and people of European ancestry reaped the main benefits from the great migration. By 1913 people in Australia, Canada, and the United States all had higher average incomes than people in Great Britain, still Europe's wealthiest nation.

✤ WESTERN IMPERIALISM

The expansion of Western society reached its apex between about 1880 and 1914. In those years, the leading European nations not only continued to send massive streams of migrants, money, and manufactured goods around the world, but also rushed to create or enlarge vast *political* empires abroad. This political empire building contrasted sharply with the economic penetration of non-Western territories between 1816 and 1880, which had left a China or a Japan "opened" but politically independent. By contrast, the empires of the late nineteenth century recalled the old European colonial empires of the seventeenth and eighteenth centuries and led contemporaries to speak of the new imperialism.

Characterized by a frantic rush to plant the flag over as many people and as much territory as possible, the new imperialism had momentous consequences. It resulted in new tensions among competing European states, and it led to wars and rumors of war with non-European powers. The new imperialism was aimed primarily at Africa and Asia. It put millions of black, brown, and yellow peoples directly under the rule of whites. How and why did whites come to rule these peoples?

The Scramble for Africa

The most spectacular manifestation of the new imperialism was the seizure of Africa, which broke sharply with previous patterns and fascinated contemporary Europeans and Americans. As late as 1880, European nations controlled only 10 percent of the African continent, and their possessions were hardly increasing. The French had begun conquering Algeria in 1830, and within fifty years substantial numbers of French, Italian, and Spanish colonists had settled among the overwhelming Arab majority.

At the other end of the continent, in South Africa, the British had taken possession of the Dutch settlements at Cape Town during the wars with Napoleon I. This takeover had led disgruntled Dutch cattle ranchers and farmers in 1835 to make their so-called Great Trek into the interior, where they fought the Zulu and Xhosa peoples for land. After 1853, while British colonies such as Canada and Australia were beginning to evolve toward self-government, the Boers, or Afrikaners (as the descendents of the Dutch in the Cape Colony were beginning to call themselves), proclaimed their political independence and defended it against British armies. By 1880 Afrikaner and British settlers, who detested each other, had wrested control of much of South Africa from the Zulu, Xhosa, and other African peoples.

European trading posts and forts dating back to the Age of Discovery and the slave trade dotted the coast of West Africa. The Portuguese proudly but ineffectively held their old possessions in Angola and Mozambique. Elsewhere over the great mass of the continent, Europeans did not rule.

Between 1880 and 1900, the situation changed drastically. Britain, France, Germany, and Italy scrambled for African possessions as if their national livelihoods depended on it. By 1900 nearly the whole continent had been carved up and placed under European rule: only Ethiopia in northeast Africa and Liberia on the West African coast remained independent. Even the Dutch settler republics of southern Africa were conquered by the British in the bloody Boer War (1899–1902). In the years before 1914, the European powers tightened their control and established colonial governments to rule their gigantic empires (Map 26.2).

In the complexity of the European seizure of Africa, certain events and individuals stand out. Of enormous importance was the British occupation of Egypt, which established the new model of formal political control. There was also the role of Leopold II of Belgium (r. 1865–1909), an energetic, strong-willed monarch with a lust for distant territory. "The sea bathes our coast, the world lies before us," he had exclaimed in 1861. "Steam and electricity have annihilated distance, and all the non-appropriated lands on the surface of the globe can become the field of our operations and of our success."[8] By 1876 Leopold was focusing on central Africa. Subsequently, he formed a financial syndicate under his personal control to send Henry M. Stanley, a sensation-seeking journalist and part-time explorer, to the Congo basin. Stanley was able to establish trading stations, sign "treaties" with African chiefs, and plant Leopold's flag. Leopold's actions alarmed the French, who quickly sent out an expedition under Pierre de Brazza. In 1880 de Brazza signed a treaty of protection with the chief of the large Teke tribe and began to establish a French protectorate on the north bank of the Congo River.

Leopold's buccaneering intrusion into the Congo area raised the question of the political fate of black Africa—Africa south of the Sahara. By 1882 when the British successfully invaded and occupied Egypt, the richest and most developed land in Africa, Europe had caught "African fever." There was a gold rush mentality, and the race for territory was on.

To lay down some basic rules for this new and dangerous game of imperialist competition, Jules Ferry of France and Otto von Bismarck of Germany arranged an international conference on Africa in Berlin in 1884 and 1885. The conference established the principle that European claims to African territory had to rest on "effective occupation" in order to be recognized by other states.

This principle was very important. It meant that Europeans would push relentlessly into interior regions from all sides and that no single European power would be able to claim the entire continent. The conference recognized Leopold's personal rule over a neutral Congo free state and declared all of the Congo basin a free trade zone. The conference also agreed to work to stop slavery and the slave trade in Africa.

The Berlin conference coincided with Germany's sudden emergence as an imperial power. Prior to about 1880, Bismarck, like many other European leaders at the time, had seen little value in colonies. Colonies reminded him, he said, of a poor but proud nobleman who wore a fur coat when he could not afford a shirt underneath. Then in 1884 and 1885 as political agitation for expansion increased, Bismarck did an abrupt about-face, and Germany established protectorates over a number of small African kingdoms and tribes in Togo, Cameroon, southwest Africa, and, later, East Africa. In acquiring colonies, Bismarck cooperated against the British with France's Ferry, who was as ardent for empire as he was for education. With Bismarck's tacit approval, the French pressed vigorously southward from Algeria, eastward from their old forts on the Senegal coast, and northward from de Brazza's newly formed protectorate on the Congo River. The object of these three thrusts was Lake Chad, a malaria-infested swamp on the edge of the Sahara Desert.

Meanwhile, the British began enlarging their West African enclaves and impatiently pushing northward from the Cape Colony and westward from Zanzibar. Their thrust southward from Egypt was blocked in the Sudan by fiercely independent Muslims, who massacred a British force at Khartoum in 1885.

A decade later another British force, under General Horatio H. Kitchener, moved cautiously and more successfully up the Nile River, building a railroad to supply arms and reinforcements as it went. Finally, in 1898 these British troops met their foe at Omdurman, where Muslim tribesmen armed with spears charged time and time again only to be cut down by the recently invented machine gun. For one smug participant, the young British officer Winston Churchill, it was "like a pantomime scene" in a play. "These extraordinary foreign figures . . . march up one by one from the darkness of Barbarism to the footlights of civiliza-

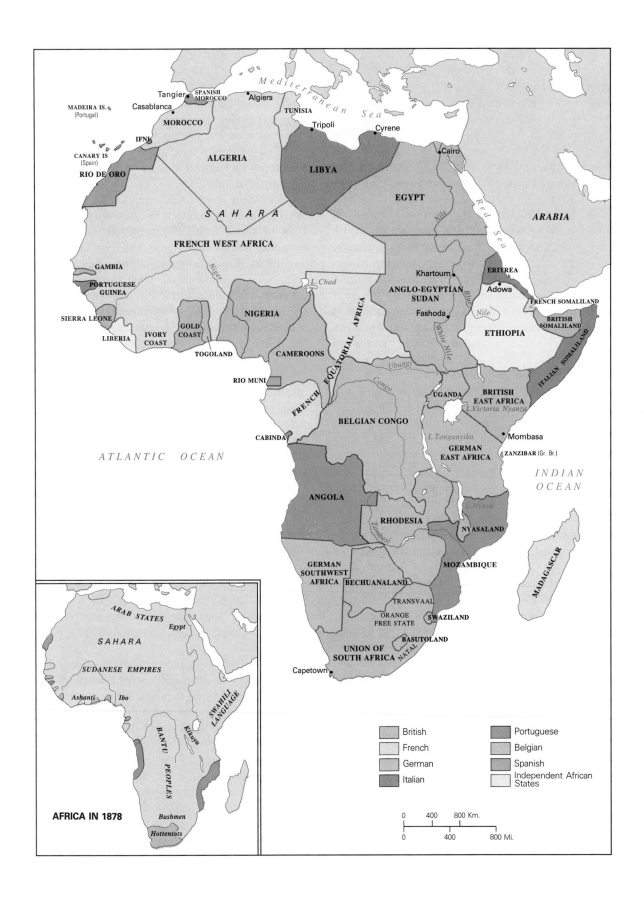

Mediterranean Sea

Tangier
Casablanca
MADEIRA IS. (Portugal)
SPANISH MOROCCO
Algiers
TUNISIA
Tripoli
Cyrene
Cairo
MOROCCO
IFNI
CANARY IS (Spain)
RIO DE ORO
ALGERIA
LIBYA
EGYPT
ARABIA

S A H A R A

FRENCH WEST AFRICA

Nile
Red Sea

L. Chad
Khartoum
ERITREA
Adowa
FRENCH SOMALILAND

GAMBIA
PORTUGUESE GUINEA
ANGLO-EGYPTIAN SUDAN
BRITISH SOMALILAND

SIERRA LEONE
NIGERIA
Fashoda
ETHIOPIA

LIBERIA
IVORY COAST
GOLD COAST
Blue Nile
White Nile

TOGOLAND
CAMEROONS
ITALIAN SOMALILAND

RIO MUNI
FRENCH EQUATORIAL AFRICA
Ubangi
Congo
UGANDA

CABINDA
BRITISH EAST AFRICA
L. Victoria Nyanza

ATLANTIC OCEAN
BELGIAN CONGO
L. Tanganyika
Mombasa
GERMAN EAST AFRICA
ZANZIBAR (Gr. Br.)

INDIAN OCEAN

ANGOLA
L. Nyasa

RHODESIA
NYASALAND

Zambesi
MOZAMBIQUE
MADAGASCAR

GERMAN SOUTHWEST AFRICA
BECHUANALAND

TRANSVAAL
SWAZILAND
ORANGE FREE STATE
BASUTOLAND

UNION OF SOUTH AFRICA
NATAL
Capetown

ARAB STATES
Egypt

SAHARA

SUDANESE EMPIRES
SWAHILI LANGUAGE

Ashanti
Ibo
Kikuyu

BANTU PEOPLES

AFRICA IN 1878
Bushmen
Hottentots

British
French
German
Italian
Portuguese
Belgian
Spanish
Independent African States

0   400   800 Km.

0   400   800 Mi.

Omdurman, 1898 European machine guns cut down the charging Muslim tribesmen again and again. "It was not a battle but an execution," said one witness. Thus the Sudan was conquered and one million square miles were added to the British Empire. *(Source: E. T. Archive)*

tion . . . and their conquerors, taking their possessions, forget even their names. Nor will history record such trash." For another, more somber English observer, "It was not a battle but an execution. The bodies were not in heaps . . . but they spread evenly over acres and acres."[9] In the end, eleven thousand brave but poorly armed Muslim tribesmen lay dead, while only twenty-eight Britons had been killed.

Continuing up the Nile after the Battle of Omdurman, Kitchener's armies found that a small French force had already occupied the village of Fashoda. Locked in imperial competition with

MAP 26.2 The Partition of Africa European nations carved up Africa after 1880 and built vast political empires. What African states remained independent?

Britain ever since the British occupation of Egypt, France had tried to beat the British to one of Africa's last unclaimed areas—the upper reaches of the Nile. The result was a serious diplomatic crisis and even the threat of war. Eventually, wracked by the Dreyfus affair (see page 854) and unwilling to fight, France backed down and withdrew its forces.

The British conquest of the Sudan exemplifies the general process of empire building in Africa. The fate of the Muslim force at Omdurman was eventually inflicted on all native peoples who resisted European rule: they were blown away by vastly superior military force. But however much the European powers squabbled for territory and privilege around the world, they always had the sense to stop short of actually fighting each other. Imperial ambitions were not worth a great European war.

barbarian lands and those who fail to participate in this great rivalry will play a pitiable role in time to come."[10]

Treitschke's harsh statement reflects not only the increasing aggressiveness of European nationalism after Bismarck's wars of German unification but also Social Darwinian theories of brutal competition among races. As one prominent English economist argued, the "strongest nation has always been conquering the weaker . . . and the strongest tend to be best." Thus European nations, which were seen as racially distinct parts of the dominant white race, had to seize colonies to show they were strong and virile. Moreover, since racial struggle was nature's inescapable law, the conquest of inferior peoples was just. "The path of progress is strewn with the wreck . . . of inferior races," wrote one professor in 1900. "Yet these dead peoples are, in very truth, the stepping stones on which mankind has risen to the higher intellectual and deeper emotional life of today."[11] Social Darwinism and harsh racial doctrines fostered imperialist expansion.

So did the industrial world's unprecedented technological and military superiority. Three aspects were crucial. First, the rapidly firing machine gun, so lethal at Omdurman in the Sudan, was an ultimate weapon in many another unequal battle. Second, newly discovered quinine proved no less effective in controlling attacks of malaria, which had previously decimated whites in the tropics whenever they left breezy coastal enclaves and dared to venture into mosquito-infested interiors. Third, the combination of the steamship and the international telegraph permitted Western powers to quickly concentrate their firepower in a given area when it was needed. Never before—and never again after 1914—would the technological gap between the West and non-Western regions of the world be so great.

Social tensions and domestic political conflicts also contributed mightily to overseas expansion, according to a prominent interpretation of recent years. In Germany, in Russia, and in other countries to a lesser extent, conservative political leaders were charged with manipulating colonial issues in order to divert popular attention from the class struggle at home and to create a false sense of national unity. Therefore, imperial propagandists relentlessly stressed that colonies benefited workers as well as capitalists, providing jobs and cheap raw materials that raised workers' standard of living.

Government leaders and their allies in the tabloid press successfully encouraged the masses to savor foreign triumphs and glory in the supposed increase in national prestige. In short, conservative leaders defined imperialist development as a national necessity, and then they used the realization of that necessity to justify the status quo and their continued hold on power.

Finally, certain special-interest groups in each country were powerful agents of expansion. Shipping companies wanted lucrative subsidies. White settlers on dangerous, turbulent frontiers constantly demanded more land and greater protection. Missionaries and humanitarians wanted to spread religion and stop the slave trade. Explorers and adventurers sought knowledge and excitement. Military men and colonial officials, whose role has often been overlooked by those who write on imperialism, foresaw rapid advancement and high-paid positions in growing empires. The actions of such groups and the determined individuals who led them thrust the course of empire forward.

Western society did not rest the case for empire solely on naked conquest and a Darwinian racial struggle or on power politics and the need for naval bases on every ocean. Imperialists developed additional arguments in order to satisfy their consciences and answer their critics.

A favorite idea was that Europeans could and should "civilize" more primitive, nonwhite peoples. (See Listening to the Past.) According to this view, nonwhites would eventually receive the benefits of modern economies, cities, advanced medicine, and higher standards of living. In time, they might be ready for self-government and Western democracy. Thus the French spoke of their sacred "civilizing mission." Rudyard Kipling (1865–1936), who wrote masterfully of Anglo-Indian life and was perhaps the most influential British writer of the 1890s, exhorted Europeans to unselfish service in distant lands:

Take up the White Man's Burden—
  Send forth the best ye breed—
Go bind your sons to exile
  To serve your captives' need,
To wait in heavy harness,
  On fluttered folk and wild—
Your new-caught, sullen peoples
  Half-devil and half-child.[12]

❖ **A Missionary School** A Swahili schoolboy leads his classmates in a reading lesson in Dar es Salaam in German East Africa before 1914, as portraits of Emperor William II and his wife look down on the classroom. Europeans argued that they were spreading the benefits of a superior civilization with schools like this one, which is unusually solid because of its strategic location in the capital city. *(Source: Ullstein Bilderdienst)*

Many Americans accepted the ideology of the white man's burden. It was an important factor in the decision to rule, rather than liberate, the Philippines after the Spanish-American War. Like their European counterparts, these Americans sincerely believed that their civilization had reached unprecedented heights and that they had unique benefits to bestow on all "less advanced" peoples. Another argument was that imperial government protected natives from tribal warfare as well as cruder forms of exploitation by white settlers and business people.

Peace and stability under European control also permitted the spread of Christianity—the "true" religion. In Africa Catholic and Protestant missionaries competed with Islam south of the Sahara, seeking converts and building schools to spread the Gospel. Many Africans' first real contact with whites was in mission schools. As late as 1942, for example, 97 percent of Nigeria's student population was in mission schools. Some peoples, such as the Ibo in Nigeria, became highly Christianized.

Such occasional successes in black Africa contrasted with the general failure of missionary efforts in India, China, and the Islamic world. There Christians often preached in vain to peoples with ancient, complex religious beliefs. Yet the number of Christian believers around the world did increase substantially in the nineteenth century, and missionary groups kept trying. Unfortunately, "many missionaries had drunk at the well of European racism," and this probably prevented them from doing better.[13]

Critics of Imperialism

The expansion of empire aroused sharp, even bitter, critics. A forceful attack was delivered in 1902, after the unpopular Boer War, by radical English economist J. A. Hobson (1858–1940) in his *Imperialism,* a work that influenced Lenin and others. Hobson contended that the rush to acquire colonies was due to the economic needs of unregulated capitalism, particularly the need of the rich to find outlets for their surplus capital. Yet, Hobson argued, imperial possessions did not pay off economically for the country as a whole. Only unscrupulous special-interest groups profited from them, at the expense of both the European taxpayer and the natives. Moreover, Hobson argued that the quest for empire diverted popular attention away from domestic reform and the need to reduce the great gap between rich and poor. These and similar arguments were not very persuasive, however. Most people then (and now) were sold on the idea that imperialism was economically profitable for the homeland, and a broad and genuine enthusiasm for empire developed among the masses.

Hobson and many other critics struck home, however, with their moral condemnation of whites imperiously ruling nonwhites. They rebelled against crude Social Darwinian thought. "O Evolution, what crimes are committed in thy name!" cried one foe. Another sardonically coined a new beatitude: "Blessed are the strong, for they shall prey on the weak."[14] Kipling and his kind were lampooned as racist bullies whose rule rested on brutality, racial contempt, and the Maxim machine gun. Henry Labouchère, a member of Parliament and prominent spokesman for this position, mocked Kipling's famous poem:

Pile on the Brown Man's burden!
And if ye rouse his hate,
Meet his old-fashioned reasons
With Maxims up to date,
With shells and Dum-Dum bullets
A hundred times plain
The Brown Man's loss must never
Imply the White Man's gain.[15]

Similarly, in *Heart of Darkness* Polish-born novelist Joseph Conrad (1857–1924) castigated the "pure selfishness" of Europeans in "civilizing" Africa; the main character, once a liberal scholar, turns into a savage brute.

Critics charged Europeans with applying a degrading double standard and failing to live up to their own noble ideals. At home Europeans had won or were winning representative government, individual liberties, and a certain equality of opportunity. In their empires Europeans imposed military dictatorships on Africans and Asians; forced them to work involuntarily, almost like slaves; and discriminated against them shamelessly. Only by renouncing imperialism, its critics insisted, and giving captive peoples the freedoms Western society had struggled for since the French Revolution would Europeans be worthy of their traditions. Europeans who denounced the imperialist tide provided colonial peoples with a Western ideology of liberation.

RESPONSES TO WESTERN IMPERIALISM

To peoples in Africa and Asia, Western expansion represented a profoundly disruptive assault. Everywhere it threatened traditional ruling classes, traditional economies, and traditional ways of life. Christian missionaries and European secular ideologies challenged established beliefs and values. Non-Western peoples experienced a crisis of identity, one made all the more painful by the power and arrogance of the white intruders.

The initial response of African and Asian rulers was to try driving the unwelcome foreigners away. This was the case in China, Japan, and the upper Sudan, as we have seen. Violent antiforeign reactions exploded elsewhere again and again, but the superior military technology of the industrialized West almost invariably prevailed. Beaten in battle, many Africans and Asians concentrated on preserving their cultural traditions at all costs. Others found themselves forced to reconsider their initial hostility. Some (such as Ismail of Egypt) concluded that the West was indeed superior in some ways and that it was therefore necessary to reform their societies and copy European achievements. Thus it is possible to think of responses to the Western impact as a spectrum, with "traditionalists" at one end, "westernizers" or "modernizers" at the other, and many shades of opinion in between. Both before and after European domination, the struggle among these groups was often intense. With time, however, the modernizers tended to gain the upper hand.

When the power of both the traditionalists and the modernizers was thoroughly shattered by superior force, the great majority of Asians and Africans accepted imperial rule. Political participation in non-Western lands was historically limited to small elites, and the masses were used to doing what their rulers told them. In these circumstances Europeans, clothed in power and convinced of their righteousness, governed smoothly and effectively. They received considerable support from both traditionalists (local chiefs, landowners, religious leaders) and modernizers (Western-educated professional classes and civil servants).

Nevertheless, imperial rule was in many ways an imposing edifice built on sand. Support for European rule among the conforming and accepting millions was shallow and weak. Thus the conforming masses followed with greater or lesser enthusiasm a few determined personalities who came to oppose the Europeans. Such leaders always arose, both when Europeans ruled directly and when they manipulated native governments, for at least two basic reasons.

First, the nonconformists—the eventual anti-imperialist leaders—developed a burning desire for human dignity. They came to feel that such dignity was incompatible with foreign rule, with its smirks and smiles, its paternalism and condescension. Second, potential leaders found in the Western world the ideologies and justification for their protest. They discovered liberalism, with its credo of civil liberty and political self-determination. They echoed the demands of anti-imperialists in Europe and America that the West live up to its own ideals.

More important, they found themselves attracted to modern nationalism, which asserted that every people had the right to control its own destiny. After 1917 anti-imperialist revolt would find another weapon in Lenin's version of Marxian socialism. Thus the anti-imperialist search for dignity drew strength from Western culture, as is apparent in the development of three major Asian countries—India, Japan, and China.

Empire in India

India was the jewel of the British Empire, and no colonial area experienced a more profound British impact. Unlike Japan and China, which maintained a real or precarious independence, and unlike African territories, which were annexed by Europeans only at the end of the nineteenth century, India

was ruled more or less absolutely by Britain for a very long time.

Arriving in India on the heels of the Portuguese in the seventeenth century, the British East India Company had conquered the last independent native state by 1848. The last "traditional" response to European rule—the attempt by the established ruling classes to drive the white man out by military force—was broken in India in 1857 and 1858. Those were the years of the Great Rebellion (which the British called a "mutiny"), when an insurrection by Muslim and Hindu mercenaries in the British army spread throughout northern and central India before it was finally crushed, primarily by loyal native troops from southern India. Thereafter Britain ruled India directly. India illustrates, therefore, for better and for worse, what generations of European domination might produce.

After 1858 India was ruled by the British Parliament in London and administered by a tiny, all-white civil service in India. In 1900 this elite consisted of fewer than 3,500 top officials, for a population of 300 million. The white elite, backed by white officers and native troops, was competent and generally well disposed toward the welfare of the Indian peasant masses. Yet it practiced strict job discrimination and social segregation, and most of its members quite frankly considered the jumble of Indian peoples and castes to be racially inferior. As Lord Kitchener, one of the most distinguished top military commanders of India, stated:

It is this consciousness of the inherent superiority of the European which has won for us India. However well educated and clever a native may be, and however brave he may prove himself, I believe that no rank we can bestow on him would cause him to be considered an equal of the British officer.[16]

When, for example, the British Parliament in 1883 was considering a major bill to allow Indian judges to try white Europeans in India, the British community rose in protest and defeated the measure. The idea of being judged by Indians was inconceivable to the Europeans, for it was clear to them that the empire in India rested squarely on racial inequality.

In spite of (or perhaps even because of) their strong feelings of racial and cultural superiority, the British acted energetically and introduced many desirable changes to India. Realizing that they needed well-educated Indians to serve as skilled

The British in India This photo suggests not only the incredible power and luxury of the British ruling class in India but also its confidence and self-satisfaction. As one British viceroy said, "We are all British gentlemen engaged in the magnificent work of governing an inferior race." *(Source: Bettmann/Hulton)*

subordinates in the government and army, the British established a modern system of progressive secondary education in which all instruction was in English. Thus through education and government service, the British offered some Indians excellent opportunities for both economic and social advancement. High-caste Hindus, particularly quick to respond, emerged as skillful intermediaries between the British rulers and the Indian people, and soon they formed a new elite profoundly influenced by Western thought and culture.

This new bureaucratic elite played a crucial role in modern economic development, which was a second result of British rule. Irrigation projects for agriculture, the world's third largest railroad network for good communications, and large tea and jute plantations geared to the world economy were all developed. Unfortunately, the lot of the Indian masses improved little, for the increase in production was eaten up by population increase.

Finally, with a well-educated, English-speaking Indian bureaucracy and modern communications, the British created a unified, powerful state. They placed under the same general system of law and administration the different Hindu and Muslim peoples and the vanquished kingdoms of the entire subcontinent—groups that had fought each other for centuries during the Middle Ages and had been repeatedly conquered by Muslim and Mongol invaders. It was as if Europe, with its many states and varieties of Christianity, had been conquered and united in a single great empire.

In spite of these achievements, the decisive reaction to European rule was the rise of nationalism among the Indian elite. No matter how anglicized and necessary a member of the educated classes became, he or she could never become the white ruler's equal. The top jobs, the best clubs, the modern hotels, and even certain railroad compartments were sealed off to brown-skinned men and women. The peasant masses might accept such inequality as the latest version of age-old oppression, but the well-educated, English-speaking elite eventually could not. For the elite, racial discrimination meant not only injured pride but also bitter injustice. It flagrantly contradicted those cherished Western concepts of human rights and equality. Moreover, it was based on dictatorship, no matter how benign.

By 1885 when educated Indians came together to found the predominately Hindu Indian National Congress, demands were increasing for the equality and self-government Britain enjoyed and had already granted white-settler colonies, such as Canada and Australia. By 1907, emboldened in part by Japan's success (see the next section), the radicals in the Indian National Congress were calling for complete independence. Even the moderates were demanding home rule for India through an elected parliament. Although there were sharp divisions between Hindus and Muslims, Indians were finding an answer to the foreign challenge. The common heritage of British rule and Western ideals, along with the reform and revitalization of the Hindu religion, had created a genuine movement for national independence.

The Example of Japan

When Commodore Perry arrived in Japan in 1853 with his crude but effective gunboat diplomacy, Japan was a complex feudal society. At the top stood a figurehead emperor; but for more than two hundred years, real power had been in the hands of a hereditary military governor, the *shogun.* With the help of a warrior-nobility known as *samurai,* the shogun governed a country of hard-working, productive peasants and city dwellers. Often poor and restless, the intensely proud samurai were humiliated by the sudden American intrusion and the unequal treaties with Western countries.

When foreign diplomats and merchants began to settle in Yokohama, radical samurai reacted with a wave of antiforeign terrorism and antigovernment assassinations between 1858 and 1863. The imperialist response was swift and unambiguous. An allied fleet of American, British, Dutch, and French warships demolished key forts, further weakening the power and prestige of the shogun's government. Then in 1867, a coalition led by patriotic samurai seized control of the government with hardly any bloodshed and restored the political power of the emperor. This was the Meiji Restoration, a great turning point in Japanese development.

The immediate, all-important goal of the new government was to meet the foreign threat. The battle cry of the Meiji reformers was "Enrich the state and strengthen the armed forces." Yet how were these tasks to be done? In an about-face that was one of history's most remarkable chapters, the young but well-trained, idealistic but flexible lead-

Japanese Industrialization   The famous Tomioka silk reeling factory pioneered with mass-production techniques and women factory workers in the 1870s. The combination shown here of European technology with native dress symbolizes Japan's successful integration of Western practices into the traditional culture of its society. *(Source: Laurie Platt Winfrey, Inc.)*

ers of Meiji Japan dropped their antiforeign attacks. Convinced that Western civilization was indeed superior in its military and industrial aspects, they initiated from above a series of measures to reform Japan along modern lines. They were convinced that "Japan must be reborn with America its mother and France its father."[17] In the broadest sense, the Meiji leaders tried to harness the power inherent in Europe's dual revolution in order to protect their country and catch up with the West.

In 1871 the new leaders abolished the old feudal structure of aristocratic, decentralized government and formed a strong unified state. Following the example of the French Revolution, they dismantled the four-class legal system and declared social equality. They decreed freedom of movement in a country where traveling abroad had been a most serious crime. They created a free, competitive, government-stimulated economy. Japan began to build railroads and modern factories. Thus the new generation adopted many principles of a free, liberal society, and, as in Europe, such freedom resulted in a tremendously creative release of human energy.

Yet the overriding concern of Japan's political leadership was always a powerful state, and to achieve this, more than liberalism was borrowed from the West. A powerful modern navy was created, and the army was completely reorganized along French and German lines, with three-year military service for all males and a professional officer corps. This army of draftees effectively put down disturbances in the countryside, and in 1877 it was used to crush a major rebellion by feudal elements protesting the loss of their privileges. Japan also borrowed rapidly and adapted skillfully the West's science and modern technology, particularly in industry, medicine, and education. Many Japanese were encouraged to study abroad, and the government paid large salaries to attract foreign experts. These experts were always carefully controlled, however, and replaced by trained Japanese as soon as possible.

By 1890, when the new state was firmly established, the wholesale borrowing of the early restoration had given way to more selective emphasis on those things foreign that were in keeping with Japanese tradition. Following the model of the German Empire, Japan established an authoritarian constitution and rejected democracy. The power of the emperor and his ministers was vast; that of the legislature, limited.

Japan successfully copied the imperialism of Western society. Expansion not only proved that Japan was strong; it also cemented the nation together in a great mission. Having "opened" Korea with the gunboat diplomacy of imperialism in 1876, Japan decisively defeated China in a war over Korea in 1894 to 1895 and took Formosa (modern-day Taiwan). In the next years, Japan competed aggressively with the leading European powers for influence and territory in China, particularly Manchuria. There Japanese and Russian imperialism met and collided. In 1904 Japan attacked Russia without warning, and after a bloody war, Japan emerged with a valuable foothold in China, Russia's former protectorate over Port Arthur (see Map 26.3). By 1910, with the annexation of Korea, Japan had become a major imperialist power, continually expanding its influence in China in spite of sharp protests from its distant Pacific neighbor, the United States.

Japan became the first non-Western country to use an ancient love of country to transform itself and thereby meet the many-sided challenge of Western expansion. Moreover, Japan demonstrated convincingly that a modern Asian nation could defeat and humble a great Western power. Many Chinese nationalists were fascinated by Japan's achievement. A group of patriots in French-ruled southern Vietnam sent Vietnamese students to Japan to learn the island empire's secret of success. Japan provided patriots in Asia and Africa with an inspiring example of national recovery and liberation.

Toward Revolution in China

In 1860 the two-hundred-year-old Manchu Dynasty in China appeared on the verge of collapse. Efforts to repel foreigners had failed, and rebellion and chaos wracked the country. Yet the government drew on its traditional strengths and made a surprising comeback that lasted more than thirty years.

Two factors were crucial in this reversal. First, the traditional ruling groups temporarily produced new and effective leadership. Loyal scholar-statesmen and generals quelled disturbances such as the great Tai Ping rebellion. The empress dowager Tzu Hsi, a truly remarkable woman, governed in the name of her young son and combined shrewd insight with vigorous action to revitalize the bureaucracy.

❖ **The Empress Dowager Tzu Hsi** drew on conservative forces, like the court eunuchs surrounding her here, to maintain her power. Three years after her death in 1908, a revolution broke out and forced the last Chinese emperor, a boy of six, to abdicate. *(Source: Courtesy of the Freer Gallery of Art, Smithsonian Institution, Washington, D.C.)*

Second, destructive foreign aggression lessened, for the Europeans had obtained their primary goal of commercial and diplomatic relations. Indeed, some Europeans contributed to the dynasty's recovery. A talented Irishman effectively reorganized China's customs office and increased the government tax receipts, while a sympathetic American diplomat represented China in foreign lands and helped strengthen the central government. Such efforts dovetailed with the dynasty's efforts to adopt some aspects of Western government and technology while maintaining traditional Chinese values and beliefs.

The parallel movement toward domestic reform and limited cooperation with the West collapsed under the blows of Japanese imperialism. The Sino-Japanese war of 1894 to 1895 and the subsequent harsh peace treaty revealed China's helplessness in the face of aggression, triggering a rush for foreign concessions and protectorates in China. At the high point of this rush in 1898, it appeared that the European powers might actually divide China among themselves, as they had recently divided Africa. Probably only the jealousy each na-

tion felt toward its imperialist competitors saved China from partition, although the U.S. Open Door policy, which opposed formal annexation of Chinese territory, may have helped tip the balance. In any event, the tempo and impact of foreign penetration greatly accelerated after 1894.

So, too, did the intensity and radicalism of the Chinese reaction. Like the leaders of the Meiji Restoration, some modernizers saw salvation in Western institutions. In 1898 the government launched a desperate "hundred days of reform" in an attempt to meet the foreign challenge. More radical reformers, such as the revolutionary Sun Yat-sen (1866–1925), who came from the peasantry and was educated in Hawaii by Christian missionaries, sought to overthrow the dynasty altogether and establish a republic.

On the other side, some traditionalists turned back toward ancient practices, political conservatism, and fanatical hatred of the "foreign devils." "Protect the country, destroy the foreigner" was their simple motto. Such conservative, antiforeign patriots had often clashed with foreign missionaries, whom they charged with undermining reverence for ancestors and thereby threatening the Chinese family and the entire society. In the agony of defeat and unwanted reforms, secret societies such as the Boxers rebelled. In northeastern China, more than two hundred foreign missionaries and several thousand Chinese Christians were killed. Once again the imperialist response was swift and harsh. Peking was occupied and plundered by foreign armies. A heavy indemnity was imposed.

The years after the Boxer Rebellion (1900–1903) were ever-more troubled. Anarchy and foreign influence spread as the power and prestige of the Manchu Dynasty declined still further. Antiforeign, antigovernment revolutionary groups agitated and plotted. Finally in 1912, a spontaneous uprising toppled the Manchu Dynasty. After thousands of years of emperors and empires, a loose coalition of revolutionaries proclaimed a Western-style republic and called for an elected parliament. The transformation of China under the impact of expanding Western society entered a new phase, and the end was not in sight.

SUMMARY

In the nineteenth century, the industrializing West entered the third and most dynamic phase of its centuries-old expansion into non-Western lands. In so doing, Western nations profitably subordinated those lands to their economic interests, sent forth millions of emigrants, and established political influence in Asia and vast political empires in Africa. The reasons for this culminating surge were many, but the economic thrust of robust industrial capitalism, an ever-growing lead in technology, and the competitive pressures of European nationalism were particularly important.

Western expansion had far-reaching consequences. For the first time in human history, the world became in many ways a single unit. Moreover, European expansion diffused the ideas and techniques of a highly developed civilization. Yet the West relied on force to conquer and rule, and it treated non-Western peoples as racial inferiors. Thus non-Western elites, often armed with Western doctrines, gradually responded to the Western challenge. They launched a national, anti-imperialist struggle for dignity, genuine independence, and modernization. This struggle would emerge as a central drama of world history after the great

European civil war of 1914 to 1918, which reduced the West's technological advantage and shattered its self-confidence and complacent moral superiority.

NOTES

1. Quoted in A. Waley, *The Opium War Through Chinese Eyes* (New York: Macmillan, 1958), p. 29.
2. Quoted in J. W. Hall, *Japan, from Prehistory to Modern Times* (New York: Delacorte Press, 1970), p. 250.
3. Quoted in R. Hallett, *Africa to 1875* (Ann Arbor: University of Michigan Press, 1970), p. 109.
4. Quoted in Earl of Cromer, *Modern Egypt* (London, 1911), p. 48.
5. Quoted in T. Blegen, *Norwegian Migration to America,* vol. 2 (Northfield, Minn.: Norwegian-American Historical Association, 1940), p. 468.
6. Quoted in I. Howe, *World of Our Fathers* (New York: Harcourt Brace Jovanovich, 1976), p. 25.
7. Quoted in C. A. Price, *The Great White Walls Are Built: Restrictive Immigration to North America and Australia, 1836–1888* (Canberra: Australian National University Press, 1974), p. 175.
8. Quoted in W. L. Langer, *European Alliances and Alignments, 1871–1890* (New York: Vintage Books, 1931), p. 290.
9. Quoted in J. Ellis, *The Social History of the Machine Gun* (New York: Pantheon Books, 1975), pp. 86, 101.
10. Quoted in G. H. Nadel and P. Curtis, eds., *Imperialism and Colonialism* (New York: Macmillan, 1964), p. 94.
11. Quoted in W. L. Langer, *The Diplomacy of Imperialism,* 2d ed. (New York: Alfred A. Knopf, 1951), pp. 86, 88.
12. Rudyard Kipling, *The Five Nations* (London, 1903), quoted by the permission of Mrs. George Bambridge, Methuen & Company, and Doubleday & Company, Inc.
13. E. H. Berman, "African Responses to Christian Mission Education," *African Studies Review* 17 (1974): 530.
14. Quoted in Langer, *The Diplomacy of Imperialism,* p. 88.
15. Quoted in Ellis, pp. 99–100.
16. Quoted in K. M. Panikkar, *Asia and Western Dominance: A Survey of the Vasco da Gama Epoch of Asian History* (London: George Allen & Unwin, 1959), p. 116.
17. Quoted in Hall, p. 289.

SUGGESTED READING

General surveys of European expansion in a broad perspective include R. Betts, *Europe Overseas* (1968); A. Thornton, *Imperialism in the Twentieth Century* (1977); T. Smith, *The Patterns of Imperialism* (1981); and W. Woodruff, *Impact of Western Man* (1967), which has an extensive bibliography. D. K. Fieldhouse has written two fine surveys, *Economics and Empire, 1830–1914* (1970) and *Colonialism, 1870–1945* (1981). G. Barraclough, *An Introduction to Contemporary History* (1964), argues powerfully that Western imperialism and the non-Western reaction to it have been crucial in world history since about 1890. J. A. Hobson's classic *Imperialism* (1902) is readily available, and the Marxist-Leninist case is effectively presented in V. G. Kieran, *Marxism and Imperialism* (1975). Two excellent anthologies on the problem of European expansion are the volume by Nadel and Curtis cited in the Notes, and H. Wright, ed., *The "New Imperialism,"* rev. ed. (1975).

Britain's leading position in European imperialism is examined in a lively way by B. Porter, *The Lion's Share* (1976); J. Morris, *Pax Britannica* (1968); and D. Judd, *The Victorian Empire* (1970), a stunning pictorial history. G. Stocking, *Victorian Anthropology* (1987), is a brilliant analysis of the cultural and racial implications of Western expansion. B. Semmel has written widely on the intellectual foundations of English expansion, as in *The Rise of Free Trade Imperialism* (1970). J. Gallagher and R. Robinson, *Africa and the Victorians: The Climax of Imperialism* (1961), is an influential reassessment. H. Brunschwig, *French Colonialism, 1871–1914* (1966), and W. Baumgart, *Imperialism: The Idea and Reality of British and French Colonial Expansion* (1982), are well-balanced studies. A. Moorehead, *The White Nile* (1971), tells the fascinating story of the European exploration of the mysterious Upper Nile. Volumes 5 and 6 of K. Latourette, *History of the Expansion of Christianity,* 7 vols. (1937–1945), examine the powerful impulse for missionary work in non-European areas. D. Headrick stresses Western technological superiority in *Tools of Empire* (1981). C. Erikson, *Emigration from Europe, 1815–1914* (1976), and R. Vecoli and S. Sinke, eds., *A Century of European Migrations, 1830–1930* (1991), are valuable general studies.

Howe and Blegen, cited in the Notes, provide dramatic accounts of Jewish and Norwegian migration to the United States. Most other migrant groups have also found their historians: M. Walker, *Germany and the Emigration, 1816–1885* (1964), and W. Adams, *Ireland and Irish Emigration to the New World* (reissued 1967), are outstanding. Langer's volumes consider the diplomatic aspects of imperialism in exhaustive detail. Ellis's well-illustrated study of the machine gun is fascinating, as is Price on the restriction of Asian migration to Australia. All these works are cited in the Notes.

E. Wolf, *Europe and the People Without History* (1982), considers, with skill and compassion, the impact of imperialism on non-Western peoples. Two unusual and provocative studies on personal relations between European rulers and non-European subjects are D. Mannoni, *Prospero and Caliban: The Psychology of Colonialization* (1964), and F. Fanon, *Wretched of the Earth* (1965), a bitter attack on white racism by a black psychologist active in the Algerian revolution. V. Ware, *Beyond the Pale: White Women, Racism and History* (1992), examines the complex role of European women in imperialism. Novels also bring the psychological and human dimensions of imperialism alive. H. Rider Haggard, *King Solomon's Mines,* portrays the powerful appeal of adventure in exotic lands; Rudyard Kipling, the greatest writer of European expansion, is at his stirring best in *Kim* and *Soldiers Three.* Joseph Conrad unforgettably probes European motives in *Heart of Darkness,* whereas André Gide, *The Immoralist,* closely examines European moral corruption in North Africa. William Boyd, *An Ice-Cream War,* a good story of British and Germans fighting each other in Africa during the First World War, is a favorite with students.

Hall, cited in the Notes, is an excellent introduction to the history of Japan. Waley, also cited in the Notes, has written extensively and well on China. I. Hsü, *The Rise of Modern China,* 2d ed. (1975), and K. Latourette, *The Chinese: Their History and Culture,* rev. ed. (1964), are fine histories with many suggestions for further reading. E. Reischauer's topical survey, *Japan: The Story of a Nation* (1981), is recommended, as are T. Huber, *The Revolutionary Origins of Modern Japan* (1981), and Y. Fukuzawa, *Autobiography* (1966), the personal account of a leading intellectual who witnessed the emergence of modern Japan.

G. Perry, *The Middle East: Fourteen Islamic Centuries* (1983), concisely surveys nineteenth-century developments and provides an up-to-date bibliography. B. Lewis, *The Middle East and the West* (1963), is a penetrating analysis of the impact of Western ideas on Middle Eastern thought. Hallett, cited in the Notes, and R. July, *A History of the African People* (1970), contain excellent introductions to Africa in the age of imperialism. J. D. Fage, *A History of Africa* (1978), is also recommended. A classic study of Western expansion from an Indian viewpoint is Panikkar's volume mentioned in the Notes. S. Wolpert, *A New History of India,* 2d ed. (1982), incorporates recent scholarship in a wide-ranging study that is highly recommended.

27

The Great Break: War and Revolution

✢ In the summer of 1914, the nations of Europe went willingly to war. They believed they had no other choice. Moreover, both peoples and governments confidently expected a short war leading to a decisive victory. Such a war, they believed, would "clear the air," and European society would be able to go on as before.

These expectations were almost totally mistaken. The First World War was long, indecisive, and tremendously destructive. To the shell-shocked generation of survivors, it was known simply as the Great War: the war of unprecedented scope and intensity. From today's perspective it is clear that the First World War marked a great break in the course of Western historical development since the French and Industrial revolutions. A noted British political scientist has gone so far as to say that even in victorious and relatively fortunate Great Britain, the First World War was *the* great turning point in government and society, "as in everything else in modern British history. . . . There's a much greater difference between the Britain of 1914 and, say, 1920, than between the Britain of 1920 and today."[1] This strong statement contains a great amount of truth, for all of Europe as well as for Britain.

John Singer Sargent's World War I painting *Gassed. (Source: By courtesy of the Trustees of the Imperial War Museum)*

- What caused the Great War?
- How did the war lead to revolution and the fall of empires?
- How and why did war and revolution have such enormous and destructive consequences?
- How did the years of trauma and bloodshed form elements of today's world, many of which people now accept and even cherish?

These are the questions this chapter will try to answer.

THE FIRST WORLD WAR

The First World War was so long and destructive because it involved all the Great Powers and because it quickly degenerated into a senseless military stalemate. Like evenly matched boxers in a championship bout, the two sides tried to wear each other down. But there was no referee to call a draw, only the blind hammering of a life-or-death struggle.

The Bismarckian System of Alliances

The Franco-Prussian War and the founding of the German Empire opened a new era in international relations. France was decisively defeated in 1871 and forced to pay a large war indemnity and give up Alsace-Lorraine. In ten short years, from 1862 to 1871, Bismarck had made Prussia-Germany—traditionally the weakest of the Great Powers—the most powerful nation in Europe (see pages 838–842). Had Bismarck been a Napoleon I or a Hitler, for whom no gain was ever sufficient, continued expansion would no doubt sooner or later have raised a powerful coalition against the new German Empire. Yet he was not. As Bismarck never tired of repeating after 1871, Germany was a "satisfied" power. Within Europe, Germany had no territorial ambitions and only wanted peace.

But how was peace to be preserved? Bismarck's first concern was to keep an embittered France diplomatically isolated and without military allies. His second concern was the threat to peace posed by the east, by Austria-Hungary and from Russia. Those two enormous multinational empires had many conflicting interests, particularly in the Balkans, where the Ottoman Empire—the "sick man of Europe"—was ebbing fast. There was a real threat that Germany might be dragged into a great war between the two rival empires. Bismarck's solution was a system of alliances (Figure 27.1) to restrain both Russia and Austria-Hungary, to prevent conflict between them, and to isolate a hostile France, which could never forget the loss of Alsace-Lorraine.

A first step was the creation in 1873 of the conservative Three Emperors' League, which linked the monarchs of Austria-Hungary, Germany, and Russia in an alliance against radical movements. In 1877 and 1878, when Russia's victories over the Ottoman Empire threatened the balance of Austrian and Russian interests in the Balkans and the balance of British and Russian interests in the Middle East, Bismarck played the role of sincere peace maker. At the Congress of Berlin in 1878, he saw that Austria obtained the right to "occupy and administer" the Ottoman provinces of Bosnia and Herzegovina to counterbalance Russian gains; at the same time independent Balkan states were carved from the disintegrating Ottoman Empire.

Bismarck's balancing efforts at the congress infuriated Russian nationalists, and this led Bismarck to conclude a defensive military alliance with Austria against Russia in 1879. Motivated by tensions with France, Italy joined Germany and Austria in 1882, thereby forming what became known as the Triple Alliance.

Bismarck continued to work for peace in eastern Europe, seeking to neutralize tensions between Austria-Hungary and Russia. In 1881 he capitalized on their mutual fears and cajoled them both into a secret alliance with Germany. This Alliance of the Three Emperors lasted until 1887. It established the principle of cooperation among all three powers in any further division of the Ottoman Empire, while each state pledged friendly neutrality in case one of the three found itself at war with a fourth power (except the Ottoman Empire).

Bismarck also maintained good relations with Britain and Italy while encouraging France in Africa but keeping France isolated in Europe. In 1887 Russia declined to renew the Alliance of the Three Emperors because of new tensions in the Balkans. Bismarck craftily substituted the Russian-German Reinsurance Treaty, by which both states promised neutrality if the other was attacked.

Bismarck's accomplishments in foreign policy after 1871 were great. For almost a generation, he maintained German leadership in international affairs, and he worked successfully for peace by managing conflicts and by restraining Austria-Hungary and Russia with defensive alliances.

The Rival Blocs

In 1890 the young, impetuous emperor William II dismissed Bismarck, in part because of the chancellor's friendly policy toward Russia since the 1870s. William then adamantly refused to renew the Russian-German Reinsurance Treaty, in spite of Russian willingness to do so. This fateful departure in foreign affairs prompted long-isolated republican

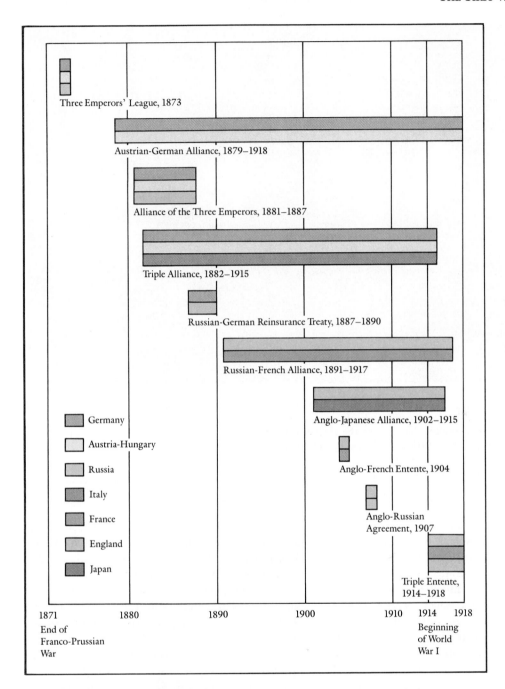

Germany
Austria-Hungary
Russia
Italy
France
England
Japan

Three Emperors' League, 1873

Austrian-German Alliance, 1879–1918

Alliance of the Three Emperors, 1881–1887

Triple Alliance, 1882–1915

Russian-German Reinsurance Treaty, 1887–1890

Russian-French Alliance, 1891–1917

Anglo-Japanese Alliance, 1902–1915

Anglo-French Entente, 1904

Anglo-Russian Agreement, 1907

Triple Entente, 1914–1918

1871
End of
Franco-Prussian
War

1880   1890   1900   1910   1914   1918

Beginning
of World
War I

✦ **FIGURE 27.1 The Alliance System After 1871** Bismarck's subtle diplomacy maintained reasonably good relations among the eastern monarchies—Germany, Russia, and Austria-Hungary—and kept France isolated. The situation changed dramatically in 1891, when the Russian-French Alliance divided the Great Powers into two fairly equal military blocs.

France to court absolutist Russia, offering loans, arms, and friendship. In both countries there were enthusiastic public demonstrations, and in St. Petersburg harbor the autocratic Alexander III stood barheaded on a French battleship while a band played the "Marseillaise," the hymn of the Revolution. A preliminary agreement between the two countries was reached in 1891, and in early 1894

❖ **The Congress of Berlin, 1878** With the Austrian representative on his right and with other participants looking on, Bismarck the mediator symbolically seals the hard-won agreement by shaking hands with the chief Russian negotiator. The Great Powers often relied on such special conferences to settle their international disputes. *(Source: The Bettmann Archive)*

France and Russia became military allies. This alliance (see Figure 27.1) was to remain in effect as long as the Triple Alliance of Austria, Germany, and Italy existed. As a result, continental Europe was dangerously divided into two rival blocs.

Great Britain's foreign policy became increasingly crucial. Long content with "splendid isolation" and no permanent alliances, Britain after 1891 was the only uncommitted Great Power. Could Britain afford to remain isolated, or would it feel compelled to take sides? Alliance with France or Russia certainly seemed highly unlikely. With a vast and rapidly expanding empire, Britain was often in serious conflict with these countries around the world.

Britain also squabbled with Germany: Emperor William II was a master of tactless public statements, and Britain found Germany's pursuit of greater world power after about 1897 disquieting. Nevertheless, many Germans and some Britons believed that their leaders would eventually formalize

the "natural alliance" they felt already united the advanced, racially related Germanic and Anglo-Saxon peoples. Alas, such an understanding never materialized. Instead, the generally good relations that had prevailed between Prussia and Great Britain ever since the mid-eighteenth century, and certainly under Bismarck, gave way to a bitter Anglo-German rivalry.

There were several reasons for this tragic development. Commercial rivalry in world markets between Germany and Great Britain increased sharply in the 1890s. Above all, Germany's decision in 1900 to expand greatly its battle fleet posed a challenge to Britain's long-standing naval supremacy. This decision coincided with the hard-fought Boer War (1899–1902) between the British and the tiny Dutch republics of South Africa, which had a major impact on British policy. British political leaders saw that Britain was overextended around the world. The Boer War also brought into the open widespread anti-British feeling as editorial writers in many nations denounced this latest manifestation of British imperialism. There was even talk of Germany, Austria, France, and Russia forming a grand alliance against the bloated but insatiable British Empire. Therefore, British leaders prudently set about shoring up their exposed position with alliances and agreements.

Britain improved its often-strained relations with the United States and in 1902 concluded a formal alliance with Japan (see Figure 27.1). Britain then responded favorably to the advances of France's skillful foreign minister, Théophile Delcassé, who wanted better relations with Britain and was willing to accept British rule in Egypt in return for British support of French plans to dominate Morocco. The resulting Anglo-French Entente of 1904 settled all outstanding colonial disputes between Britain and France.

Frustrated by Britain's turn toward France in 1904 and wanting a diplomatic victory to gain greater popularity at home, Germany's leaders decided to test the strength of the entente and drive a wedge between Britain and France. First Germany threatened and bullied France into dismissing Delcassé. However, rather than accept the typical territorial payoff of imperial competition—a slice of French jungle somewhere in Africa or a port in Morocco—in return for French primacy in Morocco, the Germans foolishly rattled their swords by insisting in 1905 on an international conference on the whole Moroccan question; nor did the Germans present precise or reasonable demands. Germany's crude bullying forced France and Britain closer together, and Germany left the resulting Algeciras Conference of 1906 empty-handed and isolated (except for Austria-Hungary).

The result of the Moroccan crisis and the Algeciras Conference was something of a diplomatic revolution. Britain, France, Russia, and even the United States began to see Germany as a potential threat, a would-be intimidator that might seek to dominate all Europe. At the same time, German

German Warships Under Full Steam As these impressive ships engaged in battle exercises in 1907 suggest, Germany did succeed in building a large modern navy. But Britain was equally determined to maintain its naval superiority, and the spiraling arms race helped poison relations between the two countries. *(Source: Bibliothèque des Arts Décoratifs/Jean-Loup Charmet)*

leaders began to see sinister plots to "encircle" Germany and block its development as a world power. In 1907 Russia, battered by its disastrous war with Japan and the revolution of 1905, agreed to settle its quarrels with Great Britain in Persia and central Asia with a special Anglo-Russian Agreement (see Figure 27.1). As a result of that agreement, Germany's blustering paranoia increased, as did Britain's thinly disguised hostility.

Germany's decision to add a large, enormously expensive fleet of big-gun battleships to its already expanding navy also heightened tensions after 1907. German nationalists, led by the extremely persuasive Admiral Alfred von Tirpitz, saw a large navy as the legitimate mark of a great world power and as a source of pride and patriotic unity. But British leaders such as Lloyd George saw it as a detestable military challenge, which forced them to spend the "People's Budget" on battleships rather than social welfare. Ongoing economic rivalry also contributed to distrust and hostility between the two nations. Unscrupulous journalists and special-interest groups in both countries portrayed healthy competition in foreign trade and investment as a form of economic warfare.

Many educated shapers of public opinion and ordinary people in Britain and Germany were increasingly locked in a fateful "love-hate" relationship between the two countries. Proud nationalists in both countries simultaneously admired and feared the power and accomplishments of their nearly equal rival. In 1909 the mass-circulation London *Daily Mail* hysterically informed its readers in a series of reports that "Germany is deliberately preparing to destroy the British Empire."[2] By then Britain was psychologically, if not officially, in the Franco-Russian camp. The leading nations of Europe were divided into two hostile blocs, both ill-prepared to deal with upheaval on Europe's southeastern frontier.

The Outbreak of War

In the early years of this century, war in the Balkans was as inevitable as anything can be in human history. The reason was simple: nationalism was destroying the Ottoman Empire and threatening to break up the Austro-Hungarian Empire. The only questions were what kinds of wars would occur and where they would lead.

Greece had long before led the struggle for national liberation, winning its independence in 1832. In 1875 widespread nationalist rebellion in the Ottoman Empire had resulted in Turkish repression, Russian intervention, and Great Power tensions. Bismarck had helped resolve this crisis at the 1878 Congress of Berlin, which worked out the partial division of Turkish possessions in Europe. Austria-Hungary obtained the right to "occupy and administer" Bosnia and Herzegovina. Serbia and Rumania won independence, and a part of Bulgaria won local autonomy. The Ottoman Empire retained important Balkan holdings, for Austria-Hungary and Russia each feared the other's domination of totally independent states in the area (Map 27.1).

After 1878 the siren call of imperialism lured European energies, particularly Russian energies, away from the Balkans. This diversion helped preserve the fragile balance of interests in southeastern Europe. By 1903, however, Balkan nationalism was on the rise once again. Serbia led the way, becoming openly hostile toward both Austria-Hungary and the Ottoman Empire. The Serbs, a Slavic people, looked to Slavic Russia for support of their national aspirations. To block Serbian expansion and to take advantage of Russia's weakness after the revolution of 1905, Austria in 1908 formally annexed Bosnia and Herzegovina, with their large Serbian, Croatian, and Muslim populations. The kingdom of Serbia erupted in rage but could do nothing without Russian support.

Then in 1912, in the First Balkan War, Serbia turned southward. With Greece and Bulgaria it took Macedonia from the Ottoman Empire and then quarreled with Bulgaria over the spoils of victory—a dispute that led in 1913 to the Second Balkan War. Austria intervened in 1913 and forced Serbia to give up Albania. After centuries, nationalism had finally destroyed the Ottoman Empire in Europe (Map 27.2). This sudden but long-awaited event elated the Balkan nationalists and dismayed the leaders of multinational Austria-Hungary. The former hoped and the latter feared that Austria might be next to be broken apart.

Within this tense context, Archduke Francis Ferdinand, heir to the Austrian and Hungarian thrones, and his wife, Sophie, were assassinated by Bosnian revolutionaries on June 28, 1914, during a state visit to the Bosnian capital of Sarajevo. The assassins were closely connected to the ultranationalist Serbian society The Black Hand. This revolutionary group was secretly supported by members of the Serbian government and was dedicated to

❖ **MAP 27.1 The Balkans After the Congress of Berlin, 1878** The Ottoman Empire suffered large territorial losses but remained a power in the Balkans.

❖ **MAP 27.2 The Balkans in 1914** Ethnic boundaries did not follow political boundaries, and Serbian national aspirations threatened Austria-Hungary.

uniting all Serbians in a single state. Although the leaders of Austria-Hungary did not and could not know all the details of Serbia's involvement in the assassination plot, they concluded after some hesitation that Serbia had to be severely punished once and for all. After nearly a month of maneuvering, on July 23 Austria-Hungary presented Serbia with an unconditional ultimatum.

The Serbian government had just forty-eight hours in which to agree to cease all subversion in Austria and all anti-Austrian propaganda in Serbia. Moreover, a thorough investigation of all aspects of the assassination at Sarajevo was to be undertaken in Serbia by a joint commission of Serbian and Austrian officials. These demands amounted to control of the Serbian state. When Serbia replied moderately but evasively, Austria began to mobilize

and then declared war on Serbia on July 28. Thus a desperate multinational Austria-Hungary deliberately chose war in a last-ditch attempt to stem the rising tide of hostile nationalism within its borders and save the existing state. The "Third Balkan War" had begun.

Of prime importance in Austria-Hungary's fateful decision was Germany's unconditional support. Emperor William II and his chancellor, Theobald von Bethmann-Hollweg, gave Austria-Hungary a "blank check" and urged aggressive measures in early July, even though they realized that war between Austria and Russia was the most probable result. They knew Russian pan-Slavs saw Russia not only as the protector but also as the eventual liberator of southern Slavs. As one pan-Slav had said much earlier, "Austria can hold her part of the

Slavonian mass as long as Turkey holds hers and vice versa."[3] At the very least a resurgent Russia could not stand by, as in the Bosnian crisis, and simply watch the Serbs be crushed. Yet Bethmann-Hollweg apparently hoped that while Russia (and therefore France) would go to war, Great Britain would remain neutral, unwilling to fight for "Russian aggression" in the distant Balkans. After all, Britain had reached only "friendly understandings" with France and Russia on colonial questions and had no alliance with either power.

In fact, the diplomatic situation was already out of control. Military plans and timetables began to dictate policy. Russia, a vast country, would require much longer to mobilize its armies than Germany and Austria-Hungary. On July 28 as Austrian armies bombarded Belgrade, Tsar Nicholas II ordered a partial mobilization against Austria-Hungary. Almost immediately he found that this was impossible. All the complicated mobilization plans of the Russian general staff had assumed a war with both Austria and Germany: Russia could not mobilize against one without mobilizing against the other. Therefore, on July 29 Russia ordered full mobilization and in effect declared general war. For, as French general Boisdeffre had said to the agreeing Russian tsar when the Franco-Russian military convention was being negotiated in 1892, "mobilization is a declaration of war."[4]

The same tragic subordination of political considerations to military strategy descended on Germany. The German general staff had also thought only in terms of a two-front war. The staff's plan for war—the Schlieffen plan, the work of Count Alfred von Schlieffen, chief of the German general staff from 1891 to 1906 and a professional military man—called for knocking out France first with a lightning attack through neutral Belgium before turning on Russia.

Thus on August 2, 1914, General Helmuth von Moltke, "acting under a dictate of self-preservation," demanded that Belgium permit German armies to pass through its territory. Belgium, whose neutrality had been solemnly guaranteed in 1839 by all the great states including Prussia, refused. Germany attacked. Thus Germany's terrible, politically disastrous response to a war in the Balkans was an all-out invasion of France by way of the plains of neutral Belgium on August 3. In the face of this act of aggression, Great Britain joined France and declared war on Germany the following day. The First World War had begun.

Reflections on the Origins of the War

Although few events in history have aroused such interest and controversy as the coming of the First World War, the question of immediate causes and responsibilities can be answered with considerable certainty. Austria-Hungary deliberately started the Third Balkan War. A war for the right to survive was Austria-Hungary's desperate, although understandable, response to the aggressive, yet understandable, revolutionary drive of Serbian nationalists to unify their people in a single state. Moreover, in spite of Russian intervention in the quarrel, it is clear that from the beginning of the crisis Germany not only pushed and goaded Austria-Hungary but was also responsible for turning a little war into the Great War by means of a sledgehammer attack on Belgium and France. Why Germany was so aggressive in 1914 is less certain.

Diplomatic historians stress that German leaders lost control of the international system after Bismarck's resignation in 1890. They felt increasingly that Germany's status as a world power was declining, while that of Britain, France, Russia, and the United States was growing. Indeed, the powers of what officially became in August 1914 the Triple Entente—Great Britain, France, and Russia—were checking Germany's vague but real aspirations as well as working to strangle Austria-Hungary, Germany's only real ally. Germany's aggression in 1914 reflected the failure of all European leaders, not just those in Germany, to incorporate Bismarck's mighty empire permanently and peacefully into the international system.

Another more controversial interpretation, which has been developed by anticonservative German historians in recent years, argues that domestic conflicts and social tensions lay at the root of Germany's increasingly belligerent foreign policy from the late 1890s onward. Germany industrialized and urbanized rapidly after 1870 and established a popularly elected parliament. But German society was not democraticized, and ultimate political power remained concentrated in the hands of the monarchy, the army, and the Prussian nobility. Determined to hold on to power and increasingly frightened before 1914 by the rising socialist movement, the German ruling class was willing to gamble on diplomatic victory and even on war as the means of rallying the masses to its side and preserving its privileged position. Historians have also discerned similar, if less clear-cut, behavior in

Great Britain, where leaders faced civil war in northern Ireland, and in Russia, where the revolution of 1905 had brought tsardom to its knees.

This stimulating debate over social tensions and domestic political factors correctly suggests that the triumph of nationalism was a crucial underlying precondition of the Great War. Nationalism was at the heart of the Balkan wars, in the form of Serbian aspirations and the grandiose pan-German versus pan-Slavic racism of some fanatics. Nationalism also drove the spiraling arms race. Broad popular commitment to "my country right or wrong" weakened groups that thought in terms of international communities and consequences. Thus the big international bankers, who were frightened by the prospect of war in July 1914, and the extreme-left socialists, who believed that the enemy was at home and not abroad, were equally out of step with national feeling. In each country the great majority of the population enthusiastically embraced the outbreak of war in August 1914. In each country people believed that their country had been wronged, and they rallied to defend it. Patriotic nationalism brought unity in the short run.

Nonetheless, the wealthy governing classes certainly underestimated the risk of war to themselves in 1914. They had forgotten that great wars and great social revolutions very often go hand in hand. Metternich's alliance of conservative forces in support of international peace and the social status quo had become only a distant memory.

The First Battle of the Marne

When the Germans invaded Belgium in August 1914, they and everyone else believed that the war would be short, for urban society rested on the food and raw materials of the world economy: "The boys will be home by Christmas." The Belgian army heroically defended its homeland, however, and fell back in good order to join a rapidly landed British army corps near the Franco-Belgian border. This action complicated the original Schlieffen plan of concentrating German armies on the right wing and boldly capturing Paris in a vast encircling movement. Moreover, the German left wing in Lorraine failed to retreat, thwarting the plan to suck French armies into Germany and then annihilate them. Instead, by the end of August, dead-tired German soldiers were advancing along an enormous front in the scorching summer heat. The neatly designed prewar plan to surround Paris

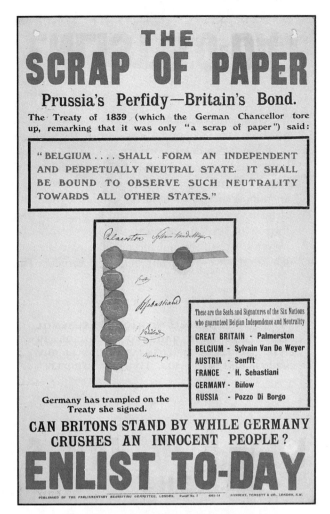

❖ **This British Poster** shows the signature page of the 1839 treaty guaranteeing the neutrality of Belgium. When German armies invaded Belgium in 1914, Chancellor Bethmann-Hollweg cynically dismissed the treaty as a "scrap of paper"—a perfect line for anti-German propaganda. *(Source: By courtesy of the Trustees of the Imperial War Museum)*

from the north and west had been thrown into confusion.

French armies totaling 1 million, reinforced by more than 100,000 British troops, had retreated in orderly fashion before Germany's 1.5 million men in the field. Under the leadership of the steel-nerved General Joseph Joffre, the French attacked a gap in the German line at the Battle of the Marne on September 6. For three days, France threw everything into the attack. At one point, the French government desperately requisitioned all the taxis of Paris to rush reserves to the troops at the front. Finally, the Germans fell back. Paris and France had been miraculously saved.

Stalemate and Slaughter

The attempts of French and British armies to turn the German retreat into a rout were unsuccessful, however, and so were moves by both sides to outflank each other in northern France. As a result, both sides began to dig trenches to protect themselves from machine gun fire. By November 1914 an unbroken line of trenches extended from the Belgian ports through northern France past the fortress of Verdun and on to the Swiss frontier.

In the face of this unexpected stalemate, slaughter on the western front began in earnest. The defenders on both sides dug in behind rows of trenches, mines, and barbed wire. For days and even weeks, ceaseless shelling by heavy artillery supposedly "softened up" the enemy in a given area (and also signaled the coming attack). Then young draftees and their junior officers went "over the top" of the trenches in frontal attacks on the enemy's line.

The cost in lives was staggering; the gains in territory, minuscule. The massive French and British offensives during 1915 never gained more than 3 miles of blood-soaked earth from the enemy. In the Battle of the Somme in the summer of 1916, the British and French gained an insignificant 125 square miles at the cost of 600,000 dead or wounded, while the Germans lost 500,000 men.

The Fruits of War The extent of carnage, the emotional damage, and the physical destruction on the western front were equally unprecedented. Once-great cathedrals standing in ruin symbolized the disaster. *(Source: UPI/Bettmann Newsphotos)*

That same year, the unsuccessful German campaign against Verdun cost 700,000 lives on both sides. British poet Siegfried Sassoon (1886–1967) wrote of the Somme offensive, "I am staring at a sunlit picture of Hell."

Terrible 1917 saw General Robert Nivelle's French army almost destroyed in a grand spring attack at Champagne. At Passchendaele in the fall, the British traded 400,000 casualties for 50 square miles of Belgian Flanders. The hero of Erich Remarque's great novel *All Quiet on the Western Front* (1929) describes one such attack:

We see men living with their skulls blown open; we see soldiers run with their two feet cut off. . . . Still the little piece of convulsed earth in which we lie is held. We have yielded no more than a few hundred yards of it as a prize to the enemy. But on every yard there lies a dead man.

Such was war on the western front.

The war of the trenches shattered an entire generation of young men. Millions who could have provided political creativity and leadership after the war were forever missing. Moreover, those who lived through the holocaust were maimed, shell-shocked, embittered, and profoundly disillusioned. The young soldiers went to war believing in the world of their leaders and elders, the pre-1914 world of order, progress, and patriotism. Then, in Remarque's words, the "first bombardment showed us our mistake, and under it the world as they had taught it to us broke in pieces." For many, the sacrifice and comradeship of the battlefield became life's crucial experience, which "soft" civilians could never understand. A chasm opened up between veterans and civilians, making the hard postwar reconstruction all the more difficult.

The Widening War

On the eastern front, slaughter did not degenerate into suicidal trench warfare. With the outbreak of the war, the "Russian steamroller" immediately moved into eastern Germany. Very badly damaged by the Germans under Generals Paul von Hindenburg and Erich Ludendorff at the battles of Tannenberg and the Masurian Lakes in August and September 1914, Russia never threatened Germany again. On the Austrian front, enormous armies seesawed back and forth, suffering enormous losses. Austro-Hungarian armies were repulsed twice by little Serbia in bitter fighting. But with the help of German forces, they reversed the Russian advances of 1914 and forced the Russians to retreat deep into their own territory in the eastern campaign of 1915. A staggering 2.5 million Russians were killed, wounded, or taken prisoner that year.

These changing tides of victory and defeat brought neutral countries into the war (Map 27.3). Italy, a member of the Triple Alliance since 1882, had declared its neutrality in 1914 on the grounds that Austria had launched a war of aggression. Then in May 1915, Italy joined the Triple Entente of Great Britain, France, and Russia in return for promises of Austrian territory. Bulgaria allied with Austria and Germany, now known as the Central Powers, in September 1915 in order to settle old scores with Serbia.

The entry of Italy and Bulgaria in 1915 was part of a general widening of the war. The Balkans, with the exception of Greece, came to be occupied by the Central Powers, and British forces were badly defeated in 1915 trying to take the Dardanelles from Turkey, Germany's ally. More successful was the entente's attempt to incite Arab nationalists against their Turkish overlords. An enigmatic British colonel, soon known to millions as Lawrence of Arabia, aroused the Arab princes to revolt in early 1917. In 1918 British armies from Egypt smashed the Ottoman Empire once and for all. In the Middle East campaign, the British drew on forces from Australia, New Zealand, and India. Contrary to German hopes, the colonial subjects of the British (and French) did not revolt but loyally supported their foreign masters. The European war extended around the globe as Great Britain, France, and Japan seized Germany's colonies.

A crucial development in the expanding conflict came in April 1917 when the United States declared war on Germany. American intervention grew out of the war at sea, sympathy for the Triple Entente, and the increasing desperation of total war. At the beginning of the war, Britain and France had established a total naval blockade to strangle the Central Powers and prevent deliveries of food and raw materials from overseas. No neutral ship was permitted to sail to Germany with any cargo. The blockade annoyed Americans, but effective propaganda about German atrocities in occupied Belgium as well as lush profits from selling war supplies to Britain and France blunted American indignation.

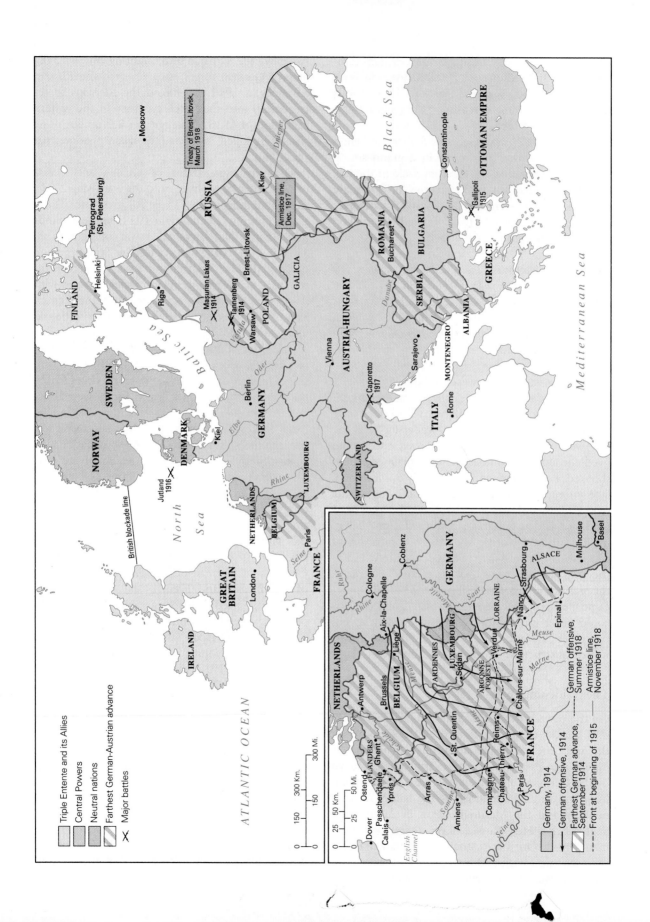

Triple Entente and its Allies

Central Powers

Neutral nations

Farthest German-Austrian advance

✕ **Major battles**

ATLANTIC OCEAN

IRELAND

GREAT BRITAIN
London

North Sea

British blockade line

Jutland 1916 ✕

NORWAY

SWEDEN

Baltic Sea

FINLAND
Helsinki

Petrograd (St. Petersburg)

Moscow

RUSSIA

Treaty of Brest-Litovsk, March 1918

Armistice line, Dec. 1917

Kiev

Dnieper

Black Sea

Constantinople

OTTOMAN EMPIRE

Gallipoli 1915 ✕

Dardanelles

GREECE

Mediterranean Sea

ALBANIA

MONTENEGRO

Rome
ITALY

Caporetto 1917 ✕

Danube

SERBIA

Sarajevo

BULGARIA

ROMANIA
Bucharest

AUSTRIA-HUNGARY

Vienna

Riga

Masurian Lakes ✕ 1914

Tannenberg 1914

Warsaw

Vistula

POLAND

GALICIA

Oder

Berlin

GERMANY

Elbe

Kiel

DENMARK

NETHERLANDS

BELGIUM

LUXEMBOURG

Rhine

SWITZERLAND

Paris
Seine

FRANCE

0   150   300 Km.
0   150   300 Mi.

NETHERLANDS

Antwerp

Brussels
BELGIUM

Ghent

Ostend

FLANDERS

Passchendaele

Ypres

Dover

Calais

English Channel

Arras

Amiens

Somme

Scheldt

Liège
Aix-la-Chapelle

Meuse

Cologne

Rhine

Ruhr

Coblenz

GERMANY

Moselle

Saar

LUXEMBOURG

ARDENNES

Sedan

ARGONNE FOREST

Verdun

LORRAINE

Strasbourg

Nancy

ALSACE

Mulhouse

Basel

Epinal

Meuse

Marne

Châlons-sur-Marne

Reims

Château-Thierry

Compiègne

St. Quentin

Aisne

Marne

Paris

Seine

FRANCE

Germany, 1914

→ **German offensive, 1914**

Farthest German advance, September 1914

--- **Front at beginning of 1915**

------- **German offensive, Summer 1918**

——— **Armistice line, November 1918**

0   25   50 Km.
0   25   50 Mi.

❖ **War in the Balkans** Serbia's tough peasant army repulsed two Austrian invasions in 1914 and forced Germany to come to Austria's aid in 1915. Reflecting the war of movement on the eastern front, this column of German cavalry is crossing the Drina river that separates the Austrian province of Bosnia and Herzegovina from southern Serbia, as Serbian villagers watch from the other side. The Austro-German force captured Belgrade and occupied Serbia. *(Source: Bibliothek Für Zeitgeschichte, Stuttgart)*

Moreover, in early 1915 Germany launched a counter-blockade using the murderously effective submarine, a new weapon that violated traditional niceties of fair warning under international law. In May 1915, after sinking about ninety ships in the British war zone, a German submarine sank the British passenger liner *Lusitania,* which was also carrying arms and munitions. More than 1,000 lives, among them 139 Americans, were lost. President Woodrow Wilson protested vigorously. Germany was forced to relax its submarine warfare for almost two years; the alternative was almost certain war with the United States.

Early in 1917, the German military command—confident that improved submarines could starve Britain into submission before the United States could come to its rescue—resumed unrestricted submarine warfare. Like the invasion of Belgium, this was a reckless gamble. British shipping losses reached staggering proportions, though by late 1917 naval strategists had come up with an effective response: the convoy system for safe transatlantic shipping. In the meantime, an embattled President Wilson had told a sympathetic Congress and people that the "German submarine warfare against commerce is a warfare against mankind." Thus the last uncommitted great nation, as fresh and enthusiastic as Europe had been in 1914, entered the world war in April 1917, almost three years after it began. Eventually the United States was to tip the balance in favor of the Triple Entente and its allies.

❖ **MAP 27.3 The First World War in Europe** The trench war on the western front was concentrated in Belgium and northern France, while the war in the east encompassed an enormous territory.

✠ THE HOME FRONT

Before looking at the last year of the Great War, let us turn our attention to the people on the home front. They were tremendously involved in the ti-

Waging Total War A British war plant strains to meet the insatiable demand for trench-smashing heavy artillery shells. Quite typically, many of these defense workers are women. *(Source: By courtesy of the Trustees of the Imperial War Museum)*

tanic struggle. War's impact on them was no less massive than on the men crouched in the trenches.

Mobilizing for Total War

In August 1914 most people had greeted the outbreak of hostilities enthusiastically. In every country the masses believed that their nation was in the right and defending itself from aggression. With the exception of a few extreme left-wingers, even socialists supported the war. Tough standby plans to imprison socialist leaders and break general strikes protesting the war proved quite unnecessary in 1914. In Germany, for example, the trade unions voted not to strike, and socialists in the Reichstag voted money for war credits in order to counter the threat of Russian despotism. A German socialist volunteered for the front, explaining to fellow members of the Reichstag that "to shed one's blood for the fatherland is not difficult: it is enveloped in romantic heroism."[5] Everywhere the support of the masses and working class contrib-

uted to national unity and an energetic war effort.

By mid-October generals and politicians had begun to realize that more than patriotism would be needed to win the war, whose end was not in sight. Each country experienced a relentless, desperate demand for men and weapons. In France, for example, the generals found themselves needing 100,000 heavy artillery shells a day, as opposed to the 12,000 they had anticipated using. This enormous quantity had to come from a French steel industry that had lost three-fourths of its iron resources in the first days of the war, when Germany seized the mines of French Lorraine. Each belligerent quickly faced countless shortages, for prewar Europe had depended on foreign trade and a great international division of labor. In each country economic life and organization had to change and change fast to keep the war machine from sputtering to a stop. And change they did.

In each country a government of national unity began to plan and control economic and social life in order to wage "total war." Free-market capitalism was abandoned, at least "for the duration." Instead, government planning boards established priorities and decided what was to be produced and consumed. Rationing, price and wage controls, and even restrictions on workers' freedom of movement were imposed by government. Only through such regimentation could a country make the greatest possible military effort. Thus, though there were national variations, the great nations all moved toward planned economies commanded by the established political leadership.

This revolutionary development would burn deeply into the twentieth-century consciousness. The planned economy of total war released the tremendous energies first harnessed by the French under Robespierre during the French Revolution. Total war, however, was based on tremendously productive industrial economies not confined to a single nation. The result was an effective—and therefore destructive—war effort on all sides.

Moreover, the economy of total war blurred the old distinction between soldiers on the battlefield and civilians at home. As President Wilson told Americans shortly after the United States entered the war, there were no armies in the traditional sense. Rather, "there are entire nations armed. Thus the men [and women] who remain to till the soil and man the factories are not less a part of the army than the men beneath the battle flags."[6] The war was a war of whole peoples and entire populations, and the loser would be the society that cracked first.

Finally, however awful the war was, the ability of governments to manage and control highly complicated economies strengthened the cause of socialism. With the First World War, socialism became for the first time a realistic economic blueprint rather than a utopian program.

Germany illustrates the general trend. It also went furthest in developing a planned economy to wage total war. As soon as war began, Walter Rathenau, the talented, foresighted, Jewish industrialist in charge of Germany's largest electrical company, convinced the government to set up the War Raw Materials Board to ration and distribute raw materials. Under Rathenau's direction, every useful material from foreign oil to barnyard manure was inventoried and rationed. Moreover, the board launched successful attempts to produce substitutes, such as synthetic rubber and synthetic nitrates. Without the spectacular double achievement of discovering a way to "fix" nitrogen present in the air and then producing synthetic nitrates in enormous quantity to make explosives, the blockaded German war machine would have stalled in a matter of months.

Food was also rationed in accordance with physical need. Men and women doing hard manual work were given extra rations. During the last two years of the war, only children and expectant mothers received milk rations. Sometimes mistakes were made that would have been funny if they had not been tragic. In early 1915 German authorities calculated that greedy pigs were eating food that hungry people needed, and they ordered a "hog massacre," only to discover later that too few pigs remained to eat an abundant potato crop. Germany also failed to tax the war profits of private firms heavily enough. This contributed to massive deficit financing, inflation, the growth of a black market, and the eventual re-emergence of class conflict.

Following the terrible battles of Verdun and the Somme in 1916, Chancellor Bethmann-Hollweg was driven from office in 1917 by military leaders Hindenburg and Ludendorff, who became the real rulers of Germany. They decreed the ultimate mobilization for total war. Germany, said Hindenburg, could win only "if all the treasures of our soil that agriculture and industry can produce are used exclusively for the conduct of War. . . . All other considerations must come second."[7] This goal, they believed, required that every German man, woman, and child be drafted into the service of the war. Thus in December 1916, military leaders rammed through the Reichstag the Auxiliary Service Law, which required all males between seventeen and sixty to work only at jobs considered critical to the war effort.

Although women and children were not specifically mentioned, this forced-labor law was also aimed at them. Many women already worked in war factories, mines, and steel mills, where they labored, like men, at the heaviest and most dangerous jobs. With the passage of the Auxiliary Service Law, many more women followed. Children were organized by their teachers into garbage brigades to collect every scrap of useful materials: grease strained from dishwater, coffee grounds, waste paper, tin cans, metal door knockers, bottles, rags, hair, bones, and so forth as well as acorns, chestnuts, pine cones, and rotting leaves. Potatoes gave way to turnips, and people averaged little more than 1,000 calories a day. Thus in Germany total war led to the establishment of history's first "totalitarian" society, and war production increased while some people starved to death.

Great Britain mobilized for total war less rapidly and less completely than Germany, for it could import materials from its empire and from the United States. By 1915, however, a serious shortage of shells had led to the establishment of the Ministry of Munitions under David Lloyd George. The ministry organized private industry to produce for the war, controlled profits, allocated labor, fixed wage rates, and settled labor disputes. By December 1916 when Lloyd George became prime minister, the British economy was largely planned and regulated. More than two hundred factories and 90 percent of all imports were bought and allocated directly by the state. Subsequently, even food was strictly rationed, while war production continued to soar. Great Britain had followed successfully in Germany's footsteps.

The Social Impact

The social impact of total war was no less profound than the economic impact, though again there were important national variations. The millions of men at the front and the insatiable needs of the military created a tremendous demand for workers. Jobs were available for everyone. This situation had seldom, if ever, been seen before 1914, when unemployment and poverty had been facts of urban

✦ **Wartime Propaganda** was skillful and effective. The poster on the left celebrates African Army Day, and tells French civilians that loyal troops from Africa and the colonies will help turn the tide against Germany. The German poster on the right draws upon a rich historical image, linking the brave German knight who slayed the dragon with an appeal to patriotic citizens to buy yet another series of war bonds. *(Source: Courtesy of the Trustees of the Imperial War Museum)*

life. This exceptional demand for labor brought about momentous changes.

One such change was greater power and prestige for labor unions. Having proved their loyalty in August 1914, labor unions became an indispensable partner of government and private industry in the planned war economy. Unions cooperated with war governments on work rules, wages, and production schedules in return for real participation in important decisions. This entry of labor leaders and unions into policy-making councils paralleled the entry of socialist leaders into the war governments.

The role of women changed dramatically. In every country large numbers of women left home and domestic service to work in industry, transportation, and offices. By 1917 women formed fully 43 percent of the labor force in Russia. The number of women driving buses and streetcars increased tenfold in Great Britain. Moreover, women became highly visible—not only as munitions workers but as bank tellers, mail carriers, even police officers.

At first, the male-dominated unions were hostile to women moving into new occupations, believing that their presence would lower wages and change work rules. But government pressure and the principle of equal pay for equal work (at least until the end of the war) overcame these objections. Women also served as nurses and doctors at the front. In general, the war greatly expanded the range of women's activities and changed attitudes toward women. As a direct result of women's many-sided war effort, Britain, Germany, and Austria granted women the right to vote immediately after the war. Women also showed a growing spirit of independence during the war, as they started to bob their hair, shorten their skirts, and smoke in public.

War also promoted greater social equality, blurring class distinctions and lessening the gap between rich and poor. This blurring was most apparent in Great Britain, where wartime hardship was never extreme. In fact, the bottom third of the population generally lived *better* than they ever had, for the poorest gained most from the severe shortage of labor. English writer Robert Roberts recalled how his parents' tiny grocery store in the slums of Manchester thrived during the war as never before when people who had scrimped to buy bread and soup bones were able to afford fancy cakes and thick steaks. In 1924 a British government study revealed that the distribution of income had indeed shifted in favor of the poorest; only half as many families lived in severe poverty as in 1911, even though total production of goods had not increased. In continental countries greater equality was reflected in full employment, rationing according to physical needs, and a sharing of hardships. There, too, society became more uniform and more egalitarian, in spite of some war profiteering.

Finally, death itself had no respect for traditional social distinctions. It savagely decimated the young aristocratic officers who led the charge, and it fell heavily on the mass of drafted peasants and unskilled workers who followed. Yet death often spared the aristocrats of labor, the skilled workers and foremen. Their lives were too valuable to squander at the front, for they were needed to train the newly recruited women and older unskilled men laboring valiantly in war plants at home.

Growing Political Tensions

During the first two years of war, most soldiers and civilians supported their governments. Even in Austria-Hungary—the most vulnerable of the belligerents, with its competing nationalities—loyalty to the state and monarchy remained astonishingly strong through 1916. Belief in a just cause, patriotic nationalism, the planned economy, and a sharing of burdens united peoples behind their various national leaders. Furthermore, each government did its best to control public opinion to bolster morale. Newspapers, letters, and public addresses were rigorously censored. Good news was overstated; bad news was repressed or distorted.

Each government used both crude and subtle propaganda to maintain popular support. German propaganda hysterically pictured black soldiers from France's African empire raping German women, while German atrocities in Belgium and elsewhere were ceaselessly recounted and exaggerated by the French and British. Patriotic posters and slogans, slanted news, and biased editorials inflamed national hatreds and helped sustain superhuman efforts.

By the spring of 1916, however, people were beginning to crack under the strain of total war. In April 1916 Irish nationalists in Dublin tried to take advantage of this situation and rose up against British rule in their great Easter Rebellion. A week of bitter fighting passed before the rebels were crushed and their leaders executed. Strikes and

❖ **Irish Nationalists** Organized in 1913 to press for Home Rule in Ireland, the un-official Irish Citizen Army was committed to complete independence from Great Britain. Shown here beneath a defiant pro-republican banner, it fought with other militant groups in the Easter Rebellion. *(Source: Lawrence Collection, National Library of Ireland, Dublin)*

protest marches over inadequate food began to flare up on every home front. Soldiers' morale began to decline. Italian troops mutinied. Numerous French units refused to fight after General Nivelle's disastrous offensive of May 1917. Only tough military justice and a tacit agreement with troops that there would be no more grand offensives enabled the new general in chief, Henri Philippe Pétain, to restore order. A rising tide of war-weariness and defeatism also swept France's civilian population before Georges Clemenceau emerged as a ruthless and effective wartime leader in November 1917. Clemenceau (1841–1929) established a virtual dictatorship, pouncing on strikers and jailing without trial journalists and politicians who dared to suggest a compromise peace with Germany.

The strains were worse for the Central Powers. In October 1916 the chief minister of Austria was assassinated by a young socialist crying, "Down with Absolutism! We want peace!"[8] The following month, when feeble old Emperor Francis Joseph died sixty-eight years after his mother, Sophia, had pushed him onto the throne in 1848 (see page 788), a symbol of unity disappeared. In spite of absolute censorship, political dissatisfaction and

conflicts among nationalities grew. In April 1917 Austria's chief minister summed up the situation in the gloomiest possible terms. The country and army were exhausted. Another winter of war would bring revolution and disintegration. "If the monarchs of the Central Powers cannot make peace in the coming months," he wrote, "it will be made for them by their peoples."[9] Both Czech and Yugoslav leaders demanded autonomous democratic states for their peoples. The British blockade kept tightening; people were starving.

The strain of total war and of the Auxiliary Service Law was also evident in Germany. In the winter of 1916 to 1917, Germany's military position appeared increasingly desperate. Stalemates and losses in the west were matched by temporary Russian advances in the east: hence the military's insistence on an all-or-nothing gamble of unrestricted submarine warfare when the Triple Entente refused in December 1916 to consider peace on terms favorable to the Central Powers.

Also, the national political unity of the first two years of war was collapsing as the social conflict of prewar Germany re-emerged. A growing minority of socialists in the Reichstag began to vote against war credits, calling for a compromise "peace without annexations or reparations." In July 1917 a coalition of socialists and Catholics passed a resolution in the Reichstag to that effect. Such a peace was unthinkable for conservatives and military leaders. So also was the surge in revolutionary agitation and strikes by war-weary workers that occurred in early 1917. When the bread ration was further reduced in April, more than 200,000 workers struck and demonstrated for a week in Berlin, returning to work only under the threat of prison and military discipline. Thus militaristic Germany, like its ally Austria-Hungary (and its enemy France), was beginning to crack in 1917. Yet it was Russia that collapsed first and saved the Central Powers—for a time.

 ## THE RUSSIAN REVOLUTION

The Russian Revolution of 1917 was one of modern history's most momentous events. Directly related to the growing tensions of World War One, it had a significance far beyond the wartime agonies of a single European nation. The Russian Revolution opened a new era. For some, it was Marx's socialist vision come true; for others, it was the triumph of dictatorship. To all, it presented a radically new prototype of state and society.

The Fall of Imperial Russia

Like its allies and its enemies, Russia embraced war with patriotic enthusiasm in 1914. At the Winter Palace, while throngs of people knelt and sang, "God Save the Tsar," Tsar Nicholas II (r. 1894–1917) repeated the oath Alexander I had sworn in 1812 and vowed never to make peace as long as the enemy stood on Russian soil. Russia's lower house, the Duma, voted war credits. Conservatives anticipated expansion in the Balkans, while liberals and most socialists believed alliance with Britain and France would bring democratic reforms. For a moment, Russia was united.

Soon the strains of war began to take their toll. Unprecedented artillery barrages used up Russia's supplies of shells and ammunition, and better-equipped German armies inflicted terrible losses. In 1915, substantial numbers of Russian soldiers were sent to the front without rifles; they were told to find their arms among the dead. There were two million Russian casualties in 1915 alone. Despite declining morale among soldiers and civilians, Russia's battered peasant army did not collapse but continued to fight courageously until early 1917.

Under the shock of defeat, Russia moved toward full mobilization on the home front. The Duma and organs of local government took the lead, setting up special committees to coordinate defense, industry, transportation, and agriculture. These efforts improved the military situation, and Russian factories produced more than twice as many shells in 1916 as in 1915. Yet there were many failures, and Russia mobilized less effectively for total war than the other warring nations.

The great problem was leadership. Under the constitution resulting from the revolution of 1905 (see pages 849–850), the tsar had retained complete control over the bureaucracy and the army. Legislation proposed by the Duma, which was weighted in favor of the wealthy and conservative classes, was subject to the tsar's veto. Moreover, Nicholas II fervently wished to maintain the sacred inheritance of supreme royal power, which, with the Orthodox church, was for him the key to Russia's greatness. A kindly, slightly stupid man, of whom a friend said he "would have been an ideal country gentleman, devoting his life to wife and children, his farms and his sport," Nicholas failed to form a close partnership with his citizens in order to fight the war more effectively. He relied instead on the old bureaucratic apparatus, distrusting the moderate Duma, rejecting popular involvement, and resisting calls to share power.

As a result, the Duma, the educated middle classes, and the masses became increasingly critical of the tsar's leadership. Following Nicholas's belated dismissal of the incompetent minister of war, demands for more democratic and responsive government exploded in the Duma in the summer of 1915. "From the beginning of the war," declared one young liberal, "public opinion has understood the character and magnitude of the struggle; it has understood that short of organizing the whole country for war, victory is impossible. But the Government has rejected every offer of help with disdain."[10] In September parties ranging from conservative to moderate socialist formed the Progressive Bloc, which called for a completely new government responsible to the Duma instead of the tsar. In answer, Nicholas temporarily adjourned the Duma and announced that he was traveling to the front in order to lead and rally Russia's armies.

His departure was a fatal turning point. With the tsar in the field with the troops, control of the government was taken over by the hysterical empress, Tsarina Alexandra, and a debauched adventurer, the monk Rasputin. A minor German princess and granddaughter of England's Queen Victoria, Nicholas's wife was a devoted mother with a sick child, a strong-willed woman with a hatred of parliaments. Having constantly urged her husband to rule absolutely, Alexandra tried to do so herself in his absence. She seated and unseated the top ministers. Her most trusted adviser was "our Friend Grigori," an uneducated Siberian preacher who was appropriately nicknamed "Rasputin"—the "Degenerate."

Rasputin began his career with a sect noted for mixing sexual orgies with religious ecstasies, and his influence rested on mysterious healing powers. Alexis, Alexandra's fifth child and heir to the throne, suffered from a rare disease, hemophilia.

❖ **Family Portrait** With husband Nicholas II standing behind, the beautiful but tense Alexandra shows one of her daughters, who could not inherit the throne, to her grandmother, Queen Victoria of Britain, and Victoria's son, the future Edward VII. European monarchs were closely related by blood and breeding before 1914. *(Source: Nicholas A. de Basily Collection, Hoover Institution)*

The tiniest cut meant uncontrollable bleeding, terrible pain, and possible death. Medical science could do nothing. Only Rasputin could miraculously stop the bleeding, perhaps through hypnosis. The empress's faith in Rasputin was limitless. "Believe more in our Friend," she wrote her husband in 1916. "He lives for you and Russia." In this atmosphere of unreality, the government slid steadily toward revolution.

In a desperate attempt to right the situation and end unfounded rumors that Rasputin was the empress's lover, three members of the high aristocracy murdered Rasputin in December 1916. The empress went into semipermanent shock, her mind haunted by the dead man's prophecy: "If I die or you desert me, in six months you will lose your son and your throne."[11] Food shortages in the cities worsened; morale declined. On March 8 women calling for bread in Petrograd (formerly St. Petersburg) started riots, which spontaneously spread to the factories and then elsewhere throughout the city. From the front the tsar ordered troops to restore order, but discipline broke down and the soldiers joined the revolutionary crowd. The Duma responded by declaring a provisional government on March 12, 1917. Three days later, Nicholas abdicated.

The Provisional Government

The March revolution was the result of an unplanned uprising of hungry, angry people in the capital, but it was joyfully accepted throughout the country. The patriotic upper and middle classes rejoiced at the prospect of a more determined and effective war effort, while workers happily anticipated better wages and more food. All classes and political parties called for liberty and democracy. They were not disappointed. As Lenin said, Russia became the freest country in the world. After generations of arbitrary authoritarianism, the provisional government quickly established equality before the law; freedom of religion, speech, and assembly; the right of unions to organize and strike; and the rest of the classic liberal program.

Yet both the liberal and moderate socialist leaders of the provisional government rejected social revolution. The reorganized government formed in May 1917, which included the fiery agrarian socialist Alexander Kerensky, refused to confiscate large landholdings and give them to peasants, fearing that such drastic action in the countryside would only complete the disintegration of Russia's peasant army. For the patriotic Kerensky as for other moderate socialists, the continuation of war was still the all-important national duty. There would be plenty of time for land reform later, and thus all the government's efforts were directed toward a last offensive in July. Human suffering and war-weariness grew, sapping the limited strength of the provisional government.

From its first day, the provisional government had to share power with a formidable rival—the Petrograd Soviet (or council) of Workers' and Soldiers' Deputies. Modeled on the revolutionary soviets of 1905, the Petrograd Soviet was a huge, fluctuating mass meeting of two to three thousand workers, soldiers, and socialist intellectuals. Seeing itself as a true grassroots revolutionary democracy, this counter- or half-government suspiciously watched the provisional government and issued its own radical orders, further weakening the provisional government. Most famous of these was Army Order No. 1, issued to all Russian military forces as the provisional government was forming.

Order No. 1 stripped officers of their authority and placed power in the hands of elected committees of common soldiers. Designed primarily to protect the revolution from some counter-revolutionary Bonaparte on horseback, Army Order No. 1 instead led to a total collapse of army discipline. Many an officer was hanged for his sins. Meanwhile, following the foolhardy summer offensive, masses of peasant soldiers began "voting with their feet," to use Lenin's graphic phrase. That is, they began returning to their villages to help their families get a share of the land, which peasants were simply seizing as they settled old scores in a great agrarian upheaval. All across the country, liberty was turning into anarchy in the summer of 1917. It was an unparalleled opportunity for the most radical and most talented of Russia's many socialist leaders, Vladimir Ilyich Lenin (1870–1924).

Lenin and the Bolshevik Revolution

From his youth, Lenin's whole life had been dedicated to the cause of revolution. Born into the middle class, Lenin became an implacable enemy of imperial Russia when his older brother was executed for plotting to kill the tsar in 1887. As a law student Lenin began searching for a revolutionary faith. He found it in Marxian socialism, which began to win converts among radical intellectuals as industrialization surged forward in Russia in the 1890s. Exiled to Siberia for three years because of socialist agitation, Lenin studied Marxian doctrines with religious intensity. After his release, this young priest of socialism joined fellow believers in western Europe. There he lived for seventeen years and developed his own revolutionary interpretations of the body of Marxian thought.

Three interrelated ideas were central for Lenin. First, turning to the early fire-breathing Marx of 1848 and the *Communist Manifesto* for inspiration, Lenin stressed that capitalism could be destroyed only by violent revolution. He tirelessly denounced all revisionist theories of a peaceful evolution to socialism as betraying Marx's message of unending class conflict. Lenin's second, more original, idea was that under certain conditions a socialist revolution was possible even in a relatively backward country like Russia. Though capitalism was not fully developed there and the industrial working class was small, the peasants were poor and thus potential revolutionaries.

Lenin believed that at a given moment revolution was determined more by human leadership than by vast historical laws. Thus was born his third basic idea: the necessity of a highly disciplined workers' party, strictly controlled by a dedicated elite of intellectuals and full-time revolutionaries like Lenin himself. Unlike ordinary workers and trade-union officials, this elite would never be seduced by short-term gains. It would not stop until revolution brought it to power.

Lenin's theories and methods did not go unchallenged by other Russian Marxists. At meetings of the Russian Social Democratic Labor party in London in 1903, matters came to a head. Lenin demanded a small, disciplined, elitist party, while his opponents wanted a more democratic party with mass membership. The Russian party of Marxian socialism promptly split into two rival factions. Lenin's camp was called *Bolsheviks,* or "majority group"; his opponents were *Mensheviks,* or "minority group." Lenin's majority did not last, but Lenin did not care. He kept the fine-sounding name Bolshevik and developed the party he wanted: tough, disciplined, revolutionary.

Unlike most other socialists, Lenin did not rally round the national flag in 1914. Observing events from neutral Switzerland, he saw the war as a product of imperialistic rivalries and as a marvelous opportunity for class war and socialist upheaval.

The March revolution was, Lenin felt, a step in that direction. Since propaganda and internal subversion were accepted weapons of total war, the German government graciously provided the impatient Lenin, his wife, and about twenty trusted colleagues with safe passage across Germany and back into Russia in April 1917. The Germans hoped that Lenin would undermine the sagging war effort of the world's freest society. They were not disappointed.

Arriving triumphantly at Petrograd's Finland Station on April 3, Lenin attacked at once. To the great astonishment of the local Bolsheviks, he rejected all cooperation with the "bourgeois" provisional government of the liberals and moderate socialists. His slogans were radical in the extreme: "All power to the soviets"; "All land to the peasants"; "Stop the war now." Never a slave to Marx-

ian determinism, the brilliant but not unduly intellectual Lenin was a superb tactician. The moment was now.

Yet Lenin almost overplayed his hand. An attempt by the Bolsheviks to seize power in July collapsed, and Lenin fled and went into hiding. He was charged with being a German agent, and indeed he and the Bolsheviks were getting money from Germany.[12] But no matter. Intrigue between Kerensky, who became prime minister in July, and his commander in chief, General Lavr Kornilov, a popular war hero "with the heart of a lion and the brains of a sheep," resulted in Kornilov's leading a feeble attack against the provisional government in September. In the face of this rightist "counterrevolutionary" threat, the Bolsheviks were rearmed and redeemed. Kornilov's forces disintegrated, but Kerensky lost all credit with the army, the only

❖ **Mass Demonstrations in Petrograd** in June 1917 showed a surge of working-class support for the Bolsheviks. In this photo a few banners of the Mensheviks and other moderate socialists are drowned in a sea of Bolshevik slogans. (*Source: Sovfoto*)

force that might have saved him and democratic government in Russia.

Trotsky and the Seizure of Power

Throughout the summer, the Bolsheviks had appealed very effectively to the workers and soldiers of Petrograd, markedly increasing their popular support. Party membership had soared from 50,000 to 240,000, and in October the Bolsheviks gained a fragile majority in the Petrograd Soviet. Moreover, Lenin had found a strong right arm— Leon Trotsky, the second most important person in the Russian Revolution.

A spellbinding revolutionary orator and independent radical Marxist, Trotsky (1879–1940) supported Lenin wholeheartedly in 1917. It was Trotsky who brilliantly executed the Bolshevik seizure of power. Painting a vivid but untruthful picture of German and counter-revolutionary plots, Trotsky first convinced the Petrograd Soviet to form a special military-revolutionary committee in October and make him its leader. Military power in the capital passed into Bolshevik hands. Trotsky's second master stroke was to insist that the Bolsheviks reduce opposition to their coup by taking power in the name, not of the Bolsheviks, but of the more popular and democratic soviets, which were meeting in Petrograd from all over Russia in early November. On the night of November 6, militants from Trotsky's committee joined with trusty Bolshevik soldiers to seize government buildings and pounce on members of the provisional government. Then they went on to the congress of soviets. There a Bolshevik majority— roughly 390 of 650 turbulent delegates—declared that all power had passed to the soviets and named Lenin head of the new government.

The Bolsheviks came to power for three key reasons. First, by late 1917 democracy had given way to anarchy: power was there for those who would take it. Second, in Lenin and Trotsky the Bolsheviks had an utterly determined and truly superior leadership, which both the tsarist government and the provisional government lacked. Third, in 1917 the Bolsheviks succeeded in appealing to many soldiers and urban workers, people who were exhausted by war and eager for socialism. With time, many workers would become bitterly disappointed, but for the moment they had good reason to believe that they had won what they wanted.

Dictatorship and Civil War

History is full of short-lived coups and unsuccessful revolutions. The truly monumental accomplishment of Lenin, Trotsky, and the rest of the Bolsheviks was not taking power but keeping it. In the next four years, the Bolsheviks went on to conquer the chaos they had helped create, and they began to build their kind of dictatorial socialist society. The conspirators became conquerors. How was this done?

Lenin had the genius to profit from developments over which he and the Bolsheviks had no control. Since summer, a peasant revolution had been sweeping across Russia as the tillers of the soil invaded and divided among themselves the great and not-so-great estates of the landlords and the church. Peasant seizure of the land—a Russian 1789—was not very Marxian, but it was quite unstoppable in 1917. Thus Lenin's first law, which supposedly gave land to the peasants, actually merely approved what peasants were already doing. Urban workers' great demand in November was direct control of individual factories by local workers' committees. This, too, Lenin rectified with a decree in November.

Unlike many of his colleagues, Lenin acknowledged that Russia had lost the war with Germany, that the Russian army had ceased to exist, and that the only realistic goal was peace at any price. That price was very high. Germany demanded in December 1917 that the Soviet government give up all its western territories. These areas were inhabited by Poles, Finns, Lithuanians, and other non-Russians—all those people who had been conquered by the tsars over three centuries and put into the "prisonhouse of nationalities," as Lenin had earlier called the Russian Empire.

At first, Lenin's fellow Bolsheviks would not accept such great territorial losses. But when German armies resumed their unopposed march into Russia in February 1918, Lenin had his way in a very close vote in the Central Committee of the party. "Not even his greatest enemy can deny that at this moment Lenin towered like a giant over his Bolshevik colleagues."[13] A third of old Russia's population was sliced away by the German meat ax in the Treaty of Brest-Litovsk in March 1918. With peace, Lenin had escaped the certain disaster of continued war and could pursue his goal of absolute political power for the Bolsheviks—now renamed Communists—within Russia.

THE RUSSIAN REVOLUTION

1914	Russia enthusiastically enters the First World War
1915	Two million Russian casualties Progressive Bloc calls for a new government responsible to the Duma rather than to the tsar Tsar Nicholas adjourns the Duma and departs for the front; strong influence of Alexandra and Rasputin on the government
December 1916	Murder of Rasputin
March 8, 1917	Bread riots in Petrograd (St. Petersburg)
March 12, 1917	Duma declares a provisional government
March 15, 1917	Tsar Nicholas abdicates without protest
April 3, 1917	Lenin returns from exile and denounces the provisional government
May 1917	Reorganized provisional government, including Kerensky, continues the war Petrograd Soviet issues Army Order no. 1, granting military power to committees of common soldiers
Summer 1917	Agrarian upheavals: peasants seize estates, peasant soldiers desert the army to participate
October 1917	Bolsheviks gain a majority in the Petrograd Soviet
November 6, 1917	Bolsheviks seize power; Lenin heads the new "provisional workers' and peasants' government"
November 1917	Lenin accepts peasant seizure of land and worker control of factories; all banks nationalized
January 1918	Lenin permanently disbands the Constituent Assembly
February 1918	Lenin convinces the Bolshevik Central Committee to accept a humiliating peace with Germany in order to safeguard the revolution
March 1918	Treaty of Brest-Litovsk: Russia loses one-third of its population Trotsky as war commissar begins to rebuild the Russian army Government moves from Petrograd to Moscow
1918–1920	Great Civil War
Summer 1918	Eighteen competing regional governments White armies oppose the Bolshevik revolution
1919	White armies on the offensive but divided politically; they receive little benefit from Allied intervention
1920	Lenin and Red armies victorious, retaking Belorussia and Ukraine

In November 1917 the Bolsheviks had cleverly proclaimed their regime only a "provisional workers' and peasants' government," promising that a freely elected Constituent Assembly would draw up a new constitution. But free elections produced a stunning setback for the Bolsheviks, who won less than one-fourth of the elected delegates. The Socialist Revolutionaries—the peasants' party—had a clear majority. The Constituent Assembly met for only one day, on January 18, 1918. It was then permanently disbanded by Bolshevik soldiers acting under Lenin's orders. Thus even before the peace with Germany, Lenin was forming a one-party government.

The destruction of the democratically elected Constituent Assembly helped feed the flames of civil war. People who had risen up for self-rule in November saw that once again they were getting dictatorship from the capital. For the next three years, "Long live the [democratic] soviets; down with the Bolsheviks" was to be a popular slogan. The officers of the old army took the lead in organizing the so-called White opposition to the Bolsheviks in southern Russia, Ukraine, Siberia, and west of Petrograd. The Whites came from many social groups and were united only by their hatred of the Bolsheviks—the Reds.

By the summer of 1918, fully eighteen self-proclaimed regional governments—several of which represented minority nationalities—were competing with Lenin's Bolsheviks in Moscow. By the end of the year, White armies were on the attack. In October 1919 it appeared they might triumph, as they closed in on Lenin's government from three sides. Yet they did not. By the spring of 1920, the White armies had been almost completely defeated, and the Bolshevik Red Army had retaken Belorussia and Ukraine. The following year, the Communists also reconquered the independent nationalist governments of the Caucasus. The civil war was over; Lenin had won.

Lenin and the Bolsheviks won for several reasons. Strategically, they controlled the center, while the Whites were always on the fringes and disunited. Moreover, the poorly defined political program of the Whites was vaguely conservative, and it did not unite all the foes of the Bolsheviks under a progressive, democratic banner. For example, the most gifted of the White generals, the nationalistic General Anton Denikin, refused to call for a democratic republic and a federation of nationalities, although he knew that doing so would help his

Vladimir Lenin Displaying his determination and skill as a revolutionary orator, Lenin in 1920 exhorts soldiers in the Red Army to defend the revolution in the last stage of the civil war. These units departing from Moscow will help retake Kiev and establish unshakable Bolshevik power in Ukraine and Belorussia. *(Source: Novosh)*

cause. Most important, the Communists quickly developed a better army, an army for which the divided Whites were no match.

Once again, Trotsky's leadership was decisive. The Bolsheviks had preached democracy in the army and elected officers in 1917. But beginning in March 1918, Trotsky as war commissar reestablished the draft and the most drastic discipline for the newly formed Red Army. Soldiers deserting or disobeying an order were summarily shot. Moreover, Trotsky made effective use of former tsarist army officers, who were actively recruited and given unprecedented powers of discipline over their troops. In short, Trotsky formed a disciplined and effective fighting force.

The Bolsheviks also mobilized the home front. Establishing "war communism"—the application of the total war concept to a civil conflict—they seized grain from peasants, introduced rationing, nationalized all banks and industry, and required everyone to work. Although these measures contributed to a breakdown of normal economic activity, they also served to maintain labor discipline and to keep the Red Army supplied.

"Revolutionary terror" also contributed to the Communist victory. The old tsarist secret police was re-established as the Cheka, which hunted down and executed thousands of real or supposed foes, such as the tsar and his family and other "class enemies." At one point shortly after the government moved from Petrograd to Moscow in March 1918, a circus clown in Moscow was making fun of the Bolsheviks to an appreciative audience. Chekists in the crowd quickly pulled out their guns and shot several laughing people. Moreover, people were shot or threatened with being shot for minor nonpolitical failures. The terror caused by the secret police became a tool of the government. The Cheka sowed fear, and fear silenced opposition.

Finally, foreign military intervention in the civil war ended up helping the Communists. After Lenin made peace with Germany, the Allies (the Americans, British, and Japanese) sent troops to Archangel and Vladivostok to prevent war material they had sent the provisional government from being captured by the Germans. After the Soviet government nationalized all foreign-owned factories without compensation and refused to pay all of Russia's foreign debts, Western governments, particularly that of France, began to support White armies. Yet these efforts were small and half-hearted. In 1919 Western peoples were sick of war, and few Western politicians believed in a military crusade against the Bolsheviks. Thus Allied intervention in the civil war did not aid the Whites effectively, though it did permit the Communists to appeal to the patriotic nationalism of ethnic Russians, in particular former tsarist army officers. Allied intervention was both too little and too much.

Together, the Russian Revolution and the Bolshevik triumph were one of the reasons the First World War was such a great turning point in modern history. A radically new government, based on socialism and one-party dictatorship, came to power in a great European state, maintained power, and eagerly encouraged worldwide revolution. Although halfheartedly constitutional monar-

chy in Russia was undoubtedly headed for some kind of political crisis before 1914, it is hard to imagine the triumph of the most radical proponents of change and reform except in a situation of total collapse. That was precisely what happened to Russia in the First World War.

THE PEACE SETTLEMENT

Victory over revolutionary Russia boosted sagging German morale, and in the spring of 1918 the Germans launched their last major attack against France. Yet this offensive failed, just as those before it had. With breathtaking rapidity, the United States, Great Britain, and France decisively defeated Germany militarily. The guns of world war finally fell silent. Then as civil war spread in Russia and as chaos engulfed much of eastern Europe, the victorious Western Allies came together in Paris to establish a lasting peace.

Expectations were high; optimism was almost unlimited. The Allies labored intensively and soon worked out terms for peace with Germany and for the creation of the peace-keeping League of Nations. Nevertheless, the hopes of peoples and politicians were soon disappointed, for the peace settlement of 1919 turned out to be a failure. Rather than creating conditions for peace, it sowed the seeds of another war. Surely this was the ultimate tragedy of the Great War, a war that directly and indirectly cost 332 billion dollars and left ten million dead and another twenty million wounded. How did this tragedy happen? Why was the peace settlement unsuccessful?

The End of the War

In early 1917 the strain of total war was showing everywhere. After the Russian Revolution in March, there were major strikes in Germany. In July a coalition of moderates passed a "peace resolution" in the Reichstag, calling for peace without territorial annexations. To counter this moderation born of war-weariness, the German military established a virtual dictatorship. The military also aggressively exploited the collapse of Russian armies after the Bolshevik Revolution. Advancing almost unopposed on the eastern front in early 1918, the German high command won great concessions from Lenin in the Treaty of Brest-Litovsk in March 1918.

With victory in the east quieting German moderates, General Ludendorff and company fell on France once more in the great spring offensive of 1918. For a time, German armies pushed forward, coming within 35 miles of Paris. But Ludendorff's exhausted, overextended forces never broke through. They were decisively stopped in July at the second Battle of the Marne, where 140,000 fresh American soldiers saw action. Adding 2 million men in arms to the war effort by August, the late but massive American intervention decisively tipped the scales in favor of Allied victory.

By September, British, French, and American armies were advancing steadily on all fronts, and a panicky General Ludendorff realized that Germany had lost the war. Yet he insolently insisted that moderate politicians shoulder the shame of defeat, and on October 4 the emperor formed a new, more liberal German government to sue for peace. As negotiations over an armistice dragged on, an angry and frustrated German people finally rose up. On November 3 sailors in Kiel mutinied, and throughout northern Germany soldiers and workers began to establish revolutionary councils on the Russian soviet model. The same day Austria-Hungary surrendered to the Allies and began breaking apart. Revolution broke out in Germany, and masses of workers demonstrated for peace in Berlin. With army discipline collapsing, the emperor abdicated and fled to Holland. Socialist leaders in Berlin proclaimed a German republic on November 9 and simultaneously agreed to tough Allied terms of surrender. The armistice went into effect on November 11, 1918. The war was over.

Revolution in Germany

Military defeat brought political revolution to Germany and Austria-Hungary, as it had to Russia. In Austria-Hungary the revolution was primarily nationalistic and republican in character. Having started the war to preserve an antinationalistic dynastic state, the Habsburg empire had perished in the attempt. In its place, independent Austrian, Hungarian, and Czechoslovak republics were proclaimed, while a greatly expanded Serbian monarchy united the south Slavs and took the name of Yugoslavia. The prospect of firmly establishing the new national states overrode class considerations for most people in east-central Europe.

The German Revolution of November 1918 resembled the Russian Revolution of March 1917. In both cases, a genuine popular uprising toppled an authoritarian monarchy and established a liberal provisional republic. In both countries, liberals and moderate socialists took control of the central government, while workers' and soldiers' councils formed a counter-government. In Germany, however, the moderate socialists won, and the Lenin-like radical revolutionaries in the councils lost. In communist terms, the liberal, republican revolution in Germany in 1918 was only half a revolution: a bourgeois political revolution without a communist second installment. It was Russia without Lenin's Bolshevik triumph.

There were several reasons for the German outcome. The great majority of Marxian socialist leaders in the Social Democratic party were, as before the war, really pink and not red. They wanted to establish real political democracy and civil liberties, and they favored the gradual elimination of capitalism. They were also German nationalists, ap-

Rosa Luxemburg A brilliant writer and a leader in the German Social Democratic party, Luxemburg scorned moderate socialism and stressed the revolutionary character of Marxism. Murdered by army officers in 1919, she was canonized by the faithful as a communist saint. *(Source: Courtesy, Centralne Archiwum KCPZPR, Warsaw, Poland)*

palled by the prospect of civil war and revolutionary terror. Moreover, there was much less popular support among workers and soldiers for the extreme radicals than in Russia. Nor did the German peasantry, which already had most of the land, at least in western Germany, provide the elemental force that has driven all great modern revolutions, from the French to the Chinese.

Of crucial importance was the fact that the moderate German Social Democrats, unlike Kerensky and company, accepted defeat and ended the war the day they took power. This act ended the decline in morale among soldiers and prevented the regular army, with its conservative officer corps, from disintegrating. When radicals headed by Karl Liebknecht and Rosa Luxemburg and their supporters in the councils tried to seize control of the government in Berlin in January, the moderate socialists called on the army to crush the uprising. Liebknecht and Luxemburg were arrested and then brutally murdered by army leaders, an act that caused the radicals in the Social Democratic party to break away in anger and form a pro-Lenin German Communist party shortly thereafter. Finally, even if the moderate socialists had followed Liebknecht and Luxemburg on the Leninist path, it is very unlikely that would have succeeded. Civil war in Germany would certainly have followed, and the Allies, which were already occupying western Germany according to the terms of the armistice, would have marched on to Berlin and ruled Germany directly. Historians have often been unduly hard on Germany's moderate socialists.

The Treaty of Versailles

The peace conference opened in Paris in January 1919 with seventy delegates representing twenty-seven victorious nations. There were great expectations. A young British diplomat later wrote that the victors "were convinced that they would never commit the blunders and iniquities of the Congress of Vienna [of 1815]." Then the "misguided, reactionary, pathetic aristocrats" had cynically shuffled populations; now "we believed in nationalism, we believed in the self-determination of peoples." Indeed, "we were journeying to Paris . . . to found a new order in Europe. We were preparing not Peace only, but Eternal Peace."[14] This general optimism and idealism had been greatly strengthened by President Wilson's January 1918 peace proposal, the Fourteen Points, which stressed na-

tional self-determination and the rights of small countries.

The real powers at the conference were the United States, Great Britain, and France, for Germany was not allowed to participate and Russia was locked in civil war and did not attend. Italy was considered part of the Big Four, but its role was quite limited. Almost immediately the three great Allies began to quarrel. President Wilson, who was wildly cheered by European crowds as the spokesman for a new idealistic and democratic international cooperation, was almost obsessed with creating the League of Nations. Wilson insisted that this question come first, for he passionately believed that only a permanent international organization could protect member states from aggression and avert future wars. Wilson had his way, although Lloyd George of Great Britain and especially Clemenceau of France were unenthusiastic. They were primarily concerned with punishing Germany.

Playing on British nationalism, Lloyd George had already won a smashing electoral victory in December on the popular platform of making Germany pay for the war. "We shall," he promised, "squeeze the orange until the pips squeak." Personally inclined to make a somewhat moderate peace with Germany, Lloyd George was to a considerable extent a captive of demands for a total victory worthy of the sacrifices of total war against a totally depraved enemy. As Kipling summed up the general British feeling at the end of the war, the Germans were "a people with the heart of beasts."[15]

France's Georges Clemenceau, "the Tiger" who had broken wartime defeatism and led his country to victory, wholeheartedly agreed. Like most French people, Clemenceau wanted old-fashioned revenge. He also wanted lasting security for France. This, he believed, required the creation of a buffer state between France and Germany, the permanent demilitarization of Germany, and vast German reparations. He feared that sooner or later Germany with its sixty million people would attack France with its forty million, unless the Germans were permanently weakened. Moreover, France had no English Channel (or Atlantic Ocean) as a reassuring barrier against German aggression. Wilson, supported by Lloyd George, would hear none of this. Clemenceau's demands seemed vindictive, violating morality and the principle of national self-determination. By April the conference was deadlocked on the German question, and Wilson packed his bags to go home.

Clemenceau's obsession with security reflected his anxiety about France's long-term weakness. In the end, convinced that France should not break with its allies because France could not afford to face Germany alone in the future, he agreed to a compromise. He gave up the French demand for a Rhineland buffer state in return for a formal defensive alliance with the United States and Great Britain. Under the terms of this alliance, both Wilson and Lloyd George promised that their countries would come to France's aid in the event of a German attack. Thus Clemenceau appeared to win his goal of French security, as Wilson had won his of a permanent international organization. The Allies moved quickly to finish the settlement, believing that any adjustments would later be possible within the dual framework of a strong Western alliance and the League of Nations (Map 27.4).

The Treaty of Versailles between the Allies and Germany was the key to the settlement, and the terms were not unreasonable as a first step toward re-establishing international order. (Had Germany won, it seems certain that France and Belgium would have been treated with greater severity, as Russia had been at Brest-Litovsk.) Germany's colonies were given to France, Britain, and Japan as League of Nations mandates. Germany's territorial losses within Europe were minor, thanks to Wilson. Alsace-Lorraine was returned to France. Parts of Germany inhabited primarily by Poles were ceded to the new Polish state, in keeping with the principle of national self-determination. Predominately German Danzig was also placed within the Polish tariff lines, but as a self-governing city under League of Nations protection. Germany had to limit its army to 100,000 men and agree to build no military fortifications in the Rhineland.

More harshly, the Allies declared that Germany (with Austria) was responsible for the war and had therefore to pay reparations equal to all civilian damages caused by the war. This unfortunate and much-criticized clause expressed inescapable popular demands for German blood, but the actual figure was not set, and there was the clear possibility that reparations might be set at a reasonable level in the future when tempers had cooled.

When presented with the treaty, the German government protested vigorously. But there was no alternative, especially considering that Germany was still starving because the Allies had not yet lifted their naval blockade. On June 28, 1919, German representatives of the ruling moderate Social Democrats and the Catholic party signed the treaty in the Sun King's Hall of Mirrors at Versailles, where Bismarck's empire had been joyously proclaimed almost fifty years before.

Separate peace treaties were concluded with the other defeated powers—Austria, Hungary, Bulgaria, and Turkey. For the most part, these treaties merely ratified the existing situation in east-central Europe following the breakup of the Austro-Hungarian Empire. Like Austria, Hungary was a particularly big loser, as its "captive" nationalities (and some interspersed Hungarians) were ceded to Rumania, Czechoslovakia, Poland, and Yugoslavia. Italy got some Austrian territory. The Turkish empire was broken up. France received Lebanon and Syria, while Britain took Iraq and Palestine, which was to include a Jewish national homeland first promised by Britain in 1917. Officially League of Nations mandates, these acquisitions of the Western powers were one of the more imperialistic elements of the peace settlement. Another was mandating Germany's holdings in China to Japan. The age of Western imperialism lived on. National self-determination remained a reality only for Europeans and their offspring.

American Rejection of the Versailles Treaty

The rapidly concluded peace settlement of early 1919 was not perfect, but within the context of war-shattered Europe it was an acceptable beginning. The principle of national self-determination, which had played such a large role in starting the war, was accepted and served as an organizing framework. Germany had been punished but not dismembered. A new world organization complemented a traditional defensive alliance of satisfied powers. The serious remaining problems could be worked out in the future. Moreover, Allied leaders had seen speed as essential for another reason: they detested Lenin and feared that his Bolshevik Revolution might spread. They realized that their best answer to Lenin's unending calls for worldwide upheaval was peace and tranquility for war-weary peoples.

There were, however, two great interrelated obstacles to such peace: Germany and the United States. Plagued by communist uprisings, reactionary plots, and popular disillusionment with losing the war at the last minute, Germany's moderate

way to a fragile truce. For this and for what came later, the United States must share a large part of the guilt.

SUMMARY

Why did World War One have such revolutionary consequences? Why was it such a great break with the past? World War One was, first of all, a war of committed peoples. In France, Britain, and Germany in particular, governments drew on genuine popular support. This support reflected not only the diplomatic origins of the war but also the way western European society had been unified under the nationalist banner in the later nineteenth century, despite the fears that the growing socialist movement aroused in conservatives. The relentlessness of total war helps explain why so many died, why so many were crippled physically and psychologically, and why Western civilization would in so many ways never be the same again. More concretely, the war swept away monarchs and multinational empires. National self-determination apparently triumphed, not only in Austria-Hungary but also in many of Russia's western borderlands. Except in Ireland and parts of Soviet Russia, the revolutionary dream of national unity, born of the French Revolution, had finally come true.

Two other revolutions were products of the war. In Russia the Bolsheviks established a radical regime, smashed existing capitalist institutions, and stayed in power with a new kind of authoritarian rule. Whether the new Russian regime was truly Marxian or socialist was questionable, but it indisputably posed a powerful, ongoing revolutionary challenge to Europe and its colonial empires.

More subtle but quite universal in its impact was an administrative revolution. This revolution, born of the need to mobilize entire societies and economies for total war, greatly increased the power of government. And after the guns grew still, government planning and wholesale involvement in economic and social life did not disappear in Europe. Liberal market capitalism and a well-integrated world economy were among the many casualties of the administrative revolution, and greater social equality was everywhere one of its results. Thus even in European countries where a communist takeover never came close to occurring, society still experienced a great revolution.

Finally, the "war to end war" did not bring peace—only a fragile truce. In the West the Allies failed to maintain their wartime solidarity. Germany remained unrepentant and would soon have more grievances to nurse. Moreover, the victory of national self-determination in eastern Europe created a power vacuum between a still-powerful Germany and a potentially mighty communist Russia. A vast area lay open to military aggression from two sides.

NOTES

1. M. Beloff, quoted in *U.S. News & World Report*, March 8, 1976, p. 53.
2. Quoted in J. Remak, *The Origins of World War I* (New York: Holt, Rinehart & Winston, 1967), p. 84.
3. Quoted in W. E. Mosse, *Alexander II and the Modernization of Russia* (New York: Collier Books, 1962), pp. 125–126.
4. Quoted in Remak, p. 123.
5. Quoted in J. E. Rodes, *The Quest for Unity: Modern Germany, 1848–1970* (New York: Holt, Rinehart & Winston, 1971), p. 178.
6. Quoted in F. P. Chambers, *The War Behind the War, 1914–1918* (London: Faber & Faber, 1939), p. 444.
7. Quoted in ibid., p. 168.
8. Quoted in R. O. Paxton, *Europe in the Twentieth Century* (New York: Harcourt Brace Jovanovich, 1975), p. 109.
9. Quoted in Chambers, p. 378.
10. Quoted in ibid., p. 110.
11. Quoted in ibid., pp. 302, 304.
12. A. B. Ulam, *The Bolsheviks* (New York: Collier Books, 1968), p. 349.
13. Ibid., p. 405.
14. H. Nicolson, *Peacemaking 1919* (New York: Grosset & Dunlap Universal Library, 1965), pp. 8, 31–32.
15. Quoted in ibid., p. 24.

SUGGESTED READING

O. Hale, *The Great Illusion, 1900–1914* (1971), is a thorough account of the prewar era. Remak's volume cited in the Notes; J. Joll, *The Origins of the First World War* (1992); and L. Lafore, *The Long Fuse* (1971), are recommended studies of the causes of the First

World War. A. J. P. Taylor, *The Struggle for Mastery in Europe, 1848–1919* (1954), is an outstanding survey of diplomatic developments, with an exhaustive bibliography. V. Steiner, *Britain and the Origins of the First World War* (1978), and G. Kennan, *The Decline of Bismarck's European Order: Franco-Russian Relations, 1875–1890* (1979), are also major contributions. K. Jarausch's *The Enigmatic Chancellor* (1973) is an important recent study on Bethmann-Hollweg and German policy in 1914. C. Falls, *The Great War* (1961), is the best brief introduction to military aspects of the war. B. Tuchman, *The Guns of August* (1962), is a marvelous account of the dramatic first month of the war and the beginning of military stalemate. G. Ritter provides an able study in *The Schlieffen Plan* (1958). J. Winter, *The Experience of World War I* (1988), is a strikingly illustrated history of the war, and A. Horne, *The Price of Glory: Verdun 1916* (1979), is a moving account of the famous siege. J. Ellis, *Eye-Deep in Hell* (1976), is a vivid account of trench warfare, whereas J. Keegan's fascinating *Face of Battle* (1976) examines soldiers and warfare in a long-term perspective. V. Brittain's *Testament of Youth,* the moving autobiography of an English nurse in wartime, shows lives buffeted by new ideas and personal tragedies. A. Marwick, *War and Change in Twentieth-Century Europe* (1990), is a useful synthesis.

F. L. Carsten, *War Against War* (1982), considers radical movements in Britain and Germany. The best single volume on the home fronts is still the one by Chambers mentioned in the Notes. Chambers draws heavily on the many fine books on the social and economic impact of the war in different countries published by the Carnegie Endowment for International Peace under the general editorship of J. T. Shotwell. M. Higonnet, J. Jensen, and M. Weitz, eds., *Behind the Lines: Gender and the Two World Wars* (1987), examines the changes that the war brought for women and for relations between the sexes. A. Marwick, *The Deluge* (1970), is a lively account of war and society in Britain; G. Feldman, *Army, Industry, and Labor in Germany, 1914–1918* (1966), shows the impact of total war and military dictatorship on Germany. Three excellent collections of essays, R. Wall and J. Winter, eds., *The Upheaval of War: Family, Work, and Welfare in Europe, 1914–1918* (1988); J. Roth, ed., *World War I* (1967); and R. Albrecht-Carrié, ed., *The Meaning of the First World War* (1965), probe the enormous consequences of the war for people and society. The debate over Germany's guilt and aggression, which has been reopened in recent years, may be best approached through G. Feldman, ed., *German Imperialism, 1914–1918* (1972), and A. Hillgruber, *Germany and the Two World Wars* (1981). M. Fainsod, *International Socialism and the World War* (1935), ably discusses the splits between radical and moderate socialists during the conflict. In addition to Erich Maria Remarque's great novel *All Quiet on the Western Front,* Henri Barbusse, *Under Fire* (1917), and Jules Romains, *Verdun* (1939), are highly recommended for their fictional, yet realistic re-creations of the war. P. Fussell, *The Great War and Modern Memory* (1975), probes all the powerful literature inspired by the war. M. Ecksteins, *Rites of Spring: The Great War and the Birth of the Modern Age* (1989), is an imaginative cultural investigation that has won critical acclaim.

R. Suny and A. Adams, eds., *The Russian Revolution and Bolshevik Victory* (1990), presents a wide range of old and new interpretations. A. Ulam's work cited in the Notes, which focuses on Lenin, is a masterful introduction to the Russian Revolution, whereas S. Fitzpatrick, *The Russian Revolution* (1982), provides a provocative reconsideration. B. Wolfe, *Three Who Made a Revolution* (1955), a collective biography of Lenin, Trotsky, and Stalin, and R. Conquest, *V. I. Lenin* (1972), are recommended. L. Trotsky himself wrote the colorful and exciting *History of the Russian Revolution* (1932), which may be compared with the classic eyewitness account of the young, pro-Bolshevik American J. Reed, *Ten Days That Shook the World* (1919). R. Daniels, *Red October* (1969), provides a clear account of the Bolshevik seizure of power, and R. Pipes, *The Formation of the Soviet Union* (1968), is recommended for its excellent treatment of the nationality problem during the revolution. D. Koenker, W. Rosenberg, and R. Suny, eds., *Party, State and Society in the Russian Civil War* (1989), probes the social foundations of Bolshevik victory. A. Wildman, *The End of the Russian Imperial Army* (1980), is a fine account of the soldiers' revolt, and G. Leggett, *The Cheka: Lenin's Secret Police* (1981), shows revolutionary terror in action. Boris Pasternak's justly celebrated *Doctor Zhivago* is a great historical novel of the revolutionary era. R. Massie, *Nicholas and Alexandra* (1971), is a moving popular biography of Russia's last royal family and the terrible health problem of the heir to the throne. H. Nicolson's study listed in the Notes captures the spirit of the Versailles settlement. T. Bailey, *Woodrow Wilson and the Lost Peace* (1963), and W. Widenor, *Henry Cabot Lodge and the Search for an American Foreign Policy* (1981), are also highly recommended. A. Mayer provocatively stresses the influence of domestic social tensions and widespread fear of further communist revolt in *The Politics and Diplomacy of Peacemaking* (1969).

German War Aims and the Treaty of Versailles

Was Germany treated too harshly by the Allies in the Treaty of Versailles? Or was Germany pursuing reckless and aggressive policies before and during the First World War, which justified the victors' attempt to restrain Germany in 1919? Politicians and historians have long debated these questions.

Fresh controversies arose in the 1960s when young German historians argued that Germany was not only especially responsible for the outbreak of the First World War but also planned to impose brutal terms on its foes after they were defeated. A newly discovered memorandum, which was prepared on September 9, 1914, by German chancellor Bethmann-Holweg after consulting with powerful business leaders, supported the young historians and attracted great interest. Bethmann-Hollweg's memorandum, which follows first, may be compared with key provisions from the famous June 28, 1919, Treaty of Versailles, excerpted second.

[The general aim is security] for the German Reich in west and east for all imaginable time. For this purpose France must be so weakened as to make her revival as a great power impossible for all time. Russia must be thrust back as far as possible from Germany's eastern frontier and her domination over the non-Russian vassal peoples [of the Russian empire] broken. . . .

1. *France.* . . . The [French iron] ore-field of Briey, which is necessary for the supply of ore for our industry, to be ceded [to Germany].

Further, a war indemnity, to be paid in installments; it must be high enough to prevent France from spending any considerable sums on armaments in the next 15–20 years.

Futhermore: a commercial treaty which makes France economically dependent on Germany, secures the French market for our exports and makes it possible to exclude British commerce from France. . . .

2. *Belgium.* . . . At any rate Belgium, even if allowed to continue to exist as a state, must be reduced to a vassal state, must allow us to occupy any militarily important ports, must place her coast at our disposal in military aspects, must become economically a German province. . . .

3. *Luxemburg.* [This country] will become a German federal state and will receive a strip of the present Belgian province of Luxemburg and perhaps the corner of Longwy [in France]. . . .

4. We must create a *central European economic association* through common custom treaties, to include France, Belgium, Holland, Denmark, Austria-Hungary, Poland, and perhaps Italy, Sweden and Norway. This association will not have any common constitutional supreme authority and all its members will be formally equal, but in practice will be under German leadership and must stabilize Germany's economic dominance over Mitteleuropa [central Europe].

5. *The question of colonial acquisitions,* where the first aim is the creation of a continuous Central African colonial empire, will be considered later . . .

7. *Holland* . . . [This country] must be left independent in externals, but be made internally dependent on us.

Article 42. Germany is forbidden to maintain or construct any fortifications either on the left bank of the Rhine or on the right bank to the west of a line drawn 50 kilometers to the East of the Rhine. . . .

Article 45. As compensation for the destruction of the coal mines in the north of France and as part payment towards the total reparation due from Germany for the damage resulting from the war, Germany cedes to France in full and absolute possession, with exclusive right of exploitation, unencumbered and free from all debts and charges of any kind, the coal mines situated in the Saar Basin. . . .

Article 49. Germany renounces in favor of the League of Nations, in the capacity of trustee, the government of the territory defined above [Saar Basin].

At the end of fifteen years . . . the inhabitants of the said territory shall be called upon to indicate the sovereignty under which they desire to be placed. . . .

Article 51. The territories [of Alsace and Lorraine] which were ceded to Germany [in 1871] . . . are restored to French sovereignty. . . .

Articles 80, 81, and 87. Germany acknowledges and will strictly respect the independence of Austria . . . [and] recognizes the complete independence of the Czecho-Slovak state . . . and of Poland. . . .

Article 116. Germany acknowledges and agrees to respect as permanent and inalienable the independence of all the territories which were part of the former Russian empire on August 1, 1914. . . .

Article 159. The German military forces shall be demobilized and reduced as prescribed hereinafter.

Article 160. . . . After that date [March 31, 1920] the total number of effectives in the Army of the States constituting Germany must not exceed 100,000 men, including officers and establishments of depots. The Army shall be devoted exclusively to the maintenance of order within the territory and to the control of the frontiers. . . .

Article 231. The Allied and Associated Governments affirm and Germany accepts the responsibility of Germany and her allies for causing all the loss and damage to which the Allied and Associated Governments and their nationals have been subjected as a consequence of the war imposed upon them by the aggression of Germany and her allies.

Article 232. The Allied and Associated Governments recognize that the resources of Germany are not adequate . . . to make complete reparation for all such loss and damage.

The Allied and Associated Governments, however, require, and Germany undertakes, that she will make compensation for all damage done to the civilian population of the Allied and Associated Power and to their property. . . .

Article 233. The amount of the above damage for which compensation is to be made by Germany shall be determined by an Inter-Allied Commission. . . . The findings of the commission as to the amount of damage

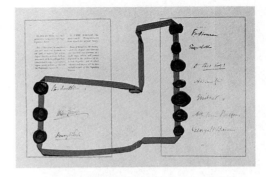

The last two pages of the Treaty of Versailles, with seals and signatures of participants. (Source: Courtesy of the Trustees of the Imperial Was Museum)

defined as above shall be concluded and notified to the German Government on or before May 1, 1921. . . .

Article 428. As a guarantee for the execution of the present Treaty by Germany, the German territory situated to the west of the Rhine, together with the bridgeheads, will be occupied by Allied and Associated troops for a period of fifteen years from the coming into force of the present Treaty.

Questions for Analysis

1. How did Bethmann-Hollweg believe Germany should treat a defeated France? A defeated Belgium?

2. How would you characterize Bethmann-Hollweg's proposals in general?

3. Locate on Map 27.4 the territories discussed in the Treaty of Versailles. (The Saar is on Map 29.1.) Were the territorial changes imposed on Germany harsh or fair? Why or why not?

4. What measures were the Allies taking to enforce the treaty?

5. Imagine you are a lawyer. Prepare a defense of Germany's actions before and during World War One.

Sources: F. Fischer, *Germany's Aims in the First World War* (New York: W. W. Norton, 1967) pp. 103–104; United States, Foreign Relations, *Treaty of Versailles, Paris Peace Conference, 1919* (Washington, D.C.: Government Printing Office, 1947).

28

The Age of Anxiety

When Allied diplomats met in Paris in early 1919 with their optimistic plans for building a lasting peace, most people looked forward to happier times. They hoped that life would return to normal after the terrible trauma of total war. They hoped that once again life would make sense in the familiar prewar terms of peace, prosperity, and progress. These hopes were in vain. The Great Break—the First World War and the Russian Revolution—had mangled too many things beyond repair. Life would no longer fit neatly into the old molds.

Instead, great numbers of men and women felt themselves increasingly adrift in a strange, uncertain, and uncontrollable world. They saw themselves living in an age of anxiety, an age of continual crisis (this age lasted until at least the early 1950s). In almost every area of human experience, people went searching for ways to put meaning back into life.

- What did such doubts and searching mean for Western thought, art, and culture?
- How did leaders deal with the political dimensions of uncertainty and try to re-establish real peace and prosperity between 1919 and 1939?
- Why did those leaders fail?

These are the questions this chapter will explore.

Dust, a painting of the Great Depression by the American painter Ben Shahn. *(Source: Courtesy, Kennedy Galleries, New York)*

UNCERTAINTY IN MODERN THOUGHT

A complex revolution in thought and ideas was under way before the First World War, but only small, unusual groups were aware of it. After the war, new and upsetting ideas began to spread through the entire population. Western society began to question and even abandon many cherished values

❖ **"The War, as I Saw It"** This was the title of a series of grotesque drawings that appeared in 1920 in *Simplicissimus,* Germany's leading satirical magazine. Nothing shows better the terrible impact of World War One than this profoundly disturbing example of expressionist art. *(Source: Caroline Buckler)*

and beliefs that had guided it since the eighteenth-century Enlightenment and the nineteenth-century triumph of industrial development, scientific advances, and evolutionary thought.

Before 1914 most people still believed in progress, reason, and the rights of the individual. Progress was a daily reality, apparent in the rising standard of living, the taming of the city, and the steady increase in popular education. Such developments also encouraged the comforting belief in the logical universe of Newtonian physics as well as faith in the ability of a rational human mind to understand that universe through intellectual investigation. And just as there were laws of science, so were

there laws of society that rational human beings could discover and then wisely act on. At the same time, the rights of the individual were not just taken for granted; they were actually increasing. Well-established rights were gradually spreading to women and workers, and new "social rights," such as old-age pensions, were emerging. In short, before World War One most Europeans had a moderately optimistic view of the world, and with good reason.

From the 1880s on, however, a small band of serious thinkers and creative writers began to attack these well-worn optimistic ideas. These critics rejected the general faith in progress and the power of the rational human mind. Their views were greatly strengthened by the experience of history's most destructive war, which suggested to many that human beings were a pack of violent, irrational animals quite capable of tearing the individual and his or her rights to shreds. There were growing pessimism and a general crisis of the mind, and an expanding chorus of thinkers, creative writers, and scientists echoed and enlarged on the themes first expressed by the small group of critics between 1880 and 1914. People did not know what to think. This disorientation was particularly acute in the 1930s, when the rapid rise of harsh dictatorships and the Great Depression transformed old certainties into bitter illusions.

No one expressed this state of uncertainty better than French poet and critic Paul Valéry (1871–1945) in the early 1920s. Speaking of the "crisis of the mind," Valéry noted that Europe was looking at its future with dark foreboding:

The storm has died away, and still we are restless, uneasy, as if the storm were about to break. Almost all the affairs of men remain in a terrible uncertainty. We think of what has disappeared, and we are almost destroyed by what has been destroyed; we do not know what will be born, and we fear the future, not without reason. . . . Doubt and disorder are in us and with us. There is no thinking man, however shrewd or learned he may be, who can hope to dominate this anxiety, to escape from this impression of darkness.[1]

In the midst of economic, political, and social disruptions, Valéry saw the "cruelly injured mind," besieged by doubts and suffering from anxieties. This was the general intellectual crisis of the twentieth century, which touched almost every field of thought. The implications of new ideas and discoveries in philosophy, physics, psychology, and literature played a central role in this crisis, disturbing "thinking people" everywhere.

Modern Philosophy

Among those thinkers in the late nineteenth century who challenged the belief in progress and the general faith in the rational human mind, German philosopher Friedrich Nietzsche (1844–1900) was particularly influential. The son of a Lutheran minister, Nietzsche rejected Christianity and became a professor of classical languages until ill health forced him to retire at an early age. Never a sys-

tematic philosopher, Nietzsche wrote as a prophet in a provocative and poetic style. His first great work in 1872 argued that ever since classical Athens, the West had overemphasized rationality and stiffled the passion and animal instinct that drive human activity and true creativity. Nietzsche went on to question all values. He claimed that Christianity embodied a "slave morality," which glorified weakness, envy, and mediocrity. In Nietzsche's most famous line, a wise fool proclaims that "God is dead," dead because He has been murdered by lackadaisical modern Christians who no longer really believe in Him. Nietzsche viewed the pillars of conventional morality—reason, democracy, progress, respectability—as outworn social and psycho-

Friedrich Nietzsche This colored photograph of the German philosopher was taken in 1882, when he was at the height of his creative powers. A brilliant iconoclast, Nietzsche debunked European values and challenged the optimistic faith in human rationality before World War One. (*Source: Archiv Für Kunst und Geschichte, Berlin*)

logical constructs whose influence was suffocating self-realization and excellence.

Nietzsche painted a dark world, foreshadowing perhaps his loss of sanity in 1889. The West was in decline; false values had triumphed. The death of God left people disoriented and depressed. The only hope for the individual was to accept the meaninglessness of human existence and then make that very meaninglessness a source of self-defined personal integrity and hence liberation. This would at least be possible for a few superior individuals, who could free themselves from the humdrum thinking of the masses and become true heroes. Little read during his active years, Nietzsche attracted growing attention in the early twentieth century, especially from German radicals who found inspiration in Nietzsche's ferocious assault on the conventions of pre-1914 imperial Germany. Subsequent generations have each discovered new Nietzsches, and his influence remains enormous to this day.

This growing dissatisfaction with established ideas before 1914 was apparent in other important thinkers. In the 1890s, French philosophy professor Henri Bergson (1859–1941) convinced many young people through his writing that immediate experience and intuition were as important as rational and scientific thinking for understanding reality. Indeed, according to Bergson, a religious experience or a mystical poem was often more accessible to human comprehension than a scientific law or a mathematical equation.

Another thinker who agreed about the limits of rational thinking was French socialist Georges Sorel (1847–1922). Sorel frankly characterized Marxian socialism as an inspiring but unprovable religion rather than a rational scientific truth. Socialism would come to power, he believed, through a great, violent strike of all working people, which would miraculously shatter capitalist society. Sorel rejected democracy and believed that the masses of the new socialist society would have to be tightly controlled by a small revolutionary elite.

The First World War accelerated the revolt against established certainties in philosophy, but that revolt went in two very different directions. In English-speaking countries, the main development was the acceptance of logical empiricism (or logical positivism) in university circles. In continental countries, where esoteric and remote logical empiricism did not win many converts, the primary development in philosophy was existentialism.

Logical empiricism was truly revolutionary. It quite simply rejected most of the concerns of traditional philosophy, from the existence of God to the meaning of happiness, as nonsense and hot air. This outlook began primarily with Austrian philosopher Ludwig Wittgenstein (1889–1951), who later emigrated to England, where he trained numerous disciples.

Wittgenstein argued in his pugnacious *Tractatus Logico-Philosophicus* (Essay on Logical Philosophy) in 1922 that philosophy is only the logical clarification of thoughts, and therefore it becomes the study of language, which expresses thoughts. The great philosophical issues of the ages—God, freedom, morality, and so on—are quite literally senseless, a great waste of time, for statements about them can neither be tested by scientific experiments nor demonstrated by the logic of mathematics. Statements about such matters reflect only the personal preferences of a given individual. As Wittgenstein put it in the famous last sentence of his work, "Of what one cannot speak, of that one must keep silent." Logical empiricism, which has remained dominant in England and the United States to this day, drastically reduced the scope of philosophical inquiry. Anxious people could find few, if any, answers in this direction.

Some looked for answers in *existentialism.* Highly diverse and even contradictory, existential thinkers were loosely united in a courageous search for moral values in a world of terror and uncertainty. Theirs were true voices of the age of anxiety.

Most existential thinkers in the twentieth century were atheists. Often inspired by Nietzsche, who had already proclaimed the death of God and called for new values, they did not believe a supreme being had established humanity's fundamental nature and given life its meaning. In the words of the famous French existentialist Jean-Paul Sartre (1905–1980), human beings simply exist: "They turn up, appear on the scene." Only after they "turn up" do they seek to define themselves. Honest human beings are terribly alone, for there is no God to help them. They are hounded by despair and the meaninglessness of life. The crisis of the existential thinker epitomized the modern intellectual crisis—the shattering of traditional beliefs in God, reason, and progress.

Existentialists did recognize that human beings, unless they kill themselves, must act. Indeed, in the words of Sartre, "man is condemned to be free." There is therefore the possibility—indeed, the necessity—of giving meaning to life through actions, of defining oneself through choices. To do so, individuals must become "engaged" and choose their own actions courageously and consistently and in full awareness of their inescapable responsibility for their own behavior. In the end, existentialists argued, human beings can overcome life's absurdity.

Modern existentialism first attained prominence in Germany in the 1920s when philosophers Martin Heidegger and Karl Jaspers found a sympathetic audience among disillusioned postwar university students. But it was in France during and immediately after World War Two that existentialism came of age. The terrible conditions of the war reinforced the existential view of and approach to life. On the one hand, the armies of the German dictator Hitler had conquered most of Europe and unleashed a hideous reign of barbarism. On the other, men and women had more than ever to define themselves by their actions. Specifically, each individual had to choose whether to join the resistance against Hitler or accept and even abet tyranny. The writings of Sartre, who along with Albert Camus (1913–1960) was the leading French existentialist, became enormously influential. Himself active in the French Resistance, Sartre and his colleagues offered a powerful answer to profound moral issues and the contemporary crisis.

The Revival of Christianity

The loss of faith in human reason and in continual progress also led to a renewed interest in the Christian view of the world. Christianity and religion in general had been on the defensive in intellectual circles since the Enlightenment, especially during the late nineteenth century, but a number of thinkers and theologians began to revitalize the fundamentals of Christianity, especially after World War One. They had a powerful impact on society. Sometimes described as Christian existentialists because they shared the loneliness and despair of atheistic existentialists, they revived the tradition of Saint Augustine. They stressed human beings' sinful nature, the need for faith, and the mystery of God's forgiveness.

This development was a break with the late nineteenth century. In the years before 1914, some theologians, especially Protestant ones, had felt the need to interpret Christian doctrine and the Bible so that they did not seem to contradict science, evolution, and common sense. Christ was therefore seen primarily as the greatest moral teacher, and the "supernatural" aspects of his divinity were strenuously played down. An important, if extreme, example of this tendency was the young Albert Schweitzer's *Quest of the Historical Jesus* (1906). A theologian and later a famous medical missionary and musician of note, Schweitzer (1875–1965) argued that while on earth Christ had been a completely natural man whose teachings had been only temporary rules to prepare himself and his disciples for the end of the world, which they were erroneously expecting. In short, some modern theologians were embarrassed by the miraculous, unscientific aspects of Christianity and turned away from them.

The revival of fundamental Christian belief after World War One was fed by rediscovery of the work of nineteenth-century Danish religious philosopher Søren Kierkegaard (1813–1855), whose ideas became extremely influential. Kierkegaard had rejected formalistic religion and denounced the worldliness of the Danish Lutheran church. He had eventually resolved his personal anguish over his imperfect nature by making a total religious commitment to a remote and majestic God.

Similar ideas were brilliantly developed by Swiss Protestant theologian Karl Barth (1886–1968), whose many influential writings after 1920 sought to re-create the religious intensity of the Reformation. For Barth, the basic fact about human beings is that they are imperfect, sinful creatures whose reason and will are hopelessly flawed. Religious truth is therefore made known to human beings only through God's grace. People have to accept God's word and the supernatural revelation of Jesus Christ with awe, trust, and obedience. Lowly mortals should not expect to "reason out" God and his ways.

Among Catholics, the leading existential Christian thinker was Gabriel Marcel (1887–1973). Born into a cultivated French family, where his atheistic father was "gratefully aware of all that . . . art owed to Catholicism but regarded Catholic thought itself as obsolete and tainted with absurd superstitions,"[2] Marcel found in the Catholic church an answer to what he called the postwar "broken world." Catholicism and religious belief provided the hope, humanity, honesty, and piety for which he hungered. Flexible and gentle, Marcel and his countryman Jacques Maritain (1882–

1973) denounced anti-Semitism and supported closer ties with non-Catholics.

After 1914 religion became much more relevant and meaningful to thinking people than it had been before the war. In addition to Marcel and Maritain, many other illustrious individuals turned to religion between about 1920 and 1950. Poets T. S. Eliot and W. H. Auden, novelists Evelyn Waugh and Aldous Huxley, historian Arnold Toyn-bee, Oxford professor C. S. Lewis, psychoanalyst Karl Stern, physicist Max Planck, and philosopher Cyril Joad were all either converted to religion or attracted to it for the first time. (See Listening to the Past.) Religion, often of a despairing, existential variety, was one meaningful answer to terror and anxiety. In the words of another famous Roman Catholic convert, English novelist Graham Greene, "One began to believe in heaven because one believed in hell."[3]

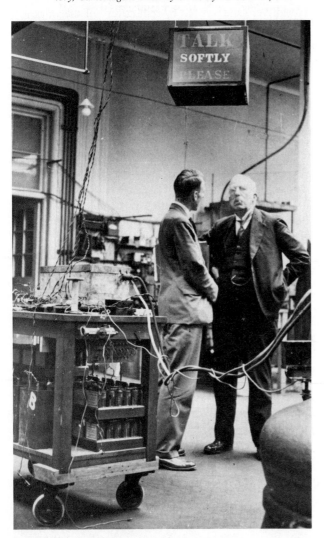

✦ **Lord Rutherford** The great physicist Ernest Rutherford split the atom in 1919 with a small device he could hold in his hands. Here he is seen with a colleague in Cambridge University's renowned Cavendish Laboratory in 1932, when scientific laboratories engaged in pure research were still relatively small. *(Source: Cavendish Laboratory, Cambridge University/C. E. Wynn-Williams)*

The New Physics

Ever since the scientific revolution of the seventeenth century, scientific advances and their implications had greatly influenced the beliefs of thinking people. By the late nineteenth century, science was one of the main pillars supporting Western society's optimistic and rationalistic view of the world. The Darwinian concept of evolution had been accepted and assimilated in most intellectual circles. Progressive minds believed that science, unlike religion and philosophical speculation, was based on hard facts and controlled experiments. Science seemed to have achieved an unerring and almost completed picture of reality. Unchanging natural laws seemed to determine physical processes and permit useful solutions to more and more problems. All this was comforting, especially to people who were no longer committed to traditional religious beliefs. And all this was challenged by the new physics.

An important first step toward the new physics was the discovery at the end of the nineteenth century that atoms were not like hard, permanent little billiard balls. They were actually composed of many far-smaller, fast-moving particles, such as electrons and protons. Polish-born physicist Marie Curie (1867–1934) and her French husband discovered that radium constantly emits subatomic particles and thus does not have a constant atomic weight. Building on this and other work in radiation, German physicist Max Planck (1858–1947) showed in 1900 that subatomic energy is emitted in uneven little spurts, which Planck called "quanta," and not in a steady stream, as previously believed. Planck's discovery called into question the old sharp distinction between matter and energy; the implication was that matter and energy might be different forms of the same thing. The old view of atoms as the stable, basic building blocks of nature, with a different kind of unbreakable atom for each of the ninety-two chemical elements, was badly shaken.

In 1905 German-born Jewish genius Albert Einstein (1879–1955) went further than the Curies and Planck in challenging Newtonian physics. His famous theory of special relativity postulated that time and space are relative to the viewpoint of the observer and that only the speed of light is constant for all frames of reference in the universe. In order to make his revolutionary and paradoxical idea somewhat comprehensible to the nonmathematical lay person, Einstein later used analogies involving moving trains. For example, if a woman in the middle of a moving car got up and walked forward to the door, she had gone, relative to the train, a half car length. But relative to an observer on the embankment, she had gone farther. The closed framework of Newtonian physics was quite limited compared to that of Einsteinian physics, which unified an apparently infinite universe with the incredibly small, fast-moving subatomic world. Moreover, Einstein's theory stated clearly that matter and energy are interchangeable and that even a particle of matter contains enormous levels of potential energy.

The 1920s opened the "heroic age of physics," in the apt words of one of its leading pioneers, Ernest Rutherford (1871–1937). Breakthrough followed breakthrough. In 1919 Rutherford showed that the atom could be split. By 1944 seven subatomic particles had been identified, of which the most important was the neutron. The neutron's capacity to pass through other atoms allowed for even more intense experimental bombardment of matter, leading to chain reactions of unbelievable force. This was the road to the atomic bomb.

Although few nonscientists understood this revolution in physics, the implications of the new theories and discoveries, as presented by newspapers and popular writers, were disturbing to millions of men and women in the 1920s and 1930s. The new universe was strange and troubling. It lacked any absolute objective reality. Everything was "relative," that is, dependent on the observer's frame of reference. Moreover, the universe was uncertain and undetermined, without stable building blocks. In 1927 German physicist Werner Heisenberg (1901–1976) formulated the "principle of uncertainty," which postulates that because it is impossible to know the position and speed of an individual electron, it is therefore impossible to predict its behavior. Instead of Newton's dependable, rational laws, there seemed to be only tendencies and probabilities in an extraordinarily complex and uncertain universe.

Moreover, a universe described by abstract mathematical symbols seemed to have little to do with human experience and human problems. When, for example, Planck was asked what science could contribute to resolving conflicts of values, his response was simple: "Science is not qualified to speak to this question." Physics, the queen of the sciences, no longer provided people easy, optimistic answers—for that matter, it did not provide any answers at all.

Freudian Psychology

With physics presenting an uncertain universe so unrelated to ordinary human experience, questions regarding the power and potential of the human mind assumed special significance. The findings and speculations of leading psychologist Sigmund Freud (see page 820), were particularly disturbing.

Before Freud, poets and mystics had probed the unconscious and irrational aspects of human behavior. But most professional, "scientific" psychologists assumed that a single, unified conscious mind processed sense experiences in a rational and logical way. Human behavior in turn was the result of rational calculation—of "thinking"—by the conscious mind. Basing his insights on the analysis of dreams and of hysteria, Freud developed a very different view of the human psyche beginning in the late 1880s.

According to Freud, human behavior is basically irrational. The key to understanding the mind is the primitive, irrational unconscious, which he called the *id*. The unconscious is driven by sexual, aggressive, and pleasure-seeking desires and is locked in a constant battle with the other parts of the mind: the rationalizing conscious (the *ego*), which mediates what a person *can* do, and ingrained moral values (the *superego*), which specify what a person *should* do. Human behavior is a product of a fragile compromise between instinctual drives and the controls of rational thinking and moral values. Since the instinctual drives are extremely powerful, the ever-present danger for individuals and whole societies is that unacknowledged

✦ **Munch: The Dance of Life**   Like his contemporary Sigmund Freud, the expressionist painter Edvard Munch studied the turmoil and fragility of human thought and action. Solitary figures struggling with fear and uncertainty dominate his work. Here the girl in white represents innocence, the tense woman in black stands for mourning and rejection, and the woman in red evokes the joy of passing pleasure. (*Source: U Nasjonalgalleriet, Oslo. Photo: Jacques Lathion*)

drives will overwhelm the control mechanisms in a violent, distorted way. Yet Freud also agreed with Nietzsche that the mechanisms of rational thinking and traditional moral values can be too strong. They can repress sexual desires too effectively, crippling individuals and entire peoples with guilt and neurotic fears.

Freudian psychology and clinical psychiatry had become an international movement by 1910, but only after 1918 did they receive popular attention, especially in the Protestant countries of northern Europe and in the United States. Many opponents and even some enthusiasts interpreted Freud as saying that the first requirement for mental health is an uninhibited sex life. Thus after the First World War, the popular interpretation of Freud reflected and encouraged growing sexual experimentation,

particularly among middle-class women. For more serious students, the psychology of Freud and his followers drastically undermined the old, easy optimism about the rational and progressive nature of the human mind.

Twentieth-Century Literature

The general intellectual climate of pessimism, relativism, and alienation was also articulated in literature. Novelists developed new techniques to express new realities. The great nineteenth-century novelists had typically written as all-knowing narrators, describing realistic characters and their relationship to an understandable, if sometimes harsh, society. In the twentieth century, most major writers adopted the limited, often confused viewpoint of a single individual. Like Freud, these novelists focused their attention on the complexity and irrationality of the human mind, where feelings, memories, and desires are forever scrambled. The great French novelist Marcel Proust (1871–1922), in his semiautobiographical *Remembrance of Things Past* (1913–1927), recalled bittersweet memories of childhood and youthful love and tried to discover their innermost meaning. To do so, Proust lived like a hermit in a soundproof Paris apartment for ten years, withdrawing from the present to dwell on the past.

Serious novelists also used the "stream-of-consciousness" technique to explore the psyche. In *Jacob's Room* (1922), Virginia Woolf (1882–1941) created a novel made up of a series of internal monologues, in which ideas and emotions from different periods of time bubble up as randomly as from a patient on a psychoanalyst's couch. William Faulkner (1897–1962), perhaps America's greatest twentieth-century novelist, used the same technique in *The Sound and the Fury* (1922), much of whose intense drama is confusedly seen through the eyes of an idiot. The most famous stream-of-consciousness novel—and surely the most disturbing novel of its generation—is *Ulysses,* which Irish novelist James Joyce (1882–1941) published in 1922. Into an account of an ordinary day in the life of an ordinary man, Joyce weaves an extended ironic parallel between his hero's aimless wanderings through the streets and pubs of Dublin and the adventures of Homer's hero Ulysses on his way home from Troy. Abandoning conventional grammar and blending foreign words, puns, bits of knowledge, and scraps of memory together in bewildering confusion, the language of Ulysses is intended to mirror modern life itself: a gigantic riddle waiting to be unraveled.

As creative writers turned their attention from society to the individual and from realism to psychological relativity, they rejected the idea of progress. Some even described "anti-utopias," nightmare visions of things to come. In 1918 an obscure German high school teacher named Oswald Spengler (1880–1936) published *The Decline of the West,* which quickly became an international sensation. According to Spengler, every culture experiences a life cycle of growth and decline. Western civilization, in Spengler's opinion, was in its old age, and death was approaching in the form of conquest by the yellow race. T. S. Eliot (1888–

1965), in his famous poem *The Waste Land* (1922), depicted a world of growing desolation, although after his conversion to Anglo-Catholicism in 1927, Eliot came to hope cautiously for humanity's salvation. No such hope appeared in the work of Franz Kafka (1883–1924), whose novels *The Trial* (1925) and *The Castle* (1926) as well as several of his greatest short stories portray helpless individuals crushed by inexplicably hostile forces. The German-Jewish Kafka died young, at forty-one, and so did not see the world of his nightmares materialize in the Nazi state.

Englishman George Orwell (1903–1950), however, had seen both that reality and its Stalinist

❖ **Virginia Woolf** Her novels captured sensations like impressionist paintings, and her home attracted a circle of artists and writers known as the Bloomsbury Group. Many of Woolf's essays dealt with women's issues and urged greater opportunity for women's creativity. *(Source: U Gisèle Freund/Photo Researchers)*

counterpart by 1949 when he wrote perhaps the ultimate in anti-utopian literature: *1984*. Orwell set the action in the future, in 1984. Big Brother—the dictator—and his totalitarian state use a new kind of language, sophisticated technology, and psychological terror to strip a weak individual of his last shred of human dignity. The supremely self-confident chief of the Thought Police tells the tortured, broken, and framed Winston Smith, "If you want a picture of the future, imagine a boot stamping on a human face—forever."[4] A phenomenal best seller, *1984* spoke to millions of people in the closing years of the age of anxiety.

❖ MODERN ART AND MUSIC

Throughout the twentieth century, there has been considerable unity in the arts. The "modernism" of the immediate prewar years and the 1920s is still strikingly modern. Manifestations of modernism in art, architecture, and music have of course been highly varied, just as in physics, psychology, and philosophy; yet there are resemblances, for artists, scientists, and original thinkers partake of the same culture. Creative artists rejected old forms and old values. Modernism in art and music meant constant experimentation and a search for new kinds of expression. And though many people find the modern visions of the arts strange, disturbing, and even ugly, the twentieth century, so dismal in many respects, will probably stand as one of Western civilization's great artistic eras.

Architecture and Design

Modernism in the arts was loosely unified by a revolution in architecture. This revolution not only gave the other arts striking new settings; it also intended nothing less than a transformation of the physical framework of urban society according to a new principle: *functionalism.* Buildings, like industrial products, should be useful and "functional": that is, they should serve, as well as possible, the purpose for which they were made. Thus architects and designers had to work with engineers, town planners, and even sanitation experts. Moreover, they had to throw away useless ornamentation and find beauty and aesthetic pleasure in the clean lines of practical constructions and efficient machinery. Viennese pioneer Adolf Loos

(1870–1933) quite typically equated ornamentation with crime, and Franco-Swiss genius Le Corbusier (1887–1965) insisted that "a house is a machine for living in."[5]

The United States, with its rapid urban growth and lack of rigid building traditions, pioneered in the new architecture. In the 1890s the Chicago school of architects, led by Louis H. Sullivan (1856–1924), used cheap steel, reinforced concrete, and electric elevators to build skyscrapers and office buildings lacking almost any exterior ornamentation. In the first decade of the twentieth century, Sullivan's student Frank Lloyd Wright (1869–1959) built a series of radically new and truly modern houses featuring low lines, open interiors, and mass-produced building materials. Europeans were inspired by these and other American examples of functional construction, such as the massive, unadorned grain elevators of the Midwest.

Around 1905, when the first really modern buildings were going up in Europe, architectural leadership shifted to the German-speaking countries and remained there until Hitler took power in 1933. In 1911 twenty-eight-year-old Walter Gropius (1883–1969) broke sharply with the past in his design of the Fagus shoe factory at Alfeld, Germany. A clean, light, elegant building of glass and iron, Gropius's new factory represented a jump right into the middle of the century.

After the First World War, the new German republic gave Gropius the authority to merge the schools of fine and applied arts at Weimar into a single, interdisciplinary school, the Bauhaus. In spite of intense criticism from conservative politicians and university professors, the Bauhaus brought together many leading modern architects, artists, designers, and theatrical innovators, who worked as an effective, inspired team. Throwing out traditional teaching methods, they combined the study of fine art, such as painting and sculpture, with the study of applied art in the crafts of printing, weaving, and furniture making. Throughout the 1920s, the Bauhaus, with its stress on functionalism and good design for everyday life, attracted enthusiastic students from all over the world. It had a great and continuing impact.

Along with Gropius, architect and town planner Le Corbusier had a revolutionary influence on the development of modern architecture. Often drawing his inspiration from industrial forms, such as

❖ **Frank Lloyd Wright: The "Falling Water" House** Often considered Wright's masterpiece, Falling Water combines modern architectural concepts with close attention to a spectacular site. Anchored to a high rock ledge by means of reinforced concrete, the house soars out over a cascading waterfall at Bear Run in western Pennsylvania. Built in 1937 for a Pittsburgh businessman, Falling Water is now open to the public and attracts 70,000 visitors each year. *(Source: Western Pennsylvania Conservancy/Art Resource)*

ocean liners, automobiles, and airplanes, Le Corbusier designed houses with flat roofs, open interior spaces, and clear, clean lines. His famous Savoy Villa at Poissy rested on concrete pillars and seemed to float on air. A true visionary, Le Corbusier sketched plans for a city of the future, with tall buildings surrounded by playgrounds and parks.

Another leader in the modern, or "international," style was Ludwig Mies van der Rohe (1886–1969), who followed Gropius as director of the Bauhaus in 1930 and immigrated to the United States in 1937. His classic Lake Shore Apartments in Chicago, built between 1948 and 1951, symbolize the triumph of steel-frame and glass-wall modern architecture, which had grown out of Sullivan's skyscrapers and German functionalism in the great building boom after the Second World War.

Modern Painting

Modern painting grew out of a revolt against French impressionism. The *impressionism* of such French painters as Claude Monet (1840–1926), Pierre Auguste Renoir (1841–1919), and Camille Pissarro (1830–1903) was, in part, a kind of "superrealism." Leaving exact copying of objects to photography, these artists sought to capture the momentary overall feeling, or impression, of light falling on a real-life scene before their eyes. By 1890, when impressionism was finally established, a few artists known as *postimpressionists,* or sometimes as *expressionists,* were already striking out in new directions. After 1905 art increasingly took on a nonrepresentational, abstract character, a development that reached its high point after World War Two.

Though individualistic in their styles, postimpressionists were united in their desire to know and depict worlds other than the visible world of fact. Like the early-nineteenth-century romantics, they wanted to portray unseen, inner worlds of emotion and imagination. Like modern novelists, they wanted to express a complicated psychological view of reality as well as an overwhelming emotional intensity. In *The Starry Night* (1889), for example, the great Dutch expressionist Vincent van Gogh (1853–1890) painted the vision of his mind's eye. Flaming cypress trees, exploding stars, and a cometlike Milky Way swirl together in one great cosmic rhythm. Paul Gauguin (1848–1903), the French stockbroker-turned-painter, pioneered in expressionist techniques, though he used them to infuse his work with tranquility and mysticism. In 1891 he fled to the South Pacific in search of unspoiled beauty and a primitive way of life. Gauguin believed that the form and design of a picture were important in themselves and that the painter need not try to represent objects on canvas as the eye actually saw them.

Fascination with form, as opposed to light, was characteristic of postimpressionism and expressionism. Paul Cézanne (1839–1906), who had a profound influence on twentieth-century painting, was particularly committed to form and ordered design. He told a young painter, "You must see in nature the cylinder, the sphere, and the cone."[6] As Cézanne's later work became increasingly abstract and nonrepresentational, it also moved away from the traditional three-dimensional perspective toward the two-dimensional plane, which has characterized so much of modern art. The expressionism of a group of painters led by Henri Matisse (1869–1954) was so extreme that an exhibition of their work in Paris in 1905 prompted shocked critics to call them *les fauves*—"the wild beasts." Matisse and his followers still painted real objects, but their primary concern was the arrangement of color, line, and form as an end in itself.

In 1907 a young Spaniard in Paris, Pablo Picasso (1881–1973), founded another movement—*cubism.* Cubism concentrated on a complex geometry of zigzagging lines and sharply angled, overlapping planes. About three years later came the ultimate stage in the development of abstract, nonrepresentational art. Artists such as the Russian-born Wassily Kandinsky (1866–1944) turned away from nature completely. "The observer," said Kandinsky, "must learn to look at [my] pictures . . . as form and color combinations . . . as a representation of mood and not as a representation of *objects.*"[7] On the eve of the First World War, extreme expressionism and abstract painting were developing rapidly not only in Paris but also in Russia and Germany. Modern art had become international.

In the 1920s and 1930s, the artistic movements of the prewar years were extended and consolidated. The most notable new developments were *dadaism* and *surrealism.* Dadaism attacked all accepted standards of art and behavior, delighting in outrageous conduct. Its name, from the French word *dada,* meaning "hobbyhorse," is deliberately nonsensical. A famous example of dadaism was a reproduction of Leonardo da Vinci's *Mona Lisa* in which the famous woman with the mysterious smile sports a mustache and is ridiculed with an obscene inscription. After 1924 many dadaists were attracted to surrealism, which became very influential in art in the late 1920s and 1930s. Surrealists painted a fantastic world of wild dreams and complex symbols, where watches melted and giant metronomes beat time in precisely drawn but impossible alien landscapes.

Refusing to depict ordinary visual reality, surrealist painters made powerful statements about the age of anxiety. Picasso's 26-foot-long mural *Guernica* (1937) masterfully unites several power-

❖ **Picasso: Guernica** In this rich, complex work a shrieking woman falls from a burning house on the far right. On the left a woman holds a dead child, while toward the center are fragments of a warrior and a screaming horse pierced by a spear. Picasso has used only the mournful colors of black, white, and gray. *(Source: Museo del Prado, Madrid. Pablo Picasso, Guernica [1937, May-early June]. Oil on canvas. © SPADEM, Paris/VAGA, New York, 1982)*

ful strands in twentieth-century art. Inspired by the Spanish Civil War, the painting commemorates the bombing of the ancient Spanish town of Guernica by fascist planes, an attack that took the lives of a thousand people—one out of every eight inhabitants—in a single night of terror. Combining the free distortion of expressionism, the overlapping planes of cubism, and the surrealist fascination with grotesque subject matter, *Guernica* is what Picasso meant it to be: an unforgettable attack on "brutality and darkness."

Modern Music

Developments in modern music were strikingly parallel to those in painting. Composers, too, were attracted by the emotional intensity of expressionism. The ballet *The Rite of Spring* by composer Igor Stravinsky (1882–1971) practically caused a riot when it was first performed in Paris in 1913 by Sergei Diaghilev's famous Russian dance company. The combination of pulsating, dissonant rhythms from the orchestra pit and an earthy representation of lovemaking by the dancers on the stage seemed a shocking, almost pornographic enactment of a primitive fertility rite.

After the experience of the First World War, when irrationality and violence seemed to pervade the human experience, expressionism in opera and ballet flourished. One of the most famous and powerful examples was the opera *Wozzeck,* by Alban Berg (1885–1935), first performed in Berlin in 1925. Blending a half-sung, half-spoken kind of dialogue with harsh, atonal music, *Wozzeck* is a gruesome tale of a soldier driven by Kafka-like inner terrors and vague suspicions of unfaithfulness to murder his mistress.

Some composers turned their backs on long-established musical conventions. As abstract painters arranged lines and color but did not draw identifiable objects, so modern composers arranged sounds without creating recognizable harmonies. Led by Viennese composer Arnold Schönberg (1874–1951), they abandoned traditional harmony and tonality. The musical notes in a given piece were no longer united and organized by a key; instead they were independent and unrelated. Schönberg's twelve-tone music of the 1920s arranged all twelve notes of the scale in an abstract, mathematical pattern, or "tone row." This pattern sounded like no pattern at all to the ordinary listener and could be detected only by a highly

had turned its back on European problems. Eastern Europe was in ferment, and no one could predict the future of communist Russia. Moreover, the international economic situation was poor and greatly complicated by war debts and disrupted patterns of trade. Yet for a time, from 1925 to late 1929, it appeared that peace and stability were within reach. When the subsequent collapse of the 1930s mocked these hopes, the disillusionment of liberals in the democracies was intensified.

Germany and the Western Powers

Germany was the key to lasting peace. Only under the pressure of the Allies' naval blockade and threat to extend their military occupation from the Rhineland to the rest of the country had Germany's new republican government signed the Treaty of Versailles in June 1919. To Germans of all political parties, the treaty represented a harsh, dictated peace, to be revised or repudiated as soon as possible. The treaty had neither broken nor reduced Germany, which was potentially still the strongest country in Europe. Thus the treaty had fallen between two stools: too harsh for a peace of reconciliation, too soft for a peace of conquest.

Moreover, with ominous implications for the future, France and Great Britain did not see eye to eye on Germany. By the end of 1919, France wanted to stress the harsh elements in the Treaty of Versailles. Most of the war in the west had been fought on French soil, and much of rich, industrialized northern France had been devastated. The expected costs of reconstruction were staggering; like Great Britain, France had also borrowed large sums from the United States during the war, which had to be repaid. Thus French politicians believed that massive reparations from Germany were a vital economic necessity. Moreover, if the Germans had to suffer to make the payments, the French would not be overly concerned. Having compromised with President Wilson only to be betrayed by America's failure to ratify the treaty, many French leaders saw strict implementation of all provisions of the Treaty of Versailles as France's last best hope. Large reparation payments could hold Germany down indefinitely, and France would realize its goal of security.

The British soon felt differently. Prewar Germany had been Great Britain's second-best market in the entire world, and after the war a healthy, prosperous Germany appeared to be essential to the British economy. Indeed, many English people agreed with the analysis of the young English economist John Maynard Keynes (1883–1946), who eloquently denounced the Treaty of Versailles in his famous *Economic Consequences of the Peace* (1919). According to Keynes's interpretation, astronomical reparations and harsh economic measures would indeed reduce Germany to the position of an impoverished second-rate power, but such impoverishment would increase economic hardship in all countries. Only a complete revision of the foolish treaty could save Germany—and Europe. Keynes's attack exploded like a bombshell and became very influential. It stirred deep guilt feelings about Germany in the English-speaking world, feelings that often paralyzed English and American leaders in their relations with Germany and its leaders between the First and the Second World War.

The British were also suspicious of France's army—momentarily the largest in Europe—and France's foreign policy. Ever since 1890, France had looked to Russia as a powerful ally against Germany. But with Russia hostile and socialist, and with Britain and the United States unwilling to make any firm commitments, France turned to the newly formed states of eastern Europe for diplomatic support. In 1921 France signed a mutual defense pact with Poland and associated itself closely with the so-called Little Entente, an alliance that joined Czechoslovakia, Rumania, and Yugoslavia against defeated and bitter Hungary. The British and the French were also on cool terms because of conflicts relating to their League of Nations mandates in the Middle East.

While French and British leaders drifted in different directions, the Allied reparations commission completed its work. In April 1921 it announced that Germany had to pay the enormous sum of 132 billion gold marks (33 billion dollars) in annual installments of 2.5 billion gold marks. Facing possible occupation of more of its territory, the young German republic, which had been founded in Weimar but moved back to Berlin, made its first payment in 1921. Then in 1922, wracked by rapid inflation and political assassinations and motivated by hostility and arrogance as well, the Weimar Republic announced its inability to pay more. It proposed a moratorium on reparations for three years, with the clear implication that thereafter reparations would either be drastically reduced or eliminated entirely.

The British were willing to accept this offer, but the French were not. Led by their tough-minded, legalistic prime minister, Raymond Poincaré (1860–1934), they decided they either had to call Germany's bluff or see the entire peace settlement dissolve to France's great disadvantage. So, despite strong British protests, France and its ally Belgium decided to pursue a firm policy. In early January 1923, French and Belgian armies began to occupy the Ruhr district, the heartland of industrial Germany, creating the most serious international crisis of the 1920s.

The Occupation of the Ruhr

The strategy of Poincaré and his French supporters was simple: since Germany was resisting and would not pay reparations in hard currency or gold, France and Belgium would collect reparations in kind—coal, steel, and machinery. If forcible collection proved impossible, France would use occupation to paralyze Germany and force it to accept the Treaty of Versailles.

Strengthened by a wave of patriotism, the German government ordered the people of the Ruhr to stop working and start passively resisting the French occupation. The coal mines and steel mills of the Ruhr grew silent, leaving 10 percent of Germany's total population in need of relief. The French answer to passive resistance was to seal off not only the Ruhr but also the entire Rhineland from the rest of Germany, letting in only enough food to prevent starvation. The French also revived plans for a separate state in the Rhineland.

By the summer of 1923, France and Germany were engaged in a great test of wills. As the German government had anticipated, French armies could not collect reparations from striking workers at gunpoint. But French occupation was indeed paralyzing Germany and its economy, for the Ruhr district normally produced 80 percent of Germany's steel and coal. Moreover, the occupation of the Ruhr turned rapid German inflation into runaway inflation. Faced with the need to support the striking Ruhr workers and their employers, the German government began to print money to pay its bills. Prices soared. People went to the store with a big bag of paper money; they returned home with a handful of groceries. German money

"Hands Off the Ruhr" The French occupation of the Ruhr to collect reparations payments raised a storm of patriotic protest in Germany. This anti-French poster of 1923 turns Marianne, the personification of French republican virtue, into a vicious harpy. *(Source: Internationaal Instituut voor Sociale Geschiedenis)*

rapidly lost all value, and so did anything else with a stated fixed value.

Runaway inflation brought about a social revolution. The accumulated savings of many retired and middle-class people were wiped out. The old middle-class virtues of thrift, caution, and self-reliance were cruelly mocked by catastrophic inflation. People told themselves that nothing had real value anymore, not even money. The German middle and lower middle classes, feeling cheated, burned with resentment. Many hated and blamed the

Western governments, their own government, big business, the Jews, the workers, and the communists for their misfortune. They were psychologically prepared to follow radical leaders in a crisis.

In August 1923, as the mark fell and political unrest grew throughout Germany, Gustav Stresemann (1878–1929) assumed leadership of the government. Stresemann adopted a compromising attitude. He called off passive resistance in the Ruhr and in October agreed in principle to pay reparations but asked for a re-examination of Germany's ability to pay. Poincaré accepted. His hard line was becoming increasingly unpopular with French citizens, and it was hated in Britain and the United States. Moreover, occupation was dreadfully expensive, and France's own currency was beginning to lose value on foreign exchange markets.

More generally, in both Germany and France power was finally passing to the moderates, who realized that continued confrontation was a destructive, no-win situation. Thus after five long years of hostility and tension, culminating in a kind of undeclared war in the Ruhr in 1923, Germany and France decided to give compromise and cooperation a try. The British, and even the Americans, were willing to help. The first step was a reasonable compromise on the reparations question.

Hope in Foreign Affairs, 1924–1929

The reparations commission appointed an international committee of financial experts headed by American banker Charles G. Dawes to re-examine reparations from a broad perspective. The committee made a series of recommendations known as the Dawes Plan (1924), and the plan was accepted by France, Germany, and Britain. German reparations were reduced and placed on a sliding scale, like an income tax, whereby yearly payments depended on the level of German economic prosperity. The Dawes Plan also recommended large loans to Germany, which could come only from the United States. These loans were to help Stresemann's government put its new currency on a firm basis and promote German recovery. In short, Germany would get private loans from the United States and pay reparations to France and Britain, thus enabling those countries to repay the large sums they owed the United States.

This circular flow of international payments was complicated and risky. And for a time it worked.

The German republic experienced a spectacular economic recovery. By 1929 Germany's wealth and income were 50 percent greater than in 1913. With prosperity and large, continual inflows of American capital, Germany easily paid about 1.3 billion dollars in reparations in 1927 and 1928, enabling France and Britain to pay the United States. In 1929 the Young Plan, named after an American businessman representing the United States, further reduced German reparations and formalized the link between German reparations and French-British debts to the United States. In this way the Americans, who did not have armies but who did have money, belatedly played a part in the general economic settlement that, though far from ideal, facilitated the worldwide recovery of the late 1920s.

This economic settlement was matched by a political settlement. In 1925 the leaders of Europe signed a number of agreements at Locarno, Switzerland. Stresemann, who guided Germany's foreign policy until his death in 1929, had suggested a treaty with France's conciliatory Aristide Briand (1862–1932), who had returned to office in 1924 after French voters rejected the bellicose Poincaré. By this treaty Germany and France solemnly pledged to accept their common border, and both Britain and Italy agreed to fight either country if it invaded the other. Stresemann also agreed to settle boundary disputes with Poland and Czechoslovakia by peaceful means, and France promised those countries military aid if they were attacked by Germany. For their efforts Stresemann and Briand shared the Nobel Peace Prize in 1926. The effect of the treaties of Locarno was far-reaching. For years, a "spirit of Locarno" gave Europeans a sense of growing security and stability in international affairs.

Hopes were strengthened by other developments. In 1926 Germany joined the League of Nations, where Stresemann continued his "peace offensive." In 1928 fifteen countries signed the Kellogg-Briand Pact, which "condemned and renounced war as an instrument of national policy." The signing states agreed to settle international disputes peacefully. Often seen as idealistic nonsense because it made no provisions for action in case war actually occurred, the pact was nevertheless a hopeful step. It grew out of a suggestion by Briand that France and the United States renounce the possibility of war between their two countries.

✦ **Berlin, the 1920s** These colorful slices of life in Berlin give a feeling for the vibrancy and complexity of the German capital after the German economy stabilized and boomed in the late 1920s. Interwar Berlin had its faults and excesses, but few ever accused the great city of being dull and uninteresting. *(Source: Berlinische Galerie Museum fur Moderne Kunst Photographie und Architektur)*

Briand was gently and subtly trying to draw the United States back into involvement with Europe. When Secretary of State Frank B. Kellogg proposed a multinational pact, Briand appeared close to success. Thus the cautious optimism of the late 1920s also rested on the hope that the United States would accept its responsibilities as a great world power and consequently contribute to European stability.

Hope in Democratic Government

Domestic politics also offered reason to hope. During the occupation of the Ruhr and the great inflation, republican government in Germany had appeared on the verge of collapse. In 1923 communists momentarily entered provincial governments, and in November an obscure nobody named Adolf Hitler leaped on to a table in a beer hall in Munich and proclaimed a "national socialist revolution." But Hitler's plot to seize control of the government was poorly organized and easily crushed, and Hitler was sentenced to prison, where he outlined his theories and program in his book *Mein Kampf* (My Struggle). Throughout the 1920s, Hitler's National Socialist party attracted support only from a few fanatical anti-Semites, ultranationalists, and disgruntled ex-servicemen. In 1928 his party had an insignificant twelve seats in the Reichstag. Indeed, after 1923 democracy seemed to take root in Weimar Germany. A new currency was established, and the economy boomed.

The moderate businessmen who tended to dominate the various German coalition governments were convinced that economic prosperity demanded good relations with the Western powers, and they supported parliamentary government at home. Stresemann himself was a man of this class, and he was the key figure in every government until his death in 1929. Elections were held regularly, and republican democracy appeared to have growing support among a majority of the Germans.

There were, however, sharp political divisions in the country. Many unrepentant nationalists and monarchists populated the right and the army. Germany's Communists were noisy and active on the left. The Communists, directed from Moscow, reserved their greatest hatred and sharpest barbs for their cousins the Social Democrats, whom they endlessly accused of betraying the revolution. The working classes were divided politically, but most supported the nonrevolutionary but socialist Social Democrats.

The situation in France had numerous similarities to that in Germany. Communists and Socialists battled for the support of the workers. After 1924 the democratically elected government rested mainly in the hands of coalitions of moderates, and business interests were well represented. France's great accomplishment was rapid rebuilding of its war-torn northern region. The expense of this undertaking led, however, to a large deficit and substantial inflation. By early 1926 the franc had fallen to 10 percent of its prewar value, causing a severe crisis. Poincaré was recalled to office, while Briand remained minister for foreign affairs. The Poincaré government proceeded to slash spending and raise taxes, restoring confidence in the economy. The

An American in Paris The young Josephine Baker suddenly became a star when she brought an exotic African eroticism to French music halls in 1925. American blacks and Africans had a powerful impact on entertainment in Europe in the 1920s and 1930s. *(Source: Bettmann/Hulton)*

franc was "saved," stabilized at about one-fifth of its prewar value. Good times prevailed until 1930.

Despite political shortcomings, France attracted artists and writers from all over the world in the 1920s. Much of the intellectual and artistic ferment of the times flourished in Paris. As writer Gertrude Stein (1874–1946), a leader of the large colony of American expatriates living in Paris, later recalled, "Paris was where the twentieth century was."[10] More generally, France appealed to foreigners and the French as a harmonious combination of small businesses and family farms, of bold innovation and solid traditions.

Britain, too, faced challenges after 1920. The wartime trend toward greater social equality continued, however, helping maintain social harmony. The great problem was unemployment. Many of Britain's best markets had been lost during the war. In June 1921 almost 2.2 million people—23 percent of the labor force—were out of work, and throughout the 1920s unemployment hovered around 12 percent. Yet the state provided unemployment benefits of equal size to all those without jobs and supplemented those payments with subsidized housing, medical aid, and increased old-age pensions. These and other measures kept living standards from seriously declining, defused class tensions, and pointed the way toward the welfare state Britain established after World War Two.

Relative social harmony was accompanied by the rise of the Labour party as a determined champion of the working classes and of greater social equality. Committed to the kind of moderate, "revisionist" socialism that had emerged before World War One (see page 858), the Labour party replaced the Liberal party as the main opposition to the Conservatives. The new prominence of the Labour party reflected the decline of old liberal ideals of competitive capitalism, limited government control, and individual responsibility. In 1924 and 1929, the Labour party under Ramsay MacDonald (1866–1937) governed the country with the support of the smaller Liberal party. Yet Labour moved toward socialism gradually and democratically, so that the middle classes were not overly frightened as the working classes won new benefits.

The Conservatives under Stanley Baldwin (1867–1947) showed the same compromising spirit on social issues. The last line of Baldwin's greatest speech in March 1925 summarized his international and domestic programs: "Give us peace in our time, O Lord." In spite of such conflicts as the 1926 strike by hard-pressed coal miners, which ended in an unsuccessful general strike, social unrest in Britain was limited in the 1920s and in the 1930s as well. In 1922 Britain granted southern, Catholic Ireland full autonomy after a bitter guerrilla war, thereby removing another source of prewar friction. Thus developments in both international relations and in the domestic politics of the leading democracies gave cause for cautious optimism in the late 1920s.

✣ THE GREAT DEPRESSION, 1929–1939

Like the Great War, the Great Depression must be spelled with capital letters. Economic depression was nothing new. Depressions occurred throughout the nineteenth century with predictable regularity, as they recur in the form of recessions and slumps to this day. What was new about this depression was its severity and duration. It struck the entire world with ever-greater intensity from 1929 to 1933, and recovery was uneven and slow. Only with the Second World War did the depression disappear in much of the world.

The social and political consequences of prolonged economic collapse were enormous. The depression shattered the fragile optimism of political leaders in the late 1920s. Mass unemployment made insecurity a reality for millions of ordinary people, who had paid little attention to the intellectual crisis or to new directions in art and ideas (Map 28.1). In desperation, people looked for leaders who would "do something." They were willing to support radical attempts to deal with the crisis by both democratic leaders and dictators.

The Economic Crisis

There is no agreement among historians and economists about why the Great Depression was so deep and lasted so long. Thus it is best to trace the course of the great collapse before trying to identify what caused it.

Though economic activity was already declining moderately in many countries by early 1929, the crash of the stock market in the United States in October of that year really started the Great Depression. The American stock market boom, which

Isaac Soyer: Employment Agency (1937) The frustration and agony of looking for work against long odds are painfully evident in this American masterpiece. The time-killing, pensive resignation, and dejection seen in the three figures are only aspects of the larger problem. One of three talented brothers born in Russia and trained as artists in New York, Isaac Soyer worked in the tradition of American realism and concentrated on people and the influence of their environment. *(Source: Collection of Whitney Museum of American Art)*

increase demand and break the vicious cycle of decline.

Along with economic effects, mass unemployment posed a great social problem that mere numbers cannot adequately express. Millions of people lost their spirit and dignity in an apparently hopeless search for work. Homes and ways of life were disrupted in millions of personal tragedies. Young people postponed marriages they could not afford, and birthrates fell sharply. There was an increase in suicide and mental illness. Poverty or the threat of poverty became a grinding reality. In 1932 the workers of Manchester, England, appealed to their city officials—a typical appeal echoed throughout the Western world:

We tell you that thousands of people . . . are in desperate straits. We tell you that men, women, and children are going hungry. . . . We tell you that great numbers are being rendered distraught through the stress and worry of trying to exist without work. . . .

If you do not do this—if you do not provide useful work for the unemployed—what, we ask, is your alternative? Do not imagine that this colossal tragedy of unemployment is going on endlessly without some fateful catastrophe. Hungry men are angry men.[12]

Mass unemployment was a terrible time bomb preparing to explode.

The New Deal in the United States

Of all the major industrial countries, only Germany was harder hit by the Great Depression, or reacted more radically to it, than the United States. Depression was so traumatic in the United States because the 1920s had been a period of complacent prosperity. The Great Depression and the response to it marked a major turning point in American history.

President Herbert Hoover (1895–1972) and his administration initially reacted to the stock market crash and economic decline with dogged optimism and limited action. In May 1930 Hoover told a group of business and farm leaders, "I am convinced that we have now passed the worst and with continued unity of effort we shall rapidly recover." When, however, the full force of the financial crisis struck Europe in the summer of 1931 and boomeranged back to the United States, people's worst fears became reality. Banks failed; unemployment soared. In 1932 industrial production fell to about 50 percent of its 1929 level. In these tragic circumstances Franklin Delano Roosevelt (1882–1945), an inspiring wheelchair-bound aristocrat previously crippled by polio, won a landslide electoral victory with grand but vague promises of a "New Deal for the forgotten man."

Roosevelt's basic goal was to reform capitalism in order to preserve it. In his words, "A frank examination of the profit system in the spring of 1933 showed it to be in collapse; but substantially everybody in the United States, in public office and out of public office, from the very rich to the very poor, was as determined as was my Administration to save it."[13] Roosevelt rejected socialism and government ownership of industry in 1933. To right the situation, he chose forceful government intervention in the economy.

In this choice, Roosevelt and his advisers were greatly influenced by American experience in World War One. During the wartime emergency, the American economy had been thoroughly planned and regulated. Roosevelt and his "brain trust" of advisers adopted similar policies to restore prosperity and reduce social inequality. Roosevelt was flexible, pragmatic, and willing to experiment. Government intervention and experimentation

were combined in some of the New Deal's most significant measures.

The most ambitious attempt to control and plan the economy was the National Recovery Administration (NRA), established by Congress right after Roosevelt took office. The key idea behind the NRA was to reduce competition and fix prices and wages for everyone's benefit. This goal required government, business, and labor to hammer out detailed regulations for each industry. Along with this kind of national planning in the private sector of the economy, the government believed it could sponsor enough public works projects to assure recovery. Because the NRA broke with the cherished American tradition of free competition and aroused conflicts among business people, consumers, and bureaucrats, it did not work well. By the time the NRA was declared unconstitutional in 1935, Roosevelt and the New Deal were already moving away from government efforts to plan and control the entire economy.

Instead, Roosevelt and his advisers attacked the key problem of mass unemployment directly. The federal government accepted the responsibility of employing directly as many people as financially possible, something Hoover had consistently rejected. Thus when it became clear in late 1933 that the initial program of public works was too small, new agencies were created to undertake a vast range of projects.

The most famous of these was the Works Progress Administration (WPA), set up in 1935. At its peak in late 1938, this government agency employed more than three million individuals. One-fifth of the entire labor force worked for the WPA at some point in the 1930s. To this day, thousands of public buildings, bridges, and highways built by the WPA stand as monuments to energetic government efforts to provide people with meaningful work. The WPA was enormously popular in a nation long schooled in self-reliance and the work ethic. The hope of a job with the government helped check the threat of social revolution in the United States.

Other social measures aimed in the same direction. Following the path blazed by Germany's Bismarck in the 1880s, the U.S. government in 1935 established a national social security system, with old-age pensions and unemployment benefits, to protect many workers against some of life's uncertainties. The National Labor Relations Act of 1935 gave union organizers the green light by declaring collective bargaining to be the policy of the United States. Following some bitter strikes, such as a sit-down strike at General Motors in early 1937, union membership more than doubled, from four million in 1935 to nine million in 1940. In general, between 1935 and 1938 government rulings and social reforms chipped away at the privileges of the wealthy and tried to help ordinary people.

Yet despite undeniable accomplishments in social reform, the New Deal was only partly successful as a response to the Great Depression. At the height of the recovery in May 1937, seven million workers were still unemployed. The economic situation then worsened seriously in the recession of 1937 and 1938. Production fell sharply, and although unemployment never again reached the fifteen million mark of 1933, it hit eleven million in 1938 and was still a staggering ten million when war broke out in Europe in September 1939.

The New Deal never did pull the United States out of the depression. This failure frustrated Americans then, and it is still puzzling today. Perhaps, as some have claimed, Roosevelt should have used his enormous popularity and prestige in 1933 to nationalize the banks, the railroads, and some heavy industry so that national economic planning could have been successful. Even though Roosevelt's sharp attack on big business and the wealthy after 1935 had popular appeal, it also damaged business confidence and made the great capitalists uncooperative. Given the low level of profit and the underutilization of many factories, however, it is questionable whether business would have behaved much differently even if the New Deal had catered to it.

It is often argued that the New Deal did not put enough money into the economy through deficit financing. Like his predecessors in the White House, Roosevelt was attached to the ideal of the balanced budget. His largest deficit was only 4.4 billion dollars in 1936. Compare this figure with deficits of 21.5 billion dollars in 1942 and 57.4 billion dollars in 1943, when the nation was prosperously engaged in total war and unemployment had vanished. By 1945 many economists were concluding that the New Deal's deficit-financed public works had been too small a step in the right direction. These Keynesian views were to be very influential in economic policy in Europe and America after the Second World War.

The Scandinavian Response to the Depression

Of all the Western democracies, the Scandinavian countries under Socialist leadership responded most successfully to the challenge of the Great Depression. Having grown steadily in number in the late nineteenth century, the Socialists became the largest political party in Sweden and then in Norway after the First World War. In the 1920s they passed important social reform legislation for both peasants and workers, gained practical administrative experience, and developed a unique kind of socialism. Flexible and nonrevolutionary, Scandinavian socialism grew out of a strong tradition of cooperative community action. Even before 1900, Scandinavian agricultural cooperatives had shown how individual peasant families could join together for everyone's benefit. Labor leaders and capitalists were also inclined to work together.

When the economic crisis struck in 1929, Socialist governments in Scandinavia built on this pattern of cooperative social action. Sweden in particular pioneered in the use of large-scale deficits to finance public works and thereby maintain production and employment. Scandinavian governments also increased social welfare benefits, from old-age pensions and unemployment insurance to subsidized housing and maternity allowances. All this spending required a large bureaucracy and high taxes, first on the rich and then on practically everyone. Yet both private and cooperative enterprise thrived, as did democracy. Some observers saw Scandinavia's welfare socialism as an appealing "middle way" between sick capitalism and cruel communism or fascism.

Recovery and Reform in Britain and France

In Britain MacDonald's Labour government and then, after 1931, the Conservative-dominated coalition government followed orthodox economic theory. The budget was balanced, but unemployed workers received barely enough welfare to live. Despite government lethargy, the economy recovered considerably after 1932. By 1937 total production was about 20 percent higher than in 1929. In fact, for Britain the years after 1932 were actually somewhat better than the 1920s had been, quite the opposite of the situation in the United States and France.

This good but by no means brilliant performance reflected the gradual reorientation of the British economy. After going off the gold standard in 1931 and establishing protective tariffs in 1932, Britain concentrated increasingly on the national, rather than the international, market. The old export industries of the Industrial Revolution, such as textiles and coal, continued to decline, but new industries, such as automobiles and electrical appliances, grew in response to British home demand. Moreover, low interest rates encouraged a housing boom. By the end of the decade, there were highly visible differences between the old, depressed industrial areas of the north and the new, growing areas of the south. These developments encouraged Britain to look inward and avoid unpleasant foreign questions.

Because France was relatively less industrialized and more isolated from the world economy, the Great Depression came late. But once the depression hit France, it stayed and stayed. Decline was steady until 1935, and a short-lived recovery never brought production or employment back up to predepression levels. Economic stagnation both reflected and heightened an ongoing political crisis. There was no stability in government. As before 1914, the French parliament was made up of many political parties, which could never cooperate for very long. In 1933, for example, five coalition cabinets formed and fell in rapid succession.

The French lost the underlying unity that had made government instability bearable before 1914. Fascist-type organizations agitated against parliamentary democracy and looked to Mussolini's Italy and Hitler's Germany for inspiration. In February 1934 French fascists and semifascists rioted and threatened to overturn the republic. At the same time, the Communist party and many workers opposed to the existing system were looking to Stalin's Russia for guidance. The vital center of moderate republicanism was sapped from both sides.

Frightened by the growing strength of the fascists at home and abroad, the Communists, the Socialists, and the Radicals formed an alliance—the Popular Front—for the national elections of May 1936. Their clear victory reflected the trend toward polarization. The number of Communists in the parliament jumped dramatically from 10 to 72, while the Socialists, led by Léon Blum, became the strongest party in France, with 146 seats. The re-

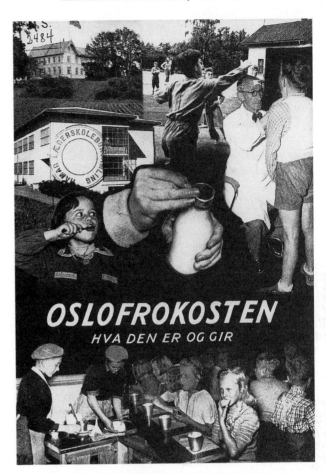

❖ **Scandinavian Socialism** championed cooperation and practical welfare measures, playing down strident rhetoric and theories of class conflict. The Oslo Breakfast, depicted in the lower part of this poster, exemplified the Scandinavian approach. It provided every schoolchild in the Norwegian capital with a good breakfast free of charge. (*Source: Universitets-biblioteket i Oslo*)

ally quite moderate Radicals slipped badly, and the conservatives lost ground to the semifascists.

In the next few months, Blum's Popular Front government made the first and only real attempt to deal with the social and economic problems of the 1930s in France. Inspired by Roosevelt's New Deal, the Popular Front encouraged the union movement and launched a far-reaching program of social reform, complete with paid vacations and a forty-hour workweek. Popular with workers and the lower middle class, these measures were quickly sabotaged by rapid inflation and cries of revolution from fascists and frightened conservatives. Wealthy people sneaked their money out of the country, labor unrest grew, and France entered a severe financial crisis. Blum was forced to announce a "breathing spell" in social reform.

The fires of political dissension were also fanned by civil war in Spain. Communists demanded that France support the Spanish republicans, while many French conservatives would gladly have joined Hitler and Mussolini in aiding the attack of Spanish fascists. Extremism grew, and France itself was within sight of civil war. Blum was forced to resign in June 1937, and the Popular Front quickly collapsed. An anxious and divided France drifted aimlessly once again, preoccupied by Hitler and German rearmament.

SUMMARY

After the First World War, Western society entered a complex and difficult era—truly an age of anxiety. Intellectual life underwent a crisis marked by pessimism, uncertainty, and fascination with irrational forces. Ceaseless experimentation and rejection of old forms characterized art and music, while motion pictures and radio provided a new, standardized entertainment for the masses. Intellectual and artistic developments that had been confined to small avant-garde groups before 1914 gained wider currency along with the insecure state of mind they expressed.

Politics and economics were similarly disrupted. In the 1920s political leaders groped to create an enduring peace and rebuild the prewar prosperity, and for a brief period late in the decade they even seemed to have succeeded. Then the Great Depression shattered that fragile stability. Uncertainty returned with redoubled force in the 1930s. The international economy collapsed, and unemployment struck millions worldwide. The democracies turned inward as they sought to cope with massive domestic problems and widespread disillusionment. Generally speaking, they were not very successful. The old liberal ideals of individual rights and responsibilities, elected government, and economic freedom, even when they managed to survive, seemed ineffective and outmoded to many. And in many countries these ideas were abandoned completely.

NOTES

1. P. Valéry, *Variety,* trans. M. Cowley (New York: Harcourt Brace, 1927), pp. 27–28.
2. Quoted in S. Hughes, *The Obstructed Path: French Social Thought in the Years of Desperation, 1930–1960* (New York: Harper & Row, 1967), p. 82.
3. G. Greene, *Another Mexico* (New York: Viking Press, 1939), p. 3.
4. G. Orwell, *1984* (New York: New American Library, 1950), p. 220.
5. C. E. Jeanneret-Gris (Le Corbusier), *Towards a New Architecture* (London: J. Rodker, 1931), p. 15.
6. Quoted in A. H. Barr, Jr., *What Is Modern Painting?,* 9th ed. (New York: Museum of Modern Art, 1966), p. 27.
7. Quoted in ibid., p. 25.
8. R. Graves and A. Hodge, *The Long Week End: A Social History of Great Britain, 1918–1939* (New York: Macmillan, 1941), p. 131.
9. Quoted in A. Briggs, *The Birth of Broadcasting,* vol. 1 (London: Oxford University Press, 1961), p. 47.
10. Quoted in R. J. Sontag, *A Broken World, 1919–1939* (New York: Harper & Row, 1971), p. 129.
11. C. P. Kindleberger, *The World in Depression, 1929–1939* (Berkeley and Los Angeles: University of California Press, 1973), p. 292.
12. Quoted in S. B. Clough et al., eds., *Economic History of Europe: Twentieth Century* (New York: Harper & Row, 1968), pp. 243–245.
13. Quoted in D. Dillard, *Economic Development of the North Atlantic Community* (Englewood Cliffs, N.J.: Prentice-Hall, 1967), p. 591.

SUGGESTED READING

Among general works, E. Wiskemann's *Europe of the Dictators, 1919–1945* (1966) and Sontag's study cited in the Notes are particularly recommended. The latter has an excellent bibliography. A. Bullock, ed., *The Twentieth Century* (1971), is a lavish visual feast combined with penetrating essays on major developments since 1900. Two excellent accounts of contemporary history—one with a liberal and the other with a conservative point of view—are R. Paxton, *Europe in the Twentieth Century* (1975), and P. Johnson, *Modern Times: The World from the Twenties to the Eighties* (1983). Crucial changes in thought before and after World War One are discussed in three rewarding intellectual histories: G. Masur, *Prophets of Yesterday*

(1961); H. S. Hughes, *Consciousness and Society* (1956); and M. Biddiss, *Age of the Masses: Ideas and Society Since 1870* (1977). R. Stromberg, *European Intellectual History Since 1789* (1986), and F. Baumer, *Modern European Thought: Continuity and Change in Ideas, 1600–1950* (1970), are recommended general surveys. W. Kaufmann, *Nietzsche* (1974), is a sympathetic and justly famous study, and S. Aschheim, *The Nietzsche Legacy in Germany, 1890–1990* (1992), considers the range of responses to the pioneering philosopher. W. Barrett, *Irrational Man: A Study in Existential Philosophy* (1958), is still useful.

N. Cantor, *Twentieth-Century Culture: Modernism to Deconstruction* (1988), is a pugnacious and stimulating survey. J. Rewald's *The History of Impressionism* (1961) and *Post-Impressionism* (1956) are excellent, as is the work by Barr cited in the Notes. P. Collaer, *A History of Modern Music* (1961), and H. R. Hitchcock, *Architecture: Nineteenth and Twentieth Centuries* (1958), are good introductions, whereas T. Wolfe, *From Bauhaus to My House* (1981), is a lively critique of modern architecture. L. Barnett, *The Universe and Dr. Einstein* (1952), is a fascinating study of the new physics. A. Storr, *Freud* (1989), and P. Rieff, *Freud* (1956), consider the man and how his theories have stood the test of time. In *Civilization and Its Discontents* (1930), which is highly recommended, S. Freud explores his theory of instinct and repression, arguing that society's necessary repression of instinctual drives will always leave people unhappy. M. White, ed., *The Age of Analysis* (1955), opens up basic questions of twentieth-century psychology and philosophy. H. Liebersohn, *Fate and Utopia in German Sociology* (1988), analyzes developments in German social science. J. Willett, *The New Sobriety: Art and Politics in the Weimar Period, 1917–1933* (1978), and P. Gay, *Weimar Culture* (1970), consider the artistic renaissance and the political culture in Germany in the 1920s. M. Marrus, ed., *Emergence of Leisure* (1974), is a pioneering inquiry into an important aspect of mass culture. H. Daniels-Rops, *A Fight for God,* 2 vols. (1966), is a sympathetic history of the Catholic church between 1870 and 1939.

G. Ambrosius and W. Hibbard, *A Social and Economic History of Twentieth-Century Europe* (1989), provides a good survey; C. Maier, *Recasting Bourgeois Europe* (1975), is an ambitious comparative study of social classes and conflicts in France, Germany, and Italy after World War One. P. Fritzsche, *Rehearsals for Fascism: Populism and Political Mobilization in Weimar Germany* (1990); R. Wohl, *The Generation of 1914* (1979); R. Kuisel, *Capital and State in Modern France: Renovation and Economic Management* (1982); and W. McDougall, *France's Rhineland Diplomacy, 1914–1924* (1978), are four more important studies on aspects of the postwar challenge. H. James, *The German Slump: Politics and Economics, 1924–1936* (1986), is excellent analysis of economic recovery and subsequent collapse. M. Childs, *Sweden: The Middle Way* (1961), applauds Sweden's efforts at social reform. W. Neuman, *The Balance of Power in the Interwar Years, 1919–1939* (1968), perceptively examines international politics after the Locarno treaties of 1925. In addition to the contemporary works discussed in the text, the crisis of the interwar period comes alive in R. Crossman, ed., *The God That Failed* (1950), in which famous Western writers tell why they were attracted to and later repelled by communism; J. Ortega y Gasset's renowned *The Revolt of the Masses* (1932); and F. A. Hayek's *The Road to Serfdom* (1944), a famous warning of the dangers to democratic freedoms.

In addition to Kindleberger's excellent study of the Great Depression cited in the Notes, there is J. Galbraith's very lively and understandable account of the stock market collapse, *The Great Crash* (1955). J. Garraty, *Unemployment in History* (1978), is noteworthy, though novels best portray the human tragedy of economic decline. W. Holtby, *South Riding* (1936), and W. Greenwood, *Love on the Dole* (1933), are moving stories of the Great Depression in England; Hans Fallada, *Little Man, What Now?* (1932), is the classic counterpart for Germany. Also highly recommended as commentaries on English life between the wars are R. Graves, *Goodbye to All That* (1957), and George Orwell, *The Road to Wigan Pier* (1972). Among French novelists, André Gide painstakingly examines the French middle class and its values in *The Counterfeiters*; Albert Camus, the greatest of the existential novelists, is at his unforgettable best in *The Stranger* (1942) and *The Plague* (1947).

A Christian View of Evil

The English philosopher C. E. M. Joad (1891–1953) stands out among intellectuals who turned toward religion in the age of anxiety. As a university student he shed his faith and became a militant rationalist who was "frequently in demand for lectures and articles which adopted an attitude hostile to revealed religion in general, and to the Christian Church in particular." Only after intense reflection did Joad retrace his steps and come to reaccept Christianity. Ever the serious intellectual, he described and analyzed his "spiritual odyssey" in closely reasoned and influential writings.

The following selection is taken from God and Evil, *published in 1942 when Hitler's empire posed the problem of human depravity in the starkest terms. Reconsidering the modern secular faith in the primacy of environmental influences and in the perfectibility of humankind, Joad found these beliefs wanting. He reaffirmed the Christian focus on sin and the need for God's grace to escape from evil and find salvation.*

There is, we are told, a revival of interest in religious matters. . . . In this revival of interest I have shared. . . . As a young man at Oxford, I participated, as was natural to my age and generation, in prolonged and frequent discussions of religion which, finding me a Christian, left me as they did many of my generation, an agnostic, an agnostic who entertained a deep-seated suspicion of all dogmatic creeds. . . .

As an agnostic, I felt convinced of two things: first, . . . within the sphere of religion that we did not and probably could not know the truth; secondly, in regard to the so-called religious truths that I had been taught, as, for example, that God created the world as stated in Genesis [and] . . . sent His Son into it to redeem mankind, that it was improbable that they were true and certain that they could not

be *known* to be true. In the confidence of this conviction I proceeded, to all intents and purposes, to turn my back upon the whole subject. . . .

It was only after the coming of the Nazis that my mind began again to turn in the direction of religion. . . . [With] the outbreak of [the Second World] war the subject leapt straight into the forefront of my consciousness where it has remained ever since. . . .

I take it [my spiritual odyssey] to be not untypical. From conversations and discussions, especially with students, I surmise that the revival of interest in religion is widespread. . . . This topical relevance of religion derives from two sources. [First, there is] the relation between religion and politics. This connection . . . subsists at all times, but in quiet times of peace it usually remains implicit. The peculiar circumstances of the last twenty-five years have, however, combined to thrust it into the foreground of men's consciousness. . . . Thus times of revolutionary political change are also times of religious questioning and discussion.

The other source of the specifically topical interest in religion is . . . the obtrusiveness of evil. [Perhaps] there is no more evil abroad in Western civilization than there was at the end of the last century, but it cannot be denied that what there is of it is more obtrusive. I am not referring to evils arising from the relation between the sexes upon which the Church has laid such exclusive stress. . . . I mean the evils of cruelty, savagery, oppression, violence, egotism, aggrandisement, and lust for power. So pervasive and insistent have these evils become that it is at times difficult to avoid concluding that the Devil has been given a longer rope than usual, . . . [and] it becomes correspondingly more difficult to explain it away by the various methods which have been fashionable during the last twenty years.

There was, for example, the explanation of evil in terms of economic inequality and injustice. Socialist writers had taught my generation that bad conditions were the cause of human wretchedness . . . and also of human wickedness. Poverty . . . was the supreme sin; supreme if only because it was the source of all the others. . . .

And the moral [of this teaching]? That evil is due to bad social conditions. Now you can reform bad social conditions by Act of Parliament, substituting comfort, cleanliness, security, and financial competence for discomfort, dirt, insecurity, and want. Therefore, presumably, you can make men virtuous . . . by Act of Parliament.

There was a later explanation of evil in terms of early psychological maltreatment and consequent psychological maladjustment. Evil, then, according to this view, was the result not of bad social, but of bad psychological conditions; not so much of an imperfect society, as of an imperfect family, an ill-directed nursery, and a wrongly run school. Reform society, said the Socialist, and evil will disappear. Reform the school and the family, the psychoanalysts added, and society will reform itself and, once again, evil will disappear. . . .

The contemporary view of evil is untenable. . . . Evil is not *merely* a by-product of unfavourable circumstances; it is too widespread and too deep-seated to admit of any such explanation; so widespread, so deep-seated that one can only conclude that what the religions have always taught is true, and that evil is endemic in the heart of man. . . . The intellectual blunder [of the comfortable and secure late-nineteenth century was] . . . denying what we had traditionally been taught, the doctrine of original sin. . . .

For the simple truth is that one cannot help oneself. . . . For one cannot help but know that one's character is *not* strong enough, one's efforts *not* efficacious, at least, that they are not, if unaided. . . . There are two alternatives [to giving in to evil].

The first, since the world is evil, is to escape from it and to find, first in withdrawal, and, as an ultimate hope, in Nirvana, the true way of life. The second is to face evil and to seek to overcome it. . . . The first is the way of the East, the second of Christianity. My temperament and disposition incline me to the second, but the second I know to be impossible

✥ The British philosopher Cyril Edwin Mitchinson Joad (1891–1953). *(Source: Hulton-Deutsch)*

unless I am assisted from without. By the grace of God we are assured, such assistance may be obtained and evil may be overcome; otherwise, there is no resource and no resistance.

Questions for Analysis

1. How did Joad account for a renewed interest in religious matters?

2. Joad concentrated on the problem of evil in human affairs. What did he mean by "evil"? Was it becoming more powerful in his time?

3. What, according to Joad, were the usual explanations for the existence of evil? What was his view of these explanations?

4. In Joad's view, how did the Christian doctrine of original sin relate to the problem of evil? How could the Christian overcome sin and evil?

Source: C. E. M. Joad, *God and Evil* (New York: Harper and Brothers, 1943), pp. 9–20, 103–104.

29

Dictatorships and the Second World War

❖ The era of anxiety and economic depression was also a time of growing strength for political dictatorship. Popularly elected governments and basic civil liberties declined drastically in Europe. On the eve of the Second World War, liberal democratic governments were surviving only in Great Britain, France, the Low Countries, the Scandinavian nations, and neutral Switzerland. Elsewhere in Europe, various kinds of "strongmen" ruled. Dictatorship seemed the wave of the future. Thus the decline in liberal political institutions and the intellectual crisis were related elements in the general crisis of European civilization.

The era of dictatorship is a highly disturbing chapter in the history of Western civilization. The key development was not only the resurgence of authoritarian rule but also the rise of a particularly ruthless and dynamic tyranny. This new kind of tyranny reached its fullest realization in the Soviet Union and Nazi Germany in the 1930s. Stalin and Hitler mobilized their peoples for enormous undertakings and ruled with unprecedented severity. Hitler's mobilization was ultimately directed toward racial aggression and territorial expansion, and his sudden attack on Poland in 1939 started World War Two.

Nazi armies were defeated by a great coalition, and today we want to believe that the era of totalitarian dictatorship was a terrible accident, that Stalin's slave labor camps and Hitler's gas chambers "can't happen again." Yet the cruel truth is that horrible atrocities continue to plague the world in our time. The Khmer Rouge inflicted genocide on its people in Kampuchea, and civil war in Bosnia led to racially motivated atrocities recalling the horrors of World War Two. And there are other examples. Thus it is all the more vital that we understand Europe's era of brutal dictatorship in order to guard against the possibility of its recurrence in the future.

Hugo Jager's photograph of a crowd of enthusiastic Hitler supporters. *(Source: Hugo Jager, Life Magazine, © Time Warner, Inc.)*

relates the radical dictatorships to the rise of modern totalitarianism. The second focuses on the idea of fascism as the unifying impulse. The third stresses the limitations of such broad generalizations and the uniqueness of each regime. Each school has strengths and weaknesses.

The concept of *totalitarianism* emerged in the 1920s and the 1930s, although it is frequently and mistakenly seen as developing only after 1945 during the cold war.[1] In 1924 Mussolini spoke of the "fierce totalitarian will" of his movement in Italy. In the 1930s many British, American, and German exiled writers used the concept of totalitarianism to link Italian and German fascism with Soviet communism under a common antiliberal umbrella. The alliance between Hitler and Stalin in 1939 reinforced this explanation.

Early writers believed that modern totalitarianism burst on the scene with the revolutionary total war effort of 1914 to 1918. The war called forth a tendency to subordinate all institutions and all classes to one supreme objective: victory. As French thinker Elie Halévy put it in 1936, the varieties of modern totalitarian tyranny—fascism, Nazism, and communism—could be thought of as "feuding brothers" with a common father: the nature of modern war.[2]

Writers such as Halévy believed that the crucial experience of World War One was carried further by Lenin and the Bolsheviks during the Russian civil war. Lenin showed how a dedicated minority could make a total effort and achieve victory over a less determined majority. Lenin also demonstrated how institutions and human rights might be subordinated to the needs of a single group—the Communist party—and its leader, Lenin. Thus he provided a model for single-party dictatorship, and he inspired imitators, including Adolf Hitler. Modern totalitarianism reached maturity in the 1930s in the Stalinist U.S.S.R. and Nazi Germany, according to this school of interpretation.

As numerous Western political scientists and historians argued in the 1950s and the 1960s, the totalitarian state used modern technology and communications to exercise complete political power. But it did not stop there. Increasingly, the state took over and tried to control just as completely the economic, social, intellectual, and cultural aspects of people's lives. Deviation from the norm even in art or family behavior could become a crime. In theory, nothing was politically neutral; nothing was outside the scope of the state.

This grandiose vision of total state control broke decisively not only with conservative authoritarianism but also with nineteenth-century liberalism and democracy. Indeed, totalitarianism was a radical revolt against liberalism. Classical liberalism, which emerged decisively in the American and French revolutions, sought to limit the power of the state and protect the sacred rights of the individual. Moreover, liberals stood for rationality, peaceful progress, economic freedom, and a strong middle class. All of that disgusted totalitarians as sentimental slop. They believed in will power, preached conflict, and worshiped violence. The individual was infinitely less valuable than the state, and there were no lasting rights, only temporary rewards for loyal and effective service. Only a single powerful leader and a single party, both unrestrained by law or tradition, determined the destiny of the totalitarian state.

Unlike old-fashioned authoritarianism, modern totalitarianism was based not on an elite but on people who had already become engaged in the political process, most notably through commitment to nationalism and socialism. Thus according to this interpretation, real totalitarian states built on mass movements and possessed boundless dynamism. Totalitarian societies were fully mobilized societies, moving toward some goal. And as soon as one goal was achieved at the cost of enormous sacrifice, another arose at the leader's command to take its place. Thus totalitarianism was in the end a *permanent* revolution, an *unfinished* revolution, in which rapid, profound change imposed from on high went on forever.

A second group of writers approached radical dictatorships outside the Soviet Union through the concept of *fascism*. A term of pride for Mussolini and Hitler, who used it to describe the supposedly "total" and revolutionary character of their movements, fascism was severely criticized by these writers and linked to reactionary forces, decaying capitalism, and domestic class conflict. Orthodox Marxists first argued that fascism was the way powerful capitalists sought to manipulate a mass movement capable of destroying the revolutionary working class and thus protect the enormous profits to be reaped through war and territorial expansion. Less doctrinaire socialists saw fascism as only one of several possible ways for the ruling class to escape from a general crisis of capitalism. Both Marxists and quasi-Marxists usually rejected the totalitarian model, discerning at least some elements of the genuine socialism they desired in communist regimes such as that of Stalin.

Scholarly interest in fascism declined in the 1950s but revived thereafter. Comparative studies of fascist movements all across Europe showed that they shared many characteristics, including extreme, often expansionist nationalism; an antisocialism aimed at destroying working-class movements; alliances with powerful capitalists and landowners; mass parties, which appealed especially to the middle class and the peasantry; a dynamic and violent leader; and glorification of war and the military. European fascism remains a product of class conflict, capitalist crisis, and postwar upheaval in these more recent studies, but the basic interpretation has become less dogmatic and more subtle and convincing.

Historians today often adopt a third approach, which emphasizes the uniqueness of developments in each country. This approach has been both reflected and encouraged in recent years by an outpouring of specialized historical studies that challenge parts of overarching interpretations like totalitarianism and fascism. This is especially true for Hitler's Germany, and a similar revaluation of Stalin's U.S.S.R. may be expected now that the fall of communism has opened the former Soviet Union's archives to new research. For this third school of historians, differences in historical patterns are often more important than striking but frequently superficial similarities.

Four tentative judgments concerning these debates seem appropriate. First, as is often the case in history, leading schools of interpretation are rather closely linked to the political passions and the ideological commitments of the age. Thus modern Western "bourgeois-liberal" observers, worried by the dual challenge of the Nazi and Soviet dictatorships, often found the totalitarian framework convincing in the 1930s and in the early cold war. At the same time Marxist, socialist, and new left writers easily saw profound structural differences between the continued capitalism in fascist countries and the socialism established in the Soviet Union.

Second, as a noted scholar has recently concluded, the concept of totalitarianism retains real value. It correctly highlights that both Hitler's Germany and Stalin's Soviet Union made an unprecedented "total claim" on the belief and behavior of their respective citizens.[3] Third, antidemocratic, antisocialist movements sprang up all over

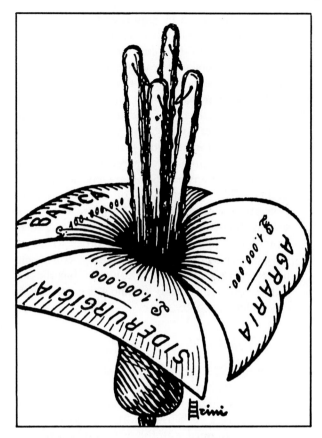

❖ **"The Flower of Fascism"** This symbolic representation by Giuseppe Scalarini stresses class conflict and violence. The petals of the fascist flower are massive contributions from banks, big business, and big landowners, which open to reveal big clubs—the violence and brutality of fascism.

Europe, but only in Italy and Germany (and some would say Spain) were they able to take power. Studies of fascist movements seeking power locate common elements, but they do not explain what fascist governments actually did. Fourth, the problem of Europe's radical dictatorships is complex and there are few easy answers.

❖ STALIN'S SOVIET UNION

Many of Lenin's harshest critics claim that he established the basic outlines of a modern totalitarian dictatorship after the Bolshevik Revolution and during the Russian civil war. If this is so, then Joseph Stalin (1879–1953) certainly finished the job. A master of political infighting, Stalin cautiously consolidated his power and eliminated his enemies in the mid-1920s. Then in 1928, as undisputed leader of the ruling Communist party, he launched the first five-year plan—the "revolution from above," as he so aptly termed it.

The five-year plans were extremely ambitious. Often incorrectly considered a mere set of economic measures to speed up the Soviet Union's industrial development, the five-year plans actually marked the beginning of a renewed attempt to mobilize and transform Soviet society along socialist lines. The ultimate goal of the plans was to generate new attitudes, new loyalties, and a new socialist humanity. The means Stalin and the small Communist party elite chose in order to do so were constant propaganda, enormous sacrifice, and unlimited violence and state control. Thus the Soviet Union in the 1930s became a dynamic, modern totalitarian state.

From Lenin to Stalin

By spring 1921 Lenin and the Bolsheviks had won the civil war, but they ruled a shattered and devastated land. Many farms were in ruins, and food supplies were exhausted. In southern Russia drought combined with the ravages of war to produce the worst famine in generations. By 1920, according to the government, from 50 to 90 percent of the population in seventeen provinces was starving. Industrial production also broke down completely. In 1921, for example, output of steel and cotton textiles was only about 4 percent of what it had been in 1913. Trotsky later wrote that the "collapse of the productive forces surpassed anything of the kind history had ever seen. The country, and the government with it, were at the very edge of the abyss."[4] The Bolsheviks had destroyed the economy as well as their foes.

In the face of economic disintegration, riots by peasants and workers, and an open rebellion by previously pro-Bolshevik sailors at Kronstadt—a rebellion that had to be quelled with machine guns—the tough but ever-flexible Lenin changed course. In March 1921 he announced the New Economic Policy (NEP), which re-established limited economic freedom in an attempt to rebuild agriculture and industry. During the civil war, the communists had simply seized grain without payment. With the NEP, Lenin substituted a grain tax on the country's peasant producers, who were permitted to sell their surpluses in free markets. Peasants were also encouraged to buy as many goods as they could afford from private traders and small

❖ **Lenin and Stalin in 1922** Lenin re-established limited economic freedom throughout Russia in 1921, but he ran the country and the Communist party in an increasingly authoritarian way. Stalin carried the process much further and eventually built a regime based on harsh dictatorship. *(Source: Sovfoto)*

handicraft manufacturers, groups that were now allowed to reappear. Heavy industry, railroads, and banks, however, remained wholly nationalized.

The NEP was shrewd and successful both politically and economically. Politically, it was a necessary but temporary compromise with the Soviet Union's overwhelming peasant majority. Flushed with victory after the revolutionary gains of 1917, the peasants would have fought to hold onto their land. With fond hopes of immediate worldwide revolution fading by 1921, Lenin realized that his government was not strong enough to take land from the peasants. As he had accepted Germany's harsh terms at Brest-Litovsk in 1918, Lenin made a deal with the only force capable of overturning his government.

Economically, the NEP brought rapid recovery. In 1926 industrial output surpassed the level of 1913, and Soviet peasants were producing almost as much grain as before the war. Counting shorter hours and increased social benefits, workers were living somewhat better than they had in the past.

As the economy recovered and the government partially relaxed its censorship and repression, an intense struggle for power began in the inner circles of the Communist party, for Lenin had left no chosen successor when he died in 1924. The principal contenders were the stolid Stalin and the flamboyant Trotsky.

The son of a shoemaker, Joseph Dzhugashvili— later known as Stalin—studied for the priesthood but was expelled from his theological seminary, probably for rude rebelliousness. By 1903 he had joined the Bolsheviks. In the years before the First World War, he engaged in many revolutionary activities in the southern Transcaucasian area of the multinational Russian Empire, including a daring bank robbery to get money for the Bolsheviks. This raid gained Lenin's attention and approval. Ethnically a Georgian, Stalin in his early writings focused on the oppression of minority peoples in the Russian Empire. He was a good organizer but a poor speaker and writer, with no experience outside of Russia.

Trotsky, a great and inspiring leader who had planned the 1917 takeover (see page 921) and then created the victorious Red Army, appeared to have all the advantages. Yet it was Stalin who succeeded Lenin. Stalin won because he was more effective at gaining the all-important support of the party, the only genuine source of power in the one-party state. Rising to general secretary of the party's Central Committee just before Lenin's first stroke in 1922, Stalin used his office to win friends and allies with jobs and promises. Stalin also won recognition as commissar of nationalities, a key position in which he governed many of the minorities in the vast Soviet Union.

The "practical" Stalin also won because he appeared better able than the brilliant Trotsky to relate Marxian teaching to Soviet realities in the 1920s. First, as commissar of nationalities he built on Lenin's idea of granting minority groups a certain degree of freedom in culture and language while maintaining rigorous political control through carefully selected local communists. Stalin could therefore loudly claim to have found a way to solve the ancient problem of ethnic demands for independence in the multinational state.

Second, Stalin developed a theory of "socialism in one country" that was more appealing to the majority of communists than Trotsky's doctrine of "permanent revolution." Stalin argued that the Russian-dominated Soviet Union had the ability to build socialism on its own. Trotsky maintained that socialism in the Soviet Union could succeed only if revolution occurred quickly throughout Europe. To many communists, especially Soviet communists, Trotsky's views seemed to sell their country short and to promise risky conflicts with capitalist countries by recklessly encouraging revolutionary movements around the world. Stalin's willingness to break with the NEP and push socialism at home appealed to young militants. In short, Stalin's theory of socialism in one country provided many in the party with a glimmer of hope in the midst of the capitalist-appearing NEP, which they had come to detest.

With cunning skill Stalin gradually achieved absolute power between 1922 and 1927. First, he allied with Trotsky's personal enemies to crush Trotsky, who was expelled from the Soviet Union in 1929 and eventually was murdered in Mexico in 1940, undoubtedly on Stalin's order. Second, Stalin aligned with the moderates, who wanted to go slow at home, to suppress Trotsky's radical followers. Third, having defeated all the radicals, he turned against his allies, the moderates, and destroyed them as well. Stalin's final triumph came at the party congress of December 1927, which condemned all "deviation from the general party line" formulated by Stalin. The dictator was then ready to launch his revolution from above—the real revolution for millions of ordinary citizens.

The Five-year Plans

The party congress of 1927, which ratified Stalin's seizure of power, marked the end of the NEP and the beginning of the era of socialist five-year plans. The first five-year plan had staggering economic objectives. In just five years, total industrial output was to increase by 250 percent. Heavy industry, the preferred sector, was to grow even faster; steel production, for example, was to jump almost 300 percent. Agricultural production was slated to increase by 150 percent, and one-fifth of the peasants in the Soviet Union were scheduled to give up their private plots and join socialist collective farms. In spite of warnings from moderate communists that these goals were unrealistic, Stalin raised them higher as the plan got under way. By 1930 economic and social change was sweeping the country.

Stalin unleashed his "second revolution" for a variety of interrelated reasons. There were, first of all, ideological considerations. Like Lenin, Stalin and his militant supporters were deeply committed to socialism as they understood it. Since the country had recovered economically and their rule was secure, they burned to stamp out the NEP's private traders, independent artisans, and few well-to-do peasants. Purely economic motivations were also important. Although the economy had recovered, it seemed to have stalled in 1927 and 1928. A new socialist offensive seemed necessary if industry and agriculture were to grow rapidly.

Political considerations were most important. Internationally, there was the old problem, remaining from prerevolutionary times, of catching up with the advanced and presumably hostile capitalist nations of the West. Stalin said in 1931, when he pressed for ever-greater speed and sacrifice, "We are fifty or a hundred years behind the advanced countries. We must make good this distance in ten years. Either we do it, or we shall go under."[5]

Domestically, there was what communist writers of the 1920s called the "cursed problem"—the problem of the peasants. For centuries, the peasants had wanted to own the land, and finally they had it. Sooner or later, the communists reasoned, the peasants would become conservative little capitalists and pose a threat to the regime. Therefore, Stalin decided on a preventive war against the peasantry in order to bring it under the absolute control of the state.

That war was *collectivization*—the forcible consolidation of individual peasant farms into large, state-controlled enterprises. Beginning in 1929, peasants all over the Soviet Union were ordered to give up their land and animals and become members of collective farms, although they continued to live in their own homes. As for the *kulaks,* the better-off peasants, Stalin instructed party workers to "liquidate them as a class." Stripped of land and livestock, the kulaks were generally not even permitted to join the collective farms. Many starved or were deported to forced-labor camps for "re-education."

Since almost all peasants were in fact poor, the term *kulak* soon meant any peasant who opposed the new system. Whole villages were often attacked. One conscience-stricken colonel in the secret police confessed to a foreign journalist, "I am an old Bolshevik. I worked in the underground against the Tsar and then I fought in the Civil War. Did I do all that in order that I should now surround villages with machine guns and order my men to fire indiscriminately into crowds of peasants? Oh, no, no!"[6]

Forced collectivization of the peasants led to economic and human disaster. Large numbers of peasants slaughtered their animals and burned their crops in sullen, hopeless protest. Between 1929 and 1933, the number of horses, cattle, sheep, and goats in the Soviet Union fell by at least half. Nor were the state-controlled collective farms more productive. The output of grain barely increased between 1928 and 1938, when it was almost identical to that of 1913. Communist economists had expected collectivized agriculture to pay for new factories. Instead, the state had to invest heavily in agriculture, building thousands of tractors to replace slaughtered draft horses. Collectivized agriculture was unable to make any substantial financial contribution to Soviet industrial development in the first five-year plan. And the human dimension of the tragedy was shocking. Collectivization created human-made famine in 1932 and 1933, and many perished. Indeed, Stalin confided to Churchill at Yalta in 1945 that ten million people had died in the course of collectivization.

Yet collectivization was a political victory of sorts. By the end of 1932, fully 60 percent of peasant families had been herded onto collective farms; by 1938, 93 percent. Regimented and indoctrinated as employees of an all-powerful state, the peasants were no longer even a potential political threat to Stalin and the Communist party. Moreover, the state was assured of grain for bread

❖ **Decorative Art in Soviet Russia** Russia had a rich tradition of icon-painting and decorative religious art, which was expected to glorify Soviet life and socialist achievements after the revolution. This beautiful lacquered lid of a wooden box was produced in the old icon-painting center of Palekh, 200 miles east of Moscow. The painter skillfully combines modern motifs, such as tractors and factories, with traditional themes of peasant life. Historians usually find considerable continuity in the midst of revolutionary change. *(Source: Novosti)*

for urban workers, who were much more important politically than the peasants. Collective farmers had to meet their grain quotas first and worry about feeding themselves second. Many collectivized peasants drew much of their own food from tiny, grudgingly tolerated garden plots that they worked in their off hours. No wonder some peasants joked, with that grim humor peculiar to a totalitarian society, that the initials then used by the Communist party actually stood for "The Second Serfdom, That of the Bolsheviks."

The industrial side of the five-year plans was more successful—indeed, quite spectacular. The output of industry doubled in the first five-year plan and doubled again in the second. Soviet industry produced about four times as much in 1937 as it had in 1928. No other major country had ever achieved such rapid industrial growth. Heavy industry led the way; consumer industry grew quite slowly. Steel production—a near-obsession with Stalin, whose name fittingly meant "man of steel" in Russian—increased roughly 500 percent between 1928 and 1937. A new heavy industrial complex was built almost from scratch in western Siberia. Industrial growth also went hand in hand with urban development. Cities rose where nomadic tribes had grazed their flocks. More than

twenty-five million people migrated to cities during the 1930s.

The great industrialization drive, concentrated between 1928 and 1937, was an awe-inspiring achievement purchased at enormous sacrifice. The sudden creation of dozens of new factories required a great increase in total investment and a sharp decrease in consumption. Few nations had ever invested more than one-sixth of their yearly net national income. Soviet planners decreed that more than one-third of net income go for investment. This meant that only two-thirds of everything being produced could be consumed by the people *and* the increasingly voracious military. The money was collected from the people by means of heavy, hidden sales taxes.

There was therefore no improvement in the average standard of living. Indeed, the most careful studies show that the average nonfarm wage apparently purchased only about *half* as many goods in 1932 as in 1928. After 1932 real wages rose slowly, so that in 1937 workers could buy about 60 percent of what they had bought in 1928.

Two other factors contributed importantly to rapid industrialization: firm labor discipline and foreign engineers. Between 1930 and 1932, trade unions lost most of their power. The government could assign workers to any job anywhere in the country, and individuals could not move without the permission of the police. When factory managers needed more hands, they called on their counterparts on the collective farms, who sent them millions of "unneeded" peasants over the years.

Foreign engineers were hired to plan and construct many of the new factories. Highly skilled American engineers, hungry for work in the depression years, were particularly important until newly trained Soviet experts began to replace them after 1932. The gigantic mills of the new Siberian steel industry were modeled on America's best. Those modern mills were eloquent testimony to the ability of Stalin's planners to harness even the skill and technology of capitalist countries to promote the surge of socialist industry.

Life in Stalinist Society

The aim of Stalin's five-year plans was to create a new kind of society and human personality as well as a strong industrial economy and a powerful army. Stalin and his helpers were good Marxian economic determinists. Once everything was owned by the state, they believed, a socialist society and a new kind of human being would inevitably emerge. They were by no means totally successful, but they did build a new society, whose broad outlines existed through the early 1980s. For the people, life in Stalinist society had both good and bad aspects.

The most frightening aspect of Stalinist society was brutal, unrestrained police terrorism. First directed primarily against the peasants after 1929, terror was increasingly turned on leading Communists, powerful administrators, and ordinary people for no apparent reason. As one Soviet woman later recalled, "We all trembled because there was no way of getting out of it. Even a Communist himself can be caught. To avoid trouble became an exception."[7] A climate of fear swept over the land.

In the early 1930s, the top members of the party and government were Stalin's obedient servants, but there was some grumbling in the party. At a small gathering in November 1932, even Stalin's wife complained bitterly about the misery of the people. Stalin showered her with insults, and she died that same night, apparently by her own hand. In late 1934 Stalin's number-two man, Sergei Kirov, was suddenly and mysteriously murdered. Although Stalin himself probably ordered Kirov's murder, he used the incident to launch a reign of terror.

In August 1936 sixteen prominent old Bolsheviks confessed to all manner of plots against Stalin in spectacular public trials in Moscow. Then in 1937 lesser party officials and newer henchmen were arrested. In addition to party members, union officials, managers, intellectuals, army officers, and countless ordinary citizens were struck down. Local units of the secret police were even ordered to arrest a certain percentage of the people in their districts. In all, at least eight million people were probably arrested, and millions never returned from prisons and forced-labor camps.

Stalin's mass purges were truly baffling, and many explanations have been given for them. Possibly Stalin believed that the old Communists, like the peasants under NEP, were a potential threat to be wiped out in a preventive attack. Yet why did leading Communists confess to crimes they could not possibly have committed? Their lives had been devoted to the party and the socialist revolution. German novelist Arthur Koestler believed that they probably confessed "in order to do a last service to the Party," the party they loved even when it was wrong. There are many other interpretations. Some prisoners were cruelly tortured and warned that their loved ones would also die if they did not confess. Some scholars argue that the purges demonstrated that Stalin was sadistic or insane, for his bloodbath greatly weakened the government and the army. Others see the terror as an aspect of the fully developed totalitarian state, which must by its nature always be fighting real or imaginary enemies. At the least, the mass purges were a message to the people: no one was secure; everyone had to serve the party and its leader with redoubled devotion.

Another aspect of life in the 1930s was constant propaganda and indoctrination. Party activists lectured workers in factories and peasants on collective farms, while newspapers, films, and radio broadcasts endlessly recounted socialist achievements and capitalist plots. Art and literature became highly political. Whereas the 1920s had seen considerable experimentation in modern art and theater, intellectuals were ordered by Stalin to become "engineers of human minds." Writers and artists who could effectively combine genuine creativity and political propaganda became the darlings of the regime. They often lived better than top members of the political elite. It became increasingly important for the successful writer and artist to glorify Russian nationalism. Russian history was rewritten so that early tsars such as Ivan the Terrible and Peter the Great became worthy forerunners of the greatest Russian leader of all—Stalin.

Stalin seldom appeared in public, but his presence was everywhere—in portraits, statues, books, and quotations from his "sacred" writings. Although the government persecuted religion and turned churches into "museums of atheism," the state had both an earthly religion and a high priest—Marxism-Leninism and Joseph Stalin.

Life was hard in Stalin's Soviet Union. The masses of people lived primarily on black bread and wore old, shabby clothing. There were constant shortages in the stores, although very heavily taxed vodka was always readily available. A shortage of housing was a particularly serious problem. Millions were moving into the cities, but the government built few new apartments. In 1940 there were approximately 4 people per room in every urban dwelling, as opposed to 2.7 per room in 1926. A relatively lucky family received one room for all its members and shared both a kitchen and a toilet with others on the floor. Less fortunate workers, kulaks, and class enemies built scrap-lumber shacks or underground dugouts in shantytowns.

Life was hard but by no means hopeless. Idealism and ideology had real appeal for many communists, who saw themselves heroically building the world's first socialist society while capitalism crumbled and degenerated into fascism in the West. This optimistic belief in the future of the Soviet Union also attracted many disillusioned Westerners to communism in the 1930s.

On a more practical level, Soviet workers did receive some important social benefits, such as old-age pensions, free medical services, free education, and day-care centers for children. Unemployment was almost unknown. Finally, there was the possibility of personal advancement.

The keys to improving one's position were specialized skills and technical education. Rapid indus-

❖ **Adult Education** Illiteracy, especially among women, was a serious problem after the Russian Revolution. This early photo shows how adults successfully learned to read and write throughout the Soviet Union. *(Source: Sovfoto)*

trialization required massive numbers of trained experts, such as skilled workers, engineers, and plant managers. Thus the state provided tremendous incentives to those who could serve its needs. It paid the mass of unskilled workers and collective farmers very low wages, but it dangled high salaries and many special privileges before its growing technical and managerial elite. This elite joined with the political and artistic elites in a new upper class, whose members were rich, powerful, and insecure, especially during the purges. Yet the possible gains of moving up outweighed the risks. Millions struggled bravely in universities, institutes, and night schools for the all-important specialized education. One young man summed it up: "In Soviet Russia there is no capital except education. If a person does not want to become a collective farmer or just a cleaning woman, the only means you have to get something is through education."[8]

Mobilizing Women in the Soviet Union

The radical transformation of Soviet society had a profound impact on women's lives. Marxists had traditionally believed that both capitalism and the middle-class husband exploited women. The Russian Revolution of 1917 immediately proclaimed complete equality of rights for women. In the 1920s divorce and abortion were made easily available, and women were urged to work outside the home and liberate themselves sexually. The most prominent Bolshevik feminist, Alexandra Kollontai, went so far as to declare that the sex act had no more significance than "drinking a glass of water." This observation drew a sharp rebuke from the rather prudish Lenin, who said that "no sane man would lie down to drink from a puddle in the gutter or even drink from a dirty glass."[9] After Stalin came to power, sexual and familial liberation was played down, and the most lasting changes for women involved work and education.

These changes were truly revolutionary. Young women were constantly told that they had to be fully equal to men, that they could and should do anything men could do. Peasant women in Russia had long experienced the equality of backbreaking physical labor in the countryside, and they continued to enjoy that equality on collective farms. With the advent of the five-year plans, millions of women also began to toil in factories and in heavy construction, building dams, roads, and steel mills in summer heat and winter frost. Yet most of the opportunities open to men through education were also open to women. Determined women pursued their studies and entered the ranks of the better-paid specialists in industry and science. Medicine practically became a woman's profession. By 1950, 75 percent of all doctors in the Soviet Union were women.

Thus Stalinist society gave women great opportunities but demanded great sacrifices as well. The vast majority of women simply *had* to work outside the home. Wages were so low that it was almost impossible for a family or couple to live only on the husband's earnings. Moreover, the full-time working woman had a heavy burden of household tasks in her off hours, for most Soviet men in the 1930s still considered the home and the children the woman's responsibility. Men continued to monopolize the best jobs. Finally, rapid change and economic hardship led to many broken families, creating further physical, emotional, and mental strains for women. In any event, the often-neglected human resource of women was ruthlessly mobilized in Stalinist society. This, too, was an aspect of the Soviet totalitarian state.

MUSSOLINI AND FASCISM IN ITALY

Mussolini's movement and his seizure of power in 1922 were an important step in the rise of dictatorships in Europe between the two world wars. Like all the future dictators, the young Mussolini hated liberalism and wanted to destroy it in Italy. But although Mussolini began as a revolutionary socialist, like Stalin, he turned against the working class and successfully sought the support of conservatives. At the same time, Mussolini and his supporters were the first to call themselves "fascists"—revolutionaries determined to create a certain kind of totalitarian state. Yet few scholars today would argue that Mussolini succeeded. His dictatorship was brutal and theatrical, but it remained a halfway house between conservative authoritarianism and modern totalitarianism.

The Seizure of Power

In the early twentieth century Italy was a liberal state with civil rights and a constitutional monarchy. On the eve of the First World War, the parliamentary regime finally granted universal male suffrage, and Italy appeared to be moving toward democracy. But there were serious problems. Much of the Italian population was still poor, and many peasants were more attached to their villages and local interests than to the national state. Moreover, the papacy, many devout Catholics, conservatives, and landowners remained strongly opposed to liberal institutions and to the heirs of Cavour and Garibaldi—the middle-class lawyers and politicians who ran the country largely for their own benefit. Relations between church and state were often tense. Class differences were also extreme, and a powerful revolutionary socialist movement had developed. Only in Italy among the main European countries did the radical left wing of the Socialist party gain the leadership as early as 1912, and only in Italy did the Socialist party unanimously oppose the war from the very beginning.[10]

The war worsened the political situation. Having fought on the side of the Allies almost exclusively for purposes of territorial expansion, the parliamentary government bitterly disappointed Italian nationalists with Italy's modest gains at Versailles. Workers and peasants also felt cheated: to win their support during the war, the government had promised social and land reform, which it did not deliver after the war.

Of great importance, the Russian Revolution inspired and energized Italy's revolutionary socialist movement. The Socialist party quickly lined up with the Bolsheviks, and radical workers and peasants began occupying factories and seizing land in 1920. These actions scared and mobilized the property-owning classes. Moreover, after the war the pope lifted his ban on participation by Catholics in Italian politics, and a strong Catholic party quickly emerged. Thus by 1921 revolutionary socialists, antiliberal conservatives, and frightened property owners were all opposed—though for different reasons—to the liberal parliamentary government.

Into these crosscurrents of unrest and fear stepped the blustering, bullying Benito Mussolini (1883–1945). Son of a village schoolteacher and a poor blacksmith, Mussolini began his political career as a Socialist leader and radical newspaper editor before World War One. In 1914, powerfully influenced by antidemocratic cults of violent action, the young Mussolini urged that Italy join the Allies, a stand for which he was expelled from the Italian Socialist party. Later Mussolini fought at the front and was wounded in 1917. Returning home,

he began organizing bitter war veterans like himself into a band of fascists—from the Italian word for "a union of forces."

At first Mussolini's program was a radical combination of nationalist and socialist demands, including territorial expansion, benefits for workers, and land reform for peasants. As such, it competed directly with the well-organized Socialist party and failed to get off the ground. When Mussolini saw that his violent verbal assaults on rival Socialists won him growing support from conservatives and the frightened middle classes, he shifted gears in 1920. In thought and action, Mussolini was a striking example of the turbulent uncertainty of the age of anxiety.

Mussolini and his growing private army of Black Shirts began to grow violent. Typically, a band of fascist toughs would roar off in trucks at night and swoop down on a few isolated Socialist organizers, beating them up and force-feeding them almost deadly doses of castor oil. Few people were killed, but socialist newspapers, union halls, and local Socialist party headquarters were destroyed. Mussolini's toughs pushed Socialists out of the city governments of northern Italy.

Mussolini, a skillful politician, refused to become a puppet of antiliberal conservatives and capitalists. He allowed his followers to convince themselves that they were not just opposing the "reds" but also making a real revolution of their own. Many believed that they were destroying parliamentary government and forming a strong, dynamic movement that would help the little people against the established interests.

With the government breaking down in 1922, largely because of the chaos created by his direct-action bands, Mussolini stepped forward as the savior of order and property. Striking a conservative note in his speeches and gaining the sympathetic neutrality of army leaders, Mussolini demanded the resignation of the existing government and his own appointment by the king. In October 1922, to force matters, a large group of Fascists marched on Rome to threaten the king and force him to call on Mussolini. The threat worked. Victor Emmanuel III (r. 1900–1946), who had no love for the old liberal politicians, asked Mussolini to form a new cabinet. Thus after widespread violence and a threat of armed uprising, Mussolini seized power "legally." He was immediately granted dictatorial authority for one year by the king and the parliament.

❖ **Mussolini** was a charismatic orator with a sure touch for emotional propaganda. He loved settings that linked fascist Italy to the glories of imperial Rome. Poised to address a mass rally in Rome at the time of Matteotti's murder, Mussolini then called for 90,000 more volunteers to join his gun-toting fascist militia. Members of the militia stand as an honor guard in front of the podium. *(Source: Popperfoto)*

The Regime in Action

Mussolini became dictator on the strength of Italians' rejection of parliamentary government coupled with fears of Soviet-style revolution. Yet what he intended to do with his power was by no means

clear until 1924. Some of his dedicated supporters pressed for a "second revolution." Mussolini's ministers, however, included old conservatives, moderates, and even two reform-minded Socialists. A new electoral law was passed giving two-thirds of the representatives in the parliament to the party that won the most votes, a change that allowed the Fascists and their allies to win an overwhelming majority in 1924. Shortly thereafter five of Mussolini's fascist thugs kidnapped and murdered Giacomo Matteotti, the leader of the Socialists in the parliament. In the face of this outrage, the opposition demanded that Mussolini's armed squads be dissolved and all violence be banned.

Although Mussolini may or may not have ordered Matteotti's murder, he stood at the crossroads of a severe political crisis. After some hesitation, he charged forward. Declaring his desire to "make the nation Fascist," he imposed a series of repressive measures. Freedom of the press was abolished, elections were fixed, and the government ruled by decree. Mussolini arrested his political opponents, disbanded all independent labor unions, and put dedicated fascists in control of Italy's schools. Moreover, he created a fascist youth movement, fascist labor unions, and many other fascist organizations. As Mussolini trumpeted his goal in a famous slogan of 1926, "Everything in the state, nothing outside the state, nothing against the state." By the end of that year, Italy was a one-party dictatorship under Mussolini's unquestioned leadership.

Yet Mussolini did not complete the establishment of a modern totalitarian state. His Fascist party never became all-powerful. It never destroyed the old power structure, as the communists did in the Soviet Union, or succeeded in dominating it, as the Nazis did in Germany. Membership in the Fascist party was more a sign of an Italian's respectability than a commitment to radical change. Interested primarily in personal power, Mussolini was content to compromise with the old conservative classes that controlled the army, the economy, and the state. He never tried to purge these classes or even move very vigorously against them. He controlled and propagandized labor but left big business to regulate itself, profitably and securely. There was no land reform.

Mussolini also drew increasing support from the Catholic church. In the Lateran Agreement of 1929, he recognized the Vatican as a tiny independent state, and he agreed to give the church heavy financial support. The pope expressed his satisfaction and urged Italians to support Mussolini's government.

Nothing better illustrates Mussolini's unwillingness to harness everyone and everything for dynamic action than his treatment of women. He abolished divorce and told women to stay at home and produce children. To promote that goal, he decreed a special tax on bachelors in 1934. In 1938 women were limited by law to a maximum of 10 percent of the better-paying jobs in industry and government. Italian women as women appear not to have changed their attitudes or behavior in any important way under fascist rule.

Mussolini's government did not pass racial laws until 1938 and did not persecute Jews savagely until late in the Second World War, when Italy was under Nazi control. Nor did Mussolini establish a truly ruthless police state. Only twenty-three political prisoners were condemned to death between 1926 and 1944. In spite of much pompous posing by the chauvinist leader and in spite of mass meetings, salutes, and a certain copying of Hitler's aggression in foreign policy after 1933, Mussolini's fascist Italy, though repressive and undemocratic, was never really totalitarian.

✤ HITLER AND NAZISM IN GERMANY

The most frightening dictatorship developed in Nazi Germany. A product of Hitler's evil genius as well as of Germany's social and political situation and the general attack on liberalism and rationality in the age of anxiety, the Nazi movement shared some of the characteristics of Mussolini's Italian model and was a form of fascism. The Nazi dictatorship smashed or took over most independent organizations, mobilized the economy, and began brutally persecuting the Jewish population. Thus Nazism asserted an unlimited claim over German society and put all final power in the hands of its endlessly aggressive leader—Adolf Hitler. In this regard Nazism was truly totalitarian.

The Roots of Nazism

Nazism grew out of many complex developments, of which the most influential were extreme nationalism and racism. These two ideas captured the mind of the young Hitler, and it was he who dominated Nazism for as long as it lasted.

Born the fourth child of a successful Austrian customs official and an indulgent mother, Adolf Hitler (1889–1945) spent his childhood in small towns in Austria. A good student in grade school, Hitler did poorly on reaching high school and dropped out at age fourteen following the death of his father. After four years of unfocused loafing, Hitler finally left for Vienna to become an artist. Denied admission to the Imperial Academy of Fine Arts because he lacked talent, the dejected Hitler stayed in Vienna. There he lived a comfortable, lazy life on his generous orphan's pension and found most of the perverted beliefs that guided his life.

In Vienna Hitler soaked up extreme German nationalism, which was particularly strong there. Austro-German nationalists, as if to compensate for their declining position in the Austro-Hungarian Empire, believed Germans to be a superior people and the natural rulers of central Europe. They often advocated union with Germany and violent expulsion of "inferior" peoples as the means of maintaining German domination of the Austro-Hungarian Empire.

Hitler was deeply impressed by Vienna's mayor, Karl Lueger (1844–1910), whom he called the "mightiest mayor of all times." Lueger claimed to be a "Christian socialist." With the help of the Catholic trade unions, he had succeeded in winning the support of the little people of Vienna for an attack on capitalism and liberalism, which he held responsible for un-Christian behavior and excessive individualism. A master of mass politics in the urban world, Lueger showed Hitler the enormous potential of anticapitalist and antiliberal propaganda.

From Lueger and others, Hitler eagerly absorbed virulent anti-Semitism, racism, and hatred of Slavs. He was particularly inspired by the racist ravings of an ex-monk named Lanz von Liebenfels. Preaching the crudest, most exaggerated distortions of the Darwinian theory of survival, Liebenfels stressed the superiority of Germanic races, the inevitability of racial conflict, and the inferiority of the Jews. Liebenfels even anticipated the breeding and extermination policies of the Nazi state. He claimed that the master race had to multiply its numbers by means of polygamy and breeding stations, while it systematically sterilized and liquidated inferior races. Anti-Semitism and racism became Hitler's most passionate convictions, his explanation for everything. The Jews, he claimed, directed an international conspiracy of finance capitalism and Marxian socialism against German culture, German unity, and the German race. Hitler's belief was totally irrational, but he never doubted it.

Although he moved to Munich in 1913 to avoid being drafted in the Austrian army, the lonely Hitler greeted the outbreak of the First World War as a salvation. He later wrote in his autobiography, *Mein Kampf*, that, "overcome by passionate enthusiasm, I fell to my knees and thanked heaven out of an overflowing heart." The struggle and discipline of war gave life meaning, and Hitler served bravely as a dispatch carrier on the western front.

When Germany was suddenly defeated in 1918, Hitler's world was shattered. Not only was he a fanatical nationalist, but war was also his reason for living. Convinced that Jews and Marxists had "stabbed Germany in the back," he vowed to fight on. And in the bitterness and uncertainty of postwar Germany, his wild speeches began to attract attention.

In late 1919 Hitler joined a tiny extremist group in Munich called the German Workers' party. In addition to denouncing Jews, Marxists, and democrats, the German Workers' party promised unity under a uniquely German "national socialism," which would abolish the injustices of capitalism and create a mighty "people's community." By 1921 Hitler had gained absolute control of this small but growing party. Moreover, Hitler was already a master of mass propaganda and political showmanship. Party members sported badges and uniforms, gave victory salutes, and marched like robots through the streets of Munich. But Hitler's most effective tool was the mass rally, a kind of political revival meeting. Songs, slogans, and demonstrations built up the tension until Hitler finally arrived. He then often worked his audience into a frenzy with wild, demagogic attacks on the Versailles treaty, the Jews, the war profiteers, and Germany's Weimar Republic.

Party membership multiplied tenfold after early 1922. In late 1923, when the Weimar Republic seemed on the verge of collapse, Hitler decided on an armed uprising in Munich. Inspired by Mussolini's recent easy victory, Hitler had found an ally in General Ludendorff of First World War fame. After Hitler had overthrown the Bavarian government, Ludendorff was supposed to march on Berlin with Hitler's support. The plot was poorly or-

ganized, however, and it was crushed by the police, backed up by the army, in less than a day. Hitler was arrested, tried, and sentenced to five years in prison. He had failed for the moment. But Nazism had been born, and it did not die.

Hitler's Road to Power

At his trial, Hitler violently denounced the Weimar Republic and skillfully presented his own program. In doing so, he gained enormous publicity and attention. Moreover, he learned from his unsuccessful revolt. Hitler concluded that he had to undermine, rather than overthrow, the government, that he had to use its tolerant democratic framework to intimidate the opposition and come to power through electoral competition. He forced his more violent supporters to accept his new strategy. He also used his brief prison term—he was released in less than a year—to dictate *Mein Kampf*. There he expounded on his basic themes: "race," with a stress on anti-Semitism; "living space," with a sweeping vision of war and conquered territory; and the leader-dictator (*Führer*), with unlimited, arbitrary power. Hitler's followers had their bible.

In the years of prosperity and relative stability between 1924 and 1929, Hitler concentrated on building his National Socialist German Workers' party, or Nazi party. By 1928 the party had 100,000 highly disciplined members under Hitler's absolute control. To appeal to the middle classes, Hitler de-emphasized the anticapitalist elements of national socialism and vowed to fight Bolshevism.

The Nazis were still a small splinter group in 1928, when they received only 2.6 percent of the vote in the general elections and twelve seats in the Reichstag. There the Nazi deputies pursued the legal strategy of using democracy to destroy democracy. As Hitler's talented future minister of propaganda, Joseph Goebbels (1897–1945), explained in 1928 in the party newspaper, "We become Reichstag deputies in order to paralyze the spirit of Weimar with its own aid. . . . We come as enemies! As the wolf breaks into the sheepfold, so we come."[11]

In 1929 the Great Depression began striking down economic prosperity, one of the barriers that had kept the wolf at bay. Unemployment jumped from 1.3 million in 1929 to 5 million in 1930; that year Germany had almost as many unemployed as all the other countries of Europe combined. Industrial production fell by one-half between 1929 and

1932. By the end of 1932, an incredible 43 percent of the labor force was unemployed, and it was estimated that only one in every three union members was working full time. No factor contributed more to Hitler's success than the economic crisis. Never very interested in economics before, Hitler began promising German voters economic as well as political and military salvation.

Hitler pitched his speeches especially to the middle and lower middle classes—small business people, office workers, artisans, and peasants. Already disillusioned by the great inflation of 1923, these people were seized by panic as bankruptcies increased, unemployment soared, and the dreaded Communists made dramatic election gains. The middle and lower middle classes deserted the conservative and moderate parties for the Nazis in great numbers.

Simultaneously, Hitler worked hard behind the scenes to win the support of two key elite groups. First, he promised big business leaders that he would restore their depression-shattered profits, by breaking Germany's strong labor movement and reducing workers' wages if need be. Second, he assured top army leaders that the Nazis would overturn the Versailles settlement and rearm Germany. Thus Hitler successfully followed Mussolini's fascist recipe. Hitler won at least the tacit approval of powerful conservatives who could have blocked his bid for power.

The Nazis also appealed strongly to German youth. Indeed, in some ways the Nazi movement was a mass movement of young Germans. Hitler himself was only forty in 1929, and he and most of his top aides were much younger than other leading German politicians. "National Socialism is the organized will of the youth," proclaimed the official Nazi slogan, and the battle cry of Gregor Strasser, a leading Nazi organizer, was "Make way, you old ones."[12] In 1931 almost 40 percent of Nazi party members were under thirty, compared with 20 percent of Social Democrats. Sixty-seven percent of Nazi members were under forty. National recovery, exciting and rapid change, and personal advancement: these were the appeals of Nazism to millions of German youths.

In the election of 1930, the Nazis won 6.5 million votes and 107 seats, which made them second in strength only to the Social Democrats, the moderate socialists. The economic and political situation continued to deteriorate, and Hitler and the Nazis kept promising that they would bring

Hitler in Opposition Hitler returns the salute of his Brown Shirts in this photograph from the third party day rally in Nuremberg in 1927. The Brown Shirts formed a private army within the Nazi movement, and their uniforms, marches, salutes, and vandalism helped keep Hitler in the public eye in the 1920s. *(Source: Courtesy, Bison Books, London)*

economy recovery and national unity. In 1932 the Nazi vote leaped to 14.5 million, and the Nazis became the largest party in the Reichstag.

Another reason Hitler came to power was the breakdown of democratic government as early as May 1930. Unable to gain the support of a majority in the Reichstag, Chancellor (chief minister) Heinrich Brüning convinced the president, the aging war hero General Hindenburg, to authorize rule by decree. The Weimar Republic's constitu-

❖ **The Mobilization of Young People** was a prime objective of the Nazi leadership. Here boys in a Nazi youth group, some of whom are only children, are disciplined and conditioned to devote themselves to the regime. *(Source: Bettmann/Hulton)*

tion permitted such rule in emergency situations, but the rather authoritarian, self-righteous Brüning intended to use it indefinitely. Moreover, Brüning was determined to overcome the economic crisis by cutting back government spending and ruthlessly forcing down prices and wages. Brüning's ultraorthodox policies not only intensified the economic collapse in Germany but also convinced the lower middle classes that the country's republican leaders were stupid and corrupt. These classes were pleased, rather than dismayed, by Hitler's attacks on the republican system. After President Hindenburg forced Brüning to resign in May 1932, the new government, headed by Franz von Papen, continued to rule by decree.

The continuation of the struggle between the Social Democrats and Communists, right up until the moment Hitler took power, was another aspect of the breakdown of democratic government. The Communists refused to cooperate with the Social Democrats, even though the two parties together outnumbered the Nazis in the Reichstag, even after the elections of 1932. German Communists (and the still complacent Stalin) were blinded by hatred of Socialists and by ideology: the Communists believed that fascism was reactionary and antirevolutionary, that Hitler's rise therefore represented the last agonies of monopoly capitalism, and that a communist revolution would soon follow his taking power. Socialist leaders pleaded, even at the Soviet Embassy, for at least a temporary alliance with the Communists to block Hitler, but to no avail. Perhaps the Weimar Republic was already too far gone, but this disunity on the left was undoubtedly another nail in the republic's coffin.

Finally, there was Hitler's skill as a politician. A master of mass propaganda and psychology, he had written in *Mein Kampf* that the masses were the "driving force of the most important changes in this world" and were themselves driven by hysterical fanaticism and not by knowledge. To arouse such hysterical fanaticism, he believed that all propaganda had to be limited to a few simple, endlessly repeated slogans. Thus in the terrible economic and political crisis, he harangued vast audiences with passionate, irrational oratory. Men moaned and women cried, seized by emotion. And many uncertain individuals, surrounded by thousands of entranced listeners, found security and a sense of belonging.

At the same time, Hitler continued to excel at dirty, back-room politics. That, in fact, brought him to power. In complicated in-fighting in 1932 he cleverly succeeded in gaining additional support from key people in the army and big business. These people thought they could use Hitler for their own advantage to get increased military spending, fat contracts, and tough measures against workers. Conservative and nationalistic politicians such as Papen thought similarly. They thus accepted Hitler's demand to join the government only if he became chancellor. There would be only two other National Socialists and nine solid conservatives as ministers, and in such a coalition government, they reasoned, Hitler could be used and controlled. On January 30, 1933, Hitler was legally appointed chancellor by Hindenburg.

The Nazi State and Society

Hitler moved rapidly and skillfully to establish an unshakable dictatorship. His first step was to continue using terror and threats to gain more power while maintaining legal appearances. He immediately called for new elections and applied the enormous power of the government to restrict his opponents. In the midst of a violent electoral campaign, the Reichstag building was partly destroyed by fire. Although the Nazis themselves may have set the fire, Hitler screamed that the Communist party was responsible. On the strength of this accusation, he convinced President Hindenburg to sign dictatorial emergency acts that practically abolished freedom of speech and assembly as well as most personal liberties.

When the Nazis won only 44 percent of the vote in the elections, Hitler immediately outlawed the Communist party and arrested its parliamentary representatives. Then on March 23, 1933, the Nazis pushed through the Reichstag the so-called Enabling Act, which gave Hitler absolute dictatorial power for four years. Only the Social Democrats voted against this bill, for Hitler had successfully blackmailed the Center party by threatening to attack the Catholic church.

Armed with the Enabling Act, Hitler and the Nazis moved to smash or control all independent organizations. Meanwhile, Hitler and his propagandists constantly proclaimed that their revolution was legal and constitutional. This deceitful stress on legality, coupled with divide-and-conquer techniques, disarmed the opposition until it was too late for effective resistance.

The systematic subjugation of independent organizations and the apparent creation of a totalitarian state had massive repercussions. The Social Democratic and Center parties were soon dissolved, and Germany became a one-party state. Only the Nazi party was legal. Elections were farces. The Reichstag was jokingly referred to as the most expensive glee club in the country, for its only function was to sing hymns of praise to the Führer. Hitler and the Nazis took over the government bureaucracy intact, installing many Nazis in top positions. At the same time, they created a series of overlapping Nazi party organizations responsible solely to Hitler.

As recent research shows, the resulting system of dual government was riddled with rivalries, contradictions, and inefficiencies. Thus the Nazi state lacked the all-compassing unity that its propagandists claimed and was sloppy and often disorganized. Yet this fractured system suited Hitler and his purposes. He could play the established bureaucracy against his private, personal "party government" and maintain his freedom of action. Hitler could concentrate on general principles and the big decisions, which he always made.

In the economic sphere, one big decision outlawed strikes and abolished independent labor unions, which were replaced by the Nazi Labor Front. Professional people—doctors and lawyers, teachers and engineers—also saw their previously independent organizations swallowed up in Nazi associations. Nor did the Nazis neglect cultural and intellectual life. Publishing houses were put under Nazi control, and universities and writers were quickly brought into line. Democratic, socialist, and Jewish literature was put on ever-growing blacklists. Passionate students and pitiful professors burned forbidden books in public squares. Modern art and architecture were ruthlessly prohibited. Life became violently anti-intellectual. As the cynical Goebbels put it, "When I hear the word 'culture' I reach for my gun."[13] By 1934 a brutal dictatorship characterized by frightening dynamism and obedience to Hitler was already largely in place.

Only the army retained independence, and Hitler moved brutally and skillfully to establish his control there, too. He realized that the army as well as big business was suspicious of the Nazi storm troopers (the SA), the quasi-military band of three million toughs in brown shirts who had fought communists and beaten up Jews before the

Nazis took power. These unruly storm troopers expected top positions in the army and even talked of a "second revolution" against capitalism. Needing to preserve good relations with the army and big business, Hitler decided that the SA leaders had to be eliminated. On the night of June 30, 1934, he struck.

Hitler's elite personal guard—the SS—arrested and shot without trial roughly a thousand SA leaders and assorted political enemies. While his propagandists spread lies about SA conspiracies, army leaders and President Hindenburg responded to the purge with congratulatory telegrams. Shortly thereafter army leaders swore a binding oath of "unquestioning obedience . . . to the Leader of the German State and People, Adolf Hitler." The SS grew rapidly. Under its methodical, inhuman leader, Heinrich Himmler (1900–1945), the SS joined with the political police, the Gestapo, to expand its network of special courts and concentration camps. Nobody was safe.

From the beginning, Jews were a special object of Nazi persecution. By the end of 1934, most Jewish lawyers, doctors, professors, civil servants, and musicians had lost their jobs and the right to practice their professions. In 1935 the infamous Nuremberg Laws classified as Jewish anyone having one or more Jewish grandparents and deprived Jews of all rights of citizenship. By 1938 roughly one-quarter of Germany's half-million Jews had emigrated, sacrificing almost all their property in order to leave Germany.

Following the assassination of a German diplomat in Paris by a young Jewish boy trying desperately to strike out at persecution, the attack on the Jews accelerated. A well-organized wave of violence destroyed homes, synagogues, and businesses, after which German Jews were rounded up and made to pay for the damage. It became very difficult for Jews to leave Germany. Some Germans privately opposed these outrages, but most went along or looked the other way. Although this lack of response reflected the individual's helplessness in a totalitarian state, it was more certainly a sign of the strong popular support Hitler's government enjoyed.

Hitler's Popularity

Hitler had promised the masses economic recovery—"work and bread"—and he delivered. Breaking with Brüning's do-nothing policies, Hitler im-

mediately launched a large public works program to pull Germany out of the depression. Work began on superhighways, offices, gigantic sports stadiums, and public housing. In 1936 Germany turned decisively toward rearmament, and government spending began to concentrate on the military. The result was that unemployment dropped steadily, from six million in January 1933 to about one million in late 1936. By 1938 there was a shortage of workers, and women eventually took many jobs previously denied them by the antifeminist Nazis. Thus everyone had work, and between 1932 and 1938 the standard of living for the average employed worker increased moderately. The profits of business rose sharply. For millions of people, economic recovery was tangible evidence in their daily lives that the excitement and dynamism of Nazi rule were based on more than show and propaganda.

For the masses of ordinary German citizens, who were not Jews, Slavs, Gypsies, Jehovah's Witnesses, communists, or homosexuals, Hitler's government meant greater equality and more opportunities. In 1933 the position of the traditional German elites—the landed aristocracy, the wealthy capitalists, and the well-educated professional classes— was still very strong. Barriers between classes were generally high. Hitler's rule introduced changes that lowered these barriers. For example, stiff educational requirements, which favored the well-to-do, were relaxed. The new Nazi elite included many young and poorly educated dropouts, rootless lower-middle-class people like Hitler who rose to the top with breathtaking speed. More generally, the Nazis tolerated privilege and wealth only as long as they served the needs of the party. Even big business was constantly ordered around, to the point that "probably never in peacetime has an ostensibly capitalist economy been directed as non- and even anti-capitalistically as the German economy between 1933 and 1939."[14]

Yet few historians today believe that Hitler and the Nazis brought about a real social revolution, as an earlier generation of scholars often argued. Millions of modest middle-class and lower-middle-class people *felt* that Germany was becoming more open and equal, as Nazi propagandists constantly claimed. But quantitative studies show that the well-educated classes held on to most of their advantages and that only a modest social leveling occurred in the Nazi years. It is significant that the Nazis shared with the Italian fascists the stereotypic view of women as housewives and mothers. Only under the relentless pressure of war did they reluctantly mobilize large numbers of German women for work in offices and factories.

Hitler's rabid nationalism, which had helped him gain power, continued to appeal to Germans after 1933. Ever since the wars against Napoleon, many Germans had believed in a special mission for a superior German nation. The successes of Bismarck had furthered such feelings, and near-victory in World War One made nationalists eager for renewed expansion in the 1920s. Thus when Hitler went from one foreign triumph to another and a great German empire seemed within reach, the majority of the population was delighted and kept praising the Führer's actions well into the war.

Not all Germans supported Hitler, however, and a number of German groups actively resisted him after 1933. Tens of thousands of political enemies were imprisoned, and thousands were executed. Opponents of the Nazis pursued various goals, and under totalitarian conditions they were never unified, a fact that helps account for their ultimate lack of success. In the first years of Hitler's rule, the principal resisters were the communists and the social democrats in the trade unions. But the expansion of the SS system of terror after 1935 smashed most of these leftists. A second group of opponents arose in the Catholic and Protestant churches. However, their efforts were directly primarily at preserving genuine religious life, not at overthrowing Hitler. Finally in 1938 (and again in 1942 to 1944), some high-ranking army officers, who feared the consequences of Hitler's reckless aggression, plotted against him, unsuccessfully.

Honoring German Women The Nazi state favored traditional roles for women, believing that they should keep house and raise families, preferably large ones. Each of these smiling mothers has done her duty and given birth to several children. In this ceremony the city of Berlin is recognizing each mother's achievement and naming itself the honorary guardian of her baby. *(Source: Archiv für Kunst und Geschichte, Berlin)*

NAZI EXPANSION AND THE SECOND WORLD WAR

Although economic recovery and somewhat greater opportunity for social advancement won Hitler support, they were only by-products of the Nazi regime. The guiding and unique concepts of Nazism remained space and race—the territorial expansion of the superior German race. As Germany regained its economic strength and as independent organizations were brought under control, Hitler formed alliances with other dictators and began expanding. German expansion was facilitated by the uncertain, divided, pacific Western democracies, which tried to buy off Hitler to avoid war.

Yet war inevitably broke out, in both the West and the East, for Hitler's ambitions were essentially unlimited. On both war fronts Nazi soldiers scored enormous successes until late 1942, establishing a horrifyingly vast empire of death and destruction. Hitler's reckless aggression also raised a mighty coalition determined to smash the Nazi order. Led by Britain, the United States, and the Soviet Union, the Grand Alliance—to use Winston Churchill's favorite term—functioned quite effectively in military terms. By the summer of 1943, the tide of battle had turned. Two years later, Germany and its allies lay in ruins, utterly defeated. Thus the terrible Nazi empire proved short-lived.

Aggression and Appeasement, 1933–1939

Hitler's tactics in international politics after 1933 strikingly resembled those he had used in domestic

1919	Treaty of Versailles; J. M. Keynes, *Economic Consequences of the Peace*
1919–1920	U.S. Senate rejects the Treaty of Versailles
1921	Germany is billed $35 billion in reparations
1922	Mussolini seizes power in Italy; Germany proposes a moratorium on reparations
January 1923	France and Belgium occupy the Ruhr; Germany orders passive resistance to the occupation
October 1923	Stresemann agrees to reparations based on Germany's ability to pay
1924	Dawes Plan: German reparations reduced and put on a sliding scale; Large U.S. loans to Germany recommended to promote German recovery; occupation of the Ruhr ends; Adolf Hitler, *Mein Kampf*
1924–1929	Spectacular German economic recovery; circular flow of international funds enables sizable reparations payments
1925	Treaties of Locarno promote European security and stability
1926	Germany joins the League of Nations
1928	Kellogg-Briand Pact renounces war as an instrument of international affairs
1929	Young Plan further reduces German reparations; crash of U.S. stock market
1929–1933	Depths of the Great Depression
1931	Japan invades Manchuria
1932	Nazis become the largest party in the Reichstag
January 1933	Hitler appointed chancellor
March 1933	Reichstag passes the Enabling Act, granting Hitler absolute dictatorial power
October 1933	Germany withdraws from the League of Nations
July 1934	Nazis murder Austrian chancellor
March 1935	Hitler announces German rearmament
June 1935	Anglo-German naval agreement
October 1935	Mussolini invades Ethiopia and receives Hitler's support
1935	Nuremburg Laws deprive Jews of all rights of citizenship
March 1936	German armies move unopposed into the demilitarized Rhineland
July 1936	Outbreak of civil war in Spain
1937	Japan invades China; Rome-Berlin Axis
March 1938	Germany annexes Austria
September 1938	Munich Conference; Britain and France agree to German seizure of the Sudetenland from Czechoslovakia
March 1939	Germany occupies the rest of Czechoslovakia; the end of appeasement in Britain
August 1939	Russo-German nonaggression pact
Sept. 1, 1939	Germany invades Poland
Sept. 3, 1939	Britain and France declare war on Germany

MAP 29.1 The Growth of Nazi Germany, 1933–1939 Until March 1939, Hitler brought ethnic Germans into the Nazi state; then he turned on the Slavic peoples he had always hated. He stripped Czechoslovakia of its independence and prepared for an attack on Poland in September 1939.

politics between 1924 and 1933. When Hitler was weak, he righteously proclaimed that he intended to overturn the "unjust system" established by the treaties of Versailles and Locarno—but only by legal means. As he grew stronger, and as other leaders showed their willingness to compromise, he increased his demands and finally began attacking his independent neighbors (Map 29.1).

Hitler realized that his aggressive policies had to be carefully camouflaged at first, for Germany's army was limited by the Treaty of Versailles to only 100,000 men. As he told a group of army commanders in February 1933, the early stages of his policy of "conquest of new living space in the East and its ruthless Germanization" had serious dangers. If France had real leaders, Hitler said, it would "not give us time but attack us, presumably with its eastern satellites."[15] To avoid such threats to his plans, Hitler loudly proclaimed his peaceful intentions to all the world. Nevertheless, he felt strong enough to walk out of a sixty-nation disarmament conference and withdraw from the League of Nations in October 1933. Stresemann's policy of peaceful cooperation was dead; the Nazi determination to rearm was out in the open.

Following this action, which met with widespread approval at home, Hitler moved to incorporate independent Austria into a greater Germany. Austrian Nazis climaxed an attempted overthrow by murdering the Austrian chancellor in July 1934. They were unable to take power, however, because a worried Mussolini, who had initially greeted Hitler as a fascist little brother, massed his troops on the Brenner Pass and threatened to fight. When in March 1935 Hitler established a general military draft and declared the "unequal" disarmament clauses of the Treaty of Versailles null and void, other countries appeared to understand the danger. With France taking the lead, Italy and Great Britain protested strongly and warned against future aggressive actions.

Yet the emerging united front against Hitler quickly collapsed. Of crucial importance, Britain adopted a policy of appeasement, granting Hitler everything he could reasonably want (and more) in order to avoid war. The first step was an Anglo-German naval agreement in June 1935 that broke Germany's isolation. The second step came in March 1936 when Hitler suddenly marched his armies into the demilitarized Rhineland, brazenly violating the treaties of Versailles and Locarno. This was the last good chance to stop the Nazis, for Hitler had ordered his troops to retreat if France resisted militarily. But an uncertain France would not move without British support, and the occupation of German soil by German armies seemed right and just to Britain. With a greatly improved strategic position, Germany handed France a tremendous psychological defeat.

British appeasement, which practically dictated French policy, lasted far into 1939. It was motivated by British feelings of guilt toward Germany and the pacifism of a population still horrified by the memory of the First World War. As in Germany, many powerful conservatives in Britain underestimated Hitler. They believed that Soviet communism was the real danger and that Hitler could be used to stop it. A leading member of Britain's government personally told Hitler in November 1937 that it was his conviction that Hitler "not only had accomplished great things in Germany itself, but that through the total destruction of Communism in his own country . . . Germany rightly had to be considered as a Western bulwark against Communism."[16] Such rigid anticommunist feelings made an alliance between the Western powers and Stalin unlikely.

As Britain and France opted for appeasement and the Soviet Union watched all developments suspiciously, Hitler found powerful allies. In 1935 the bombastic Mussolini decided that imperial expansion was needed to revitalize Italian fascism. From Italian colonies on the east coast of Africa, he attacked the independent African kingdom of Ethiopia. The Western powers and the League of Nations piously condemned Italian aggression—a posture that angered Mussolini—without saving Ethiopia from defeat. Hitler, who had secretly supplied Ethiopia with arms to heat up the conflict, supported Italy energetically and thereby overcame Mussolini's lingering doubts about the Nazis. The result in 1936 was an agreement on close cooperation between Italy and Germany, the so-called Rome-Berlin Axis. Japan, which had been expanding into Manchuria since 1931, soon joined the Axis alliance.

At the same time, Germany and Italy intervened in the long, complicated Spanish Civil War, where their support eventually helped General Francisco Franco's fascist movement defeat republican Spain. Spain's only official aid came from the U.S.S.R., for public opinion in Britain and especially in France was hopelessly divided on the Spanish question.

In late 1937, while proclaiming peaceful intentions to the British and their gullible prime minister, Neville Chamberlain, Hitler told his generals his real plans. His "unshakable decision" was to crush Austria and Czechoslovakia at the earliest possible moment as the first step in his long-contemplated drive to the east for living space. By threatening Austria with invasion, Hitler forced the Austrian chancellor in March 1938 to put local Nazis in control of the government. The next day German armies moved in unopposed, and Austria became two more provinces of Greater Germany (see Map 29.1).

Simultaneously, Hitler began demanding that the pro-Nazi, German-speaking minority of western Czechoslovakia—the Sudetenland—be turned over to Germany. Yet democratic Czechoslovakia was prepared to defend itself. Moreover, France had been Czechoslovakia's ally since 1924; and if France fought, the Soviet Union was pledged to

❖ **Cartoonist David Low's** biting criticism of appeasing leaders appeared shortly after Hitler remilitarized the Rhineland. Appeasement also appealed to millions of ordinary citizens, who wanted to avoid at any cost another great war. *(Source: Cartoon by David Low. Reproduced by permission of London Evening/Solo Standard)*

help. As war appeared inevitable—for Hitler had already told the leader of the Sudeten Germans that "we must always ask so much we cannot be satisfied"—appeasement triumphed again. In September 1938 Chamberlain flew to Germany three times in fourteen days. In these negotiations, to which the U.S.S.R. was deliberately not invited, Chamberlain and the French agreed with Hitler that the Sudetenland should be ceded to Germany immediately. Returning to London from the Munich conference, Chamberlain told cheering crowds that he had secured "peace with honor . . . peace for our time." Sold out by the Western powers, Czechoslovakia gave in.

Confirmed once again in his opinion of the Western democracies as weak and racially degenerate, Hitler accelerated his aggression. In a shocking violation of his solemn assurances that the Sudetenland was his last territorial demand, Hitler's armies occupied the Czech lands in March 1939, while Slovakia became a puppet state. The effect on Western public opinion was electrifying. For the first time, there was no possible rationale of self-determination for Nazi aggression since Hitler was seizing Czechs and Slovaks as captive peoples. Thus when Hitler used the question of German minorities in Danzig as a pretext to confront Poland, a suddenly militant Chamberlain declared that Britain and France would fight if Hitler at-

tacked his eastern neighbor. Hitler did not take these warnings seriously, and thus he decided to press on.

In an about-face that stunned the world, Hitler offered and Stalin signed a ten-year Nazi-Soviet nonaggression pact in August 1939 whereby each dictator promised to remain neutral if the other became involved in war. Even more startling was the attached secret protocol, which ruthlessly divided eastern Europe into German and Soviet zones, "in the event of a political territorial reorganization." Although this top-secret protocol sealing the destruction of Poland and the Baltic states became known only after the war, the nonaggression pact itself was enough to make Britain and France cry treachery, for they, too, had been negotiating with Stalin. But Stalin had remained distrustful of Western intentions. Moreover, Britain and France had offered him military risk without gain, whereas Hitler had offered territorial gain without risk. For Hitler, everything was set. He told his generals on the day of the nonaggression pact, "My only fear is that at the last moment some dirty dog will come up with a mediation plan." On September 1, 1939, German armies and warplanes smashed into Poland from three sides. Two days later Britain and France, finally true to their word, declared war on Germany. The Second World War had begun.

Hitler's Empire, 1939–1942

Using planes, tanks, and trucks in the first example of a *blitzkrieg,* or "lightning war," Hitler's armies crushed Poland in four weeks. While the Soviet Union quickly took its part of the booty—the eastern half of Poland and the Baltic states of Lithuania, Estonia, and Latvia—French and British armies dug in in the west. They expected another war of attrition and economic blockade.

In spring 1940 the lightning war struck again. After occupying Denmark, Norway, and Holland, German motorized columns broke through southern Belgium, split the Franco-British forces, and trapped the entire British army on the beaches of Dunkirk. By heroic efforts the British withdrew their troops but not their equipment.

France was taken by the Nazis. Aging marshal Henri-Philippe Pétain formed a new French government—the so-called Vichy government—to accept defeat, and German armies occupied most of France. By July 1940 Hitler ruled practically all of western continental Europe; Italy was an ally and the Soviet Union, a friendly neutral. Only Britain, led by the uncompromising Winston Churchill (1874–1965), remained unconquered. Churchill proved to be one of history's greatest wartime leaders, rallying the British with stirring speeches, infectious confidence, and bulldog determination.

Germany sought to gain control of the air, the necessary first step for an amphibious invasion of Britain. In the Battle of Britain, up to a thousand German planes attacked British airfields and key factories in a single day, dueling with British defenders high in the skies. Losses were heavy on both sides. Then in September Hitler angrily and foolishly changed his strategy, turning from military objectives to indiscriminate bombing of British cities in an attempt to break British morale. British factories increased production of their excellent fighter planes, anti-aircraft defense improved with the help of radar, and the heavily bombed people of London defiantly dug in. In September and October 1940, Britain was beating Germany three to one in the air war. There was no possibility of immediate German invasion of Britain.

In these circumstances, the most reasonable German strategy would have been to attack Britain through the eastern Mediterranean, taking Egypt and the Suez Canal and pinching off Britain's supply of oil. Moreover, Mussolini's early defeats in Greece had drawn Hitler into the Balkans, where

Germany quickly conquered Greece and Yugoslavia while forcing Hungary, Rumania, and Bulgaria into alliances with Germany by April 1941. This reinforced the logic of a thrust into the eastern Mediterranean. But Hitler was not a reasonable person. His lifetime obsession with a vast eastern European empire for the master race irrationally dictated policy. By late 1940 he had already decided on his next move, and in June 1941 German armies suddenly attacked the Soviet Union along a vast front. With Britain still unconquered, Hitler's decision was a wild, irrational gamble epitomizing the violent, unlimited, and ultimately self-destructive ambitions of Nazism.

Faithfully fulfilling all obligations under the Nazi-Soviet pact and even ignoring warnings of impending invasion, Stalin was caught off guard. Nazi armies moved like lightning across the steppe. By October 1941 Leningrad was practically surrounded, Moscow was besieged, and most of Ukraine had been conquered; yet the Soviets did not collapse. When a severe winter struck German armies outfitted in summer uniforms, the invaders were stopped.

While Hitler's armies dramatically expanded the war in Europe, his Japanese allies did the same in Asia. Engaged in a general but undeclared war against China since 1937, Japan's rulers had increasingly come into diplomatic conflict with the Pacific basin's other great power, the United States. When the Japanese occupied French Indochina in July 1941, the United States retaliated by cutting off sales of vital rubber, scrap iron, oil, and aviation fuel. Tension mounted further, and on December 7, 1941, Japan attacked the U.S. naval base at Pearl Harbor in Hawaii. Hitler immediately declared war on the United States, even though his treaty obligations with Japan did not require him to initiate this course of action.

While Japanese forces advanced swiftly into Southeast Asia after the crippling surprise attack at Pearl Harbor, Hitler and his European allies continued the two-front war against the Soviet Union and Great Britain. Not until late 1942 did the Nazis suffer their first major defeats. In the meantime, Hitler ruled a vast European empire stretching from the outskirts of Moscow to the English Channel. Hitler and the top Nazi leadership began building their "New Order," and they continued their efforts until their final collapse in 1945. In doing so, they showed what Nazi victory would have meant.

Hitler's New Order was based firmly on the guiding principle of Nazi totalitarianism: racial imperialism. Within this New Order, the Nordic peoples—the Dutch, Norwegians, and Danes—received preferential treatment, for they were racially related to the Germans. The French, an "inferior" Latin people, occupied the middle position. They were heavily taxed to support the Nazi war effort but were tolerated as a race. Once Nazi reverses began to mount in late 1942, however, all the occupied territories of western and northern Europe were exploited with increasing intensity. Material shortages and both mental and physical suffering afflicted millions of people.

Slavs in the conquered territories to the east were treated with harsh hatred as "subhumans." At the height of success in 1941 to 1942, Hitler painted for his intimate circle the fantastic details of a vast eastern colonial empire where Poles, Ukrainians, and Russians would be enslaved and forced to die out, while Germanic peasants resettled the resulting abandoned lands. Himmler and the elite corps of SS volunteers struggled loyally, sometimes against the German army, to implement part of this general program even before victory was secured. In parts of Poland, the SS arrested and evacuated Polish peasants to create a German "mass settlement space." Polish workers and Soviet prisoners of war were transported to Germany, where they did most of the heavy labor and were systematically worked to death. The conditions of Soviet slave labor in Germany were so harsh that four out of five Soviet prisoners did not survive the war.

✤ **Prelude to Murder** This photo captures the terrible inhumanity of Nazi racism. Frightened and bewildered families from the soon-to-be-destroyed Warsaw ghetto are being forced out of their homes by German soldiers for deportation to concentration camps. There they face murder in the gas chambers. *(Source: Roger-Viollet)*

Finally, Jews were condemned to extermination, along with Gypsies, Jehovah's Witnesses, and captured communists. By 1939 German Jews had lost all their civil rights, and after the fall of Warsaw the Nazis began deporting them to Poland. There they and Jews from all over Europe were concentrated in ghettos, compelled to wear the Jewish star, and turned into slave laborers. But by late 1941 Himmler's SS was beginning to carry out the "final solution of the Jewish question"—the murder of every single Jew. As Marco Nahon wrote in *Birkenau,* the chilling account of his nightmare ordeal as a Jewish deportee from Greece, many Jews in small towns could hardly imagine the enormity of the crime that lay before them. (See Listening to the Past.) Yet all over Hitler's empire, Jews were systematically arrested, packed like cattle onto freight trains, and dispatched to extermination camps.

There the victims were taken by force or deception to "shower rooms," which were actually gas chambers. These gas chambers, first perfected in the quiet, efficient execution of seventy thousand mentally ill Germans between 1938 and 1941, permitted rapid, hideous, and thoroughly bureaucratized mass murder. For fifteen to twenty minutes came the terrible screams and gasping sobs of men, women, and children choking to death on poison gas. Then, only silence. Special camp workers quickly yanked the victims' gold teeth from their jaws and cut off their hair for use as chair stuffing. The bodies were then cremated, or sometimes boiled for oil to make soap, while the bones were crushed to produce fertilizers. At Auschwitz–Birkenau, the most infamous of the Nazi death factories, as many as twelve thousand human beings were slaughtered each day. On the turbulent Russian front, the SS death squads forced the Jewish population to dig giant pits, which became mass graves as the victims were lined up on the edge and cut down by machine guns. The extermination of European Jews was the ultimate monstrosity of Nazi racism and racial imperialism. By 1945 six million Jews had been murdered.

The Grand Alliance

While the Nazis built their savage empire, the Allies faced the hard fact that chance, rather than choice, had brought them together. Stalin had been cooperating fully with Hitler between August 1939 and June 1941, and only the Japanese attack on Pearl Harbor in December 1941 and Hitler's immediate declaration of war had overwhelmed powerful isolationism in the United States. The Allies' first task was to overcome their mutual suspicions and build an unshakable alliance on the quicksand of accident. By means of three interrelated policies they succeeded.

First, President Roosevelt accepted Churchill's contention that the United States should concentrate first on defeating Hitler. Only after victory in Europe was achieved would the United States turn toward the Pacific for an all-out attack on Japan, the lesser threat. Thus, the United States promised and sent large amounts of military aid to Britain and the U.S.S.R., and American and British forces in each combat zone were tightly integrated under a single commander. America's policy of "Europe first" helped solidify the anti-Hitler coalition.

Second, within the European framework the Americans and the British put immediate military needs first. They consistently postponed tough political questions relating to the eventual peace settlement and thereby avoided conflicts that might have split the alliance until after the war.

Third, to further encourage mutual trust, the Allies adopted the principle of the "unconditional surrender" of Germany and Japan. This policy of unconditional surrender cemented the Grand Alliance because it denied Hitler any hope of dividing his foes. It probably also discouraged Germans and Japanese who might have tried to overthrow their dictators in order to make a compromise peace. Of great importance for the postwar shape of Europe, it meant that Soviet and Anglo-American armies would almost certainly come together to divide all of Germany, and most of the Continent, among the victorious allies.

The military resources of the Grand Alliance were awesome. The strengths of the United States were its mighty industry, its large population, and its national unity. Even before Pearl Harbor, President Roosevelt had called America the "arsenal of democracy" and given military aid to Britain and the Soviet Union. Now the United States geared up rapidly for all-out war production and drew heavily on a generally cooperative Latin America for resources. It not only equipped its own armies but also eventually gave its allies about 50 billion dollars in arms and equipment. Britain received by far the most, but about one-fifth of the total went to the Soviet Union in the form of badly needed trucks, planes, and munitions.

Too strong to lose and too weak to win standing alone, Britain continued to make a great contribution as well. The British economy was totally and effectively mobilized, and the sharing of burdens through rationing and heavy taxes on war profits maintained social harmony. Moreover, as 1942 wore on Britain could increasingly draw on the enormous physical and human resources of its empire and of the United States. By early 1943 the Americans and the British were combining small aircraft carriers with radar-guided bombers to rid the Atlantic of German submarines. Britain, the impregnable floating fortress, became a gigantic front-line staging area for the decisive blow to the heart of Germany.

As for the Soviet Union, so great was its strength that it might well have defeated Germany without Western help. In the face of the German advance, whole factories and populations were successfully evacuated to eastern Russia and Siberia. There war production was reorganized and expanded, and the Red Army was increasingly well supplied. The Red Army was also well led, for a new generation of talented military leaders quickly arose to replace those so recently purged. Most important of all, Stalin drew on the massive support and heroic determination of the Soviet people, especially those in the central Russian heartland. Broad-based Russian nationalism, as opposed to narrow communist ideology, became the powerful unifying force in what was appropriately called the "Great Patriotic War of the Fatherland."

Finally, the United States, Britain, and the Soviet Union were not alone. They had the resources of much of the world at their command. And, to a greater or lesser extent, they were aided by a growing resistance movement against the Nazis throughout Europe, even in Germany. Thus although Ukrainian peasants often welcomed the Germans as liberators, the barbaric occupation policies of the Nazis quickly drove them to join and support behind-the-lines guerrilla forces. More generally, after the U.S.S.R. was invaded in June 1941, communists throughout Europe took the lead in the underground resistance, joined by a growing number of patriots and Christians. Anti-Nazi leaders from occupied countries established governments-in-exile in London, like that of the "Free French" under the intensely proud General Charles De Gaulle. These governments gathered valuable secret information from resistance fighters and even organized armies to help defeat Hitler.

The Tide of Battle

Barely halted at the gates of Moscow and Leningrad in 1941, the Germans renewed their offensive against the Soviet Union in July 1942. This time they drove toward the southern city of Stalingrad in an attempt to cripple communications and seize the crucial oil fields of Baku. Reaching Stalingrad, the Germans slowly occupied most of the ruined city in a month of incredibly savage house-to-house fighting.

❖ **"For the Motherland's Sake, Go Forward, Heroes"** Joining the historic Russian warrior and the young Soviet soldier in the common cause, this poster portrays the defense of the nation as a sacred mission and illustrates the way Soviet leaders successfully appealed to Russian nationalism during the war. *(Source: Library of Congress)*

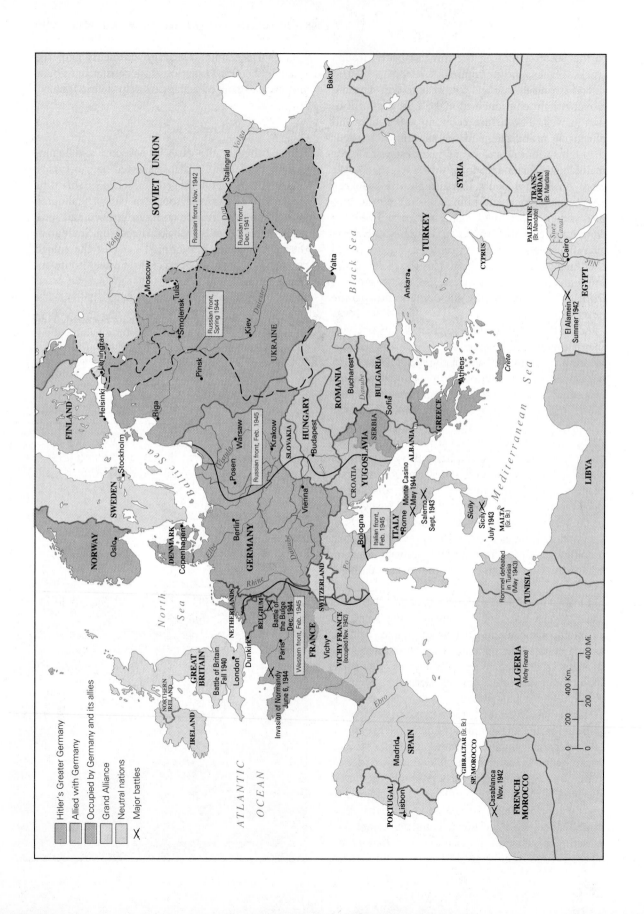

Then in November 1942, Soviet armies counterattacked. They rolled over Rumanian and Italian troops to the north and south of Stalingrad, quickly closing the trap and surrounding the entire German Sixth Army of 300,000 men. The surrounded Germans were systematically destroyed, until by the end of January 1943 only 123,000 soldiers were left to surrender. Hitler, who had refused to allow a retreat, had suffered a catastrophic defeat. In the summer of 1943, the larger, better-equipped Soviet armies took the offensive and began moving forward (Map 29.2).

In late 1942 the tide also turned in the Pacific and in North Africa. By late spring 1942, Japan had established a great empire in East Asia (Map 29.3). Unlike the Nazis, the Japanese made clever appeals to local nationalists, who hated European imperial domination and preferred Japan's so-called Greater Asian Co-prosperity Sphere.

Then in the Battle of the Coral Sea in May 1942, Allied naval and air power stopped the Japanese advance and also relieved Australia from the threat of invasion. This victory was followed by the Battle of Midway Island, in which American pilots sank all four of the attacking Japanese aircraft carriers and established American naval superiority in the Pacific. In August 1942 American marines attacked Guadalcanal in the Solomon Islands. Badly hampered by the policy of "Europe first"—only 15 percent of Allied resources were going to fight the war in the Pacific in early 1943—the Americans, under General Douglas MacArthur and Admiral Chester Nimitz, and the Australians nevertheless began "island hopping" toward Japan. Japanese forces were on the defensive.

In North Africa the war had been seesawing back and forth since 1940. In May 1942 combined German and Italian armies under the brilliant General Erwin Rommel attacked British-occupied Egypt and the Suez Canal for the second time. After a rapid advance, they were finally defeated by British forces at the Battle of El Alamein, only 70 miles from Alexandria. In October the British counterattacked in Egypt, and almost immediately thereafter an Anglo-American force landed in Morocco and Algeria. These French possessions, which were under the control of Pétain's Vichy French government, quickly went over to the side of the Allies.

Having driven the Axis powers from North Africa by the spring of 1943, Allied forces maintained the initiative by invading Sicily and then mainland Italy. Mussolini was deposed by a war-weary people, and the new Italian government publicly accepted unconditional surrender in September 1943. Italy, it seemed, was liberated. Yet Mussolini was rescued by German commandos in a daring raid and put at the head of a puppet government. German armies seized Rome and all of northern Italy. Fighting continued in Italy.

Indeed, bitter fighting continued in Europe for almost two years. Germany, less fully mobilized for war than Britain in 1941, applied itself to total war in 1942 and enlisted millions of German women and millions of prisoners of war and slave laborers from all across occupied Europe in that effort. Between early 1942 and July 1944, German war production actually tripled. Although British and American bombing raids killed many German civilians, these raids were surprisingly ineffective from a military point of view. Also, German resistance against Hitler failed. After an unsuccessful attempt on Hitler's life in July 1944, thousands of Germans were brutally liquidated by SS fanatics. Terrorized at home and frightened by the prospect of unconditional surrender, the Germans fought on with suicidal stoicism.

On June 6, 1944, American and British forces under General Dwight Eisenhower landed on the beaches of Normandy in history's greatest naval invasion. Having tricked the Germans into believing that the attack would come near the Belgian border, the Allies secured a foothold on the coast of Normandy. In a hundred dramatic days, more than two million men and almost a half-million vehicles pushed inland and broke through German lines. Rejecting proposals to strike straight at Berlin in a massive attack, Eisenhower moved forward cautiously on a broad front. Not until March 1945 did American troops cross the Rhine and enter Germany.

The Soviets, who had been advancing steadily since July 1943, reached the outskirts of Warsaw by August 1944. For the next six months they

✦ **MAP 29.2 World War Two in Europe** The map shows the extent of Hitler's empire at its height, before the battle of Stalingrad in late 1942 and the subsequent advances of the Allies until Germany surrendered on May 7, 1945.

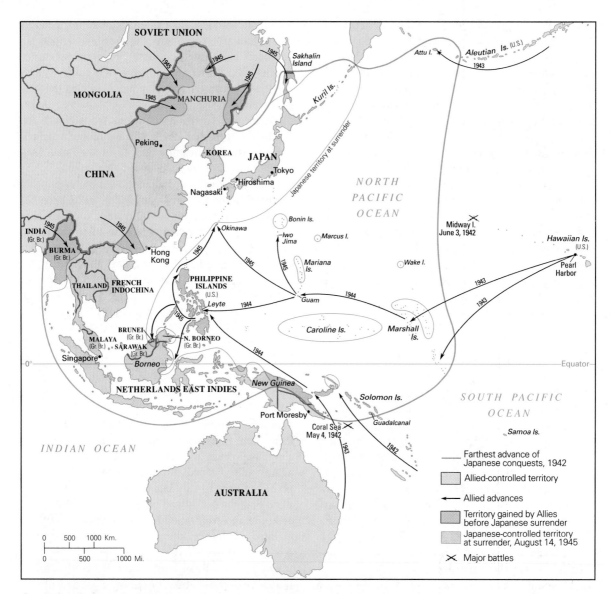

MAP 29.3 **World War Two in the Pacific** Japanese forces overran an enormous territory in 1942, which the Allies slowly recaptured in a long bitter struggle. As this map shows, Japan still held a large Asian empire in August 1945, when the unprecedented devastation of atomic warfare suddenly forced it to surrender.

moved southward into Rumania, Hungary, and Yugoslavia. In January 1945 Red armies again moved westward through Poland, and on April 26 they met American forces on the Elbe River. The Allies had closed their vise on Nazi Germany and overrun Europe. As Soviet forces fought their way into Berlin, Hitler committed suicide in his bunker, and on May 7 the remaining German commanders capitulated.

Three months later, the United States dropped atomic bombs on Hiroshima and Nagasaki in Japan. Mass bombing of cities and civilians, one of the terrible new practices of World War Two, had ended in the final nightmare—unprecedented human destruction in a single blinding flash. The Japanese surrendered. The Second World War, which had claimed the lives of more than fifty million soldiers and civilians, was over.

SUMMARY

The Second World War marked the climax of the tremendous practical and spiritual maladies of the age of anxiety, which led in many lands to the rise of dictatorships. Many of these dictatorships were variations on conservative authoritarianism, but there was also a fateful innovation—a new kind of dictatorship that was exceptionally dynamic and theoretically unlimited in its actions.

When apprehensive middle-class liberals in the West faced the rise of these new dictatorships, they often focused on their perceived similarities. Liberals fastened on the violent, profoundly antiliberal, and apparently totalitarian character of these brutal challengers, linking the one-party socialism of Lenin and Stalin with the one-party fascism of Mussolini and Hitler. In contrast, the political left usually insisted on the differences between the revolutionary socialist tradition—triumphing, however imperfectly, in the Bolsheviks' Soviet Union—and the reactionary and capitalist nature of European fascist movements and fascist governments in Italy and Germany. As the dramatic struggles of the 1930s and the Second World War (and early cold war) fall into a longer historical perspective and as more research adds new insights, a growing number of historians are stressing the limitations of both the totalitarian and fascist models and concentrating instead on the uniqueness of developments in each regime.

To be sure, recent scholarship on fascism has demonstrated the great importance of antisocialism and conservative support in Mussolini's and Hitler's rise to power and in the subsequent policies of their governments. The ideological divide between antisocialist fascists and antifascist socialists was enormous. It is also clear that both Nazi activists and fire-eating communists believed that their own regimes and societal systems were mortal enemies. Certainly Hitler thought so, and he acted on his fanatical convictions.

❖ **The City of Nagasaki** A second atomic bomb struck Nagasaki on August 9, 1945, three days after the first giant fireball incinerated Hiroshima. Approximately 75,000 Japanese were killed or injured at Nagasaki. In this grim photo, taken about a month after the attack, a Japanese survivor pushes his bicycle along a path cleared through the ruins. *(Source: UPI/Bettmann Newsphotos)*

At the same time, Hitler's Nazism appears increasingly as a uniquely evil and nihilistic system. Nazism had fascist origins, but German fascism in power ultimately presented only superficial similarities with fascism in Italy. As for Hitler's Germany and Stalin's U.S.S.R., both asserted a total claim on the lives of their citizens, posed ambitious goals, and demanded popular support. This combination gave both dictatorships their awesome power and dynamism. That dynamism was, however, channeled in quite different directions. Stalin and the Communist party aimed at building their kind of socialism and the new socialist personality at home. Hitler and the Nazi elite aimed at unlimited territorial and racial aggression on behalf of a master race; domestic recovery was only a means to that end.

Nazi racism and unlimited aggression made war inevitable, first with the western European democracies, then with hated eastern neighbors, and finally with the United States. Plunging Europe into the ultimate nightmare, unlimited aggression unwittingly forged a mighty coalition that smashed the racist Nazi empire and its leader. In the words of the ancient Greeks, he whom the gods would destroy, they first make mad.

Notes

1. I. Kershaw, *The Nazi Dictatorship: Problems and Perspectives of Interpretation,* 2d ed. (London: Edward Arnold, 1989), pp. 20–23.
2. E. Halévy, *The Era of Tyrannies* (Garden City, N.Y.: Doubleday, 1965), pp. 265–316, esp. p. 300.
3. Kershaw, *The Nazi Dictatorship,* p. 34.
4. Quoted in P. C. Roberts, "'War Communism': A Re-examination," *Slavic Review* 29 (June 1970): 257.
5. Quoted in A. G. Mazour, *Soviet Economic Development: Operation Outstrip, 1921–1965* (Princeton, N.J: Van Nostrand, 1967), p. 130.
6. Quoted in I. Deutscher, *Stalin: A Political Biography,* 2d ed. (New York: Oxford University Press, 1967), p. 325.
7. Quoted in H. K. Geiger, *The Family in Soviet Russia* (Cambridge, Mass.: Harvard University Press, 1968), p. 123.
8. Quoted in ibid., p. 156.
9. Quoted in B. Rosenthal, "Women in the Russian Revolution and After," in *Becoming Visible: Women in European History,* ed. R. Bridenthal and C. Koonz (Boston: Houghton Mifflin, 1976), p. 383.
10. R. Vivarelli, "Interpretations on the Origins of Fascism," *Journal of Modern History* 63 (March 1991): 41.
11. Quoted in K. D. Bracher, "The Technique of the National Socialist Seizure of Power," in *The Path to Dictatorship, 1918–1933,* ed. T. Eschenburg et al. (Garden City, N.Y.: Doubleday, 1966), p. 117.
12. Quoted in K. D. Bracher, *The German Dictatorship: The Origins, Structure and Effects of National Socialism* (New York: Praeger, 1970), pp. 146–147.
13. Quoted in R. Stromberg, *An Intellectual History of Modern Europe* (New York: Appleton-Century-Crofts, 1966), p. 393.
14. D. Schoenbaum, *Hitler's Social Revolution: Class and Status in Nazi Germany, 1933–1939* (Garden City, N.Y.: Doubleday, 1967), p. 114.
15. Quoted in Bracher, *The German Dictatorship,* p. 289.
16. Quoted in ibid., p. 306.

Suggested Reading

The historical literature on fascist and totalitarian dictatorships is rich and fascinating. Kershaw's work cited in the Notes provides an excellent recent survey of this literature, includes extensive bibliographical references, and is highly recommended. H. Arendt, *The Origins of Totalitarianism* (1951), is a classic interpretation. E. Weber, *Varieties of Fascism* (1964), stresses the radical social aspirations of fascist movements all across Europe. F. L. Carsten, *The Rise of Fascism* (1982), and W. Laqueur, ed., *Fascism* (1976), are also recommended. Z. Sternhell, *Neither Right Nor Left: Fascist Ideology in France* (1986), is important and stimulating, stressing the antiliberal and antisocialist origins of fascist thinking in France.

R. Stites, *The Women's Liberation Movement in Russia: Feminism, Nihilism, and Bolshevism, 1860–1930* (1978); S. Fitzpatrick, *Cultural Revolution in Russia, 1928–1931* (1978); and the works by Geiger and Deutscher cited in the Notes are all highly recommended, as is Deutscher's sympathetic three-volume study of Trotsky. R. McNeal, *Stalin: Man and Ruler* (1988), is useful. S. Cohen, *Bukharin and the Bolshevik Revolution* (1973), examines the leading spokesman of moderate communism, who was destroyed by Stalin. R. Conquest, *The Great Terror* (1968), is an excellent account of Stalin's purges of the 1930s. A. Solzhenitsyn, *The Gulag Archipelago* (1964), passionately condemns Soviet police terror, which

Solzhenitsyn tracks back to Lenin. Arthur Koestler, *Darkness at Noon* (1956), is a famous fictional account of Stalin's trials of the Old Bolsheviks. R. Medvedev, *Let History Judge* (1972), is a penetrating and highly recommended history of Stalinism by a Russian dissident, which may be compared with the excellent synthesis by M. Lewin, *The Making of the Soviet System* (1985). R. Conquest, *The Harvest of Sorrow* (1986), authoritatively recounts Soviet collectivization and the human-made famine. Three other remarkable books are J. Scott, *Behind the Urals* (1973), an eyewitness account of an American steelworker in the Soviet Union in the 1930s; S. Alliluyeva, *Twenty Letters to a Friend* (1967), the amazing reflections of Stalin's daughter, who chose twice to live in the United States before returning home; and M. Fainsod, *Smolensk Under Soviet Rule* (1958), a unique study based on communist records captured first by the Germans and then by the Americans.

A. De Grand, *Italian Fascism: Its Origins and Development* (1989); A. Lyttelton, *The Seizure of Power* (1987); and E. R. Tannebaum, *The Fascist Experience* (1972), are excellent studies of Italy under Mussolini. D. Mack Smith, *Mussolini* (1982), is authoritative. Ignazio Silone, *Bread and Wine* (1937), is a moving novel by a famous opponent of dictatorship in Italy. E. Morante, *History* (1978), a fictional account of one family's divergent reactions to Mussolini's rule, is recommended. Two excellent books on Spain are H. Thomas, *The Spanish Civil War* (1977), and E. Malefakis, *Agrarian Reform and Peasant Revolution in Spain* (1970). In the area of foreign relations, G. Kennan, *Russia and the West Under Lenin and Stalin* (1961), is justly famous; A. L. Rowse, *Appeasement* (1961), powerfully denounces the policies of the appeasers. R. Paxton, *Vichy France* (1973), tells a controversial story extremely well, and J. Lukac, *The Last European War* (1976), argues provocatively that victory by Hitler could have saved Europe from both Soviet and American domination.

On Germany, F. Stern, *The Politics of Cultural Despair* (1963), and W. Smith, *The Ideological Origins of Nazi Imperialism* (1986), are fine complementary studies on the origins of Nazism. Bracher's *The German Dictatorship,* cited in the Notes, remains the best single work on Hitler's Germany. It may be compared with the important work by M. Brozat, *The Nazi State* (1981), and with W. Shirer, *The Rise and Fall of the Third Reich* (1960), a gripping account of an American journalist who experienced Nazi Germany firsthand. J. Fest, *Hitler* (1974), and A. Bullock, *Hitler: A Study in Tyranny* (1964), are engrossing biographies of the Führer. In addition to *Mein Kampf, Hitler's Secret Conversations, 1941–1944* (1953) reveals the dictator's wild dreams and beliefs. I. Kershaw, *The "Hitler Myth": Image and Reality in the Third Reich* (1987), is a provocative reassessment of the limits of Hitler's power. M. Mayer, *They Thought They Were Free* (1955), probes the minds of ten ordinary Nazis and why they believed Hitler was their liberator. A. Speer, *Inside the Third Reich* (1970), contains the fascinating recollections of Hitler's wizard of the armaments industry. C. Koonz, *Mothers in the Fatherland: Women, the Family, and Nazi Politics* (1987), and D. Peukert, *Inside Nazi Germany: Conformity, Opposition, and Racism in Everyday Life* (1987), are pioneering forays into the social history of the Nazi era. G. Mosse, *Toward the Final Solution* (1978), is a powerful history of European racism. Moving accounts of the Holocaust include A. Mayer, *Why Did the Heavens Not Darken? The "Final Solution" in History* (1989); M. Gilbert, *The Holocaust: The History of the Jews During the Second World War* (1985); and L. Dawidowicz, *The War Against the Jews, 1933–1945* (1975). M. Marrus, *The Holocaust in History* (1987), is an excellent interpretive survey by a leading authority. Especially recommended is E. Weisel, *Night* (1961), a brief and very compelling autobiographical account of a young Jew in a Nazi concentration camp. Jørgen Haestrup, *Europe Ablaze* (1978), is a monumental account of wartime resistance movements throughout Europe, and A. Frank, *The Diary of Anne Frank,* is a remarkable personal account of a young Jewish girl in hiding during the Nazi occupation of Holland.

J. Campbell's *The Experience of World War II* (1989) is attractively illustrated and captures the drama of global conflict, as does G. Keegan, *The Second World War* (1990). G. Wright, *The Ordeal of Total War, 1939–1945* (1990), and C. Emsley, *World War II and Its Consequences* (1990), are also recommended. B. H. Liddell Hart, *The History of the Second World War* (1971), is an overview of military developments. G. Weinberg, *The Foreign Policy of Hitler,* 2 vols. (1970, 1980), is an excellent detailed account of the diplomatic origins and course of World War Two from the German perspective. Three dramatic studies of special aspects of the war are A. Dallin, *German Rule in Russia, 1941–1945* (1981), which analyzes the effects of Nazi occupation policies on the Soviet population; L. Collins and D. La Pierre, *Is Paris Burning?* (1965), a best-selling account of the liberation of Paris and Hitler's plans to destroy the city; and J. Toland, *The Last Hundred Days* (1966), a lively account of the end of the war.

LISTENING TO THE
PAST

Witness to the Holocaust

The Second World War brought mass murder to the innocent. The Nazis and their allies slaughtered six million Jews in addition to about five million Slavs, gypsies, Jehovah's Witnesses, homosexuals, and mentally ill. On the Russian front some Jews were simply mowed down with machine guns, but most Jews were arrested in their homelands and taken in freight cars to unknown destinations, which were in fact extermination camps. The most infamous camp—really two camps on different sides of a railroad track—was Auschwitz-Birkenau in eastern Poland. There two million people were murdered in gas chambers.

The testimony of camp survivors helps us comprehend the unspeakable crime known to history as the Holocaust. One eye-witness was Marco Nahon, a Greek Jew and physician who escaped extermination at Auschwitz-Birkenau along with several thousand other slave laborers in the camp. The following passage is taken from Birkenau: The Camp of Death, *which Nahon wrote in 1945 after his liberation. Conquered by Germany in 1941, Greece was divided into German, Italian, and Bulgarian zones of occupation. The Nahon family lived in Dimotika in the Bulgarian zone.*

Early in March 1943, disturbing news arrives from Salonika [in the German occupation zone]: the Germans are deporting the Jews [of Salonika]. They lock them up in railway cattlecars . . . and send them to an unknown destination—to Poland, it is said. . . . Relatives and friends deliberate. What can be done in the face of this imminent threat? . . . My friend Vitalis Djivré speaks with conviction: "We must flee, cross over into Turkey at once, go to Palestine, Egypt—anywhere at all—but leave immediately.". . . A few friends and I held a completely different opinion. . . . [I say that] I am not going to emigrate. They are going to take us away to Germany or Poland [to work]? If so, I'll work. . . . It is certain that the Allies will be the victors, and once the war is over, we'll go back home. . . .

Until the end we were deaf to all the warnings. . . . [None of the warnings] would be regarded as indicating the seriousness of the drama in preparation. But does not the human mind find inconceivable the total extermination of an innocent population? In this tragic error lay the main cause, the sole cause, of our perdition. . . .

On Monday May 10, 1943, the bugles awaken us at a very early hour. We [have already been arrested and] today we are leaving for Poland. . . . As soon as a freight car has been packed to capacity with people, it is quickly locked up, and immediately the remaining passengers are pushed into the next one. . . .

Every two days the train stops in some meadow in open country. The car doors are flung open, and the whole transport spreads out in the fields. Men and women attend to their natural needs, side by side, without any embarrassment. Necessity and common misfortune have made them part of one and the same family. . . .

We are now in a small station in Austria. Our car door half opens; a Schupo [German police officer] is asking for the doctor. . . . He leads me to the rear of the convoy and shuts me inside the car where the woman is in labor. She is very young; this is her first child. The car, like all the others, is overcrowded. The delivery takes place in deplorable conditions, in front of everybody—men, women, and children. Fortunately, everything turns out well, and a few hours later a baby boy comes into the world. The new mother's family is very happy and passes candy around. Surely no one realizes that two days later the mother and her baby and more than half of the company will pass through the chimney of a crematorium at Birkenau.

It is May 16, 1943. We have reached the end of our journey [and arrived at Auschwitz-Birkenau]. The train stops along a wooden platform. Through the openings of the cars we can see people wearing strange costumes of blue and white stripes [the prisoners who work in the camp]. We immediately notice that they are doing nothing voluntarily but are moving and acting on command. . . . The people in stripes . . . line us up five by five, the women on one side, the men on the other. I lose sight of my wife and little girl in the crowd. I will never see them again.

They make us march, swiftly as always, before a group of [German] officers. One of them, without uttering a word and with the tip of his forefinger, makes a rapid selection. He is, as we know later on, the Lagerarzt, the SS medical doctor of the camp [the notorious Dr. Mengele]. They call him here the "Angel of Death." [Mengele divides the men into two groups: those who are young and sturdy for work in the camp, and those who are old, sick, and children. The women are also divided and only healthy young women without children are assigned to work. All those not selected for work] are immediately loaded on trucks and driven off somewhere. Where? Nobody knows yet. . . .

[After being assigned to a crude windowless barrack,] we must file before the . . . scribes, who are responsible for receiving and registering the transport. Each prisoner must fill out a form in which he relinquishes his identity and becomes a mere number. . . . I am given the number 122274. My son, who is next, gets 122275. This tattoo alarms us terribly. . . . Each one of us now comes to realize in the deepest part of his conscious being, and with a bitter sense of affliction, that from this moment on he is no more than an animal. . . .

After our meal [of watery soup] Léon Yahiel, a veteran among the Lager inmates, . . . gives us this little speech: "My friends, here you must . . . forget your families, your wives, your children. You must live only for yourselves and try to last as long as possible." At these words our spirits plunge into grief and despair. Forget about our families? The hint is unmistakable. Our minds are confused. . . .

❖ Deporters getting off the coaches at Auschwitz. *(Source: Hulton Deutsch Collection Limited)*

Our families taken away from us forever? No, it is humanly not conceivable that we should pay such a penalty without having done anything to deserve it, without any provocation.

What miserable wretches we prisoners are! We have no idea that while we entertain these thoughts, our wives, our children, our mothers and our fathers have already ceased to exist. They have arrived at Auschwitz this morning, healthy and full of life. They have now been reduced to smoke and ashes.

Questions for Analysis

1. How did the Jews of Dimotika react in early 1943 to the news of Jews being deported? Why?

2. Describe the journey to Auschwitz-Birkenau. Did those on the train know what was awaiting them there?

3. How did the Nazis divide the Jews at Auschwitz-Birkenau? Why?

4. What did you learn from Nahon's account? What parts of his testimony made the greatest impression on you?

Source: Slightly adapted from M. Nahon, *Birkenau: The Camp of Death,* trans. J. Bowers (Tuscaloosa: University of Alabama Press, 1989), pp. 21, 23, 33–39.

CHAPTER

30

Recovery and Conflict, 1945–1968

✥ The total defeat of the Nazis and their allies in 1945 laid the basis for one of Western civilization's most remarkable recoveries. A battered western Europe dug itself out from under the rubble and fashioned a great renaissance in the postwar era, which lasted into the late 1960s. The United States also made solid progress. The Soviet Union became more humane and less dictatorial.

Yet there was also a tragic setback. The Grand Alliance against Hitler gave way to an apparently endless "cold war" in which conflict between East and West threatened world peace and domestic politics. In the 1960s, as sharp criticism from the noncommunist left revived and the United States intervened massively in the bitter civil war in Vietnam, political discontent increased dramatically and brought radical challenges. In 1968 the established order tottered in both the communist East and the capitalist West. But it did not fall. The revolutionary surges were broken and diffused as a new and different era emerged.

✥ ✥ ✥ ✥ ✥ ✥ ✥ ✥ ✥

The reality of the Berlin Wall, grim symbol of postwar division in Europe. *(Source: Sahm Doherty/Liaison)*

- What were the causes of the cold war, the most disappointing development of the postwar era?

- How and why, in spite of the tragic division of the Continent into two hostile camps, did western Europe recover so successfully from the ravages of war and Nazism?

- To what extent did communist eastern Europe and the United States experience a similar recovery?

- How and why did European empires collapse and Asian and African peoples gain political independence?

- How did people live in the postwar era, and why did a revolutionary surge build and break in the 1960s?

These are the questions this chapter will seek to answer.

✤ THE COLD WAR, 1942–1953

In 1945 triumphant American and Soviet soldiers came together and embraced on the banks of the Elbe River in the heart of vanquished Germany. At home in the United States and in the Soviet Union, the soldiers' loved ones erupted in joyous celebration. Yet victory was flawed. The Allies could not cooperate politically in peace making. Motivated by different goals and hounded by misunderstandings, the United States and the Soviet Union soon found themselves at loggerheads. By the end of 1947, Europe was rigidly divided. It was West versus East in a cold war that eventually engulfed the entire world.

The Origins of the Cold War

The most powerful allies in the wartime coalition—the Soviet Union and the United States—began to quarrel almost as soon as the unifying threat of Nazi Germany disappeared. The hostility between the Eastern and Western superpowers brought bitter disappointment to millions of people, but it was not really so surprising. It was the sad but logical outgrowth of military developments, wartime agreements, and long-standing political and ideological differences.

In the early phases of the Second World War, the Americans and the British made military victory their highest priority. They consistently avoided discussion of Stalin's war aims and the shape of the eventual peace settlement. This policy was evident in December 1941 and again in May 1942 when Stalin asked the United States and Britain to agree to the Soviet Union's moving its western border of 1938 farther west at the expense of Poland, in effect ratifying the gains that Stalin had made from his deal with Hitler in 1939.

Stalin's request ran counter to the moralistic Anglo-American Atlantic Charter of August 1941. In good Wilsonian fashion, the Atlantic Charter had called for peace without territorial expansion or secret agreements and for free elections and self-determination for all liberated nations. In this spirit, the British and Americans declined to promise Polish territory to Stalin. He received only a military alliance and no postwar commitments. Yet the United States and Britain did not try to take advantage of the Soviet Union's precarious position in 1942 because they feared that hard bargaining would anger Stalin and encourage him to consider making a separate peace with Hitler. They focused instead on the policy of unconditional surrender to solidify the alliance.

By late 1943 as Allied armies scored major victories, specific issues related to the shape of the postwar world could no longer be postponed. The conference that Stalin, Roosevelt, and Churchill held in the Iranian capital of Teheran in November 1943 thus proved of crucial importance in determining subsequent events. There, the "Big Three" jovially reaffirmed their determination to crush Germany and searched for the appropriate military strategy. Churchill, fearful of the military dangers of a direct attack and anxious to protect Britain's political interests in the eastern Mediterranean, argued that American and British forces should follow up their North African and Italian campaigns with an indirect attack on Germany through the Balkans (see Map 29.2). Roosevelt, however, agreed with Stalin that an American-British frontal assault through France would be better. This agreement was part of Roosevelt's general effort to meet Stalin's wartime demands whenever possible, and it had momentous political implications. It meant that the Soviet and the American-British armies would come together in defeated Germany along a north-south line and that only Soviet troops would liberate eastern Europe. Thus the basic shape of postwar Europe was emerging even as the fighting continued. Real differences over questions such as Poland were carefully ignored.

When the Big Three met again in February 1945 at Yalta on the Black Sea in southern Russia, advancing Soviet armies were within 100 miles of Berlin. The Red Army had occupied not only Poland but also Bulgaria, Rumania, Hungary, part of Yugoslavia, and much of Czechoslovakia. The temporarily stalled American-British forces had yet to cross the Rhine into Germany. Moreover, the United States was far from defeating Japan. Indeed, the U.S. military believed that the invasion and occupation of Japan would cost one million American casualties—an estimate that contributed to the subsequent decision to drop atomic bombs

❖ **The Big Three** In 1945 a triumphant Winston Churchill, an ailing Franklin Roosevelt, and a determined Joseph Stalin met at Yalta in southern Russia to plan for peace. Cooperation soon gave way to bitter hostility. *(Source: F.D.R. Library)*

in order to save American lives. In short, the Soviet Union's bargaining position was strong and America's was weak.

There was little the increasingly sick and apprehensive Roosevelt could do but double his bet on Stalin's peaceful intentions. It was agreed at Yalta that Germany would be divided into zones of occupation and would pay heavy reparations to the Soviet Union in the form of agricultural and industrial goods, though many details remained unsettled. At American insistence, Stalin agreed to declare war on Japan after Germany was defeated. He also agreed to join the proposed United Nations, which the Americans believed would help preserve peace after the war; it was founded in April 1945 in San Francisco.

For Poland and eastern Europe—"that Pandora's Box of infinite troubles," according to U.S.

secretary of state Cordell Hull—the Big Three struggled to reach an ambiguous compromise at Yalta: eastern European governments were to be freely elected but pro-Soviet. As Churchill put it at the time, "The Poles will have their future in their own hands, with the single limitation that they must honestly follow in harmony with their allies, a policy friendly to Russia."[1] The Yalta compromise over eastern Europe broke down almost immediately. Even before the Yalta conference, Bulgaria and Poland were controlled by communists who had arrived home with the Red Army. Minor concessions to noncommunist groups thereafter did not change this situation. Elsewhere in eastern Europe, pro-Soviet "coalition" governments of several parties were formed, but the key ministerial posts were reserved for Moscow-trained communists.

At the postwar Potsdam conference of July 1945, the long-ignored differences over eastern Europe finally surged to the fore. The compromising Roosevelt had died and been succeeded by the more determined President Harry Truman (1884–1972), who demanded immediate free elections throughout eastern Europe. Stalin refused point-blank. "A freely elected government in any of these East European countries would be anti-Soviet," he admitted simply, "and that we cannot allow."[2]

Here, then, is the key to the much-debated origins of the cold war. American ideals, pumped up by the crusade against Hitler, and American politics, heavily influenced by millions of voters from eastern Europe, demanded free elections in Soviet-occupied eastern Europe. Stalin, who had lived through two enormously destructive German invasions, wanted absolute military security from Germany and its potential Eastern allies once and for all. Suspicious by nature, he believed that only communist states could be truly dependable allies, and he realized that free elections would result in independent and possibly hostile governments on the Soviet Union's western border. Moreover, by the middle of 1945 there was no way short of war that the United States and its Western allies could determine developments in eastern Europe, and war was out of the question. Stalin was bound to have his way.

West Versus East

The American response to Stalin's exaggerated conception of security was to "get tough." In May 1945 Truman abruptly cut off all aid to the U.S.S.R. In October he declared that the United States would never recognize any government established by force against the free will of its people. In March 1946 former British prime minister Churchill ominously informed an American audience in Fulton, Missouri, that an "iron curtain" had fallen across the Continent, dividing Germany and all of Europe into two antagonistic camps. Emotional, moralistic denunciations of Stalin and the communist Soviet Union emerged as part of American political life. Yet the United States also responded to the popular desire to "bring the boys home" and demobilized with great speed. When the war against Japan ended in September 1945, there were 12 million Americans in the armed forces; by 1947 there were only 1.5 million, as opposed to 6 million for the Soviet Union. Some

historians have argued that American leaders believed that the atomic bomb gave the United States all the power it needed; but getting tough really meant talking tough.

Stalin's agents quickly reheated what they viewed as the "ideological struggle against capitalist imperialism." The large, well-organized Communist parties of France and Italy obediently started to uncover American plots to take over Europe and challenged their own governments with violent criticisms and large strikes. The Soviet Union also put pressure on Iran and Turkey, and while Greek communists battled Greek royalists, another bitter civil war raged in China. By the spring of 1947, it appeared to many Americans that Stalin wanted much more than just puppet regimes in Soviet-occupied eastern Europe. He seemed determined to export communism by subversion throughout Europe and around the world.

The United States responded to this challenge with the Truman Doctrine, which was aimed at "containing" communism in areas already occupied by the Red Army. Truman told Congress in March 1947, "I believe it must be the policy of the United States to support free people who are resisting attempted subjugation by armed minorities or by outside pressure." To begin, Truman asked Congress for military aid to Greece and Turkey. Then in a famous speech in June 1947, Secretary of State George C. Marshall urged Americans to offer Europe economic aid and help it rebuild its shattered economy. (See Listening to the Past.) Marshall's proposal became the basis of the Marshall Plan, one of the most successful foreign policy initiatives in U.S. history.

Stalin refused Marshall Plan assistance for all of eastern Europe. He purged the last remaining noncommunist elements from the coalition governments of eastern Europe and established Soviet-style, one-party communist dictatorships. The seizure of power in Czechoslovakia in February 1948 was particularly brutal and antidemocratic, and it greatly strengthened Western fears of limitless communist expansion, beginning with Germany. Thus when Stalin blocked all traffic through the Soviet zone of Germany to Berlin, the former capital, which the occupying powers had also divided into sectors at the end of the war, the Western Allies decided to respond firmly but not provocatively. Rejecting calls from some hotheads for the American army to "shoot its way to Berlin," Allied forces began flying hundreds of planes over the Soviet roadblocks around the clock, supplying provisions to the people of West Berlin and thwarting Soviet efforts to swallow up the West Berliners. After 324 days the Soviets backed down and called off their Berlin blockade: containment seemed to work. In 1949, therefore, the United States formed an anti-Soviet military alliance of Western governments: the North Atlantic Treaty Organization (NATO). Established as a regional alliance for self-defense and featuring American troops stationed permanently in Europe, NATO was designed to contain Stalin by effectively protecting western Europe from the possibility of Soviet attack. Stalin countered by tightening his hold on his satellites, later united in the Warsaw Pact. Europe was divided into two hostile blocs.

In late 1949 communists triumphed in China, frightening and angering many Americans, some of whom saw an all-powerful worldwide communist conspiracy extending even into the upper reaches of the American government. When the Soviet-backed communist forces of northern Korea invaded southern Korea in 1950, President Truman acted swiftly. American-led U.N. armies intervened, and for the next three years they were engaged in savage fighting in the Korean War. The cold war had spread around the world and become very hot.

The rapid descent from victorious Grand Alliance to bitter cold war was intimately connected with the tragic fate of eastern Europe. After 1932, when the eastern European power vacuum invited Nazi racist imperialism, the appeasing Western democracies mistakenly did nothing. They did, however, have one telling insight: how, they asked themselves, could they unite with Stalin to stop Hitler without giving Stalin great gains on his western borders? After Hitler's invasion of the Soviet Union, the Western powers preferred to ignore this question and hope for the best. But when Stalin later began to claim the spoils of victory, the United States began to protest and professed outrage. This belated opposition quite possibly encouraged even more aggressive measures by the always-suspicious Stalin, and it helped explode the quarrel over eastern Europe into a global confrontation. This Soviet-American confrontation became institutionalized, and it lasted for decades despite intermittent periods of relaxation.

❖ **The Berlin Airlift** Standing in the rubble of their bombed-out city, a German crowd in the American sector awaits the arrival of a U.S. transport plane flying in over the Soviet blockade in 1948. The crisis over Berlin was a dramatic indication of growing tensions among the Allies, which resulted in the division of Europe into two hostile camps. *(Source: Walter Sanders,* LIFE MAGAZINE © *Time Inc.)*

✤ THE WESTERN RENAISSANCE

With the cold war dividing Europe into two blocs, the future appeared bleak on both sides of the iron curtain. Economic conditions were the worst in generations. Politically, Europe was weak and divided, a battleground for cold war ambitions. Moreover, European empires were crumbling in the face of nationalism in Asia and Africa. Yet Europe recovered, and the Western nations led the way. In less than a generation, western Europe initiated major social reforms and joined the United States in achieving unprecedented economic prosperity. Moreover, western Europe began moving toward genuine unity and regained much of its traditional prominence in world affairs. It was an amazing rebirth—a true renaissance in the West.

The Postwar Challenge

After the war, economic conditions in western Europe were terrible. Simply finding enough to eat was a constant problem. Runaway inflation and black markets testified to severe shortages and hardship. The bread ration in Paris in 1946 was little more than it had been in 1942 under Nazi occupation. Many people believed that Europe was quite simply finished. Prominent British historian Arnold Toynbee felt that, at best, western Europeans might seek to civilize the crude but powerful Americans, somewhat as the ancient Greeks had civilized their Roman conquerors.

Suffering was most intense in defeated Germany. The major territorial change of the war had moved the Soviet Union's border far to the west. Poland was in turn compensated for this loss to the Soviets with land taken from Germany (Map 30.1). To solidify these changes in boundaries, thirteen million people were driven from their homes in eastern Germany (and other countries in eastern Europe) and forced to resettle in a greatly reduced Germany. The Soviets were also seizing factories and equipment as reparations, even tearing up railroad tracks and sending the rails to the Soviet Union.

In 1945 and 1946, conditions were not much better in the Western zones, for the Western Allies also treated the German population with great severity at first. By February 1946 the average daily diet of a German in the Ruhr had been reduced to two slices of bread, a pat of margarine, a spoonful of porridge, and two small potatoes. Countless Germans sold prized possessions to American soldiers to buy food. By the spring of 1947, refugee-clogged, hungry, prostrate Germany was on the verge of total collapse and threatening to drag down the rest of Europe.

Yet western Europe was not finished. The Nazi occupation and the war had discredited old ideas and old leaders. All over Europe many people were willing to change and experiment in hopes of building a new and better Europe out of the rubble. New groups and new leaders were coming to the fore to guide these aspirations. Progressive Catholics and revitalized Catholic political parties—the Christian Democrats—were particularly influential.

In Italy the Christian Democrats emerged as the leading party in the first postwar elections in 1946, and in early 1948 they won an absolute majority in the parliament in a landslide victory. Their very able leader was Alcide De Gasperi, a courageous antifascist and former Vatican librarian firmly committed to political democracy, economic reconstruction, and moderate social reform. In France, too, the Catholic party provided some of the best postwar leaders, such as Robert Schuman. This was particularly true after January 1946 when General Charles De Gaulle, the inspiring wartime leader of the Free French, resigned after having re-established the free and democratic Fourth Republic. With Germany partitioned by the cold war, a radically purified Federal Republic of Germany (as West Germany was officially known) found new and able leadership among its Catholics. In 1949 Konrad Adenauer, the former mayor of Cologne and a long-time anti-Nazi, began his long, highly successful democratic rule; the Christian Democrats became West Germany's majority party for a generation. In providing effective leadership for their respective countries, the Christian Democrats were inspired and united by a common Christian and European heritage. They steadfastly rejected authoritarianism and narrow nationalism and placed their faith in democracy and cooperation.

The socialists and the communists, active in the resistance against Hitler, also emerged from the war with increased power and prestige, especially in France and Italy. They, too, provided fresh leadership and pushed for social change and economic reform with considerable success. In the immediate postwar years, welfare measures such as family al-

MAP 30.1 Europe After the Second World War Both the Soviet Union and Poland took land from Germany, which the Allies partitioned into occupation zones. Those zones subsequently formed the basis of the east and the west German states, as the iron curtain fell to divide both Germany and Europe. Austria was detached from Germany and also divided into four occupation zones. But the Soviets subsequently permitted Austria to be unified as a neutral state.

lowances, health insurance, and increased public housing were enacted throughout much of Europe. In Italy social benefits from the state came to equal a large part of the average worker's wages.

In France large banks, insurance companies, public utilities, coal mines, and the Renault auto company were nationalized by the government. Britain followed the same trend. The voters threw out Chur-

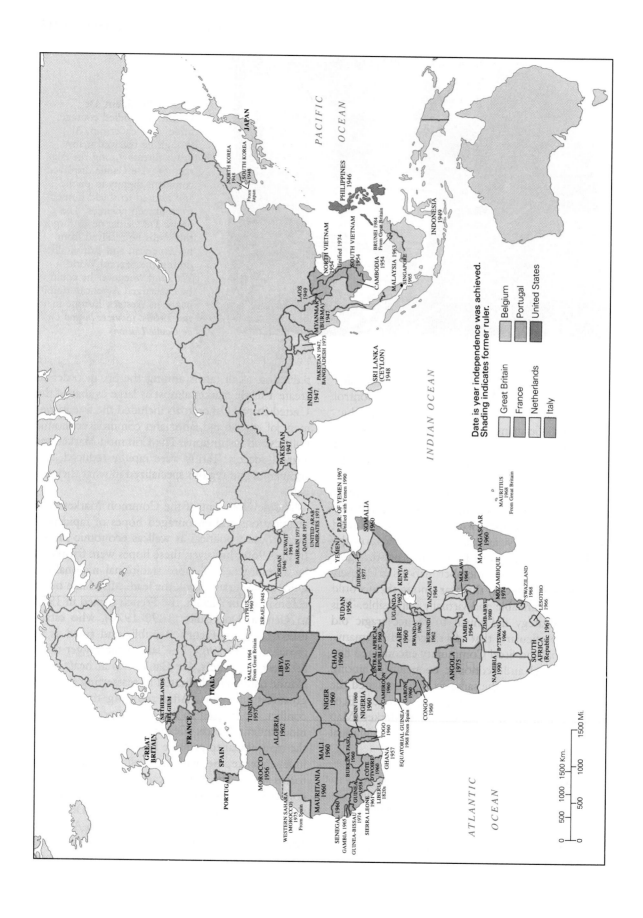

PACIFIC
OCEAN

JAPAN

NORTH KOREA
1948

SOUTH KOREA 1948
From Japan

PHILIPPINES
1946

NORTH VIETNAM
1954

Unified 1974

BRUNEI 1984
From Great Britain

SOUTH VIETNAM
1954

CAMBODIA
1954

INDONESIA
1949

MALAYSIA 1963

SINGAPORE
1963

LAOS
1949

MYANMAR
(BURMA) 1947

PAKISTAN 1947
BANGLADESH 1973

INDIA
1947

SRI LANKA
(CEYLON)
1948

INDIAN OCEAN

PAKISTAN
1947

YEMEN

P.D.R. OF YEMEN 1967
Unified with Yemen 1990

UNITED ARAB
EMIRATES 1971

QATAR 1971

BAHRAIN 1971

KUWAIT
1961

JORDAN
1946

SOMALIA
1960

ISRAEL 1948

CYPRUS
1960

MALTA 1964
From Great Britain

DJIBOUTI
1977

KENYA
1963

MADAGASCAR
1960

MALAWI
1964

MOZAMBIQUE
1974

SWAZILAND
1968

MAURITIUS
1968
From Great Britain

UGANDA
1962

TANZANIA
1964

ZAMBIA
1964

ZIMBABWE
1980

LESOTHO
1966

RWANDA
1962

BURUNDI
1962

ZAIRE
1960

CENTRAL AFRICAN
REPUBLIC 1960

SUDAN
1956

LIBYA
1951

CHAD
1960

NIGER
1960

CAMEROON
1960

GABON
1960

CONGO
1960

NAMIBIA
1990

B'TSWANA
1966

SOUTH
AFRICA
(Republic 1961)

ANGOLA
1975

GREAT
BRITAIN

NETHERLANDS

BELGIUM

FRANCE

ITALY

SPAIN

PORTUGAL

TUNISIA
1957

ALGERIA
1962

MOROCCO
1956

WESTERN SAHARA
(MOROCCO)
1975
From Spain

MAURITANIA
1960

MALI
1960

SENEGAL 1960

GAMBIA 1965

GUINEA-BISSAU
1974

GUINEA
1958

SIERRA LEONE
1961

LIBERIA
1820s

BURKINA FASO
1960

CÔTE
D'IVOIRE
1960

GHANA
1957

TOGO
1960

BENIN 1960

NIGERIA
1960

EQUATORIAL GUINEA
1968 From Spain

ATLANTIC
OCEAN

Date is year independence was achieved.
Shading indicates former ruler.

Great Britain   Belgium

France   Portugal

Netherlands   United States

Italy

0   500   1000 1500 Km.

0   500   1000   1500 Mi.

mit the scheduled advent of majority rule within the Common Market, and he forced his partners to accept many of his views. Thus throughout the 1960s, the Common Market thrived economically but remained a union of sovereign states.

Decolonization

The postwar era saw the total collapse of colonial empires. Between 1947 and 1962, almost every colonial territory gained independence. Europe's long expansion, which had reached a high point in the late nineteenth century, was completely reversed (Map 30.3). The spectacular collapse of Western political empires fully reflected old Europe's eclipsed power after 1945. Yet the new nations of Asia and Africa were deeply influenced by Western ideas and achievements, so that the "westernization" of the world rushed forward even as European empires passed into history.

Modern nationalism, with its demands for political self-determination and racial equality, spread from intellectuals to the masses in virtually every colonial territory after the First World War. Economic suffering created bitter popular resentment, and thousands of colonial subjects had been unwillingly drafted into French and British armies. Nationalist leaders stepped up their demands. By 1919 one high-ranking British official was mournfully writing, "A wave of unrest is sweeping over the Empire, as over the rest of the world. Almost every day brings some disturbance or other at our Imperial outposts."[4] The Russian Revolution also encouraged the growth of nationalism, and the Soviet Union verbally and militarily supported nationalist independence movements.

Most Europeans regarded their empires very differently after 1945 than before 1914, or even before 1939. Empire had rested on self-confidence and a sense of righteousness; Europeans had believed their superiority to be not only technical and military but also spiritual and moral. The horrors of the Second World War, the near-destruction of

❖ **MAP 30.3 The New States in Africa and Asia** Divided primarily along religious lines into two states, British India led the way to political independence in 1947. Most African territories achieved statehood by the mid-1960s, as European empires passed away, unlamented.

Western civilization, and Japan's demonstration that white Europeans were not invincible vanquished such complacent arrogance and gave opponents of imperialism the upper hand in Europe. After 1945 most Europeans were willing to let go of their colonies more or less voluntarily and to concentrate on rebuilding at home.

India, Britain's oldest, largest, and most lucrative nonwhite possession, played a key role in decolonization and the end of empire. Nationalist opposition to British rule coalesced after the First World War under the leadership of British-educated lawyer Mohandas "Mahatma" Gandhi (1869–1948), who preached nonviolent "noncooperation" with the British. Indian intellectuals effectively argued the old liberal case for equality and self-determination. In response, Britain's rulers gradually introduced political reforms and limited self-government. When the war ended, independence followed very rapidly. The new Labour government was determined to leave India, radicals and socialists had always opposed imperialism, and the heavy cost of governing India had become an intolerable financial burden. The obstacle to India's independence posed by conflict between India's Hindu and Muslim populations was resolved in 1947 through the creation of two states, predominantly Hindu India and Muslim Pakistan.

If Indian nationalism drew on Western parliamentary liberalism, Chinese nationalism developed and triumphed in the framework of Marxist-Leninist ideology. In the turbulent early 1920s, a broad alliance of nationalist forces within the Soviet-supported *Guomindang* (*Kuomintang,* or National People's party) was dedicated to unifying China and abolishing European concessions. But in 1927 Chiang Kai-shek (1887–1975), the successor to Sun Yat-sen (see page 893) and the leader of the Guomindang, broke with his more radical communist allies, headed by Mao Zedong (Mao Tse-tung), and tried to destroy them.

In 1931, to escape Guomindang armies closing in for the kill, Mao (1893–1976) led his followers on an incredible 5,000-mile march to remote northern China and built up an independent power base there. Even war against the Japanese army of occupation could not force Mao and Chiang to cooperate. By late 1945 their long-standing quarrel had erupted in civil war. Stalin gave Mao some aid, and the Americans gave Chiang much more. Winning the support of the

✤ **The Glorification of Mao Zedong** Leading the Communists to victory and establishing a strong unified state, Mao exercised an extraordinary influence on Chinese history and was worshiped as though he was a demigod in the mid-1960s. Waving their fists and the "Little Red Book," a collection of slogans and teachings of Mao, these followers are singing praises to the leader as they stand before his portrait. *(Source: Roger Pic)*

peasantry by promising to expropriate the big landowners, the tougher, better-organized communists forced the Nationalists to withdraw to the island of Taiwan (formerly known as Formosa) in 1949.

Mao and the communists united China's 550 million inhabitants in a strong centralized state, expelled foreigners, and began building a new society along Soviet lines, with mass arrests, forced-labor camps, and ceaseless propaganda. The peasantry was collectivized, and the inevitable five-year plans concentrated successfully on the expansion of heavy industry.

Most Asian countries followed the pattern of either India or China. Britain quickly gave Sri Lanka (Ceylon) and Burma independence in 1948;

the Philippines became independent of the United States in 1946. The Dutch attempt to reconquer the Dutch East Indies was unsuccessful, and in 1949 Indonesia emerged independent.

The French sought to re-establish colonial rule in Indochina, but despite American aid, they were defeated in 1954 by forces under the communist and nationalist guerrilla leader Ho Chi Minh (1890–1969), who was supported by the U.S.S.R. and China. At the subsequent international peace conference in Geneva, French Indochina gained independence. Vietnam was divided into two hostile zones, a communist north under Ho Chi Minh and an anticommunist south, pending unification on the basis of internationally supervised free elections. But the elections were never held, and civil war soon broke out between the north and the south.

In Africa, Arab nationalism was an important factor in the ending of empire. Sharing a common language and culture, Arab nationalists were also loosely united by their opposition to the colonial powers and to the migration of Jewish refugees to Palestine. The British, whose occupation policies in Palestine were condemned by Arabs and Jews, by Soviets and Americans, announced their withdrawal from Palestine in 1948. The United Nations voted for the creation of two states, one Arab and one Jewish. The Arab countries immediately attacked the new Jewish nation and suffered a humiliating defeat. In the course of the fighting, thousands of Arab refugees fled from the territory that became the Jewish state of Israel.

Many of these Arab refugees refused to accept defeat. They vowed to fight on until the state of Israel was destroyed or until they established their own independent Palestinian state. These Palestinian refugees also sought the support of existing Arab states, claiming that Israel was the great enemy of Arab interests and Arab nationalism. The Arab-Israeli conflict was destined to outlive the postwar era. Only in 1993 did Palestinians and Israelis move hesitantly toward peace.

The Arab defeat in 1948 triggered a nationalist revolution in Egypt in 1952, where a young army officer named Gamal Abdel Nasser (1918–1970) drove out the pro-Western king. In 1956 Nasser abruptly nationalized the Suez Canal, the last symbol and substance of Western power in the Middle East. Infuriated, the British and French, along with the Israelis, invaded Egypt. This was, however, to be the dying gasp of imperial power: the moralistic, anti-imperialist Americans joined with the Soviets to force the British, French, and Israelis to withdraw.

The failure of the Western powers to unseat Nasser in 1956 in turn encouraged Arab nationalists in Algeria. That country's large French population considered Algeria an integral part of France. It was this feeling that made the ensuing war so bitter and so atypical of decolonization. In the end, General De Gaulle, who had returned to power as part of a movement to keep Algeria French, accepted the principle of Algerian self-determination. In 1962, after more than a century of French rule, Algeria became independent and the European population quickly fled.

In most of Africa south of the Sahara, decolonization proceeded much more smoothly. Beginning in 1957, Britain's colonies achieved independence with little or no bloodshed and then entered a very loose association with Britain as members of the British Commonwealth of Nations. In 1958 the clever De Gaulle offered the leaders of French black Africa the choice of a total break with France or immediate independence within a kind of French commonwealth. All but one of the new states chose association with France. African leaders did so because they identified with French culture and because they wanted aid from France. The French, buoyed up by economic growth and political recovery, were eager to help—provided their former colonies would accept close ties with France on French terms. As in the past, the French and their Common Market partners, who helped foot the bill, saw themselves as continuing their civilizing mission in black Africa. More important, they saw in Africa untapped markets for their industrial goods, raw materials for their factories, outlets for profitable investment, and good temporary jobs for their engineers and teachers. The British acted somewhat similarly, especially after they finally joined the Common Market in 1973.

As a result, western European countries actually managed to increase their economic and cultural ties with their former African colonies in the 1960s and 1970s. Above all, they used the lure of special trading privileges with the Common Market and heavy investment in French- and English-language education to enhance a powerful Western presence in the new African states. This situation led a variety of leaders and scholars to charge that western Europe (and the United States) had imposed a system of neocolonialism on the former colonies.

According to this view, neocolonialism was a system designed to perpetuate Western economic domination and undermine the promise of political independence, thereby extending to Africa (and much of Asia) the neocolonial subordination that the United States had established in Latin America after the political revolutions of the early nineteenth century. At the very least, enduring influence in black Africa testified to western Europe's resurgent economic and political power in international relations.

America's Civil Rights Revolution

As in western Europe, the Second World War cured the depression in the United States and brought about a great economic boom. Unemployment practically vanished and personal income doubled as the well-being of Americans increased dramatically. Despite fears that peace would bring renewed depression, conversion to a peacetime economy went smoothly. The U.S. economy then proceeded to advance fairly steadily for a long generation.

Prosperity helps explain why postwar domestic politics consisted largely of modest adjustments to the status quo until the early 1960s. The upset victory of Democratic presidential candidate Harry Truman in 1948 demonstrated that Americans had no interest in undoing Roosevelt's social and economic reforms. Congress proceeded to increase social security benefits, subsidize middle- and lower-class housing, and raise the minimum wage. These and other liberal measures consolidated the New Deal. In 1952 the Republican party and the voters turned to General Dwight D. Eisenhower (1890–1969), a national hero and moderate.

The federal government's only major new undertaking during the Eisenhower years was the interstate highway system, a suitable symbol of the basic satisfaction of the vast majority. Some Americans feared, however, that the United States was becoming a "blocked society," obsessed with stability and incapable of wholesome change. This feeling contributed in 1960 to the election of the young John F. Kennedy (1917–1963), who promised to "get the country moving again." President Kennedy captured the popular imagination, revitalized the old Roosevelt coalition, and modestly expanded existing liberal legislation before he was struck down by an assassin's bullet on November 22, 1963.

The American government spared no expense to turn a theoretical possibility into a practical reality. The Manhattan Project ballooned into a mammoth crash program that went forward in several universities and special laboratories. The most important of these was the newly created laboratory at Los Alamos in the wilds of New Mexico, which assembled a team of brilliant American and European scientists. After three years of intensive effort, the first atomic bomb was successfully tested in July 1945. In August 1945 two bombs were dropped on Hiroshima and Nagasaki, thereby ending the war with Japan.

The atomic bomb showed the world both the awesome power and the heavy moral responsibilities of modern science and its high priests. As one Los Alamos scientist exclaimed as he watched the first mushroom cloud rise over the American desert, "We are all sons-of-bitches now!"[10]

The spectacular results of directed research during World War Two inspired a new model for science—"Big Science." By combining theoretical work with sophisticated engineering in a large organization, Big Science could attack extremely difficult problems, from better products for consumers to new and improved weapons for the military. The assumption was that almost any conceivable technical goal might be attained.

Big Science was extremely expensive, requiring large-scale financing from governments and large corporations. Equipment grew ever more complex and expensive because many advances depended directly on better instruments. The trend toward bigness was particularly pronounced in atomic physics, perhaps the most prestigious and influential area of modern science. When Rutherford first "split the atom" in 1919, his equipment cost only a few dollars; the accelerators used in high-energy

❖ **Atomic Weapons** were the ultimate in state-directed scientific research. In this photo the awesome mushroom cloud of an American atomic bomb rises over the Pacific island of Bikini. (*Source: U.S. Department of Energy*)

Top managers ar
fore represented th
of salaried specialist
often with backgrou
ing, these experts ir
classes, even the
realistic, they wei
efficiency and pract
lems. Everywhere s
crats passed on the
advanced education
rare instances could
had attained. Thus
based largely on sp
education, was mo
cure than the old p

The structure of
more flexible and (
from farms and th
decline in one of
least mobile group
technological chan
ceased to expand, a
collar and service
employees bore a
middle class of sala
workers, who were
specialized.

While a dema
big bureaucracies
divisions, Europea
class tensions with
forms. Many of th
unemployment be
age pensions—sim
measures first pio
before the First W
new.

Britain's Labou
mediately after 19
sive national healt
ernments followed
on the system, pa
free medical care
the total cost.

Most countries
ances—direct gove
them raise their cl
many poor famili
pean government
built inexpensive
families and indi

experiments while the atomic bomb was being built were in the 100,000-dollar range. By 1960 the cost had jumped to 30 million dollars. These big accelerators did an amazingly good job of prying atoms apart, and ever-more-sophisticated observations demanded ever-more-powerful and costly accelerators in the postwar period.

Even ordinary science became big and expensive by historical standards. The least costly laboratory capable of doing useful research in either pure or applied science required around 200,000 dollars a year in the 1960s.

Populous, victorious, and wealthy, the United States took the lead in Big Science after World War Two. Between 1945 and 1965, spending on scientific research and development in the United States grew five times as fast as the national income. By 1965 fully 3 percent of all income in the United States was being spent on scientific research and development, and fully three-quarters of all funds spent in the United States were coming from the government. It was generally accepted that government should finance science heavily, in both the "capitalist" United States and the "socialist" Soviet Union.

One reason for the similarity was that science was not demobilized in either country after the war. Scientists remained a critical part of every major military establishment, and a large portion of all postwar scientific research went for "defense." New weapons such as rockets, nuclear submarines, and spy satellites demanded breakthroughs no less remarkable than those of radar and the first atomic bomb. After 1945 roughly one-quarter of all men and women trained in science and engineering in the West—and perhaps more in the Soviet Union—were employed full time in the production of weapons to kill other humans.

Sophisticated science, lavish government spending, and military needs all came together in the space race of the 1960s. In 1957 the Soviets used long-range rockets developed in their nuclear weapons program to put a satellite in orbit. In 1961 they sent the world's first cosmonaut circling the globe. Breaking with President Eisenhower's opposition to an expensive space program, President Kennedy made an all-out U.S. commitment to catch up with the Soviets and land a crewed spacecraft on the moon "before the decade was out." Harnessing pure science, applied technology, and up to 5 billion dollars a year, the Apollo Pro-

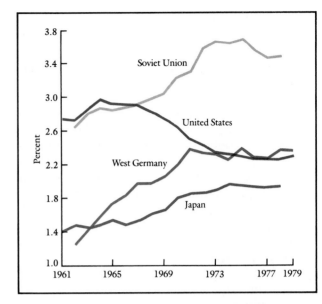

❖ **Figure 31.1 Research and Development Expenditures as a Percentage of GNP in the United States, Soviet Union, West Germany, and Japan, 1961–1979** While the United States spent less of its national income on research and development after the early 1960s, European nations and Japan spent more. This helped Europe and Japan narrow or even close the technological gap that had existed after the end of World War Two. (*Source: Data Resources, Inc.*)

gram achieved its ambitious objective in 1969. Four more moon landings followed by 1972.

The rapid expansion of government-financed research in the United States attracted many of Europe's best scientists during the 1950s and 1960s. Thoughtful Europeans lamented this "brain drain" and feared that Europe was falling hopelessly behind the United States in science, technology, and the most dynamic industrial sectors of the late twentieth century.

In fact, a revitalized Europe was already responding to the American challenge, pooling their efforts on such Big Science projects as the *Concorde* supersonic passenger airliner and the peaceful uses of atomic energy. By 1974 many European nations were devoting a substantial percentage of their income to research and development and were in the process of achieving equality with the United States in many fields of scientific endeavor (Figure 30.1).

The rise of Big Science and of close ties between science and technology greatly altered the lives of scientists. The scientific community grew much

larger than ever befo
times as many scien
America in 1975 as i
gists, engineers, and
after 1945, in part be
them.

One consequence
its high degree of s
possibly master a br
medicine, which was
dividing into new spe
tense specialization
rates at which both b
and practical applicati

Highly specialized
nologists normally ha
team, which complete
style of modern scier
scientists were like pr
dividuals who had to
Modern scientists and
players on American
great atomic physics l
outside Geneva reser
thousand people—sci
kind of support pers
therefore went on in
tions. The individual
a great machine, a m

The advent of large
in Europe and the U
gence of a new grou
search administrators
research, managed pe
politicians and large c
funds was always inte

Many science man
reaucrats. In the lat
turned increasingly t
environmental concer
alarm about undesiral
cal advance. The gro
suggested how scient
ated the entire societ

Modern science b
competitive. This con
in Nobel Prize–winne
book *The Double He*
Watson and an Engli
ered the structure of
ity. A brash young Ar
Watson seemed almc

it had tripled again to forty-four million as car ownership was democratized and came within the range of better-paid workers.

Europeans took great pleasure in the products of the "gadget revolution" as well. Like Americans, Europeans filled their houses and apartments with washing machines, vacuum cleaners, refrigerators, dishwashers, radios, TVs, and stereos. The purchase of these and other consumer goods was greatly facilitated by installment purchasing, which allowed people to buy on credit. Before the Second World War, Europeans had rarely bought "on time." But with the expansion of social security safeguards, reducing the need to accumulate savings for hard times, ordinary people were increasingly willing to take on debt. This change had far-reaching consequences.

Leisure and recreation occupied an important place in consumer societies. Indeed, with incomes rising and the workweek shrinking from roughly forty-eight hours right after the war to about forty-one hours by the early 1970s, leisure became big business. In addition to ever-popular soccer matches and horse races, movies, and a growing addiction to television, individuals had at their disposal a vast range of commercialized hobbies, most of which could soak up a lot of cash. Newsstands were full of specialized magazines about everything from hunting and photography to gourmet cooking and antique collecting. Interest in "culture," as measured by attendance at concerts and exhibitions, also increased. Even so, the commercialization of leisure through standardized manufactured products was striking.

The most astonishing leisure-time development in the consumer society was the blossoming of mass travel and tourism. Before the Second World War, travel for pleasure and relaxation had been a rather aristocratic pastime. Most people had neither the time nor the money for it. But with month-long paid vacations required by law in most European countries, and widespread automobile ownership, beaches and ski resorts came within the reach of the middle class and many workers. By the late 1960s, packaged tours with cheap group flights and bargain hotel accommodations were making even distant lands easily accessible. One-fifth of West Germany's population traveled abroad each year. A French company grew rich building imitation Tahitian paradises around the world. At Swedish nudist colonies on secluded West African beaches, office workers from Stockholm fleetingly worshiped the sun in the middle of the long northern winter. Truly, consumerism had come of age.

Youth and the Counter-Culture

Economic prosperity and a more democratic class structure had a powerful impact on youth. The bulging cohort of youth born after World War Two developed a distinctive and very international youth culture. Self-consciously different in the late 1950s, this youth culture became increasingly oppositional in the 1960s, interacting with a revival of leftist thought to create a "counter-culture" that rebelled against parents, authority figures, and the status quo.

Young people in the United States took the lead. American college students in the 1950s were docile and often dismissed as the "Silent Generation," but some young people did revolt against the conformity and boredom of middle-class suburbs. These "young rebels" wore tightly pegged pants and idolized singer Elvis Presley and actor James Dean. The "beat" movement of the late 1950s expanded on the theme of revolt, and Jack Kerouac vividly captured the restless motion of the beatniks in his autobiographical novel *On the Road*. People like Kerouac clustered together in certain urban areas, such as the Haight Ashbury district of San Francisco or the Near North Side of Chicago. There the young (and the not-so-young) fashioned a highly publicized subculture that blended radical politics, unbridled personal experimentation (with drugs and communal living, for example), and new artistic styles. This subculture quickly spread to major American and western European cities.

Rock music helped tie this international subculture together. Rock grew out of the black music culture of rhythm and blues, which was flavored with country and western to make it more accessible to white teenagers. The mid-1950s signaled a breakthrough as Bill Hailey called on record buyers to "Rock Around the Clock" and Elvis Presley warned them to keep off of his "Blue Suede Shoes." In the 1960s the Beatles thrilled millions of young people, often to their parents' dismay. Like Elvis, the Beatles suggested personal and sexual freedom that many older people found disturbing.

It was Bob Dylan, a young folk singer turned rock poet with an electric guitar, who best expressed the radical political as well as cultural aspirations of the "younger generation." In a song that became a rallying cry, Dylan sang that "the times they are a'changing."[11] The song captured the spirit of growing alienation between the generation whose defining experience had been World War II and the generation ready to reject the complacency of the 1950s. Increasing discontent with middle class conformity and the injustices of racism and imperialism fueled the young leaders of social protest.

Dylan and other radical folk rock singers encouraged and reflected a growing spirit of rebellion. "You don't need a weatherman to know which way the wind is blowing," Dylan sang. No doubt about it: the wind was blowing, blowing toward revolution.

Certainly the sexual behavior of young people, or at least some young people, appeared to change dramatically in the 1960s and into the 1970s. More young people engaged in intercourse, and they did so at an earlier age. For example, a 1973 study reported that only 4.5 percent of West German youths born in 1945 and 1946 had experienced sexual relations before their seventeenth birthday but that 32 percent of those born in 1953 and 1954 had done so.[12] Perhaps even more significant was the growing tendency of young unmarried people to live together in a separate household on a semipermanent basis, with little thought of getting married or having children. Thus many youths, especially middle-class youths, defied social custom, claiming in effect that the long-standing monopoly of married couples on legitimate sexual unions was dead.

Several factors contributed to the emergence of the international youth culture in the 1960s. First, mass communications and youth travel linked countries and continents together. Second, the postwar baby boom meant that young people became an unusually large part of the population and could therefore exercise exceptional influence on society as a whole. Third, postwar prosperity and greater equality gave young people more purchasing power than ever before. This enabled them to set their own trends and mass fads in everything from music to chemical stimulants. Common patterns of consumption and behavior fostered generational loyalty. Finally, prosperity meant that good jobs were readily available. Students and young job seekers had little need to fear punishment from straight-laced employers for unconventional behavior.

But why did the youth culture practically fuse with the counter-culture in opposition to the established order in the 1960s? This question has

The Beatles in Concert The older generation often saw sexual license and immorality in the group's frank lyrics and suggestive style. But in comparison with all that came after them in the world of pop music, the Beatles were sentimental and wholesome, as this concert scene suggests. *(Source: Fred Ward/Black Star)*

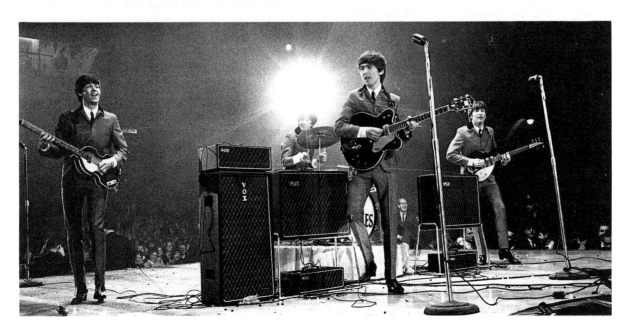

called for negotiations with North Vietnam and announced that he would not stand for re-election.

But who would succeed him? Robert Kennedy, the former president's brother, joined McCarthy and Vice-President Hubert Humphrey in the Democratic primaries. Preaching new initiatives for the poor and opposing the war, Kennedy won in the California primary, but he was immediately gunned down by an assassin. Humphrey—Johnson's defender and anointed successor—received the Democratic nomination after a stormy convention in Chicago. The effort to radically alter the Democratic party had failed.

Elected president by a razor-slim margin in 1968, a conservative Richard Nixon (1913–1994) sought to gradually disengage America from Vietnam and the accompanying national crisis. Restating the long-standing American objective of containing communism in Vietnam, Nixon used American military power more effectively, scaling back search-and-destroy missions on the ground and bombing Vietcong sanctuaries in Cambodia. Nixon simultaneously pursued peace talks with the North Vietnamese. Suspending the draft, so hated on college campuses, Nixon cut American forces in Vietnam from 550,000 to 24,000 in four years, as the cost of the war dropped from 25 billion dollars a year under Johnson to 3 billion dollars under Nixon.

Moreover, President Nixon launched a daring flank attack in diplomacy. He journeyed to China in 1972 and reached a spectacular, if limited, reconciliation with Communist China. In doing so, Nixon took advantage of China's growing fears of the Soviet Union and exploited tensions between the Communist giants. Thus Nixon's opening to China undermined North Vietnam's position

Fortified by the overwhelming endorsement of the American people in his 1972 electoral triumph, President Nixon and Secretary of State Henry Kissinger finally reached a peace agreement with North Vietnam in January 1973. The agreement allowed remaining American forces to complete their withdrawal from South Vietnam, while the United States reserved the right to resume bombing of North Vietnam if the accords were broken. Fighting declined markedly in South Vietnam, where the South Vietnamese army appeared to hold its own against the Vietcong. In the United States the storm of crisis seemed past. The forces of radical change had lost, and the conservatives had reasserted their control.

Europe and Student Revolution in France

In Europe conservative forces also survived a wave of student-inspired protest and radicalism. Students in western Europe shared with their American counterparts a rejection of materialism and a belief that the postwar society was repressive and badly flawed. They, too, saw naked American aggression in Vietnam. But student protests in western Europe also highlighted more general problems of youth, education, and a society of specialists.

In contrast to the United States, high school and university educations in Europe had been limited for centuries to a small elite. That elite consisted mainly of young men and women from the well-to-do classes, along with a sprinkling of scholarship students from humbler origins. Whereas 22 percent of the American population was going on to some form of higher education in 1950, only 3 to 4 percent of western European youths were doing so. Moreover, European education was still directed toward traditional fields: literature, medicine, law, and pure science. Its basic goal was to pass on culture and pure science to an elite, and with the exception of law and medicine, applied training for specialists was not considered important.

After World War Two, public education in western Europe began to change dramatically. Enrollments skyrocketed. By 1960 at least three times as many students were going to some kind of university as had attended before the war, and the number continued to rise sharply until the 1970s. The Netherlands had 10,000 university students in 1938 and 100,000 in 1960. In France 14 percent of young people went to a university in 1965, as opposed to 4.5 percent in 1950. Reflecting the development of a more democratic class structure and a growing awareness that higher education was the key to success, European universities gave more scholarships and opened their doors to more students from the lower–middle and lower classes. Finally, in response to the expansion of science and technology, the curriculum changed. All sorts of new, practical fields—from computer science to business administration—appeared alongside the traditional liberal arts and sciences.

The rapid expansion of higher education created problems as well as opportunities for students. Classes were badly overcrowded, and there was little contact with professors. Competition for grades became intense. Moreover, although more practical areas of study were added, they were added less quickly than many students wanted. Thus many students felt that they were not getting the kind of education they needed for jobs in the modern world and that basic university reforms were absolutely necessary.

At the same time, some reflective students warned of the dangers of narrowly trained experts. They feared that universities would soon do nothing but turn out docile technocrats both to stock and to serve "the establishment." Others of a Marxian persuasion saw the class of trained specialists they expected to enter as the new exploited class in society. The remedy to this situation, both groups believed, was "participation"—the democratization of decision making *within* large, specialized bureaucratic organizations. Only in this way would such organizations serve real human needs and not merely exploit the individual and the environment. Thus the often unrealistic student radicals tried to answer a vital question: how was the complex new society of specialized experts to be made humane and responsive?

The many tensions within the exploding university population came to a head in the late 1960s and early 1970s. Following the American example, European university students rose to challenge their university administrations and even their governments. The most far-reaching of these revolts occurred in France in 1968. It began at the stark new University of Nanterre in the gloomy industrial suburbs of Paris. The movement quickly spread to the hallowed halls of the medieval Sorbonne in the heart of Paris. Students occupied buildings and took over the university. This takeover led to violent clashes with police, who were ordered in to break up a demonstration that was fast becoming an uprising.

Most students demanded both changes in the curriculum and a real voice in running the univer-

❖ **Student Rebellion in Paris** These rock-throwing students in the Latin Quarter of Paris are trying to force education reforms and even to topple De Gaulle's government. Throughout May 1968 students clashed repeatedly with France's tough riot police in bloody street fighting. De Gaulle remained in power, but a major reform of French education did follow. *(Source: Bruno Barbey/Magnum)*

sity. Some student radicals went further, linking the attack on French universities to new left critiques of capitalism. Daniel Cohn-Bendit, the most famous of these student leaders, denounced modern universities in class terms as "factories of privilege":

The present educational structure ensures that the majority of working-class children are barred not only from the bourgeois society we are trying to overthrow, but also from the intellectual means of seeing through it. . . . The mediocrity of university teaching is no accident, but reflects the life style of a civilization in which culture itself has become a marketable commodity and in which the absence of all critical faculties is the safest guarantee of profitable specialization of university studies.[14]

The student radicals appealed to France's industrial workers for help. Rank-and-file workers ignored the advice of their cautious union officials, and a more or less spontaneous general strike spread across France in May 1968. It seemed certain that President De Gaulle's Fifth Republic would collapse. In fact, De Gaulle stiffened, declaring he was in favor of university reforms and higher minimum wages but would oppose "bedwetting." Securing the firm support of French army commanders in West Germany, he moved troops toward Paris and called for new elections. Thoroughly frightened by the protest-turned-upheaval and fearful that a successful revolution could lead to an eventual communist takeover, the masses of France voted for a return to law and order. De Gaulle and his party scored the biggest electoral victory in modern French history. Workers returned to work and the minirevolution collapsed.

Yet the proud De Gaulle and the confident, if old-fashioned, national political revival he represented had been cruelly mocked. In 1969 a tired and discouraged President De Gaulle resigned, and within a year he was dead. For much of the older generation in France, and indeed throughout western Europe, the student revolution of 1968 signaled the end of illusions and the end of an era. Social stability and material progress had resulted once again in conflict and uncertainty.

Reform in Czechoslovakia

In the wake of Khrushchev's reforms in the Soviet Union, the 1960s brought modest liberalization and more consumer goods to eastern Europe. The satellite countries, especially Poland and Rumania,

gained somewhat greater national autonomy, and many hoped for further progress. Czechoslovakia moved more slowly, but in January 1968 it began making up for lost time. The reform elements in the Czechoslovak Communist party gained a majority and voted out the long-time Stalinist leader in favor of Alexander Dubček (b. 1921). Ushering in an exciting period of thaw and rebirth in the famous "Prague Spring" of 1968, Dubček's government launched a series of major economic and political initiatives that fascinated observers around the world.

Educated in Moscow, Dubček was a dedicated communist. But he and his allies within the party were also idealists who believed that they could reconcile genuine socialism with personal freedom and internal party democracy. Thus local decision making by trade unions, managers, and consumers replaced rigid bureaucratic planning. Censorship was relaxed, and mindless ideological conformity gave way to exciting free expression. Intellectuals, students, and the general population responded enthusiastically, and the reform program proved enormously popular. Czechoslovakia had been eastern Europe's only advanced industrial state before the Second World War, and Dubček was reviving traditions that were still deeply cherished.

Although Dubček remembered the lesson of Soviet troops crushing the Hungarian revolution of 1956 and proclaimed his loyalty to the Warsaw Pact of communist states, the determination of the Czech reformers to build "socialism with a human face" frightened hard-line communists. These fears were particularly strong in Poland and East Germany, where the leaders knew full well that they lacked popular support. Moreover, the Soviet Union feared that a liberalized Czechoslovakia would eventually be drawn to neutralism or even to the democratic West. Thus the Eastern bloc countries launched a concerted campaign of intimidation against the Czech leaders, but Dubček's regime refused to knuckle under. The Soviet response was brutal. In August 1968, 500,000 Soviet and allied eastern European troops suddenly occupied Czechoslovakia.

The Czechs made no attempt to resist militarily. The Soviets immediately arrested Dubček and the other top leaders and flew them to Moscow, where they were forced to surrender to Soviet demands. Gradually but inexorably the reform program was abandoned and its supporters removed from office. Thus the Czechoslovak experiment in humanizing

❖ **The End of Reform** In August 1968 Soviet tanks rumbled into Prague to extinguish Czechoslovakian efforts to build a humane socialism. Here people watch the massive invasion from the sidewalks, knowing full well the suicidal danger of armed resistance. *(Source: Joseph Koudelka PP/Magnum)*

communism and making it serve the needs of ordinary citizens failed.

Shortly after the Czechoslovak invasion, Brezhnev declared the so-called Brezhnev Doctrine, according to which the Soviet Union and its allies had the right to intervene in any socialist country whenever they saw the need. Predictably, the occupation of Czechoslovakia raised a storm of protest. Many Communist parties in western Europe were harshly critical, partly out of conviction and partly out of a desire to limit their electoral losses. But the occupation did not seriously alter ongoing Western efforts to secure better relations with the Eastern bloc countries. The reason was simple: the West considered Czechoslovakia to be part of the U.S.S.R.'s sphere of influence, for better or worse. Thus the empire that Stalin had built remained solidly in place in 1968, and most observers believed it would last for the foreseeable future.

SUMMARY

The recovery of Europe after World War Two was one of the most striking chapters in the long, uneven course of Western civilization. Although the dangerous tensions of the cold war frustrated fond hopes for a truly peaceful international order, the transition from imperialism to decolonization proceeded rapidly, surprisingly smoothly, and without serious damage to western Europe. Instead, as eastern Europe fell under harsh one-party communist rule, genuine political democracy gained unprecedented strength in western Europe, and rapid economic progress marked a generation.

Fundamental social changes accompanied the political recovery and economic expansion of the postwar years. Pure science combined with applied technology, often under government direction, to fulfill the loftiest hopes of its enthusiasts and achieve amazing success. The triumphs of applied science contributed not only to economic expansion but also to a more fluid, less antagonistic class structure, in which specialized education was the high road to advancement, regardless of political system. The shining accomplishments of the postwar era seemed to realize the promise in Western society's fateful embrace of the "dual revolution," which had begun in France and England in the late eighteenth century and which had been momentarily halted by the agonies of the Great Depression and horrors of Nazi dictatorship.

An international youth culture also emerged in the 1960s. Many young college students in Europe and the United States joined forces with opponents of the Vietnam War, and they revolted against boring prosperity, omnipresent bureaucracy, and perceived Western imperialism. These student revolts shattered smug complacency and shook governments in the United States and France. But in both countries, and in Czechoslovakia as well, the would-be revolutionaries failed. On both sides of the iron curtain frightened conservatives regained control as widespread disillusionment signaled the passing of the soaring 1960s and the end of the postwar era. The parallels between 1968 and 1848, that other great year of failed revolutions and subsequent reaction, were very striking.

NOTES

1. Quoted in N. Graebner, *Cold War Diplomacy, 1945–1960* (Princeton, N.J.: Van Nostrand, 1962), p. 17.
2. Quoted in ibid.
3. Quoted in J. Hennessy, *Economic "Miracles"* (London: Andre Deutsch, 1964), p. 5.
4. Quoted in R. von Albertini, "The Impact of Two World Wars on the Decline of Colonialism," *Journal of Contemporary History* 4 (January 1969): 17.
5. Quoted in S. E. Morison et al., *A Concise History of the American Republic* (New York: Oxford University Press, 1977), p. 697.
6. Quoted in H. Smith, *The Russians* (New York: Quadrangle Books/New York Times, 1976), p. 303.
7. Quoted in D. Treadgold, *Twentieth Century Russia*, 5th ed. (Boston: Houghton Mifflin, 1981), p. 442.
8. Quoted in I. Deutscher, "The U.S.S.R. Under Khrushchev," in *Soviet Society*, ed. A. Inkeles and K. Geiger (Boston: Houghton Mifflin, 1961), p. 41.
9. Quoted in J. Ziman, *The Force of Knowledge: The Scientific Dimension of Society* (Cambridge: Cambridge University Press, 1976), p. 128.
10. Quoted in S. Toulmin, *The Twentieth Century: A Promethean Age*, ed. A. Bullock (London: Thames & Hudson, 1971), p. 294.
11. Quoted in N. Cantor, *Twentieth Century Culture: Modernism to Deconstruction* (New York: Peter Lang, 1988), p. 252.
12. M. Mitterauer, *The History of Youth* (Oxford: Basil Blackwell, 1992), p. 40.
13. Quoted in Morison et al., p. 735.
14. Quoted in C. Black, *Rebirth: A History of Europe Since World War II* (Boulder, Colo.: Westview Press, 1992), pp. 364–365.

SUGGESTED READING

A good introduction to international politics is provided by W. Keylor, *The Twentieth Century: An International History* (1984), which has extensive, up-to-date bibliographies. An excellent way to approach wartime diplomacy is through the accounts of the statesmen involved. Great leaders and matchless stylists, Winston Churchill and Charles De Gaulle both wrote histories of the war in the form of memoirs. Other interesting memoirs are those of Harry Truman (1958); Dwight Eisenhower, *Crusade in Europe* (1948); and Dean Acheson, *Present at the Creation* (1969), a beautifully written defense of American foreign policy in the early cold war. W. A. Williams, *The Tragedy of American Diplomacy* (1962), and W. La Feber, *America, Russia, and the Cold War* (1967), claim, on the contrary, that the United States was primarily responsible for the conflict with the Soviet Union. Two other important studies focusing on American policy are J. Gaddis, *The United States and the Origins of the Cold War* (1972), and D. Yergin, *Shattered Peace: The Origins of the Cold War and the National Security Council* (1977). V. Mastny's thorough investigation of Stalin's war aims, *Russia's Road to the Cold War* (1979), is recommended.

Two important general studies with extensive bibliographies are W. Laqueur, *Europe in Our Time: A History, 1945–1992* (1992), and P. Johnson, *Modern Times: The World from the Twenties to the Eighties* (1983). Black, listed in the Notes, and R. Mayne, *The Recovery of Europe, 1945–1973* (1973), are also recommended surveys. P. Lane, *Europe Since 1945: An Introduction* (1985), is an interesting combination of text and political documents. T. White, *Fire in the Ashes* (1953), is a vivid view of European resurgence and Marshall Plan aid by an outstanding journalist. I. Unger and D. Unger, *Postwar America: The United States Since 1945* (1989), and W. Leuchtenberg, *In the Shadow of FDR: From Harry Truman to Ronald Reagan* (1989), ably discuss developments in the United States. Postwar economic and social developments are analyzed in G. Ambrosius and W. Hibbard, *A Social and Economic History of Twentieth-Century Europe* (1989), and F. Tipton and R. Aldrich, *An Economic and Social History of Europe from 1939 to the Present* (1986).

F. R. Willis, *France, Germany, and the New Europe, 1945–1967* (1968), is useful for postwar European diplomacy. Three outstanding works on France are

J. Ardagh, *The New French Revolution* (1969), which puts the momentous social changes since 1945 in human terms; S. Bernstein, *The Republic of de Gaulle, 1958–1969* (1993); and D. L. Hanley et al., eds., *France: Politics and Society Since 1945* (1979). On West Germany, H. Turner, *The Two Germanies Since 1945: East and West* (1987), and W. Patterson and G. Smith, eds., *The West German Model: Perspectives on a Stable State* (1981), are good introductions. R. Dahrendorf, *Society and Democracy in Germany* (1971), is a classic interpretation. The spiritual dimension of West German recovery is probed by Günter Grass in his world-famous novel *The Tin Drum* (1963), as well as in the novels of Heinrich Böll. H. S. Hughes, *The United States and Italy* (1968), is a good introduction to modern Italian history. A. Marwick, *British Society Since 1945* (1982), and A. H. Halsey, *Change in British Society* (1981), are good on postwar developments. F. Zweig, *The Worker in an Affluent Society* (1961), probes family life and economic circumstances in the British working class on the basis of extensive interviews. R. E. Tyrrell, ed., *The Future That Doesn't Work* (1977), is a polemical but absorbing attack on British socialism. R. von Albertini, *Decolonialization* (1971), is a good history of the decline and fall of European empires, as is T. von Laue, *The World Revolution of Westernization: The Twentieth Century in Global Perspective* (1987), a stimulating interpretation. The tremendous economic problems of the newly independent countries of Asia and Africa are discussed sympathetically by B. Ward, *Rich Nations and Poor Nations* (1962), and R. Heilbroner, *The Great Ascent* (1953).

Z. Brzezinski, *The Grand Failure: The Birth and Death of Communism in the Twentieth Century* (1989), is a readable overview by a leading American scholar. H. Seton-Watson, *The East European Revolution* (1965), is a good history of the communization of eastern Europe, and S. Fischer-Galati, ed., *Eastern Europe in the Sixties* (1963), discusses major developments. P. Zinner's *National Communism and Popular Revolt in Eastern Europe* (1956) and *Revolution in Hungary* (1962) are excellent on the tragic events of 1956. W. Connor, *Socialism, Politics and Equality: Hierarchy and Change in Eastern Europe and the USSR* (1979), and J. Hough and M. Fainsod, *How the Soviet Union Is Governed* (1978), are important general studies. A. Amalrik, *Will the Soviet Union Survive Until 1984?* (1970), is a fascinating interpretation of Soviet society and politics in the 1960s by a Russian who paid for his criticism with prison and exile. A. Lee, *Russian Journal* (1981), and Smith, cited in the Notes, are excellent journalistic, yet comprehensive reports by perceptive American observers.

Ziman's volume cited in the Notes, which has an excellent bibliography, is a penetrating look at science by a leading physicist. C. P. Snow's widely discussed book, *The Two Cultures and the Scientific Revolution* (1963), explores the gap between scientists and nonscientists. A. Bramwell, *Ecology in the Twentieth Century: A History* (1989), examines negative aspects of technical and industrial development. J. Ellul, *The Technological Society* (1964), is also highly critical of technical progress. D. S. Landes, *The Unbound Prometheus: Technological Change and Industrial Development in Western Europe from 1750 to the Present* (1969), remains enthusiastic. Two more stimulating works on technology are J. J. Servan-Schreiber, *The World Challenge* (1981), and H. Jacoby, *The Bureaucratization of the World* (1973).

In addition to previously mentioned country studies, A. Simpson, *The New Europeans* (1968), provides a good guide to Western society in the 1960s. Mitterauer and Cantor, both cited in the Notes, are excellent on the youth culture and the trends that made it possible. W. Hampton, *Guerrilla Minstrels: John Lennon, Joe Hill, Woodie Guthrie, Bob Dylan* (1986), is highly recommended. L. Wylie, *Village in the Vauclause* (1964), and P. J. Hélias, *The Horse of Pride* (1980), provide fascinating pictures of life in the French village. A. Kriegel's *The French Communists* (1972) and *Eurocommunism* (1978) are also recommended. D. Caute, *The Year of the Barricades: A Journey Through 1968* (1988), is a high-energy account that brings the upheavals to life. A. Touraine, *The May Movement* (1971), is sympathetic toward the French student revolt; noted sociologist R. Aron, in *The Elusive Revolution* (1969), is highly critical. Two outstanding works on the Vietnam War are N. Sheehan, *A Bright and Shining Lie: John Paul Vann and America in Vietnam* (1988), and A. Short, *The Origins of the Vietnam War* (1989). Among the many books to come out of the Czechoslovak experience in 1968, three are particularly recommended: H. Schwartz, *Prague's 200 Days: The Struggle for Democracy in Czechoslovakia* (1969); I. Svitak, *The Czechoslovak Experiment, 1968–1969* (1971); and Z. Zeman, *Prague Spring* (1969).

George Marshall's Plan for European Recovery, 1947

Although commencement speeches are usually quickly forgotten, the following address by Secretary of State George C. Marshall at the Harvard University graduation ceremonies on June 5, 1947, was a famous exception. Signaling a historic U.S. initiative, Marshall analyzed Europe's desperate economic conditions and proposed a program of American aid—the Marshall Plan.

Marshall offered U.S. aid to all European governments willing to cooperate, and the Soviet Union joined in early European efforts to draw up a collective response to the American proposal. But Joseph Stalin, probably fearing American domination and wanting to conceal the Soviet Union's terrible economic position, refused to provide the detailed data that western Europeans (and Americans) deemed essential for effective coordination. Marshall Plan aid went only to western Europe, accelerating the division of Europe and the onset of the cold war.

I need not tell you gentlemen that the world situation is very serious. That must be apparent to all intelligent people. . . .

In considering the requirements for the rehabilitation of Europe, the physical loss of life, the visible destruction of cities, factories, mines, and railroads was correctly estimated, but it has become obvious during recent months that this visible destruction was probably less serious than the dislocation of the entire fabric of the European economy. For the past ten years conditions have been highly abnormal. The feverish preparation for war and more feverish maintenance of the war effort engulfed all aspects of national economies. Machinery has fallen into disrepair or is entirely obsolete. . . . In many countries, confidence in the local currency has been severely shaken. The breakdown of the business structure of Europe during the war was complete. Recovery has been seriously retarded by the fact that two years after the close of hostilities a peace settlement with Germany and Austria has not been agreed upon. But even given a more prompt solution of these difficult problems, the rehabilitation of the economic structure of Europe quite evidently will require a much longer time and a greater effort than had been foreseen.

[One aspect of the situation in Europe is that] the farmer has always produced the foodstuffs to exchange with the city dweller for the other necessities of life. [But now] the town and city industries are not producing adequate goods to exchange with the food-producing farmer. [Thus farmers and peasants keep the food they produce, and] meanwhile people in the cities are short of food and fuel. So the governments are forced to use their foreign money and [dollar] credits to procure these necessities abroad. This process exhausts the funds which are urgently needed for reconstruction. [Thus a very serious situation is rapidly developing, and the modern exchange economy is in danger of breaking down.]

The truth of the matter is that Europe's requirements for the next three or four years of foreign food and other essential products—principally from America—are so much greater than her present ability to pay that she must have substantial additional help or face economic, social, and political deterioration of a very grave character.

The remedy lies in breaking the vicious circle and restoring the confidence of the European people in the economic future of their own countries and of Europe as a whole. The manufacturer and the farmer throughout wide areas must be able and willing to exchange their products for currencies the continuing value of which is not open to question.

Aside from the demoralizing effect on the world at large and possibilities of disturbances arising as a result of the desperation of the people concerned, the consequences to the economy of the United States should be apparent to all. It is logical that the United States should do whatever it is able to do to assist in the return of normal economic health in the world, without which there can be no political stability and no assured peace. Our policy is directed not against any country or doctrine but against hunger, poverty, desperation, and chaos. Its purpose should be the revival of a working economy in the world so as to permit the emergence of political and social conditions in which free institutions can exist. Such assistance, I am convinced, must not be on a piecemeal basis as various crises develop. Any assistance that this Government may render in the future should provide a cure rather than a mere palliative. Any government that is willing to assist in the task of recovery will find full cooperation, I am sure, on the part of the United States Government. Any government which maneuvers to block the recovery of other countries cannot expect help from us. Furthermore, governments, political parties, or groups which seek to perpetuate human misery in order to profit therefrom politically or otherwise will encounter the opposition of the United States.

It is already evident that, before the United States Government can proceed much further in its efforts to alleviate the situation and help start the European world on its way to recovery, there must be some agreement among the countries of Europe as to the requirements of the situation and the part those countries will take in order to give proper effect to whatever action might be taken by this Government. It would be neither fitting nor efficacious for this Government to undertake to draw up unilaterally a program designed to place Europe on its feet economically. This is the business of the Europeans. The initiative, I think, must come from Europe. The role of this country should consist of friendly aid in the drafting of a European program and of later support of such a program so far as it may be practical for us to do so. The program should be a joint one, agreed by a number of, if not all, European nations.

An essential part of any successful action on the part of the United States is an understanding on the part of the people of America of the character of the problem and remedies to be applied. Political passion and prejudice should have no part. With foresight, and a

German poster promoting Marshall Plan aid. *(Source: Bundesarchiv, Koblenz)*

willingness on the part of our people to face up to the vast responsibility which history has clearly placed upon our country, the difficulties I have outlined can and will be overcome.

Questions for Analysis

1. Why, according to Marshall, was the European economy on the verge of a breakdown? What was the specific financial problem?

2. What kind of responses did Marshall want Americans and Europeans to make? Why?

3. Do you find any evidence of tensions between the United States and the Soviet Union in Marshall's speech? What evidence?

4. What assumptions did Marshall make about the relationship between economics and politics? What caused upheaval and instability, according to Marshall?

Source: Slightly adapted from G. Marshall, "Address at Harvard University, June 5, 1947," *A Decade of American Foreign Policy: Basic Documents, 1941–1949,* U.S. Senate Document 123, 81st Cong., 1st sess., (Washington, D.C.: Government Printing Office, 1950), pp. 1268–1270.

31

The Recent Past, 1968 to the Present

Sometime during the late 1960s or early 1970s, the postwar era came to an end. With fits and starts, a new age opened, as postwar certitudes such as domestic political stability and social harmony evaporated and intense political conflict, culminating in the upheavals of 1968, re-emerged. A second break came with expanding roles for women, which interacted with a powerful "second wave" of feminist thought and action and resulted in major changes for women and gender relations. These changes dated from the late 1960s and gathered momentum in the 1970s. Above all, the astonishing postwar economic advance, unparalleled in its rapidity and consistency, came to an abrupt halt. Old, almost forgotten problems such as high unemployment, expensive energy, and international monetary instability suddenly resurfaced, and the buoyant self-confidence of the postwar era disappeared.

The end of the postwar era also signaled renewed efforts to reduce cold war tensions in Europe and to liberalize communist eastern Europe. With a revitalized West Germany taking the initiative, these efforts achieved some success in the early 1970s, and after renewed cold war competition, they reached fruition after 1985. The Soviet Union entered a period of sweeping change. Communist rule collapsed in the satellite states of eastern Europe in 1989 and in the Soviet Union itself in 1991. The long cold war between East and West came to a spectacular end, providing a welcome counterbalance to the serious economic difficulties that continued to fester after a generation.

A Russian soldier in front of Parliament in August, 1991, celebrating the defeat of the military coup. *(Source: Andy Hernandez/Sipa Press)*

- Why, after a generation, did the world economy shift into reverse gear, and what were some of the social consequences of that shift?

- How did expanding horizons for women encourage and reflect the second wave of the women's movement, and what were some of the consequences of these interrelated developments?

1043

- What were the most striking political developments within the nations of the Atlantic alliance, and how did West Germany take the initiative in trying to negotiate an enduring reconciliation with its communist neighbors?
- How did these changes interact with the evolution of the Soviet bloc, and what led to the astonishing collapse of communism and dictatorship in eastern Europe?

These are the fundamental questions that the chapter will address. We will close the chapter with some reflections on the future.

✤ THE TROUBLED ECONOMY

The energy crisis that struck Europe and the United States in the early 1970s looms large in the sudden transition from the almost automatic growth of the postwar era to a time of serious and recurring economic difficulties, which has lasted to the present. The first surge in oil prices in 1973 stunned the international economy, and the second surge in 1979 led in the early 1980s to the deepest recession since the 1930s. The collapse of the postwar monetary system in 1971 and the rapid accumulation of international debts also caused heavy long-term damage. Another painful slump struck North America and Europe in the early 1990s. The social consequences of harder times were profound and many-sided.

Money and Oil

During the Second World War, British and American leaders were convinced that international financial disorder after 1918 had contributed mightily to economic instability in the 1920s, the Great Depression, and renewed global warfare. These leaders were determined not to repeat their mistakes, and in the Bretton Woods Agreement of 1944 they laid the foundations for a new international monetary system, which proved instrumental in the unprecedented postwar boom.

Saudi Riches Saudi Arabia has enormous oil reserves, making it one of the most influential members of the Organization of Petroleum Exporting Countries (OPEC) and giving it one of the world's highest per capita incomes. Oil has also made rich men of Prince Fahd and King Khalid, shown here. *(Source: Robert Azzi/Woodfin Camp & Associates)*

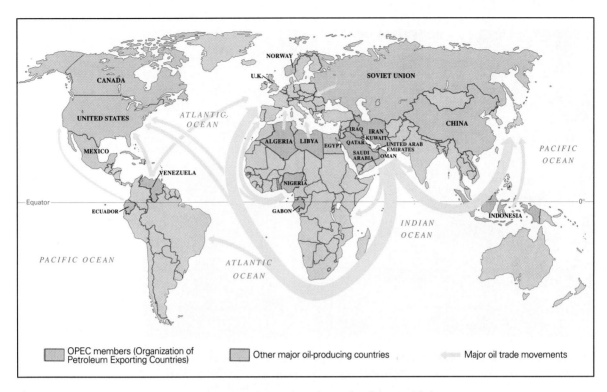

◆ **MAP 31.1 OPEC and the World Oil Trade** Though much of the world depends on imported oil, Western Europe and Japan are OPEC's biggest customers. What major oil exporters remain outside of OPEC?

The new system, operating through the World Bank and the International Monetary Fund, was based on the American dollar, which was supposed to be "as good as gold" because foreign governments could always exchange dollars for gold at 35 dollars an ounce. The United States proceeded to make needed dollars readily available to the rest of the world, so readily that by early 1971 it had only 11 billion dollars in gold left in government vaults and Europe had accumulated 50 billion American dollars. The result was a classic, long-overdue "run on the bank" in 1971 as foreigners panicked and raced to exchange their dollars for gold at 35 dollars an ounce. President Richard Nixon then decided to stop the sale of American gold. The price of gold proceeded to soar on world markets, and the value of the dollar declined. Fixed rates of exchange were abandoned, and great uncertainty replaced postwar predictability in international trade and finance. Prices for primary products, such as wheat or copper, began to rise rapidly in world markets.

The most serious example of the new trend was the dramatic reversal in the price and availability of energy. As described in Chapter 22, coal-fired steam engines broke the bottleneck of chronically inadequate energy in the late-eighteenth-century economy, making possible the Industrial Revolution and improved living standards in the nineteenth century. In the twentieth century, petroleum proved its worth, and the great postwar boom was fueled by cheap oil, especially in western Europe. Cheap oil from the Middle East permitted energy-intensive industries—automobiles, chemicals, and electric power—to expand prodigiously and lead other sectors of the economy forward. More generally, cheap oil and cheap energy encouraged businesses to invest massively in machinery and improved technology. This investment enabled workers to produce more and allowed a steady rise in the standard of living without much inflation.

In the 1950s and 1960s, the main oil-exporting countries, grouped together in the Arab-

❖ **The Egyptian-Israeli Peace Treaty** of 1979 is celebrated in front of the White
House by the men who made it possible: Egypt's President Anwar al-Sadat, U.S.
President Jimmy Carter, and Israeli Prime Minister Menachem Begin. Egypt recog-
nized Israel's right to exist and established normal diplomatic relations, while Israel
agreed to withdraw from Egyptian territory occupied in the Six-Day War of 1967.
(Source: Sipa Press)

dominated Organization of Petroleum Exporting
Countries (OPEC), had watched the price of crude
oil decline consistently compared to the price of
manufactured goods as the Western oil companies
vigorously expanded production and kept prices
low to win users of coal to petroleum (Map 31.1).
President Nasser of Egypt argued that Arab countries should find a way to push up these low oil
prices in order to increase their revenues and also
strike at Israel and its Western allies. But Egypt
lacked oil and Nasser failed. Colonel Muammar
Khadafy of Libya proved more successful. He won
important concessions from Western nations and
oil companies in the early 1970s, and his example
activated the OPEC countries. In 1971 OPEC for
the first time presented a united front against the
powerful multinational oil companies and obtained
a solid price increase. The stage was set for a revolution in energy prices during the fourth Arab-
Israeli war in October 1973.

The war began on the solemn Sabbath celebration of Yom Kippur, or the Day of Atonement, the
holiest day in the Jewish calendar. Egypt and Syria
launched a surprise attack on an unsuspecting Israel, breaking through defense positions and destroying a large part of the Israeli air force. In
response to urgent pleas, the United States airlifted
2.2 billion dollars' worth of its most sophisticated
weapons to Israel, which accepted a cease-fire after
its successful counterattack had encircled much of
the Egyptian army. Surprisingly, the Yom Kippur
War eventually led to peace between Egypt and
Israel. Egypt's initial military victories greatly enhanced the power and prestige of General Anwar
Sadat (1918–1981), Nasser's successor. This advantage enabled the realistic Sadat to achieve in
1979 the negotiated settlement with Israel that he
had long desired.

In the first days of the war, the Arab (and non-
Arab) oil producers in OPEC placed an embargo
on oil shipments to the United States and the
Netherlands in retaliation for their support of Israel. These producers also cut production and
raised prices by 70 percent, ostensibly to prevent

Europe from sharing oil with the United States. In reality, greed and a desire for revenge against the West took over: a second increase in December, after the cease-fire, meant that crude oil prices quadrupled in less than a year. It was widely realized that OPEC's brutal action was economically destructive not only to the West but also to most of the global economy. Yet the world's major powers did nothing. The Soviet Union was a great oil exporter and benefited directly, while a cautious western Europe looked to the United States for leadership. But the United States was immobilized, its attention absorbed by the Watergate crisis. Thus governments, companies, and individuals were left to deal piecemeal and manage as best they could with the so-called oil shock—a "shock" that really turned out to be an earthquake.

Inflation, Debt, and Unemployment

Coming close on the heels of upheaval in the international monetary system, the price revolution in energy sources plunged the world into its worst economic decline since the 1930s. The energy-intensive industries that had driven the economy up in the 1950s and 1960s now dragged it down in the mid-1970s. Yet while industrial output fell, soaring energy costs sent prices surging. "Stagflation"—the unexpected combination of economic stagnation and rapid inflation—developed to bedevil the public and baffle economists. Unemployment rose, while productivity and living standards declined.

But no downturn lasts forever, and by 1976 a modest recovery was in progress. People were learning to save energy, turning down thermostats and buying smaller cars. Optimists argued that the challenge of redesigning lifestyles to cope with expensive energy actually represented a great opportunity. It would force people to use natural resources more efficiently and do less damage to the environment.

Iran's Islamic revolution in 1978 and 1979 confounded these hopes, at least in the short run. Iranian oil production collapsed, OPEC again doubled the price of crude oil, and the world economy succumbed to its second oil shock. Once again, unemployment and inflation rose dramatically before another recovery began in 1982, driven by a reversal in oil prices, falling interest rates, and large U.S. trade and budget deficits. But the recovery

was very uneven. In the summer of 1985, the unemployment rate in western Europe rose to its highest levels since the Great Depression. Fully nineteen million people were unemployed. Although unemployment declined somewhat in the late 1980s, large numbers of people remained out of work. The 1990s opened with renewed recession in the United States and in Europe, where it was more severe. U.S. recovery was painfully slow until late 1993.

Many means were devised in the 1970s to measure the troubled economy, but perhaps none was more telling than the "misery index." First used with considerable effect by candidate Jimmy Carter in the 1976 U.S. presidential debates, the misery index combined rates of inflation and unemployment in a single, powerfully emotional number. Figure 31.1 presents a comparison of misery indexes for the United States and the Common Market countries between 1970 and 1986. As may be

❖ **FIGURE 31.1 The Misery Index, 1970–1986** Combining rates of unemployment and inflation provided a simple but effective measure of economic hardship. This particular index represents the sum of two times the unemployment rate plus the inflation rate, reflecting the widespread belief that joblessness causes more suffering than higher prices. EEC = European Economic Community, or Common Market countries. *(Source: OECD data, as given in* The Economist, *June 15, 1985, p. 69.)*

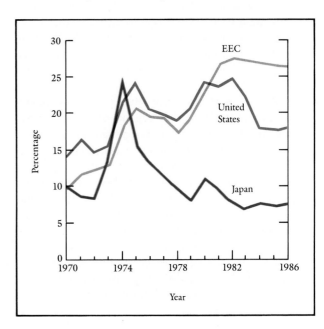

seen, "misery" increased on both sides of the Atlantic, but the increase was substantially greater in western Europe, and it remained so in the early 1990s. Higher unemployment in Europe helps explain why these hard times—often referred to by Europeans simply as "the crisis"—probably had an even greater psychological impact on Europeans than on Americans.

Nor was the Soviet bloc spared. Both the Soviet Union and the satellite states of its eastern European empire did less and less well: annual rates of economic growth fell from 6 to 7 percent in the late 1960s to 2 to 3 percent in 1980. This performance was no worse than that of most Western countries, but it mocked the long-standing propaganda boast that communist countries would "catch and surpass the capitalistic West." In the early 1980s many economies in the Soviet bloc began to decline, preparing one of the underlying conditions for the collapse of communism at the end of the decade.

Debts and deficits piled up quickly in the troubled economies of the 1970s and 1980s. In the first place, the price hikes of 1973 required a massive global transfer of wealth to the OPEC countries from both rich and poor nations. Like individual consumers suddenly faced with a financial emergency, countries scrambled to borrow in order to pay their greatly increased fuel bills. Poor countries, especially, turned to the big private international banks. These banks received deposits—the so-called petrodollars—from OPEC members and lent them back out to poor countries so that these nations could pay their oil bills. This circular flow averted total collapse, but there was a high price to pay in the form of a rapid expansion of international debt.

Rich nations also went on a borrowing binge. Almost everywhere they ran up big debts to pay for imported oil and also to maintain social welfare services as their economies declined and tax receipts fell. Western consumers also joined the race for ever-higher levels of debt. Borrowing to buy before prices rose seemed smart in the 1970s, and that attitude carried over into the 1980s. Like burgeoning government debt, a record-high level of consumer debt was a two-edged sword. It sustained current economic activity but quite possibly posed serious repayment problems, an appropriately ambiguous reflection of the troubled economy.

Some Social Consequences

The most pervasive consequences of this recent economic stagnation were probably psychological and attitudinal. Optimism gave way to pessimism; romantic utopianism yielded to sober realism. This drastic change in mood—a complete surprise only to those who had never studied history—affected states, institutions, and individuals in countless ways.

To be sure, there were heartbreaking human tragedies—lost jobs, bankruptcies, homelessness, and mental breakdowns. But on the whole, the welfare system fashioned in the postwar era prevented mass suffering and degradation. Extended benefits for the unemployed, pensions for the aged, free medical care for the needy, surplus food and special allowances for parents with children—all these and a host of lesser supports did their part. The responsive, socially concerned national state undoubtedly contributed to the preservation of political stability and democracy in the face of economic difficulties that might have brought revolution and dictatorship in earlier times.

The energetic response of governments to social needs helps explain the sharp increase in total government spending in most countries during the 1970s and 1980s. In 1982 western European governments spent an average of more than 50 percent of gross national income, as compared to only 37 percent fifteen years earlier. In the United States, the combined share of federal, state, and local government expenditures rose from 31 to 35 percent in the same years. The role of government in everyday life became more important.

In all countries, people were much more willing to see their governments increase spending than raise taxes. This imbalance contributed to the rapid growth of budget deficits, national debts, and inflation. By the late 1970s, a powerful reaction against government's ever-increasing role had set in, however, and Western governments were gradually forced to introduce austerity measures to slow the seemingly inexorable growth of public spending and the welfare state.

Part of a broad cultural shift toward greater conservatism, growing voter dissatisfaction with government and government spending helped bring Margaret Thatcher (b. 1925) to power in Britain in 1979 and contributed to the 1980 election of Ronald Reagan (b. 1911) as president of the United States. Thatcher had some success in slowing government spending and in "privatizing" industry—that is, in selling off state-owned companies to private investors. Little noticed abroad but of great social significance, Thatcher's Conservative government encouraged low- and moderate-income renters in state-owned housing projects to buy their apartments at rock-bottom prices. This privatization initiative created a whole new class of property owners, thereby eroding the electoral base of Britain's socialist Labour party.

Ronald Reagan's success in the United States was more limited and less enduring. With widespread popular support and the agreement of most congressional Democrats as well as Republicans, Reagan in 1981 pushed through major cuts in income taxes all across the board, although the largest dollar reductions went to the wealthy and well-to-do, who paid the most income taxes. (According to a 1993 study by the Internal Revenue Service, the richest 1 percent of all Americans paid 17.6 percent of all federal income taxes in 1979 and 24.6 percent in 1991, at the end of the Reagan-Bush era.)

But Reagan failed miserably at cutting government spending, which increased as a percentage of national income in the course of his presidency. Reagan's obsession with the Soviet threat and his extravagant military buildup were partly responsible, but spending on social programs also grew rapidly. First, the harsh recession of the early 1980s required that the government spend more on unemployment benefits, welfare benefits, and medical treatment for the poor. Second, Reagan's crude antiwelfare rhetoric mobilized the liberal opposition to defend the poor and eventually turned many moderates against him. Thus the budget deficit and the U. S. government debt soared, tripling in a decade. Assigning blame for this colossal failure in public policy became a staple of American politics and contributed to the subsequent repudiation of Reagan and his successor, George Bush (b. 1924). In 1992 a sharply critical Bill Clinton (b. 1946) ran for president and won on a platform promising significantly higher income taxes on the richest 1 percent of Americans as well as lower budget deficits.

The striking but temporary exception to the trend toward greater frugality was François Mitterand (b. 1916) of France. After his election as president in 1981, Mitterand led his Socialist party and Communist allies on a lurch to the left, launching a vast program of nationalization and public investment designed to spend France out of economic stagnation. By 1983 this attempt had clearly failed. Mitterand's Socialist government was then compelled to impose a wide variety of austerity measures and to maintain those policies for the rest of the decade.

Yet the French economy limped and sputtered under Mitterand's austerity as it had under his recklessness. In early 1993 frustrated French voters gave a coalition of conservatives and moderates an overwhelming victory, as the Socialist party suffered total defeat and the once-powerful Communists were reduced almost to fringe party status. With industrial production and national income declining in France (and in Germany, Italy, and Spain, among others), and with unemployment climbing to a new high of 10.7 percent in the European Community in October 1993, the new French government faced a great challenge. The hard times that began in the West in 1973 were continuing.

When governments were forced to restrain spending, Big Science (see pages 1026–27) was often singled out for cuts, unless (while the cold war lasted) its ties to the military were very direct. The problems of the atomic physics lab CERN and its American counterparts were a good example. Formed to pool western European efforts in high-energy particle physics, CERN did succeed in stealing the lead from the United States in this exciting but esoteric and uncommercial field. But the costs were truly enormous. In the 1980s CERN was increasingly attacked as an extravagant misallocation of scarce resources at a time when new fields, such as computers and genetic research, were bursting with scientific opportunities that offered mouth-watering commercial applications.

CERN's troubles encouraged the Reagan administration and its political allies to begin construction in Texas of a much grander and more expensive atom smasher. But costs soared far above estimates and public criticism mounted. In 1993 the U.S. Congress canceled the project and simply abandoned it—a 7-billion-dollar concrete folly scarring the prairie.

More generally, tighter funding for Big Science accelerated the ongoing computer revolution. That revolution thrived on the diffusion of ever-cheaper computational and informational capacity to small research groups and private businesses, which were both cause and effect of the revolution itself. Big organizations lost some of their advantages as small firms and even individuals became able to link electronically with their region and most of the world. By the 1990s a student with an inexpensive personal computer had the power of a 1950s mainframe that had filled a room and cost hundreds of thousands of dollars. From fax machines to new cars, computer technology was everywhere.

Individuals felt the impact of austerity at an early date, for, unlike governments, they could not pay their bills by printing money and going ever further into debt. The energy crisis of the 1970s forced them to reexamine not only their fuel bills but also the whole pattern of self-indulgent materialism in the postwar era. The result in both Europe and North America was a leaner, tougher lifestyle, featuring more attention to nutrition and a passion for exercise. Correspondingly, there was less blind reliance on medical science for good health and a growing awareness that individuals had to accept a large portion of the responsibility for illness and disease. More people began to realize that they could substantially increase their life spans simply by eating regular meals, sleeping seven or eight hours each night, exercising two or three times a week, maintaining moderate weight, forgoing smoking, and using alcohol only in moderation. A forty-five-year-old American male who practiced three or fewer of these habits in the late 1970s could expect to live to be sixty-seven; one who adhered to five or six could expect to live eleven more years, to age seventy-eight.

Economic troubles also strengthened existing trends within the family. Both men and women were encouraged to postpone marriage until they had put their careers on a firm foundation, so the age of marriage rose sharply for both sexes in many Western countries. Indeed, the very real threat of unemployment—or "underemployment" in a dead-end job—seemed to shape the outlook of a whole generation. The students of the 1980s were serious, practical, and often conservative. As one young woman at a French university told a reporter in 1985, "Jobs are the big worry now, so

❖ **"The New Poor"** Economic crisis and prolonged unemployment in the early 1980s reduced the status of many people from modest affluence to harsh poverty, creating a class of new poor. This photograph captures that human tragedy. After two years of unemployment, this homeless French office worker still dresses up and looks for work. But he must sleep each night in a makeshift shelter for the destitute. *(Source: Dennis Stock/Magnum)*

everyone wants to learn something practical."[1] In France as elsewhere, it was an astonishing shift from the romantic visions and political activism of the late 1960s.

Harder times meant that ever-more women entered or remained in the workforce after they married. In the United States, 66 percent of all married women held jobs in 1986, as opposed to 55 percent in 1979 and 46 percent in 1973. New attitudes related to personal fulfillment were one reason for the continuing increase, especially for well-educated, upper-middle-class women. But for the vast majority of married women—the four-fifths who fell below the top 20 percent—economic necessity also played a major role.

Many wives in poor and middle-class families simply had to work outside the home because after 1973 the average husband was earning less after the effects of continuous inflation were taken into account. The average inflation-adjusted wage for men in the United States (in 1986 dollars) declined to 26,000 dollars in 1986, as opposed to 26,700 dollars in 1979 and 28,600 dollars in 1973. The percentage decline for the large group of American men with a high school diploma or less education was substantially greater in these years.[2] As in the preindustrial era, the wife's earnings provided the margin of survival for millions of hard-pressed families.

✤ THE CHANGING LIVES OF WOMEN

The growing emancipation of women in Europe and North America was unquestionably one of the most significant changes of the recent past. This growing emancipation had distant roots, going back at least to the eighteenth-century Enlightenment. The French Revolution then stimulated the first systematic program of women's rights and gender equality. Pioneering feminists led by Olympe de Gouges and Mary Wollstonecraft demanded that "the Rights of Women be respected . . . [and] JUSTICE for one-half of the human race." Although the revolutionary era actually reduced women's rights in practical terms, the idea of gender equality was launched.

In the later nineteenth century the first wave of an organized women's movement won some modest rights, mainly for middle-class women (see pages 816–817). World War One also brought some advances. Lenin and the communists made equality between the sexes a fundamental principle (but not a practice) of Soviet life, and women secured the right to vote in most Western countries after 1918. Yet many gains that women had won in the workplace during the First World War were lost in the 1920s and 1930s, as returning male workers, conservative and fascist ideologies, and the shortage of jobs in the Great Depression all acted against women and the expansion of their rights.

The economic expansion after World War Two brought few measures that were designed specifically to help women. Yet young women in most Western (and communist) countries shared fully in the postwar education revolution and became better educated than ever before. They took advantage of the need for trained experts in a more fluid society and moved into areas of employment formerly closed to them. More married women began to work for wages outside the home, which had a major impact on many life experiences.

These everyday experiences interacted with the emergence of a second wave of feminist thought and action. This second wave of the women's movement first assumed real significance in the late 1960s, gathered strength in the next decade, and won major victories in the 1970s and 1980s. The firm demands of the second wave contrasted sharply with the quiescent women's movement of the postwar years after 1945.

Thus a variety of forces converged in the recent past to make women more equal and independent, less confined and stereotyped. This transformation has affected not only women but also gender relations and families, both of which have probably experienced some fundamental reorientations. This becomes apparent if we examine women's traditional role in the home, women's new roles outside the home in recent years, and the development of the women's movement.

Marriage and Motherhood

Before the Industrial Revolution, most men and women married late, and substantial numbers never married at all. Once a woman was married, however, she normally bore several children, of whom a third to a half would not survive to adulthood. Moreover, many women died in childbirth. With the growth of industry and urban society, people began to marry earlier, and fewer remained unmarried. As industrial development led to higher incomes and better diets, more children survived to adulthood, and population grew rapidly in the nineteenth century. By the late nineteenth century, contraception within marriage was spreading.

In the twentieth century, and especially after World War Two, these trends continued. In the postwar era, women continued to marry earlier. In Sweden, for example, the average age of first marriage dropped steadily from twenty-six in the early 1940s to twenty-three in the late 1960s. Moreover, more than nine out of ten women were marrying at least once, usually in their early twenties. Marriage was never more in vogue than in the generation after the Second World War. The triumph of romantic attraction over financial calculation seemed complete, and perhaps never before had young couples expected so much emotional satisfaction from matrimony.

After marrying early, the typical woman in Europe, the United States, and Canada had her children quickly. Whereas women in the more distant past very often had children as long as they were fertile, women in Europe and North America were having about 80 percent of their children before age thirty. As for family size, the baby boom that lasted until the early 1960s made for a fairly rapid population growth of 1 to 1.5 percent per year in many European countries. In the 1960s, however, the long-term decline in birthrates resumed. Surveys of the period in northern and western Europe began to reveal that most women believed that two, instead of three, children were ideal.

Women must have 2.1 children on average if total population is to remain constant over the long term. The number of births fell so sharply in the 1960s that total population practically stopped growing in many European countries. By the mid-1970s more people were dying each year than were being born in Austria, East Germany, West Germany, and Luxembourg, where total numbers actually declined. Very low or even negative population growth continued in western Europe into the 1990s. The United States followed the same trend: the birthrate declined from twenty-five for each thousand of population in 1957 to fifteen per thousand in 1973, and it recovered slightly thereafter only because the baby-boomers were reaching child-bearing age, not because individual women were having more children. Since the American death rate remained practically unchanged in these

years, the rate of population growth from natural increase (that is, excluding legal and illegal immigration) dropped by two-thirds, from 1.5 percent to 0.6 percent per year between the 1950s and the 1970s. The population of Africa, Latin America, and much of Asia was still growing very rapidly from natural increase, but that was certainly not true for most European countries and countries of predominately European ancestry.

The culmination of the trends toward early, almost-universal marriage and small family size in wealthy societies had revolutionary implications for women. An examination of these implications suggests why the emancipation of women—sooner or later—was almost assuredly built into the structure of modern life.

The main point is that motherhood occupied a much smaller portion of a woman's life than at the beginning of this century. The average woman's life expectancy at birth increased from about fifty years in 1900 to about seventy-five years in 1970. At the same time, women were increasingly compressing childbearing into the decade between their twentieth and thirtieth birthdays, instead of bearing children until their late thirties. By the early 1970s about half of Western women were having their last baby by the age of twenty-six or twenty-seven. When the youngest child trooped off to kindergarten, the average mother still had more than forty years of life in front of her.

This was a momentous change. Throughout history male-dominated society insisted on defining most married women (and most young unmarried women) as mothers (and potential mothers). And motherhood was very demanding: pregnancy followed pregnancy, and there were many children to nurse, guide, and bury. In recent years, however, the period devoted to having babies and caring for young children represented at most one-seventh of the average woman's life. Motherhood had become a relatively short phase in most women's total life span. Perhaps a good deal of the frustration that many women felt in the late 1960s and 1970s was due to the fact that their traditional role as mothers no longer absorbed the energies of a lifetime, and new roles in the male-dominated world outside the family were opening up too slowly.

A related revolutionary change for women was that the age-old biological link between sexual intercourse and motherhood was severed. As is well known, beginning in the early 1960s many women chose to gain effective control over pregnancy with oral contraceptives and intrauterine devices. They no longer relied on undependable males and their undependable methods. Less well known are certain physiological facts that help explain why many women in the industrialized countries did elect to practice birth control at some point in their lives.

Women in the postwar era were capable of having children for many more years than their forebears. The age of *menarche*—the age at which girls begin to menstruate and become fertile—had dropped from about seventeen years in the early nineteenth century to about thirteen years by the 1970s. At the same time, the age of onset of menopause rose. At the beginning of the eighteenth century, menopause occurred on average at about age thirty-six; it now occurred at about fifty. These physiological changes over time are poorly understood, but they were apparently due to better diets and living standards, which also substantially increased people's height and size. In any event, modern women increasingly chose to separate their sexual lives from their awesome reproductive power, which had grown with the lengthening of the time in which they were capable of bearing children. In doing so, these women became free to pursue sensual pleasure for its own sake. The consequences of this development will continue to work themselves out for a long time.

Women at Work

For centuries before the Industrial Revolution, ordinary women were highly productive members of society. They often labored for years before marriage to accumulate the necessary dowry. Once married, women worked hard on farms and in home industries while bearing and caring for their

◆ **Britain's Women on the March** After World War Two, more and more women entered the labor market as full-time workers. Although most Western women had full political rights by this time, they continued to struggle for equal pay and economic rights, as these marchers through London's Piccadilly Square demonstrate. *(Source: Globe Photos)*

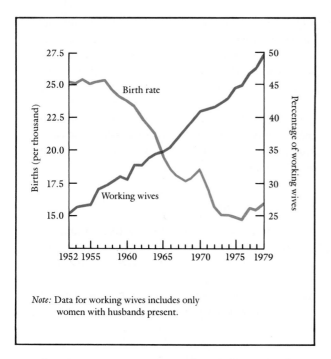

Note: Data for working wives includes only women with husbands present.

❧ **FIGURE 31.2 The Decline of the Birthrate and the Increase of Working Wives in the United States, 1952–1979** The challenge of working away from home encouraged American wives to prefer fewer children and helped to lower the birthrate.

large families. With the growth of modern industry and large cities, young women continued to work as wage earners. But once a poor woman married, she typically stopped working in a factory or a shop, struggling instead to earn money at home by practicing some low-paid craft as she looked after her children. In the middle classes, it was a rare and tough-minded woman who worked outside the home for wages, although charity work was socially acceptable.

From the beginning of the twentieth century and especially after World War Two, the situation changed dramatically once again. Opportunities for women of modest means to earn cash income within the home practically disappeared. Piano teachers, novelists, and part-time typists still worked at home as independent contractors, but the ever-greater complexity of the modern wage-based economy and its sophisticated technology meant that almost all would-be wage earners had to turn elsewhere. Moreover, because child care took less of married women's lives, it often appeared that the full-time mother-housewife had

less economic value for families. Thus the reduction of home-centered work and child care resulted in a sharp rise across Europe and North America in the number of married women who became full-time and part-time wage earners outside the home.

The trend went the furthest in eastern Europe before the collapse of communism. In the Soviet Union, most married women worked outside the home; there women accounted for almost half of all employed persons in the postwar era. In non-communist western Europe and North America, there was a good deal of variety, depending on whether married women had traditionally worked outside the home, as in France or Sweden, or stayed at home, as in Belgium and Switzerland. Nevertheless, the percentage of married women in the workforce began rising in 1950 from a range for different countries of roughly 20 to 25 percent. The rise accelerated in the late 1960s and reached a range of 45 to 70 percent in recent years. The experience of the United States was fairly typical. As Figure 31.2 suggests, the percentage of working wives increased from 25 percent in 1950 to 35 percent in 1967 and 66 percent in 1986.

The rising employment of married women was undoubtedly a powerful force in the drive for women's equality and emancipation. Take the critical matter of widespread discrimination between men and women in pay, occupation, and advancement. The young unmarried woman of sixty or a hundred years ago was more inclined to accept such injustices. She was conditioned to think of them as temporary nuisances and to look forward to marriage and motherhood for fulfillment. In the postwar era and recent past, a married wage earner in her thirties gradually developed a totally different perspective. She saw employment as a permanent condition within which she, like her male counterpart, sought not only income but also psychological satisfaction. Sexism and discrimination grew loathsome and evoked the sense of injustice that drives revolutions and reforms. When powerful voices arose to challenge the system, they found support among young working women.

Rising employment for married women was a factor in the decline of the birthrate (see Figure 31.2). Women who worked outside the home had significantly fewer children than women of the same age who did not. Moreover, survey research showed that young women who had held jobs and intended to do so again revised downward the number of children they expected to have after the first lovable but time-consuming baby was born. One reason was obvious: raising a family while holding down a full-time job was a tremendous challenge and often resulted in the woman's being grossly overworked. The fatiguing, often frustrating multiple demands of job, motherhood, and marriage simply became more manageable with fewer children.

Another reason for the decline of the birthrate was that motherhood interrupted a woman's career. Many women in Western countries stayed at home for a minimum of two or three years while their children were small. The longer the break in employment, the more a woman's career suffered. Good, affordable day care became a major demand for ever-more women, a demand that could be realized through organization and group action.

The Women's Movement

The 1970s marked the birth of a revitalized grass-roots, broad-based movement devoted to promoting the interests of women. Three basic reasons accounted for this major development. First, ongoing changes in the underlying pattern of work and motherhood created novel conditions and new demands, as has just been suggested. Second, a vanguard of feminist intellectuals articulated a powerful critique of gender relations, which stimulated many women to rethink their assumptions and challenge the status quo. Third, taking a lesson from the civil rights movement in the United States and worldwide student protest against the Vietnam War, dissatisfied individuals recognized that they had to band together if they were to influence politics and secure fundamental reforms.

The first and one of the most influential major works produced by the second wave was *The Second Sex* (1949) by the French writer and philosopher Simone de Beauvoir (1908–1986). Characterizing herself as a "dutiful daughter" of the bourgeoisie in childhood, the adolescent Beauvoir came to see her pious and submissive mother as foolishly renouncing any self-expression outside of home and marriage and showing Beauvoir the dangers of a life she did not want. A brilliant university student, Beauvoir began at the Sorbonne a complex and generally fruitful relationship with an equally gifted classmate, future philosopher Jean-Paul Sartre, who became her lifelong intellectual companion and sometime lover.

Beauvoir analyzed the position of women within the framework of existential thought (see pages 938–939). She argued that women—like all human beings—were in essence free but that they had almost always been trapped by particularly inflexible and limiting conditions. (See Listening to the Past.) Only by means of courageous action and self-assertive creativity could a woman become a completely free person and escape the role of the inferior "other" that men had constructed for her gender. Drawing on history, philosophy, psychology, biology, and literature, Beauvoir's massive investigation inspired a generation of women intellectuals.

❖ **Simone de Beauvoir** Shown here in her Paris apartment a year before her death in 1986, de Beauvoir combined the erudition of the scholar with the psychological sensitivity of the novelist in her famous study of women and women's issues, *The Second Sex.* De Beauvoir's love of books and ideas is clearly evident. A small stepladder serves as overflow bookcase and coat hanger. *(Source: Gerard Gastaud/Sipa Press)*

One such woman was Betty Friedan (b. 1924), who played a key role in reopening a serious discussion of women's issues in the United States. Unlike Beauvoir, who epitomized French individualism in believing that each woman had to chart her own course, Friedan reflected the American faith in group action and political solutions. As a working wife and the mother of three small children in the 1950s, Friedan became acutely aware of the conflicting pressures of career and family. Conducting an in-depth survey of her classmates at Smith College fifteen years after their graduation, she concluded that many well-educated women shared her growing dissatisfaction. In her pathbreaking study *The Feminine Mystique* (1963), Friedan identified this dissatisfaction as the "problem that has no name." According to Friedan, the cause of this nameless problem was a crisis of identity. Women were not permitted to become mature adults and genuine human beings. Instead, they were expected to conform to a false, infantile pattern of femininity and live (like Beauvoir's mother) for their husbands and children. In short, women faced what feminists would soon call *sexism,* a pervasive social problem that required drastic reforms.

When long-standing proposals to treat sex discrimination as seriously as race discrimination fell again on deaf ears, Friedan took the lead in 1966 in founding the National Organization for Women (NOW) to press for women's rights. NOW flourished, growing from seven hundred members in 1967 to forty thousand in 1974. Many other women's organizations of varying persuasions rose to follow NOW in Europe and the United States. Throughout the 1970s, a proliferation of publications, conferences, and institutions devoted to women's issues reinforced the emerging international movement.

Although national peculiarities abounded, this movement generally shared the common strategy of entering the political arena and changing laws regarding women. First, advocates of women's rights pushed for new statutes in the workplace: laws against discrimination, "equal pay for equal work," and measures such as maternal leave and affordable day care designed to help women combine careers and family responsibilities. Second, the movement concentrated on gender and family questions, including the right to divorce (in some Catholic countries), legalized abortion, the needs of single parents (who were usually women), and protection from rape and physical violence. In al-most every country, the effort to decriminalize abortion served as a catalyst in mobilizing an effective, self-conscious women's movement (and in creating an opposition to it, as in the United States).

In countries that had long placed women in a subordinate position, the legal changes were little less than revolutionary. In Italy, for example, new laws abolished restrictions on divorce and abortion, which had been strengthened by Mussolini and defended energetically by the Catholic church in the postwar era. By 1988 divorce and abortion were common in Italy, which had the lowest birthrate in Europe. More generally, the sharply focused women's movement of the 1970s won new rights for women. The movement became more diffuse in the 1980s and early 1990s, however, a victim of both its successes and the resurgence of an antifeminist opposition.

The accomplishments of the women's movement encouraged mobilization by many other groups. Homosexual men and lesbian women pressed their own demands, organizing politically and calling for an end to legal discrimination and social harassment. People with physical disabilities joined together to promote their interests. In Europe minority nationalities, such as the Basque people straddling the border dividing France and Spain, and immigrant groups, such as the Algerians in France and the Turks in Germany, also asserted themselves and demanded more rights and greater autonomy. Thus many subordinate groups challenged the dominant majorities, and the expansion and redefinition of human liberty—one of the great themes of modern Western and world history—continued.

THE ATLANTIC ALLIANCE

The break between the postwar era and the recent past in international politics is not immediately obvious, for the cold war continued to dominate world affairs after 1970. Yet while the cold war continued to rage outside Europe and generally defined superpower relations between the Soviet Union and the United States, an enormous step toward genuine peace was being taken in Europe. This step reduced East-West tensions in central Europe and thereby helped set the stage for the spectacular conclusion of the cold war in 1989 and the new Europe of the 1990s.

❖ **Willy Brandt in Poland, 1970** Chancellor Brandt's gesture at the Warsaw memorial to the Jewish victims of Nazi terrorism was criticized by some West Germans but praised by many more. This picture reached an enormous audience, appearing in hundreds of newspapers in both the East and the West. *(Source: Bilderdienst Süddeutscher Verlag)*

Germany's Eastern Initiative

The turning points of history are sometimes captured in dramatic moments rich in symbolism. So it was in December 1970 when West German chancellor Willy Brandt (1913–1992) flew to Poland for the signing of a historic treaty of reconciliation. Brandt laid a wreath at the tomb of the Polish unknown soldier and another at the monument commemorating the armed uprising of Warsaw's Jewish ghetto against occupying Nazi armies, after which the ghetto was totally destroyed and the Jewish survivors sent to the gas chambers. Standing before the ghetto memorial, a somber Brandt fell to his knees and knelt as if in prayer. "I wanted," Brandt said later, "to ask pardon in the name of our people for a million-fold crime which was committed in the misused name of the Germans."[3]

Brandt's gesture at the Warsaw ghetto memorial and the treaty with Poland were part of his policy of reconciliation with eastern Europe. Indeed, Brandt aimed at nothing less than a comprehensive peace settlement for central Europe and a new resolution of the "German question." That weighty question had first burst on the European scene with the modern nationalism of the French Revolution. How could fragmented Germany achieve political unity, and what role would a powerful, unified Germany play in the international order? "Resolved" in a certain fashion by Bismarck's wars of unification, the question was posed again in the twentieth century when an aggressive Germany tried twice to conquer Europe. Agreed on crushing Hitler and de-Nazifying Germany during the Second World War, the wartime Allies then found themselves incapable of working together, and bitter divisions over the treatment of defeated Germany contributed mightily to the beginning of the cold war. Germany was divided into two antagonistic states by 1949, and the German question continued to fester as national unity disappeared.

The Federal Republic of Germany (West Germany) was the larger of the two states, with forty-five million inhabitants, as opposed to eighteen million in the communist German Democratic Republic (East Germany). Formed out of the American, British, and French zones of occupation and based on freely expressed popular sovereignty, the Federal Republic claimed that the communist dictatorship installed by the Soviets lacked free elections and hence any legal or moral basis. While concentrating on completing a metamorphosis from defeated enemy to invaluable ally within NATO and the Common Market, West Germany refused to accept the loss of German territory taken by Poland and the Soviet Union after 1945. West Germany also sought with some success to undermine the East German communist regime in the postwar era. Between 1949 and 1954, it welcomed with open arms 2.3 million East German refugees seeking political freedom and economic opportunity, and the Democratic Republic limped along while the Federal Republic boomed.

But the building of the Berlin Wall in 1961 (see page 1008) dramatically changed the situation. The wall sealed the refugees' last escape route through West Berlin and allowed East Germany to stabilize and eventually become the world's most prosperous communist country.

As the popular socialist mayor of West Berlin, Willy Brandt understood the significance of the Berlin Wall and the lack of an energetic U.S. response to its construction. He saw the painful limitations of West Germany's official hard line toward communist eastern Europe in the acceptance of the status quo by the United States and its allies. Thus Brandt became convinced that a revitalized West Germany needed a new foreign policy, just as the German Social Democratic party he headed had abandoned doctrinaire Marxian socialism to become a broad-based opposition party following the Second World War. After a long battle and two bitter electoral defeats in the 1960s, Brandt became foreign minister in a coalition government in 1966 and won the chancellorship in 1969.

Brandt's victory marked the Federal Republic's political coming of age. First, it brought Germany's Social Democrats to national power for the first time since the 1920s and showed that genuine two-party political democracy had taken firm hold. Second, it was a graphic indication of West Germany's newfound liberalism and political tolerance, for the gravel-voiced Brandt was a very unconventional German leader. Illegitimate son of a poor, unwed shopgirl, and a fire-breathing socialist in his youth, Brandt had fled to Norway in the 1930s and had fought against Nazi Germany in the Second World War. Yet the electorate judged the man

himself, turning a deaf ear to smears and innuendoes about treason and low birth. Third, Brandt showed that West Germany, postwar Europe's economic giant and political dwarf, was now both able and willing to launch major initiatives in European affairs.

The essence of Brandt's policy was to seek genuine peace and reconciliation with the communist East, as Konrad Adenauer had already done in the 1950s with France and the West. Brandt negotiated treaties with the Soviet Union, Poland, and Czechoslovakia that formally accepted existing state boundaries and the loss of German territory to Poland and the Soviet Union (see Map 30.1) in return for a mutual renunciation of force or the threat of force. Using the imaginative formula of "two German states within one German nation," Brandt's government also broke decisively with the past and entered into direct relations with East Germany, aiming for modest practical improvements rather than reunification, which at that point was completely impractical.

Brandt constantly reiterated that none of these changes affected the respective military alliances of NATO and the Warsaw Pact. Yet by boldly establishing "normal relations" with the communist East, West Germany turned another page not only on its ever-more-distant Nazi past but also on cold war conflicts in central Europe. Thus West Germany's eastern peace settlement contributed to a great reduction in East-West tensions. And with the German question apparently resolved, West Germany had freed itself to assume without reservations a leadership role in Europe.

Détente or Cold War?

Brandt's bold initiatives were viewed with some suspicion by the United States, long accustomed to calling the tune for its western allies. Secretary of State Henry Kissinger warned President Nixon that Brandt might encourage West German neutrality and undermine American influence in western Europe and the strength of NATO. Kissinger and Nixon therefore sought to avoid such consequences by placing Brandt's eastern initiatives in a broader, American-led framework of reducing East-West tensions in the early 1970s.

This policy was known as *détente,* or the progressive relaxation of cold war tensions worldwide. Thus Nixon's ambiguous policy of phased withdrawal from Vietnam was sold as a part of détente, although it was designed mainly to end the conflict over the Vietnam War in the United States (see pages 1032–34). And with South Vietnamese forces seeming to hold their own against communist guerrillas in 1973, the storm of crisis in the United States seemed past.

Instead, as the Arab oil embargo unhinged the international economy, the United States reaped the Watergate whirlwind in the form of a profound constitutional crisis. Like some other earlier American presidents, Nixon authorized spying activities that went beyond the law. But he did so in an atmosphere characterized by the theft and subsequent publication of a huge series of secret government documents known as the "Pentagon Papers." He then went further than his predecessors by authorizing special units to use various illegal means to stop the leaking of government secrets to the press. One such group broke into the Democratic party headquarters in Washington's Watergate complex in June 1972 and was promptly arrested. Eventually, the media and the machinery of congressional investigation turned the break-in and later efforts to hush up the bungled job into a great moral issue. In 1974 a beleaguered Nixon was forced to resign in disgrace as the political crisis in the United States reached its culmination.

The consequences of renewed political crisis during the Watergate affair were profound. First, the scandal resulted in a major shift of power away from the presidency and toward Congress, especially in foreign affairs. Therefore, as American aid to South Vietnam diminished in 1973 and as an emboldened North Vietnam launched a general invasion against South Vietnam in early 1974, first President Nixon and then President Gerald Ford stood by because Congress refused to permit any American response. After more than thirty-five years of battle, the Vietnamese communists unified their country in 1975 as a harsh dictatorial state—a second consequence of the U.S. crisis. Third, the belated fall of South Vietnam in the wake of Watergate shook America's postwar pride and confidence. Generally interpreted as a disastrous American military defeat, the Vietnam experience left the United States divided and uncertain. Only gradually did the country recover a sense of purpose in world affairs.

As American self-confidence and influence in world affairs declined, the policy of détente reached its apogee with the Conference on Security and Cooperation in Europe. This thirty-five-nation summit opened deliberations in Helsinki, Finland, in 1973 and after long negotiations it concluded a final agreement in 1975. The Helsinki conference included all European nations (except isolationist Albania), the United States, and Canada, and its Final Act contained important elements of a general European peace treaty, like those signed at Vienna in 1815 and at Versailles in 1919. The Final Act formally stated that Europe's existing political frontiers, including those separating the two Germanies, could not be changed by force, and it provided for increased East-West economic and cultural relations as well. Thus the Atlantic alliance solemnly accepted the territorial status quo in eastern Europe as well as the Soviet Union's gains from World War Two. In return for this major concession, the Soviet Union and its allies agreed to numerous provisions guaranteeing the human rights and political freedoms of their peoples. The Final Act was a compromise embodying Western concerns for human rights and Soviet preoccupations with military security and control of eastern Europe. Optimists saw a bright new day breaking in international relations.

These hopes gradually faded in the later 1970s. The Soviet Union and its eastern allies generally ignored the human rights provisions of the Helsinki agreement in dealing with their citizens. And although the consequences of the eastern policy that Brandt had launched had greatly reduced tensions in Europe, East-West political competition remained very much alive in Africa, Asia, and Central America. Many Americans became convinced that the Soviet Union was taking advantage of détente, steadily building up its military might and pushing for political gains in Africa, Asia, and Latin America. Having been expelled from Egypt by Anwar Sadat after the 1973 war with Israel, the Soviets sought and won toeholds in South Yemen, Somalia, and, later, Ethiopia. Supporting guerrilla wars against the Portuguese in Angola and Mozambique, the Soviet Union was rewarded with Marxian regimes in both countries.

But it was in Afghanistan that Soviet action seemed most contrary to the spirit of détente. The Soviet Union had large Islamic majorities in its central Asian republics and had long been interested in its Islamic neighbor, Afghanistan. In April 1978 a pro-Soviet coup established a Marxian regime there. This new government soon made itself unpopular, and rebellion spread through the countryside. To preserve communist rule, the Soviet

Union in December 1979 suddenly airlifted crack troops to Kabul, the capital, and occupied Afghanistan with 100,000 men. Alarmed by the scale and precision of the Soviet invasion, many Americans feared that the oil-rich states of the Persian Gulf would be next and searched for an appropriate response.

President Jimmy Carter tried to lead the Atlantic alliance beyond verbal condemnation, but among the European allies only Great Britain dutifully fell into line and followed the American policy of economic sanctions against the Soviet Union. France, Italy, and especially West Germany argued that the Soviets' deplorable action in Afghanistan should not be turned into an East-West confrontation. In spite of the growing controversy over Soviet missiles on the continent (see below), European leaders were determined to salvage as much as possible of détente within Europe.

The Atlantic alliance showed the same lack of concerted action when an independent trade union rose in Poland. After the declaration of martial law in Poland in December 1981, western Europe refused again to follow the United States in imposing economic sanctions against Poland and the Soviet Union. Some observers concluded that the alliance had lost the will to think and act decisively in relations with the Soviet bloc. Others noted that occasional dramatic differences within the alliance reflected the fact that the Common Market and the United States had drifted apart and become economic rivals.

Yet despite very real disagreements, the Atlantic alliance, formed in the late 1940s to check Soviet expansion in Europe, endured and revitalized itself in the 1980s. The U.S. military buildup launched by Jimmy Carter in his last years in office was accelerated by President Ronald Reagan, who was swept into office in the 1980 election by the wave of patriotism following an agonizing hostage crisis in Iran and by general dissatisfaction with soaring inflation and sky-high gasoline prices. The new American leadership was convinced that the military balance had tipped in favor of the Soviet Union, which Reagan anathematized as the "evil empire." Increasing defense spending rapidly, the Reagan administration concentrated especially on nuclear arms and an expanded navy as keys to a resurgence of American power in the post-Vietnam era.

A broad swing in the historical pendulum toward greater conservatism gave Reagan important allies in western Europe. New leaders in both Great Britain and West Germany generally shared Reagan's conviction that the Soviet Union remained a dangerous threat.

In Great Britain a strong-willed Margaret Thatcher became prime minister in 1979 after a year of bitter strikes had eroded support for the ruling socialist Labour party. Raised in a family of prosperous grocery store owners, the ambitious and talented Thatcher studied chemistry and then law at Oxford. Marrying a wealthy businessman upon graduation and starting a family, Thatcher quickly achieved success as a lawyer and then entered politics. Becoming the leader of the Conservatives in 1975 and leading her party to victory in 1979, Thatcher saw herself as a brave champion of middle-class values, wide-open capitalism, and frugal government. Welcoming the deep recession of the early 1980s as a way to break inflation and humble Britain's powerful unions, Thatcher infuriated the left, and by 1982 she had become widely unpopular.

But Thatcher bounced back, using to her own advantage the kind of hard-line military position that she often urged on a willing Ronald Reagan. After Argentine forces in 1982 invaded and occupied the Falkland (or Malvinas) Islands, a lonely British possession 500 miles off the coast of Argentina, Thatcher acted decisively. She rejected all compromise, whipped up British patriotism, and sent the fleet to retake the Falklands. In less than two months, the 1,800 Falkland islanders and their 600,000 sheep were "liberated" by British marines, enabling Thatcher to win a solid electoral victory in 1983. Continuing her tough social policies and working well with Reagan, Thatcher was a strong advocate for a revitalized Atlantic alliance.

The situation was more complicated in West Germany. Brandt's eastern initiative was continued by his successor, Helmut Schmidt (b. 1918), who was also a Social Democrat. But like other western leaders, Schmidt had to react when the Soviet Union began installing on its own territory a new medium-range nuclear missile aimed at western Europe in 1977. Reluctantly, and despite large protest demonstrations in the late 1970s, Schmidt agreed that NATO's forces had to be strengthened and that some medium-range American cruise missiles had to be deployed by NATO in western Europe. But Schmidt and his American allies differed on the details. Only after a distinctly pro-American Helmut Kohl (b. 1930) came to power with the conservative Christian Democrats in 1982 did West Germany and the United States once again effectively coordinate military policy toward the Soviet bloc.

Passing from détente to confusion to regeneration, the Atlantic alliance bent, but it did not break. In doing so, Western society gave indirect support to ongoing efforts to liberalize authoritarian communist states in eastern Europe, efforts that after repeated defeats finally burst through in spectacular fashion in the late 1980s.

✥ THE SOVIET BLOC

Occasional differences within the NATO alliance on how to treat the Soviet bloc reflected not only shifts in Soviet conduct in foreign affairs but also ambiguities in the course of developments within eastern Europe itself. On the one hand, attempts to liberalize the system continued, and the brutality of the Stalinist era was never re-established after Nikita Khrushchev fell from power in 1964. These changes encouraged Western hopes of gradual liberalization and of a more democratic, less threatening Soviet eastern Europe.

On the other hand, hard facts frequently intervened to undermine these hopes. In addition to periodic threats and military action, the Soviet Union repeatedly demonstrated that it remained a harsh and aggressive dictatorship that paid only lip service to egalitarian ideology and was determined to uphold its rule throughout eastern Europe. Periodic efforts to achieve fundamental political change were doomed to failure sooner or later. Or so it seemed to most Western experts into the middle of the 1980s.

And then Mikhail Gorbachev burst on the scene. The new Soviet leader opened an era of reform that was as sweeping as it was unexpected. Many believed that Gorbachev would soon fall from power and that his reforms would fail in the Soviet Union. In fact, the scope of reform expanded, became more radical, and eventually culminated in revolution in eastern Europe in 1989. Communism collapsed, falling even in the Soviet Union. The peoples of eastern Eastern made a decisive breakthrough toward greater personal freedom and political democracy, although many problems remained.

Facilitated initially by Gorbachev's initiatives, the triumph of reform and democratic revolution in

✥ **Margaret Thatcher and Ronald Reagan** meet at the White House on an official state visit. The two leaders worked well together, united by a fierce determination to oppose communism abroad and to reduce spending on social programs at home. *(Source: Brad Markel/Liaison)*

eastern Europe was based on powerful historical forces. Above all, reform and revolution were the results of long-standing campaigns to humanize communism and of a social transformation in the Soviet Union. That transformation made rigid one-party dictatorship counterproductive and probably obsolete.

The Soviet Union to 1985

The 1968 invasion of Czechoslovakia (see pages 1036–37) was the crucial event of the Brezhnev era, a period that actually lasted beyond the aging leader's death in 1982 until the emergence in 1985 of Gorbachev. The invasion demonstrated unmistakably the intense conservatism of the Soviet Union's ruling elite and its determination to maintain the status quo in the Soviet bloc.

Indeed, the aftermath of intervention in Czechoslovakia also brought a certain re-Stalinization of the U.S.S.R. But now dictatorship was collective rather than personal, and coercion replaced uncontrolled terror. This compromise seemed to suit the leaders and a majority of the people, and the Soviet Union appeared stable in the 1970s and early 1980s.

A slowly rising standard of living for ordinary people contributed to stability, although the economic crisis of the 1970s greatly slowed the rate of improvement, and long lines and innumerable shortages persisted. The enduring differences between the life of the elite and the life of ordinary people also reinforced the system. Ambitious individuals still had tremendous incentive to do as the state wished in order to gain access to special, well-stocked stores; to attend special schools; and to travel abroad.

Another source of stability was the enduring nationalism of ordinary Great Russians. Party leaders successfully identified themselves with Russian patriotism, stressing their role in saving the country during the Second World War and protecting it now from foreign foes, including eastern European "counter-revolutionaries." Moreover, the politically dominant Great Russians, who are concentrated in the central Russian heartland and in Siberia (which are formally designated as the Russian Federation) and who also held through the Communist Party the commanding leadership positions in the non-Russian republics, constituted less than half of the total Soviet population. The Great Russians generally feared that greater freedom and open political competition might therefore result in demands for autonomy and even independence not only by eastern European nationalities but also by the non-Russian nationalities of the smaller republics and the autonomous regions within the Soviet Union itself. Thus liberalism and democracy generally appeared as alien political philosophies designed to undermine the U.S.S.R.'s power and greatness.

The strength of the government was expressed in the re-Stalinization of culture and art. Free expression and open protest disappeared. In 1968 when a small group of dissenters appeared in Red Square to protest the invasion of Czechoslovakia, they were arrested before they could unfurl their banners. This proved to be the high point of dissent, for in the 1970s Brezhnev and company made certain that Soviet intellectuals did not engage in public protest. Acts of open nonconformity and protest were severely punished, but with sophisticated, cunning methods.

Most frequently, dissidents were blacklisted and thus rendered unable to find a decent job since the government was the only employer. This fate was enough to keep most in line. More determined but unrenowned protesters were quietly imprisoned in jails or mental institutions. Celebrated nonconformists such as Aleksandr Solzhenitsyn were permanently expelled from the country. Once again, Jews were persecuted as a "foreign" element, though some were eventually permitted to emigrate to Israel. As the distinguished Russian dissident historian Roy Medvedev explained in the mid-1970s:

The technology of repression has become more refined in recent years. Before, repression always went much further than necessary. Stalin killed millions of people when arresting 1,000 would have enabled him to control the people. Our leaders . . . found out eventually that you don't have to put people in prison or in a psychiatric hospital to silence them. There are other ways.[4]

Eliminating the worst aspects of Stalin's dictatorship strengthened the regime, and rule by a self-perpetuating communist elite in the Soviet Union appeared to be quite solid in the 1970s and early 1980s.

Yet beneath the dreary immobility of political life in the Brezhnev era the Soviet Union was experiencing profound changes. As a perceptive British journalist put it in 1986, "The country went through a social revolution while Brezhnev slept."[5] Three aspects of this revolution, which was seldom appreciated by Western observers at the time, were particularly significant.

First, the growth of the urban population, which had raced forward at breakneck speed in the Stalin years, continued rapidly in the 1960s and 1970s. In 1985 two-thirds of all Soviet citizens lived in cities, and one-quarter lived in big cities (see Map 31.2). Of great significance, this expanding urban population lost its old peasant ways, exchanging them for more education, better job skills, and greater sophistication.

Second, the number of highly trained scientists, managers, and specialists expanded prodigiously, increasing fourfold between 1960 and 1985. Thus the class of well-educated, pragmatic, and self-confident experts, which played such an important role in restructuring industrial societies after World War Two (see pages 1028–29), developed rapidly in the Soviet Union. Moreover, leading Soviet scientists and technologists sought membership in the international "invisible college" of their disciplines, like their colleagues in the West. Correspondingly, they sought the intellectual freedom necessary to do significant work, and they often obtained it because their research had practical (and military) value.

Third, education and freedom for experts in their special areas helped foster the growth of Soviet public opinion, just as the reading revolution of the eighteenth century had encouraged the development of independent public opinion in France. Educated people read, discussed, and formed definite ideas about social questions. And if caution dictated conventional ideas (at least in public), many important issues could be approached and debated in "nonpolitical" terms. Developing definite ideas on such issues as environmental pollution or urban transportation, educated urban people increasingly saw themselves as worthy of having a voice in society's decisions, even its political decisions. This, too, was part of the quiet transformation that set the stage for the Gorbachev era.

Solidarity in Poland

Gorbachev's reforms interacted with the growth of popular protest in the Soviet Union's satellite empire. Developments in Poland were most striking and significant. There workers joined together en masse to fight peacefully for freedom and self-determination, while the world watched in amazement. Crushed in the short run but refusing to admit defeat, Polish workers waged a long campaign that inspired and reflected a powerful reform current in eastern Europe.

Poland was an unruly satellite from the beginning. Stalin said that introducing communism to Poland was like putting a saddle on a cow. Efforts to saddle the cow—really a spirited stallion—led to widespread riots in 1956 (see pages 1023–24). As a result, Polish communists dropped efforts to impose Soviet-style collectivization on the peasants and to break the Roman Catholic church. Most agricultural land remained in private hands, and the Catholic church thrived. With an independent peasant agriculture and a vigorous church, the communists failed to monopolize society.

They also failed to manage the economy effectively. Even the booming 1960s saw little eco-

Kalinin Avenue in Moscow, 1978 This broad boulevard teeming with pedestrians captures some of the spirit of life in large Soviet cities in the 1970s. It suggests how the transformation of a complex, well-educated society rushed forward even as Brezhnev slept and the Communist oligarchy squelched all open dissent. *(Source: TASS/ Sovfoto)*

nomic improvement. When the government suddenly announced large price increases right before Christmas in 1970, Poland's working class rose again in angry protest. Factories were occupied and strikers were shot, but a new communist leader came to power nevertheless. The government then wagered that massive inflows of Western capital and technology, especially from Willy Brandt's rich and now-friendly West Germany, could produce a Polish "economic miracle" that would win popular support for the regime. Instead, bureaucratic incompetence coupled with worldwide recession had

❖ **Lech Walesa and Solidarity**
An inspiration for fellow workers at the Lenin Shipyards in
the dramatic and successful
strike against the Communist
bosses in August 1980,
Walesa played a key role in
Solidarity before and after it
was outlawed. Speaking here
to old comrades at the Lenin
Shipyards after Solidarity was
again legalized in 1988,
Walesa personified an enduring opposition to Communist
rule in eastern Europe.
(Source: Merrillon/Liaison)

put the economy into a nose dive by the mid-
1970s. Workers, intellectuals, and the church became increasingly restive. Then the real Polish miracle occurred: Cardinal Karol Wojtyla, archbishop
of Cracow, was elected pope in 1978. In June
1979 he returned from Rome for an astonishing
pilgrimage across his native land. Preaching love of
Christ and country and the "inalienable rights of
man," Pope John Paul II drew enormous crowds
and electrified the Polish nation. The economic
crisis became a moral and spiritual crisis as well.

In August 1980 as scattered strikes to protest
higher meat prices spread, the sixteen thousand
workers at the gigantic Lenin Shipyards in Gdansk
(formerly known as Danzig) laid down their tools
and occupied the showpiece plant. As other workers along the Baltic coast joined "in solidarity," the
strikers advanced truly revolutionary demands: the
right to form free trade unions, the right to strike,
freedom of speech, release of political prisoners,
and economic reforms. After eighteen days of ship-
yard occupation, as families brought food to the
gates and priests said mass daily amid huge over-
head cranes, the government gave in and accepted
the workers' demands in the Gdansk Agreement.
In a state where the Communist party claimed to
rule on behalf of the proletariat, a working-class
revolt had won an unprecedented victory.

Led by feisty Lenin Shipyards electrician and
devout Catholic Lech Walesa (b. 1943), the workers proceeded to organize their free and demo-

cratic trade union. They called it "Solidarity."
Joined by intellectuals and supported by the
Catholic church, Solidarity became the union of a
nation. By March 1981 it had a membership of 9.5
million, of 12.5 million who were theoretically
eligible. A full-time staff of forty thousand linked
the union members together as Solidarity published its own newspapers and cultural and intellectual freedom blossomed in Poland. Solidarity's
leaders had tremendous, well-organized support,
and the threat of calling a nationwide strike gave
them real power in ongoing negotiations with the
communist bosses.

But if Solidarity had power, it did not try to take
power in 1981. History, the Brezhnev Doctrine,
and virulent attacks from communist neighbors all
seemed to guarantee the intervention of the Red
Army and a terrible bloodbath if Polish communists "lost control." Thus the Solidarity revolution
remained a "self-limiting revolution" aimed at defending the cultural and trade-union freedoms won
in the Gdansk Agreement without directly challenging the communist monopoly of political
power.

Solidarity's combination of strength and moderation postponed a showdown. The Soviet Union,
already facing sharp criticism for its European missile policy and condemned worldwide for its invasion of Afghanistan, played a waiting game of
threats and pressure. After a crisis in March 1981
that followed police beatings of Solidarity activists,

Walesa settled for minor government concessions, and Solidarity again dropped plans for a massive general strike. This marked a turning point. Criticism of Walesa's moderate leadership and calls for local self-government in unions and factories grew. Solidarity lost its cohesiveness. The worsening economic crisis also encouraged grassroots radicalism and frustration: a hunger-march banner proclaimed, "A hungry nation can eat its rulers."[6] With an eye on Western and especially West German opinion leaders, who generally preferred tyranny to instability in eastern Europe (although they seldom admitted this fact), the Polish communist leadership shrewdly denounced Solidarity for promoting economic collapse and provoking Soviet invasion. In December 1981 Communist leader General Wojciech Jaruzelski suddenly struck in the dead of subfreezing night, proclaiming martial law, cutting all communications, arresting Solidarity's leaders, and "saving" the nation.

Outlawed and driven underground, Solidarity fought successfully to maintain its organization and to voice the aspirations of the Polish masses after 1981. Part of the reason for the union's survival was the government's unwillingness (and probably its inability) to impose full-scale terror. Moreover, in schools and shops, in factories and offices, millions decided to continue acting as if they were free, even though they were not. Therefore, cultural and intellectual life remained extremely vigorous in spite of renewed repression. At the same time, the faltering Polish economy, battered by the global recession of the early 1980s and crippled by a disastrous brain drain after 1981, continued to deteriorate. Thus popular support for outlawed Solidarity remained strong and deep under martial law in the 1980s, preparing the way for the union's resurgence toward the end of the decade.

The rise and survival of Solidarity showed again the fierce desire of millions of eastern Europeans for greater political liberty. The union's strength also demonstrated the enduring appeal of cultural freedom, trade-union rights, patriotic nationalism, and religious feeling. Not least, Solidarity's challenge encouraged fresh thinking in the Soviet Union, ever the key to lasting change in the Eastern bloc.

Reform in the Soviet Union

Fundamental change in Russian history has often come in short, intensive spurts, which contrast vividly with long periods of immobility. We have studied four of these spurts: the ambitious "westernization" of Peter the Great in the early eighteenth century (see pages 578–579), the great reforms connected with the freeing of the serfs in the mid-nineteenth century (see pages 846–848), the Russian Revolution of 1917 (see pages 919–924), and Stalin's wrenching "revolution from above" in the 1930s (see pages 973–976). To this select list of decisive transformations, we must now add the era of reform launched by Mikhail Gorbachev in 1985. Gorbachev's initiatives brought political and cultural liberalization in the Soviet Union, and they then permitted democracy and national self-determination to triumph spectacularly in the old satellite empire and eventually in the Soviet Union itself.

As we have seen, the Soviet Union's communist elite seemed secure in the early 1980s as far as any challenge from below was concerned. The long-established system of administrative controls continued to stretch downward from the central ministries and state committees to provincial cities, and from there to factories, neighborhoods, and villages. At each level of this massive state bureaucracy, the overlapping hierarchy of the Communist party, with its 17.5 million members, continued to watch over all decisions and manipulate every aspect of national life. Organized opposition was impossible, and average people simply left politics to the bosses.

Yet the massive state and party bureaucracy was a mixed blessing. It safeguarded the elite, but it also promoted apathy in the masses. Discouraging personal initiative and economic efficiency, it was also ill-suited to secure the effective cooperation of the rapidly growing class of well-educated urban experts. Therefore, when the ailing Brezhnev finally died in 1982, his successor, the long-time chief of the secret police, Yuri Andropov (1914–1984), tried to invigorate the system. Andropov introduced modest reforms to improve economic performance and campaigned against worker absenteeism and high-level corruption. Relatively little came of these efforts, but they combined with a sharply worsening economic situation to set the stage for the emergence in 1985 of Mikhail Gorbachev (b. 1931), the most vigorous Soviet leader in a generation.

Trained as a lawyer and working his way up as a Communist official in the northern Caucasus, where he caught the attention of Andropov and other senior party members, Gorbachev was smart, charming, and tough. As long-time Soviet foreign minister Andrei Gromyko reportedly said, "This man has a nice smile, but he has got iron teeth."[7] Gorbachev was also an idealist. He believed in communism, but he realized it was failing. He (and his intelligent, influential wife, Resa, a dedicated professor of Marxist-Leninist thought) wanted to

Newly Elected President Mikhail Gorbachev vowed in his acceptance speech before the Supreme Soviet, the U.S.S.R.'s parliament, to assume "all responsibility" for the success or failure of *perestroika.* Previous parliaments were no more than tools of the Communist party, but this one actively debated and even opposed government programs. *(Source: Vlastimir Shone/Gamma-Liaison)*

save the Soviet system by improving it with fundamental reforms. And Gorbachev realized full well that success at home required better relations with the West, for the endless waste and senselessness of the arms race had had a disastrous impact on living standards in the Soviet Union.

In his first year in office, Gorbachev attacked corruption and incompetence in the bureaucracy, and he consolidated his power by packing the top level of the party with his supporters. He attacked alcoholism and drunkenness, which were deadly scourges of Soviet society. More basically, he elaborated his ambitious reform program.

The first set of reform policies was designed to transform and restructure the economy, which produced too much for the military and which was falling ever further behind that of the West as it failed to provide for the real needs of the Soviet population. To accomplish this economic "restructuring," this *perestroika,* Gorbachev and his supporters permitted freer prices, more independence for state enterprises, and the setting up of profit-seeking private cooperatives to provide personal services for consumers. These reforms initially produced some improvements, but shortages then grew as the economy stalled at an intermediate point between central planning and free-market mechanisms. By 1990 Gorbachev's timid economic initiatives had met with very little success, posing a serious threat to his leadership and the entire reform program.

Gorbachev's bold and far-reaching campaign "to tell it like it is" was much more successful. Very popular in a country where censorship, dull uniformity, and outright lies had long characterized public discourse, the newfound "openness," or *glasnost,* of the government and the media marked an astonishing break with the past. A disaster such as the Chernobyl nuclear accident in 1986, which devastated part of Ukraine and showered Europe with radioactive fallout, was investigated and reported with honesty and painstaking thoroughness. The works of long-banned and vilified émigré writers sold millions of copies in new editions, while denunciations of Stalin and his terror became standard fare in plays and movies. Thus initial openness in government pronouncements quickly went further than Gorbachev intended and led to something approaching free speech and free expression, a veritable cultural revolution.

Democratization was the third element of reform. Beginning as an attack on corruption in the

Communist party and as an attempt to bring the class of educated experts into the decision-making process, it led to the first free elections in the Soviet Union since 1917. Gorbachev and the party remained in control, but a minority of critical independents were elected in April 1989 to a revitalized Congress of People's Deputies. Many top-ranking communists who ran unopposed saw themselves defeated as a majority of angry voters struck their names from the ballot. Millions of Soviets then watched the new congress for hours on television as Gorbachev and his ministers saw their proposals debated and even rejected.

Democratization also encouraged demands for greater autonomy by non-Russian minorities, especially in the Baltic region and in the Caucasus. These demands certainly went beyond what Gorbachev had envisaged. In April 1989 troops with sharpened shovels charged into a rally of Georgian separatists in Tbilisi and left twenty dead. But whereas China's Communist leaders brutally massacred similar prodemocracy demonstrators in Beijing in June 1989 and reimposed rigid authoritarian rule, Gorbachev drew back from repression. Thus nationalist demands continued to grow in the non-Russian Soviet republics.

Finally, the Soviet leader brought and acted on "new political thinking" to the field of foreign affairs. He withdrew Soviet troops from Afghanistan, encouraged reform movements in Poland and Hungary, and sought to reduce East-West tensions. Of enormous and immediate importance, Gorbachev pledged to respect the political choices of the peoples of eastern Europe. He thereby repudiated the Brezhnev Doctrine, which had arrogantly proclaimed the right of the Soviet Union and its allies to intervene at will in eastern Europe. By 1989 it seemed that, if Gorbachev held to his word, the tragic Soviet occupation of eastern Europe might well wither away, taking the long cold war with it once and for all.

The Revolutions of 1989

Instead, history accelerated, and 1989 brought a series of largely peaceful revolutions throughout eastern Europe (Map 31.2). These revolutions overturned existing communist regimes and ended the Communist party's monopoly of power. Revolutionary mass demonstrations led to the formation of provisional governments dedicated to democratic elections, human rights, and national rejuvenation. Watched on television in the Soviet Union and around the world, these stirring events marked the triumph and the transformation of the long-standing reform movement we have been considering in this chapter.

Solidarity and the Polish people again led the way. In 1988 widespread labor unrest, raging inflation, and the outlawed Solidarity's refusal to cooperate with the military government had brought Poland to the brink of economic collapse. Profiting from Gorbachev's tolerant attitude and skillfully mobilizing forces, Solidarity pressured Poland's frustrated communist leaders into another round of negotiations that might work out a sharing of power to resolve the political stalemate and the economic crisis. The subsequent agreement legalized Solidarity again after eight long years. The agreement also declared that a large minority of representatives to the Polish parliament would be chosen by free elections in June 1989. The Communist party was still guaranteed a majority, but Solidarity won every single contested seat in an overwhelming victory. On July 4, 1989, Solidarity members jubilantly entered the 460-member Polish parliament, the first freely elected opposition in a communist country. A month later the editor of Solidarity's weekly newspaper was sworn in as the first noncommunist leader in eastern Europe since Stalin used Soviet armies to impose his system there after the Second World War.

Hungary followed Poland. Hungary's Communist boss, János Kádár, had permitted liberalization of the rigid planned economy after the 1956 uprising in exchange for political obedience and continued communist control. In May 1988 in an effort to hang on to power by granting modest political concessions, the party replaced Kádár with a reform Communist. But growing popular resistance rejected piecemeal progress, forcing the Communist party to renounce one-party rule and schedule free elections for early 1990. Welcoming Western investment and moving rapidly toward multiparty democracy, Hungarians gleefully tore down the barbed-wire "iron curtain" with Austria and opened their border to East German refugees.

As thousands of dissatisfied East Germans began pouring into Hungary, before going on to immediate resettlement in thriving West Germany, growing economic dislocation and huge candlelight demonstrations brought revolution in East Berlin. The Berlin Wall was opened, and people danced

and his family and tried to seize the Soviet government in August 1991. But the attempted coup collapsed in the face of massive popular resistance, which rallied in Moscow around Boris Yeltsin, the popularly elected president of the Russian Federation. Gorbachev was rescued and returned to power as head of the Soviet Union.

The leaders of the coup wanted to preserve communist power and the multinational Soviet Union, but they succeeded only in destroying both. An anticommunist revolution swept the Russian Federation as the Communist party was outlawed and its property confiscated. Locked in personal and political duel with Gorbachev, Yeltsin and his liberal allies declared Russia independent and withdrew from the Soviet Union. All the other Soviet republics followed suit; the Soviet Union—and Gorbachev's job—ceased to exist on December 25, 1991 (Map 31.3). Of course, the independent republics of the old Soviet Union were bound together by innumerable ties. A loose but indispensable confederation, christened the Commonwealth of Independent States, was established in 1992, but its future was anything but clear. Above all, many historians speculated that the new Russia, which often harkened back to nationalistic and prerevolutionary symbols, would eventually seek to reclaim the tsarist inheritance and bring the supposedly independent states of the commonwealth under Moscow's control.

Developments in the early 1990s did little to end such speculation, for three reasons. First, ethnic tensions abounded in the Commonwealth of Independent States, and localized civil war threatened to spread from Georgia and Armenia. Second, the Russian economy continued to decline, leading to rapid inflation and intense hardship for millions of ordinary people. Third, ethnic conflict, economic collapse, and political stalemate encouraged millions of dissatisfied Russians to vote against the democratic reforms in the general elections of December 1993. The old communists made a strong comeback, and a flamboyant ultranationalist named Vladimir Zhirinovsky captured a surprisingly large share of the vote. The ultimate fate of Russia and the states of the old Soviet Union remained uncertain.

✛ THE FUTURE IN PERSPECTIVE

What about the future? For centuries astrologers and scientists, experts and ordinary people, have sought to answer this question. Although it may seem that the study of the past has little to say about the future, the study of history over a long period is actually very useful in this regard. It helps put the future in perspective.

Certainly, history is full of erroneous predictions, a few of which we have mentioned in this book.

✛ **"A Strong President, a Strong Russia"** That is the message on the poster on the left, as these Yeltsin supporters urge the Russian president to stand firm and provide strong leadership. The new Russia faces enormous challenges, but it has already made truly remarkable progress toward personal freedom and democratic government. *(Source: Haviv/Saba)*

♦ **Map 31.3 The End of the Soviet Union** After the attempt in August 1991 to depose Gorbachev failed, an anticommunist revolution swept the Soviet Union. Led by Russia and Boris Yeltsin, the republics that formed the Soviet Union declared their sovereignty and independence. Most of the fifteen republics then formed a loose confederation with an uncertain future, the Commonwealth of Independent States.

Yet lack of success has not diminished the age-old desire to look into the future. Self-proclaimed experts even pretend that they have created a new science of futurology. With great pomposity they often act as if their hunches and guesses about future human developments are inescapable realities. Yet the study of history teaches healthy skepticism regarding such predictions, however scientific they may appear. Past results suggest that most such predictions will simply not come true or not in the anticipated way. Thus history provides some psychological protection from the fantastic visions of modern prognosticators.

This protection has been particularly valuable in recent years because many recent projections into the future have been quite pessimistic, just as they were very optimistic in the 1950s and 1960s. Many people in the Western world have feared that con-

ditions are going to get worse rather than better. For example, there have been fears that trade wars will permanently cripple the world economy, that pollution will destroy the environment, and that the traditional family will disappear. Until recently, many experts and politicians were predicting that the energy crisis—in the form of skyrocketing oil prices—meant disaster in the form of lower standards of living at best and the collapse of civilization at worst. Then some of these same experts worried that the unexpectedly sharp decline in oil prices in the early 1980s would bankrupt both low-income oil producers, such as Mexico, and the large American banks that had lent them so much money. In fact, both the oil producers and the big banks muddled through and show few signs of collapsing. It is heartening to know that most such dire predictions do not prove true, just as the same

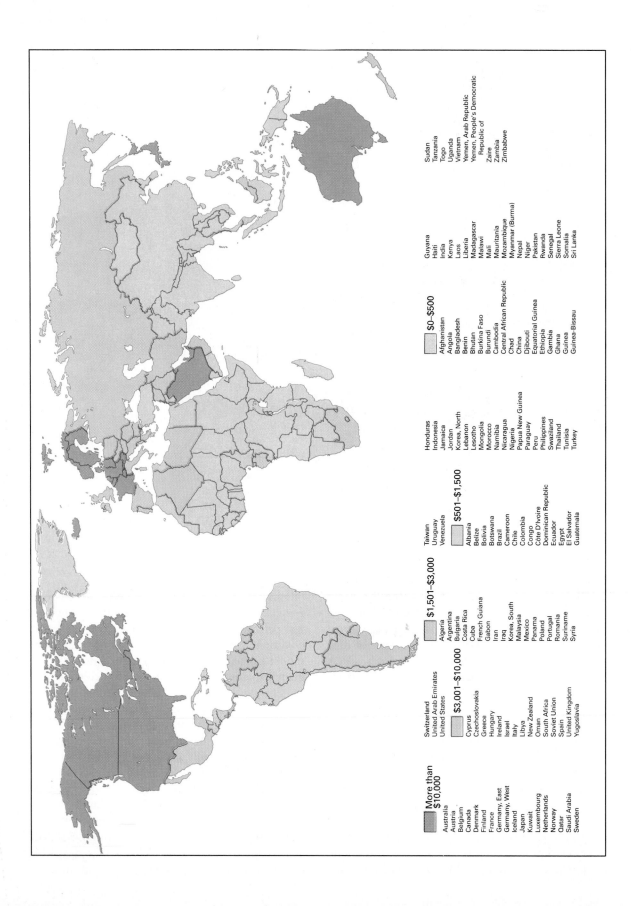

knowledge of likely error is sobering in times of optimistic expectations.

One of the more frightening and pessimistic predictions recently in vogue has been that the northern nations of Europe and North America will increasingly find themselves locked in a life-and-death struggle with the poor, overpopulated southern nations of Africa, Asia, and South America. This North-South conflict, it has been predicted, will replace the old cold war struggle of East and West with a much more dangerous, international class and racial conflict of rich versus poor, white versus nonwhite. Such, it is said, is the bitter legacy of Western imperialism.

As Map 31.4 shows, there is indeed an enormous gap between the very wealthy nations of western Europe and North America and the very poor nations of much of Africa and Asia. Yet closer examination does not reveal a growing split between two sharply defined economic camps. On the contrary, there are five or six distinct categories of nations in terms of income level. Several countries in eastern Europe form something of a middle-income group, despite their serious economic problems and long decades of communist dictatorship and mismanagement. So do the major oil-exporting states, which are still behind the wealthier countries of western Europe. Poverty in parts of Latin America is severe, but, as the map shows, standards of living are substantially higher there than in much of Africa and Asia, both of which encompass considerable economic variation.

When we consider differences in culture, religion, politics, and historical development, the supposed split between rich and poor nations breaks down still further. Thus a global class war between rich and poor appears unlikely in the foreseeable future. A more reasonable expectation is continuing pressure to reduce international economic differences through taxation and welfare measures, as has already occurred domestically in the wealthy nations. Such pressure may well bring at least modest success, for the wealthy nations generally realize that an exclusively Western (or Northern) viewpoint on global issues is unrealistic and self-defeating. The true legacy of Western imperialism is one small world.

⊹ **MAP 31.4 Estimated GNP per Capita Income in the Early 1980s**

It is this that made the nuclear arms race so ominous. Not only did the United States and the Soviet Union accumulate unbelievably destructive, ever-expanding nuclear arsenals, but Great Britain, France, China, and India all also unlocked the secret of "the bomb," and probably Israel and South Africa did so as well. Other countries became equipped or desired to "go nuclear." Thus some gloomy experts predicted that twenty or thirty states might have nuclear weapons by the end of the century. In a world plagued by local wars and ferocious regional conflicts, these experts concluded that nuclear war is almost inevitable and speculated that the human race is an "endangered species."

Yet such predictions and the undeniable seriousness of the arms race jolted Western populations out of their customary fatalism regarding nuclear weapons. Efforts to reduce or even halt the nuclear buildup in the Soviet Union and the NATO alliance made some real progress. Above all, the Gorbachev era in the Soviet Union opened the way to new thinking and genuine superpower cooperation on nuclear arms questions. This cooperation accelerated after the fall of communism in eastern Europe. Germany formally promised never to build nuclear arms as part of the price of German unification. Organized efforts to stop maverick states, such as Iraq or North Korea, from getting nuclear weapons have been going forward. An optimist can hope that these efforts and worldwide concern represent the global political will necessary to control nuclear proliferation in the future.

Whatever does or does not happen, the study of history puts the future in perspective in other ways. We have seen that every age has its problems and challenges. Others before us have trod these paths of crisis and uncertainty. This knowledge helps save us from exaggerated self-pity in the face of our own predicaments.

Perhaps our Western heritage may even inspire us with pride and measured self-confidence. We stand, momentarily, at the end of the long procession of Western civilization. Sometimes the procession has wandered, or backtracked, or done terrible things. But it has also carried the efforts and sacrifices of generations of toiling, struggling ancestors. Through no effort of our own, we are the beneficiaries of those sacrifices and achievements. Now that it is our turn to carry the torch onward, we may remember these ties with our forebears.

To change the metaphor, we in the West are like a card player who has been dealt many good cards. Some of them are obvious, such as our technical and scientific heritage or our commitments to human rights and the individual. Others are not so obvious, sometimes half-forgotten, or even hidden up the sleeve. Think, for example, of the Christian Democrats, the moderate Catholic party that emerged after World War Two to play such an important role in the western European renaissance. And in the almost miraculous victory of peaceful revolution in eastern Europe in 1989—in what the Czech playwright-turned-president Václav Havel called "the power of the powerless"—we see again the regenerative strength of the Western ideals of individual rights, representative government, and nationhood in the European homeland. We hold a good hand.

Our study of history, of mighty struggles and fearsome challenges, of shining achievements and tragic failures, gives a sense of what is the essence of life itself: the process of change over time. Again and again we have seen how peoples and societies evolve, influenced by ideas, human passions, and material conditions. As surely as anything is sure, this process of change over time will continue as the future becomes the present and then the past. And students of history are better prepared to make sense of this unfolding process because they have already observed it. They know how change is rooted in existing historical forces, and their projections will probably be better than many of the self-serving speculations of futurologists. Students of history are also prepared for the new and unexpected in human development, for they have already seen great breakthroughs and revolutions. They have an understanding of how things really happen.

Notes

1. *Wall Street Journal,* June 25, 1985, p. 1.
2. S. Rose and D. Fasenfest, *Family Income in the 1980s: New Pressures on Wives, Husbands and Young Adults* (Washington, D.C.: Economic Policy Institute, 1988), pp. 5–8.
3. Quoted in Kessing's Research Report, *Germany and East Europe Since 1945: From the Potsdam Agreement to Chancellor Brandt's "Ostpolitik"* (New York: Charles Scribner's Sons, 1973), pp. 284–285.
4. Quoted in H. Smith, *The Russians* (New York: Quadrangle Books/New York Times, 1976), pp. 455–456.
5. M. Walker, *The Waking Giant: Gorbachev's Russia* (New York: Pantheon Books, 1987), p. 175.
6. T. G. Ash, *The Polish Revolution: Solidarity* (New York: Charles Scribner's Sons, 1983), p. 186.
7. Quoted in *Time,* January 6, 1986, p. 66.

Suggested Reading

Many of the studies cited in the Suggested Reading for Chapter 30 are of value for the years since 1968 as well. Journalistic accounts in major newspapers and magazines are also invaluable tools for an understanding of recent developments. Among general works, W. Laqueur, *Europe in Our Time, A History, 1945–1992* (1992), and F. Gilbert, *The End of the European Era: 1890 to the Present* (1991), are particularly helpful with their even-handed accounts and extensive, up-to-date bibliographies. The culture and politics of protest are provocatively analyzed in H. Hughes, *Sophisticated Rebels: The Political Culture of European Dissent, 1968–1987* (1988). B. Jones, *The Making of Contemporary Europe* (1980), is a good brief account; G. Parker, *The Logic of Unity* (1975), analyzes the forces working for and against European integration. D. Swann, *The Economics of the Common Market* (1984), carries developments into the 1980s. L. Barzini, *The Europeans* (1983), draws engaging group portraits of the different European peoples and is strongly recommended. On West Germany, H. Turner, *The Two Germanies Since 1945: East and West* (1987), and L. Whetten, *Germany's Ostpolitik* (1971), are useful introductions. Willy Brandt eloquently states his case for reconciliation with the East in *A Peace Policy for Europe* (1969). W. Laqueur, *The Germans* (1985), is a highly recommended contemporary report by a famous historian doubling as a journalist. P. Jenkins, *Mrs. Thatcher's Revolution: The End of the Socialist Era* (1988), and D. Singer, *Is Socialism Doomed? The Meaning of Mitterrand* (1988), are provocative studies on Great Britain and France in the 1980s.

For developments in Poland, M. Kaufman, *Mad Dreams, Saving Graces: Poland, a Nation in Conspiracy* (1989), carries developments through the summer of 1989, whereas R. Leslie, *The History of Poland Since 1863* (1981), provides long-term perspective. T. Ash's book cited in the Notes is the best early study of Solidarity, and it and more recent books by Ash are highly recommended. They may be compared with a less sympathetic account by N. Ascherson, *The Polish August: The Self-Limiting Revolution* (1982). A. Bramberg, ed., *Poland: Genesis of a Revolution* (1983), is a valuable collection of documents, with extensive commentary.

On the Soviet Union, in addition to works cited in Chapter 30, D. Shipler, *Russia: Broken Idols, Solemn Dreams* (1983), is a solid report by an American journalist, whereas A. Shevchenko, *Breaking with Moscow* (1985), is the altogether fascinating autobiography of a top Soviet diplomat who defected to the United States. A. De Porte, *Europe Between the Superpowers: The Enduring Balance* (1979), and J. Hough and M. Fainsod, *How the Soviet Union Is Governed* (1979), are major scholarly studies of the Soviet Union in the Brezhnev era. S. White, *Gorbachev and After* (1991), is good analysis of changes in the Soviet Union. M. Lewin, *The Gorbachev Phenomenon: A Historical Interpretation* (1988), is excellent on the origins of the reforms; Walker's book cited in the Notes is a fascinating eyewitness account of Soviet life in the mid-1980s. B. Eklof, *Soviet Briefing: Gorbachev and the Reform Period* (1989), focuses on 1987, a critical year. The *New York Times* provided excellent coverage of the revolutions of 1989 and continues to examine carefully fast-breaking developments in eastern Europe and in the Soviet Union.

Among innumerable works on recent economic developments, L. Thurow, *The Zero-Sum Society* (1981), is an interesting example of early 1980s pessimism in the United States, and it may be compared with the engaging and informative work by J. Eatwell, *Whatever Happened to Britain? The Economics of Decline* (1982). W. Rostow, *The World Economy: History and Prospect* (1977), is a massive scholarly tome by a perennial optimist, and P. Hawkins, *The Next Economy* (1983), contains intelligent insights that merit consideration by the ordinary citizen. Three major intellectual works, which are rather somber in their projections, are R. Heilbroner, *An Inquiry into the Human Prospect* (1974), and J. Revel, *The Totalitarian Temptation* (1977) and *How Democracies Perish* (1983). An interesting recent work, F. Fukuyama, *The End of History and the Last Man* (1992), illustrates the general euphoria after the collapse of communism, arguing that democratic capitalism has defeated all its competitors.

General studies on women include B. Smith, *Changing Lives: Women in European History Since 1700* (1989), which provides a good overview and a current bibliography. E. Sullerot, *Women, Society and Change* (1971), is an outstanding introduction to women's evolving role after 1945; R. Patia, ed., *Women in the Modern World* (1967), compares women's situations in many countries. Two extremely influential books on women and their new awareness are S. de Beauvoir, *The Second Sex* (1962), and B. Friedan, *The Feminine Mystique* (1963). These may be compared with C. Lasch, *Haven in a Heartless World* (1977), and A. Cherlin, *Marriage, Divorce, Remarriage* (1981), which interpret changes in the American family. P. Robinson, *The Modernization of Sex* (1976), tells the fascinating story of the American investigators who helped change public attitudes by studying human sexual relations "scientifically."

On feminism and the women's movement, see N. Cott, *The Grounding of Modern Feminism* (1987). J. Lovenduski, *Women and European Politics: Contemporary Feminism and Public Policy* (1986), provides an extremely useful comparative study of similar developments in different countries. The women's movement in Italy is considered in L. Birnbaum, *Liberazione de la Donna* (1986), which is written in English despite the Italian title. C. Duchen, *Feminism in France: From May '68 to Mitterrand* (1986), is also recommended. L. Appignanesi, *Simone de Beauvoir* (1988), is a readable study of the life and thought of the famous thinker. Good studies on British women include E. Wilson, *Only Halfway to Paradise: Women in Postwar Britain, 1945–1968* (1980), and M. Barrett, *Women's Opposition Today* (1980). U. Frevert, *Women in German History: From Bourgeois Emancipation to Sexual Liberation* (1989), is both learned and engaging. Two good studies on Soviet women before the collapse of communism are F. DuPlessix Gray, *Soviet Women* (1989), and T. Mamonova, ed., *Women and Russia* (1986). C. Goldin, *Understanding the Gender Gap: An Economic History of American Women* (1989), provides a provocative economic analysis of women's issues.

A Feminist Critique of Marriage

Having grown up in Paris in a middle-class family and become a teacher, novelist, and intellectual, Simone de Beauvoir (1908–1986) turned increasingly to feminist concerns after World War Two. Her most influential work was The Second Sex *(1949), a massive declaration of independence for contemporary women.*

As an existentialist, de Beauvoir believed that all individuals must accept responsibility for their lives and strive to overcome the tragic dilemmas they face. Studying the experience of woman since antiquity, de Beauvoir argued that man had generally used education and social conditioning to create a dependent "other," a negative nonman who was not permitted to grow and strive for freedom.

Marriage—on the man's terms—was part of this unjust and undesirable process. De Beauvoir's conclusion that some couples could establish free and equal unions was based in part on her experience with philosopher Jean-Paul Sartre, de Beauvoir's encouraging companion and sometime lover.

Every human existence involves transcendence and immanence at the same time; to go forward, each existence must be maintained, for it to expand toward the future it must integrate the past, and while intercommunicating with others it should find self-confirmation. These two elements—maintenance and progression—are implied in any living activity, and for *man* marriage permits precisely a happy synthesis of the two. In his occupation and his political life he encounters change and progress, he senses his extension through time and the universe; and when he is tired of such roaming, he gets himself a home, a fixed location, and an anchorage in the world. At evening he restores his soul in the home, where his wife takes care of his furnishings and children and guards the things of the past that she keeps in store. But she has no other job than to maintain and provide for life in pure and unvarying generality; she perpetuates the species without change, she ensures the even rhythm of the days and the continuity of the home, seeing to it that the doors are locked. But she is allowed no direct influence upon the future nor upon the world; she reaches out beyond herself toward the social group only through her husband as intermediary.

Marriage today still retains, for the most part, this traditional form. . . . The male is called upon for action, his vocation is to produce, fight, create, progress, to transcend himself toward the totality of the universe and the infinity of the future; but traditional marriage does not invite woman to transcend herself with him; it confines her in immanence, shuts her up within the circle of herself. She can thus propose to do nothing more than construct a life of stable equilibrium in which the present as a continuance of the past avoids the menaces of tomorrow—that is, construct precisely a life of happiness. . . .

In domestic work, with or without the aid of servants, woman makes her home her own, finds social justification, and provides herself with an occupation, an activity, that deals usefully and satisfyingly with material objects—shining stoves, fresh, clean clothes, bright copper, polished furniture—but provides no escape from immanence and little affirmation of individuality. . . . Few tasks are more like the torture of Sisyphus than housework, with its endless repetition: the clean becomes soiled, the soiled is made clean, over and over, day after day. The housewife wears herself out marking time: she makes nothing, simply perpetuates the present. She never senses conquest of a positive Good, but rather indefinite struggle against negative Evil. . . . Washing, ironing, sweeping, ferreting out rolls of lint from under wardrobes—all this halting of decay is also the denial of life; for time simultaneously creates and destroys, and only its negative aspect concerns the housekeeper. . .

Thus woman's work within the home gives her no autonomy; it is not directly useful to society, it does not open out on the future, it produces nothing. It takes on meaning and dignity only as it is linked with existent beings who reach out beyond themselves, transcend themselves, toward society in production and action. That is, far from freeing the matron, her occupation makes her dependent upon husband and children; she is justified through them; but in their lives she is only an inessential intermediary. . . .

The tragedy of marriage is not that it fails to assure woman the promised happiness—there is no such thing as assurance in regard to happiness—but that it mutilates her; it dooms her to repetition and routine. The first twenty years of woman's life are extraordinarily rich, as we have seen; she discovers the world and her destiny. At twenty or thereabouts mistress of a home, bound permanently to a man, a child in her arms, she stands with her life virtually finished forever. Real activities, real work, are the prerogative of her man: she has mere things to occupy her which are sometimes tiring but never fully satisfying. . . .

Marriage should be a combining of two whole, independent existences, not a retreat, an annexation, a flight, a remedy. . . . The couple should not be regarded as a unit, a closed cell; rather each individual should be integrated as such in society at large, where each (whether male or female) could flourish without aid; then attachments could be formed in pure generosity with another individual equally adapted to the group, attachments that would be founded upon the acknowledgment that both are free.

This balanced couple is not a utopian fancy: such couples do exist, sometimes even within the frame of marriage, most often outside it. Some mates are united by a strong sexual love that leaves them free in their friendships and in their work; others are held together by a friendship that does not preclude sexual liberty; more rare are those who are at once lovers and friends but do not seek in each other their sole reasons for living. Many nu-

Simone de Beauvoir at home in Paris, June, 1985. *(Source: Gerard Gastand/Sipa Press)*

ances are possible in the relations between a man and a woman: in comradeship, pleasure, trust, fondness, co-operation, love, they can be for each other the most abundant source of joy, richness, and power available to human beings.

Questions for Analysis

1. How did de Beauvoir analyze marriage and marriage partners in terms of existential philosophy?

2. To what extent does a married woman benefit from a "traditional" marriage, according to de Beauvoir? Why?

3. What was de Beauvoir's solution to the situation she described? Was her solution desirable? Realistic?

4. What have you learned about the history of women that supports or challenges de Beauvoir's analysis? Include developments since World War Two and your own reflections.

Source: Simone de Beauvoir, *The Second Sex,* trans. H. M. Parshley. Copyright © 1952 and renewed 1980 by Alfred A. Knopf, Inc. Reprinted by permission of the publisher.

TIMELINE

A History of Western Society: A Brief Overview

	Government	Society and Economy
3200 B.C.	Dominance of Sumerian cities in Mesopotamia, ca 3200–2340 Unification of Egypt; Archaic Period, ca 3100–2660 Old Kingdom of Egypt, ca 2660–2180 Dominance of Akkadian empire in Mesopotamia, ca 2331–2200 Middle Kingdom in Egypt, ca 2080–1640	Neolithic Peoples rely on settled agriculture, while others pursue nomadic life, ca 7000–ca 3000 Development of wheeled transport in Mesopotamia, by ca 3200 Expansion of Mesopotamian trade and culture to the north into the south of modern Turkey, the west into the modern Middle East, and the east into modern Iran, ca 2600
2000 B.C.	Babylonian empire in Mesopotamia, ca 2000–1595 Hyksos "invasion" of Egypt, ca 1640–1570 Hittite empire in Asia Minor, ca 1600–1200 Kassites overthrow Babylonians, ca 1595 New Kingdom in Egypt, ca 1570–1075	First wave of Indo-European migrants, by 2000 Extended commerce in Egypt, by ca 2000 Horses introduced into western Asia, by ca 2000
1500 B.C.	Third Intermediate Period in Egypt, ca 1100–700 Unified Hebrew Kingdom under Saul, David, and Solomon, ca 1025–925	Use of iron increases in western Asia, by ca 1300–1100 Second wave of Indo-European migrants, by ca 1200
1000 B.C.	Hebrew Kingdom divided into Israel and Judah, 925 Rise and Fall of Assyrian empire, ca 900–612 Phoenicians found Carthage, 813 Kingdom of Kush conquers and reunifies Egypt, 8th c. Medes conquer Persia, 710 Cypselus becomes tyrant at Corinth, ca 650 Babylon wins independence from Assyria, 626 Dracon's laws on homicide at Athens, ca 621 Peisistratus becomes tyrant of Athens, ca 561 Cyrus the Great conquers Medes, founds Persian Empire, 550 Solon's reforms at Athens, ca 549 Persians complete conquest of ancient Near East, 521–464 Reforms of Cleisthenes in Athens, 508	Concentration of landed wealth in Greece, ca 750–600 Greek overseas expansion, ca 750–550 Beginning of coinage in western Asia, ca 640

Religion and Philosophy	Science and Technology	Arts and Letters
Growth of anthropomorphic religion in Mesopotamia, ca 3000–2000 Emergence of Egyptian polytheism and belief in personal immortality, ca 2660 Spread of Mesopotamian and Egyptian religious ideas as far north as modern Anatolia and as far south as central Africa, ca 2600	Development of wheeled transport in Mesopotamia, by ca 3200 Use of widespread irrigation in Mesopotamia and Egypt, ca 3000 Construction of the first pyramid in Egypt, ca 2600	Sumerian cuneiform writing, ca 3200 Egyptian hieroglyphic writing, ca 3100
Emergence of Hebrew monotheism, ca 1700 Mixture of Hittite and Near Eastern religious beliefs, ca 1595	Construction of the first ziggurats in Mesopotamia, ca 2000 Widespread use of bronze in the ancient Near East, ca 1900 Babylonian mathematical advances, ca 1800	Epic of Gilgamesh, ca 1900 Code of Hammurabi, ca 1790
Exodus of the Hebrews from Egypt into Palestine, 13th c. Religious beliefs of Akhenaten, ca 1367	Hittites introduce iron technology, ca 1400	Phoenicians develop alphabet, ca 1400 Naturalistic art in Egypt under Akhenaten, ca 1367 Hymn to Aton, ca 1350 Egyptian Book of the Dead, ca 1300
Era of the prophets in Israel, ca 1100-500 Intermixture of Etruscan and Roman religious cults, ca 753–509 Growing popularity of local Greek religious cults, ca 700 B.C.–A.D. 337 Babylonian captivity of the Hebrews, 586–539	Babylonian astronomical advances, ca 750–400	Beginning of the Hebrew Bible, ca 9th c. Traditional beginning of the Olympic Games, 776 Babylonian astronomical advances, ca 750-400 Homer, traditional author of the *Iliad* and *Odyssey*, ca 700 Hesiod, author of the *Theogony* and *Works and Days*, ca 700 Archilochos, lyric poet, 648 Aeschylus, first significant Athenian tragedian, 525/4–456

	Government	Society and Economy
500 B.C.	Ionian Revolt from Persia, 499–494 Battle of Marathon, 490 Xerxes' invasion of Greece, 480–479 Athenian establishment of the Delian Confederacy, 478/7 Publication of the Twelve Tables in Rome, 451/0 Valerio-Horatian laws in Rome, 449 Peloponnesian War, 431–404 Rome captures Veii, 396 Gauls sack Rome, 390 Roman expansion in Italy, 390–290 Theban hegemony in Greece, 371–362 Macedonian conquest of Greece, 338 Conquests of Alexander the Great, 334–323 Punic Wars, 264–146 Reforms of the Gracchi, 133–121	Building of the Via Appia begins in Italy, 312 Growth of Hellenistic trade and cities, ca 300–100 Roman overseas expansion, ca 282–146 Beginning of Roman silver coinage, 269 Growth of slavery, decline of small farmers in Rome, ca 250–100 Agrarian reforms of the Gracchi, 133–121
100 B.C.	Dictatorship of Sulla, 88–79 Civil war in Rome, 78–27 Dictatorship of Caesar, 45–44 Principate of Augustus, 31 B.C. – A.D. 14	Reform of the Roman calendar, 46
300	Constantine removes capital of Roman empire to Constantinople, ca 315 Visigoths defeat Roman army at Adrianople (378), signaling massive German invasions into the empire Bishop Ambrose refuses to yield cathedral church of Milan to Theodosius, thereby asserting church's independence from the state, 380 Death of emperor Romulus Augustus marks end of Roman empire in the West, 476 Clovis issues Salic law of the Franks, ca 490	Growth of Serfdom in Roman empire, ca 200–500 Economic contraction in Roman empire, 3rd c.
500	Law Code of Justinian, 529 Dooms of Ethelbert, king of Kent, ca 604 Spread of Islam across Arabia, the Mediterranean region, Spain, North Africa, and Asia as far as India, ca 630–733	Gallo-Roman aristocracy intermarries with Germanic chieftains Decline of towns and trade, ca 500–700 Agrarian economy predominates in the West, ca 500–1500
700	Charles Martel defeats Muslims at Tours, 733 Pippin III anointed king of the Franks, 754 Charlemagne secures Frankish crown, r. 768–814	Height of Muslim commercial activity, ca 700–1300

Religion and Philosophy	Science and Technology	Arts and Letters

Pre-Socratic philosophers, 5th c.

Socrates and his emphasis on ethics, 469–399

Plato, founder of the Academy, 429–347

Diogenes, leading proponent of Cynicism, ca 412–323

Aristotle, founder the Peripatetic school, 384–322

Epicurus, founder of the school named after him, 340–270

Zeno, founder of Stoic philosophy, 335–262

Emergence of Mithraism, ca 300

Spread of Hellenistic mystery religions, 2nd c.

Greek cults brought to Rome, ca 200

Hippocrates, formal founder of medicine ca 430

Aristotle, advances in political science, physics, and ethics, 384–322

Theophrastus, founder of botany, ca 372–288

Aristarchos of Samos, advances in astronomy, ca 310–230

Euclid codifies geometry, ca 300

Herophilus, discoveries in medicine, ca 300–250

Archimedes, works on physics and hydrologics, ca 287–212

Sophocles, tragedian who used his plays to explore moral and political problems, ca 496–406

Euripides, the most personal of the Athenian tragedians, ca 480–406

Thucydides, historian of the Peloponnesian War, ca 460–400

Aristophanes, the greatest writer of Old Comedy, ca 457–ca 385

Herodotus, the father of history, ca 450

Mithraism spreads to Rome, 27 B.C.–A.D. 270

Dedication of the Ara Pacis Augustae, 9

Traditional birth of Jesus, ca 3

Pliny the Elder, student of natural history, 23 B.C.–A.D. 79

Frontinus, engineering advances in Rome, 30 B.C.–A.D. 104

Virgil, author of the *Aeneid* and *Georgics*, 70–19

Livy, author of the great history of the Roman republic, ca 59 B.C.–A.D. 17

Ovid, elegant writer of elegiacs and Roman customs, 43 B.C.–A.D. 17

Constantine legalizes Christianity, 312

Theodosius declares Christianity the official state religion, 380

Donatist heretical movement at its height, ca 400

St. Augustine, *The City of God*, ca 425

Clovis adopts Roman Christianity, 496

St. Jerome publishes the Latin *Vulgate*, late 4th c.

St. Augustine, *Confessions*, ca 390

Byzantines preserve Greco-Roman culture, ca 400–1000

Boethius, *The Consolation of Philosophy*, ca 520

Rule of St. Benedict, 529

Monasteries established in Anglo-Saxon England, 7th c.

Muhammad preaches reform, ca 610

Publication of the Qu'ran, 651

Synod of Whitby, 664

Using watermills, Benedictine monks exploit energy of fast-flowing rivers and streams

Heavy plow and improved harness facilitate use of multiple-ox teams; harrow widely used in northern Europe

Boethius, *The Consolation of Philosophy*, ca 520

Justinian constructs church of Santa Sophia, 532–537

Pope St. Gregory (the Great) publishes *Dialogues, Pastoral Care, Moralia*, 590–604

Missionary work of St. Boniface in Germany, ca 710–750

Iconoclastic controversy in Byzantine empire, 726–843

Pippin III donates Papal States to the papacy, 756

Byzantines successfully use "Greek fire" in naval combat against Arab fleets attacking Constantinople, 673, 717

Lindisfarne Gospel Book, ca 700

Bede, *Ecclesiastical History of the English Nation*, ca 700

Beowulf, ca 700

Carolingian Renaissance, ca 780–850

	Government	Society and Economy
800	Imperial coronation of Charlemagne, Christmas 800 Treaty of Verdun, 843 Viking, Magyar, and Muslim invasions complete disintegration of Carolingian empire; growth of feudalism, ca 845–900	Byzantine commerce and industry, ca 800–1000 Viking invasions and unstable conditions lead to vast increase of serfdom
1000	Seljuk Turks conquer Muslim Baghdad, 1055 Norman conquest of England, 1066 Penance of Henry IV at Canossa, 1077	Agrarian economy predominates in the West, 1000–1500 Height of Muslim commerce and industry, ca 900–1300 Decline of Byzantine free peasantry, ca 1025–1100 Growth of towns and trade in the West, ca 1050–1300 Domesday Book, 1086
1100	Henry I of England, r. 1100–1135 Louis VI of France, r. 1108–1137 Frederick I of Germany, r. 1152–1190 Henry II of England, r. 1154–1189 Thomas Becket murdered, December 1170 Philip Augustus of France, r. 1180–1223	Henry I of England establishes the Exchequer, 1130 Beginnings of the Hanseatic League, 1159
1200	Spanish victory over Muslims at Las Navas de Tolosa, 1212 Battle of Bouvines, July 1214 Frederick II of Germany and Sicily, r. 1212–1250 Magna Carta, 1215 Louis IX of France, r. 1226–1270 Mongols destroy Baghdad and end the Abbasid caliphate, 1258 Edward I of England, r. 1272–1307 Philip IV (the Fair) of France, r. 1285–1314 War opens between England and France, 1296	Economic revival, growth of towns, clearing of wasteland contribute to great growth of personal freedom, 13th c. Agricultural expansion leads to population growth, ca 1225–1300
1300	Philip IV orders arrest of Pope Boniface at Anagni, 1303 Hundred Years' War, 1337–1450 Political chaos in Germany, ca 1350–1450 Merchant oligarchies or despots rule Italian city-states	European economic depression, ca 1300–1450 Black Death begins ca 1347; returns intermittently until 18th c. Height of the Hanseatic League, 1350–1450 Peasant and working class revolts: Jacquerie (France, 1358), Ciompi (Florence, 1378), Peasants (England, 1381)
1400	Appearance of Joan of Arc, 1429–1431 Medici domination of Florence begins, 1434	Population decline, peasants' revolts, high labor costs contribute to decline of serfdom in Western Europe

Religion and Philosophy	Science and Technology	Arts and Letters
Foundation of abbey of Cluny, 909 Byzantine conversion of Russia, late 10th c.	Stirrup and nailed horseshoes become widespread in shock combat Paper, invented in China ca 2nd c., enters Europe through Muslim Spain in 10th c. Spain develops paper industry, 10th c.	Byzantines develop the Cyrillic script, late 10th c.
Avicenna, Arab translator of Greek science, medicine, mathematics, d. 1037 Beginning of reformed papacy, 1046 Schism between Roman and Greek Orthodox churches, 1054 Pope Gregory VII, 1073–1085 Peter Abelard, 1079–1142 St. Bernard of Clairvaux, 1090–1153 First Crusade, 1095–1099	Arab conquests bring new irrigation methods, cotton cultivation, and manufacture to Spain, Sicily, southern Italy	Romanesque style in architecture and art, ca 1000–1200 *Song of Roland*, ca 1095 Muslim musicians introduce stringed instruments, lute, rebec; ancestors of violin
Beginnings of universities, ca 1100–1300 Concordat of Worms ends investiture controversy, 1122 Height of Cistercian monasticism, 1125–1175 Aristotle's works translated into Latin, ca 1140–1260 Jerusalem falls to Muslims; start of the Third Crusade, 1187 Pope Innocent III, 1198–1216	In castle construction Europeans, copying Muslim and Byzantine models, erect rounded towers and crenelated walls Windmill invented, ca 1180 Some monasteries, such as Clairvaux and Canterbury Cathedral Priory, supplied by underground pipes with running water and indoor latrines; elsewhere these very rare until 19th c.	*Rubaiyat of Umar Khayyam*, ca 1120 Dedication of abbey church of Saint-Denis launches gothic style, June 1144 Hildegard of Bingen (1098–1179) produces theological treatises, ca 1150 Court of troubador poetry, especially that of Chretian de Troyes, circulates widely
Crusaders capture Constantinople (Fourth Crusade), 1204 Maimonides, d. 1204 Founding of Franciscan Order, 1210 Fourth Lateran Council, 1215 Founding of Dominican Order, 1216 Thomas Aquinas (1225–1274) marks height of Scholasticism Pope Boniface VIII, 1294–1303	*Notebooks* of Villard de Honnecourt, a master mason (architect) a major source for gothic engineering, ca 1250 Development of double-entry bookkeeping in Florence and Genoa, ca 1250–1340 Venetians purchase secrets of glass manufacture from Syria, 1277 Mechanical clock invented, ca 1290	*Parzifal, Roman de la Rose, King Arthur and the Round Table* celebrate virtues of knighthood Height of gothic style, ca 1225–1300
Babylonian Captivity of the papacy, 1307–1377 John Wyclif, ca 1330–1384 Great Schism in the papacy, 1377–1418	Edward III of England uses cannon in siege of Calais, 1346	Patrarch, 1304–1374 Paintings of Giotto, ca 1305–1337 Dante, *Divine Comedy*, ca 1310 Boccaccio, *The Decameron*, ca 1350 Jan van Eyck, 1366–1441 Brunelleschi, 1377–1446 Chaucer, *Canterbury Tales*, ca 1385–1400
Council of Constance, 1414–1418 Pragmatic Sanction of Bourges, 1438 Expulsion of Jews from Spain, 1492	Water-powered blast furnaces operative in Sweden, Austria, the Rhine Valley, Liège, ca 1400 Leonardo Fibonacci's *Liber Abaci* (1202) popularizes use of Hindu-	Masaccio, 1401–1428 Botticelli, 1444–1510 Leonardo da Vinci, 1452–1519 Albrecht Dürer, 1471–1528

	Government	Society and Economy
1400 (cont.)	Princes in Germany consolidate power, ca 1450–1500 Ottoman Turks under Mahomet II capture Constantinople, May 1453 Wars of the Roses in England, 1453–1471 Ferdinand and Isabella of Spain capture Granada, the last Muslim stronghold, January 1492 French invasion of Italy, 1494	Christopher Columbus reaches the Americas, October 1492 Portuguese gain control of East Indian spice trade, 1498–1511
1500	Charles V, Holy Roman Emperor, 1519–1556 Imperial sack of Rome, 1527 Philip II of Spain, r. 1556–1598 Revolt of the Netherlands, 1566–1609 St. Bartholemew's Day massacre, August 24, 1572 Defeat of the Spanish Armada, 1588 Henry IV of France issues Edict of Nantes, 1598	Balboa discovers the Pacific, 1513 Magellan's crew circumnavigates the earth, 1519–1522 Spain gains control of Central and South America, ca 1520–1550 Peasants' Revolt in Germany, 1524–1525 "Times of Troubles" in Russia, 1598–1613
1600	Thirty Years' War, 1618–1648 Richelieu dominates French government, 1624–1643 Frederick William, Elector of Brandenburg, r. 1640–1688 English Civil War, 1642–1649 Louis XIV, r. 1643–1715 Peace of Westphalia, 1648 The Fronde in France, 1648–1660	Chartering of British East India Company, 1600 Famine and oppressive taxation lead to widespread revolts in Western Europe, ca 1600–1650 Continuing decline of serfdom in Western Europe, ca 1600–1650 English Poor Law, 1601 Chartering of Dutch East India Company, 1602 Height of Dutch commercial activity, ca 1630–1665
1650	Protectorate in England, 1653–1658 Leopold I, Habsburg emperor, r. 1658–1705 Treaty of the Pyrenees, 1659 Restoration of English monarchy, 1660 Siege of Vienna, 1683 Revocation of Edict of Nantes, 1685 Glorious Revolution in England, 1688–1689 Peter the Great of Russia, r. 1689–1725	Height of mercantilism in Europe, ca 1650–1750 Principle of peasants' "hereditary subjugation" to their lords affirmed in Prussia, 1653 Colbert's economic reforms in France, ca 1663–1683 Cossack revolt in Russia, 1670–1671

Religion and Philosophy	Science and Technology	Arts and Letters
	Arabic numerals, "a major factor in the rise of science in the Western world" Paris and largest Italian cities paved streets, making cleaning possible Printing and movable type, ca 1450	Michelangelo, 1475–1564 Raphael, 1483–1520 Rabelais, ca 1490–1553
Lateran Council attempts reforms of church abuses, 1512–1517 Machiavelli, *The Prince*, 1513 Concordat of Bologna, 1516 Thomas More, *Utopia*, 1516 Martin Luther publishes the *Ninety-Five Theses*, 1517 Castiglione, *The Courtier*, 1528 Henry VIII of England breaks with Rome, 1532–1534 Anabaptists control Munster, 1534 Ignatius Loyola establishes the Society of Jesus, 1540 John Calvin establishes a theocracy in Geneva, 1541 Angela Merici establishes the Ursuline Order, first religious order for education of women, 1544 Council of Trent, 1545–1563 Peace of Augsburg, 1555 Thomas Hobbes, 1588–1679 René Descartes, 1596–1650	Copernicus, *On the Revolutions of the Heavenly Bodies*, 1543 Francis Bacon, 1561–1626 Galileo, 1564–1642 Johannes Kepler, 1571–1630 William Harvey, 1578–1657	Erasmus, *The Praise of Folly*, 1509 Cervantes, 1547–1616 Baroque movement in the arts, ca 1550–1725 Shakespeare, 1564–1616 Rubens, 1577–1640 Michel de Montaigne, *Essays,* 1598 Diego Velazquez, 1599–1660
Huguenot revolt in France, 1625	Frances Bacon, *The Advancement of Learning*, 1605 Robert Boyle, 1627–1691 Anton Leeuwenhoek, 1632–1723	Rembrandt van Rijn, 1606–1669 Golden Age of Dutch culture, 1625–1675 Jan Vermeer, 1632–1675 Jean Baptiste Racine, 1639–1699
Patriarch Nikon's reforms split Russian Orthodox church, 1652 Test Act in England excludes Roman Catholics from public office, 1673 Revocation of Edict of Nantes, 1685 James II attempts to restore Roman Catholicism as state religion, 1685–1688 Montesquieu, 1689–1755 Locke, *Second Treatise on Civil Government*, 1690 Pierre Bayle, *Historical and Critical Dictionary*, 1697	Jethro Tull (1674–1741) encourages innovation in English agriculture Newton, *Principia Mathematica*, 1687 Newcomen develops steam engine, 1705	Construction of baroque palaces and remodeling of capital cities throughout central and eastern Europe, ca 1650–1725 J.S. Bach, 1685–1750 Fontenelle, *Conversations on the Plurality of Worlds*, 1686 The Enlightenment, ca 1690–1790 Voltaire, 1694–1778

	Government	Society and Economy
1900	Russo-Japanese War, 1904–1905 Revolution in Russia, 1905 Balkin wars, 1912–1913	Women's suffrage movement, England, ca 1900–1914 Social welfare legislation, France, 1904, 1910; England, 1906–1914 Agrarian reforms in Russia, 1907–1912
1914	World War One, 1914–1918 *Lusitania* sinks, 1915 Easter Rebellion, 1916 U.S. declares war on Germany, 1917 Bolshevik Revolution, 1917–1918 Treaty of Versailles, 1919	Planned economies in Europe, 1914 Auxiliary Service Law in Germany, 1916 Bread riots in Russia, March 1917
1920	Mussolini seizes power, 1922 Forced collectivization in the Soviet Union, 1929 Stalin uses police terrorism, ca 1929–1939 Hitler becomes chancellor of Germany, 1933 Rome-Berlin Axis, 1936 Nazi-Soviet Non-Aggression Pact, 1939 World War Two begins, 1939	New Economic Policy in the Soviet Union, 1921 Dawes Plan for reparations and recovery, 1924 The Great Depression, 1929–1939 Rapid industrialization in Soviet Union, 1930s Roosevelt's "New Deal," 1933 National Recovery Administration, 1935
1940	Japan bombs Pearl Harbor, 1941 War in Europe ends, 1945 United Nations, 1945 Cold War era begins, 1947 Fall of colonial empires, 1947–1962 Communist government in China, 1949 Korean War, 1950–1953 "De-Stalinization" in Soviet Union, 1955–1962	The Holocaust, 1941–1945 Marshall Plan, 1947 Organization of European Economic Cooperation, 1948 European economic progress, ca 1950–1969 European Coal and Steel Community, 1952 European Economic Community, 1957
1960	The Berlin Wall, 1961 Cuban missile crisis, 1962 United States in Vietnam, ca 1961–1973 Student rebellion in France, 1968 Détente, 1970s Soviet intervention in Afghanistan, 1979	Civil rights movement in United States, 1960s Collapse of postwar monetary system, 1971 OPEC oil price increases, 1973 and 1979 Stagflation, 1970s International Women's Movement, 1970s
1980	U.S. military buildup, 1980s Solidarity in Poland, 1980 Gorbachev begins reforms in the Soviet Union, 1985 Revolutions in Eastern Europe, 1989–1990 End of Soviet Union, 1991	Growth of debt, 1980s Gorbachev implements perestroika, 1985 Economic crisis in Poland, 1988 Unification of East and West Germany, 1989

Religion and Philosophy	Science and Technology	Arts and Letters
Separation of church and state, France, 1901–1905 Jean-Paul Sartre, 1905–1980	Max Planck develops quantum theory, ca 1900 First airplane flight, 1903 Einstein develops relativity theory, 1905–1910	"Modernism" ca 1900–1929 Conrad, *Heart of Darkness,* 1902 Cubism in art, ca 1905–1930 Marcel Proust, *Remembrance of Things Past,* 1913–1927
Schweitzer, *Quest of the Historical Jesus,* 1906	Submarine warfare, 1915 Ernest Rutherford splits the atom, 1919	Oswald Spengler, *The Decline of the West,* 1918
Emergence of modern existentialism, 1920s Wittgenstein, *Essay on Logical Philosophy,* 1922 Revival of Christianity, 1920s and 1930s	"Heroic age of physics," 1920s First major public broadcasts in Great Britain and the United States, 1920 Werner Heisenberg, "principle of uncertainty," 1927 Talking movies, 1930 Radar system in England, 1939	Walter Gropius, the Bauhaus, 1920s Dadaism and Surrealism in art, 1920s Virginia Woolf, *Jacob's Room,* 1922 James Joyce, *Ulysseus,* 1922 T. S. Eliot, *The Waste Land,* 1922 Erich Remarque, *All Quiet on the Western Front,* 1929 Pablo Picasso, *Guernica,* 1937
Simone de Beauvoir, *The Second Sex,* 1949 Communists fail to break Catholic Church in Poland, 1950s	J. Robert Oppenheimer, 1904–1967 "Big Science" in the United States, ca 1940–1970 U.S. drops atomic bombs on Japan, 1945 James Watson and Francis Crick discover structure of DNA molecule, 1953 Russian satellite in orbit, 1957	Cultural purge in Soviet Union, 1946–1952 Ludwig Mies van der Rohe, Lake Shore Apartments, 1948–1951 George Orwell, *1984,* 1949 Boris Pasternak, *Doctor Zhivago,* 1956 The "beat" movement in the United States, late 1950s
Catholic Church opposes the legalization of divorce and abortion, 1970 to present Pope John Paul II electrifies Poland, 1979	European Council for Nuclear Research (CERN), 1960 Space race, 1960s Russian cosmonaut first to orbit globe, 1961 American astronaut first person on the moon, 1969	The Beatles, 1960s Alexander Solzhenitsyn, *One Day in the Life of Ivan Denisovitch,* 1962 Betty Friedan, *The Feminine Mystique,* 1963 J.J. Servan-Schreiber, *The American Challenge,* 1967
Revival of religion in Soviet Union, 1985 to present	Reduced spending on Big Science, 1980s Computer revolution continues, 1980s and 1990s	Solzhenitsyn returns to Russia, 1994

Index

G

Philosophy: pessimism in, 936–939; logical empiricism, 938; existentialism, 938–939. *See also* Existentialism; Intellectual activity

Physics, 940–941; law of conservation of energy, 821; thermodynamics as, 821. *See also* Science

Picasso, Pablo, 946

Pickford, Mary, 948

Piedmont, Italy, 834

Pilsudski, Joseph, 969

Pissarro, Camille, 946

Pius VII (Pope), 716

Pius IX (Pope), 836; doctrine of papal infallibility, 851

Planck, Max, 940, 941

Planned economies, 913

Plantations, slavery and, 843

Poets and poetry: Blake, 744; Wordsworth, 744–745, 772–773; Coleridge, 772, 773; English romantic, 772–773; romantic, 772–773; French romantic, 773; Goethe, 773; Scott, 773; Hugo, 773–774; Pushkin, 774; Lamartine, 784; Bjornson, 879; Kipling, 886; Sassoon, 909; Valéry, 937; Auden, 940; Eliot, 940; Akhmatova, 1021

Poincaré, Raymond, 951, 952, 954

Poland, 927, 1010, 1036; Russia and, 759–761, 760 (map); French mutual defense pact with, 950; guarantees of, 952; Hitler's attack on, 967; conservative authoritarianism in, 969; Hitler and, 989 (map); German invasion of, 991, 992; Big Three compromise on, 1007; collectivized agriculture in, 1022; revolution in (1956), 1023–1024; German reconciliation with, 1057; West Germany and, 1057–1058; trade union movement in, 1060; Solidarity movement in, 1063–1065

Police terrorism: in Soviet Union, 976; Mussolini and, 981. *See also* Secret police

Political activism: during Vietnam War, 1033; women's movement and, 1056

Political nationalism, 766–767

Political parties: under Nazis, 985; after Second World War, 1013

Politics: revolution in, 691–723; First World War and, 915–917; U.S. rejection of Versailles Treaty and, 928–930; Hitler and, 984–985

Poorhouses, 746

Poor Laws (England), reform of, 779

Popes: Pius VII, 716; Rome and, 834; Pius IX, 836, 851; Leo XIII, 854;

Mussolini and, 981; John Paul II, 1064

Popular Front, in France, 961–962

Population: and Industrial Revolution, 727, 735–737; composition of Austrian Empire, 764 (map); Malthus on, 765; Ricardo on, 765; of cities, 796; urban sanitation and, 797; transportation and movement of, 867; great migration and, 874–875; birthrates and, 1052

Port Arthur, 892

Portugal: France and, 719; African imperialism of, 880, 882; conservative dictator in, 968; conservative authoritarianism in, 969

Positivism, 822

Postimpressionism, 946

Potato crop, failure in Ireland, 780, 781–782

Potsdam conference, 1008

Poverty, 1050, 1072 (map), 1073; living conditions and, 798–799; wealth and, 805; unemployment and, 958; in United States, 1020–1021

Power, *see* Energy; Nuclear power

Prague, 787; revolt in, 788

Prague Spring (1968), 1036

Pregnancy, 814

Presley, Elvis, 1030

Price controls, 1012

Private property, 698

Production: worldwide crisis in, 957; British recovery in, 960; in U.S., 960; in Soviet Union, 974

Professions, middle classes and, 806–807

Progress: belief in, 936–937; literary notions of, 943

Progressive Bloc, in Russia, 917

Prokofiev, Sergei, 1021

Proletarians, socialism and, 858

Proletariat, Marx on, 770

Propaganda: in First World War, 914, 915; films and, 949; radio and, 949; in Soviet Union, 976–977

Prostitution, 814–815; middle classes and, 813

Protective tariffs: in Germany, 851; in Britain, 961

Protestantism: in Germany, 851; Britain, Ireland, and, 855

Protest movements: in United States, 1032–1034; students and, 1032–1036; in Europe, 1034–1036. *See also* Reform movements

Proudhon, Pierre Joseph, 769

Proust, Marcel, 943

Prussia, 758; Napoleon I and, 717; railroads in, 742; Poland, Saxony,

and, 759–761, 760 (map); Holy Alliance and, 761–762; German Confederation and, 762; liberalism in, 788–789; as German kingdom, 788–790; Bismarck and, 789, 838–842; war with Denmark, 789–790; distribution of income in, 805; nationalism in, 838; Austrian war with, 839–840; Franco-Prussian War and, 841–842; in German Empire, 850; war with France, 900. *See also* Germany

Psychology and psychiatry: psychoanalysis, 820; Freud and, 941–942

Public health, 798–799; bacterial revolution and, 799–800

Public opinion, Napoleon III and, 834

Public transportation, *see* Mass public transportation; Transportation

Puddling furnace, 734

Pushkin, Aleksander, 774

Putting-out system, 729

Q

Quadruple Alliance, 720, 758–761

Quakers, 744

Quantum physics, 940

Quest of the Historical Jesus (Schweitzer), 939

Quo Vadis (movie), 948

R

Race and racism: imperialism and, 886; colonial India and, 890; totalitarian dictatorships and, 967; and Hitler, 981–982, 993–994; of Hitler, 993–994; in United States, 1020. *See also* Blacks; Slaves and slavery

Radar, 995, 1025

Radical dictatorships, totalitarianism and fascism, 969–971

Radicalism, 763–770; of American Revolution, 698; Metternich's attacks on, 762–763; Three Emperors' League against, 900; in Germany, 951–952; Popular Front and, 961. *See also* Protest movement; Reform movements; Student protests

Radio, 949

Raft of the Medusa, The (Géricault), 771

Railroads: in England, 734–735; governments and, 742; in Russia, 848; trade and, 867

Rasputin, Grigori, 918

Rathenau, Walter, 913

Rationality, 936–937